Brexit, Union, and Disunion

This book provides a critical analysis of Brexit, placing it in the broader context of the historical development of the British Constitution and earlier disputes as to the meaning of statehood, sovereignty, and territorial boundaries. Some of the greatest challenges posed by the UK's withdrawal from the EU are those it places on the British Constitution, which is already 'unsettled' and under strain. This book investigates this impact, but also uniquely locates Brexit in the broader context of historically significant British 'acts of union or disunion' – such as the loss of former US colonies and British Empire, and the place of Scotland and Ireland in the Union. These precedents help us understand how a British constitutional identity has been shaped or dismantled by legal concepts of union or sovereignty.

Sionaidh Douglas-Scott is Anniversary Chair in Law at Queen Mary University of London, formerly Professor of European and Human Rights Law, University of Oxford. Her past roles include Special Advisor, Scottish Parliament External & European Relations committee, 2015–2017; Major Leverhulme fellow, 2018–2021; LAPA fellow Princeton University, 2020–2021.

Law in Context

Since 1970, the Law in Context series has been at the forefront of a movement to broaden the study of law. The series is a vehicle for the publication of innovative monographs and texts that treat law and legal phenomena critically in their cultural, social, political, technological, environmental and economic contexts. A contextual approach involves treating legal subjects broadly, using materials from other humanities and social sciences, and from any other discipline that helps to explain the operation in practice of the particular legal field or legal phenomena under investigation. It is intended that this orientation is at once more stimulating and more revealing than the bare exposition of legal rules. The series includes original research monographs, coursebooks and textbooks that foreground contextual approaches and methods. The series includes and welcomes books on the study of law in all its contexts, including domestic legal systems, European and international law, transnational and global legal processes, and comparative law.

Books in the Series

Acosta: *The National versus the Foreigner in South America: 200 Years of Migration and Citizenship Law*
Alaattinoğlu: *Grievance Formation, Rights and Remedies*
Ali: *Modern Challenges to Islamic Law*
Alyagon Darr: *Plausible Crime Stories: The Legal History of Sexual Offences in Mandate Palestine*
Anderson, Schum & Twining: *Analysis of Evidence, 2nd Edition*
Ashworth: *Sentencing and Criminal Justice, 6th Edition*
Barton & Douglas: *Law and Parenthood*
Baxi, McCrudden & Paliwala: *Law's Ethical, Global and Theoretical Contexts: Essays in Honour of William Twining*
Beecher-Monas: *Evaluating Scientific Evidence: An Interdisciplinary Framework for Intellectual Due Process*

Brexit, Union, and Disunion

The Evolution of British Constitutional Unsettlement

SIONAIDH DOUGLAS-SCOTT
Queen Mary University of London

CAMBRIDGE
UNIVERSITY PRESS

CAMBRIDGE
UNIVERSITY PRESS

Shaftesbury Road, Cambridge CB2 8EA, United Kingdom

One Liberty Plaza, 20th Floor, New York, NY 10006, USA

477 Williamstown Road, Port Melbourne, VIC 3207, Australia

314–321, 3rd Floor, Plot 3, Splendor Forum, Jasola District Centre, New Delhi – 110025, India

103 Penang Road, #05–06/07, Visioncrest Commercial, Singapore 238467

Cambridge University Press is part of Cambridge University Press & Assessment, a department of the University of Cambridge.

We share the University's mission to contribute to society through the pursuit of education, learning and research at the highest international levels of excellence.

www.cambridge.org
Information on this title: www.cambridge.org/9781108841788

DOI: 10.1017/9781108894951

First published 2023

A catalogue record for this publication is available from the British Library

A Cataloging-in-Publication data record for this book is available from the Library of Congress

ISBN 978-1-108-84178-8 Hardback
ISBN 978-1-108-79534-0 Paperback

Contents

Figures

Note on cover: The map on the cover ['England, Scotland and Ireland, or the British Isles'] was produced by the Flemish cartographer, Abraham Ortelius, and is part of his late 16th century atlas *Theatrum Orbis Terrarum*. Therefore, it is notably by a continental European, and the land mass on its far left, of France and Flanders, indicate Britain's proximity to continental Europe. The fact that the mapmaker chose a west rather than north orientation for Britain also may be unsettling, resonating with the constitutional unsettlement that is a theme of this book.

Introduction

On 23 June 2016, a majority of the UK electorate who voted in the EU in-out referendum voted to leave the EU. This was a defining moment in the constitutional law and politics of the UK. Undoubtedly, exiting the EU has had legal, economic, and social effects within the UK, as well as in remaining EU States. But Brexit is as much about the British Constitution as it is about economics and relations with continental Europe. This book investigates the impact of Brexit on the British Constitution, but also locates Brexit in the broader context of historically significant British acts of union or disunion, drawing lessons from such past experience.

Constitutional Inadequacy

Brexit gave rise to a wide range of constitutional challenges and conundrums, which included: the role of 'advisory' referendums in Britain's Constitution; confusion over the UK's constitutional requirements for starting the EU withdrawal process; the respective roles of the UK Parliament and government in Britain's EU withdrawal; the position of the devolved nations in the Brexit process and the future of the territorial State; the extent and nature of domestic legislative changes necessary to complete Brexit, especially the increase of extensive executive powers; and the extent to which human rights will enjoy domestic protection post-Brexit.

All this has happened at a time of constitutional turbulence and disorder. Brexit has challenged a Constitution that was already 'unsettled'[1] (and it has since been further unsettled by COVID-19 regulations and the death of a long-reigning monarch).

The British Constitution has long been characterized as resting on the sovereignty of Parliament, and as unwritten, flexible, uncodified in nature, with political conventions and ministerial accountability often taking the place of hard law. However, this was a Constitution whose very uncodified and sometimes tacit nature was nonetheless supposed to give rise to a holistic

[1] N Walker, 'Our Constitutional Unsettlement' (2014) Public Law 529.

constitutional identity. There is no single document comprising the British Constitution, which instead is a blend of primary and secondary legislation, legally unenforceable conventions, arcane and opaque royal prerogatives, and insubstantial usages and understandings.

Much of the blame for the articulation of exceptionalism, flexibility and pride in the uncodified British Constitution must lie with Albert Venn Dicey, whose work, *The Law of the Constitution*, first published in 1885, set out what he perceived to be the main tenets of the Constitution. According to Dicey, the main pillars were parliamentary sovereignty, the rule of law and constitutional conventions – but in Dicey's opinion, 'The[e] secret source of strength is the absolute omnipotence, the sovereignty of Parliament.'[2] The other doyen of Victorian constitutionalism, Walter Bagehot, famously divided the Constitution into two parts – the 'dignified' and 'efficient'. Bagehot maintained that a disguised republic that had 'insinuated itself beneath the folds of monarchy', and that the function of the monarch was to 'disguise' the real working of government. Indeed, he claimed that the 'efficient secret of the English[3] Constitution' lay in the very close union and nearly complete fusion of executive and legislative powers. Both Dicey's and Bagehot's constitutional 'secrets' can prove highly damaging today. Unlimited parliamentary sovereignty acts as a straitjacket, making it impossible to protect key principles by constitutional entrenchment and closing off other constitutional models such as federalism. Bagehot's 'efficient secret' has come close to enabling executive sovereignty.

Dicey and Bagehot drew on earlier constitutional writing which stressed an organic English tradition of gradual evolution, continuity and preservation, traceable back to the 'Glorious' Revolution of 1688. The nineteenth-century historian and legislator, Thomas Babington Macaulay, wrote that, 'We owe this singular happiness, under the blessing of God, to a wise and noble constitution.'[4] To be sure, there was resistance to this celebration of the Constitution, from Tom Paine, for example. Nonetheless, Bagehot and Dicey continue to dominate English constitutional law to this day. And Dicey's work is seen by many as the nearest thing to a codified Constitution in Britain.

However, this organic Constitution underwent a gradual reform process in recent decades. These constitutional developments affected sovereignty and lines of authority. The changes included EU membership; the 1998 Human Rights Act; devolution in Scotland, Wales and Northern Ireland; removal of most hereditary peers from the House of Lords; and the increasing use of referendums as instruments of constitutional change. All this rendered the Constitution (and Britain) less unitary and more heterogeneous, more willing

[2] AV Dicey, *England's Case against Home Rule* (3rd ed., 1887) 168.

[3] Notably, Bagehot entitled his work, first published in 1867, *The English Constitution*. Dicey also referred, throughout *The Law of the Constitution*, to the *English* Constitution. Both works, however, cover the whole UK.

[4] Lord Macaulay and Lady Trevelyan (eds.), *Speeches: The Complete Writings of Lord Macaulay* (New York, 2004) II, 219.

to recognize centres of power elsewhere, without however bringing any cohesion or consolidation of constitutional form. Indeed, it was questionable whether all of this constitutional activity amounted to a major disruption likely to transform the nature of Britain's Constitution, or was simply a further evolution of Britain's flexible Constitution. For this activity had an ad hoc, disorderly feel to it.

EU membership undoubtedly played a crucial role in this constitutional transformation. This went hand in hand with developments undermining law's connection with the State. Post-sovereign approaches argue that States now share their powers with supra-State, sub-State, and trans-State systems. Neil MacCormick famously contended that 'sovereignty and sovereign states, and the inexorable linkage of law with sovereignty and the state, have been but the passing phenomena of a few centuries, that their passing is by no means regrettable …'[5]

However, Brexit challenges this recent vision of post-sovereignty. Perhaps, the most common constitutional idea to feature in Brexit debates was a reassertion of national sovereignty, of 'taking back control'. Yet, this is an anachronistic notion of sovereignty, and too simplistic. It fails to capture the way in which pooling sovereignty in one area may actually empower a State. Indeed, Brexit could imperil the very national sovereignty its advocates believe it will bring about. This is because, as well as threatening Britain's economic security, it risks empowering the executive at the expense of Parliament, and shattering the stability of the UK by threatening the peace settlement in Northern Ireland and provoking a further independence referendum in Scotland.

The 2016 EU referendum placed Britain's constitutional system under great strain, as well as providing it with uncommon public attention (including high-profile lawsuits such as *Miller*). Indeed, Peter Hennessey stated, shortly after the EU Referendum: 'The referendum was like a lightening flash illuminating a political and social landscape long in the changing … we need to look at our internal constitutional arrangements – the relationships between the nations, regions and localities of the United Kingdom.'[6] Most strikingly, the Brexit process has shed light on the inadequacies of the Constitution. As Blick and Hennessey comment, 'A key characteristic of the British constitution is the degree to which the good governance of the UK has relied on the self-restraint of those who carry it out.' But they concluded that the self-restraint is now missing, and those in charge are 'Good Chaps no more'.[7]

[5] N MacCormick, 'Beyond the Sovereign State' (1993) 56 MLR 1.

[6] House of Lords, Hansard 05 July 2016, Volume 773, at column 1963.

[7] A Blick and P Hennessy 'Good Chaps No More? Safeguarding the Constitution in Stressful Times' (2019): https://consoc.org.uk/wp-content/uploads/2019/11/FINAL- Blick-Hennessy-Good-Chaps-No-More.pdf. Maybe they somewhere include 'chapesses'. See also, P Hennessey, 'Our Sense of Decency Survived the War. It Won't Survive This', *The Times*, 8 September 2019, www.thetimes.co.uk/article/our-sense-of-decency-survived-the-war-it-wont-survive-this-3m9skzd79

And yet, there is little evidence that Brexit will provide a 'constitutional moment' in which a common solution will be found to these constitutional conundrums. It is doubtful whether a federal UK or codified Constitution will emerge, however much new constitutional arrangements are needed to deal with Brexit. Advocates of Scottish independence, or a united Ireland, are unlikely to have enthusiasm for an arrangement that would entrench them in the UK, even if it provided entrenched legal procedures to protect devolved nations within the State. And those satisfied with Brexit are unlikely to desire a codified Constitution or federal option, given that a desire for strong parliamentary sovereignty motivated their euroscepticism in the first place. Such distinct political identities militate against a comprehensive approach that could enable the British Constitution to deal with issues of disputed authority and the legacy of Brexit. In these circumstances, the outcome of the Brexit referendum provides a severe constitutional challenge for Britain.

Constitutional Amnesia

And yet, this is not the first time that Britain has encountered challenges to its very constitutional identity. Past 'acts of union and disunion',[8] such as the loss of British colonies in North America and British Empire; the admission of Scotland and Ireland into the union and then departure, or possible departure (Scotland); and the UK's EU membership since 1973, all provide precedents which help us understand how a British constitutional identity has been shaped or dismantled by law, and how law has determined issues of union, sovereignty and devolution of power. There are lessons to be learned from surprisingly similar past situations, although past examples of constitutional transformations are all too rarely invoked. Such constitutional amnesia may be a useful shield for obfuscating an unsettling imperial past involving violence, dark acts and an ugly history of colonialism. Nonetheless, there are surely ways to retrieve and re-examine the constitutional legacies of empire without falling into an unrealistic and unwholesome nostalgia.

About 75–100 years ago, many of the most noted British constitutional theorists examined the structures of the British Empire and Commonwealth (i.e. A Berriedale-Keith, Ivor Jennings, KC Wheare). More recently, those interested in transnational constitutionalism and legal pluralism have looked at the structures of the EU. But comparisons are rarely made (except perhaps by historians such as Linda Colley). And in not doing so, British legal scholars have missed something interesting. Arguments over the nature of constitutional arrangements – such as whether the British East India Company had sovereignty over parts of India, or whether the British Parliament could legislate for the entirety of the empire, raise interesting comparisons with contemporary discussions over where sovereignty lies in the EU.

[8] L Colley, *Acts of Union and Disunion* (Profile Books, 2014).

Furthermore, debates in the late nineteenth/early twentieth centuries over Irish Home Rule prefigured contemporary debates about Scottish independence. England, Scotland, Wales, and Ireland have a long history together. Questions over the union and how to manage UK unity are hardly new. However, past considerations, such as the early twentieth century exploration of 'Home Rule All Round', are infrequently revisited. The British seem ignorant of their constitutional history.

Britain's past abounds with acts of a constitutional nature across the globe, including constitution-making and managing constitutional transitions. All sorts of relationships between Britain and its overseas territories existed, and many of those territories, such as Australia and Canada, applied federalism while still within the British Empire. In contrast, there was little enthusiasm for federalism within the UK. Indeed, there existed a curiously bifurcated approach to Britain's Constitution. This indicates that the constitutional law applying within Britain was understood as differing from that which applied in Britain's then colonies and overseas territories, although this was never made explicit, and indeed, such a bifurcated approach conflicted with many of Britain's actions in the past. And, although many scholars in those overseas territories have analysed those constitutional relationships in great detail, there has been far less consideration from British theorists as to the impact of Britain's empire on the British Constitution as it applied in the UK.

Instead, commentaries on the British Constitution have often employed an 'exceptionalist' narrative, one that views Britain's uncodified Constitution, and its historical evolution, as unique and unparalleled, but nonetheless a blessing and infinitely preferable to 'foreign' Constitutions. Such a characterization is, however, unfortunate, because it hinders the ability to capture contemporary developments with constitutional language. As Bell noted, the nature of our devolutionary arrangements differs from the UK's 'dominant narrative of constitutional reform as a process that has involved continuity rather than rupture.'[9]

And once we look a little more closely, we see that a dominant narrative of peaceful continuity and exceptionalism is an *English* account that fits less happily with arrangements in other parts of the UK. Northern Ireland has certainly not enjoyed a long, peaceful history of gradually evolving constitutional affairs. Scotland possesses its distinct legal system, a different understanding of unionism, and frequently evokes a distinct constitutional tradition – as expressed in the 1989 Claim of Right and Constitutional Convention, and more recent independence initiatives. In these circumstances, the traditional narrative of unlimited parliamentary sovereignty appears less as a shared constitutional doctrine, and more as a device to manage and suppress other peoples – such as Scots, Irish, Welsh, and in the past, colonists.

****

[9] C Bell, 'Constitutional Transitions: The Peculiarities of the British Constitution and the Politics of Comparison' (2014) PL 458.

Therefore, this book has two main leitmotifs: *constitutional inadequacy* and *constitutional amnesia*. They come together in the phenomenon of Brexit. The remaining ten chapters of this book are divided into two parts. The first part examines five specific case studies, or 'acts of union and disunion'. The second concentrates on five themes of particular relevance to Brexit, alert to the relevance of the historical case studies to these themes. This 'Introduction' provides a summary of some of the main ideas and conclusions explored in these chapters.

This is not a book about Brexit as such, but a book about how the British Constitution has been affected by Brexit, and about how Britain's constitutional past is of relevance to Britain's latest act of disunion, Brexit. There are of course already many works which deal with legal aspects of Brexit, and this book certainly aims to capture the legal, political and constitutional changes of Brexit. However, this book also seeks to derive historical comparisons from Britain's constitutional past and earlier challenges regarding Statehood, sovereignty and territorial boundaries. Academic and disciplinary boundaries within law have been sufficiently solid that there has been little crossover between those working on EU law and those studying the law of the Commonwealth, Empire, Scottish devolution or Irish independence. Yet the challenge of Brexit is that it raises so many questions pertinent to all of these situations. One notable conclusion is that the British were never clear (perhaps deliberately, perhaps not so) as to what they meant by sovereignty. But they have been too willing to enforce this inchoate idea of sovereignty by force and/or unprincipled activity – a response often both damaging to those on the receiving end, and to Britain itself.

PART I: FIVE CASE STUDIES OF ACTS OF UNION AND DISUNION

I examine five case studies which reveal Britain's constitutional contingencies and complexities. Each of these studies examines Britain's role in relation to a wider community (Colonial and Revolutionary North America, Empire, Commonwealth, EU, ECHR) or a smaller one (Scotland, Ireland) in the context of a historically significant act of union or disunion. The point of this exercise is to map and analyse change at critical moments in British constitutional history. A legal-historical excursus enriches our understanding of concepts, compelling us to reconsider the meaning not only of union, sovereignty and differentiation within a broader polity, but also how law can facilitate these.

I often use the term 'Britain' loosely as a collective term for the four disparate nations of Scotland, England, Wales, and (Northern) Ireland, while recognizing that the 'UK', while being the official State in international law, is a more recent designation.

1. Scotland: The union of Scotland and England was the founding act of the UK in 1707, and consensually agreed between two sovereign parties. Scotland was never a colony of England and post-union retained considerable autonomy, including its distinct and separate legal and education systems and Church. As a result of the 1707 union, the UK Parliament (which was not simply the

English Parliament enlarged) came into being. The doctrine of unlimited parliamentary sovereignty is not accepted by everyone in Scotland, where there exists an alternative Scottish tradition of popular sovereignty, and the belief that Scotland's place in the UK union rests on its consent.

Since devolution in 1998, Scotland has developed some progressive constitutional forms, as well as more pro-European inclinations that challenge the unitary constitutional approaches of London. Brexit, however, has placed the UK union under strain, and there have been demands for a second Scottish Independence referendum. Surprisingly, despite the threat of Scottish independence, there has been little debate about what the 'Union' or 'Britain' is or should be.

2. *Ireland:* The legal and constitutional relationship between Ireland and England (and latterly Britain) was unclear for many centuries. Although Ireland enjoyed a good deal of legislative sovereignty under Grattan's Parliament from 1782, the Acts of Union in 1801 set up direct rule from Westminster. During the nineteenth century, there was a campaign and draft legislation for Irish Home Rule (which Dicey, an ardent unionist, vehemently opposed). This campaign is worth reconsidering in the Brexit/Scottish independence context, given the varied legal and constitutional arrangements that were explored and vigorously debated. However, Home Rule never came about, rendered pointless by subsequent events. Since the Belfast/Good Friday Agreement and devolution in 1998, Northern Ireland has a had a variegated but pragmatic settlement of consociation and compromise quite different from the traditional British constitutional settlement. The EU has played its role in the peace process, providing structures for its continuation. Brexit now presents considerable challenges for Northern Ireland and the Republic.

(The situation for Scotland, Northern Ireland, and Wales, especially post-devolution, and with regard to Brexit, is also considered further below in this Introduction).

3. *The US – The Loss of Britain's First Empire:* From 1764 to 1776, the British Empire confronted a political crisis for which there was no constitutional precedent. The issue was parliamentary sovereignty – the authority of the British Parliament over America. The Declaratory Act of 1766 asserted the right of the UK Parliament to legislate for the colonies 'in all cases whatsoever'. Yet, the British case for parliamentary sovereignty was not particularly clear, and eminent English politicians and lawyers, such William Pitt the Elder and Lord Camden, argued that Parliament had no ability to tax the American colonies. By 1774, most American spokesmen argued that Parliament exercised no authority over internal affairs in America. In 1776, the American colonies declared their independence and a war of independence ensued, that Britain lost.

But what could explain this disagreement over sovereignty between Britain and America? Both parties were British subjects, generally reading the same provisions of law. This chapter looks to several factors for explanation. These include the fact of Britain's uncodified Constitution, which ensured that it would be unclear which laws were in any case 'constitutional'. There was also the issue of how the British Constitution applied in the colonies. Did it apply in the same way as in mainland Britain, or was there a separate set of constitutional principles for the British Empire? The dominant view in Britain was that the colonies were a subordinate extension of the British State. In this way, the British Empire was understood as a single State – composed of single people, one Constitution, and one king – and British authority was conflated with parliamentary authority, national sovereignty with parliamentary sovereignty. This view, however, was contested in the colonies, which asserted that only the existence of a shared monarch connected American colonies legally to Britain and to each other. This suggested that colonial assemblies were comparable to Parliament. The 1603 union of the Crowns of Scotland and England was used to support this argument – that a monarch could reign over two countries, each with autonomy and separate parliaments. Indeed, the American constitutional theorist, McIlwain, went so far as to argued that, 'The true constitution of Britain was not unitary, but federal.'[10] There was, however, no acceptance of this in Britain, where the doctrine of undivided and unlimited sovereignty was increasingly employed by those in power.

4. British Empire/Commonwealth[11]*:* Britain at one time ruled over virtually a quarter of the globe's territory and population. Many late nineteenth-century textbooks asserted that Parliament's supreme law-making power applied throughout the empire.

However, the reality of empire undermined that. As Disraeli stated of the empire, 'No Caesar or Charlemagne ever presided over a domain so peculiar.' There was no legal definition of the British Empire and it possessed no explicit constitutional meaning. The constitutional law of the British Empire really was no clearer than it had been for the American colonies in the eighteenth century. For the empire was diverse and incoherent. Terminology was not very clear. The terms 'colony', 'dominion', 'possession' 'plantation', and other expressions were used in different ways at different times. Indeed, an anti-formalist attitude tended to prevail – often eschewing formal law in favour of informal assurances, customs and conventions. There was no attempt to establish a uniform legal code. The empire included 'an extraordinary range of constitutional, diplomatic, political, commercial and cultural relationships'[12] with at least eleven diverse species of government: Crown colonies of rule (including the huge 'sub-empire' of India); settlement colonies (mostly self-governing by the late nineteenth century); protectorates; condominia (like the Sudan); mandates (after 1920); naval and military fortresses (like Gibraltar and Malta);

[10] C McIlwain, 'The Historical Background of Federal Government', in R Pound, *Federalism as a Democratic Process* (1942).

[11] 'Commonwealth' here is used to denote later configurations of the British Empire as applying to self-governing Dominions from the nineteenth century, and not to 'The Commonwealth of Nations' as it now exists.

[12] J Darwin, *The Empire Project: The Rise and Fall of the British World-System, 1830–1970* (Cambridge University Press, 2009) at 1.

'occupations' (like Egypt and Cyprus); treaty-ports and 'concessions' (such as Shanghai, which was the most famous); 'informal' colonies of commercial pre-eminence (like Argentina); 'spheres of interference' like Iran, Afghanistan, and the Persian Gulf; and private trading companies – that is, the East India Company, whose claim to sovereignty over swathes of India was not defeated until well into the nineteenth century. Indeed, as one reviewer noted, 'There is scarcely a constitutional experiment known to modern practice (except, perhaps, the Russian Soviet) which is not to be found in one or other of the Constitutions of the Empire.'[13]

Indeed, it was impossible for Westminster to bind nearly a quarter of the globe with its legislation. The colonies and overseas territories were not represented in Westminster. The situation was not akin to the EU Parliament, in which British citizens had directly elected MEPs, in a Parliament with a co-decision or veto on legislation. The colonies' own legislatures, their own people on the ground, really determined what was going on, except in a few cases. And the sovereignty of the Parliament in London was only one of many types of sovereignty that existed. Much of the British Empire lent itself to a more pluralistic type of sovereignty – one that was divided, shared and indeterminate. Benton and Ford identified a 'middle power' at work in British colonies, which included the judges, magistrates, and commissioners who applied a form of legal governance of the colonies, often very much of their own, creating a vernacular Constitution.[14] What this definitely was not, was the reach of some imperial parliamentary sovereignty. And this meant that the empire lacked unity, and pluralistic tendencies flourished.

Indeed, it was likely that *power* was the only unifying factor underlying the empire, aided no doubt by British naval supremacy, and the fact that, in the nineteenth century, global communications were predominantly in British hands. However, that power could not be derived from a unified, coherent account of legal and political sovereignty. And power by itself lacks legitimacy – it must be validated by something else – which is where sovereignty becomes relevant, in providing that grounding. Yet, the claims of sovereignty made by the empire were often mutually self-contradictory.

5. The EU and ECHR: Dislike of 'eurolegalism' arguably defined a certain type of euroscepticism. In contrast, Britain, with its uncodified Constitution, has sometimes appeared to disdain law. British nonchalance, or indifference to legal rules, is sometimes displayed by those considering Britain's future post-Brexit – that is, expressing the view that trade deals and new arrangements can be made without cumbersome and legally binding treaties. However, this nonchalant stance rests on dangerously inaccurate assumptions and is not backed up by facts. Both the UK's membership of the EU and Brexit were accomplished by law. Furthermore, treaties are essential elements of the international

[13] E Jenks (1938) 20(4) Journal of Comparative Legislation and International Law 304.

[14] L Benton and L Ford, *Rage for Order* (Harvard University Press, 2016).

legal order and if ignored, Britain risks its reputation and future ability to benefit from international agreements.

Some decades ago, Lord Bingham noted that the Common Law was not an isolated island, and that English law had always shown a receptiveness to 'the experience and learning of others', citing as historic examples Pollock, Maitland, and the famous 1772 *Somersett's case* (which held that slavery could not be legally permitted in Britain) in which not only the work of Justinian, Grotius, Puffendorf, and Stair was cited, but also practice in innumerable countries. Lord Bingham expressed the hope that 'the 1990s will be remembered as the time when England – and I emphasise England – ceased to be a legal island, bounded to the north by the Tweed, and joined, or more accurately rejoined, the mainstream of European legal tradition …'[15]

Brexit might appear to have set back that optimism. However, British relations with continental Europe are deep and historical. British lawyers played a very strong role in the creation and founding of the European Convention on Human Rights (ECHR), so the rights of the ECHR (now incorporated in the Human Rights Act) are not alien, foreign devices. Furthermore, Britain was not forced into EEC membership, but joined voluntarily, persisting after its first two applications were rejected by General de Gaulle, because it perceived that it would be socially and economically enriched by such membership – a perception that turned out to be accurate. EU membership also provided an external support system for UK devolution, facilitating common approaches within the UK and conciliation between the UK and Ireland. The EU and ECHR provided external guarantees and entrenchment of human rights, many of which are now at risk post-Brexit.

Seeley suggested that the British built up an empire and then decolonized in a 'fit of absence of mind'.[16] The same may be true of Brexit, where Britain has risked leaving the EU in a state of insouciance as to the consequences.

PART II: FIVE THEMES

These five themes have been selected as of particular salience in Brexit debates. They are also analysed in light of the arguments and conclusions of the five case studies.

6. Sovereignty: Sovereignty is obviously key in the Brexit context, and in many ways lies at the core of this book's argument – a main part of which is that Britain has never been able to justify its assertion of unlimited parliamentary sovereignty. This book endorses the view that the doctrine of parliamentary sovereignty no longer carries the weight that Dicey accorded it, nor should

[15] T Bingham, '"There Is a World Elsewhere": The Changing Perspectives of English Law', in *The Business of Judging* (Oxford University Press, 2000) 87.

[16] J Seeley 'We Seem, as It Were, to Have Conquered and Peopled Half the World in a Fit of Absence of Mind', in *The Expansion of England* (Cambridge University Press, 1883).

it. Indeed, Dicey was himself inconsistent, and, in his energetic opposition to Irish Home Rule, was prepared to depart from the application of parliamentary sovereignty. In 1913, Dicey contended that if Asquith's Home Rule Bill for Ireland were enacted, it 'it would be justifiable to oppose it if necessary by armed rebellion'. If the doctrine of parliamentary sovereignty was compromised even by its greatest exponent, there is all the more reason to recognize its inconsistencies and the folly of adhering to it in all circumstances.

And in any case, Dicey's theory is not watertight historically. Unlimited parliamentary sovereignty does not have such a long pedigree. Although it has some roots in the 1688 Revolution, it became widely accepted only in the eighteenth or even nineteenth century. In 1610, Sir Edward Coke declared the right of common law courts to adjudge an Act of Parliament void, if 'against common right and reason, or repugnant'.

Westminster sovereignty is also territorially challenged. The union between Scotland and England of 1706/7 was actually founded on a treaty and based on consent. It was a union of two Parliaments, and it has been unclear to many Scots why the 'English' doctrine of parliamentary sovereignty should reign supreme. Many Scots of various political persuasions adhere to an indigenous Scottish tradition of popular sovereignty claimed to date back to the 1320 Declaration of Arbroath. Furthermore, Irish legal history reveals that Parliament's authority over Ireland was for centuries unclear. In 1720, the UK Parliament passed a Declaratory Act, asserting complete authority over Ireland, but this was repealed by Grattan's Parliament in 1782, a time when Ireland had considerable legislative freedom and sovereignty. Although Ireland was joined in parliamentary union with Britain (from 1801 to 1922), sovereignty continued to be discussed during debates over three (attempted) Home Rule Bills for Ireland, and when the bulk of Ireland gained independence as the Irish Free State in 1922, vestiges of sovereignty, such as allegiance to the British Crown, and appeals to the judicial Privy Council, were over time eradicated. And of course, as already mentioned, sovereignty in the British Empire was diffuse and indeterminate.

However, it might be argued that EU membership posed the greatest challenge to UK parliamentary sovereignty. Under the European Communities Act (ECA) 1972, the UK Parliament gave effect to the UK's EEC obligations in national law. Section 2(4) ECA required all UK statutes to be read and given effect consistently with EU law, a provision later confirmed as providing national courts with the power to disapply statutory provisions – which challenges the traditional notion of parliamentary sovereignty. Therefore, Britain did not retain *absolute* parliamentary sovereignty during its EU membership, given the ECA. However, it never lost its *external* sovereignty (i.e. what is frequently described as 'national' sovereignty, whereby a country is sovereign and recognized as independent by the international community) as Britain voluntarily joined the EEC, and also voluntarily exited, with Brexit. But Parliament did constrain its own sovereignty through the ECA, and although that Act has now been repealed by Brexit, there is no reason why Parliament should not place further constraints on its own sovereignty in future.

Lastly, parliamentary sovereignty, understood in its absolutist form, enables constitutional abuses, often translating into an application of executive sovereignty. There is, it seems, nothing that a government with a parliamentary majority may not do: abolish human rights legislation, reduce civil liberties, constrict the opportunities for judicial review, even abolish the Scottish and Welsh Parliaments, notwithstanding recent Westminster legislation, which claims for them a 'permanent' status (because, if we take the doctrine of unconstrained Westminster sovereignty at face value, then Parliament could always pass another law, repealing earlier legislation). Dicey himself acknowledged that, 'Parliamentary sovereignty … was an instrument well adapted for the establishment of democratic despotism.' It is time that Britain dispensed with the doctrine of absolute parliamentary sovereignty.

7. Union and Disunion: What impact has the UK's status as a union had on its stance on sovereignty and its approach to acts of union and disunion? What can we learn by comparing the UK to other unions such as the EU, USA or Austria-Hungary? How do unions differ from empires, given that all can be multicultural, multi-ethnic and diverse?

Unions take a variety of forms and it is not always clear what species of legal entity one is dealing with. They need not require a unitary State and may exist along a spectrum of State connectivity, from an affiliation of separate States, through to their complete fusion.

Neither the union of the EU nor of the UK are ancient unions, although the EU is obviously more recent. But the UK itself only dates from 1707. The UK union is voluntary in nature, and (unlike in the case of some Constitutions) there is no legislation prohibiting secession by one part of the UK, nor any constitutional provision asserting and mandating constitutional integrity. This chapter argues that it is preferable to understand the UK as a 'Union State' – that is, a State where the centre does not directly control every part of the territory – rather than unitary in nature, because there are different constitutional arrangements in different parts of the UK. The UK union has been characterized in terms of 'family resemblance', in that it cannot be reduced to one thing which all its parts have in common.[17] Indeed, strictly speaking, the union is not singular but plural – three separate unions, or a 'State of unions'. Whereas the England & Wales union is an incorporating one, constitutionally at least, with Welsh identity taking shape through Welsh culture and language rather than a separate Welsh legal system; the Anglo-Scottish union left key areas within a sphere of Scottish autonomy: and the union with Northern Ireland is different again, having most recently incorporated a form of governance – consociationalism – not

[17] M Keating, 'Written Evidence, House of Lords Constitution Committee', *The Union and Devolution* (2015–2016, HL Paper 149).

to be found elsewhere in the UK. So, an understanding of the union in one part of the UK may not work for its other nations.

What are the factors that tend to prompt disunion? First, disunion very often occurs as the result of war, or serious economic shock. Second, imbalanced unions tend to be weak. This is often so where one territory is much larger than other parts of the union, and/or when there is asymmetry between different parts. Third, a further propulsion towards breakup may be the behaviour of the central government, if it insists on concentrating power in the centre, refusing greater self-government for some of its nations or territories, or favouring one nation over another. Unions tend to do better if they are more elastic and less constraining. But current understandings of UK parliamentary sovereignty make such elasticity very difficult for the UK union. The doctrine of unlimited sovereignty places an almost insurmountable barrier to resolution of issues threatening the union today, particularly those of devolution. It renders federalism challenging, and any recasting of the House of Lords as an effective Chamber of the nations and regions highly problematic.

8. Federalism, Devolution, and Differentiation: Although Britain acknowledges its four 'nations', sub-state autonomy is limited by devolution, which supposedly leaves Westminster parliamentary sovereignty unaffected, constrained only by the ambiguous Sewel convention.

Does devolution permit differentiation? A survey of differentiation in the EU, including partial secession in the case of Greenland, illustrates that differentiated relationships between the EU and parts of States, although rare, are possible. The Scottish Government published its proposals for a differentiated solution for Scotland post Brexit, in *Scotland's Place in Europe*. Nonetheless, the UK Government rejected this approach, instead embracing a unitary and top-down approach. However, the Northern Ireland Brexit Protocol maintains a different regime for Northern Ireland, effectively keeping it in the EU, so there is some inconsistency.

The word 'federal' is not unheard of in the UK. In the late nineteenth/early twentieth century, British Imperial federalists argued the empire must 'federate or disintegrate'. But the imperial federation movement did not succeed. Nor did its close relation, the 'Home Rule All Round' movement for the UK in the early twentieth century. However, the UK faces similar dilemmas today in coping with competing centripetal and centrifugal forces. Devolution transfers power from the centre without relinquishing sovereignty. This distinguishes it from federalism, in which sovereignty is usually divided between a federal centre and various state territories. Post-Brexit, some of those troubled by the UK's constitutional future, who fear the union will shatter, but do not favour independence for the devolveds, have suggested a federal UK.

The main obstacles to federalism in the UK appear to be the 'England problem' and parliamentary sovereignty. It has long been recognized that the disproportionate size of one federal unit can destabilize federalism because it can affect the capacity of other territorial units to influence central government.

However, the main obstacle lies with an insistence on preserving absolute parliamentary sovereignty in the UK. Dicey insisted that 'limited sovereignty' was a 'contradiction in terms' and that federalism was 'absolutely foreign to the historical and, so to speak, instinctive policy of English constitutionalists.'[18] But there is no reason why sovereignty must be understood only as unlimited and indivisible. Dicey was, of course, a thoroughgoing unionist, who argued vigorously against all three Home Rule Bills for Ireland. But we also know that Dicey was willing to compromise his principles on parliamentary sovereignty by proposing a referendum, or even rebellion, to ensure that Home Rule did not become law.

However, post-Brexit, another problem for federalism arises. Even if federalism were somehow to prove practically possible in the UK, it would not address specific post-Brexit challenges, such as the fact that Scotland might wish EU membership. Hard borders separate EU from non-EU members, and a hard border between England and Scotland, for example, could prove difficult to manage in a federal system.

9. Democracy and the rise of the referendum in the UK: The enduring legacy of nineteenth-century constitutionalism hampers the effective realization of democracy in the UK. Bagehot's eulogizing of the fusion of the executive and legislature now appears to grant far too much power to the government, given the context of parliamentary sovereignty and a 'first past the post system' (FPTP) electoral system. There also seems to be a misconception – especially among certain tabloids – that democracy is safeguarded by the government (termed by the Johnson leadership 'The People's Government') which, because it locates its authority in a majority in Parliament, somehow represents the people. Thus, a challenge to government policy can be represented as a challenge to democracy, and those who find the government's conduct unlawful, such as the High Court in *Miller I*, can be represented as 'enemies of the people'.

This is a false and misleading interpretation of democracy, which is a far richer and more complex notion than one which requires merely that power should be exercised by a majority of elected representatives. Democracy also requires that individuals and minorities have certain fundamental protections from majoritarian interests. This is especially so with Britain's FPTP, where legislation prejudicing minority groups (especially groups lacking electoral rights) can be passed by parliamentary votes not even representing a majority of the electorate. The threats to EU citizens after Brexit, or to the Windrush generation, come to mind.

These perversions of democracy have been exacerbated by vagueness as to the role of direct democracy (and how it relates to popular sovereignty) and more specifically, referendums in the UK. The UK Cabinet Manual (which in the absence of a codified Constitution, is the closest the UK comes to a statement of its constitutional principles) does not specify the role of referendums

[18] AV Dicey, *The Law of the Constitution* (Macmillan, 8th ed., 1915) xv.

in British governance, nor suggest that a referendum vote might override other constitutional principles.[19] However, the Brexit referendum, although advisory in status, was nonetheless perceived as binding and implemented. If referendums are to become a more frequent feature of British constitutional practice, there is an urgent need for clear principles regarding their use to be articulated.

Neither popular sovereignty, nor referendums are axiomatic elements of the British Constitution. Yet, referendums have increasingly become popular tools of constitutional management in the UK. It is notable that States that do employ referendums circumscribe them with strict requirements. However, in Britain, belief in unlimited parliamentary sovereignty prevents entrenching such requirements, rendering the British Constitution vulnerable to unprincipled, major constitutional change.

10. Human Rights: Human rights have had a fragile status in Britain, given the overpowering doctrine of parliamentary sovereignty, which has enabled a parliamentary majority to achieve any policy in the absence of entrenched constitutional protections. Plans to repeal the 1998 Human Rights Act are evidence of this. Dicey wrote that parliamentary sovereignty was tempered by the rule of law in the UK, but it is unclear from his work how the rule of law could operate to override the will of a despotic parliamentary majority.

Brexit adds to this precarity, by removing EU human rights protection from UK law (which had something close to an entrenched status, while the UK was an EU member), and that of the EU Charter in particular. This calculated deletion of fundamental rights – involved in the deliberate exclusion of the EU Charter of Fundamental Rights from UK law post-Brexit – is almost unparalleled in the Western world (although perhaps the US Supreme Court's *Dobbs* decision, which removed the protected status of the right to abortion from US constitutional law, comes close, at least for that right).

Much of this book concerns Britain's constitutional history, and its resonances for the issues of UK union, devolution and Britain's relations with Europe. It may be helpful for some readers to briefly summarize this history and development here.

EVOLUTION OF THE UK

The UK introduced devolution in 1998 as a means of according greater autonomy to its constituent nations.[20] Before 1998, the UK was a fairly centralized State, but with some diversity due to its different historical relationships with Scotland, Wales and (Northern) Ireland. Wales had been absorbed into the English legal and administrative system by the sixteenth century (starting with

[19] *The Cabinet Manual: A Guide to the Laws, Conventions and Rules on the Operation of Government* (Cabinet Office, London, 2011).

[20] Namely, Scotland, Wales, and Northern Ireland. But not everyone would agree with the characterization of Northern Ireland as a 'nation'. While many unionists see Northern Ireland

the campaigns of Edward I in the thirteenth century and achieving a complete political union with England under Tudor legislation from 1536 to 1542). Under the Wales and Berwick-on-Tweed Act 1746, law in England was deemed to include Wales.

Scotland was an independent State until 1707 (although there had been a union of the Crowns of England and Scotland from 1603), when it chose to enter into a union with England. Under that union, Scotland retained its separate legal and education systems and Church, and parliamentary sovereignty was simply not mentioned in the Acts of Union of 1706/7. Ireland was different again, having first been subject to constraints and supervision from London, although Parliament's authority over Ireland was contested and for 20 years from 1782, Ireland had considerable legislative sovereignty. However, from 1801, Ireland was in an Act of Union with the UK, until, following a war of independence, the greater part of Ireland in 1922 acquired Dominion status – a constitutional compromise between the British authorities and Irish nationalist rebels who had demanded a complete break from the UK. In 1937, the 1922 Dominion Constitution was replaced by Ireland's existing Constitution. However, Northern Ireland remained in the UK, operating an early form of devolution, until its Parliament, Stormont, was abolished in 1972, and direct rule by Westminster established.

There are also British islands, including the Channel Islands, and the Isle of Man, which have a peculiar almost semi-federal, constitutional status. Jersey and Guernsey (the major Channel Islands) and the Isle of Man are not part of the UK (but nor are they British colonies) but instead Crown Dependencies (which means that the British Crown has ultimate responsibility for them) and each has its own legislature, executive, courts and system of law. Their constitutional relationship with the Westminster Parliament is uncertain and they possess considerable autonomy. They are not part of the Commonwealth of Nations, nor were EU members, although enjoyed distinct trading relationships with it.

In contrast, Gibraltar is a British Overseas Territory (on the southern tip of Spain), not officially part of the UK, self-governing in all matters but foreign affairs (which included the EU), and unlike the Channel Islands and Isle of Man, formerly a member of the EU. Although Gibraltar voted overwhelmingly to remain in the EU in the 2016 Referendum, it was compelled to leave the EU with the UK. Spain has also claimed sovereignty over Gibraltar, although polling revealed this to be against the wishes of the people of Gibraltar.

A note on terminology may also be useful. The 'United Kingdom' denotes the political union between England and Wales, Scotland, and Northern Ireland, and is the official term for the State in international law. 'Great Britain' applies only to Scotland, England and Wales. The 'British Isles' is a geographic

as part of the UK, and thus deny it status as a 'nation', some nationalists desire it to be part of a united Ireland, and also deny it the status of a 'nation'.

term, denoting the islands of Great Britain and Ireland, including the Irish Republic. The people of the Irish Republic are, however, not British, a term which today relates only to the UK, although was used in the past in the context of the British Empire. In this book, 'England' is used only to apply to England and not to include other nations of the UK. Many, notably Bagehot and Dicey, have however used it in this sense.

Devolution

By 1973, the *Kilbrandon Report on the Constitution* suggested that representative institutions be set up in Scotland and Wales.[21] But, due to the addition of a last minute threshold requirement, the 1979 devolution referendums in Scotland and Wales were lost. It took almost another 20 years for devolution to come to Scotland, Wales and Northern Ireland. This resulted in the 1998 Devolution Acts, which consisted of the Scotland Act 1998, the Government of Wales Act 1998, and the Northern Ireland Act 1998, which domestically implemented much of the 1998 Belfast/Good Friday Agreement.

Although initially, these devolution settlements differed from each other, subsequent amendments changed this (although devolution has always operated somewhat differently in Northern Ireland). Perhaps (over-simplifying matters) we might summarize the present situation in the following way. First, each devolved nation has a devolved parliament or assembly with legislative powers, elected on a wholly or partial proportional representation basis, and a devolved government. Second, these legislative powers are limited in number, with certain matters reserved to the Westminster Parliament. Devolved funding is provided largely through the Block Grant, which apportions funds from the UK's Consolidated Fund (the aggregate tax revenue from all four nations) and devolved governments can choose how to spend this according to policy priorities. Changes to the allocation of this funding are calculated by the Barnett Formula, which is based on changes to 'comparable' public services in England. Although most taxes are set by the central government in London, devolved governments also have tax raising powers of their own – so, for example, about 31 per cent of total tax revenue is now devolved to Scotland. Third, there exists no completely autonomous sphere of self-rule within the devolved nations, as UK sovereignty has been preserved in all matters to the UK Parliament. In this way, devolution was crafted to protect parliamentary sovereignty. Nonetheless, the Sewel Convention was generally applied, according to which Westminster 'will not normally legislate with regard to devolved matters' without the consent of the devolved parliaments, and indeed, this convention was written into legislation in the Scotland Act 2016 and Wales Act 2017. Yet, since Brexit, the status of the Sewel convention has become questionable,

[21] Royal Commission on the Constitution 1969–1973, vol. 1 Report, HMSO, London 1973 (Cmnd 5460).

and the lack of devolved parliamentary consent was ignored when major Brexit legislation was passed in Westminster.[22]

However, England, the largest of the four nations, lacks its own Parliament. This was seen as giving rise to the 'West Lothian Question' (named after the West Lothian constituency, whose MP, Tam Dalyell, raised the issue) whereby MPs elected to Westminster from devolved nations could vote on matters in England (such as education) which were devolved competences in Scotland, Wales, and Northern Ireland, and so on which English MPs had no vote for those territories. In 2015, a new procedure for 'English votes for English laws' (EVEL) was introduced by means of changes to the standing orders of the House of Commons. It gave English MPs a veto power over legislation concerning England only and was not a form of devolution to England. It was in any case abandoned in July 2021, and, to date, there has been little demand for English devolution. The problem of how, if at all, England fits within devolution, is sometimes referred to as 'the English question'.

On the one hand, devolution might appear to challenge parliamentary sovereignty. Very generally speaking, a 'reserved powers' model of devolution now operates in Scotland, Wales and Northern Ireland. This means that all legislative power is devolved except those matters expressly reserved to the UK. This resulted in considerable self-rule by devolved institutions. In this respect, UK devolution looked to have given rise to something akin to the 'self-rule' of federalism, with 'quasi sovereign' institutions in its devolved territories.

Yet on the other hand, UK devolution always lacked the 'shared rule' that characterizes federalism. Reserved areas tend to overlap with powers that are often shared under federalism. But, with devolution, all the reserved powers are exercised by London, and relations between the UK government and devolved governments remain almost entirely informal, based on Concordats, memoranda of understanding, and a somewhat dysfunctional Joint Ministerial Committee of executives that rarely met before Brexit. Devolved institutions lack enforceable legal powers in these areas. Even legislative relations between Westminster and the devolved parliaments are regulated by the informal 'Sewel convention' – which, even after its translation into legislation, was nevertheless held by the UK Supreme Court, almost inexplicably, to be nonetheless a mere convention and not legally enforceable.[23] This lack of shared rule means that, for example, devolveds seem to be in a weak situation when it comes to international affairs, including Brexit but also treaties more generally. This absence of shared rule also means that the UK government has over the past few years refused to accept that Scotland might have any power to hold another

[22] The EU Withdrawal Act 2018 was adopted without the legislative consent of Scotland; the EU Withdrawal Agreement Act 2020 adopted without the legislative consent of Scotland, Wales and Northern Ireland. Both the Scottish and Welsh Parliaments refused legislative consent to the Internal Market Act 2020 and EU-UK Future Relationship Act 2020.

[23] *Miller* v. *Secretary of State for Exiting the European Union* [2017] UKSC 5, at [146].

independence referendum, insisting this falls with reserved powers and is for the UK government alone to determine.

All in all, there is something to be said for the term 'Schrodinger's devolution', namely, 'the idea that, since 1999, Scotland, Wales and Northern Ireland both have and have not experienced fundamental constitutional change, on which claims to territorial autonomy can be founded.'[24]

The Problem of Brexit for Devolution

UK devolution took place after the UK joined the EEC (now EU) in 1973, and EU membership insulated devolved nations from a unitary UK wide approach. Keating neatly summarized the situation:

> The UK was, until 2016, evolving as plurinational union in a characteristically British way. There was an increased understanding that it is not a unitary state. The Sewel Convention, while not binding in law, was observed in practice. The system had survived the challenge of a referendum on independence in Scotland without legal order breaking down. The political agenda in Scotland was moving back to social and economic questions. The divisive issue of sovereignty had been put into suspension in Northern Ireland, although a deep division remained between the two communities. The question of England has not been fully addressed but was not pressing.[25]

However, Brexit shook this up, endangering both devolution and the UK union itself. In the referendum on the UK's EU membership, the UK as a whole voted to leave. In contrast, 62 per cent of Scotland's voting electorate, and 56 per cent of those voting in Northern Ireland, voted to remain. Yet, the devolved nations had no formal role in the Article 50 withdrawal proceedings, and thus no means of ensuring that their constitutional interests were protected. Unlike amendments to federal Constitutions, there was no requirement for devolved participation in or consent to this major constitutional change. The devolveds were similarly unable to play any important part in the Brexit negotiations due to the relations with the EU being treated as a foreign policy matter and thus a reserved power for the UK government.

However, although the UK government declared that the UK would leave the EU as one State, the Northern Ireland Protocol complicated things.[26] The prospect of a post-Brexit external border between an EU State (Ireland) and non-EU territory (Northern Ireland) was a fearful reminder of the role that border played in the violent recent past, during 'the Troubles'. There is also a

[24] M Sandford and C Gormley-Heenan, '"Taking Back Control", the UK's Constitutional Narrative and Schrodinger's Devolution', (2020) 73(1) Parliamentary Affairs 110.

[25] M Keating, 'The UK's Evolving Constitution', in *La Evolución de los Modelos Territoriales* (Paloma Requejo, 2018) 177.

[26] Revised Protocol on Ireland and Northern Ireland included in the Withdrawal Agreement, 17 October 2019, TF50 64 (2019).

certain irony in this predicament – in the 2016 EU Referendum, the majority in Northern Ireland voted to remain in the EU, but it was the Brexit-supporting DUP (that supported former UK Prime Minister Theresa May in power from 2017 to 2019) that urged a troublesome hard Brexit, and subsequently became incensed by the inescapable result of that approach.

The Northern Ireland predicament was 'solved' by the Protocol attached to the Withdrawal Agreement agreed between the EU and Boris Johnson's government in 2019, (after Theresa May's earlier solution of the 'Backstop'[27] was rejected). UK (then) Prime Minister, Boris Johnson, deliberately opted to put a border between Great Britain and Northern Ireland rather than take an alternative option of keeping the UK in the EU Customs Union. This led to a fragmentation of the UK's Internal Market, with Northern Ireland applying different rules. Unionists in Northern Ireland became very dissatisfied with the Protocol, and this led to violent incidents. For its part, the EU was not satisfied with the UK's enforcement of the Protocol and started legal action. The situation seems precarious and unsettled, although may be ameliorated if the 2023 'Windsor Framework' on the Protocol is implemented. Yet, there appear no palatable outcomes. A hard border across Ireland would be ruinous for the peace process. The only other resolution would appear to be greater unity for Northern Ireland – either with the UK (by placing a hard border across Ireland) or with the Republic – through a unification referendum under the conditions of the Good Friday Agreement.[28] Either course of action would inflame a sizeable proportion of those in Northern Ireland.

***

Brexit has revealed many flaws in Britain's aged Constitution. Too many of its uncodified rules and conventions are unclear or ambiguous, including many of serious national importance. This book explores these uncertainties, and also why so many of them should be attributed to constitutional inadequacy. But it also looks at the historical roots for Britain's constitutional transformations, which have often been obscured by constitutional amnesia. The conclusion is that, without some sort of new constitutional settlement, both the Constitution, and the union itself, are at risk.

[27] The 'backstop' was an insurance policy that guaranteed no hard Irish border after Brexit by keeping the UK inside a single EU-UK customs territory until a trade deal could be struck with the EU.

[28] s1 Northern Ireland Act 1998 (implementing Belfast/Good Friday Agreement).

Part I

Five Case Studies of Acts of Union and Disunion

1

Scotland

Union and Devolution

The United Kingdom of Great Britain[1] came into being on 1 May 1707 after separate Acts of Union were adopted and given royal assent by both the Scottish and English Parliaments. Therefore, this Union is not an ancient creation, but a construction of just over 300 years.[2] Before that, Scotland and England were independent States. However, the structure and status of the 1707 Union is somewhat ambiguous, not least in legal terms, and the earlier part of this chapter considers its rather elusive nature.

1.1 Background and Context

The 1707 Union was not the first Union achieved between Scotland and England. A Union of Crowns had been in existence since 1603, when James VI of Scotland came to the throne of England on the death of the childless Queen Elizabeth, thus becoming England's first King James.

James was, however, ambitious for closer relations between the two countries, seeking a more formal union of Parliaments as well as of the Crowns, suggesting this as a 'consummation' of a marriage. He even set up a Commission in 1604 to consider a deeper union between the two State but this project failed.[3] The objections came principally (but not only) from the English, who did not want to share their economic benefits with the Scots, and could generally only countenance a subjugation of Scots law to English law. Indeed, James had already delivered a speech to the English Parliament in 1607, lauding the common law of England as 'the best of any Law in the world'.[4] But a union of laws was not acceptable in Scotland. Nonetheless, the idea of further union was in motion, and was supported by Francis Bacon,[5] whose writings were to reappear later in the century, when union was being taken more seriously.

[1] This is how the Articles of Union refer to Britain.

[2] Linda Colley, *Britons: Forging the Nation* (Yale University Press, 1992).

[3] Alain Wijffels, 'A British *ius commune*? A Debate on the Union of the Laws of Scotland and England during the First Years of James VI/I's English Reign' (2002) 6 Edinburgh LR 315.

[4] I James, *The Workes of the Most High and Mighty Prince, James* (London, 1616) 511–514 and 553.

[5] See e.g. Bacon's 1603 memorandum, *A Brief Discourse Touching the Happy Union of the Kingdoms of England and Scotland.*

Under the Union of the Crowns, England and Scotland remained separate kingdoms, each with separate legal systems and political structures. There was virtually no statute law regulating it. What Union there was, came about by Proclamation, an instance of the royal prerogative, such as when James styled himself King of 'Great Britain' rather than of England and Scotland separately.[6] The status of Scots in England and English in Scotland (known as 'postnati') was not settled by any Act of Parliament but by the English courts in *Calvin's case* in 1608,[7] in which Chief Justice Coke ruled that a child born in Scotland, after the King's accession to the English throne, being the King's subject, had the same rights as Englishmen.

Scotland and England retained their own separate courts, legal systems and administrations. However, the King resided in London, rarely if at all visiting Scotland, and this situation favoured English concerns and interests. Nonetheless, the Union of the Crowns managed to function until Charles I alienated the Scots by interfering with the Scottish Church, imposing an Anglican book of common prayer on them. Scots reacted to Charles' attempt to impose religious homogeneity by drawing up a national Covenant in 1638, which reaffirmed the Presbyterian faith. In 1643, the covenanters formed an alliance with the English Parliament, which strengthened the parliamentary side in the Civil War. In fact, Union of Scotland and England subsequently came about from 1652, but it was a Cromwellian one, imposed by conquest, whereby Scotland's Parliament and sovereignty were both extinguished, when Scotland was incorporated by Cromwell into a British republic, the Commonwealth.

Nor was the Restoration under Charles II from 1660 particularly beneficial for Scotland, even although Scotland regained her Parliament, independent statehood and sovereignty. For brevity's sake, we will only note here that the adoption of the English Navigation Acts in 1660, which restricted trade to and from the colonies to *English* ships, provided no exception for Scotland, and thus excluded her from benefits of such trade. The Glorious Revolution of 1688 ousted the Stuart King James VII/II – a convert to Roman Catholicism who had succeeded Charles II – from both countries, replacing him with William of Orange and Mary his wife (and James VII/II's Protestant daughter). A national Convention in Edinburgh voted a Claim of Right[8] of 1689, just as the English Parliament had adopted a Bill of Rights in 1688. Both documents set out a catalogue of abuses committed by James VII/II. However, whereas the English Bill of Rights used the fiction of 'abdication' as justification for offering the throne to William, the Scottish Claim of Right declared that James had by virtue of

6 B Galloway, *The Union of England and Scotland 1603–1608* (Edinburgh: John Donald, 1986) at 20–22 and 60–61.

7 *Calvin's Case*, 6 James I [1608].

8 David Edward ('Scotland's Magna Carta: The Claim of Right and the Common Law' (2015) 6 UK SC Yearbook, 8) also notes that the Claim of Right is 'significantly different from the English Bill of Rights'.

his 'violation of the lawes and liberties of the kingdome', '*forfeited* the right to the crown' (emphasis added). The Claim of Right is considered to reflect the philosophy of sixteenth-century George Buchanan[9] which asserted that all political power derived from the people, and that the monarch is obligated by the conditions under which they assumed the throne. William and Mary, when offered the Crown of Scotland in 1689, were obliged to accept it on the terms of the Claim of Right, including that the monarch's prerogatives be subject to the rule of law.

1.1.1 Constitutional Reasons

Many of the roots of the Acts of Union lay in the constitutional changes of the Glorious Revolution. Scottish historian, McKechnie, endorsed Macaulay's[10] account of how the monarchy's powers were gradually eviscerated by the English Parliament, and of how the King was forced to appoint a ministry to satisfy parliamentarians. Yet, if the King was more constrained by his ministers in London, he was also less able to satisfy his Scottish subjects. Indeed, McKechnie contended that, in the reign of William and Mary, Scotland, 'while still nominally free and independent, was practically in a worse position than any British self-governing colony at the present day.'[11] For unlike colonial dominion parliaments that could call colonial governments to account, this was not the case with pre-1707 Scotland, which was largely governed from London. Even where the Scottish Privy Council itself exercised governing powers, it had little responsibility to the Scottish Parliament.

Nonetheless, the Scottish Parliament also began to show its weight, and in 1690 abolished the 'Lords of the Articles'. This was a committee of the Scottish Parliament, appointed by the King and under executive control, with prime responsibility for framing and initiating legislation. Its abolition thus removed a dominant executive control over Scottish legislation.

1.1.2 Famine, Betrayal, Darien, and the Succession

However, factors other than constitutional changes were also relevant. The 1690s were hard years in Scotland. Catastrophic harvest failures caused widespread famine. There were other ruinous events. The Scottish Darien venture of 1699–1701, an attempt to find a trading settlement in Darien, at the isthmus of Panama, proved a complete failure, beset by financial mismanagement and tropical disease. There was a huge loss of life and perhaps as much as

[9] Buchanan's *De Jure Regni apud Scotos* 1579 was considered so dangerous that it was burned by Oxford University in 1683.

[10] TB Macaulay, *The History of England from the Accession of James II, vol iii*, (Cambridge Library collection, first published 1849).

[11] The 'present day' being 1907 when McKechnie wrote the article; W McKechnie, 'The Constitutional Necessity for the Union of 1707' (1907) 5 Scottish Historical Review 56.

one quarter of Scotland's wealth was lost in this venture.[12] However, it could not escape notice that the Darien company had received no help from King William, who in 1699 issued a proclamation banning English subjects from dealing with the Darien colony in any way. Whatever the causes of the Darien calamity, it was perceived by many Scots as exacerbated by the shortcomings of the Union of the Crowns, whereby the King would place English concerns ahead of Scottish ones.

More generally, Scottish trade was not flourishing under the Union of the Crowns. There was very little free trade between England and Scotland, and the Navigation Acts were enforced against the Scots, leaving only an illicit trade with American colonies. Debate continues[13] whether economics sparked Scotland's desire for union, but there was clearly a hope in Scotland for an opening of English markets to them.

Trade was not the only thorny problem, however. There was also the issue of succession to the throne. England and Scotland shared a common monarch and Anne, Mary's (Protestant) younger sister and daughter of James VII/II, had failed to produce an heir. The fear was that, on Anne's death, the throne might devolve to the Catholic son of deposed James VII/II (by his second marriage), thus putting the Protestant line at risk. So, in 1700, the English Parliament adopted the Act of Settlement,[14] whereby, should Anne die without heir, then her successor would not be Catholic James or his son – 'the Old Pretender' – but the next Protestant in line, Sophia Electress of Hannover (or her heirs), who was then the elderly grandchild of James VI by his daughter Elizabeth. This English Act of Settlement had no force in Scotland, nor were the Scots consulted about it. However, when Scotland failed to act similarly and define a successor, the English feared a possible succession in Scotland of the 'Old Pretender', aided by French support (England was at war with France in the 1690s and 1700s). This, as much as anything, turned English minds in favour of a greater union in Scotland, as a means to secure a Hanoverian succession.

The Jacobite cause in Scotland, however, was complicated. Both James VII/II and his son were Catholic. Scotland was heavily Presbyterian. But Jacobite support, while threatening the Protestant ascendancy, did not derive only from Catholics. It was also supported by Episcopalians (part of the Anglican Communion), who had been alienated by both the establishment of radical Presbyterianism in Scotland, and by the abolition of bishops there. Jacobitism also had an undoubtedly romantic element, benefiting from the fable of 'the lost cause', the notion that 'the king shall enjoy his own again'.[15]

[12] See Douglas Watt, *The Price of Scotland: Darien, Union and the Wealth of Nations* (Edinburgh: Luath Press, 2007).

[13] TC Smout, *Scottish Trade on the Eve of the Union, 1660–1707* (Edinburgh: Edinburgh University Press, 1963); CA Whatley with D Patrick, *The Scots and the Union* (Edinburgh: Edinburgh University Press, 2006) 11.

[14] Act of Settlement 1700, 13 Will 3.

[15] A traditional ballad, originally a Cavalier song from the English Civil War, that became a popular Jacobite song.

Another attempt was made at union between the two nations in 1702 but nothing came of it. So, the succession was still a problem, and the English began to realize that, in order to settle that issue, some sweetener must be offered Scotland, most likely admitting Scots into England's trading system.

1.1.3 Legislation of the Scottish Parliament in 1703 and 1704

But relations were to get worse before union could be achieved. Some provocative legislation took place on both sides of the border, which helps explain the direction Union ultimately took. In 1703, the Scottish Parliament adopted *An Act anent* [concerning] *Peace and War.* This asserted the Scottish Parliament's right to declare war and make peace, abolishing the monarch's royal prerogative in this area, ensuring Scotland would not be forced into foreign wars on England's account. In effect, it was a move towards a more federal model of organization.

In 1704, the Scottish Parliament then adopted an *Act of Security for the Kingdom,*[16] asserting Scotland's right to determine succession to the Scottish Crown. This Act mandated that the Claim of Right be read to any new monarch before administration of the coronation oath (and also provided that free trade between England and Scotland was a condition of Scotland agreeing any Hanoverian succession). Without agreeing these limitations, any succeeding monarch might forfeit the Crown. Much influence on this Act is attributed to Andrew Fletcher of Saltoun,[17] now revered as a Scottish patriot. Nonetheless, the Queen (somewhat reluctantly) gave her royal assent to the Act, although the clause on free trade was omitted (although had been approved by the Scottish Parliament).

The Scottish Parliament also passed the Wine and Wool Acts, in 1704. The Wine Act permitted trade with France during the war (between England and France) and the Wool Act permitted the export of wool from Scotland but not its import. Both were seen by the English as hostile legislation. And, in the meantime, Scotland had not agreed the Hanoverian succession. Perhaps, relations between Scotland and England reached their lowest point in 1705, when an English ship, the *Worcester*, was seized in Leith on charges of piracy of a Darien ship, and its captain and two of its crew, were publicly executed in Leith, although quite possibly innocent.

1.1.4 The English 'Aliens Act'

It was felt that these aggressive (to English eyes) Scottish statutes needed some response. In 1705, Westminster legislated an *Act for the effectual securing of the Kingdom of England from the apparent dangers that might arise from several*

[16] Act of Security, Parl. Scot., xi, 1

[17] See A Fletcher, *Account of a Conversation Concerning the Right Regulation of Government* (Edinburgh, 1703).

acts lately passed by the Parliament of Scotland (aka 'Aliens Act'). This Bill in its Preamble called for 'a nearer and more complete union'. But it also contained a threatening follow up, warning that, if Scotland had not appointed commissioners, or accepted the Hanoverian succession, by Christmas Day 1705, then it would suffer severe economic penalties, and Scots in England (unless domiciled there) would be treated as aliens. Notably, this threat, that Scots might be declared aliens in England, conflicted with *Calvin's case*. According to Devine, this Act was 'a naked piece of economic blackmail'.[18]

However, by 1705, a treaty of Union was becoming a more attractive prospect to Scotland, (mainly due to perceived economic benefits rather than agreement on Hanoverian succession). And thus, the Scots agreed to start negotiations, and the threatening sections in the Aliens Act were repealed.

1.2 Negotiating and Drafting the Articles and Acts of Union

The Union of 1707 took place against a background of European war, economic crisis, and worries over the succession. Devine describes the 1707 union as 'a marriage of convenience founded on pragmatism, realpolitik, competing national patriotisms.'[19] But the parties achieved two major goals – for the 2nd Article of Union secured the British Union on the Hanoverian succession, and the 4th Article provided Scots with freedom of trade with England and its colonies.

The process started, however, with the surprising 1705 motion in the Scottish Parliament that Queen Anne select the thirty-one commissioners to represent Scotland in negotiations for Union. This ensured the likeliness of their approving a treaty according to the English goal of incorporating Scotland and unifying the two Parliaments. Why this motion was approved is unclear, although some suggest that the Duke of Hamilton, a Jacobite and leader of the anti-unionist cause in the Scottish Parliament, was bribed by the English.[20] George Lockhart of Carnwarth, a Jacobite, and thus a somewhat isolated Scottish commissioner in 1706, later dated Scotland's 'ruine' from this point.[21] In February 1706, Anne named thirty-one commissioners for Scotland, nearly all in favour of union and allies of Lord Queensberry (a major 'court' or royalist, in the Edinburgh Parliament, who was to steer through the Act of Union there). In April 1706, the thirty-one English commissioners were appointed, mostly Whigs intent on securing a Hanoverian succession, Lord Godolphin (English Treasurer, credited with steering the Act of Union through Westminster) prominent among them. Daniel Defoe was sent to Edinburgh as an agent and generally promoted the unionist cause, publishing

[18] T Devine, *Independence or Union: Scotland's Past and Scotland's Present* (Penguin, 2017) at 19.
[19] Devine, *Independence or Union*, 3.
[20] M Fry, *The Union: England, Scotland and the Treaty of 1707* (Birlinn, 2013) 179.
[21] D Szechi (ed.), *'Scotland's Ruine:' Lockhart of Carnwath's Memoirs of the Union* (Aberdeen: Association for Scottish Literary Studies, 1995) 172.

The History of the Union of Great Britain in 1709, 10 years before *Robinson Crusoe*, for which he is now more widely known.

A procedure for the negotiations was agreed, whereby Scottish and English commissioners debated separately, maintaining secrecy and communicating only in writing. If necessary, all commissioners could meet around an enormous table in the Westminster 'cockpit.' The session began on 22 April 1706.

1.2.1 Main Points of Negotiation

1.2.1.1 A United British Kingdom (Articles I–III)

A federal union was initially proposed by the Scottish commissioners. This had already been mooted in Scotland (i.e. by William Seton of Pitmeddon in the Scottish Parliament) although in the early eighteenth century there was no great precision in the use of this term. However, there was no appetite for a federal union in England, where federalism was seen as perpetuating weak and divisive government. The English instead focussed on an 'incorporating' union, unifying the Parliaments, coupled with securing the succession. And this was what was ultimately achieved (in Articles I–III Articles of Union.)

1.2.1.2 Trade (Article IV)

The Scottish commissioners insisted on free trade, not only with England, but with all its colonies, and also the protection of the Navigation Acts. Article IV settled this. Perhaps one of the most significant clauses in the Union treaty was that abolishing internal customs barriers, given that such barriers were retained by other European countries until much later (Austria until 1775 and France until 1790).[22] The British Government in London, and Westminster Parliament, would in future regulate trade.

1.2.1.3 'The Equivalent' (Article XV)

Finance was an issue. The burden of tax was higher in England, which had imposed additional taxes to fund its European wars, but also collected its taxes more effectively than Scotland. A homogenized system under Union would therefore raise Scotland's tax burden. To render this more bearable, commissioners agreed that a sum known as the 'Equivalent' would be transferred to Scotland to compensate for financial loss caused by Union. Opinions on the 'Equivalent' differ, but it was described by Lockhart as a 'mighty bait, a swingeing bribe'.[23]

1.2.1.4 Preservation of Distinct Legal Systems (Articles XVIII–XX)

James VI/I had suggested a Union whereby the English common law might replace the Scottish legal system. This was not on the table now. The two

[22] Colley, *Britons*, 38.

[23] G. Lockhart, *Letters of George Lockhart of Carnwath 1698-1732* (printed for Scottish History Society, 1989) volume I.

countries possessed, and continue to possess, distinct systems of law. Whereas the English 'common law' was largely precedent based, Scots law was notably influenced by Roman law, and much of it organized in the 1681 *Institutes* of Lord Stair (President of the Scottish Court of Session). Scots law also drew a distinction between public and private right – a distinction preserved under Union, with Scottish public law much more amenable to change by the Great Britain Parliament than private law.

In general, Scottish laws, with the exception of those on trade and customs, would remain in force, unless contrary to the Union treaty. Additionally, English courts were barred from reviewing decisions of the Scottish courts. However, this last stipulation was ambiguous, in that it omitted to rule out any appeal from the Court of Session to the House of Lords. And indeed, such a right did in fact develop within a few years of Union.

1.2.1.5 Parliamentary Representation (Article XXII)

This presented the commissioners with a knotty problem. How could an integration of parliaments be achieved between two nations so disparate and unequal in nature? How many Scots should sit in the Westminster Parliament? Should the composition of this Parliament for Great Britain be determined anew, or should Westminster simply absorb new Scottish members? This issue motivated the only joint session of commissioners, on 12 June 1706.

The English opening proposal was very low – it would have added only 13 Scots to the existing 513 English MPs in Westminster. Eventually a compromise was reached, with a total of 45 Scottish MPs to be added to the House of Commons and 16 Scottish peers to the House of Lords. In this way, the total of Scottish constituencies was reduced by 2/3 and 90 per cent of Scottish nobleman were excluded from Westminster. English representation in both Houses was left untouched.

1.2.1.6 Agreement

A final draft of the Articles of Union was adopted on 22 July 1706, only three months after negotiations had opened – very speedy for what in effect has been described as 'a Constitution' for a new State.[24] The draft was signed by all commissioners with the exception of Lockhart, for Scotland, and the Archbishop of York, for England. Notably, however, nothing had been agreed at this stage about the Scottish Kirk or Church, and we will return to this. But what had been achieved was a framework document that would effectuate the existence of a new State, the United Kingdom of Great Britain.

But the agreed Articles left many questions unanswered. The nature of this united Parliament had not been set out in the Articles (was it sovereign?), nor indeed the legal nature of the United Kingdom of Great Britain itself. Was it

[24] N MacCormick, 'Does the United Kingdom Have a Constitution? (1978) 29 N. Ir. Legal Q. 1.

truly an 'incorporating' union, and if so, what did that mean? These questions will be considered below.

1.2.2 Ratification

The draft Articles might have been adopted by the commissioners, but until they had been ratified by both Parliaments, there could be no Union. The process of ratification began in the Scottish Parliament, which was seen as presenting the greater obstacle. Notably, however, a text of the Bill was only provided to that Parliament in October 1707, leaving no time for scrutiny before the session began. It has been said by historians that there was much opposition to Union in Scotland generally.[25] There is also the suggestion that bribery played its part in Scottish ratification – with nobles 'bought and sold with English gold' as the Burns poem recites.[26] Nonetheless, several amendments were achieved by the Scottish Parliament, not the least important concerning the Presbyterian kirk.

1.2.2.1 Act of Security for the Kirk

Notably, the Presbyterian Kirk had been excluded from the text of the Articles of Union. This did not satisfy Scots, and quite possibly Union might never have been achieved if it had not provided security for the kirk – Dicey and Rait certainly expressed this view.[27] The kirk occupied a singularly important place in Scotland. But by 1706, the Presbyterian church in Scotland felt under threat from a prospective Jacobite restoration. Although Union might seem attractive to Presbyterians because of England's Protestant church, it was felt that the Church of England and secular State were too interfused, with bishops sitting in the House of Lords, and the monarch as Head of the Church. In contrast, the Presbyterian church, although it is the national Church of Scotland, is not established and there are no bishops. Scotland adhered to a constitutional doctrine of two swords, one wielded by the State, and the other by the kirk, with ultimate supremacy vested in neither.[28] Indeed, the Scottish Parliament had in the 1690s guaranteed Presbyterian governance of the Church, giving the Church of Scotland the ability to adopt its own legal Acts.

Reverend William Carstares,[29] moderator of the Church of Scotland in 1706, pushed the case for an Act of Security for the Kirk, in order to guarantee its

[25] E.g. Fry, *The Union*, chapters 5 & 6; Devine, *Independence or Union*, chapters 1–3.

[26] Robert Burns' 1791 poem *Such a Parcel of Rogues in a Nation.*

[27] AV Dicey and RS Rait, *Thoughts on the Union between England and Scotland* (London, 1920) 247, 252–254.

[28] See G Cowie, 'Establishment, Schism and the Kirk: Assessing the Relationship between Scots Law and the Presbyterian Churches in Scotland', LLB dissertation at https://glasgow.academia.edu/GraemeCowie; and DM Walker, *A Legal History of Scotland* (Edinburgh: T&T Clark, 1995) iii at 248. This concept of the two swords, representing two kingdoms, one spiritual, one temporal, was earlier expressed in the papal bull of Pope Boniface VIII in 1302: the *Unam Sanctam.*

[29] Fry: 'no man did more to make Edinburgh a cradle of the Enlightenment' (Fry, *The Union*, 238).

status. And so, an 'Act for Securing the Protestant Religion and Presbyterian Church Government in Scotland' was adopted by the Scottish Parliament in January 1707. This Act was incorporated into the Acts of the Scottish and English Parliaments by which the Treaty of Union was ratified. A similar Act securing the status of the Church of England was adopted for England.[30]

Therefore, two independent churches were to be secured in one State. This was undoubtedly unusual in the Europe of its time, in which Statehood was linked to religious identity. Admittedly both churches were Protestant, which has been identified as a unifying feature of British identity.[31] However, Fry describes 'a sort of creeping federalism in having two different rival Churches', suggesting this as one reason 'why Union never produced one nation'.[32] Perpetual security for the Kirk also appeared to be drafted as a fundamental provision of Union legislation: to 'be held and observed in all time comeing as a fundamental and essential condition of any Treaty or Union to be concluded betwixt the two Kingdoms without any alteration thereof or derogation thereto in any sort forever'. And so, although the Scottish Parliament was to end, the role of the Church of Scotland's General Assembly was intended to continue forever, and to operate as a constitutional check or balance.

1.2.2.2 Ratification

Aside from provision for security of the Scottish Kirk, the other Articles of Union had to be ratified by the Scottish Parliament. Article IV on trade was easily passed, but other provisions proved more contentious. Regarding Article III, on the Union of Parliaments, Andrew Fletcher had queried how Scottish interests might be protected when Scottish representatives were to be such a small minority in Westminster. Hamilton (who proved so weak in advocating the antiunion cause) had argued that Scottish MPs at Westminster should be able to exercise a veto on matters fundamental to Union, but this came to nothing, with the pro-unionist, governing party returning that there must simply be trust in the English, as there was no possibility of a Scottish veto.[33]

And with that, the Scottish Parliament adopted the *Act Ratifying and Approving the Treaty of Union of the Two Kingdoms of Scotland and England*.[34] After the Scottish Parliament had legislated, the matter came before the English Parliament, where legislation for an Act of Union was quickly adopted,[35] and all Scots amendments accepted.

[30] 'An Act for securing the Church of England as by Law established' (The Act of 6 Anne 1706).

[31] Colley, *Britons*, chapter 1. [32] Fry, *The Union*, chapter 6.

[33] See e.g. Sir John Clerk of Penicuik, *History of the Union of Scotland and England*, D Duncan (ed.) (Edinburgh, 1993).

[34] Union with England Act 1706, APS XI, 406, c 7.

[35] Union with Scotland Act 1706, c. 11 (Regnal. 6_Ann).

1.2.3 Why Did Scotland Agree to Union?

How did it happen that the independent Scottish Parliament of 1703 voted itself out of existence three years later by a clear majority?[36] Indeed, in the autumn of 1706, when debates began in the Scottish Parliament over ratification, there was still so much rioting and opposition to Union that the Marquess of Queensberry, steering the debates for the Scottish Government, had needed a military escort to Parliament House.

One reason why opposition to Union failed is that it was ill-organized and disunited, encompassing both Jacobite members, and also Presbyterians such as Andrew Fletcher, who inclined to republicanism, and certainly did not want the return of a Catholic Stuart. They could not agree over the succession. Economic matters were also pressing, and, according to McKechnie, 'The status quo had become intolerable, and the only question at the commencement of Queen Anne's reign was as to the form the inevitable change should take.'[37]

Indeed, there seemed little alternative to union. Sir Alexander Seton of Pitmedden, a Lord Justiciary and commissioner, in a well-known speech of 1706, had considered possible alternatives: 'That we continue under the same sovereign with England, with limitations on his prerogative as king of Scotland; that the two kingdoms be incorporated into one; or that they be entirely separated'.[38]

Seton's first alternative – that both countries continue but with limitations on the sovereign's prerogative (as countenanced in the Scottish Act of Security) – would in effect have been a 'divided sovereignty', whereby a central authority in London could not dictate terms to Scotland. But would it have been possible to agree such an arrangement? It was the Scottish Act of Security, which contained such limitations, which had after all worried the English and led to the Aliens Act. Seton's third alternative of a complete separation also carried risks. Continued Jacobite activity, with French support, was not something the English were happy to contemplate. A failure to agree the Hanoverian succession looked likely to provoke war a 'war of the British succession' with England. The possible outcome would have been conquest of Scotland by England, or a very unfavourable forced union.

Not all agree that the 1707 union was inevitable, but counterfactual history is a hard business (and perhaps not best adopted by lawyers). In Scotland the last word fell to Chancellor Seafield: *'now there's ane end of ane auld sang'*.[39]

[36] Devine, *Independence or Union*, 20.
[37] McKechnie, 'The Constitutional Necessity for the Union of 1707', 60.
[38] Quoted in Daniel Defoe, *A History of the Union between England and Scotland* (London, 1786) 232.
[39] Quoted e.g. in R Watson, *The Literature of Scotland* (Macmillan, 2006) at 161.

1.3 Legal Effect

> Pierre Trudeau … said that for Canada to share a continent with the United States was like a man having to share a bed with an elephant.[40]

1.3.1 Introduction

The meaning, effects and consequences of that Union, most particularly the legal ones, now fall to be considered.

This new Union of 1707 was a complex arrangement. Neil MacCormick[41] usefully summarized the Articles of Union. *Firstly*, provisions setting out what was common to the whole of Great Britain, which included the Crown, the flag, the Executive and the bicameral Westminster Parliament. The Union would encompass a single market, customs union (the largest then in existence) and common currency. *Secondly*, equally important is what would remain separate. There would continue to be separate and distinct legal systems and national churches, as well as civic institutions and local government. Unless incompatible with Union, all pre-existing Scots law would remain, although the Great Britain Parliament could amend Scots law in future. However, the Parliament would, under Article XVIII, have no capacity to amend those Scots laws concerning private right 'except for evident utility of the subjects within Scotland'. *Thirdly*, there were transitional provisions, including those implementing a new tax regime for Scotland, as well as those compensating Scotland for incurring some of the English national debt. And *finally*, Article XXV underlined the fundamental status and supremacy of the Articles of the new Union: 'That all Laws and Statutes in either Kingdom so far as they are contrary to or inconsistent with the Terms of these Articles or any of them shall from and after the Union cease and become void.'[42]

1.3.2 How Best to Define the Anglo-Scottish *Union*?

Walker described it as 'complicated', and for Colin Kidd it is 'a somewhat mysterious entity'.[43] Three distinct questions arise. First, by what legal documents was the Union constituted; second, what was the status of this Union; and third, should it be referred to as a *Treaty* or *Acts* of Union?

[40] Quoted in, e.g., Paul Henderson Scott, *Still in Bed with an Elephant* (Saltire, 1998) at 1.

[41] N MacCormick, *The English Constitution, the British State, and the Scottish Anomaly* (British Academy Lecture, 1997).

[42] This might appear to be an attempt at entrenchment – see further below.

[43] D Walker, 'The Union and the Law' (2007) Journal of the Law Society of Scotland; Colin Kidd, *The Union and the Constitution* (History and Policy Papers, September 2012).

1.3.2.1 By What Legal Documents Was the Union Constituted?

Properly speaking, the Union agreement comprises three distinct documents:

1. The Articles (or Treaty) of Union agreed between Commissioners appointed to negotiate the Union
2. The Union with England Act 1707 passed by the Scottish Parliament *and*
3. The Union with Scotland Act 1706 passed by the English Parliament.[44]

But there is disagreement among lawyers as to whether it was the Articles of Union, or Acts of Parliament, that defined the Union. This will be further considered below.

1.3.2.2 What Was the Status of the Union?

Was the Union a merger, or completely new State? Dicey[45] stressed that this was an 'incorporating' union, arguing that, although a new State had in name been created, what in substance took place was the absorption of the smaller (Scotland) into the larger (England). However, Scottish legal academic, TB Smith, argued that what occurred was in fact the incorporation of two existing States into a third which had no prior existence – an unusual occurrence.[46] However, this raises an interesting question. What would happen if Scotland were to become independent? Would Great Britain thereby cease to exist? This issue was raised in the run up to the Scottish independence referendum in 2014 and most, but not all, commentators agreed that England and Wales would still constitute the state of Great Britain.[47]

1.3.2.3 International Aspects of Union

This leads to the third question. Should we refer to the Union as the Treaty of Union, rather than the Act or Acts of Union? For there to be a treaty, there must be an international agreement between sovereign powers. This does seem to have been the case. Prior to Union, both England and Scotland were independent, sovereign States. The agreement satisfied international law requirements for a treaty.[48] Both Parliaments purported to have ratified a 'treaty.'[49]

[44] The dates are a bit confusing. The Scottish Act of Union preceded the English one, but is dated 1707, because the two countries were using different calendars.

[45] AV Dicey and RS Rait, *Thoughts on the Union between England and Scotland* (London, 1920).

[46] TB Smith, 'The Union of 1707 as Fundamental Law' [1957] Public Law 99; also E Wicks, 'A New Constitution for a New State? The 1707 Union of England and Scotland', (2001) LQR 117, 109–126.

[47] See A Boyle and J Cameron, *Annex A: Opinion: Referendum on the Independence of Scotland – International Law Aspects Part IV* (Scotland Analysis, UK Government, 2013).

[48] See now Vienna Convention 1969, Article 2(1)(a); also Lord McNair, *Law of Treaties* (Oxford University Press, 1961) 40.

[49] See Defoe's description of Queen Anne twice visiting the negotiations and enquiring after the progress of 'the Treaty' (*History of the Union* (1709), Part 2, at 47).

The Articles themselves refer to 'this Treaty', and 'Article' is the technical term for a provision in a treaty, rather than 'section' which is used in statutes. However, although Smith concluded there had been a treaty, he believed that such treaty as an obligation *jure gentium* subsisted only until May 1, 1707, when 'by merger the parties to the treaty ceased to exist.'[50] And, thereafter, for Smith, a new State came into being. For Walker, the Union was an agreement made in 1706–1707, not by the Parliaments, but by the commissioners. On the other hand, Mitchell considered only the two Acts of Parliament to be determinative because 'not merely were the Articles of Union amended, but those Articles were of no effect unless absorbed in this legislative compact.'[51]

1.3.2.4 The Status of the Union

In summarizing this short survey of diverse views, one might describe the Union as an aggregate of the Articles of Association, both Acts of Union (and the incorporated Acts for the Security of the Church of Scotland and Church of England). We could accurately state that a treaty on union was signed and ratified, although the situation thereafter becomes complex because the two independent signing States ceased to exist when the Union came into existence. But it has to be acknowledged that this is not a very promising beginning – the legal status of the Union between Scotland and England is somewhat mysterious and unclear.

1.3.3 A Revolution, by Consent or Not?

According to Smith, 'the British Parliament was the creation of the terms of Union – by what was in effect a revolution by consent.'[52] What might this mean, and was there really a revolution (whether by consent or other means) in 1707?

In common parlance, we might understand a revolution as a fundamental change in political organization, encompassing the overthrow, or renunciation, of one government or ruler and the substitution of another.[53] The Union of 1707 certainly appears outside the usual course of legal events because it terminated the existence of two independent States, thus occasioning a decisive break with the past. But was this a revolution? The problem is that its lead up does not look revolutionary. The Union had been provided for by law, from the provisions for the parliamentary commissioners negotiating the Articles of Union, to the Acts of Union that ratified those Articles.

According to Kelsen, a legal order will be revolutionary if its Constitution cannot be derived from, or authorized by, the previous legal order. However, because the United Kingdom of Great Britain was brought into being by

50 Smith, 'The Union of 1707 as Fundamental Law', 99.
51 JDB Mitchell, *Constitutional Law* (2nd ed., 1968) at 72.
52 Smith, 'The Union of 1707 as Fundamental Law', 99, 111.
53 *Merriam-Webster* online dictionary.

two quite separate sets of legal acts –both of Scotland and England – there is, in Kelsonian terms, no 'single chain of validity' to 'a historically first Constitution'.[54] But in that case, there was a fresh start, the creation of a new State of Great Britain, even if not a forcible overthrow of the old regimes, then at least a 'revolution by consent', as characterized by Smith. And in Kelsonian terms, it would mean that the historically first Constitution of Great Britain was indeed that established by the Anglo-Scottish Treaty and Acts of Union of 1707. And indeed, according to de Smith, the Articles of Union 'provided a rudimentary framework of a written constitution.'[55]

1.3.4 Are (Some of) the Articles/Acts of Union 'Fundamental' in Status?

Are some provisions fundamental law, that is possessing some sort of entrenched status, making them hard to override? Certainly, it has been argued that Parliament was 'born unfree', created and bound by a higher law (namely provisions of Union).[56]

Parliamentary sovereignty has overshadowed discussions of British constitutional law, but, in the early eighteenth century, the concept of a 'fundamental law' was not unheard of.[57] The words of Union legislation itself suggest that at least some of it was intended to be 'fundamental'. Provisions of the Acts securing the Protestant religion are expressed as 'a fundamentall and essentiall Condition of the said Treaty or Union', and, together with the Articles of Union themselves ordained 'to be and continue in all time coming the sure and perpetuall foundation of ane compleat and intire Union.' Even Dicey had to acknowledge that, 'The legislators who passed these Acts assuredly intended to give to certain provisions of them more than the ordinary effect of statutes.'[58] Moreover, in *MacCormick*, the Lord Advocate, defending the UK Government's case, conceded that Parliament had no lawful power to amend or repeal fundamental terms of the Union, such as those protecting Scotland's independent legal system[59] – quite a concession to make.

[54] H Kelsen, *General Theory of Law and State* (tr. A. Wedberg, 1945).

[55] De Smith, *Constitutional and Administrative Law* (2nd ed., 1973) at 74. But see Wicks, 'A New Constitution for a New State?', at 117, who argues that they are not sufficiently detailed to form a Constitution.

[56] JDB Mitchell, *Constitutional Law* (2nd ed., 1968) 69. See further, on the fundamental status of some Articles: Smith, 'The Union of 1707 as Fundamental Law', 99; N MacCormick, 'Does the United Kingdom Have a Constitution?' (1978) 29 NILQ 1; M Upton, 'Marriage Vows of the Elephant: The Constitution of 1707' (1989) 105 LQR 79; A O'Neill, 'A Tale of Two Constitutions' (1997) 26 SLT 205; JD Ford, 'The Legal Provisions in the Acts of Union' (2007) 66 CLJ 140. Defoe, *History of the Union*, pt 2, 73–74, 246.

[57] On use of 'fundamental law' in Scotland, see J Goodare, *State and Society in Early Modern Scotland* (Oxford, 1999) 19–22; For England, see J Gough, *Fundamental Law in English Constitutional History* (1961); also Robert Wylie, *A Letter Concerning the Union, with Sir George Mackenzie's Observations and Sir John Nisbet's Opinion upon the Same Subject* (1706).

[58] A-V Dicey, *The Law of the Constitution* (Macmillan, 9th ed., 1950) 88–91.

[59] *MacCormick* v. *Lord Advocate* 1953 SC 396, at 411.

1.3.4.1 Have Provisions in Practice Been Treated as Fundamental?

Nonetheless, there is disagreement over how much of the Union agreement has been violated or repealed. Legislation was adopted post-Union early in the early eighteenth century, namely the 1708 Treason Act, 1711 Toleration Act, 1711 Patronage Act and 1713 Malt Tax Act, all of which allegedly violated the terms of Union.[60] At one end of the spectrum of opinions is Munro, who claims that 'almost all of the articles and sections of the legislation have been repealed in whole or in part.[61] This may seem an extreme claim, but undoubtedly those provisions which required professors of Scottish universities to be recognized Presbyterians (Article XXV) were repealed by the Universities (Scotland) Acts 1853 and 1932. However, Middleton argued that just because Parliament had repealed provisions of Union it did that follow that Parliament had the legal power to do so. Smith on the other hand argued this as an example of reform by consent. And it is the case that, under international law, consent to a breach of a treaty allows the treaty to remain in force.[62] At the other end is Mitchell who argues that it is 'doubtful if there has as yet been any breach.'[63]

However, it is also undeniable that the Articles of Union differ in nature, depending on the extent to which they permit repeal or amendment. As Smith argues, with reference to Lord Cooper's opinion in *MacCormick* v. *Lord Advocate*, there exist three main types of provision. First, some Articles, (such as Article XVIII: 'no alteration be made in Laws which concern private Right, except for evident utility of the subjects within Scotland') made provision for subsequent amendment. A second group was drafted to exclude subsequent modification, for example by using the terms 'forever after' or 'in all time coming.' The remaining provisions (i.e. XX and XXI) are inconclusively drafted.

1.3.4.2 Challenging the Classic View of Parliamentary Sovereignty

If some terms in the Union agreement are truly fundamental, this threatens the Diceyan view of parliamentary sovereignty. However, although Dicey acknowledged the intention of the drafters of the Acts of Union to give some special status to their terms, he personally viewed the Union Acts as like any other legislation: 'neither the Act of Union with Scotland, nor the Dentists Act, 1878 has more claim than the other to be considered a supreme law.'[64] For Dicey, continuing parliamentary sovereignty was a matter of logic: 'a sovereign power cannot, while retaining its sovereign character, restrict its own powers

[60] Upton ('Marriage Vows of the Elephant', at 93) provides a list of statutes accused of violating the terms of the Union, although concludes that only the Universities (Scotland) Acts 1853 and 1932 in fact constitute breaches.

[61] C Munro, *Studies in Constitutional Law* (2nd ed., 1999) 67.

[62] KWB Middleton, 'New Thoughts on the Union' (1954) 66 JR 37, 43; Smith, 'The Union of 1707 as Fundamental Law', 113; also Article 60(1) Vienna Convention.

[63] Mitchell, *Constitutional Law* (2nd ed., 1968) 73.

[64] AV Dicey, *An Introduction to the Study of the Law of the Constitution* (London: Macmillan, 10th ed., 1959) 145.

by particular enactment .... "Limited Sovereignty" in short, is, in the case of a Parliamentary as of every other sovereign, a contradiction in terms.'[65] But why must sovereignty be understood only as unlimited and indivisible in nature? Many other commentaries understand it very differently.[66] Dicey's answer was that sovereignty had always been understood in this way in England: 'The historical reason why Parliament has never succeeded in passing immutable laws ... lies deep in the history of the English people and in the peculiar development of the English constitution.'[67] But this, even if true, this is a different claim, and can only be a contingent fact, distinguishable from Dicey's claim for logical truth.

In any case, it is unclear that the English Parliament (or the Scottish Parliament[68]) was sovereign in the sense of absolute and illimitable in 1707. With the Glorious Revolution came a recognition that statute law should take priority over the royal prerogative, as the supreme form of law in England. Yet we search in vain in the 1689 Bill of Rights, or the Acts of Union, for a recognition that the English Parliament was sovereign as understood by Dicey, namely illimitable. It was Dicey, writing almost two centuries later, who argued that Parliament was sovereign and illimitable. But judicial precedents for Dicey's view are somewhat sparse.[69]

Furthermore, an important challenge to the Diceyan view was posed by Lord Cooper (the Lord President of the Court of Session) in *MacCormick*: why should the new Parliament bear only English characteristics? According to Lord Cooper,

> I have difficulty seeing why it should have been supposed that the new parliament of Great Britain must inherit all the peculiar characteristics of the English parliament but none of the Scottish parliament, as if all that happened in 1707 was that Scottish representatives were admitted to the parliament of England.[70]

Lord Cooper was giving judgment in the case of *MacCormick* v. *Lord Advocate*. In 1953 John MacCormick, a well-known Scottish Nationalist (operating outside of the SNP) brought an action against the Crown adopting the title of Elizabeth II, arguing that although she was the second Queen Elizabeth of England, she was the *first* Queen Elizabeth of the United Kingdom. The Court of Session dismissed the case, on the basis that the Queen's title was derived from her prerogative powers and not therefore justiciable. However,

[65] Ibid., 68.

[66] Divisible sovereignty was well understood by the Framers of the US Federal Constitution. *See The Federalist* No. 39 (J. Madison).

[67] Dicey, *An Introduction to the Study of the Law of the Constitution*, at 91.

[68] On Scottish constitutional law pre-union, David Walker, *A Legal History of Scotland Vol. III* (T&T Clark 1997) chapter 2.

[69] These include: *Edinburgh & Dalkeith Ry.* v. *Wauchope* [1842] 1 Bell App. Cas. 252; *Vauxhall Estates Ltd.* v. *Liverpool Corporation* [1932] 1 KB 733; *Pickin* v. *British Railways Board* [1974] A.C. 765.

[70] *MacCormick* v. *Lord Advocate* [1953] SC 396, at 411.

in giving judgment, Lord Cooper (who was also an eminent legal historian and former Unionist (i.e. Conservative) politician) stated that: 'The principle of the unlimited sovereignty of Parliament is a distinctively English principle'. This stimulated a different, non Diceyan interpretation of the British Constitution, especially among Scottish jurists, such as TB Smith, and Neil MacCormick,[71] who was John MacCormick's son.

Lord Cooper's view was not unanimously shared south of the border. For example, Wade, in the editorial introduction to post-1953 editions of Dicey's *Law of the Constitution* was somewhat dismissive of Lord Cooper's remarks:

> All this means only that Lord Cooper regarded the Act of Union as a fundamental part of constitutional law and that he regretted that the state of the law was such that even a fundamental provision was subject to alteration by Act of Parliament which the courts were bound to accept. It is indeed somewhat surprising that an understandable expression of patriotism on the part of a great Scottish judge should have been erected into a serious challenge to the doctrine of parliamentary sovereignty in the United Kingdom.[72]

A further, different, argument was added by supporters of the orthodox view, who contended that, even if the Acts of Union were intended as fundamental law, things have since changed, and unqualified parliamentary sovereignty has now become the fundamental principle of British constitutional law. For Wade it is 'too late' to invoke Articles of Union as binding on the Westminster Parliament.[73] [But why is it 'too late'? Who decides this?]

In any event, there is at least a case to be made that England's former constitutional law was no longer uniquely controlling after 1707. JDB Mitchell famously contended that the British Parliament, as a product of Union, was 'born unfree'.[74] And Smith wrote that he found himself 'unable to accept the view of those English constitutional lawyers who hold that the terms of Union have no more force than an ordinary Act of Parliament'[75] Smith argued that contrary claims derived from the assumption that the British Parliament is the English Parliament with some additional Scottish members, but the same powers as the former English Parliament.[76] Neil MacCormick agreed, arguing that 'Those who treated Britain as England writ large … override moral and legal commitments in the Treaty.'[77]

There are, nonetheless, contrary views. For Munro, the Union Parliament continued to depend on prior English custom. For Scott, all that remained was

[71] Professor Sir Neil MacCormick (1941–2009), Regius Professor of Public Law at Edinburgh, also became an SNP Member of the European Parliament.

[72] Wade, *Introduction to the Study of the Law of the Constitution*, at Lxvi.

[73] HWR Wade, *Constitutional Fundamentals* (1980) at 33.

[74] JDB Mitchell *Constitutional Law* (2nd ed., 1968).

[75] Smith, 'The Union of 1707 as Fundamental Law', at 110.

[76] Smith notes: 'Article III clearly contemplates a new Parliament, as does Article XXII' (Smith, 'The Union of 1707 as Fundamental Law', 111).

[77] N MacCormick, 'Does the United Kingdom Have a Constitution?' (1978) 29 NILQ 1, at 2.

the English Parliament 'unchanged, apart from its new name and the addition of the Scottish members.'[78] Smith's response was that 'The fact that the internal organization of Parliament is based on pre-Union English practice … cannot justify the assumption that its legislative powers extend beyond those conferred by the constituent agreement of 1707.'[79]

In conclusion, opinions differ as to whether any provisions of the Act of Union have fundamental status. Smith was clearly of the view that some were such. And indeed, it should be stressed that most of the crucial provisions have in substance been respected.[80]

1.3.5 The Role of the Courts

But what should the courts do if faced with an Act of Parliament that appears to violate fundamental terms of the Union? Should they refuse to apply it? The problem is that the Articles and Acts of Union (rather like the now defunct 1972 European Communities Act) contain no specific provisions detailing what courts should do in such situations. There is no easy answer and in any case no caselaw in which courts have explicitly refused to give effect to legislation on the grounds that it violated the terms of Union.[81]

In *MacCormick*, Lord President Cooper reserved opinion as to whether the Court of Session might review legislation on ground of its violation of Articles of Union, and in 1975, Lord Keith reached a similar conclusion in *Gibson* v. *Lord Advocate. Gibson* concerned fishing rights and EEC law. The issue was whether s 2(1) ECA violated laws 'which concern private right' under Article XVIII in Scotland, because it impliedly derogated from exclusive rights to fish within Scottish waters, thus altering the law other than 'for the evident utility of subjects within Scotland.' The action failed, because the right at issue was deemed a public not a private law right. However, Lord Keith also stated that: 'Like Lord President Cooper, I prefer to reserve my opinion on what the question would be if the United Kingdom Parliament passed an Act purporting to abolish the Court of Session or the Church of Scotland or to substitute English law for the whole body of Scots private law …'[82]

More recently, in 1991, in *Pringle, Petitioner*,[83] the issue of the constitutional effect of fundamental provisions in the Act of Union again arose. *Pringle* concerned payment of the hugely unpopular 'poll tax', a charge introduced

[78] C Munro, *Studies in Constitutional Law* (2nd ed., Oxford: Oxford University Press, 1999) 65–66; PH Scott, *1707 – The Union of Scotland and England* (Edinburgh: Chambers, 1979) 52.

[79] Smith, 'The Union of 1707 as Fundamental Law', 111.

[80] C Turpin and A Tomkins, *British Government and the Constitution* (Cambridge University Press, 2012) at 227.

[81] In earlier cases, such issues were aired but not determined – e.g *Minister of Prestonkirk* v. *Earl of Wemyss* [1808]; *Earl of Kinnoul* v. *Presbytery of Auchterarder* [1838] 16 D. 661; *Laughland* v. *Wansbrough Paper Co.* [1921] SLT 341.

[82] *Gibson* v. *Lord Advocate* [1975] SC 136, at 144.

[83] *Pringle, Petitioner*, [1991] SLT 330.

under the 1987 Abolition of Domestic Rates Etc. (Scotland) Act, (a piece of Westminster legislation opposed by Scottish MPs and only adopted on the votes of English MPs, the year before[84] it was introduced in England[85]). *Pringle* used the *nobile officium*[86] remedy of the Court of Session to seek relief from liability to pay the poll tax. The argument was that its imposition contravened Article IV Act of Union because Scots would be at a disadvantage to the rest of the UK. This failed, because the court found no disadvantage for Scots (given that, unlike England, they no longer had to pay domestic rates) but once again, the court did not completely reject the argument that a UK Act of Parliament might be invalid for violating a term in the Act of Union. Lastly, in *Lord Gray's Motion*, Lord Hope stated that 'the argument that the legislative powers of the new Parliament of Great Britain were subject to restrictions expressed in the Union agreement cannot be dismissed as entirely fanciful.'[87]

The caselaw, therefore, is inconclusive. The problem is that the issue has never been squarely faced. In *MacCormick*, the issue was held non-justiciable, and in *Gibson*, not a matter of private right. Yet, just as one should not rule out the possibility that British courts might refuse recognition to a statute that, for example, abolished judicial review altogether,[88] so in an equivalent extreme case – that is, one attempting to abolish the separate Scottish legal system – might courts deny constitutionality to legislation that contravened the most fundamental principles of Union? But these would be very extreme cases.

1.3.6 Separate Legal Systems

Article XVIV of the Treaty of Union ensured that Scotland's legal system would continue as a separate jurisdiction, with separate courts (but not separate legislatures, at least until 1999). Clashes have inevitably arisen with English law, and although these separate legal systems exist within one State, (distinct) private international law systems have had to govern these conflicts.

In the Scottish case of *Orr Ewing's Trustees*, Lord President Inglis held, 'The judicatories of Scotland and England are as independent of each other within their respective territories, as if they were the judicatories of two foreign states.'[89]

[84] Legislation was often introduced in Scotland a year earlier than England, creating a perception that Scotland was a test subject.

[85] Where it was also to prove highly unpopular, sparking riots. The measure was soon repealed for the whole UK and the council tax introduced instead.

[86] The *nobile officium* concerns the court's equitable jurisdiction to provide exceptional remedies in cases of necessity. It was notably used in 2019 to challenge the prorogation of Parliament in *Cherry QC MP and others* v. *Advocate General for Scotland* [2019] CSIH 49.

[87] [2000] SC (HL) 46, 59.

[88] See e.g. Lord Hope (obiter) in *AXA General Insurance Limited* v. *The Lord Advocate* [2012] 1 A.C. 868.

[89] *Orr Ewing* v. *Orr Ewing's Trs* [1884] 11 R 600, at 629. The same position is adopted in England, see e.g. *Stuart* v. *Bute* [1861] 4 Macq 1, at 49, per Lord Campbell LC: '[A]s to judicial

1.4 After 1707

1.4.1 The Aftermath

On 1 May 1707, there was rejoicing and church bell ringing in London when the Union came into being. In Scotland, spirits were not so high, and the story is that the bells of St Giles in Edinburgh rang 'why should I be sad on my wedding day?' There was no immediate economic miracle in Scotland, and the English were slow to pay the 'Equivalent'. But customs and excise began to be enforced with an increased efficacy in Scotland, so that many felt worse off than before Union. The independent Scottish State had been extinguished. Even if Andrew Fletcher of Saltoun had famously said, 'If man may make all the ballads he should not care who should make the laws of a nation?', Fletcher himself left Scotland after the Union came into being, going first to London. (Indeed, many Scots began moving to London to further their careers.) Fletcher's last words were supposedly and famously, 'Lord have mercy upon my poor countrey that is so barbarously oppressed!'[90]

In early years following the Union, discontent and opposition increased in Scotland. A Tory government had replaced the Whig coalition in London in 1710, and from 1712, several provocative laws were passed in Parliament. The 1712 Toleration Act permitted more freedom to the Episcopalian minority in Scotland, if they agreed to pray for the (future) Hanoverian king. The 1712 Patronage Act re-established the right of Scottish landowners, instead of the local congregation, to nominate parish ministers. This seemed to conflict with the self-understanding of Presbyterianism and to be an intrusion of the State on the privileges of the Scottish Kirk.[91] This conflict eventually led to the 'Great Disruption' of 1843 which formed the Free Church of Scotland. Furthermore, the Christmas Observance Act of 1712 removed the ban on Christmas celebrations in Scotland (banned since 1575) to the great displeasure of the Scottish Church. All this legislation led to criticism that the Church of Scotland lacked sufficient protections in the Treaty of Union. These aggravating measures appeared to risk the very continued existence of Union.

jurisdiction, Scotland and England, although politically under the same Crown, and under the supreme sway of one legislature, are to be considered as independent foreign countries, unconnected with each other.'

90 'Letters of Andrew Fletcher of Saltoun and his Family 1717–16', vol. X (Scottish History Society, 1965).

91 See further the 1838 *Auchterarder case* which concerned the 1838 Court of Session judgement that the Presbyterian Kirk, itself having been established by statute, was the creature of the State. As Harold Laski wrote of this, 'The real head and centre of the whole problem was thus the theory of parliamentary sovereignty .... For the courts there could not be such a thing as a fundamental law. They could not ... announce that lay patronage was an ecclesiastical question, and therefore within the competence of the general assembly, for so to do would be not only to question the sovereignty of parliament, but also, implicitly, to admit that the general assembly was a coordinate legislature with parliament.' H Laski, 'The Political Theory of the Disruption' (1916) 10 American Political Science Review 437, 459. Also, Lord Rodger of Earlsferry, *The Courts, The Church and The Constitution: Aspects of the Disruption of 1843* (Edinburgh, 2008).

This dissatisfaction only increased with the Malt Tax Act in 1713, which considerably increased the price of ale in Scotland, appearing to breach Article XIV Treaty of Union. In response, Scottish parliamentarians introduced their own attempt to dissolve the Union. But this failed, lost by only a small number of proxy votes.[92]

However, a new threat presented itself in the 1715 Jacobite rebellion of the 'Old Pretender'. This was potentially the most threatening of all Jacobite rebellions. Whereas, previously, support for the Stuarts had been religious and dynastic, now Jacobites sought to present themselves as championing Scottish freedom and independence. However, the rising failed to defeat the (smaller) Crown forces at the battle of Sheriffmuir, and the initiative was lost, partly due to incompetent leadership, and so the putative James VIII/III was forced back to France.

1.4.2 'Britons'?

Nonetheless, the failure of both the attempted dissolution of Union, and the 1715 Jacobite rebellion, should not be attributed to any strong feeling of 'Britishness'. As Linda Colley writes, 'this was a union of policy and not of affection.' Colley also describes the Great Britain of this time as 'like the Christian doctrine of the Trinity, both three and one and altogether something of a mystery.'[93]

Colley's argument is that[94] a sense of Britishness came to be developed as a result of a sense of *dissimilarity* from those beyond Britain, especially the French. France had for long been England's main enemy and rival, although Thomas Carlyle commented that Scottish culture up to the date of the Union had been essentially French.[95] This gradually changed after 1707, as Britons (including Scots) came to identify with the Protestant faith, against Catholicism. Indeed, Colley highlights the extent to which this identification and division of religion was formalized in law.[96] Up to 1829, British Catholics were not permitted to vote and were banned from all state offices and Parliament. For most of the eighteenth century, Catholics suffered from punitive taxation, were prohibited from possessing arms, and suffered great prejudice in access to education, the right to property and religious freedom. This anti-Catholicism was also embraced by a driven group of Scottish Presbyterians, who understood Union as a means of eradicating Catholic influence. Furthermore, a Stuart restoration was perceived as not only threatening a Catholic religious revival, but also freedom itself. For liberty, and the British Constitution, were also viewed as linked to Protestantism, and the Constitution was, as Colley writes, perceived to be

[92] See further https://thehistoryofparliament.wordpress.com/2013/05/31/there-has-been-all-along-something-odd-in-this-affair-the-malt-tax-and-the-1713-attempt-to-repeal-the-union/
[93] Colley, *Britons*, at 15. [94] Ibid., at 17.
[95] *Works of Thomas Carlyle*, vol. 6: 'Miscellanies', at 27. [96] Colley, *Britons*, at 19.

'unique, splendid and sovereign, the hard-won prerogative of a free Protestant people.'[97]

Ultimately, the Jacobite Catholic cause was seen to threaten not only the stability of the constitutional order, but also the country more generally, through the risk of violence, civil war, and destruction of trade. For another important element of Britishness was the embrace of commerce and trade, the growth of what Napoleon came to refer to as 'a nation of shopkeepers'.

And so, little by little, in the course of the eighteenth century, perceptions in Scotland of the benefits of Union changed.[98] For the most part, Scotland was left semi-independent, sufficiently distant, but benefiting from Union in commerce and foreign affairs, even if the tax burden weighed more heavily. The Union started to gain a greater stability. The Scottish Parliament no longer existed, but Edinburgh maintained its role as a centre of law and administration. Scotland enjoyed a great deal of legal, religious, and administrative autonomy, and to be sure, the Enlightenment did much to increase Scotland's standing in cultural matters. On the other hand, talented Scots gained access to important official positions in England, often at the expense of English, quite a few of whom (e.g. John Wilkes) came to resent Scottish influence. Scotland was increasing in prosperity, and often faring better than England. Aside from the Scottish Enlightenment, Scotland could claim superiority over England in universities (five to England's two), education generally, and the medical professions. Scots also played a significant role in Empire, which after all, became well-known as the 'British' and not 'English' empire. Many Scotsmen joined the army, especially working in India, with the East India company, and making their fortune there.

1.4.3 Scottish Governance up to Devolution in 1998

Following the 1707 Union, Scottish administration was absorbed into that of Great Britain and based in London. Scotland's independent legal system and Church remained and there was also administrative decentralization for matters such as health, education and prisons, and local government boards were established in Scotland in the nineteenth century. A new system was introduced in 1885 with a Secretary for Scotland appointed as head of the new Scottish Office in Whitehall. However, for many, the notion of a Scottish Office in London appeared a contradiction in terms, and, in 1939 the Scottish Office moved to Edinburgh (although continued to maintain a branch in London).[99]

In 1883, the Scottish Home Rule Association was founded, and in 1913 a Home Rule Bill for Scotland was introduced into Parliament by Scottish Liberal

[97] Ibid., at 49.

[98] On Unionism in general, see Colin Kidd, *Union and Unionisms* (Cambridge University Press, 2008).

[99] See further David Milne, *The Scottish Office* (George Allan and Unwin, 1957).

MP, William Cowan. Cowan stated that, 'At nineteen out of twenty General Elections since 1832 Scotland has returned a Liberal majority to Parliament, and ... that body advocates without reserve Scottish Home Rule', concluding that, 'Is it any wonder Scotland is tired and demands a parliament of her own?'[100] The Scottish Home Rule Bill was designed along similar lines to Irish Home Rule and would revive the Scottish Parliament, although the principle of Westminster parliamentary sovereignty would be maintained. However, the Bill was not adopted due to the onset of the First World War, and although it returned in the 1920s, the impetus was lost and Scottish nationalism was a diminished force until the SNP gained its first seat in Westminster in 1945. In 1978, the UK Labour Government introduced the Scotland Bill, with provision for a referendum on a Scottish Assembly.[101] However, this Bill contained a provision (in s.85)[102] requiring 40 per cent of the Scottish electorate to vote for devolution for it to be implemented. In the event, although a majority voted for an Assembly, the 40 per cent threshold was not reached, and so devolution did not take place.

By 1998, the Scottish Secretary of State had many responsibilities, encompassing a wide range of Scottish affairs, and the Scottish Office employed about 10,000 civil servants. During the twentieth century, the House of Commons developed special procedures for legislation relating only to Scotland, Northern Ireland, and Wales. A Scottish Grand Committee was established in the House of Commons, comprising all MPs representing Scottish constituencies, to debate bills relating exclusively to Scotland, as well as a Select Committee on Scottish Affairs. Nonetheless, these special procedures were embedded in the Westminster Parliament, within the centralized blueprint of the unitary State.

1.5 A Distinct Constitutional Tradition?

1.5.1 Changing Views of Union

By 1907, on the 200th anniversary of the 1707 Union, it seems that Scots generally took a positive view of Union.[103] However, by half a century or so later, views were changing. Union was more likely to be seen as a corrupt bargain, achieved by politicians and other figures in pursuit of their own self-interest, and a victory of English managerial politics and control. Nationalism was on the rise in Scotland.

[100] See further Government of Scotland Bill 1913.

[101] This roughly followed the recommendations of the 1973 Kilbrandon report (The Royal Commission on the Constitution 1969–1973) (Cmnd 5460, 1973).

[102] Sometimes called a 'wrecking amendment', this provision (opposed by the Government) was inserted as a result of pressure by backbench Labour MP George Cunningham (of Scottish origin, but opposed to devolution).

[103] See e.g. Peter Hume Brown (ed.), *The Union of 1707* (Glasgow, 1907).

1.5.2 A Scottish Tradition of Popular Sovereignty?

Many in England seem unaware of the claim to a distinct Scottish constitutional tradition, considerably different from the English doctrine of parliamentary sovereignty. The Scottish tradition looks to *popular* sovereignty, and traces its origins back in history: to the Declaration of Arbroath in 1320; the doctrines of early modern theorists such as George Buchanan; and Claim of Right of 1689. The interchange between the English and Scottish traditions is unclear, but it is unlikely that the British Constitution can simply be interpreted as the English tradition writ large.

The Declaration of Arbroath of 1320 is often referenced,[104] especially since its 700th anniversary in April 2020. This Declaration was written in Latin by Scottish barons to Pope John XXII, requesting that he recognize Scotland's independence from England, and also recognize Robert Bruce (excommunicated in 1319) as Scotland's lawful king. The document is often credited as the origin of concepts of popular sovereignty because it declared that Bruce was '*King, not only by right of succession according to our laws and customs, but also with the due consent of us all.*' Nonetheless, one might question the extent to which popular sovereignty and 'the people' are validated by this document. As with the English Magna Carta, this was a document signed by wealthy nobles, not by all the people. It was eight years before the Pope responded and reversed Bruce's excommunication, and the Declaration enjoyed near obscurity for a couple of centuries, while in contrast, the theory of divine right of kings enjoyed a resurgence under the Stuarts.

George Buchanan (described by Neil MacCormick as 'the greatest of the Scottish contributors to the European renaissance … and perhaps our first articulate theorist of sovereignty'[105]) had been principle tutor to the young King James VI in Scotland. Buchanan's 1578 *De Iure Regni Apud Scotos* ('The Law of Kingship Among the Scots'[106]) was a short treatise explaining the Scottish Constitution. In this treatise, Buchanan sanctioned the assassination of a tyrant, and he included Mary Queen of Scots in this definition, seeing her as ruling only in her own interest. His thesis was that the law was above the monarch, and that Scotland had not behaved egregiously in deposing Mary. Buchanan declared that 'The judge has his authority from the law, not the law from the judge.'[107] Neil MacCormick argued that, prior to Union, Scotland had

[104] This document had an interesting influence in the US. Many of the signatories to the American Declaration of Independence were of Scottish descent. Thomas Jefferson claimed Robert Bruce as an ancestor, and encountered the Declaration of Arbroath during his education at the college of William and Mary under William Small, who was a Scotsman.

[105] N MacCormick, 'Stands Scotland Where She Did?: New Unions for Old in These Islands' (2000) 35 Irish Jurist 1–16, 9.

[106] RA Mason and MS Smith, *A Dialogue on the Law of Kingship amongst the Scots: A Critical Edition and Translation of George Buchanan's De Jure Regni apud Scotos Dialogus* (Ashgate, 2004).

[107] Ibid., at 33, 143.

been sufficiently influenced by Buchanan to embrace a constitutional commitment to some type of popular sovereignty, contending that:

> The old Scottish constitution, as Scots authorities like George Buchanan were very insistent, was never a constitution based on conquest. Hence the Ius Regni, the law of the kingdom, could never be interpreted as constituting an absolute monarchy, but only as authorizing a limited one dependent on popular assent.[108]

After Union, it was unclear to what extent the older Scottish tradition of popular sovereignty had been overtaken by English conceptions of parliamentary sovereignty. However, by the late twentieth century, this older tradition of popular sovereignty was recognized more clearly. The Campaign for a Scottish Assembly was formed in 1980, and in 1988, produced *A Claim of Right for Scotland*. This took its name from the 1689 Claim of Right, stating that 'parliamentary government under the present British constitution had failed Scotland'.[109] This report was produced at a time of increasing political dissonance between England and Scotland. Since 1979, conservative majorities had formed governments in London, but conservative representation had been greatly reduced in Scotland (so that by 1997, no conservative MPs were returned for Scotland) leading to a perception of a lack of legitimacy of UK governments over Scotland. A Convention was established in 1989 to draw up plans for a Scottish Parliament with Canon Kenyon Wright as its executive chairman, declaring 'the sovereign right of the Scottish people to determine the form of government best suited to their needs'.[110] Members of the Scottish Constitutional Convention included most political parties, as well as STUC, churches, business and grass roots organizations. However, the SNP withdrew, after expressing concern that the Convention would not consider Scottish independence. The Conservative Party also took no part, being opposed to a devolved Parliament for Scotland. The Constitutional Convention's 1990 interim report claimed that parliamentary sovereignty was 'a constitutional fiction which cloaks the effective exercise of sovereign power by the governing political party'.[111] The Convention's 1995 report, *Scotland's Parliament, Scotland's Right,* formed the basis of the UK Government's White Paper proposals, *Scotland's Parliament*, in 1997. (Indeed, many members of the 1997 UK Labour Government had been signatories to the Claim of Right.)

One may summarize the above by noting distinct constitutional principles in England and Scotland. However, it would be a mistake to ascribe adherence

[108] N MacCormick, *Questioning Sovereignty* (Oxford University Press, 1999) 55. But MacCormick's interpretation of Buchanan has been criticized as a selective interpretation. Colin Kidd, *Subverting Scotland's Past: Scottish Whig Historians and the Creation of an Anglo-Scottish Identity: 1689–1830* (Cambridge University Press, 2003) 19–20.

[109] *Report of the Constitutional Steering Committee of the Campaign for a Scottish Assembly* (Edinburgh, 1988) at 1.1

[110] Scottish Constitutional Convention: *Towards Scotland's Parliament* (1990) 10.

[111] *Towards Scotland's Parliament,* 16.

to popular sovereignty and the Claim of Right only to Scottish nationalist politicians. As noted, many politicians of the Labour, Liberal and other political parties subscribed to these principles, and they were embraced by the 1997 Labour Government as the foundation for the new Devolution settlement – an event that might even be seen in the words of US constitutional law theorist, Bruce Ackerman, as a 'constitutional moment'.[112] The Scottish Constitutional Convention should also be considered in tandem with other campaigns and demonstrations against the UK Government in Scotland, such as poll tax revolts. These have collectively been characterized as organized rejections of the UK Government's legitimacy in Scotland, comparable to the rebellions in the American colonies in 1773 after the Tea Act, whereby 'the act of imposing an unpopular tax where there was defective representation in the context of questionable legitimacy is similar'.[113]

1.5.3 Britain as a 'Union' Rather Than 'Unitary' State?

An important question is whether the UK should be described as a 'Union State' rather than unitary in nature. Aileen McHarg describes the 'union' State as 'one in which, because of the way the state emerged historically, heterogeneity of governance arrangements between constituent regions or nations has become a normal and persistent feature.'[114] Although the concept of union is widely used in constitutional studies to refer to the consolidation of existing units into one, it is not the same as a unitary State, a term which implies a constitutional order with a single, unrivalled, legal competence, which places a central agency in a position of unequivocal authority. In contrast, within a union State, different parts of that State may understand the Constitution in different ways.

Britain might better be described as a 'Union' State, as there is a strong argument that it lacks an unequivocal, unitary sovereignty.[115] This is a significant contention, as it challenges the argument that sovereignty rests entirely with the Westminster Parliament. Lord Steyn's obiter comment in *Jackson* v. *Attorney General*[116] that 'the settlement contained in the Scotland Act 1998 … point[s] to

112 B Ackerman, *We the People Vol. I: Foundations* (Harvard University Press, 1993) arguing that Constitutional moments deviate from ordinary politics and involve decisions of 'the People' overthrowing preceding ruling arrangements.

113 P Speirs, *Scotland's Challenge to Parliamentary Sovereignty: Can Westminster Abolish the Scottish Parliament Unilaterally?* (University of Glasgow, LL.M(R) thesis, 2015) at 50.

114 A McHarg, 'Public Law in Scotland: Difference and Distinction', in A McHarg and T Mullen (eds.), *Public Law in Scotland* (Avizandum Publishing Ltd, 2006) 1–22, 16. See also N Walker, 'Beyond the Unitary Conception of the United Kingdom Constitution?' (2000) *PL* 384; S Rokkan and D Urwin, *Economy, Territory, Identity: Politics of West European Territories* (SAGE Publications, 1983).

115 But the Devolution Acts 1998 assert parliamentary sovereignty. s28(7) Scotland 1998 Act provides: 'This section does not affect the power of the Parliament of the United Kingdom to make laws for Scotland.'

116 *Jackson* v. *Attorney General* [2005] UKHL 56, Lord Steyn, at para. 102.

a divided sovereignty' bolsters this view (although many traditionalists would contest this point). There exist different constitutional settlements in the different parts of the UK. Indeed, James Mitchell described the UK since devolved government as 'a state of unions.'[117] Michael Keating argues that the UK is better conceived as a 'plurinational' rather than a 'multinational' State, because its people have plural national identities.[118] The continuation of separate civic institutions, legal system and cultural heritage in Scotland, along with the historical tradition of a right of the Scottish people to self-determination, and the recognition of the UK as a Union State, point towards the Union as a continuing agreement between two independent nations, Scotland and England. This, in turn, suggests that, should one of these nations no longer wish to continue the Union, then it has a right to terminate the agreement, and revert to its former status as an independent State.

1.6 Devolution

Devolution came to Scotland with the Scotland Act 1998. At the same time, devolution was also introduced in Wales and Northern Ireland (Government of Wales Act 1998, Northern Ireland Act 1998). The 1998 Scotland Act was preceded by a 1997 UK Government White Paper, *Scotland's Parliament*,[119] and gave effect to that White Paper with no great changes. A referendum was held in Scotland on 11 September 1997, in which 74 per cent of those voting supported the creation of a Scottish Parliament.

The Scotland Act 1998 sets out the main provisions of Scottish devolution and has been described as 'on any view a monumental piece of constitutional legislation.'[120] This Act devolved primary legislative power, as well as executive functions, to the Scottish Parliament and Scottish Government.[121] Although since the Acts of Union, Scotland had retained a certain amount of autonomy (notably in its church, legal, and education systems) it lacked its own legislative autonomy (in contrast to Quebec, e.g., which had gained this in the British North America Act 1867).

The purpose of devolution was to give further powers to Scotland. Yet devolution falls short of a federal system of governance, in which separate spheres of sovereignty exist. All the leading UK political parties accepted devolution, some more willingly than others. The Scottish National Party (SNP) continued to campaign for independence, while working with devolution, and since 2007, has been either in government, or in minority government, in Scotland. In

117 J Mitchell, 'The Westminster Model and the State of Unions' (2010) 63 Parliamentary Affairs, 85–88.

118 M. Keating, *Plurinational Democracy: Stateless Nations in a Post-Sovereignty Era* (Oxford University Press, 2001) 26–27.

119 *Scotland's Parliament*, Cm 3658, 24 July 1997.

120 *Martin* v. *HM Advocate* [2010] UKSC 10, 2010 SC (UKSC) 40, at 44 per Lord Walker.

121 From 2007, previously Scottish 'Executive'.

June 2009, the Calman Commission report, *Serving Scotland Better: Scotland and the United Kingdom in the 21st Century*, concluded that devolution had generally functioned successfully, and recommended increasing fiscal autonomy for Scotland, and much of its report was implemented by the Scotland Act 2012. However, more substantial changes were introduced by the Scotland Act 2016, implemented after the 2014 Scottish independence referendum resulted in a 55/45 per cent split for remaining in the UK. Since then, with Brexit, there have been calls for another independence referendum in Scotland. All of this will be discussed further below.

The Scotland Act 1998 (s37) provides that: 'The Union with Scotland Act 1706 and the Union with England Act 1707 have effect subject to this Act.' This does not mean the Acts of Union became irrelevant since devolution. The Acts are still on the statute book, and much of them continue to be relevant law.[122] The Scotland Act does not appear to infringe any fundamental provisions in the Acts of Union. Indeed, the argument that the UK is a union, based on consent of its parties, continues to be made, most notably in arguments for a second independence referendum. On the other hand, it might be asked whether provisions, such as the 'eternal' ones in the Act of Union, create problems for independence? For example, it might seem that devolution has become a pathway to independence in Scotland. If the UK Union itself were to terminate, and Scotland withdraw, what then of arguments deriving from the 'fundamental' and eternal status of Union legislation? So, devolution and its law may be replacing the older and different nature of the 1707 settlement.

1.6.1 The Scottish Parliament and Government

The Scottish unicameral Parliament sits at Holyrood in Edinburgh and met for the first time on 12 May 1999. However, opinions vary as to whether this Parliament is totally new. At its first session, SNP member Winnie Ewing, stated, 'the Scottish Parliament, adjourned on 25th day of March in the year 1707, is hereby reconvened'.[123]

The Scottish Parliament presently has 129 members (MSPs) now elected for a fixed term of five years. Part I Scotland Act 1998 sets out the process by which they are elected, which is through a mixed, or additional, member system (AMS), whereby each voter has two different votes, comprising a 'First Past the Post' and proportional representation element. This AMS system has often resulted in a coalition, or minority government, and also often produced a different political administration from that in London for the UK overall. The Scottish Parliament devises its own procedures and much of its work is done through committees, which, among other things,

[122] They were pleaded, e.g., by the Scottish intervention in the *Miller* case.

[123] '12 May 1999: Winnie Ewing Reconvenes the Scottish Parliament'. *BBC News*.

scrutinize legislation and the Scottish Government. Under s28(2) Scotland Act a Bill is adopted as an Act of the Scottish Parliament (ASP) 'when it has been passed by the Parliament and has received Royal Assent.' Roughly speaking, the stages in the Scottish Parliament's legislative procedure tally with the second reading, committee stage and third reading of Westminster Bills. But there is of course, no equivalent to the House of Lords' function as a revising Chamber. The Scottish Parliament has only limited legislative powers and may not legislate incompatibly with EU law (while the UK was an EU member) and ECHR rights, nor may it legislate on matters reserved to Westminster.

Power was also devolved to a separate Scottish Government by s53 Scotland Act 1998, so the powers of UK Whitehall ministers have been decreased. The Scottish Government follows a 'Cabinet style', comprising the First Minister (nominated by the Parliament), other ministers, and Scottish law officers (Lord Advocate and Solicitor General for Scotland). However, a Secretary of State for Scotland continues to exist in the UK Cabinet, albeit with reduced responsibilities. Further, s87 Scotland Act created a new office, that of Advocate General for Scotland (a member of the UK Government), who advises the UK Government on Scots law.

Some of the funding for the Scottish Government comes from the 'block grant' transferred from the UK Treasury to the Scottish Ministers. This block grant is calculated according to the 'Barnett formula'[124] first devised in 1978, which equalizes funding across the UK and aims to give each devolved nation the same per person change in funding as that agreed for comparable government services in England. Therefore, this block grant is not actually based on the needs of Scotland. There have been many calls for change or removal of the Barnett formula, but deciding what to replace it with has not been easy. In any event, over the past 10 years, the funding system has changed due to increased devolution of tax raising powers to Scotland, with block grant funding commensurately reduced – but the Barnett formula itself remains.

1.7 A Reserved Powers Model

UK devolution generally now operates on a 'reserved powers' model.[125] This has the effect that everything not specifically set out in statute as 'reserved' to Westminster is assumed to be devolved. Schedule 5 Scotland Act 1998 specifies the 'reserved matters' outside the competence of the Scottish Parliament. 'General reservations' under Part I of Schedule 5 include: under s1 the Constitution

[124] See further, M Keep, 'The Barnett Formula', House of Commons Briefing Paper 7386, 23 January 2020.

[125] Welsh devolution has followed this model since the Wales Act 2017. Northern Ireland devolution also has some variations.

(including the Crown and UK Union); under s7 foreign affairs (including EU and other international organizations, regulation of international trade and international development aid); under s8 the Civil Service; under s9 defence and armed forces; under s10 Treason. Under Part II of Schedule 5, 'specific reservations' are made for financial and economic matters; immigration and nationality; national security, official secrets and terrorism; competition; insolvency; consumer protection; energy; coal, oil and gas; nuclear energy; social security; employment; broadcasting. However, exceptions to reserved areas have been created. For example, Scotland has fiscal powers that have been devolved under the 2012 and 2016 Scotland Acts, allowing the Scottish Parliament to set all income tax rates and bands (except the personal allowance, which remains reserved).

As Lord Hope stated in the *Imperial Tobacco* case, there exists a common theme in reserved matters:

> It is that matters in which the UK as a whole has an interest should continue to be the responsibility of the UK Parliament at Westminster. They include matters which are affected by its treaty obligations and matters that are designed to ensure that there is a single market within the United Kingdom for the free movement of goods and services.[126]

As a corollary, matters not reserved to the UK and so devolved to Scotland, include Scots private law and criminal law; the prosecution service, police and prisons; the judiciary and the court system; agriculture, forestry and fisheries; economic development, tourism, roads and transport; planning and environmental protection; education and training; health; local government, social work and housing; and sport and the arts. The 2012 and 2016 Scotland Acts devolved sone further areas including tax, stamp duty, abortion law and air passenger duty.

The list of reserved matters may be altered by transferring additional powers to the Scottish Parliament by Order in Council under s30 Scotland Act 1998, if both the Scottish and UK Parliaments agree. This is what happened regarding the holding of the first Scottish independence referendum in 2014.

The reserved powers model, whereby it is those powers reserved to the centre that are specified, is also found in federal and confederal jurisdictions. For example, the US federal Constitution 10th Amendment states: 'powers not delegated to the United States by the Constitution, nor prohibited by it to the States, are reserved to the States respectively, or to the people.' This model was also to be found in the practices of the British Empire, although a division of powers between the 'imperial' Parliament in London and colonial legislatures in London was never clearly set out.[127]

[126] *Imperial Tobacco Ltd* v. *Lord Advocate* [2012] UKSC 61, para. 29.

[127] See David Torrance, 'Reserved Matters in the United Kingdom' (House of Commons briefing paper CBP 8544, 2019) 7.

1.7.1 Restrictions on Competence of the Scottish Parliament

According to s29(1), 'An Act of the Scottish Parliament is not law so far as any provision of the Act is outside the legislative competence of the Parliament.' And notably, s28(7) Scotland Act 1998 explicitly upholds the power of the UK Parliament to legislate for Scotland, so preserving the notion of unlimited UK parliamentary sovereignty.

The Scottish Parliament is therefore a legislature of limited competence. It must not legislate on reserved matters nor in breach of ECHR rights, nor formerly EU law. s31(1) Scotland Act 1998 requires the Scottish minister promoting a Bill to state that its provisions are within legislative competence, and s31(2) imposes the same duty on the Presiding Officer of the Parliament (who functions in a similar way to the Speaker of the House of Commons). UK ministers also possess a veto power under s35 Scotland Act 1998 where they have reasonable grounds to believe a Bill incompatible with international obligations, or defence or national security, or modifies the law on reserved matters so as to have an adverse effect. ASPs may, in the final instance, be struck down by the courts. Under s33(1) Scotland Act, the Advocate General, Lord Advocate or the Attorney General may refer the question of whether a Bill would be within legislative competence to the Supreme Court.

1.7.2 The Sewel Convention

From the outset, it was agreed that it might at times be expedient if the UK Parliament could legislate on a devolved matter (e.g. if homogeneous legislation were needed for the whole UK.) And so, Lord Sewel made the now famous statement at the time of the Scotland Act's debate in the House of Lords: 'we would expect a convention to be established that Westminster would not normally legislate with regard to devolved matters in Scotland without the consent of the Scottish Parliament'.[128]

Thus the 'Sewel Motion', or Legislative Consent Motion (LCM) was born. In the earlier days of devolution, such motions were quite frequently used, and consent given. In 2016, the convention was given a statutory basis by the Scotland Act 2016. The weakness of this statutory provision was shown up when the Supreme Court judged that it was still only a convention in status,[129] and after that, when the EUWA 2018, and WAA 2020, were both adopted by Westminster in the absence of legislative consent from the Scottish Parliament. This is discussed further below.

1.8 The 2014 Independence Referendum

Initially, the Scottish Parliament was controlled by pro-union parties, usually Labour and Liberal Democrat, in coalition. However, the SNP gained a historic victory in the 2011 Scottish Parliament elections, giving them the

[128] HL Deb vol. 592, col 791, 21 July 1998.

[129] *R (Miller)* v. *Secretary of State for Exiting the European Union* [2017] UKSC 5.

majority to request a referendum on independence, which had been a pledge in their manifesto. (Although, at that time, there was also strong public support for 'devo max', namely, much greater devolution stopping short of complete independence, but the UK Government refused to allow this on the referendum ballot.)

By 2011, the Scottish Government was presenting the case for Scottish independence in terms of democratic self-determination, legitimacy, and sovereignty. Arguments based on any notion of ethnic or cultural essence were eschewed, the focus instead being on civic nationalism and independence derived from the sovereign will of people living and working in Scotland. Given that England has 84 per cent of the total UK population it was hard to see how Scottish voters could have any meaningful influence on UK elections. Devolution had not made sufficient inroads into this situation because many significant policies – such as foreign policy and finance – were still reserved matters.

1.8.1 The Section 30 Order

(Then) UK Prime Minister, David Cameron, acknowledged the SNP's victory in 2011, and publicly accepted that it was for the Scottish people to decide on Scotland's future. Nonetheless, the UK Government contested the Scottish Parliament's competence to legislate for an independence referendum.[130] In contrast, the Scottish Government maintained that the Scottish Parliament did possess the relevant legislative competence.[131]

In the event, neither view was conclusively adopted, and the issue was settled in another way when the UK and Scottish Governments signed the Edinburgh Agreement in 2012. Under that Agreement, the UK Government drafted an Order in Council (a 'section 30 order') granting the Scottish Parliament the necessary powers to hold an independence referendum, on or before 31 December 2014.

1.8.2 The Referendum

The competence issue being settled, the Scottish Parliament then adopted two pieces of legislation making possible a referendum on Scottish Independence: the Scottish Independence Referendum (Franchise) Act 2013 and the Scottish Independence Referendum Act 2013. The Franchise Act provided that all persons entitled to vote in local government and Scottish Parliament elections could vote in the referendum, along with 16- and 17-year olds. This proved relatively uncontroversial and the only disagreement concerned the Act's bar

[130] UK Government: *Scotland's Constitutional Future*, available at: www.gov.uk/government/uploads/system/uploads/attachment_data/file/39248/Scotlands_Constitutional_Future.pdf

[131] *Your Scotland, Your Referendum*, paras. 1.5–1.9.

on prisoner voting.[132] The Scottish Independence Referendum Act 2013 set out other substantive terms of the referendum. It confirmed the date of the referendum (18 September 2014) and the specific question to be asked ('Should Scotland be an independent country?') and also set out the rules for official campaigns to follow.

On 26 November 2013, the Scottish Government published *Scotland's Future,* its guide to an independent Scotland. In the event of a 'yes' vote, the Scottish Government planned for an 'Independence Day' on 24 March 2016, with elections for an independent Scottish Parliament in May 2016. Some Scottish Government proposals which proved particularly controversial included: the continued use of sterling via a formal currency union with rUK (namely, England, Wales and Northern Ireland); maintaining NATO membership; and negotiating membership of the EU on the same terms as the UK then had.[133] These proposals were dependent on securing agreement with rUK, the EU and other international organizations, for which the Scottish Government set the target of negotiating and implementing the arrangements within a proposed 18-month transition period to March 2016.[134]

A key issue was the institutional changes to be introduced following independence. The Scottish Government proposed an interim Constitution, to be followed by an 'inclusive and participative' process for replacing it with a permanent written Constitution. The Bill for the interim Constitution proclaimed popular sovereignty.[135] As well as the above, a transfer of power from Westminster to Holyrood was also foreseen as necessary to empower the Scottish Parliament to officially enact independence and adopt legislation on all policy areas formerly reserved to Westminster.

The Scottish Independence Referendum took place on 18 September 2014, and the turnout of 84.6 per cent was the highest recorded for a UK election or referendum since the January 1910 general election (which preceded the introduction of universal suffrage). The proposition 'Should Scotland be an independent country?' was rejected by a margin of 10.6 per cent.

1.9 Scotland Act 2016

On 7 September 2014, shortly before the independence referendum, a YouGov poll had suggested 51 per cent of Scots favoured independence. In reaction, on 16 September 2014, immediately before the referendum vote, the leaders

[132] In *Moohan* v. *Lord Advocate* UKSC 2014 the UK Supreme Court upheld the Court of Session decision that the ban on prisoner voting was lawful (because ECtHR caselaw – *Hirst* v. *UK (No2)* [2005] – applied only to elections and not referendums).

[133] See further S Douglas-Scott, 'Scotland, Secession, and the European Union', in A McHarg, T Mullen, A Page, and N Walker (eds.), *The Scottish Independence Referendum: Constitutional and Political Implications* (Oxford University Press, 2016).

[134] *Scotland's Future,* 'Preface', at x.

[135] Scottish Government, *The Scottish Independence Bill: A Consultation on an interim Constitution for Scotland* (2014) clause 3.

of the three largest unionist parties (Conservative, Labour, Liberal Democrat) gave a 'Vow' to the Scottish electorate,[136] that in the event of a 'No' vote there would be further devolution of power to Scotland, including a guarantee that the Scottish Parliament would be permanent.

However, when he stood outside 10 Downing street, the morning after the referendum vote, David Cameron clarified that further Scottish devolution would only come after the next general election, and linked it to changes for England, saying, 'We have heard the voice of Scotland and now the millions of voices of England must be heard'.[137] This suggested further powers for Scotland were dependent not only on the next election, but also a broader constitutional settlement preventing Scottish MPs voting on England only issues. (Unlike the other three nations, England lacks its own dedicated Parliament.) So the stubborn 'West Lothian' question re-emerged.[138]

In October 2015, the UK House of Commons adopted new parliamentary procedures[139] enabling 'English Votes for English Laws' (or EVEL) supposedly to mitigate the 'West Lothian' problem. However, these were quietly abandoned in July 2021. There is no obvious solution to the asymmetric patterns of devolution in the UK, an element which has caused ill-feeling and may have contributed to the rise of English nationalism. And notably, both EVEL and the Brexit referendum were Conservative election manifesto pledges in 2015 – both unsatisfactory remedies for rising English nationalism. There has been no attempt to find a comprehensive constitutional settlement for the UK.

1.9.1 An Overview of the Scotland Act 2016

A Commission was set up in late 2014, shortly after the referendum vote, headed by Lord Smith of Kelvin, to oversee the further devolution commitments such as those in the 'Vow'. A little later, the Smith Commission produced a report recommending some areas for further devolution, and that 'UK legislation will state that the Scottish Parliament and Scottish Government are permanent institutions.'[140] The fear that Westminster might seek to abolish a Scottish Parliament predated 1998 devolution. And the fear was not without reason, for the Greater London Council had been abolished by Margaret Thatcher by the UK Local Government Act 1985.

[136] Published on the front page of the *Daily Record* (Scotland's highest circulating newspaper).

[137] 'David Cameron raises West Lothian question after Scotland vote: 'English votes for English laws', *The Guardian*, 19 September 2014.

[138] Named after Labour MP for West Lothian, Tam Dalyell, who in the 1970s protested that, post any devolution, Scottish MPs in the UK Parliament might have a decisive voice in legislation on matters concerning England only, whereas English MPs would no longer participate in devolved legislation. (A similar argument surfaced during home rule debates for Ireland.) See further, R Hazell (ed.), *The English Question* (Manchester University Press, 2006).

[139] House of Commons Standing Orders 83J–83X.

[140] *Report of the Smith Commission for further devolution of powers to the Scottish Parliament* (27 November 2014).

Many of the Smith Commission recommendations were incorporated into the Scotland Act 2016. These new powers would, in the view of the UK Government, transform Holyrood into a 'powerhouse Parliament'.[141] Some additional powers were devolved, giving the Scottish government greater powers to raise income tax. Perhaps most notably, the 2016 Act provided in s1 that, 'The Scottish Parliament and the Scottish Government are a permanent part of the United Kingdom's constitutional arrangements' and in s2 put the Sewel Convention on a statutory basis.

1.9.2 The 'Constitutional Clauses'

1.9.2.1 Section 1 Scotland Act 2016

This reads:

> *Permanence of the Scottish Parliament and Scottish Government*
>
> (1) The Scottish Parliament and the Scottish Government are a permanent part of the United Kingdom's constitutional arrangements.
>
> (2) The purpose of this section is, with due regard to the other provisions of this Act, to signify the commitment of the Parliament and Government of the United Kingdom to the Scottish Parliament and the Scottish Government.
>
> (3) In view of that commitment it is declared that the Scottish Parliament and the Scottish Government are not to be abolished except on the basis of a decision of the people of Scotland voting in a referendum.

Notably however, this crucial section of the Scotland Act 2016 is only located in section 63A of the now amended Scotland Act 1998, where it might easily be missed. Most significantly perhaps, this new section is also only a declaration of political intent ('to signify the commitment of the Parliament and Government of the United Kingdom'). Indeed, it is hard to attribute any other constitutional effect to the section, given the UK Government's adherence to parliamentary sovereignty which might seem to rule out any entrenchment of the sort necessary to ensure a permanent devolved Parliament in the UK.[142]

Furthermore, two notable statements were made about parliamentary sovereignty during its legislative passage. The Advocate General (Richard Keen QC) in closing the third reading of the Bill in the House of Lords, claimed that no restriction had been placed on Parliament's sovereignty.[143] Also, Lord Hope, (who had given a key opinion in *R (Jackson)* v. *Attorney General* – albeit obiter – appearing to place some qualifications on parliamentary sovereignty)

[141] 'Cameron: Holyrood Can Become a Powerhouse Parliament', *BBC News Online*, 2 October 2015.

[142] E.g. M Elliott, 'The Draft Scotland Bill and the Sovereignty of the UK Parliament', *Public Law for Everyone blog*, 22 January 2015; C Himsworth, 'Legislating for Permanence and a Statutory Footing' (2016) 20 Edinburgh LR 361. Although see K Campbell, 'The Draft Scotland Bill and Limits in Constitutional Statutes' (30 January 2015) UK Const. L. Blog.

[143] HL Deb, 21 March 2016, col 2071.

affirmed his loyalty to the principle of parliamentary sovereignty.[144] So it is questionable just what section 1 actually achieved legally.

1.9.2.2 Section 2 Scotland Act 2016

Section 2 put the 'Sewel convention' on some sort of[145] statutory basis. As a constitutional convention it was previously seen as being politically, as opposed to legally binding. However, s2 Scotland Act 2016 inserts a new subsection (8) into s28 Scotland Act 1998, which now reads: 'But it is recognized that the Parliament of the United Kingdom will not normally legislate with regard to devolved matters without the consent of the Scottish Parliament', although s28(7) still states that 'This section does not affect the power of the Parliament of the United Kingdom to make laws for Scotland'.

However, it seems that s2 Scotland Act 2016 does not transform the convention into a statutory obligation. The Supreme Court held in *Miller* that the Sewel Convention has no *legal* force, ruling that s2 Scotland Act 2016 was not intended to convert Sewel into a justiciable legal rule, but rather to 'entrench it as a convention.'[146] But an 'entrenched convention' is a puzzling notion in the absence of any method of enforcing compliance with it, and a controversial decision in the context of the delicate state of UK-Scottish constitutional politics, which provided the context for the enactment of the Scotland Act 2016. The Supreme Court explained that its finding was compelled by the wording in the Scotland Act itself, because 'We would have expected Westminster to have used other words if it were seeking to convert a convention into a legal rule justiciable by the courts.'[147] But it does seem strange to include a provision in legislation that is not intended to create any legal effect. So once again, it was questionable that anything had been achieved legally.

But there are other problems with the wording of s2 Scotland Act. First, what is meant by the term 'normally'? This word was described by the House of Lords Constitution Committee as 'unusual in legislation', but 'seems to make clear that Parliament will still have the legal power to legislate for Scotland, even on devolved matters, without the consent of the Scottish Parliament'.[148] But surely, if 'normally' just means what the UK Government interprets it as, then it is unhelpful or redundant? And so it proved. Substantial pieces of Brexit legislation, the EUWA 2018, and the EU WAA 2020, were passed without the legislative consent of the Scottish Parliament. A second complaint was that the

[144] Although, elsewhere, Lord Hope stated (of Article XIX Act of Union 1707) that: 'As a student at Edinburgh University many years ago, I was taught that the provision in those terms was fundamental law and in that respect the UK Parliament did not have absolute sovereignty.' HL Deb, 24 November 2015, col 617.

[145] The term 'some sort of' is used advisedly, given disagreements over the status of s 2, and the finding in *Miller*.

[146] *Miller*, judgement of the majority, at para. 149. [147] Ibid., at para. 148.

[148] House of Lords Constitution committee, *Proposals for the Devolution of Further Powers to Scotland* (n. 3) para. 72.

new statutory provision referred only to 'devolved matters.' This was felt to misrepresent the scope of the Sewel convention, which had evolved to cover both devolved policy areas and situations where the UK Parliament varied the legislative competence of the Scottish Parliament or Government.[149] This latter use was not included in s2 Scotland Act 2016. So, the scope of the UK government obligation in s28(8) is in any case unclear.

And thus concludes this discussion of the Scotland Act 2016. Notwithstanding the 2014 referendum, there was no far-reaching attempt to get to grips with both devolution and diversity, nor to think through and support counterbalancing, central elements that might bind the UK together. The combination of the ad hoc response in the 2016 Scotland Act, along with EVEL, was a partial, poorly thought out approach, stoking up future problems.

1.10 Judicial Review and Devolution

1.10.1 Introduction

How have the courts addressed questions of the Scottish Parliament's competence? 'Hard' judicial review (namely that in which a court can invalidate primary legislation) of Westminster statutes has not traditionally been possible under 'classic' interpretations of Britain's Constitution, in which the doctrine of parliamentary sovereignty prevails. However, this has not applied in the case of subordinate legislatures. For example, judicial review of legislation of the former Northern Ireland Parliament (1922–1972) was possible, although rare.[150] Since then, judicial review of legislation on certain grounds has been possible in the post 1998 devolution settlements. This availability of more searching judicial review tells us something about how devolution has changed the nature of law in the UK.

By the late 1990s, the idea that democratically enacted statutes might be reviewable no longer seemed so controversial in the UK. Even Westminster statutes could be set aside if they conflicted with EU law, as the *Factortame* case had shown.[151] Further, the 1988 Claim of Right for Scotland had declared the popular sovereignty of the Scottish people, thus circulating the notion that the power to legislate is limited and derives from the people. Constitutional review by the courts has since then become an important aspect of the devolution settlement in Scotland.

One early question[152] was that of the *status* of Acts of the Scottish Parliament. Should they be treated as primary legislation, because they are the output of an

[149] UK Government Devolution Guidance Note 10 (DGN10) https://assets.publishing.service.gov.uk/government/uploads/system/uploads/attachment_data/file/60985/post-devolution-primary-scotland.pdf

[150] For an example of a successful challenge see *Ulster Transport Authority* v. *James Brown & Sons Ltd* [1953] NI 79.

[151] *R* v. *Secretary of State for Transport, ex parte Factortame (no. 2)* [1991] 1 All ER 70.

[152] E.g. *Adams* v. *Scottish Ministers* [2004] SC 665 and *Whaley* v. *Watson* [2000] SC 340.

elected, democratic Parliament, or, alternatively, as analogous to local authority decisions, because devolved Parliaments are subordinate in status? In *AXA General Insurance Ltd*, the UK Supreme Court held that ASPs cannot be challenged as if they were decisions of a subordinate public body, and so they could not be reviewed on common law grounds of irrationality or unreasonableness. However, because the Scottish Parliament does not enjoy the sovereignty of the Crown in Parliament, its legislation could be amenable to some common law supervision'[153] – but only in the most exceptional circumstances.[154] In this way, common law conditions for judicial review of ASPs are not so far from those some judges have suggested might apply to Westminster primary legislation. (An exceptional rule of law review of Westminster statutes was suggested in the dicta of Baroness Hale, Lord Steyn and Lord Hope in *Jackson* v. *Attorney General*.[155]) So, while the Scottish Parliament can be distinguished from Westminster, courts have stressed what the Scottish Parliament has *in common* with the Westminster Parliament, namely its status as a democratic legislature with the legitimacy that follows from that.

But what of the Scotland Act itself, the legislation that established the Scottish Parliament? In 2002, in the Northern Ireland *Robinson* case, the House of Lords (judicial Chamber) held that the Devolution Acts were in effect Constitutions, to be interpreted 'generously and purposively'.[156] This looked like a rather radical departure. However, both the Court of Session and UK Supreme Court later rejected this approach. Although the Supreme Court held in *H* v. *Lord Advocate*,[157] that the Scotland Act, as a constitutional statute,[158] could not be impliedly repealed, in *Imperial Tobacco* Lord Reed stated:

> The Scotland Act is not a constitution, but an Act of Parliament. There are material differences. The context of the devolution of legislative and executive power within the United Kingdom is evidently different from that of establishing a constitution for an independent state such as Jamaica or Barbados, or a British overseas territory such as Bermuda.[159]

1.10.2 Statutory Grounds of Review

The Scottish Parliament may be a democratically elected body but it is constrained by statute, mainly under ss 28 and 29 Scotland Act.

153 *AXA General Insurance Ltd* v. *HM Advocate* [2011] UKSC 46 per Lord Hope, at para. 47.
154 This approach was carried forward in *Imperial Tobacco Ltd* [2012] SLT 749 at para. 58.
155 *Jackson* v. *Attorney General* [2005] UKHL 56.
156 *Robinson* v. *Secretary of State for Northern Ireland* [2002] UKHL 32, 11, especially the opinion of Lord Hoffmann.
157 [2013] 1 AC 413.
158 Following Lord Justice Laws' obiter dictum in *Thoburn* [2002] EWHC 195 (Admin).
159 *Imperial Tobacco Ltd* v. *Lord Advocate* [2012] CSIH 9 2012 SC 297 at [71], per Lord Reed.

s29(2)d provides that ASPs must not be incompatible with the ECHR nor (while the UK was an EU member) with EU law. Although the democratic credentials of the Scottish Parliament were stressed by the Supreme Court in *AXA*, it is nonetheless constrained far more strongly by ECHR rights than Westminster. This means that any ASP incompatible with ECHR rights is 'not law', whereas statutes enacted by Westminster may only declared 'incompatible' with the ECHR by the courts under s4 HRA and cannot be invalidated by the courts for violation of the Human Rights Act 1998. Section 29(2)(d) also stated that the Scottish Parliament could not act incompatibly with EU law. Since 1 February 2020, the UK has left the EU, but under EUWA 2018, devolved legislatures are still bound by 'retained EU law', although the UK Parliament, and UK ministers, are free to amend it. The opposition of the Scottish government to Brexit legislation is considered further below.

Secondly, what have been termed 'federal'[160] (although this may be a bit of a misnomer, given the UK is not a federal State) restrictions apply, namely those which determine the division of competences between the UK and Scottish levels of government. S29(2)(b) provides that Scottish Parliament legislation will be outside competence if it relates to a reserved matter. Although most earlier challenges to ASPs were based on ECHR rights, there has been increasing litigation alleging that Scottish legislation trespassed on matters reserved to Westminster. But the line between reserved and devolved matters can be rather difficult to draw. When considering whether a provision relates to a reserved matter the courts must determine this 'by reference to the purpose of the provision, having regard (among other things) to its effect in all the circumstances' (s29(3) SA). Further, s 101(2) Scotland Act provides that ASPs are to be 'read as narrowly as is required for it to be within competence, if such a reading is possible.'

Some federal jurisdictions, especially Canada, have taken a 'pith and substance' approach to competence, seeking out the essential character of the law, and its true meaning and purpose,[161] looking at the statute as a whole. However this approach was not followed wholeheartedly by the UK Supreme Court.[162] *In Imperial Tobacco*, Lord Hope said that the 'pith and substance' test was unnecessary because the Devolution Acts did not use that phrase and provided their own rubric for interpretation, thus suggesting that the UK test for division of powers should not be compared to those in a federal jurisdiction. Generally, the Supreme Court has held that a provision will be outside competence if it has a 'more than a loose or consequential connection to a reserved matter' – a phrase that was used in 2010 in *Martin*,[163] and repeated in other cases since.

160 C McCorkindale, A McHarg, and PF Scott, 'The Courts, Devolution, and Constitutional Review' (2017) 36 Univ. of Queensland LJ 289–310.

161 *General Motors of Canada Ltd* v. *City National Leasing* [1989] 1 SCR 641 Supreme Court of Canada.

162 Lord Hope in *Martin* v. *HM Advocate* [2010] UKSC 10, para. 15, and in *Imperial Tobacco*, para. 13.

163 Lord Walker in *Martin* v. *HM Advocate* [2010] UKSC 10, para. 49, endorsed by L Hope in *Imperial Tobacco*, also *Christian Institute* v. *Lord Advocate* [2016] UKSC 51.

In March 2018, the Scottish Parliament adopted the *UK Withdrawal from the European Union (Legal Continuity) (Scotland) Act 2018* by 95 votes to 32. This Bill shared its structure and approach with the UK EUWA 2018,[164] seeking to complement it. However, it diverged from the EUWA in some areas, for example, it did not exclude the EU Charter of Fundamental Rights, and allowed Scotland to keep pace with EU developments in future. It also, in its s17 (in contrast to the UK EUWA), required consent of Scottish ministers should UK Ministers wish to alter or repeal retained EU law within devolved areas. This Bill was challenged by the UK government and the lawsuit made constitutional history – being the first ASP referred to the UK Supreme Court by the Attorney General under s33 Scotland Act 1998, a procedure that constitutes a type of 'abstract', rather than 'concrete' review. Later in 2018, the Supreme Court, applying the familiar test of whether a provision had 'more than a loose or consequential connection to a reserved matter' found only s17 outside of the Scottish Parliament's competence,[165] due to enactments in the EUWA (subsequent to the adoption of the Scottish Continuity legislation), which prohibited the EUWA's own modification. However, it is hard not to conclude that the Continuity Bill was competent when adopted by the Scottish Parliament. If so, surely it follows that the UK Government may challenge any devolved legislation it dislikes, thus suspending its application while the matter is *sub judice*, and in the meantime adopt its own 'protected legislation', which by coming into force automatically trumps the devolved legislation.

In 2021, the UK Supreme Court upheld the UK Government's challenge to two Bills adopted by the Scottish Parliament on grounds they exceeded the Scottish Parliament's powers. Both Bills implemented treaties into Scots law, one incorporating the UN Convention on the Rights of the Child, the other the European Charter of local self-government. Although both Bills were unanimously approved by MSPs and certified by the Presiding Officer as within the Scottish Parliament's powers, the Court held that both Bills placed obligations on UK ministers that exceeded devolved powers.[166] Significantly, the Supreme Court found that provisions in the Bills would modify s28(7) SA in what Elliott describes as 'a highly unconvincing judgement that reads the Scottish Devolution settlement unnecessarily narrowly.'[167] This significant judgement on legislative competence was perhaps a harbinger of how the Supreme Court would determine the competence of a future Scottish independence referendum Bill.

164 The EUWA is discussed further below.

165 *A Reference by the Attorney General and the Advocate General for Scotland* [2018] UKSC 64. The term 'Bill' is used because, although it was adopted by the Parliament, royal assent had been suspended until litigation was concluded.

166 *Reference by the Attorney General and the Advocate General for Scotland* [2021] UKSC 42

167 M Elliott and N Kilford, 'Devolution in the Supreme Court: Legislative Supremacy, Parliament's 'Unqualified' Power, and 'Modifying' the Scotland Act', U.K. Const. L. Blog (15 October 2021).

1.10.3 Role of the UK Supreme Court

These judgements prompt questions as to the Supreme Court's growing role in devolution jurisprudence. The UK Supreme Court has been the final court of appeal for devolution disputes since 2009.[168] When it hears devolution issues, the Supreme Court sits as a UK court, rather than a Scottish (or English and Welsh, or Northern Irish) court. Yet, Scots law is different to English law, and each of the three devolution settlements is in turn different from each other, perhaps undermining the concept of a uniform devolution jurisprudence,[169] let alone a uniform constitutional law. Since 2017, the UK Supreme Court has sometimes sat in Edinburgh, Belfast and Cardiff, perhaps in an attempt to counteract a perception that the Court might be too London centred and England dominated.

Originally it was the Judicial Committee of the Privy Council (JCPC) that determined devolution disputes. The JCPC was thought to be well placed for this role, having been a court of last resort for many Commonwealth jurisdictions in the past, and having served this function under the Government of Ireland Act 1920. However, both the SNP and the Liberal Democrats were unhappy with this arrangement,[170] seeking to amend the 1998 Scotland Bill to provide for a constitutional court whose judges would be institutionally independent from the House of Lords and English domination. As this chapter has explored, a different Scottish constitutional tradition has evolved, which is sometimes difficult to square with orthodox English theories of parliamentary sovereignty. And so, a dominance of English judges[171] determining devolution cases might seem problematic.

1.10.4 Conclusions

Therefore, ASPs are reviewable by the courts which may declare their provisions ultra vires, thus distinguishing them from Acts of the Westminster Parliament. Notably, in a 2018 lecture, Lady Hale stated that 'the only conclusion I can draw is that devolution of legislative – as opposed to executive – power turns the United Kingdom Supreme Court into a genuinely constitutional court.'[172] Nonetheless, the caselaw on constitutional review of ASPs is somewhat equivocal. Sometimes, the approach seems to be a constitutional one, approaching the Scottish Parliament as a democratically elected primary legislator, established

168 Constitutional Reform Act 2005, s. 40.

169 See David Feldman, 'None, One or Several: Perspectives on the UK's Constitution(s)' (2005) 64.

170 See HC Deb vol. 312, cols 203–215, 12 May 1998 (SNP).

171 Section 28(8) Constitutional Reform Act provides that: 'In making selections for the appointment of judges of the Court the commission must ensure that between them the judges will have knowledge of, and experience of practice in, the law of each part of the United Kingdom.' In practice, there have usually been two Scottish members of the Court.

172 'Devolution and The Supreme Court – 20 Years On', Scottish Public Law Group 14 June 2018.

by a constitutional statute. On the other hand, the Supreme Court seems to have also rejected the federal 'pith and substance' test, and cleaved to an absolutist view of Westminster parliamentary sovereignty in its more recent judgements.

If Scotland had voted for independence in 2014, a Constitutional Convention would have been assembled to draft a written Constitution which limited the sovereignty of legislative acts.[173] The role of judges to determine constitutional meaning, and if necessary invalidate 'ordinary' legislative acts for non-compliance with the Constitution, tends to become augmented with written Constitutions, as it has been in the US, since the decision of *Marbury* v. *Madison*. The outlier is the Westminster Parliament.

1.11 Devolution and Parliamentary Sovereignty

How then does devolution interact with parliamentary sovereignty? According to Dicey, parliamentary sovereignty prevents the Scotland Act (or Acts of Union) having any special entrenched status. They are for Dicey, ordinary Acts, open to implied or express repeal just like any other Act of Parliament. Diceyan doctrine holds that Westminster parliamentary sovereignty has been unqualified by devolution. Section 28(7) Scotland Act asserts the power of the UK Parliament to make laws for Scotland. Thus, is certainly not federalism, and denies full sovereignty to Scotland, even within the sphere of devolved matters.

However, not all have taken the view that Westminster parliamentary sovereignty has been left untouched. In 1998, Vernon Bogdanor suggested that, following devolution, Parliamentary supremacy 'will become merely a nebulous right to supervise the Scottish Parliament, together with the right under pathological circumstances, to abolish it.'[174] The apparent devolution challenge to parliamentary sovereignty is enlarged by competing claims of the popular sovereignty of the Scottish people, asserted to have the right to determine their political setup. This is enhanced by the idea, also prevalent in Scotland, of the UK as a voluntary union, dissolvable at will by either party.

Yet in practice, things are more complicated. Neither legal doctrine nor political practice have been particularly clear. This was illustrated by the apparent failure to translate the Sewel convention into a legislative obligation. For a long time, the British Constitution has celebrated its uncodified, apparently 'flexible' nature, one composed a much of political practices, conventions and usages as hard legal rules. Yet, legally unenforceable conventions depend on trust, willing compliance and good faith if the Constitution is to work effectively. There is less of that trust in operation now we are witnessing the demise

[173] See *Scotland's Future: Your Guide to an Independent Scotland* (2013) 332, 334–335.

[174] V Bogdanor, 'Devolution: The Constitutional Aspects', in *Constitutional Reform in the United Kingdom* (University of Cambridge Centre for Public Law, 1998) at 12.

of what Hennessey describes as the 'good chaps'[175] account of government. But equally, if constitutional conventions are vague and nebulous, so are the legal rules. What is the status of Westminster parliamentary sovereignty? As explained in Chapter 6, its basis is somewhat mysterious.

1.12 Brexit

1.12.1 Background

This unsettled constitutional situation was further complicated by Brexit, which hit the UK like a 'lightning bolt'.[176] During the Scottish independence referendum campaign, the pro-UK, 'Better Together' side notably raised the issue of EU membership. They suggested that the only way Scotland's EU membership would be assured was by remaining in the UK, and that an independent Scotland's application for EU membership could take years, with no guarantee of success. Thus, in voting against independence, many Scots might have thought they were securing EU membership. This proved not to be the case.

In the 2016 EU referendum, in which overall the UK voted by 51.9 per cent to leave the EU, Scotland voted by 62 per cent to remain. (This was a bigger margin than the 55 per cent of voting Scots voting to remain in the UK in 2014.) The EU Single Market was the main destination for Scotland's international exports, and, according to a 2016 report by the Fraser of Allander Institute, Brexit will have a significant negative impact on the Scottish economy, resulting in a GDP lower by 2–5 per cent, and employment lower by 1–3 per cent, than if the UK remained in the EU.[177] The Scottish government argued that it was undemocratic for Scotland to be driven out of the EU against its will. Yet, within the constraints of Britain's constitutional arrangements, it has been difficult for Scotland to forge a different relationship with the EU from the rest of the UK. The current devolution settlement treats EU negotiations as 'reserved' matters, giving Scotland few legal rights in the EU withdrawal process. Nonetheless, efforts were made within Scotland to explore whether it could remain in the EU Single Market. The Scottish Government published *Scotland's Place in Europe*[178] in December 2016, well before the UK Government had concretized its position, stating a desire to maintain the benefits of EU membership for Scotland.

1.12.2 A UK 'Union' Approach

Although foreign policy, which includes relations with the EU, is reserved to the UK government, it is too simplistic to state that devolved administrations

175 See e.g. 'Good Chaps No More? Safeguarding the Constitution in Stressful Times' by Andrew Blick and Peter Hennessy (2019) Constitution Society. Maybe Hennessey somewhere includes chapesses – I haven't been able to confirm.

176 Peter Hennessey, House of Lords, Hansard 5 July 2016, Volume 773, column 1963.

177 Fraser of Allander Institute: 'Long-Term Economic Implications of Brexit: A Report for the Scottish Parliament' (October 2016).

178 Available at www.gov.scot/publications/scotlands-place-europe/

have no interest in EU matters. A large part of EU law relates to devolved competences – as a result, devolved governments had an important role in implementing and applying EU law. Additionally, many areas of EU law straddle devolved and reserved competences.[179]

However, notwithstanding Scottish aspirations, in her Lancaster House speech[180] in January 2017 (then Prime Minister) Theresa May stated that the UK would leave both the Single Market and the Customs Union. No mention was made in the UK Government's letter triggering Article 50 TEU[181] of any particular arrangements for Scotland (although Northern Ireland was singled out as a special case), so it seemed that the UK Government rejected the Scottish Government's proposals. Nor were the contents of the Article 50 notification shared with the Scottish Government prior to its publication. This left little space for Scotland to protect its interests in the withdrawal process, where it was the UK Government that did the negotiating, embracing a unitary and top-down approach, excluding devolved governments from the negotiation process.[182] However, the archetype of 'unitary' State has been undermined by two decades of devolution in the UK.[183]

1.12.2.1 The UK Internal Market

In the past, EU law constrained its member States to legislate in compliance with the EU Internal Market. Yet, in the absence of EU common principles, barriers to trade within the UK may materialize. Federal States have had to make provision to ensure policy harmonization. For example, the US commerce clause states that the US Congress shall have power 'To regulate Commerce with foreign Nations, and among the several States, and with the Indian Tribes.'[184] How would Britain manage its Internal Market post Brexit?

An earlier UK Government Brexit White Paper argued for national 'common frameworks'.[185] But the 2020 UK Internal Market Act is the main vehicle to provide a basic framework for the UK Internal Market and to prevent trade barriers within it. The Act relies on two major principles – mutual recognition and non-discrimination. Although devolveds may set their own regulations in devolved areas, the mutual recognition provision prevents them from applying these to goods and services already marketed in other parts of the UK (also extending to goods imported into the UK from third countries). The

[179] E.g. immigration, which is reserved, may impact on health policy, which is devolved.
[180] *The Government's Negotiating Objectives for Exiting the EU: PM Speech*, 17 January 2017.
[181] *Prime Minister's letter to Donald Tusk triggering Article 50*, 29 March 2017.
[182] Such intra-UK government machinery as exists, including the EU formation of the Joint Ministerial Committee, JMC(E) were perceived by the devolveds as weak, sidelined, and as functioning inadequately.
[183] See e.g. R Hazell and R Rawlings, *Devolution, Law Making and the Constitution* (Imprint Academic, 2005).
[184] United States Constitution (Article I, Section 8, Clause 3).
[185] UK Government: 'Legislating for the United Kingdom's Withdrawal from the European Union' at 27, para. 4.4.

non-discrimination principle prohibits devolved governments from discriminating against goods and services from other parts of the UK.

Overall, devolved Governments view the Act as weakening their ability to legislate in devolved areas, and, according to Michael Russell MSP, 'radically undermining the powers and democratic ability of the Scottish Parliament.'[186] Furthermore, the 2020 Internal Market Act provides the UK Government with spending powers in many devolved areas, thus compromising their ability to take credit for funding policy innovations within their territories.

1.12.3 The *Miller* Litigation and the Sewel Convention

In *Miller*, the UK Supreme Court determined that the UK Government may not trigger Article 50 by use of the prerogative alone. The devolution aspects of this case have been, however, somewhat under-analysed.

The Scottish Government intervened in *Miller*, arguing that any Parliamentary legislation authorizing the UK Government to trigger Article 50 would require the consent of the Scottish Parliament as it would necessitate amending the Devolution Statutes. So, the status of the Sewel convention was at issue. However, the Supreme Court in *Miller* held that, notwithstanding its incorporation in the Scotland Act 2016, the measure remains a convention, not a legally enforceable obligation, and in fact the European Union (Notification of Withdrawal) Act 2017 was adopted without any legislative consent motion(s) having been requested or adopted.

The Scottish Government also argued in *Miller* that triggering Article 50 by unilateral act of the Crown would be contrary to the Claim of Right 1689 and Act of Union 1706. The Claim of Right argument contended that government only has such powers as expressly granted to it by the people in representative assembly. The Scottish Government also argued that the UK's withdrawal from the EU would result in modifications to Scots private law (e.g. employment and consumer rights derived directly from EU law) not for the evident utility of the Scottish people (and so contrary to Article XVIII Act of Union) – especially given that 62 per cent of the Scottish Referendum vote was for Remain. Both of these arguments failed, but nonetheless, drawing on these statutes illustrates that Scotland and England have different constitutional traditions, and historically different views of the Crown's privileges. The Supreme Court's judgement in *Miller* has been criticized for assuming 'that the 19th century English constitutional tradition as formulated/invented by Dicey – is the fount and only origin of the contemporary United Kingdom constitution.'[187]

[186] M Russell, *After Brexit: The UK Internal Market Act and Devolution* (Scottish Government, 8 March 2021).

[187] A O'Neill, 'The Miller Decision: Legal Constitutionalism Ends Not with a Bang, but a Whimper' (2017/2/03) VerfBlog.

1.12.4 The EU Withdrawal Act 2018 and the EU Withdrawal Agreement Act 2020

As if to press home the impact of the *Miller* ruling, Westminster also adopted the 2018 EUWA without the consent of the Scottish Parliament. The EUWA provides the apparatus for the huge revision of the UK legal system necessary as a consequence of the UK's exit from the EU. This is 'a legal undertaking of a type and scale that is unique and unprecedented.'[188] The EUWA provides for continuity by preserving EU law as it exists immediately before Brexit, converting it into domestic (or 'retained EU') law, and then, where necessary, granting UK Government ministers huge law-making powers to repeal or amend it. It also provided for repeal of the ECA 1972.

Importantly for this chapter, the EUWA set out important and controversial provisions – sections 10, 11 & 12, along with schedules 2 & 3 – regarding devolution. Most controversial is s12 EUWA, which, to summarize a convoluted provision, enables the UK Government unilaterally to limit devolved powers in areas of retained EU law. And so, the Scottish Parliament refused to grant its consent to the relevant sections of the EUWA, which was nonetheless adopted in Westminster.

A Withdrawal Agreement[189] was agreed between the EU and the UK government on 17 October 2019 and entered into force on 1 February 2020, after the UK Parliament had adopted the EU WAA 2020 and the EU had approved it. From that date, the UK was no longer an EU member, although there was a transition period until 31 December 2020, during which most EU law continued to apply in the UK. The WAA was notably adopted without the consent of any of the devolved legislatures. According to Ian Blackford, MP, and SNP leader at Westminster: 'We are faced with a situation which is completely unprecedented when the government in Edinburgh, Belfast and in Cardiff has not given consent to this act of parliament. That completely contravenes the devolution settlement.'[190]

1.13 Conclusions

1.13.1 A Second Scottish Independence Referendum?

At time of writing, much is uncertain. But Brexit has, to date, involved a forceful centralization. Given that England is so much larger that Scotland,

[188] Per House of Lords Constitution Committee, *European Union (Withdrawal) Bill*, 29 January 2018, HL 69 2017–19, p. 3.

[189] *Agreement on the withdrawal of the United Kingdom of Great Britain and Northern Ireland from the European Union and the European Atomic Energy Community*, 2019/C 384 OJ C 384, 12 November 2019.

[190] 'Boris Johnson's Brexit Bill Becomes Law', *The Guardian*, 23 January 2020.

Wales and Northern Ireland, and English Government is merged into UK Government, this seems to empower England over the devolved nations. In late 2019, the Scottish Government published *Scotland's Right to Choose: Putting Scotland's Future in Scotland's Hands,* stating its commitment to 'an agreed, legal process … which will be accepted as legitimate in Scotland, the UK as a whole, and by the international community.' This document cited as grounds for an independence referendum: Scots' sovereign right to determine their own constitutional future; a material change in circumstances since the 2014 referendum, (namely Brexit, despite the desire of majority of Scottish voters to remain, and effects of Brexit on Scotland); and the existence of a mandate for a referendum derived from electoral victories at the 2016 Holyrood election, and 2017 and 2019 Westminster elections. After the SNP won forty-eight of Scotland's fifty-nine seats in the UK General Election in December 2019, Nicola Sturgeon claimed there was a 'renewed, refreshed and strengthened mandate' for another referendum, and requested a 'section 30 order' from the UK Government for the power to hold an independence referendum. This was, however, rejected in January 2020 by Prime Minister Boris Johnson.[191]

Although the Covid pandemic meant that moves towards independence were on hold for a while, nonetheless, opinion polls in 2020 consistently showed support for Scottish independence at around or over 50 per cent, with one poll showing a record high of 58 per cent. The Scottish Parliament adopted referendum legislation in 2020,[192] setting out the general rules and applicable franchise for all referendums in Scotland. In January 2021, the SNP produced a 'routemap' to independence, followed by a draft independence referendum Bill in March 2021, which it committed to enact if an SNP Government were re-elected with a majority to do so. In the May 2021 Scottish Parliament elections, the SNP fell one seat short of an overall majority, although together with the Green party MSPs, an overall majority for independence exists in the Scottish Parliament. But the UK Government continued to state that it would refuse to grant a s30 order – a refusal that seems somewhat ironic, given that the UK Government has often cast the 'will of the people' as crucial (necessitating the honouring of the Brexit non-binding referendum). Nicola Sturgeon has also stressed the importance of popular consent. In an SNP conference speech, Sturgeon stated that Brexit had included

> a process to allow Northern Ireland to decide if and for how long it will stay aligned to the single market and customs union … Wales will have voted to leave. England will have voted to leave. Northern Ireland will be given a say over its future. Scotland will be the only country in the UK to be taken out

[191] Boris Johnson's rejection, 14 January 2020: https://assets.publishing.service.gov.uk/government/uploads/system/uploads/attachment_data/file/857586/Nicola_Sturgeon_20200114.pdf

[192] The Referendums (Scotland) Act 2020 and The Scottish Elections (Franchise & Representation) Act 2020.

> of the EU against our will and with no say over our future relationship with Europe.[193]

However, after deadlock and UK Government rejection of the s30 route, in June 2022, the Scottish Government launched new steps in the campaign for independence.[194] It started by issuing a series of papers, under the umbrella of *Building a New Scotland*,[195] intended to increase popular support for independence. The centrepiece, however, was an independence referendum Bill, issued on 28 June 2022, but not then introduced into the Scottish Parliament, because the Scottish Lord Advocate, Dorothy Bain, immediately referred[196] the Bill to the UK Supreme Court under Schedule 6 Scotland Act 1998 with the question:

> Does the provision of the proposed Scottish Independence Referendum Bill that provides that the question to be asked in a referendum would be 'Should Scotland be an independent country?' relate to reserved matters? In particular, does it relate to: (i) the Union of the Kingdoms of Scotland England (Para 1b Sched. 5); and/or (ii) the Parliament of the United Kingdom (para 1c. Sched 5).

Although it is somewhat unusual to refer a Bill that is not yet law, the Supreme Court rejected the UK Government's contention that the action was 'premature'[197] (because the Bill had not yet been passed by the Scottish Parliament) and the action was scheduled for hearing on 11 and 12 October 2022. The First Minister also announced that if the Bill were found within legislative competence, then the Scottish Government would immediately introduce the Bill so that the referendum could proceed on 19 October 2023.

1.13.1.1 Scottish Independence in the UK Supreme Court

On 23 November 2022, the UK Supreme Court gave judgement on the legal viability of a second Scottish independence referendum.[198] The Supreme Court held that the Scottish Parliament lacked the legal competence to adopt legislation for a second independence referendum, because such legislation would relate to matters reserved to the UK under schedule 5 Scotland Act 1998

[193] Available at www.snp.org/nicola-sturgeons-address-to-snp19/

[194] 'Next steps in independence referendum set out', 28 June 2022, at www.gov.scot/news/next-steps-in-independence-referendum-set-out/

[195] See further www.gov.scot/newscotland/

[196] Reference by the Lord Advocate to the Supreme Court – available at www.gov.scot/binaries/content/documents/govscot/publications/strategy-plan/2022/07

[197] In *Keatings* v. *Advocate-General* [2021] CSIH 25, the Scottish Court of Session refused a declaration that the Scottish Parliament had the power to hold a referendum on Scottish independence, stating that the application was 'premature, hypothetical and academic', given that no referendum Bill had been introduced to the Scottish Parliament.

[198] *Reference by the Lord Advocate of Devolution Issues under Paragraph 34 of Schedule 6 to the Scotland Act 1998.*

(namely, the Union of the Kingdoms of Scotland and England and/or the UK Parliament).

The core of the case came with the Court's determination that a referendum Bill would relate to reserved matters. Well-known caselaw, such as the 2010 *Martin* v. *Her Majesty's Advocate*, established that a statutory provision relates to a reserved matter if it has something more than 'a loose or consequential connection' with it. Under section 29(3) Scotland Act 1998, this should be determined by reference to the purpose of the provision (i.e. the proposed referendum) having regard to its effect in all the circumstances. The Lord Advocate argued that the draft Bill was a 'consultative referendum' whose 'purpose' was, in the very words of the draft Bill itself, 'to make provision for ascertaining the views of the people of Scotland on whether Scotland should be an independent country'.[199] In this way, the Lord Advocate argued that a consultative referendum would not 'relate to' the reserved matter of the Union, in more than the 'loose or consequential' sense required by caselaw. However, the Court disagreed, finding that, even if the referendum had no immediate legal consequences, it would still have important political consequences, and more than a loose or consequential connection with the reserved matters of the Union of Scotland and England and the sovereignty of the UK Parliament.

Overall, perhaps the Supreme Court's decision was not very surprising. For a start, only five Supreme Court judges (Lord Reed, Lady Rose, Lord Lloyd-Jones, Lord Sales, and Lord Stephens) sat to hear it – not the full Court of 11 who heard the *Miller I* and *Miller/Cherry* Brexit cases. Therefore, although this case was noted as important by Lord Reed, it was not seen as meriting a hearing by a full Supreme Court. Further, although the Supreme Court found against the UK Government in both *Miller* cases –which might have appeared encouraging to the Scottish Government – those cases can be distinguished. Lord Reed, himself Scottish in origin and legal training, is now President of the UK Supreme Court, which was not the case in the *Miller* disputes, and the 'Reed Court' appears to take a somewhat different judicial approach from preceding Supreme Court configurations. As Conor Gearty has argued,[200] the Reed Court is more formalist in approach, adopting a close reading of legal texts in preference to broader arguments (such as those of relevance to Scottish independence which rest on the principle of democracy, or on unincorporated human rights such as self-determination). Furthermore, in both *Miller* cases, the beneficiary was the UK Parliament, and parliamentary sovereignty – a doctrine that the Supreme Court, and particularly Lord Reed, is unlikely to apply to the Scottish Parliament.

[199] *Reference by the Lord Advocate to the Supreme Court – available at www.gov.scot/binaries/content/documents/govscot/publications/strategy-plan/2022/07*

[200] C Gearty, 'In the Shallow End', LRB, 27 January 2022.

Furthermore, the Supreme Court has tended to view the devolution settlement narrowly, which does not favour the Scottish Government's arguments for independence. In *Miller I*, the Court found the Sewel Convention (that the UK Parliament 'will not normally legislate with regard to devolved matters without the consent of the Scottish Parliament') to be only a political convention and thus legally unenforceable, despite its having been legislated in section 2 2016 Scotland Act. In the 2018 *Scottish Continuity Bill* case and 2021 *UN Rights of the Child* case (decided unanimously by the Supreme Court, and in which four out of the five judges in the 2022 referendum case sat), the Court also approached Scottish devolution narrowly (not 'generously and purposively', as it had devolution legislation in the much earlier *Robinson* case[201]) – finding that the Scotland Act 'must be interpreted in the same way as any other statute'. Therefore, they concluded that it could not be applied in a way that undermined the sovereignty of the Westminster Parliament.

And finally, in *Miller I*, the Supreme Court took a broad approach to the 'effect' of actions – finding the prerogative could not be used to trigger Article 50 TEU to start the process of leaving the EU, because its practical effect would lead to the repeal of the ECA 1972, and only Parliament could repeal legislation, not the Government. Therefore, it is unsurprising that the Court considered that even a consultative referendum could have wide effects, even if not legal ones, because it might ultimately lead to the breakup of the UK.

1.13.1.2 What Follows?

The Supreme Court's judgement is not startling. However, it does leave Scotland in a potentially frustrating constitutional position. The UK Union has been recognized as voluntary,[202] and Scotland's right to self-determination stressed, including by UK Government ministers. Nonetheless, Scotland's First Minister, Nicola Sturgeon, suggested that losing in the Supreme Court 'will clarify that any notion of the UK as a voluntary union of nations is a fiction and that that the UK is a partnership of equals is false.'[203] And absent UK political support, it is hard to see how Scotland's rights can be exercised in a way that would garner legal recognition from the international community.

Nicola Sturgeon had already declared that, if the Supreme Court were to find a draft Bill outside Holyrood powers, then the SNP would fight the next

[201] *Robinson* v. *Secretary of State for Northern Ireland and Others*, [2002] UKHL 32.

[202] For example, 'as a nation, [the Scots] have an undoubted right to national self-determination; thus far they have exercised that right by joining and remaining in the Union. Should they determine on independence no English party or politician would stand in their way.' Margaret Thatcher, *The Downing Street Years* (Harper Collins, 1993) at 624.

[203] Scottish Government, 'Next Steps in Independence Referendum Set Out', 28 June 2022

UK General Election as a 'de facto' referendum on the 'single question' of whether Scotland should be independent. Although such a strategy has had some past uses (such as when Sinn Fein regarded its overwhelming 1918 General Election victory as providing a mandate to issue its Declaration of Independence) its efficacy has also been doubted by some, including SNP members, and future SNP independence strategy appeared itself clouded, when Nicola Sturgeon herself resigned, in February 2023, to the surprise of many, and Hamza Yousaf was elected SNP leader, and Scottish First Minister.

It has also been argued that, absent any s30 order, the Scottish Government might make a unilateral declaration of independence. Such declarations are not illegal under international law, as was recognized by the 2010 *Advisory Opinion* of the ICJ in the case of Kosovo.[204] However, there is no absolute guarantee a UDI would receive recognition by international community, and indeed, Kosovo did not receive recognition by all countries. The consequences of proclaiming independence in a context viewed as illegal by the central State have been painfully obvious, given the custodial sentences of key Catalonian politicians who proclaimed independence. A further argument has been that SNP members in Westminster might use organized parliamentary obstruction – that is, filibusters, countless amendments, challenges to chairs, and nominations to committees – to hold up matters in the House of Commons. Such tactics were used by Charles Stewart Parnell in the late nineteenth century when arguing for Irish Home Rule,[205] although did not achieve Home Rule, which was successively blocked at Westminster.

However, and more broadly, as Joanna Cherry KC MP has suggested, there are clear advantages to taking the 'wider constitutional context'[206] of Scotland–England relations into account, rather than focussing solely on the issue of whether the Scottish Parliament has the power to hold an independence referendum under a devolution settlement barely 25 years old. The constitutional relationship between England and Scotland was founded on the Treaty of Union, a consensual Union concluded between two sovereign States, which established the United Kingdom of Great Britain. Under this Union, Scotland continued with its own separate civic institutions, legal system, church and cultural heritage. This indicates that Union is a continuing agreement between two independent nations.

Indeed, a separate intervenor brief[207] was submitted by the SNP to the Supreme Court case, which made additional arguments based on the right

[204] 'Accordance with International Law of the Unilateral Declaration of Independence in Respect of Kosovo', 22 July 2010, ICJ 141.

[205] M Keating, 'Parnell's Lessons for Scottish Nationalism in Westminster and Beyond', 25 July 2018, available at www.centreonconstitutionalchange.ac.uk/opinions/parnells-lessons-scottish-nationalism-westminster-and-beyond

[206] J Cherry, 'Here's the Facts on the Scottish Independence Case at the UK Supreme Court', *The National*, 13 October 2022.

[207] Available here: www.snp.org/the-snps-supreme-court-submission-on-the-independence-referendum/

of the Scottish people to self-determination, and to democracy. These arguments were dismissed by the Supreme Court, which held that the right to self-determination was not at issue. However, the right to self-determination should not be dismissed so quickly. It is a fundamental and inalienable right, located in Article 1 UN Covenant, and, although this Covenant has not been incorporated into domestic law, the SNP brief argued that UK statutes (such as the 1998 Scotland Act) should be interpreted compatibly with the UK's international law commitments. Many UK Prime Ministers and politicians, including Margaret Thatcher, have acknowledged that the Union is a voluntary one, and that Scotland has a right to self-determination. Therefore, through its own conduct over many years, the UK Government has generated an expectation allowing for independence in principle. This situation clearly distinguishes the UK from States such as Spain, Article 2 of whose Constitution declares 'the indissoluble unity of the Spanish nation', or the US, whose Supreme Court in 1868, in *Texas* v. *White*, held that there was no right to state secession.[208]

Furthermore, as the UK Supreme Court itself acknowledged in *Miller/Cherry* 'The legal principles of the constitution are not confined to statutory rules, but include constitutional principles developed by the common law'. Democracy is a key constitutional principle, and yet the UK Government has undermined democracy by ignoring the SNP's 2021 manifesto pledge and its endorsement by the Scottish people, as well as the January 2020 Scottish Parliament vote for an independence referendum.

These points based on self-determination and democracy may be supplemented by legal arguments based on consent, change of circumstances and the requirement to negotiate in good faith. Together, these arguments make a case that the UK Government's refusal to negotiate the independence issue with Scotland is unreasonable. To be sure, such arguments must be supported by evidence that the Scottish people desire to exercise their right to self-determination and leave the Union. If this were not so, the Scottish Government would itself be violating the principle of democracy. The clearest way to demonstrate this would be by a referendum on independence, and that is why referendums have been the focus of so much discussion to date. But its existence could be demonstrated in other ways, such as at a General Election.

Indeed, Scotland is in a constitutionally frustrating and somewhat anomalous position. The Union is acknowledged to be voluntary and not forced, and Scotland's right to self-determination has been stressed, including by UK Government ministers. And yet, without UK political support, it is difficult to see how Scotland's rights can be exercised. And so, the issue of Scottish independence is not dead, just as the issue of Irish independence was not forgotten when successive Irish Home Rule Bills failed in Westminster in the nineteenth

[208] *Texas* v. *White*, 74 U.S. 700 [1868].

century. But the issue perhaps moves to a broader legal, political and constitutional stage, one with a longer history than the Devolution Acts.

1.14 Contrasting Views

This chapter has revealed different understandings of British Constitutional law to be at issue. One unitary view, that of the UK Government, argues that parliamentary sovereignty requires that final authority remains with Westminster, leaving Scottish claims a moral and political, but not legal force. A contrasting view interprets the Acts of Union as a pact between two States, dependent on consent. It identifies a conception of popular, rather than parliamentary, sovereignty that applies in Scotland. It might however be questioned whether the claim to popular sovereignty is actually an enforceable claim? If so, Scotland should be able to exercise that right and should not depend on the permission of the UK Parliament to do so. But it is harder to identify a legally recognized right of Scotland to self-determination in the UK Constitution, although there exists no UK prohibition on secession, nor unlike Article 2 Spanish Constitution, any stipulation of the unity of the State.

For all the talk in 2014, of the potential for the Scottish Parliament to become 'the most powerful devolved parliament in the world', the UK is not a federal State in the sense of having legally guaranteed powers granted to the devolved authorities. It also has no legally guaranteed shared powers, as is the case in many federal States (and given the disparity in size between England and the other devolved nations, conceiving how shared powers might function is problematic). This concentration of sovereignty in Westminster presents a problem when a devolved nation takes a different view on Brexit, as Scotland has done, and cannot then protect its interests. Brexit has brought these issues into sharp focus, without however suggesting any solution.

Indeed, Brexit has been allowed to compress parliamentary sovereignty into an executive sovereignty that, by imposing a uniform approach, threatens the UK Union. There is little evidence that Brexit will provide a 'constitutional moment' in which a common solution will be found to these constitutional conundrums. It seems unlikely that a federal UK or written Constitution will emerge, however much new constitutional arrangements are needed. Advocates of Scottish independence, or a united Ireland, have little enthusiasm for an arrangement that would entrench them in the UK, even if it provided authoritative procedures protecting different national communities within the State. And those satisfied with Brexit are unlikely to desire a written Constitution or federal option, given that a desire for strong parliamentary sovereignty motivated their Euroscepticism in the first place.

However, even if Scotland were to become independent, then what remained of the UK Union (rUK) would be an irregular assemblage of England, Wales and Northern Ireland (if Northern Ireland remained in the Union). What would be the basis of that Union? A study of Scotland has revealed that the somewhat adventitious approach to Union reaches its limits when it is revealed to be detrimental to the interest of one of the parties (usually the weaker one). Given the somewhat ad hoc way in which devolution has developed to date, there has been no attempt to address Britain's constitutional status in a more principled way. Whether Scotland remains in the Union or not, there is an urgent need for a constitutional rethink and restructure.

2

Ireland

2.1 Early Days: Ireland and England

Ireland and the UK have a long backstory – even longer if one considers the relationship between Ireland and England. Yet for only a small part of that period (1801–1921) was Ireland actually part of the UK. Since then, it became first a Free State, and then from 1937 an independent republic. But prior to 1801, Ireland's status is challenging to classify. For many in England, Ireland was an English colony,[1] and any unrest there to be suppressed with violence. However, Ireland was also characterized as a distinct regime, with its own traditions and laws. And, although there may have been colonial aspects to past Irish governance, to identify it as a 'colony' is to demean and misinterpret its relationship with Britain.

Before, 1171, when Henry II imposed his rule there, Ireland was made up of disparate tribal kingdoms. Henry came armed with a papal bull (the 'Laudabiliter) issued by Pope Adrian IV in 1155, which apparently proclaimed Henry's right to enter and govern Ireland to impose order. It has since been asserted that this Bull was a fabrication[2] – perhaps classifiable as the 'Original Sin' in the relationship of England to Ireland, furnishing a justification for invasion, one in a long series of such pretexts.

Nonetheless, Henry imposed his rule, taking the title of Lord of Ireland, and arrogating Dublin, Wexford and their surroundings as what became known as the 'English pale.' Outside of that area, the Irish kings continued their kingdoms as vassals of the king of England. Royal government in Ireland was modelled on England, and it was claimed that Henry II established an Irish Parliament. However, Ireland was not incorporated into England, and its government was left to a Lord Lieutenant. Indeed, from 1172 to the Act of Union in 1800, reigning sovereigns spent only nine months in Ireland.

[1] E.g. M Hechter, *Internal Colonialism: The Celtic Fringe in British National Development* (London: RKP, 1975).

[2] E.g. A Duggan, 'The Making of a Myth: Giraldus Cambrensis, Laudabiliter, and Henry II's Lordship of Ireland' (2007) 4 Studies in Medieval and Renaissance History 249.

2.1.1 Poynings' Law

Over the next 300 years or so, the legal relationship between England and Ireland was ill-defined, and a vexed question was whether English legislation could in fact bind Ireland. Confusion was not dispelled by the fact that the medieval English Parliament was a very different entity from now, and the king was often seen as the sole authority for legislation. Lawsuits such as the *Merchants of Waterford Case*[3] illustrated the difficult constitutional relationship between the two Parliaments, and Sir Edward Poynings, an Englishman, was sent by Henry VII as Lord Deputy to Ireland, and in December 1494, the Irish Parliament at Drogheda adopted Poynings' Law.[4]

Poynings' Law notably provided that all English statute law was to be binding in Ireland. But Poynings' Law is best known for its chapter IV, which mandated that the Irish Parliament could not be convened without royal approval, and that all Irish Bills must be sent to the English Crown for approval. Poynings' Law was an extraordinary piece of legislation, disempowering the Irish Parliament, but most extraordinary was that the Irish Parliament itself *voluntarily* adopted Poynings' Law. (Perhaps a contributing factor was that Poynings' Law commences with a clause (or threat) that all property granted by the Crown since 1327 was to be cancelled unless the Irish complied). Poynings' Law was to remain in force until finally amended, by 'Grattan's Parliament', in 1782. For 300 years, the Irish legislature was debilitated and forced into a convoluted and time-consuming procedure by England.

2.1.2 The 'Kingdom of Ireland'

In 1534, Henry VIII declared the Church of England independent from the Roman Catholic Church and papal supremacy. Therefore, given that English rule in Ireland had supposedly been legitimated by the Pope, a new basis for its legitimation was required. So, in 1541, the Crown of Ireland Act[5] was passed by both the English and Irish Parliaments. This statute established Ireland as a dependent kingdom, 'appertayning or belonging' to the 'imperial crown of England.'

In 1560, the Elizabethan Acts of Supremacy and Uniformity, passed in the Irish Parliament, imposed an Anglican church settlement on Ireland. Conflict was particularly fierce under the English force led by Walter Raleigh and his half-brother Humphrey Gilbert (the path to whose tent was lined with decapitated heads of opponents) whose brutal action at

[3] YB 2 Rich. III, fol. 11; YB 1 Hen. VII, fol. 2. Also WJ Johnston, 'English Legislature and the Irish Courts' (1924) 40 LQR 91.

[4] 10 Hen. 7, ch. 9 [1495]. Also J Kelly, *Poynings' Law and the Making of Law in Ireland, 1660–1800* (Dublin: Four Courts, 2007).

[5] 33 Henry VIII, c. 1.

Smerwick in 1580 ranked with the 1572 St Bartholomew's Day massacre in Paris. Nonetheless, attempts to convert a majority of Irish to Protestantism failed. This Irish policy also was very costly, impoverishing the Crown, with effects to be felt in the seventeenth-century struggles between Crown and Parliament.

2.1.3 Seventeenth-Century England and Ireland

James VI/I, already the monarch of the 'union of the crowns' of England and Scotland, authorized the plantation of Ulster, the most northernmost province of Ireland, by English and Scots, an action that was to prove fateful later in Ireland's history.

After the execution of King Charles I in 1649, Oliver Cromwell was appointed commander-in-chief of Ireland. Cromwell's conquest of Ireland was ferocious in suppressing all Catholic and royalist opposition, including its 1649 massacres of Irish garrisons at Drogheda and Wexford. An Act of Settlement for Ireland was passed in 1652, confiscating the land of those supporting the royalist cause, and giving it to Cromwellian soldiers and supporters, causing a radical shift in land ownership. From 1653, a union of England, Scotland and Ireland was established, and Britain was briefly ruled by a codified Constitution – the 'Instrument of Government', with Cromwell as Lord Protector of a unified commonwealth (although there was no formal Act of Union between Britain and Ireland). A single Parliament in London existed, with 30 representatives each from Ireland and Scotland. The Restoration of Charles II in 1660 nullified the Commonwealth parliamentary union. But this did not end the land question. The Acts of Settlement (1662) and of Explanation (1665) were adopted by the Irish Parliament, and by the late 1670s, Catholics were in possession of about 1/3 of Irish land (still down on the 2/3 it had been in 1641). Then, in 1673 the Test Act was passed by the English Parliament, with the purpose of excluding all non-Anglicans from official positions.

Yet things changed again when James VII/II, who had converted to Catholicism, became king in 1685. His reign did not last long, and he was ousted from England by William III in 1688. However, James fled via France to Ireland, where a new Irish Parliament had assembled, in which 224 out of 230 members were Catholic. This new Parliament – sometimes called 'popish' or 'patriot' Parliament – adopted an Act of Recognition in 1689, acknowledging James' right to the Crown of Ireland, followed by a Land Settlement Act and a Declaratory Act, declaring Westminster had no right to adopt laws for Ireland (one of several proclamations of Irish autonomy, followed by those of Molyneux, Swift and Grattan, who were, however, Protestants). However, Poynings' Law was not repealed (due to James' opposition) and the subsequent complete Jacobite defeat made these earlier Acts worthless.

2.2 The Protestant Ascendancy

2.2.1 'The Glorious' Revolution

One might note that, although it has been a longstanding British tradition to characterize the 'Glorious Revolution' of 1688–9 as 'bloodless', in Ireland this was certainly not so. James was finally defeated by William III at the Battle of the Boyne on 12 July 1690, but his supporters continued fighting until defeat at Aughrim, and surrender at Limerick in 1691. The treaty of Limerick terminated war, but was not ratified by the Irish Parliament until 1697, and even then, articles of toleration for Catholics were omitted. Soon after, the English Parliament legislated that Acts of the Irish Parliament under King James were illegal.[6] Membership of the Irish Parliament was to be limited to Protestants.

Thus 'Ascendancy Ireland' – oligarchic government based on an Anglo-Irish (Protestant) landowning class – became established. This class included neither Catholics, nor Protestants of other denominations (such as Scots Presbyterians associated with the Ulster Plantation of 1606–1609, nor the Cromwellian soldiers who received land for service). This Anglo-Irish ascendancy was a minority in population terms, although it controlled the majority of land.

2.2.2 Penal/Popery Laws

At the turn of the eighteenth century, Ireland, like England, had a common law system, and this was a time when 'Englishmen congratulated themselves on enjoying rights and benefits in law that could not be overridden at the whim of kings and ministers …'[7] However, such benefits, if they in fact existed, were considerably less conspicuous in Ireland. This was largely due to severe Penal laws there – to the extent that, by 1759, John Bowes, the Irish Lord Chancellor, stated that '[t]he law does not suppose any such person to exist as an Irish Catholic.'[8] These Penal laws[9] were a series of measures that constrained all aspects of a Catholic's existence (Figure 2.1) – restricting their freedom of religion, education, political and property rights, and sometimes also those of Protestant dissenters. According to Edmund Burke, these were, 'a machine … as well fitted for the oppression, impoverishment and degradation of a people,

[6] According to J Swift MacNeill (*The Constitutional and Parliamentary History of Ireland till the Union*, Dublin: The Talbot Press, 1917, at 59), 'All the Acts … of this Parliament were ordered by William's Parliament to be burned by a clause in an Act unmaking its legislation.'

[7] D Lemmings (ed.), *The British and Their Laws in the Eighteenth Century* (Woodbridge UK: Boydell Press, 2005) 1.

[8] S. Connolly, *Religion, Law and Power: The Making of Protestant Ireland 1660–1760* (Oxford: Clarendon, 1992) 231.

[9] Similar laws were adopted in England, whose Parliament adopted the Clarendon Code (1661–1665) and the Test Act (1673), which required holders of public office to take oaths of loyalty and to receive the sacrament of the Church of England. However, Catholics were a very small minority in England, but the vast majority of the population in Ireland.

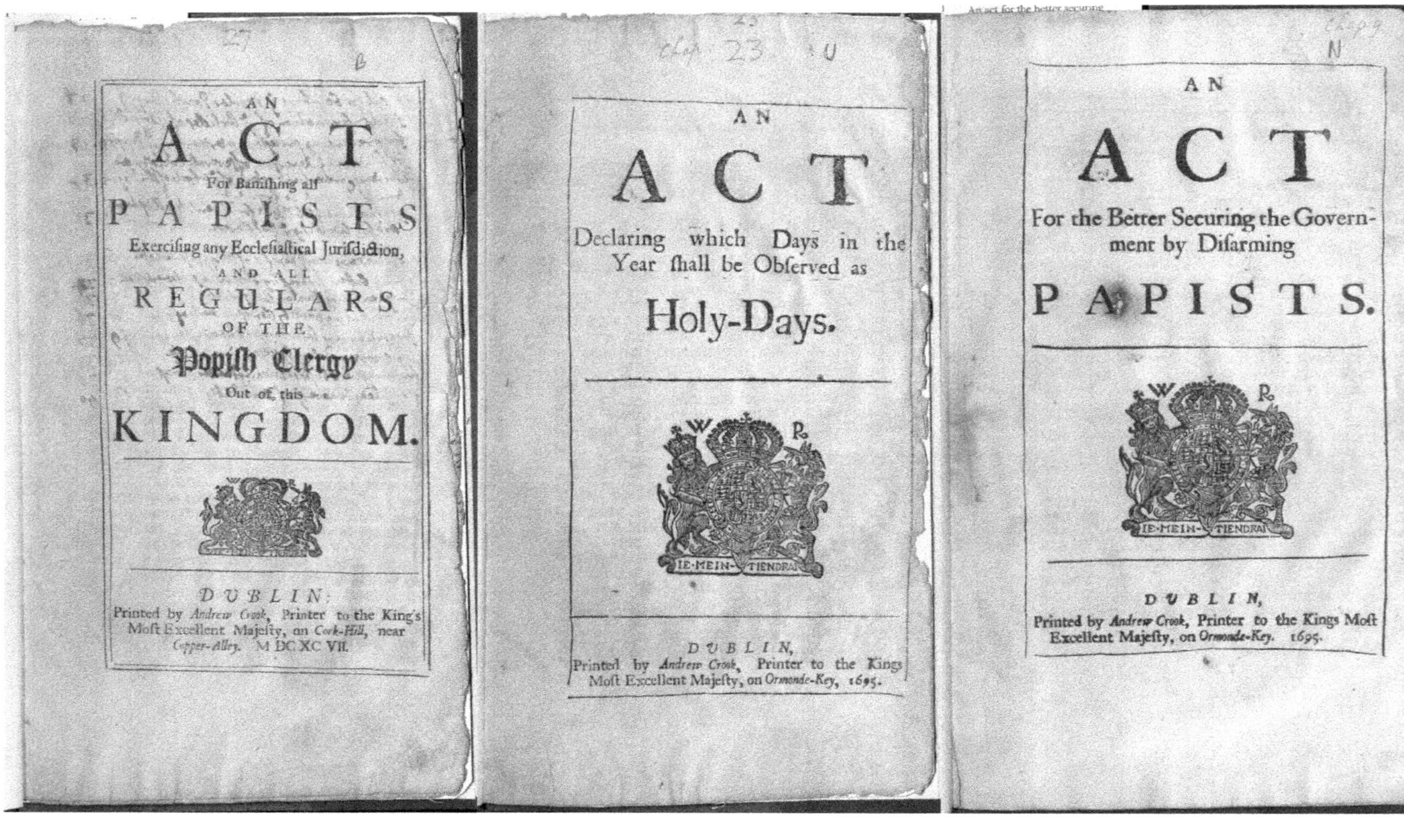
AN
ACT
For Baniſhing all
PAPISTS
Exerciſing any Eccleſiaſtical Juriſdiction,
AND ALL
REGULARS
OF THE
Popiſh Clergy
Out of this
KINGDOM.
DUBLIN:
Printed by Andrew Crook, Printer to the King's Moſt Excellent Majeſty, on Cork-Hill, near Copper-Alley. M DC XC VII.

AN
ACT
Declaring which Days in the Year ſhall be Obſerved as
Holy-Days.
DUBLIN,
Printed by Andrew Crook, Printer to the Kings Moſt Excellent Majeſty, on Ormonde-Key, 1695.

AN
ACT
For the Better Securing the Government by Diſarming
PAPISTS.
DUBLIN,
Printed by Andrew Crook, Printer to the Kings Moſt Excellent Majeſty, on Ormonde-Key. 1695.

Figure 2.1 Examples of Penal laws

and the debasement in them of human nature itself, as ever proceeded from the perverted ingenuity of man.'[10]

Penal laws against Catholics were passed nearly every year from the reign of William and Mary until well into the eighteenth century. The most notable (but only a small sample) can be classified in the following way.

Laws banning Catholics from civil and political office, and the franchise: Catholics had been barred from most public offices, including the legal professions and Irish and English Parliaments (with some periods of respite) from 1603, and this was reaffirmed on several occasions from 1697.[11] Catholics were banned from marrying Protestants,[12] and the 1728 Disenfranchising Act denied all Catholics the vote.[13]

Religion: The 1697 'Bishops' Banishment Act' ordered all bishops and members of Catholic religious orders to leave Ireland and set draconian penalties should they not do so.[14] Parish priests were not banished, but had to register with the government, risking banishment if they did not do so.

Education: The 1695 Act banned anyone from sending their child to a foreign 'popish' university, college school or household 'beyond the seas' for education, on pain of forfeiting their land and estates.[15] It also banned Catholics from keeping schools within Ireland, and encouraged informants – who stood to gain one half of forfeited land.

Land and property: 'An Act for the Better Securing the Government, by Disarming Papists' (1695) prohibited Catholics from owning weapons or horses worth more than £5.[16] A highly significant penal law was the 1703 Act to Prevent the Further Growth of Popery,[17] also known as the 'Gavelkind' Act. This banned inheritance by primogeniture among Catholics, so land had to be divided equally between all sons. Catholics were also banned from inheriting land from Protestants, from buying land, and holding a lease for longer than 31 years. These gavelkind provisions were effectively enforced, emasculating the Catholic gentry.

Although there was no general prohibition of Catholic religious worship, altogether, these laws comprised a remarkable catalogue of repression and discrimination. Perhaps most notorious was the 1719 Irish Bill legislating for the castration of unregistered Catholic priests (although there was also an attempt to legislate in 1721 for the whipping of nuns). This was approved and recommended by the Irish Privy Council. However, the castration clause was removed by the English Privy Council, and in the end the whole legislation was rejected on return to Ireland.[18]

[10] E Burke, 'Tracts on the Popery Laws', in P Langford, *The Writings and Speeches of Edmund Burke*, vol. 9 (Oxford: Oxford University Press, 1981–) 437.

[11] 10 Will III c.13 (1698); 6 Ann c 6 (1707); 2 Geo I c.10 (1715). [12] 9 Will III c.3 (1697).

[13] 1 Geo II c.9 (1728). [14] 9 Will III cl (1697). [15] 7 Will 3 c4 (1695).

[16] 7 Will 3 c 5 (1695). [17] 2 Ann c.6 (1703).

[18] WEH Lecky, *A History of Ireland in the Eighteenth Century* (Ireland: Longmans, Green, and Company, 1892) 153.

The noted (Protestant) Irish historian, WEH Lecky, wrote that it would be impossible 'for any Irish Protestant whose mind is not wholly perverted by religious bigotry, to look back without shame and indignation to the Penal Code.'[19] He also argued that England should share the blame, given that the Penal laws were passed when the English/British Parliament had complete control of the Irish Parliament. More recently, Maureen Wall has likened the Penal laws to South Africa's former apartheid legislation.[20] Although Connolly suggested[21] that the Penal laws were not implemented as stringently as the strongly expressed fears of 'popery' might have implied, even if this were so, the aim of this oppressive raft of legislation was to ensure an unchallenged Protestant ascendancy, giving this one tenth of the population extraordinary dominance, and a monopoly over government. The Penal laws effectively excluded Catholics from participation in politics, as they were disenfranchised until 1793, and ineligible for Parliament or high office until 1829.

2.2.3 Molyneux

In the eighteenth century, argument for greater autonomy from Britain came from influential Protestants rather than Catholics. William Molyneux's *The Case of Ireland's Being Bound by Acts of Parliament in England, Stated* was published in Dublin in 1698. This challenged the English Parliament's power to legislate for Ireland, and also the claim of the English House of Lords to be ultimate court of appeal in Irish cases. Molyneux was an Irish Protestant, MP, lawyer, and also a strong supporter of William III, so can hardly be cast as a rebel insurgent against the Crown.

Molyneux argued that Ireland had not been conquered but instead voluntarily submitted to Henry II. Nonetheless, Molyneux also argued in the alternative that, even if Ireland were conquered, that was insufficient to provide Henry with title to Ireland, and that the Irish (of the 1690s) were largely descendants of those who had come over with Henry, and they possessed all the rights of Englishmen. Molyneux argued that prior to 1649,[22] English legislation for Ireland had only been binding in Ireland when re-enacted there, and that Ireland should be recognized as a separate kingdom, subject only to the king, and independent of the English Parliament. Molyneux also relied on natural law and natural rights, using the arguments of John Locke,[23] with

[19] WEH Lecky, *Leaders of Public Opinion in Ireland* (Ireland: Longmans, Green, and Company, 1903) 124.

[20] M Wall, *Catholic Ireland in the Eighteenth Century* (Dublin: Geography Publications, 1989).

[21] Connolly, *Religion, Law and Power*, 263.

[22] From the 1640s, the English Long Parliament began legislating for Ireland, and in 1649 declared 'the people of England and of all the dominions and territories thereunto belonging are … a Commonwealth.'

[23] John Locke *Second Treatise*, chapter 16.

whom he had been in correspondence. Molyneux's *Case* was highly influential and went through many editions, becoming a key text for Irish patriotism, along with the works of Jonathan Swift and Henry Grattan. Molyneux was himself influenced by notable earlier Irish assertions. In 1641, the Irish House of Commons issued a *Declaration* completely denying the authority of the English Parliament over the Irish, and Patrick Darcy, a Catholic member of Irish House of Commons, delivered the *Argument* in support of this *Declaration*, shortly thereafter.[24]

However, in 1698 the English Parliament approved a unanimous resolution against the *Case* declaring, 'that the said Book was of dangerous consequence to the crown and people of England, by denying [their authority] to bind the kingdom and people of Ireland.'[25] The *Case* did, however, become influential in the eighteenth century in colonial America, where many of its arguments were seen as valuable precedents, in particular rejection of the claim of the British Parliament to bind those who were not represented in it.

2.2.4 *Annesley* v. *Sherlock*, the Two Houses of Lords, and the Declaratory Act 1720

However, the contested issue of Westminster parliamentary sovereignty did not go away. The English/British Parliament continued to legislate on Irish matters until in 1720 it passed the Declaratory Act, which explicitly stated that Westminster had the right to pass laws 'to bind the people and kingdom of Ireland'.[26] The catalyst had been *Annesley v Sherlock*,[27] a dispute over which of the two Houses of Lords, in Dublin and Westminster, had the final say over Ireland. Section 2 Declaratory Act stated: 'That the house of lords of Ireland have not … any jurisdiction to judge of, affirm or reverse any judgment, sentence or decree, given or made in any court within the said kingdom'.

However, s1 of the Declaratory Act went beyond any judicial disputes to declare that the king in Parliament, 'had, hath and of right ought to have full power and authority to make laws and statutes of sufficient force and validity, to bind the kingdom and people of Ireland.' Why was this provision added? According to Philip Yorke (a future English Lord Chancellor, and grandfather of the later Yorke who presided over the 1766 Declaratory Act for North America), 'it deprived the Lords of Ireland from the exercise

[24] *A Declaration setting forth How, and by what Means, the Laws and Statutes of England…came to be of Force in Ireland;* An *Argument Delivered by Patricke Darcy, Esquire, 9 Iunii,* 1641.

[25] Parliamentary History, (1698) v 1181.

[26] 6 Geo. I c. 5. 'An Act for the Better Securing the Dependency of Ireland upon the Crown of Great Britain.'

[27] Twenty-one J'ls of the House of Lords [Great Britain] [1718] 55.

of a power to which they had no right, and which, if granted them, would of consequence make that kingdom independent of Great Britain.'[28] The aim was to straighten out a constitutional principle English law had never made clear.

For Irish patriots, what became known as 'the sixth of George I' was viewed as an outrage for many years to come.[29] In theory, the implications of the Declaratory Act appeared immense. In practice, government in Ireland went on, much as before. Nonetheless, the Declaratory Act 1720 was repeated almost word for word when the British Parliament passed the Declaratory Act for the American colonies in 1766, where it was similarly resented. But in that case, the results were very different.

2.3 The Constitution of 1782

2.3.1 General Introduction

Therefore, Catholics in Ireland were completely locked out of public life by the Penal laws. Presbyterians in Ulster also had very little power. Power in Ireland was in the hands of a small Anglo-Irish Protestant elite. The next major constitutional events in Ireland occurred later in the eighteenth century, with the developments of 'The Constitution of 1782' and 'Grattan's Parliament'. Things had begun to change by 1759 when Henry Flood took a seat in the Irish Parliament and organized an effective opposition (the Patriots). However, Flood's standing was diminished when he accepted a seat in the Irish Privy Council in 1775, and thereafter, Henry Grattan took over as leader of the Patriot party. Grattan was a member of the Anglo-Irish elite, an Irish MP from 1775, lawyer who had studied in the Middle Temple, and who pushed for independent status for Ireland.

By the later 1770s, the American Revolution was greatly influencing Irish affairs. Indeed, there were notable similarities between the position of the American colonies and that of Ireland. Benjamin Franklin had visited Dublin in 1771, suggesting co-operation between Ireland and America. In 1779, in the face of growing pressure in Ireland for the non-importation of British goods, Lord North was forced to remove the commercial restrictions Ireland suffered when trading with Britain and its colonies. By 1782, there was sufficient pressure on the British government, shaken by its losses in the American war, to make further concessions. These led to the 'Constitution of 1782', which involved considerable amendments to Poynings' Law, and repeal of the Declaratory Act.

[28] W Hayton, 'The Stanhope/Sunderland Ministry and the Repudiation of Irish Parliamentary Independence' (1998) 113 *English Hist Review* 610.

[29] E.g. Swift, *A Letter to the Whole People of Ireland* (Dublin: John Harding, 1724), 15.

2.3.2 Poynings' Law and Repeal of the Declaratory Act

It will be remembered that under Poynings' Law all proposed Irish legislation had to be submitted to both the Irish and British Privy Councils for approval. In 1782, Poynings' Law was amended (but not repealed) by 'An Act to Regulate the Manner of Passing Bills, and to Prevent Delays in Summoning of Parliaments.'[30] This was an Irish Statute, sometimes known as Yelverton's Law, after its sponsor, Barry Yelverton, a leading Patriot constitutional lawyer. The old procedure (known as 'heads of Bills') was abolished, and the Irish Privy Council no longer had any role in proceedings. Nonetheless, Irish Bills still required Royal Assent.

The other major reform was repeal of the 1720 Declaratory Act by the Repeal Act of 1782.[31] This was an Act of the British Parliament, adopted in Westminster after the resignation of Lord North's Ministry, which had presided over defeat in the American War of Independence. There were also reforms to the position of Catholics, for example allowing Catholics who had taken the oath of allegiance to become teachers, buy and bequeath land in the same way as Protestants, and abolishing obsolete provisions of the Penal Code. But Catholics were still excluded from political rights. A further Act[32] declared that Irish judges should hold office, as in England, during good behaviour and not at the behest of the sovereign. A Habeas Corpus Act was also introduced for the first time (although suspended in 1793, when the British feared rebellion in Ireland).

This was all seen as a major success for Grattan, who was voted a grant of £50,000 by the Irish House of Commons, along with a residence. In April 1782, Grattan declared: 'I found Ireland on her knees. She is now a nation. In that character I hail her, and … I say, *Esto perpetua*!'[33]

2.3.3 The Renunciation Act

However, while Gratton was content enough with repeal of the Declaratory Act, Flood desired the British to go further, demanding they take the positive step of renouncing any right at all to legislate for Ireland. Repeal was insufficient for Flood, who insisted that it was:

> an undeniable principle of law that the mere repeal of a declaratory Act does not renounce the principle of it, and … that nothing but a final renouncing of the principle of this law is adequate to our security. With regard to this law of George I… What is the title of the law? It is an Act for the better securing of the dependency of Ireland. On the face of it, therefore, it imports expressly

[30] 21 & 22 Geo. III c. 47. [31] 22. Geo. III c. 53. [32] 21 & 22 Geo. III c. 50.

[33] GP Gooch, 'Grattan's Parliament', in JH Morgan (ed.), *The New Irish Constitution* (London: Hodder and Stoughton, 1912) 269.

> that dependency did before exist, and that, by consequence, it must continue till expressly renounced....[34]

The British passed another statute – the Irish Appeals Act 1783 (or 'Renunciation Act'), which provided that complete legislative and judicial independence for Ireland 'should be established and ascertained for ever ... and at no time be questioned or be questionable.'[35]

2.3.4 Ireland and Sovereignty up to the Acts of Union

These developments merit further analysis. Can we be more precise about the question of Irish sovereignty? Ireland was a separate kingdom according to the 1541 Crown of Ireland Act, although this had not stopped it being described as a colony and Ireland's trade had been regulated by the English Navigation Acts, just as had that of the American colonies. In 1778, British MP William Pulteney referred to 'Britain's colonies in America, Ireland and Canada.'[36] Indeed, although a separate kingdom, Ireland often appeared to have less autonomy than some British colonies, such as Virginia and Jamaica, where attempts to introduce the equivalent of Poynings' Law in the late seventeenth century had failed.

Up to 1782, relations between the British and Irish Parliaments were determined by two statutes, both designed to make the Irish legislature subordinate. The 1494 Poynings' Law required all Irish Bills to be first approved by the Privy Council in London. The 1720 Declaratory Act asserted the right of the British Parliament 'to make laws and statutes of sufficient force and validity to bind the kingdom and people of Ireland'. For Blackstone (who believed Ireland *conquered* by Henry II), Ireland was clearly subordinate.[37]

However, Blackstone's critics challenged his understanding of Irish history, denying a conquest of Ireland had ever taken place, as well as attacking his understanding of the British Constitution which accorded absolute power to Parliament. Charles Francis Sheridan (Irish government official and brother of politician and playwright, Richard Brinsley Sheridan) criticised Blackstone's work on the Constitution as, 'confused, inconsistent, and ... frequently absurd.' Sheridan stressed that one of his reasons for writing was to warn off politicians from replicating in Ireland the unsuccessful American policy of Lord North, which he saw as a salutary example of the destructive consequences of Blackstone's doctrine of sovereignty.[38]

So, whose argument is the more persuasive? Those, such as Blackstone, asserting absolute parliamentary sovereignty, or their opponents, such as

[34] *Irish Debates*, I, 417–418. [35] 23 George III c. 8

[36] D Kanter, *The Making of British Unionism* (Dublin: Four Courts Press, 2009) 23, fn 8.

[37] Blackstone, *Commentaries* I, section IV.

[38] CF Sheridan, *Observations of the Doctrine Laid Down by Sir William Blackstone*, In a Letter to Sir William Blackstone (Dublin, 1779) 3.

Molyneux or Sheridan, who resisted the claims of absolute Westminster sovereignty? A closer look at the changes of the 1782 Irish Constitution provides some further material with which to address this question. We will consider two contrasting views.

First, US legal historian, John Phillip Reid,[39] considered the problem of what could be achieved by repeal of the 1720 Declaratory Act. For Reid, asking the British Parliament to repeal the Act appeared to be a recognition of that Parliament's sovereignty. Reid seems to follow Flood's arguments that a Declaratory Act appears to declare something that already exists, and so, just as making a Declaratory Act does not alter the law, neither could its unmaking alter the law. Instead, Henry Flood had demanded that the British Parliament renounce the Irish Declaratory Act, which it did. However, Reid departed from Flood, finding him on unconvincing constitutional ground, because Reid believed neither repeal of the Declaratory Act, nor the Renunciation Act, could do anything more than impose a moral obligation on British Parliaments in the future (because he believed a future Parliament might enact a new Declaratory Act). Therefore, for Reid, the only solution for Americans was to declare their independence from Britain.

In contrast, there is the argument of English jurist, WR Anson, perhaps better known for classic textbooks on contract and constitutional law. In 1886, however, Anson published a contribution to the debate over the (then) Government of Ireland Bill, in the Law Quarterly Review.[40] Anson's quest was to determine whether inalienable parliamentary sovereignty had continued between repeal of the Declaratory Act and the 1800 Act of Union. By repeal of the Declaratory Act, the British Parliament purported to transfer legislative sovereignty to the Irish Parliament. Yet, Anson noted, if we concede the theory that no Parliament may bind its successor, then it follows that Irish parliamentary independence could have been ended by simply re-enacting the Declaratory Act. However, Anson observed that, in introducing this repealing legislation to Parliament, neither Fox nor Shelburne suggested that Westminster would keep the right to legislate for Ireland. Nor, Anson stresses, did any of those who enabled the Act of Union insist that Westminster had retained sovereignty over Ireland after the 1782 repeal. Anson particularly noted Pitt's statement that, by repealing the Declaratory Act, 'the power of the British Parliament of making laws for Ireland was given up.'[41] Anson was a unionist, whose focus was to argue that what had been the case for the repeal of the Declaratory Act must also be so for the 1886 Government of Ireland Bill, and thus, sovereignty would be surrendered.

[39] JP Reid: *Constitutional History of the American Revolution: The Authority of Law*, 'The Renunciation Solution' (Wisconsin University Press, 1993).

[40] WR Anson, 'Government of Ireland Bill and the Sovereignty of Parliament' (1886) 2 LQR 427.

[41] Ibid., 438.

This argument, coming from a convinced unionist and adherent of parliamentary sovereignty, is very interesting, for it suggests that the British Parliament *had given up* sovereignty in 1782 (*a fortiori* with the Renunciation Act) – a view in line with Dicey's assertion that sovereignty may be renounced.[42] It also suggests that, even for a traditionalist such as Anson, a sort of federal arrangement such as that in the first Home Rule Bill, whereby sovereignty could be divided, was conceivable if not desirable.

2.3.5 Conclusions

The 1782 constitutional changes occurred when the British Government feared Irish rebellion after the experience in America. But the 1782 Constitution lasted only 18 years until the Acts of Union in 1800, although some at the time thought that the changes were intended to be permanent. The Constitution of 1782 might have appeared a great victory for Irish independence. However, although the Irish legislature might have gained much freedom, perhaps to the extent of achieving its distinct sovereignty from Westminster, the Irish Executive were still appointed by and accountable to the British Government, not the Irish Parliament. This made tension between the Irish Parliament and both executives very likely. And the Irish system of patronage, which compromised the electoral system, was still rotten.

2.4 The Acts of Union[43]

2.4.1 The Road to Union

It is perplexing that in both Scotland and Ireland, union with England, and eradication of their respective parliaments, took place shortly after both these parliaments had grown to their most assertive.[44] The Scottish Parliament had just escaped from royal control by abolishing the Lords of the Articles in 1688–1689, and the Irish Parliament had won its legislative independence in 1782. But such flexing of political muscles suited England in neither case, which feared the consequences of a more powerful neighbour on their border. Thoughts turned to union.

A union of Ireland and England had been pondered early in the eighteenth century, but got nowhere. There was also some discussion of an imperial union,[45] comprising Britain, Ireland and colonies, although this too was discontinued after the American revolution. After 1783, William Pitt, the new

[42] See further for Dicey's view, chapter 4 on the British Empire.

[43] E.g. PM Geoghegan, *The Irish Act of Union: A Study of High Politics 1798–1801* (Dublin: Gill & Macmillan, 1999). D Keogh and K Whelan (eds.), *Acts of Union: The Causes, Contexts and Consequences of the Act of Union* (Dublin: Four Courts, 2001).

[44] Alvin Jackson, *The Two Unions* (Oxford: Oxford University Press, 2011) 69.

[45] See Kanter, *The Making of British Unionism 1740–1848*, 23 et seq.

British Prime Minister, formulated his 'commercial propositions' to tempt Ireland into a commercial union with Britain, but this was voted down in the British House of Commons, a bitter failure for Pitt, who increasingly disliked the 1782 Irish Constitution. However, the (relatively modest) Irish Catholic Relief Act of 1793 was passed.[46] This statute enfranchised Catholics on the same terms as Protestants (i.e. if they owned or rented property worth £2 per annum), as well as allowing them on juries, in the magistracy, and to commissions in the Army and Navy. They could also now obtain degrees in Dublin University and bear arms. This Act abolished many of the oppressive Penal laws, but it did not, however, permit Catholics to stand for Parliament (unless they took the oath of supremacy). Catholics were still excluded from the offices of Lord Lieutenant, Chief Secretary, Chancellor of the Exchequer, and other senior official positions. So, this was unfinished business.

All this should also be seen in the wider context of the French Revolution, Britain's war with France, and the growth of emancipatory and liberal ideas. Paine's *Rights of Man* was published in Ireland in 1791, and became very influential. Wolfe Tone, a young Protestant barrister previously exiled in America, in 1791 established the radical political group, 'United Irishmen,' which urged the unity of north and south in recognition of a common nationalist cause. In 1798, an uprising orchestrated by the United Irishmen was brutally suppressed and Wolfe Tone court-martialled and found guilty, although took his own life in prison before he could be executed. Most commentators agree that the Acts of Union were prompted by the British need for greater security, rather than concern for better Irish governance.[47] Unlike the Acts of Union with Scotland, which had brought definite economic advantages for Scotland, Ireland had already secured much free trade in 1779. So, Union looked to benefit the Irish much less than it had the Scots.

2.4.2 Union

With effect from 1 January 1801, the Irish and British Acts of Union came into effect. The Parliament of Ireland was dissolved, and the kingdoms of Ireland and Great Britain merged into one 'United Kingdom'. The Irish Constitution of 1782, which had seemed so radical, had lasted only 18 years. Grattan himself, a strong opponent of Union, had retired from the Irish Parliament in 1797, ill and demoralized (although he was to return to the united Parliament from 1805, and fight for Catholic emancipation).

Jackson notes that contemporary accounts stressed the role of bribes, venality, and the preferment of offices in the achievement of Union.[48] Furthermore,

46 'For the Relief of his Majesty's Roman Catholic Subjects of Ireland' 33 George III c.21

47 E.g. I Mclean, *What's Wrong with the British Constitution?* (Oxford: Oxford University Press, 2009) 78.

48 *The Two Unions*, 99.

in 1997, David Wilkinson uncovered newly released material (apparently stored in secret service funds), revealing actual expenditure on the Irish union campaign.[49] Geoghegan argued that, 'What is clear is that a major cover-up was initiated after the passing of the Union to prevent any exposure of the illegal methods that had been approved.'[50] Cornwallis, Irish Lord Lieutenant of the time, complained that: 'I despise and hate myself every hour for engaging in such dirty work, and am supported only by the reflection that without an Union the British Empire must be dissolved.'[51] Cornwallis was probably not the only official to feel uncomfortable. Chief Secretary Castlereagh suffered the first of several nervous breakdowns in 1801.

It also seems that Irish Catholics were won over by the promise of further emancipation – a promise that was not however kept. King George III took the view that emancipation was incompatible with his coronation oath and vetoed Catholic emancipation, and Pitt, Cornwallis and Castlereagh who had proffered such emancipation, resigned in February 1801. And, as a result, the Union came to be seen as illegitimate by most Irish Catholics from the outset.

There is also the question of what impact Union had on the notion of Britishness. It did not help that that so many in England professed to know so little about Ireland, and such claims of ignorance continued for many years – including by Dicey, in his copious writings against home rule. Such acknowledged ignorance, however, did not prevent disparagement of Ireland. During his time as Chief Secretary in Ireland, Peel adjudged Ireland to be a wild country inhabited by a people 'drunk on the pursuit of violence and unrest.'[52] Such sentiments were neither conducive to solidarity nor to evolution of a British identity. Insurrection Acts were enforced on many occasions in Ireland, and habeas corpus suspended from 1797–1802 and 1803–1806.

2.4.3 The Terms of the Acts

The main motivation seems to have been security driven – with the goal of embedding Ireland in a unitary British State. Originally, it seems that the intention was to establish two commissions to negotiate Union, as for the 1707 Union. However, the terms of Union were determined instead by government ministers not parliamentary commissioners. The Union Agreement was therefore negotiated in Ireland by Lord Lieutenant Cornwallis and Chief Secretary Viscount Castlereagh (a highly reactionary figure when British Foreign Secretary from

49 D Wilkinson, '"How Did They Pass the Union?": Secret Service Expenditure in Ireland, 1799–1804' (1997) 82 *History* 223.

50 P Geoghegan, 'An Act of Power & Corruption?' (2000) *History Ireland* 8.

51 Gooch, 'Grattan's Parliament', 277. This was the same Cornwallis, who in command of British forces, surrendered to the Americans at Yorktown in 1781.

52 Peel to Liverpool, 15 October 1813, *Peel Papers*, BL Add. MS 40285.

1812 to 1822). By June 1800, Union legislation had completed all parliamentary stages, having cleared the Irish Commons on a vote of 158–115.

Two identical statutes were passed in the British and Irish Parliaments – the British Union with Ireland Act 1800, and the Irish Act for the Union of Great Britain and Ireland 1800.[53] These Acts created the United Kingdom of England, Wales, Scotland and Ireland. They came into force on 1 January 1801, and from that date, the Irish Parliament in Dublin was abolished.

Each Act contained eight Articles. Articles I–IV provided for the political aspects of Union. Article I stated: 'Great Britain and Ireland to be united for ever from 1 Jan. 1801.' Under Article II, succession to the Crown was to continue as 'at present', according to existing laws. Article III created a united Parliament, and Article IV set out its parliamentary representation. Existing Westminster parliamentarians were to be joined by 28 Irish temporal peers, four (rotating) bishops of the Church of Ireland, and 100 MPs[54] (about 1/5 of the House of Commons' total representation). The remaining 84 Irish parliamentary boroughs were disfranchised. It seems that all were pocket boroughs, and their patrons received £15,000 in compensation for the loss of what was considered their property. [In 1800, the Irish population was about 5 million – i.e. about half that of Great Britain – and the Scottish population only about 1.6 million. However, things were to change radically, with the dramatic fall of the Irish population in the Famine, and the huge growth of the Scots population in the nineteenth century, so Scots would come to be underrepresented in Westminster in contrast to Ireland]. Article V originally united the established Church of England and Church of Ireland into one Protestant Episcopal Church (since repealed). Article VI established a Customs Union and free trade. Article VII stated that Ireland would contribute 2/17 to UK expenditure, which then represented the ratio of Irish to British foreign trade (but is generally regarded as unduly burdensome to Ireland.[55]) Article VIII dealt with legal and judicial aspects of the Union. All laws in force at the time of Union, as well as the courts of either kingdom, were to remain, subject only to changes by the UK Parliament. The two Treasuries were later united in 1817 and Irish and British taxation became standardized.

The Acts of Union were somewhat under-studied, at least until the late twentieth century,[56] when the 2000 bicentenary of the Acts stimulated scholarship. The 1800 Union was often described as an 'incorporating' union[57] (and it also removed the appellate jurisdiction of the former Irish House of Lords). But although the two parliaments might at least be merged, the two Executives

[53] British Parliament (39 & 40 Geo. 3 c. 67); Irish Parliament (40 Geo. 3 c.38).

[54] In 1800, the Irish House of Lords had 247 members and its House of Commons 300. Kanter, *The Making of British Unionism*, 20.

[55] JC Beckett, *The Making of Modern Ireland* (London: Faber & Faber, 1966) 282.

[56] Several works have been published since, including M Brown, PM Geoghegan, and J Kelly (eds.), *The Irish Act of Union, 1800: Bicentennial Essays* (Dublin: Irish Academic Press, 2003).

[57] E.g. K. Theodore Hoppen, 'An Incorporating Union?' (2008) 123 *English Hist. Review* 328.

were not (unlike in the case of Scotland). Lord Redesdale (Lord Chancellor of Ireland from 1802 to 1806) complained that: 'Those who contrived the union … seem to have thought only of carrying that measure without considering how the machine was to work afterwards …. The consequence is that, in many parts, the machine cannot work at all.'[58]

Too little thought was given to governance. Indeed, according to Scottish radical MP, Joseph Hume, up to the present (i.e. 1823) 'Ireland had been governed as our slave colonies were, by a viceroy and colonial establishment; and Jamaica might be called, with as much propriety, a part of the United Kingdom as Ireland.'[59] And so the Irish Government continued to be administered from the semi-colonial Viceregal court in Dublin Castle, remaining under the direction of the Lord Lieutenant (or Viceroy) and Chief Secretary, unlike Scotland, whose government had been absorbed into the British government at time of Union. The Irish Parliament was sold to the Bank of Ireland (with the stipulation that the interior be reconstructed to remove any traces of the Irish Parliament[60]). Irish parliamentarians moved to Westminster and Irish politics lost any coherence. Although in Scotland, Union became generally regarded as successful in the later eighteenth and nineteenth centuries, this perception of success did not develop in Ireland, with the exception of Ulster. Union did not give rise to any immediate prosperity in Ireland and only lasted a little over 120 years. Many factors contributed to the opposition to it – including the lack of Catholic relief until 1830, the terrible Famine, and the Land system in Ireland.

2.5 Catholic Emancipation

Although Catholics were excluded from public office in both Britain and Ireland until 1829, in Ireland Catholics made up the bulk of the population, the laws were more draconian, and the Irish land tenure system was a disgrace of its own.

Britain has sought to present itself as tolerant country, a stronghold of liberty, respecting freedom of religion in contrast with continental autocrats such as Louis XIV, Napoleon, and Hitler. And yet the Whig narrative of the evolution of a progressive and enlightened Constitution is undermined by the earlier vision of the 'Protestant Constitution',[61] which was seen as prevailing only after a long struggle with Catholicism. It included the following features: the Coronation Oath vowed to maintain the Protestant religion, and the Act of Settlement maintained a Protestant succession; taking a seat in Parliament

[58] Redesdale to W Wickham, 30 January 1806, in *The Manuscripts of JB Fortsecue Esq.* (1912) 25.

[59] Hansard (25 June 1823), 2nd series ix, 1216.

[60] Beckett, *The Making of Modern Ireland*, 284.

[61] E.g. D Bateman, 'The Fall of the Protestant Constitution', in *Disenfranchising Democracy* (Cambridge: Cambridge University Press, 2018); GFA Best, 'The Protestant Constitution and Its Supporters, 1800–1829' (1958) 8 *Transactions of the Royal Historical Society* 105.

required an oath that excluded Catholics, and Bishops of the Church of England sat (and still do) in the House of Lords. Further, the Toleration Act of 1689 excluded both atheists and Catholics from its ambit, and John Locke, famous for his works on religious toleration, nonetheless rejected toleration for Catholics. When anti-Catholic Penal laws were liberalized in 1778, these modest steps sparked the Gordon Riots – the worst riots in modern British history, in which about 1000 people were killed, and the damage caused to London would only be exceeded by the Blitz.[62] Some also believed that Britain owed its Empire to the Protestant settlement. One reviewer opined that, 'England was now Protestant ... and with that Protestantism began her prosperity. And what a prosperity! Where has the world anything to show to it?'[63]

And yet, change was to come: 1829 brought Catholic emancipation, 1837 replacement of Church tithes, and 1869 disestablishment of the (Protestant) Church of Ireland. And by the early twentieth century, the land tenure system had been largely rectified by legislation. A key factor in Catholic emancipation was the involvement of the 'Liberator' Daniel O'Connell,[64] a young Irish Catholic lawyer. O'Connell founded the Catholic Association in 1823, for the purpose of adopting 'all such legal and constitutional measures as may be most useful to obtain Catholic Emancipation'. O'Connell's campaign was remarkable for its discipline, organization and ability to intimidate the British Government without any resort to force. O'Connell himself stood in 1828 as parliamentary candidate for County Clare, but, as a Catholic was prevented from taking his seat. In 1829, after the Catholic Emancipation Act became law, O'Connell was re-elected to the same seat unopposed. O'Connell was, however, ultimately unsuccessful in his aim of repealing the Act of Union. This would have to wait nearly 100 years.

Peel and Wellington, in charge of the British government of the time, were conservatives and faithful Anglicans, so their conversion to Catholic emancipation might appear somewhat surprising. Both of them however, had experience of Ireland – and feared the risk to peace, order, and the British Empire, should such relief not take place. Yet, even if Peel and Wellington had been converted to Catholic relief, there was official opposition from elsewhere. King George III had always insisted Catholic emancipation would violate his coronation oath, and his son George IV (although he appeared to have no religious scruples) had been influenced by his brother, the Duke of York, a notorious anti-Catholic bigot. Others took the King's coronation oath seriously. Best[65] suggests this is because the oath was seen as providing a check

[62] L Colley, *Britons: Forging the Nation 1707–1837* (Yale University Press, 1992) 23; George Rudé, 'The Gordon Riots' (1956) 6 *Transactions of the Royal Historical Society* 93.

[63] *British Magazine*, March 1832, 40 f.

[64] E.g. P Geoghegan, *King Dan: The Rise of Daniel O'Connell 1775–1829* (Ireland: Gill and Macmillan, 2008); and P Geoghegan, *Liberator: The Life and Death of Daniel O'Connell, 1830–1847* (Ireland: Gill and Macmillan, 2010).

[65] Best, 'The Protestant Constitution and Its Supporters'.

on parliamentary sovereignty. For if Parliament were omnicompetent, what might stop a future Parliament eradicating other aspects of the Protestant Constitution? In this light, the constitutional position of the king was seen, in Wellington's language, as the 'last entrenchment'. However, such a view surely misunderstands the British Constitution, implying a status for the monarch as a separate branch of the legislature, equal with the Houses of Parliament, which is certainly not the case – at least not since 1688.

Notwithstanding George IV's newly found religious scruples, Catholic Emancipation was achieved in the UK by the Roman Catholic Relief Act 1829.[66] Parliament also repealed the 1672 Test Act in Ireland and those Penal laws still in force there. Catholics could now sit in Parliament, and were eligible for most public offices, although no Catholic could become Lord Chancellor in England or Lord Lieutenant in Ireland, nor could they be admitted to Oxford and Cambridge universities. The Irish electorate became more fully moored within the Union, and Westminster was to become the locus of conflicts over the future of Ireland in the shape of Home Rule Bills later in the century. However, Catholic emancipation was accompanied in Ireland by the Parliamentary Elections (Ireland) Act 1829, which disenfranchised the Forty Shilling Freeholders of Ireland, raising by a huge amount the economic qualifications for voting there. This wiped out most of the Irish electorate – registered voters fell from over 200,000 to under 40,000,[67] and hardly increased Irish faith in British integrity.

Did Catholic emancipation really achieve a fundamental change to the British Constitution? Revisionist historians might wish to portray it as 'a constitutional revolution',[68] emasculating the Anglican supremacy. But to accept this claim would be to overplay belief in the Protestant Constitution. Whigs and progressive-minded supporters of Catholic relief had already reinterpreted the British constitutional tradition, placing a greater emphasis on civil and religious liberty at its centre.[69] And very soon, many were ridiculing this old view of the Protestant Constitution – Bagehot, only 30 years on, wondered at how anyone could have been so absurd.[70]

However, if repeal and emancipation did not signify a constitutional revolution, it did radically affect politics, splitting the Tory party, ushering in an era of Whig reform (which included the Great Reform Act of 1832 – carried by the votes of Irish MPs) which was to alter the franchise and political geography of Britain.

66 An 'Act for the Relief of His Majesty's Roman Catholic Subjects', 10 Geo. 4 c. 7.

67 Since 1793, any man renting or owning land worth 40 (i.e. £2) could vote in Ireland. See KT Hoppen, '*Elections, Politics, and Society in Ireland*' (Oxford: Clarendon Press, 1984) 1.

68 Mark Koyama, 'Catholic Emancipation as a Constitutional Revolution' medium.com, 6 April 2019; JCD Clark, *English Society 1688–1832* (Cambridge: Cambridge University Press, 2nd ed., 2000) 90, 409.

69 E.g. John Russell, *An Essay on the History of the English Government and Constitution* (London, 1821).

70 '*Biographical Studies* (London, 1881) 1.

Many 'Ultra' Tories refused to forgive Peel and Wellington – in Cambridge, notices were posted proclaiming 'Our Protestant Constitution and the Ancient Institutions of My Country for ever!' as well as those declaring the Tory leaders 'are our enemies.... Impeach them.'[71] Peel would return to office as Prime Minister in the 1840s, only to be ousted after another high-profile *volte face*, concerning the Corn Laws, which was to have even greater consequence for Tory party unity. And that change of mind would also be partly prompted by Irish affairs – in that case, the question of how to handle the Great Famine. Moreover, Catholic emancipation had fanned the flames of Protestant resurgence in Ulster, where in Ballybay, a brawl took place between militant Orangemen and Catholics.

In conclusion, the episode of Catholic emancipation provides a timely reminder of the hostility often shown to those considered to be alien. As Rowan Williams writes: 'If nothing else, the story of anti-'Popery' in Britain is an object lesson in how a narrative of the murderous religious or ideological alien is created and sustained, both deliberately and unthinkingly, even in the face of ample evidence.'[72]

2.6 The Great Famine

The Great Famine has been described as a 'cataclysmic turning point in Irish demographic and economic history.'[73] It devastated Ireland from 1845 to 1849 (possibly longer). 'Devastated' is an appropriate word, because, although one cannot be precise, it is likely that between one to three million people died.[74] At least one million Irish emigrated to North America, and just as many crossed to Great Britain. According to the British Census Commissioners, the population of Ireland in 1841 was 8,175,124, but by 1851 had fallen to 6,552,385, by 1891 it was 4.7 million, and it fell even more in the earlier twentieth century. The general consensus is that the Famine was caused by potato crop failures due to an airborne fungus or 'blight' (*Phytophthora infestans*).[75] Ireland was especially vulnerable to this blight due to its very high reliance on the potato, which was often the only food for the very poor – about 3 million people.

When early reports of the blight reached the British Government in autumn 1845, the then Prime Minister, Sir Robert Peel, set up a Commission to examine the issue, and also adopted legislation repealing the Corn Laws (so cheaper grain could be imported). These laws had been introduced in 1815 to maintain

71 National Archives, HO 44/19/ff. 112.

72 R Williams, 'What the Story of Catholic Persecution in Britain Can Teach Us about Populism and Prejudice', *The New Statesman*, 4 July 2018.

73 K O'Rourke, 'Did the Great Irish Famine Matter?' (1991) 51 *J Econ Hist*. 1. Also C Kinealy, *A Death-Dealing Famine: The Great Hunger in Ireland* (London: Pluto Press, 1997); Cecil Woodham-Smith, *The Great Hunger: Ireland 1845–1849* (London: Hamish Hamilton, 1962).

74 C O' Grada, *The Great Irish Famine* (Cambridge: Cambridge University Press, 1995) 48.

75 In 1845, there was a partial failure of the potato crop, and in 1846, 1848, and 1849 total failures. P Solar, 'The Great Famine Was No Ordinary Subsistence Crisis', in E. Margaret Crawford (ed.), *Famine: The Irish Experience* (Edinburgh: John Donald, 1989) 112.

British corn at an artificially high price by imposing high tariffs on imported grain. However, although the Irish Famine may have given Peel support for Corn Law repeal, the main reasons for repeal were not Irish policy, but English politics. From 1838, a very vigorous Anti-Corn-Law-League had emerged in Britain. Nonetheless, the repeal of the Corn Laws made Peel extremely unpopular and he was forced out of office and the Tory party split for a long time. While in office, Peel had appointed Charles Trevelyan (earlier in the Indian Civil Service – and thus following a familiar path for Victorian officials – but by then Assistant Secretary of the Treasury) as overseer of famine relief in Ireland, and Trevelyan became notorious for his conduct of this office.

Peel's government was replaced by that of the Whigs/Liberals,[76] under Lord John Russell. By 1846, the real hardship had begun, but the Whig government was a strong supporter of laissez-faire economics, and content to let Trevelyan (who made no secret of the fact that he did not wish the Irish to become overly dependent on the British Government) take full charge. In 1848, an armed uprising against the British occurred, instigated by the Irish nationalist group, 'Young Ireland'. The year 1848 was known as 'the year of revolutions' in Europe, and the group had been emboldened by popular rebellions in Paris, Vienna, Sicily, Milan and Venice, where some governments had been forced out of office. But the Irish rebellion failed. The British, aware of the risk of insurrection, had transferred troops to Ireland, as well as adopting many repressive measures, that is suspending Habeas Corpus in Ireland, imposing martial law, and passing the Treason Felony Act, which made criticism of the Crown, or Parliament, a crime punishable with deportation to Australia.

The Irish population was depleted not just by famine deaths but by a large amount of emigration (the largest ever mass emigration from one island). America had been a majority Protestant country until then, but the large amount of Irish migrants began to change that.[77] Some Irish emigrants became highly influential, decrying the horrors of the Famine. These included John Mitchel, who wrote: 'potatoes failed in like manner all over Europe, yet there was no famine save in Ireland.... The Almighty, indeed, sent the potato blight, but the English created the famine.'[78]

2.6.1 The Blameworthiness of the British Government

Why did it prove so difficult to relieve the suffering caused by the Famine? Various attempts have been made to explain Ireland's vulnerability, including identifying the Irish land system as responsible.[79] Land in Ireland was mainly

[76] The term 'Liberal' was first officially used in 1867, although in currency before that.

[77] Indeed, in America militant anti-Catholics set up a new political party (nicknamed the 'Know-Nothings') aiming to curtail Irish immigration and prevent them becoming American citizens.

[78] J Mitchel, *The Last Conquest of Ireland (Perhaps)*, P Maume (ed.), (UCD Press, 2005) at 219.

[79] CE Smith, *The Land-Tenure System in Ireland: A Fatal Regime* (1993) *Marquette L Rev* 469; Woodham-Smith, *The Great Hunger*, 20.

owned by absentee landlords and rented out, giving tenants no protection from eviction or large rent increases. As a result, tenants relied on potatoes, which could be farmed on small plots, for their subsistence. Other crops, usually grain, were exported in vast quantities to pay the excessive rents.

Most explanations have, however, laid a great deal of blame on British Government of the time, for its failure to handle the Famine effectively, either because it engaged in deliberate genocide of the Irish,[80] or (more likely) by its incompetence and neglect of Irish suffering. Although there was some financial provision, the predominant approach of the British Government was reluctance to get involved with Irish matters, supported by the belief that 'natural' means – private enterprise, the free market – would resolve the problem. In any case, after 1849, the British Government took no more steps to manage the Famine and left the Irish to cope with it themselves. Trevelyan, head of administration for Famine Relief (who was later responsible for significant civil service reforms in Britain) is surely most likely to be remembered for his infamous statement that:

> Judgment of God ... sent the calamity to teach the Irish a lesson, that calamity must not be too much mitigated.... The real evil with which we have to contend is not the physical evil of the Famine, but the moral evil of the selfish, perverse and turbulent character of the [Irish] people.[81]

In all his time in office, Trevelyan was to visit Ireland only once, and then Dublin, which was removed from the worst of the Famine. However, not all Government officials shared Trevelyan's view. For example, Lord Lieutenant Clarendon stated: 'it is enough to drive one mad, day after day.... I don't think there is another legislature in Europe that would disregard such suffering as now exists in the west of Ireland.'[82]

2.6.2 Failure of the Union

How did the fact of Ireland's being in a Union with Britain affect the British Government's conduct of Famine relief? According to Charles Trevelyan, the Union did not create a general duty on the British government to provide financial support:

> ... the disease was strictly local and the cure was to be obtained only by the application of local remedies.... The west and south of Ireland was the peccant part. The owners and holders of land in these districts had permitted or encouraged the growth of the excessive population, which depended upon the

[80] This theory was held by John Mitchel (*The Last Conquest of Ireland (Perhaps)*). But few now subscribe to it – although AJP Taylor, reviewing Woodham-Smith's *The Great Hunger*, [publ as 'Genocide' in Taylor, *Essays in English History*, (London: Penguin, 1976)] compared the Famine to Belsen.

[81] Trevelyan, *The Irish Crisis* (London: Macmillan, 1883 ed.), 97.

[82] Cited in P Gray, *Famine, Land and Politics* (Dublin: Irish Academic Press, 1998) at 314.

> precarious potato, and they alone had it in their power to restore society to a safe and healthy state ...[83]

Furthermore, there had been a press campaign in Britain to turn public opinion against the Irish. The weekly magazine *Punch* provides a good illustration of how such campaigns could affect public perceptions of the Union. In the earlier stages of the famine in October 1846, *Punch* published a cartoon, *Union is Strength*, in which John Bull, representing England, was pictured giving a basket of bread and a shovel to the Irish peasants, with the caption: 'Here are a few things to go on with Brother, and I'll soon put you in a way to earn your own living.'

But the magazine's approach soon changed, and every government loan to the Irish was denounced as placing more burdens on the respectable poor of England. And so, a different cartoon appeared – *The English Labourer's Burden; or the Irish Old Man of the Mountain* (referencing the tale of Sinbad the sailor) in which a spindly, sickly English labourer was portrayed, struggling to carry on his shoulders a gleeful Irish peasant who bears a sack of gold.[84]

But this view was certainly not shared by everyone, and the British Government's response was condemned as contravening the very principle of Union by the radical Irish MP for Rochdale, William Sharman Crawford: 'The Act of Union was framed on the principle of combined responsibility. The Union itself was forced on Ireland; but England, having taken Irish poverty into partnership, could not now repudiate the results of that connexion ... if the Union was to be maintained, the principle of united responsibility must be its basis'.[85]

Others saw government aid as derogatory. The Archbishop of Tuam, John MacHale, wrote to Prime Minister Russell, contrasting the £50,000 granted for famine relief with £20 million compensation given in 1833 to West Indies slave-owners on the abolition of slavery there, and describing the government's refusal of aid to Ireland as a denial of the Union:

> When famine walks ... then we are told: 'You have no claim on us; sink or swim; look to yourselves, and rely on your own resources.' Would such be the language to Yorkshire in the days of a vengeful visitation?.... It is only Ireland that can be flattered with the name of a Union, when giving her heart's blood to the prosperity of the empire; and then, in her inanition, to be abandoned to starvation![86]

[83] *The Irish Crisis*, 108.

[84] See P Gray, 'Punch and the Great Famine' (1993) 2 *History Ireland*. Also *The Times* expressed itself thus in March 1847: 'We have to change the very nature of a people born and bred from time immemorial in inveterate indolence, improvidence, disobedience, and consequently destitution.' And *The Spectator* went even further, 'We need not fill up "the Serbonian bog of Irish destitution" with our hard-earned store of sovereigns, nor make roads to nowhere, nor build work-houses for people to lie down and die in; and it is that conviction which makes the Englishman suddenly tighten his flowing purse-strings', 19 May 1849.

[85] *Hansard*, 1 March 1849, 103: 49

[86] B O'Reilly, *John MacHale, Archbishop of Tuam* (New York: Fr Pustet, 1890) 618.

The example of Tory MP, Isaac Butt, is a revealing illustration of how perceptions changed radically. Butt was Irish, Anglican, sympathetic to the Orange order and originally a fervent supporter of the Union. However, the Great Famine changed his views. In 1847, he wrote:

> What can be more absurd, what can be more wicked, than for men professing attachment to an imperial constitution to answer claims now put forward for state assistance to the unprecedented necessities, by talking of Ireland being a drain on the *English* treasury. The exchequer is the exchequer of the United Kingdom .... If the Union be not a mockery, there exists no such thing as an English treasury.... If, bearing our share of all imperial burdens—when calamity falls upon us we are to be told that we then recover our separate existence as a nation, just so far as to disentitle us to the state assistance which any portion of the nation visited with such a calamity had a right to expect from the governing power? If Cornwall had been visited with the scenes that have desolated Cork, would similar arguments have been used?[87]

In contrast, Trevelyan concluded *The Irish Crisis* on a positive note, writing (with no apparent irony) that, 'our humble but sincere, conviction is that the time of Ireland's regeneration is at last come. ...' and that 'we may not relax our efforts until Ireland fully participates in the social health and physical prosperity of Great Britain, which will be the true consummation of our union.'[88]

By the end of the Famine, Irish agriculture had become more diverse, and the potato ceased to be dominant in the Irish diet. However, it is difficult to deny that the British Government's handling of the Famine greatly impaired belief in the Union and its legitimacy. According to O'Farrell, 'The ultimate test of any government is – can it, as an absolute minimum, provide the basic needs of those it governs? Put to that test by the famine of 1845–1849, the government of the Union failed.'[89] Many nationalists saw the Famine as evidence of the British Government's animosity to Ireland, and anti-British hostility grew as a result. In 1919, De Valera and Sinn Féin petitioned the US Congress for recognition of the Irish State, and included in their case statistical arguments as to how Ireland's economic position had been held back by the Act of Union.[90]At the negotiations for the 1921 Anglo-Irish treaty, Sinn Féin argued the Union of Ireland with Britain had been particularly calamitous, involving many famines, and they attributed this to the lack of a domestic Irish Parliament.

87 Isaac Butt, 'A Voice for Ireland – The Famine in the Land' (1847) 29/172 *Dublin University Magazine* 514–515.

88 *The Irish Crisis*, 199, 201.

89 P O'Farrell, *Ireland's English Question* (New York: Schocken Books, 1971) 107.

90 *Ireland's Request to the Government of the USA for Recognition as a Sovereign Independent State* (Dublin, 1919).

2.7 Home Rule

Repeal of the Union had been unsuccessfully advocated by Daniel O'Connell, but generally opposed in Westminster in the earlier nineteenth century. However, from the 1880s, Irish Home Rule (not the same thing as repeal) became a major constitutional issue. Three Home Rule bills were presented in Westminster in 1886, 1893, and 1912. On each occasion, Irish Home Rulers held the balance of power in Westminster and were able to bargain for Home Rule legislation in return for supporting the Liberal party. But all three bills failed, one way or another, and all were met with Unionist opposition. The 1886 bill was defeated in the House of Commons, the 1893 Bill was rejected by the House of Lords, and the 1912 Bill, although it passed in 1914, met with serious resistance from Ulster unionists, and then was suspended due to the First World War. A very different world existed after the War, and the 1914 Act was abandoned, and replaced by the 1920 Government of Ireland Act, which ended up only applying in Northern Ireland, while the rest of Ireland broke free, to form the Irish Free State. The first part of this section on home rule presents a brief chronology and context for the main Home Rule legislation. This is followed by a more detailed legal/constitutional analysis.

Daniel O'Connell died in 1847, and after the 1848 armed uprising failed, the British Government responded coercively, suspending Habeas Corpus, and the more notable Young Irelanders were captured and transported, or emigrated – often to achieve an important stature overseas. Charles Gavan Duffy was to become Premier of the Australian province of Victoria, and John Mitchel escaped from transportation in Australia to the US, where he wrote forceful denunciations of British handling of the Famine. Indeed, Irish nationalism was greatly encouraged, both verbally and financially, by the support of American Irish. In 1858, the Irish Republican Brotherhood, more popularly known as the Fenians,[91] was established, and looked to achieve Irish separation by force, believing constitutional means had failed.

In 1868, William Gladstone became Prime Minister for the first time, and famously declared it his mission to pacify Ireland. He had announced the intention to take the axe to the tree of the Irish problem in its three branches – church, land, and education[92] (but did not support home rule at that stage). The 1869 Irish Church Act (whose membership included of course neither Catholics nor Ulster Presbyterians) disestablished the Church of Ireland. Tackling the unfair land system in Ireland proved harder and lasted into the twentieth century. In 1850, a Tenant League was established for land reform, and the Irish Land League was founded in 1879, using boycott and no-rent campaigns. A series of Land Acts were passed in Parliament[93] and eventually, by 1929, 97.4 per cent of the land had transferred to Irish farmers. Electoral

[91] 'Fenian' appears to originate with founder John O'Mahony, and derives from Fianna, the military force led by Fionn MacCuchail (Finn MacCool), a heroic warrior of Celtic legend.

[92] *Speeches of WE Gladstone MP* (London: Simpkin, Marshall & Co, October 1868) at 85.

[93] R Walsh and L O'Fox Mahoney, 'Land Law, Property Ideologies and the British–Irish Relationship' (2018) 47 *Common Law World Review* 15.

reform was also crucial (as indeed it was in Great Britain). The franchise was considerably extended in the Electoral Reform Act of 1867 and a secret ballot introduced in 1872. The Reform Act of 1884 enfranchised even more voters, and from 1885, Ireland elected about 4/5 of her MPs as Home Rulers, who very often held the balance of power in the House of Commons.

Isaac Butt, a (Protestant) Tory MP, established the Home Rule Association in 1870, and his own conversion to home rule, had (as already noted), grown out of his anger at British handling of the Famine. 'Home Rule' was potentially a less aggressive term than 'Repeal' (and although Butt referred to this scheme as federalism,[94] his plan was in fact for a subordinate Irish Parliament, with Westminster sovereignty left intact). Nonetheless, as with O'Connell, Butt's suggestions were heavily defeated in Parliament. In 1880, Charles Stewart Parnell (son of a wealthy Anglo-Irish Protestant landowner and an American mother) President of the Irish Land League, and an Irish MP, took over the Home Rule party, changing its name to the Irish Parliamentary party. In 1884, Parnell imposed a strict party whip, requiring party MPs to vote together in Parliament on all occasions. In the 1885 election, the party increased its representation in Westminster to 85 MPs.[95] He and his party also used various tactics – filibustering, obstruction – to disrupt proceedings in Westminster. Parnell is famous for declaring: 'No man has the right to fix the boundary to the march of a nation. No man has a right to say to his country: 'thus far shalt thou go and no further'.[96]

However, in 1882, Lord Frederick Cavendish, the new Chief Secretary for Ireland, was murdered in Phoenix Park, Dublin. Although Parnell expressed outrage and denounced the crime, the British responded with yet another Coercion Act, and outbursts of violence continued.

2.7.1 The Government of Ireland (Home Rule) Bill 1886

In January 1885, the Conservatives were defeated by a combination of Liberals and Irish Home Rulers, and Gladstone became Prime Minister for the third time but relied on votes of Irish MPs to get legislation through the House. Gladstone had not earlier supported home rule, seeing it as threatening disintegration of the British Empire,[97] but by now had been converted, believing home rule the only way to avoid a serious crisis in Ireland.

94 Isaac Butt, *Home Government for Ireland: Irish Federalism!* (Dublin, 1870).

95 Interestingly, Parnell had urged Irish in Britain to support the Tories at the 1885 election, partly thinking that, if the 'English right' accepted home rule, it would have a better chance of becoming law (given Tories controlled the House of Lords which then had a veto on legislation). (D Gwynn, 'John Redmond and English Politicians' (1932) 81 *Irish Quarterly Review* 22.) And it was the Tories who had earlier, in the administrations of Peel and Derby, granted home rule to the colonies.

96 E.g. Robert Kee, *The Laurel and the Ivy: The Story of Charles Stewart Parnell and Irish Nationalism* (London: Hamish Hamilton,1993).

97 J Kendle, *Ireland and the Federal Solution: The Debate over the UK Constitution* (Kingston Ontario: McGill-Queen's University Press, 1989) 32.

This was a Government Bill, drafted by Gladstone,[98] not by Irish Home Rulers, who although supporting it, would have preferred more autonomy than the Bill allowed. The Bill was in many ways modelled on the British North America Act of 1867 – legislation for Canada. It provided for an Irish Parliament and Executive (responsible to the Irish Parliament) in Dublin. But the Bill restricted an Irish Parliament's legislative powers more than Canada's. Irish MPs were to be excluded from the British Parliament, which would retain control of foreign policy, defence, coinage and customs and excise. Irish legislators could only sit if Westminster if the issue were changes to the Home Rule legislation itself. However, there was no explicit affirmation of parliamentary sovereignty in the Bill – a fact that provoked great criticism.[99] The Home Rule Bill was accompanied by a Land Purchase Bill, which would have bought out nearly all of the landlord class in Ireland. However, the Bill did not address opposition to home rule in Ulster.

The Bill was defeated by 343 votes to 313 in the House of Commons and the Land Purchase Bill withdrawn after its first reading. 93 votes against home rule had come from the Liberal party itself. As a result, Gladstone's government fell, and the Liberal party split, with its anti-home rule members, including the former radical but now imperialist Joseph Chamberlain, joining a unionist alliance with the conservatives. It seems, however, that opposition to home rule was predominantly English: 3/5 of Scottish members and 5/6 of Welsh supported Gladstone.[100] Nonetheless, as a result of this split, the Conservatives were able to hold office for most of 1886 to 1905. And Parnell's star was to shine less brightly. A series of articles appeared in *The Times*, attacking Parnell and home rule, and accusing him of complicity in the Phoenix Park murders. *The Times* also published a letter from Dicey, attacking Parnellism as 'violence masked under the form of constitutional agitation.'[101] But in 1890, the 'Parnell Commission' of three High Court judges exonerated Parnell, and evidence in *The Times* articles was shown to be a fabrication.[102] Parnell's reputation rose again, but shortly thereafter, Parnell was cited in a divorce case, and died suddenly, in 1891, aged only 45.

2.7.2 The Second Home Rule Bill 1893

Gladstone regained office for a fourth term as Prime Minister in 1892, and in 1893, aged 83, introduced a second Home Rule Bill into the House of Commons. This legislation was, unlike the 1886 Bill, not drafted by Gladstone alone, but

[98] *Papers of WE Gladstone*, BL, Files 44, 770–744, 772.
[99] Including Anson in (1886) 2 LQR 427, already mentioned.
[100] Beckett, *The Making of Modern Ireland*, 398.
[101] *The Times*, December 23, 1890.
[102] It seems the Conservative government earlier supported *The Times* attack on Parnell, attempting to discredit him – see further FSL Lyons, 'Parnellism and Crime' (1974) 24 Transactions of Royal Historical Society, at 127.

by a Cabinet committee, which also included James Bryce, and John Morley (Chief Secretary for Ireland). This legislation also differed significantly from the 1886 Bill, in that it made provision for 80 Irish MPs at Westminster (voting on all matters), and also proclaimed (Westminster) parliamentary sovereignty in its Preamble. This did not protect it from attack, however. Ulster unionist members bitterly opposed it. Joseph Chamberlain derided the attempt to preserve parliamentary sovereignty, and Lord Randolph Churchill assailed the Bill as 'extravagant and grotesque.'[103]

This time the Bill made it through the House of Commons where Gladstone was assured of a majority (debate lasted 85 sittings) by a vote of 307 to 267, but was strongly rejected by the unelected (and in 1893 very largely hereditary) House of Lords – by 419 to 41. Gladstone resigned and was not to hold office again.[104] A Unionist coalition was to hold office from 1895 to 1906. This coalition rejected political autonomy for Ireland, believing it would lead to disintegration of the British Empire, and instead proposed to counter the home rule impulse by continued force in Ireland (such as the Crime Acts introduced by Arthur Balfour).[105] However, it did institute some reforms for Ireland, culminating with the 1903 Wyndham's Act, that enabled greater land purchase by small tenants. Such a policy was sometimes known as 'constructive' unionism.[106]

2.7.3 The Third Home Rule Bill 1912 and After

2.7.3.1 The Bill's Content; Clashes with the House of Lords; Government of Ireland Act 1914

The year 1906 saw a huge 'Liberal landslide', and Liberals did not need Irish votes to pass their legislation. For some years, home rule was not a central concern, and the Liberal government focussed on social reforms (i.e. introduction of old age pensions) and rearmament to meet the increasing German threat. But their Budget was rejected by the Conservative dominated House of Lords and so they called a general election. The Liberals lost their outright majority and became again reliant on Irish votes, now led by John Redmond (as well as on those of the new, small, Parliamentary Labour Party) – which meant that home rule was back on the agenda. The Parliament Act 1911 was passed, providing for the abolition of the House of Lords veto – but only after intervention from the new King George V, and the threat to create many new Liberal peers. The 1911 Parliament Act provided that any Bill passed three years in succession by the House of Commons would become law upon royal assent, regardless

[103] 8 Parl. Deb., HC (4th ser.) (1893) 1611 and 1730.

[104] The Liberal party however remained in power (with Gladstone replaced by Lord Rosebery as Prime Minister) until 1896.

[105] Balfour was (Conservative) Prime Minister from 1902 to 1905.

[106] E.g. C Reid, 'An Experiment in Constructive Unionism' (2014) 129 English Historical Review 332.

of the position of the House of Lords. This meant that a Home Rule Bill could now be adopted without fear of its rejection by the House of Lords.[107]

Therefore, a third Home Rule Bill was introduced in 1912, This Bill provided for a bi-cameral Irish Parliament, along with reduced Irish representation (42 MPs) in Westminster. However, it explicitly provided for the Irish Parliament's sovereignty to be restricted, with Britain retaining permanent control over defence and foreign policy, customs & excise, and control over the police force for six years; and it prohibited the Irish Parliament legislating on religious matters. Its first clause read: 'Notwithstanding the establishment of the Irish Parliament or anything contained in this Act, the supreme power and authority of the Parliament of the United Kingdom shall remain unaffected and undiminished over all persons, matters and things within His Majesty's Dominions.' This Bill became law in 1914 but was suspended because of the outbreak of the Great War on 4 August 1914.[108]

2.7.3.2 Insurrection in Ulster; The Ulster Covenant; Brink of Civil War

However, the prospect that Irish Home Rule might ultimately be achieved sparked robust resistance from Ulster Unionists. The leader of the Unionist Party in Ireland was Edward Carson, the Dublin-born MP for Trinity College, who was also the barrister (and later Lord of Appeal) who had cross-examined Oscar Wilde in the libel suit that destroyed Wilde. Carson argued in Parliament that the Bill was an attempted betrayal of Ulster and demanded, 'What argument is there that you can raise for giving Home Rule to Ireland that you do not equally raise for giving Home Rule to that Protestant minority in the north east province?'[109] In September 1912, nearly half a million in Ulster signed a 'Solemn League and Covenant' (the name emulating the seventeenth-century Scottish Covenant) committing them to resist the establishment of a parliament in Dublin by all means. Their threat was enhanced by mobilization of a private army, the Ulster Volunteers, which proclaimed the right to use force, and should an Irish Parliament be forced on them, 'to refuse to recognize its authority.'[110] They were supported by Conservative Party leader, Andrew Bonar Law, a Presbyterian sympathetic to Ulster Unionism, who also declared that, 'there are things stronger than parliamentary majorities', and there was 'no length of resistance to which Ulster can go in which I would not be prepared to support them.'[111] He was not their only supporter. Dicey, who had proclaimed the rule of law to be a pillar of the British Constitution,

[107] The House of Lords had also vetoed other Liberal legislation – e.g. the 1906 Education Bill, legislation for Scotland in 1907, and 1908 Licensing Bill. This action was generally considered in breach of the Constitution.

[108] Government of Ireland Act, 1914, 4 & 5 Geo. 5 c. 90 (UK); Suspensory Act, 1914, 4 & 5 Geo. 5 c. 88 (UK).

[109] 53 Parl. Deb., HC (5th ser.) (1913) 1474.

[110] Alvin Jackson, *Ireland 1798–1998* (Chichester: Wiley-Blackwell Ltd, 2010) 246.

[111] R Blake, *The Unknown Prime Minister* (London: Allen & Unwin, 1955) 130.

along with parliamentary sovereignty, signed the Ulster Covenant, and thus pledged himself to armed resistance,[112] and FE Smith, Lord Chancellor from 1919 to 1922, also fervently supported the Orange agitation. Notably, this agitation also fragmented Irish unionism, focussing an intense Ulster unionism in the north-east, and a much looser, disparate unionism in the south. Ulster also gained some cultural support – for example, Edward Elgar (although a Roman Catholic) and Rudyard Kipling signed the Covenant, and Kipling penned the verses, 'Ulster 1912'.

By 1913, the Ulster Volunteer Force were a well-equipped army of 100,000 men – and the Ulster Unionist Council had declared itself a provisional government in September 1913, should the Home Rule Bill become law. Irish nationalists were less united. The parliamentary party relied on the eventual success of the Home Rule Bill, but others responded by forming their own militia – the Irish Volunteers. Both unionists and nationalists were importing weapons from abroad and Ireland seemed on the brink of civil war. In July 1914, the King called a conference at Buckingham Palace on whether Ulster should be permanently excluded from the Home Rule Bill. However, nothing came of this, and within weeks the First World War had erupted, and the Home Rule legislation was suspended, never to be revived for all of Ireland.

2.7.4 What Was Understood by 'Home Rule'?

But 'Home Rule' was understood in several, quite different ways. Some Irish nationalists desired a return to the old Irish Parliament terminated by the Acts of Union. In 1885, Parnell had sent Gladstone his 'Proposed Constitution' which he described as 'a modification of Grattan's parliament so as to meet the democratic progress of the age.'[113]

2.7.4.1 'Ireland as Canada'

However, Gladstone looked elsewhere for inspiration for Home Rule legislation. He considered existing examples of unions in Europe, such as between Sweden and Norway, Denmark and Iceland, Austria and Hungary, and Russia and Finland. He scrutinized federalism in the USA. But he also considered the situation in various parts of the British Empire, and, in particular, the confederation of Canadian provinces under the British North America Act 1867, a Westminster statute. What became known as 'responsible government' had developed in some colonies from the mid-nineteenth century. Under this arrangement, colonial governments were allowed to manage colonial affairs and were in turn responsible to domestically elected assemblies. This had occurred more as a matter of practice than of law, a matter of mutual trust and shared interests.

[112] RFV Heuston, *Essays in Constitutional Law* (London: Stevens, 2nd ed., 1964) 2–3.

[113] HCG Matthew, *Gladstone* (Oxford: Oxford University Press, 1995) 479.

Gladstone had himself been Colonial Secretary for a brief period and became a strong supporter of responsible government. In the first Home Rule Bill, Gladstone provided what Ward describes as 'essentially a constitution for a self-governing colony'.[114] The Irish Parliament was to be subordinate to Westminster, and, as with colonies, Ireland was to send no MPs to Westminster, except to vote on amendments to home rule legislation itself. Executive authority was to rest with a Lord Lieutenant, who like a colonial governor, would have a range of powers, subject to instructions from the monarch. In 1886, *The Times* described Gladstone's plans as '*Ireland as Canada*'.[115] As early as 1870 Isaac Butt had suggested that, 'Why should not the self-government which has made Canada contented and loyal be equally successful in Ireland in attaining the same results?'[116] In contrast, Joseph Chamberlain opined in Parliament that, 'Canada is loyal and friendly to this country. Ireland, I am sorry to say, at the present time, is not loyal and cannot be called friendly.'[117]

It was common to find Canadian dominion status and Irish home rule treated as similar notions.[118] But there were identifiable differences. Dominion legislatures had greater autonomy – for example, in defence, taxation, currency and trade – than that envisaged for the Irish Parliament. Dominions were autonomous jurisdictions of the British Empire, with greater sovereignty than a colony, even if it was not until the 1931 Statute of Westminster, that their status was sufficiently clarified to be described as sovereign States.[119] Ireland, even under home rule, would still have been part (even if semi-autonomous) of the sovereign UK. This confusion between dominion and home rule was further problematized by Goldwin Smith in 1887, when he queried whether the colonial model for Ireland was the relation of a Canadian province such as Ontario to Canada or the relationship of Canada to the UK. Either way, Smith could foresee problems – for if Ireland were in the position of Ontario, it would be necessary to reconstruct the UK as a federation, a constitutional rearrangement that went well beyond home rule legislation, whereas if Ireland were truly like Canada, this could lead to Irish independence, for, according to Smith, Canada 'is in progress towards independence, and has now almost reached the goal.'[120] Indeed, even before the First World War, many believed that dominions were gradually developing into sovereign States, something the British Government would not have considered for Ireland.[121] In any case, the

114 A Ward, 'Models of Government and Anglo-Irish Relations' (1988) 20 *Albion* 26.

115 *The Times*, 16 April 1886, at 9. 116 *Irish Federalism!*, at 81.

117 *Hansard* 3 (9 April 1886) ccciv, 1194.

118 A Ward, *Ireland and Anglo-American Relations, 1899–1921* (London: Weidenfeld and Nicolson for the London School of Economics and Political Science, 1969), 19–20; LS Amery, 'Home Rule and the Colonial Analogy', in S. Rosenbaum (ed.), *Against Home Rule: The Case for the Union* (London: Frederick Warne, 1912) 129.

119 See further T Mohr, 'The Statute of Westminster: An Irish Perspective' (2013) 30 *Law and History Review* 750.

120 Smith, 'The Canadian Constitution' (July 1887) 52 Contemporary Review 2–3.

121 E.g. Duncan Bell, *The Idea of Greater Britain* (Princeton: Princeton University Press, 2007) 1–5.

colonial model was not necessarily apposite. Ireland could not be compared to colonial settlers in a far-away country, but was a distinct and ancient nation in its own right.

2.7.4.2 Federalism

This brings us to federalism which, in the nineteenth century, was sometimes seen as a solution to the Irish question. The Liberal MP, William Sharman Crawford, had urged the case for federalism. On occasions, O'Connell had described himself as a federalist.[122] Butt had even published a paper called *Irish Federalism!* in 1870, although in the course of the 1870s, he came to speak of his proposals as home rule. The perceived advantage of federalism was, as O'Connell had noted, its capacity for shared governance of matters such as foreign and defence policy in a federative or imperial parliament.

However, the UK in the nineteenth century considered itself a unitary State, and many wanted nothing to do with federalism. Dicey, in the 'Introduction' to the eighth edition of *Law of the Constitution* in 1915, insisted that, '[i]n England, which is after all by far the most important part of the kingdom, the idea of federalism has hitherto been totally unknown.'[123] This was somewhat ingenuous, as federalism was developing in British colonies such as Canada, and British people could easily read about federalism in the famous US *Federalist papers*, which were frequently cited in nineteenth century debates about the status of Canada, Australia and South Africa. Alexis de Tocqueville's *Democracy in America* was readily available, as was James Bryce's *The American Commonwealth*, and JS Mill's *Considerations on Representative Government* included a chapter on 'Federal Representative Governments'.

2.7.4.3 'Home Rule All Round'

Distaste for federalism did not stop thoughts of 'Home Rule all round' in the early twentieth century.[124] In 1879, during his Midlothian campaign, Gladstone had stated, 'If we can make arrangements under which Ireland, Scotland, Wales, portions of England, can deal with questions of local and special interest to themselves more efficiently than Parliament now can, that, I say, will be the attainment of a great national good'.[125] In 1912, Winston Churchill (then a Liberal MP) was engaged on a proposal of 'Home Rule All Round', with devolved assemblies for Scotland, Wales and the English 'regions'.[126] Such a project was seen as avoiding the problem of imbalance in the UK, if Ireland

[122] O'Day, *Irish Home Rule* (Manchester University Press, 1998) 18.

[123] *Introduction to the Study of the Law of the Constitution*, lxxxviii. This introduction is from the original 1915 printing.

[124] See, especially on this, JE Kendle, *Ireland and the Federal Solution*, chapter 3.

[125] Quoted in V Bogdanor 'The Liberal Party and the Constitution' (2007) 54 Journal of Liberal History 6.

[126] JE Kendle, 'The Round Table Movement and "Home Rule All Round"' (1968) 11 Historical Journal 342.

was given home rule but other parts of the country were not. At one point, an amendment of the 1912 Irish Home Rule Bill contained a system devised by Lloyd George for Grand Committees in England, Scotland and Wales, which were to have the same wide legislative powers as those offered to Ireland. In consequence, the Bill's title was to be Government of Ireland and House of Commons (Devolution of Business) Bill. But this amendment was dropped from the Bill's final draft, although the notion of Home Rule all round remained under consideration, and some expanded this notion to propose a federal British Empire, of Britain and the self-governing dominions.[127]

But neither federalism nor Home Rule all round took off in the UK. Part of the problem was the situation that still exists today, even after devolution in Scotland, Wales and Northern Ireland – what to do with England, which as a single unit is far too large in population to rank equally with the other nations of the UK. But even more problematic was the division of attachment in Ireland, with a large proportion of unionists in Ulster highly antagonistic to home rule. Already, prior to the First World War, there were proposals to divide Ireland into two self-governing jurisdictions of the UK. However, there existed no serious pressure for home rule in Scotland, Wales, or the English regions at this time,[128] nor any sustained advocacy of federalism in the UK.

2.7.4.4 The Persistent Problems of Home Rule Legislation

Three issues proved particularly resistant to resolution, partly explaining why Irish home rule legislation continued to fail at Westminster.[129]

The first issue concerned Irish representation at Westminster. The problem was this – if the Irish no longer had seats in Westminster, they could have no role in decisions affecting the UK overall. Their status would be comparable to colonial legislatures, and also appear to be taxation without representation. On the other hand, if there were Irish MPs at Westminster, then how to prevent them from not only participating in UK matters concerning them – such as defence or foreign policy – but also other British matters, for which the Irish would have their own Parliament? This latter problem persisted into the twentieth and twenty-first centuries, where it was renamed the 'West Lothian problem' in the context of Scottish devolution. This problem was never adequately resolved in home rule legislation. The 1886 Bill excluded Irish MPs from Westminster, making provision only for their inclusion on amendments

[127] But not all imperial federalists agreed – e.g. Philip Kerr concluded that 'Federalism for the Empire, and Federalism for the United Kingdom are two entirely distinct ideas.' See Kendle, 'The Round Table Movement', 339.

[128] Both a 'Scottish Home Rule Association' and a Welsh equivalent 'Cymru Fydd', were founded in 1886. These never enjoyed such electoral success as Irish home rule. See N Kane, A Study of the Debate on Scottish Home Rule, 1886–1914 (PhD thesis, University of Edinburgh, 2015) and KO Morgan, *Wales in British Politics, 1868–1922* (Cardiff: University of Wales Press, 1963).

[129] See Ward, 'Models of Government and Anglo-Irish Relations', for a deeper analysis.

to home rule legislation itself. In contrast, the 1893 Home Rule Bill made provision for 80 Irish MPs at Westminster, but originally with the right to vote only on 'imperial matters', although the Bill was amended to provide full voting rights for Irish MPs. Later home rule legislation compromised – Asquith's 1912 Bill included full voting rights for Irish MPs, but only allowed half the representation Ireland's population would have justified. This problem is hard to resolve in the absence of a federal arrangement for the UK. The latest attempt at its resolution was the now defunct EVEL, or English votes for English Laws procedure.

A second problem for home rule was that of the financial relationship between Britain and Ireland. Was London to maintain control over Irish taxes and customs duties? Anything less was seen as a threat to the integrity of the UK. As a result, no home rule legislation provided Ireland with any substantial taxation powers, thus creating a perceived democratic deficit. Once again, we seen parallels with devolution to other parts of the UK in the late twentieth/ early twenty-first centuries.

A third problem was the nature of the constitutional relationship between Ireland and the UK. Many perceived it essential for Britain to possess ultimate parliamentary sovereignty. The Irish Lord Lieutenant was also to be the agent of the Crown, maintaining Crown prerogatives, rather than the Irish government dealing directly with the Crown. This would have been similar to the arrangements under colonial Constitutions. But what then would have been the level of autonomy left to Ireland? Some argued that ultimate parliamentary sovereignty and prerogative power need never be asserted – for example, James Bryce maintained in 1893 that the prerogative would be 'a power to be kept in reserve, only to be used if the gravest case should arise'. John Redmond stated that the royal prerogative was a 'sword which often is most powerful while sheathed.'[130] In contrast, Dicey contended that Britain's relations with a self-governing Ireland would rest on a 'series of understandings and mutual concessions' which were likely to be in short supply between the two countries. This is a situation we have seen replicated recently, with the Sewel Convention sidelined in Brexit legislation.

2.7.5 Dicey, Ireland, and Parliamentary Sovereignty

Why give space to the English jurist AV Dicey in a chapter on Ireland? Because Dicey has so long dominated understandings of British constitutional law, and being strongly opposed to home rule in Ireland, has colonized the debate from the English side.[131] But it is worth re-evaluating his view. Dicey was a very

[130] Bryce, *Parliamentary Debates*, 14 February 1893, 4th series, v. 8, col. 14; J Redmond, 'Notes on the Home Rule Bill: The Mutual Safeguards' (1893) 163 Contemporary Review 312.

[131] E.g. AV Dicey, *England's Case against Home Rule* (London: J Murray, 1886), *Letters on Unionist Delusions* (London: Macmillan, 1887), *The Verdict* (London: Cassell & CO., 1889), *A Leap in the Dark: A Criticism of the Principles of Home Rule as Illustrated by the Bill of 1893*

committed unionist who, by 1911, was describing himself as 'a fanatic' on the union.[132] His *Law of the Constitution* was first published in 1885, when home rule was much discussed. However, Dicey's specific response to the 1886 Home Rule Bill was his book, *England's Case against Home Rule*, which argued the case for preserving parliamentary sovereignty and dismissed federal arrangements as unsuitable for Britain. He wrote a further book, *A Leap in the Dark*, criticizing the 1893 Home Rule Bill, writing that '[n]ever before was a nation so strangely advised by such bewildered counsellors to take for so little apparent reason so desperate a leap in the dark.'[133]

Dicey argued that sovereignty by its nature had to be illimitable and non-delegated, although he acknowledged that sovereignty might be surrendered (by dissolution or by transfer and absorption into another body as with the Acts of Union between England and Scotland).[134] He wrote that 'I entertain the firmest conviction that any scheme for Home Rule in Ireland involves dangerous if not fatal innovations on the Constitution of Great Britain.'[135] Nor was Dicey any more willing to embrace the colonial model for Ireland favoured by Gladstone in 1886. Dicey believed conventions (non-legal rules) regulated and ensured responsible government in the Dominions, noting that, 'A complicated political arrangement is kept in tolerable working order by a series of understandings and of mutual concessions. If either England or Victoria were not willing to give and take the connection between England and the colony would not last a month.'[136] For Dicey, Britain could neither apply parliamentary sovereignty nor the royal prerogative against any contrary will of a self-governing colony. Britain's supremacy was ensured by mutual trust and conventions. And in the case of Ireland, he believed a coalition of Liberals and Irish nationalists could not be relied on to apply those conventions adequately – and so it could not provide stable government and threatened the dissolution of the UK.

2.7.5.1 A Conflict between the Rule of Law and Parliamentary Sovereignty? Dicey Embraces the Referendum

For Dicey, the rule of law and parliamentary sovereignty were key principles of the British Constitution. The rule of law should restrain the abuse of power.[137] However Dicey, in the *Law of the Constitution*, also described Parliament as 'an absolutely sovereign legislature' which therefore 'cannot be bound by any law.'[138] And so commentators have often noted a tension between these two

(London: J Murray, 1893), *A Fool's Paradise* (London: J Murray, 1913). R Cosgrove, *The Rule of Law: Albert Venn Dicey, Victorian Jurist* (Chapel Hill: UNC Press, 1980).

132 Dicey, letter to Walter Long, 4 July 1911, Walter Long papers BL. Kendle, *Ireland and the Federal Solution*, 131.

133 *A Leap in the Dark* (2nd ed., 1911) at 193.

134 *Law of the Constitution*, 65 n 1.

135 *England's Case*, vii.

136 AV Dicey, 'Ireland and Victoria' (1886) 49 Contemporary Review 171–172.

137 *Law of the Constitution* (9th ed., 1952) 188, 193.

138 *Law of the Constitution*, 39, 40.

principles. For if Parliament is truly omnicompetent, no law can restrain it. Yet, Dicey himself argued that the rule of law and parliamentary sovereignty were not in conflict, but sustained through the practice of constitutional conventions, as a matter of tacit consent. But on this, Dicey's argument was unclear, controversial, and unsatisfactory.[139]

Indeed, by the twentieth century, Dicey seemed to be embracing neither parliamentary sovereignty, nor the rule of law, at least where Ireland was concerned. For what was he to do when facing the potential consequences of unlimited parliamentary sovereignty – a Liberal Government that would use that sovereignty to enact home rule for Ireland? After the Parliament Act 1911, the House of Lords no longer possessed a determinative veto over any legislation. Dicey disapproved of the Parliament Act, but had to concede that the People's Budget (the original impetus for House of Lords reform) was not the right subject matter for defence of the privileges of the upper Chamber. Dicey's solution was to turn to *political* rather than legal sovereignty – to the political sovereignty of the people, as expressed in a referendum, as opposed to the legal sovereignty of Parliament, as expressed in home rule legislation.[140] His aim was to provide a check on the parliamentary control by the Liberal party in its home rule legislation. By the time Asquith's Home Rule Bill was introduced in 1912, Dicey had concluded that, unless a general election or referendum was held on the specific question of Ulster and home rule, the government had lost its constitutional authority.

But surely use of a referendum undermines the unbounded parliamentary sovereignty that Dicey had been so keen to stress – indeed, does so more than the granting of home rule and a domestic parliament to Ireland? Dicey, however, was not the only member of the English establishment to deride the 1912 Home Rule Bill. The jurist Anson, by then Warden of All Souls college Oxford, and a Privy Councillor, described that Home Rule Bill as 'an outrage which takes us outside the accustomed bounds of political obligation', and Anson participated in plans to disrupt parliamentary debates on the grounds that 'the Government has tried us beyond the limits of human endurance'.[141] By 1913, Dicey was writing that armed resistance by Ulster to home rule could be both a right and a duty.[142] Moreover, in 1914, Dicey became a member of the executive committee of British Covenanters, taking their oath, that should home rule be passed, 'I shall hold myself justified in taking or supporting any action that may be effective to prevent it being

139 Heuston referred to Dicey's discussion (in *LOTC*) on 'Relations between Parliamentary Sovereignty and the Rule of Law' as 'a curiously tortuous chapter' (Heuston, 'Sovereignty', in AG Guest (ed.), *Oxford Essays in Jurisprudence*, at 199).

140 AV Dicey, 'Ought the Referendum to be Introduced into England?' (1890) 57 The Contemporary Review 489–511.

141 H Tulloch, 'AV Dicey and the Irish Question: 1870–1922' (1980) 15 *Irish Jurist* 160.

142 Dicey to Strachey, 16 September 1909, *Strachey Papers* (St Loe Strachey was editor of the Unionist *Spectator*).

put into operation, and more particularly to prevent the armed forces of the Crown being used to deprive the people of Ulster of their rights as citizens of the United Kingdom'.[143]

In pledging himself to rebellion by the Covenant was not Dicey thereby undermining representative democracy and the rule of law? But Dicey had already written, of the second Home Rule Bill, 'The present is exactly a crisis at which we may override the practices to save the principles of the constitution.'[144] Dicey urged a Referendum Act which would itemise a number of laws that could not be altered by Parliament without a referendum (Dicey himself would have included Electoral Reform Legislation, The Act of Union of 1800 and the new Referendum Bill). But such a measure, if effective, would undermine parliamentary sovereignty, and instil new fundamental principles into the Constitution by way of entrenchment – the very consequences Dicey had himself predicted for home rule. These factors surely render Dicey an unreliable guide to the British Constitution and undermine contemporary claims to unlimited parliamentary sovereignty deriving from his theory.

2.7.6 Bryce

However, if Dicey is to be discussed in this chapter, then so must James Bryce, who played an important but very different role in the home rule debates, although has now become somewhat forgotten. Bryce was an Ulster-born Scottish Presbyterian, who became a noted jurist, historian and MP (and later, Chief Secretary for Ireland, and British Ambassador in Washington, DC). Bryce was interested in the Irish question long before 1886, and, in spite of his Ulster background, became convinced that home rule was necessary for Ireland, writing in 1884 that,

> We have tried for more than eighty years … to work upon the fiction that England, Scotland and Ireland are one country, one people: and that, where the wishes of the majority of the inhabitants of the United Kingdom differ from those of the majority of the inhabitants of Ireland, the former shall prevail. The attempt has broken down. The fiction must be abandoned.[145]

In 1880, Bryce became Liberal MP for Tower Hamlets, and was a key figure in promoting Gladstone's 1886 Home Rule Bill, also editing a book of essays on home rule.[146] Bryce did not believe parliamentary sovereignty would be surrendered in the 1886 Bill (unlike Dicey and Anson, both convinced unionists who opposed the Bill). The 1886 Government of Ireland Bill made no explicit

143 Dicey, *A Fool's Paradise*, 116, 127. 144 Dicey, *A Leap in the Dark*, at 199.

145 J Bryce, *England and Ireland* (London, 1884). Also HAL Fisher, *James Bryce* (London: Macmillan, 1927).

146 J Bryce (ed.), *Handbook of Home Rule* (London, 1887).

reservation of sovereignty to Parliament, but nor did it formally renounce sovereignty, as had the 1782 Irish Renunciatory Act. Nonetheless, as we have seen, Anson believed that, under this Bill, the British Constitution would be fundamentally changed.[147] In 1782, Parliament had repealed the 1719 Declaratory Act to grant Ireland an independent legislature, and Anson argued that 'By this repeal, the British Parliament professed to hand over its legislative sovereignty to the Irish Parliament' thus illustrating that an 'Act of the British Parliament was capable of raising the Irish Legislature from complete dependence to complete independence.'[148] Dicey shared Anson's view that the 1886 Bill would abdicate parliamentary sovereignty. Bryce, however, rejected this claim, maintaining that the authority of Parliament would not be limited by law, but subject to conventions, and limited by mutually acceptable behaviour.[149] For Bryce, the British Parliament would retain the right to legislate, but must be trusted not to exercise its legal rights. But this turned on mutual understandings, and moral obligations, not on hard law. Bryce's argument stressed actual practice rather than abstract legal sovereignty. However, Bryce's contention that Parliament would retain legal sovereignty, even if the Bill's workability depended on practical observance of conventions, may seem unsatisfactory in the present era, which has seen conventions such as Sewel flouted – for those reasons, Bryce's theorizing on parliamentary sovereignty is not embraced here. It is no part of this text to advocate an unlimited parliamentary sovereignty that cannot be disposed of.

However, other aspects of Bryce's thought remain valuable. The failure of the 1886 Bill provided Bryce with the chance to finish his work on *The American Commonwealth*, a huge three volume work, published in 1888, which focussed in particular on the American Constitution. In his advocacy of home rule in 1886, Bryce frequently referenced America, arguing that Ireland could be like the (then) 38 American states, which possessed supreme legislative power within their own sphere. Bryce's work on the American system also led him to specify a new classification of Constitutions – that of rigid and flexible – with the British Constitution as an example of a flexible Constitution.[150] Rigid Constitutions have specific, more taxing procedures for constitutional amendments, and it was then believed that federal arrangements required a rigid Constitution. However, for Bryce, home rule could combine federalism with a more flexible constitutionalism, thus rendering it something possible in the UK – a more nuanced approach than Dicey.

[147] Anson, 'The Government of Ireland Bill' (1886) *LQR* 427, considered earlier.

[148] 'The Government of Ireland Bill' at 437. [149] Hansard, vol. cccv, col. i.

[150] James Bryce, 'Flexible and Rigid Constitutions' and 'The Action of Centripetal and Centrifugal Forces on Political Constitutions', in *Studies in History and Jurisprudence* (Oxford: Clarendon Press, 1901).

2.7.7 The British Constitution and the 'Irish Question'

From the last quarter of the nineteenth century, up until 1921, the Irish question dominated and polarized politics in the UK. Although apparently an Irish question, it also raised fundamental questions about the nature of the British Constitution. Indeed, Dicey commented, ironically in 1885, on MPs newfound interest in the Constitution: 'It really is too amusing … Suppose we advertise a series of lectures next term on the Constn [sic] for statesmen and politicians.'[151] On the one hand was the opinion of those, such as Dicey, who asserted that sovereignty could not be divided, and that home rule would begin the fragmentation and hence the destruction of the British Empire. Others countered this, stressing the importance of Irish interests, and also rejecting the notion that a relatively modest Home Rule Bill could destroy parliamentary sovereignty.

Those issues raised by the Irish question in the late nineteenth century remain highly pertinent today. These include questions of whether sovereignty must be absolute, or whether it can be divided, as in federalism; whether the UK State would dissolve if power were removed from Westminster; and when it is permissible to hold a referendum. This debate continues, in the twenty-first century, with arguments over the impact of Scottish, Welsh, and Northern Irish devolution, as well as of former EU membership, on parliamentary sovereignty. And the question of partition, and of borders, is of course, highly relevant today. Home Rule can also be seen in the context of a wider debate as to governance – both of empires and of multinational States.

2.8 The Anglo-Irish Treaty

Suspension of the 1914 Act proved fatal to home rule in Ireland. The underground Irish Republican Brotherhood was rejuvenated and directed the 1916 Easter Rising. This uprising, led by Patrick Pearse, and aided by the Irish Volunteer Force, dealt a fatal blow to home rule, when Irish nationalists occupied public buildings in Dublin and argued for secession and independence from the UK. The rising was seen by Ulster unionists as an act of treason, and home rulers, such as John Edmond, also condemned it. However, public opinion was not so hostile to the Rising, especially after it was brutally suppressed by the British, who introduced martial law and executed its leaders. A critical turning point came with the 1918 General Election, in which all adult men, and some women, could now vote. In the south of Ireland, the new nationalist party, Sinn Féin, won the great majority of seats, but refused to

[151] Dicey to Bryce 10 April 1886, ms Bryce 2 76–81 Bodleian. Such comments are also redolent of increased interest in the British Constitution caused by Brexit. See Peter Hennessey's comments noted in the Introduction.

send any MPs to Westminster, instead arguing for an independent Parliament in Dublin. Sinn Féin members (other than the many who had been arrested) declared independence on 19 January 1919, and proclaimed the establishment of an Irish Republic.

Just as with the US in 1776, the Irish Declaration of Independence did not result in the immediate recognition of a new State. Between 1919 and 1921, a fierce, paramilitary war of independence took place in Ireland. The Irish Volunteers transformed into the Irish Republican Army and were backed by Sinn Féin. However, there was no engagement of armies, and fighting between British and Irish took place on the level of skirmishes and assassinations, with atrocities on both sides. In 1920, Westminster passed the Government of Ireland Act, which established two governments – one in Belfast with jurisdiction over six north-eastern counties and the other in Dublin with jurisdiction over the remainder, both with limited devolved powers. This was unacceptable in the south, and the fighting continued and, in August 1920, the British introduced the Restoration of Order in Ireland Act, including internment without trial, a practice that was to be used again and again in Ireland. However, both loyalties and government were divided, with two separate administrations across Ireland. Sinn Féin had won local government elections across southern Ireland in 1920, and State functions, such as law enforcement and tax collecting were taken over by them. In some places, a separate court system, known as the Sinn Féin or Dáil courts, was set up, and Irish Republican police replaced the Royal Irish constabulary.

By the middle of 1921, over 1300 had died fighting, yet victory seemed no closer, and the British Government was willing to seek a political, rather than military, settlement, and a truce was concluded, in effect from 11 July 1921. Late in 1921, the 'Articles of Agreement for a Treaty between Great Britain and Ireland' were signed by British and Irish representatives in London. This agreement provided for 26 counties of 'Southern Ireland' to become the 'Irish Free State' which would have Dominion status (i.e. remain part of the British Empire, but distinct and independent from the UK). Following this, the Irish Free State (Agreement) Act 1922 was passed in Westminster, which in effect recognized secession for all of Ireland except Northern Ireland.

2.8.1 Process

The desired settlement for the Irish was a sovereign, united Irish Republic. This did not happen. De Valera's (now President of Ireland)[152] preferred position

[152] The Dáil Éireann had declared him President of Ireland in August 1921 – under the 1919 Dáil Constitution. De Valera declined to attend negotiations in London, fearing that, whatever the settlement, it would prove unpalatable to many Irish.

had been 'external association', of Ireland with the Commonwealth – whereby Ireland would recognize the Crown as Head of the Commonwealth but not as Irish Head of State. However, the British would not agree this, viewing 'external association' as extremely debilitating to the Empire.

Nonetheless, an agreement was concluded in the early hours of 6 December 1921. There had been considerable differences among the Irish negotiators, and British Prime Minister, Lloyd George, with some cynicism, played on these, with an ultimatum of an 'immediate and terrible war', if all the Irish delegation did not sign the document right then.[153] However, the treaty was viewed as a defeat by those republicans who desired full sovereignty for Ireland, given that Ireland would remain a monarchy with its government conducted in the name of the British Crown. On the other hand, Michael Collins (by then Irish Minister for Finance) argued that the treaty provided Ireland not with 'the ultimate freedom that all nations desire, but the freedom to achieve it',[154] and for a great many Irish people, it brought hope of an end to the violence that had marked the Anglo-Irish war. The treaty was narrowly approved in the Dáil by 64:57 (and also passed comfortably in Westminster) but a significant minority followed de Valera, who publicly rejected its terms, and civil war erupted among nationalists in 1922–1923.

The 'Articles of Agreement for a Treaty between Great Britain and Ireland' are usually referred to as a treaty – that is, an international agreement between States. However, even although Lloyd George declared to Parliament that: 'It is an Agreement in the nature of a Treaty, exactly in the same way as the "Articles of Agreement" entered into by the Act of Union was called a Treaty by both parties in this House,'[155] some British officials argued it could not be a treaty, as Ireland was, at that time, still part of the UK in law. The Irish vehemently rejected this contention and registered it with the League of Nations in 1924.[156] In the event, the term 'Articles of Agreement for a Treaty' was somewhat of a compromise between the two approaches. The Anglo-Irish Agreement was published in the League of Nations Treaty series, but also published were the official protests to treaty status made by the UK, along with the rejoinder by the Irish Free State.

2.8.2 Terms

Under the Anglo-Irish Treaty, 26 counties of Southern Ireland became the self-governing 'Irish Free State'. The treaty provided for a Governor-General to represent the British Crown in Free State affairs and required all elected

153 Dáil Debates (21 September 1922) vol. 1 col 545 (WT Cosgrave).

154 Dáil Debate (19 December 1921) vol. T No. 6.

155 Hansard, (HC), (15 December 1921), vol. 149, col. 128. [But of course Ireland was not part of the UK before the Act of Union.]

156 Similar differences occurred in the case of the 1998 Belfast/Good Friday Agreement.

Irish representatives to swear an oath of allegiance to the Crown before taking their seat in the Dublin Parliament. Ireland had considerable autonomy, including the power to tax, regulate foreign trade, build up a standing army and reasonable autonomy in foreign policy. However, Britain retained its four strategically important naval bases in Ireland (compromising Irish neutrality in any future war). Interestingly, the Acts of Union were repealed in neither jurisdiction at that time, although no longer applied in the Irish Free State.[157]

Articles 1 and 2 were foundational. Article 1 declared that Ireland would have 'the same constitutional status in the Community of Nations known as the British Empire as the Dominion of Canada, the Commonwealth of Australia, the Dominion of New Zealand and the Union of South Africa,' and Article 2 that Ireland's position in relation to the Imperial Parliament and Government and otherwise 'shall be that of the Dominion of Canada'. However, Dominion status was at this point in time still evolving and imprecise. In particular, it was unclear if it would provide Ireland with the 'stepping stone' to greater freedom, as Collins had suggested. Ireland was partitioned and provision made for a Boundary Commission to be established. Article 15 dealt with relations between the Free State and Northern Ireland, and Article 16 prohibited either parliament from legislating to restrict freedom of religion – thereby attempting to set in place institutional mechanisms to prevent possible future sectarian divides.

2.8.3 Implementation

Provision for immediate implementation was set out in Articles 17 and 18, which were, however, rather vaguely drafted, and two controversial issues arose,[158] both essentially concerning ratification. Article 18 simply stated that the treaty, 'if approved shall be ratified by the necessary legislation.' But just what was 'the necessary legislation'? This issue is redolent of the disagreement over the necessary 'constitutional requirements' to be satisfied for a State to leave the EU under Article 50 TEU, which led to the *Miller* case.

The first issue was that Westminster legislation appeared necessary to authorize the founding of the Provisional Irish Government and transfer government functions by Order-in-Council. In the event, the Irish conceded the need for this, and the relevant UK legislation, the 1922 Irish Free State (Agreement) Act, was passed. During the transitional period, essential State apparatus was transferred to the Provisional Government. For example, Dublin Castle was handed over on 16 January 1922 and post boxes were repainted green from red.

[157] The Union with Ireland Act 1800 is still on the UK statute book (although amended) but applicable only to Northern Ireland. In Ireland, both Acts of Union were repealed in 1962 and 1983.

[158] See J McColgan, 'Implementing the 1921 Treaty: Lionel Curtis and Constitutional Procedure' (1977) 20 Irish Hist Studies 316.

The second issue concerned the new Constitution for the Free State. The Irish delegation had assumed Irish institutions alone would have responsibility for this, and that the Constitution would be indigenous in nature. But this went beyond any autonomy allowed to British Dominions to date, which required an Act of the Imperial Parliament to legitimize the Constitution. The British view was that the UK Parliament must ratify both the Treaty and the new Constitution, or the Irish Constitution would lack legitimacy. Indeed, Westminster rejected the first draft of the Irish Constitution and only adopted the Irish Free State (Constitution) Act 1922 on 5 December 1922. By this time, the British coalition government had fallen, and a conservative government, led by Andrew Bonar Law, had to complete the last stages of the transitional period, which expired on 6 December 1922.

As a result of these disagreements, there was confusion over exactly when the Irish Free State was founded. This is unfortunate, because legal certainty is clearly vital for knowing when a new State comes into being. Some observers, such as Hugh Kennedy (later Chief Justice of the Irish Supreme Court) considered the Free State to have come into being with the adoption of the (UK) Irish Free State (Agreement) Act on 31 March 1922.[159] Other commentaries went back further, suggesting the Declaration of Independence and meeting of the first Dáil Éireann on 21 January 1919 as dates for the foundation of the new Irish State.[160] However, Mohr argues the later date of 6 December 1922 as the foundation of the Free State, citing in evidence events such as the formal opening of the Oireachtas (Irish Parliament) on that date, contact from other Dominions welcoming Ireland, and confirmation in various newspaper articles, such as the *Irish Times* whose headline stated, 'December 6 – Birth of Irish Free State'.[161]

2.8.4 Aftermath

With the conclusion of the Anglo-Irish Treaty in December 1921 the violent Anglo-Irish war, was over. However, war was not over in Ireland, for an Irish civil war soon erupted in 1922–1923 among Irish nationalists themselves, over whether to accept the treaty. The partition of Ireland has often been identified as the cause of the Irish civil war. It was undoubtedly a factor, but both sides, pro and anti-treaty, claimed to be against partition, so its role was clearly complex. In fact, it appears the civil war was fought over sovereignty as much as partition. The transcripts of three days of private session Dáil debates over the treaty illustrate that the division came not over partition, but over the oath of allegiance.[162] The civil war led to the foundation of two new political

159 Judgment of Kennedy in *In re Reade* [1927] IR 31.

160 Leo Kohn, *The Constitution of the Irish Free State* (Dublin: Allen and Unwin, 1932) 36.

161 *Irish Times*, 6 December 1922, 4. T Mohr, 'Law and the Foundation of the Irish State on 6 December 1922' (2018) 59 Irish Jurist. (Mohr argues that Kennedy argued an earlier date so the Irish Constitution could be understood as an Irish creation.)

162 See further R Fanning, *Éamon de Valera: A Will to Power* (London: Faber & Faber, 2015).

parties – the pro-Treaty *Cumann na nGaedheal* (forerunner of the *Fine Gael* party) led by William Cosgrave; and *Fianna Fáil*, led by Eamon de Valera, which parted company from *Sinn Féin* in 1926, and came to power in 1932.

2.8.5 Northern Ireland

Under Article 12 of the Anglo-Irish treaty, Ulster (six counties in Northern Ireland[163]) opted-out of the Free State and remained part of the UK, albeit with devolved government under the 1920 Government of Ireland Act. As was stated by the later 'Kilbrandon' Royal Commission on the Constitution:

> Northern Ireland, by one of history's choicest ironies, is the one place where Liberal home rule ideas were ever put into practice-and by a solidly Unionist government. It can truly be said to have been given a constitution that it did not want and that was designed for another place.[164]

In the Boundary Agreement of 1925, the Free State abandoned its claims to Northern Ireland territory, in return for termination of its obligations for imperial debt. The frontier settled in the 1920 Government of Ireland Act was confirmed.[165] However, successive southern Irish governments refused to recognize this agreement as a final settlement of the question.[166] Indeed, in Irish public opinion, the Boundary Commission report took its place as a betrayal along with the 1691 Treaty of Limerick and the failure to immediately follow up the Act of Union with Catholic emancipation.

2.8.6 Sovereignty, Self-determination, and Statehood

The Irish initially sought full sovereignty and complete independence from Britain. This was not, however, achieved. While Dominion status might offer Ireland considerable domestic self-government, it did not then seem to conclusively provide an internationally recognized sovereignty. Irish envoys had sought a hearing at the 1919 Peace conference in Versailles. A feature of this conference (in addition to the aim of a peace treaty and reparations from Germany) had been the ambition of then US President, Woodrow Wilson, to construct a new international order on principles beneficial to the self-determination of small nations. Sinn Féin had hoped to profit from this, but the Irish envoys were unable to get a hearing in Versailles.[167]

163 Three Ulster counties (Donegal, Moneghan, and Cavan), where the nationalist vote was stronger, were excluded from Northern Ireland.

164 Royal Commission on the Constitution 1969–1973 (Cmnd. 5460, 1973) para 1249.

165 Ireland (Confirmation of Agreement) Act, 1925, 15 & 16 Geo. V c. 77; Treaty (Confirmation of Amending Agreement) Act, 1925.

166 Article 2 Eire 1937 Constitution originally read: 'The national territory consists of the whole island of Ireland, its islands and the territorial seas.'

167 Sinn Féin, *The Case of Ireland*, (1919) Sinn Féin series, no. 12 IR 94109 P90.

Arthur Griffith, former Sinn Féin leader and treaty delegate, had argued that the Act of Union was unconstitutional and that Ireland had its own ancient Constitution. According to Griffith, this Constitution had been concretized in Grattan's Parliament and given expression in the 1782 Renunciation Act, which functioned as a treaty between Ireland and Great Britain. Griffith also insisted that the Sinn Féin victories in the 1918 general election were an exercise of the inherent right to self-determination which had brought Union with Britain to an end. Griffith compared the result of the 1918 Irish election with the 1861 *Ausgleich*, which joined Hungary to the Austrian empire only by the retention of a common monarch. The journal *Nationality* further argued that Union 'has meant purely and simply English domination over every phase of our national life, a domination more bitter and more unfortunate, than any experienced by small nations within the Austro-Hungarian empire.'[168]

The terms of the Anglo-Irish treaty frustrated Sinn Féin's arguments for Irish self-determination. The treaty declared Ireland's status as a member of the Empire, a Dominion, not a republic or a fully independent sovereign State. However, although legally, the treaty might seem to weaken nationalists' hopes for sovereignty, as things were to turn out, this was not so. The Irish Free State was in 1931 admitted to the Council of the League of Nations – so it was treated internationally as an independent State. And Ireland's desire to secede from the Commonwealth, although not recognized by the British until 1949, was accepted by other Commonwealth members in the 1930s. So even if, in legal terms, Ireland was not fully sovereign, in practical terms it looked like it, and it became increasingly so as years went by.

2.8.7 The 1931 Statute of Westminster, Sovereignty, and Ireland

The Statute of Westminster was an Act of the UK Parliament, but it legislated what had already been determined at the Imperial Conferences of 1926 and 1930. The Report of the Imperial Conference of 1926, often known as the Balfour Declaration, declared:

> They [the Dominions] are autonomous communities within the British Empire, equal in status, in no way subordinate one to another in any aspect of their domestic or external affairs, though united by a common allegiance to the Crown, and freely associated as members of the British Commonwealth of Nations.... Every self-governing member of the Empire is now the master of its destiny. In fact, if not always in form, it is subject to no compulsion whatever.... Equality of status, so far as Britain and the Dominions are concerned, is thus the root principle governing our inter-Imperial relations.[169]

168 *Nationality* (edited by Griffith) 18 January 1919; also P Maume, 'The Ancient Constitution: Arthur Griffith and His Intellectual Legacy to Sinn Féin' (1995) 10 Irish Political Studies 125.

169 Imperial Conference, 1926, Summary of Proceedings, 14–15. Status of Great Britain and the Dominions.

The 1931 Statute of Westminster was a direct result of this conference. It explicitly provided that no law passed by the Parliament of a Dominion should be void on ground of repugnancy to the law of England, and also that a Dominion Parliament should have the power to repeal or amend any Act of the UK Parliament in so far as that Act was part of the law of the Dominion.

Ireland was at that time eager to effect full autonomy from Britain, most particularly by terminating its obligation to the Crown and ultimate appeal to the Privy Council. The Statute of Westminster appeared to permit the Oireachtas to amend even the 1921 Anglo-Irish Treaty. So much was affirmed by the Privy Council in *Moore* v. *Attorney-General for the Irish Free State* (1935).[170] But did the Statute of Westminster itself still function as an imperial root for Dominion autonomy, or were Dominions now effectively sovereign and autochthonous?[171] The question then was, from where did Irish sovereignty derive? If fully sovereign, Dominions would even be able to repeal the Statute of Westminster itself – a view held by Sir Ivor Jennings.[172] Notably, the question of the status of the Statute of Westminster was raised both in Irish Seanad Debates and in the Privy Council. In the Seanad, Patrick McGilligan compared the situation to the USA – remarking that it was unthinkable that the UK should legislate for the USA.[173] And when the question was put in the Privy Council, in *British Coal Corp* v. *the King*, the issue of revocation of the Statute of Westminster was acknowledged as legally possible but rejected on the basis 'that is theory and has no relation to realities'.[174] The retort to this was that Privy Council rulings were not binding on the Irish Courts.[175]

2.8.8 Was the Free State Constitution a British or Irish Creation?

However, many Irish jurists claimed Ireland had possessed sovereignty even prior to 1931, and that the validity of the Irish Free State Constitution[176] derived from the sovereignty of the Irish people. This argument entailed that by 1922, Westminster was no longer competent to legislate for the Irish Free State. The upshot of such an argument was that the Statute of Westminster could not apply to the Irish Free State. Therefore, Ireland's 1922 Constitution could be viewed

170 [1935] AC 494. Although in *Moore*, the Privy Council (specifically, Lord Sankey, the Lord Chancellor) also declared that prior to the Statute of Westminster, the Irish Free State Parliament could not have repealed or amended the Treaty, because the Colonial Laws Validity Act forbade this.

171 'Constitutional autochthony' relates to asserting an indigenous Constitution. See P Oliver, 'Constitutions, Autochthonous', in R Grote, F Lachenmann, and R Wolfrum (eds.), *Max Planck Encylopedia of Comparative Constitutional Law* (Oxford University Press, 2017).

172 I Jennings, 'The Statute of Westminster and Appeals to the Privy Council' (1936) 52 *LQR* 187.

173 Fourteen *Seanad Debates* 1651–1652 (23 July 1931). The Seanad is the upper House of the Irish Parliament (and the Dáil the lower).

174 *British Coal Corporation* v. *R* [1935] AC 500, 520.

175 Jennings, 'The Statute of Westminster and Appeals to the Privy Council' at 184. Notably, the Free State Government refused to recognize the PC's jurisdiction in *Moore*.

176 E.g. B Farrell, 'The Drafting of the Irish Free State Constitution' (1970) Irish Jurist; L Cahillane, *Drafting the Irish Free State Constitution* (Manchester University Press, 2016).

as the only source of constitutional law in the Irish Free State. Nonetheless, according to Wheare, 'The whole legal foundation of the Constitution of 1922 is, indeed, a matter of "irreconcilable dispute."'[177]

The Irish Provisional Government appointed a committee in January 1922 to draft the new Constitution, which included Hugh Kennedy (later to become Attorney-General and Chief Justice of the Supreme Court) and Darrell Figgis, a notable literary figure. All committee members aspired to move away from the British constitutional system, being insistent on popular sovereignty rather than parliamentary sovereignty or royal prerogative, and earlier drafts played down the role of the Crown and failed to mention the parliamentary oath. This was unacceptable to the British (Lloyd George accused the drafters of creating 'a republic in disguise'[178]) and, after the British made clear to the Irish that war was the alternative to agreement,[179] the Constitution was amended. Westminster adopted legislation[180] in 1922 recognizing the legitimacy of the Irish Free State and its Constitution, and the Irish Parliament enacted the Constitution into law.[181] So there were two separate Acts, of two distinct Parliaments. Caselaw of the Irish Supreme Court confirmed that an Irish Constituent Assembly created the 1922 Constitution.[182] In contrast, the Privy Council held that the Constitution was created by Westminster legislation.[183] It is doubtful that either court would reverse this jurisprudence.

It is difficult to deny British influence, given the redrafting of the Constitution required by the British in summer 1922 (and it was Hugh Kennedy himself, together with British Lord Chief Justice Hewart, who did much of the redrafting in London[184]). On the other hand, Hewart was unable to persuade Kennedy to remove[185] what became Article 2 of the Free State Constitution, on popular sovereignty. And notably it was Kennedy, who had prepared the memorandum, 'Observations on the Criticisms of the British Government on the Draft Irish Constitution,' which emphasized that Ireland, unlike other Dominions had not been colonized, and that although for the British, the Crown might be associated with popular acclamation, for Ireland it was a 'symbol of tyranny'.[186]

In the event, it is likely that at least some of the ambiguity as to the origins of both of the Constitution, and the Free State itself, were deliberate, to allow each

177 KC Wheare, *The Statute of Westminster and Dominion Status* (Oxford: Clarendon Press, 1938) 101.

178 JM Curran, *The Birth of the Irish Free State 1921–1923* (University of Alabama Press, 1980) 204.

179 L Cahillane, 'An Insight into the Irish Free State Constitution' (2014) 54 American Journal of Legal History 19.

180 Irish Free State (Agreement) Act 1922; Irish Free State Constitution Act 1922.

181 Constitution of the Irish Free State (*Saorstát Eireann*) Act, 1922.

182 *State (Ryan)* v. *Lennon* [1935] IR 170.

183 *Moore* v. *Attorney-General for the Irish Free State* [1935] IR 472 and [1935] AC 484.

184 T Mohr, 'British Involvement in the Creation of the First Irish Constitution' (2008) 30 Dublin University LJ 166.

185 Ibid.: TNA-PRO CAB 43/1 SFB 28th Conclusions.

186 Curran, *The Birth of the Irish Free State,* 210. CAB23/30 at 149.

State to maintain its dignity, as well as to reconcile two competing principles: parliamentary sovereignty and constitutional autochthony. However, Mohr's conclusion is that suspicions of British influence 'had the effect of stigmatising the 1922 Constitution with the mark of being a British imposition. This was a blemish that the Constitution of the Irish Free State would never escape. Eventually, this stain would settle its fate.'[187]

2.8.9 Novel Features of the Constitution

The 1922 Irish Constitution differed in some substantial ways from the British Constitution, notably in providing for constitutional judicial review by including fundamental rights; and in its provisions for referendums and popular initiative. It also laid out in Article 2 that all power was derived from the Irish people, and so did not subscribe to the principle of parliamentary sovereignty. As Ward has written, 'Ostensibly it created an Irish constitutional monarchy, but by force of will the Provisional Government ensured that key republican values were written into constitutional law for the first time, including popular sovereignty, parliamentary control of the war power, and entrenched civil rights.'[188]

The Irish Constitutional Committee had, early on its work, studied other Constitutions, and was particularly interested in the 1919 German Weimar Constitution, which guaranteed many fundamental rights, as well as referendums, and was then considered to be the most democratic Constitution in existence.[189] Popular sovereignty featured prominently in these Constitutions, and according to Cahillane, 'was one way of ensuring an autochthonous constitution. The declaration of popular sovereignty was also seen by the people as a Republican aspect of the Constitution; a sign that the Irish Free State was not going to be controlled by the Crown.'[190] Provision for both fundamental rights and for judicial review was a significant innovation. However, when the 1922 Constitution first came into force, Ireland was undergoing a civil war, and martial law had been introduced, so such 'hard' judicial review rarely if ever took place.[191]

2.8.10 Amendments

A further innovative element of the 1922 Constitution was its requirement, in Article 50, that future amendments be subject to a referendum (requiring a 2/3

[187] 'British Involvement in the Creation of the First Irish Constitution'.

[188] Ward, *The Irish Constitutional Tradition*, 187.

[189] E.g. O Kirchheimer, 'Weimar – And What Then? An Analysis of a Constitution', in F Burin and K Shell (eds.), *Politics, Law and Social Change* (New York: Columbia University Press, 1969). However, the Weimar Constitution itself was overridden, and Hitler rose to power.

[190] L Cahillane, 'The Influence of the Post-war European Constitutions on the Constitution of the Irish Free State' (2011) 15 Eur Jl Comp Law 4.

[191] JM Kelly, *Fundamental Rights in the Irish Law and Constitution* (Dublin: Allen Figgis, 2nd ed., 1967).

'supermajority') other than those in the first eight years of the Constitution's existence. However, this initial simpler amendment power was used to allow substantial amendments by parliamentary majority only, without referendum, including amendments to extend the eight-year period itself specified in Article 50. And so, the 1922 Constitution was undermined, and rendered very flexible, and easily amended – like the British Constitution. This looked more like parliamentary than popular sovereignty.

In this way, simple constitutional amendments achieved what has been described as a 'dismantling of the 1922 Constitution'.[192] The Constitution was easily amended to remove the requirement of oath taking, and end appeals to the Privy Council, as well as doing away with all references to the Crown.[193] In 1936, The Executive Authority (External Relations) Act 1936 vested executive authority in the Irish government, associating the Crown only with Irish external affairs (and thus could be seen as the fulfilment of de Valera's proposal for 'external association' in 1921).

In conclusion, in any case, what was clear was that by 1931, Ireland was legally able to repeal and amend both the Treaty and its 1922 Constitution. One argument derived this freedom from the Statute of Westminster, that is British law. The other derived it from Irish sovereignty and the Irish Constitution itself.

2.8.11 British Perspectives

The Irish Free State was established as a Dominion, remaining within the British Empire, whereas it had previously been in a Union with Great Britain as part of the UK. The UK had lost nearly one-third of its territory – the biggest loss since the American revolution.

In Britain, the fear was expressed that greater Irish autonomy and independence would lead to calls for independence elsewhere in the Empire. Winston Churchill described the Lloyd George government's turn from military force to conciliation in Ireland as the most 'complete and sudden … reversal of policy' in modern British political history.[194] This reversal was not because the British Government became convinced of the rightness of the Irish cause, but simply down to political expediency. A prolonged and brutal military campaign in Ireland was not only too costly and unbearable after the depredations of the Great War, but also unlikely to impress those members of the international community (especially the US) already critical of Britain's conduct in Ireland. And Michael Collins had observed that the Versailles Peace Conference gave

[192] G Hogan, 'Introduction to the Origins of the Irish Constitution,' Royal Irish Academy (Dublin, 2012).

[193] The Constitution (Removal of Oath) Act, 1933; The Constitution (Amendment No. 22) Act, 1933; The Constitution (Amendment No. 27) Act, 1936.

[194] WS Churchill, *The World Crisis: The Aftermath* (London: Butterworth, 1929) 290.

to Sinn Féin an 'opportunity to … call the attention of the world to the denial of our claim', rejecting 'the convenient British doctrine that we were a British province' and, thus 'a domestic question'.[195]

International reaction to the Anglo-Irish treaty was generally positive, appearing to improve the reputation of the British Empire, and the British Government took advantage of this. For example, Sir Samuel Hoare, Cabinet member at the time declared:

> The British Empire does not surrender to anyone.… We are so strong that we can make big and generous concessions such as no small and weak country would dare to make. We are making a peace with Ireland, not because we have to make a peace, but because we wish to make a peace.[196]

But for other MPs, the treaty was 'an ignoble surrender to rebellion, assassination and outrage' as well as a 'humiliation' for 'a great nation' and 'the Empire'.[197] British attitudes, whether those of the government, or of those who viewed the treaty as a surrender, frequently derived from a sense of superiority, reliant on British imperial ideology.[198] But there were also some grounds for fearing Ireland's transition out of the Union was part of a much bigger development, that of the breakup of the Empire. The actuality of Irish rebellion at last forcing Britain to conciliation and negotiation was not lost in other parts of the Empire, especially in India, where in 1922 there were calls from the Swarajya Party formed by Motihal Nehru and C. R. Das for transition to Dominion status. But overall, what was notable was the lack of British reflection on what had led to the loss of much of Ireland.

And, as time passed, the Free State altered its domestic law to remove those parts of it linking it to Britain – such as its allegiance to the Crown, and the requirement of appeals in the last instance to the Privy Council – so that it gradually withdrew from the Commonwealth. Other Commonwealth countries came to wish to do the same, and when, on gaining its independence, India declared itself a republic, the question arose whether as a republic, it might continue to be a Commonwealth member. By the 1949 London Declaration, India was allowed to remain in the Commonwealth, as a republic, on the basis of an adjustment to the notion of 'external association' first proposed by de Valera in 1921. This proposal involved the situation whereby the British monarch was head of the association (or Commonwealth) but not necessarily of the Head of State of its members.[199]

[195] Michael Collins, *The Path to Freedom* (Dublin: The Talbot Press, 1922) 84, 88.

[196] Hansard, HC, 14 December 1921, vol. 149 cc6–26.

[197] Rear-Admiral Adair HC, 14 December 1921, vol. 149 cc48–124; Sir William Davison, HC, 14 December 1921, vol. 149 cc48–124.

[198] Seán Donnelly, 'Ireland in the Imperial Imagination' (2019) 27 *Irish Studies Review* 499.

[199] N Mansergh, 'Ireland: The Republic Outside the Commonwealth' (1952) 28 *International Affairs* 277.

2.9 1937 Constitution and After

In 1932, a new Fianna Fáil government was formed, led by Éamon de Valera. The way was prepared for a new Constitution (the *Bunreacht na hÉireann*[200]), drafted by the Irish Government, approved by the *Dáil* on 14 June 1937, and confirmed by the electorate in a referendum, and so founded on popular sovereignty of the Irish people.[201] According to Wheare, this was 'a revolution in law', that broke off any attempt to derive the legitimacy of Irish law through Westminster legislation.[202]

The Free State was no more and the Constitution referred to Eire or Ireland, without of course, the measures concerning the Crown, oath, Governor General and Dominion status. Instead, it provided for a President of Ireland, elected by direct vote of the people, and bound, save as otherwise provided, to act in accordance with the advice of the Prime Minister. Article 1 of the 1937 Constitution unequivocally affirms the sovereignty of the Republic of Ireland. It also included provisions on fundamental rights, but unlike the 1922 Constitution, put them beyond the power of the Oireachtas to amend or repeal. In general, the 1937 is a rigid Constitution, albeit easier to amend than the US federal Constitution.

However, the new Constitution had its contentious elements The Preamble notably declared itself 'In the Name of the Most Holy Trinity, from Whom is all authority and to Whom, as our final end, all actions both of men and States must be referred' which might seem to compromise popular sovereignty. The special place of the Roman Catholic Church was entrenched by Article 44.1.2,[203] although it was not established as the State church. Article 41.2 related to the position of women in the home and drew much criticism.[204] Moreover, Article 2 proclaimed the national territory to be 'the island of Ireland.' No mention was made of Northern Ireland. Only after the Good Friday Agreement of 1998 did Ireland remove its claim to Northern Ireland from the text of the Constitution.

2.9.1 Ireland Leaves the Commonwealth

In 1948, the Dáil adopted The Republic of Ireland Act, terminating Ireland's association with the Commonwealth. The UK Ireland Act, 1949, provided, in

[200] Which translates as Basic Law of Ireland. See further D Keogh and A McCarthy, *The Making of the Irish Constitution 1937* (Dublin: Mercier Press, 2007).

[201] Although it did not achieve huge popular support in the referendum. 38.6 per cent of the electorate voted in favour, 29.6 per cent against and 31.8 per cent abstained or spoiled their votes – D Morgan, *Constitutional Law of Ireland* (Dublin: Round Hall Press, 1985) at 29.

[202] Wheare, *The Statute of Westminster and Dominion Status*, 276.

[203] Removed by referendum in 1973.

[204] Article 41.2 stated: 'the State recognizes that by her life within the home, woman gives to the State a support without which the common good cannot be achieved. The State shall, therefore, endeavour to ensure that mothers shall not be obliged by economic necessity to engage in labour to the neglect of their duties in the home.'

s1, that 'the part of Ireland heretofore known as Eire ceased ... to be part of His Majesty's dominions' and also that, in future, Eire was to be known in all UK legislation as 'the Republic of Ireland'. However, s2 provided that, for the purposes of any UK law, the Republic of Ireland was not to be a foreign country, and the provisions of the British Nationality Act, 1948, defined aliens in such a manner as to exclude citizens of the Republic of Ireland.

2.10 Northern Ireland

2.10.1 Historical Background

Northern Ireland remained part of the UK, but with a devolved government under the Government of Ireland Act 1920. The demographic consequence of partition was for many years to create a Catholic minority in Northern Ireland that lacked political power. Ulster Unionist parties maintained a majority in government, and in 1929 proportional representation was abolished for parliamentary elections. By 1973, the Royal Commission on the Constitution noted that: 'a large section of the community [was] always in a minority, without any share in government or any prospect of securing a share in government.'[205]

Northern Ireland thus became a separate self-governing jurisdiction, with its own Assembly (at Stormont), Executive and Lord Lieutenant/Governor. However, s4 of the Government of Ireland Act 1920 excluded whole areas from its jurisdiction, including: the Crown, making of war and peace, the armed forces, treaties and foreign relations, treason and naturalization, overseas trade, coinage, granting of titles, and 'any other matter which by this Act is declared to be a reserved matter'. A convention arose that Westminster would only legislate on matters transferred to Northern Ireland if invited to do so. In spite of this, s75 of the Government of Ireland Act clearly maintained Westminster parliamentary sovereignty over all areas. (In this respect, the scheme looked like contemporary devolution.) But, as public lawyers acknowledged, Northern Ireland's status was unclear, and, according to Geoffrey Sawer, the Government of Ireland Act 1920 had created 'an odd sort of federal situation.'[206] Nonetheless, the mechanisms established under the Government of Ireland Act 1920 continued to function until suspended in 1972 by Britain as a result of 'The Troubles'.

2.10.1.1 The Troubles

Partition was opposed by the nationalist minority in Northern Ireland, many of whom aspired to a united Ireland, and tensions between nationalists and unionists grew. These tensions erupted in 'The Troubles', a 30-year period of violent conflict starting in the late 1960s over the constitutional status of

[205] Royal Commission on the Constitution 1969–1973 (Cmnd. 5460, 1973) 1268.

[206] G Sawer, *Modern Federalism* (London: Watts & Co., 1969) 57.

Northern Ireland. Direct rule of Northern Ireland from London was introduced in 1972. British troops were stationed in Northern Ireland, and there was a forceful police presence. Much emergency legislation was introduced to deal with the terrorist situation and the rule of law came under strain.[207] Nationalist and unionist communities were segregated, but there was still great conflict and bloodshed between the two. In March 1973, a referendum was held to decide whether Northern Ireland should remain in the UK.[208] This poll was, however, boycotted by most Catholics and nationalists, but of those who voted, an overwhelming majority wanted to keep the status quo. The 1985 Anglo-Irish Agreement set up the Anglo-Irish Intergovernmental Conference, which aspired to promote cross-border co-operation with Irish Republic. It was however, opposed by Unionist MPs and the disturbances continued until a ceasefire was reached in the 1990s and the Belfast/Good Friday Agreement of 1998 concluded.

2.10.2 The Peace Process and the Belfast/Good Friday Agreement 1998

By the 1990s, the situation was changing. In late 1993, the Downing Street Declaration announced that the UK had no 'selfish strategic or economic' interest in Northern Ireland. In 1994, the IRA declared a complete cessation of military activities, which was followed by a comparable announcement from Loyalist paramilitaries. From 1996, multiparty negotiations between the UK and Irish governments ran for two years and resulted in the Belfast/Good Friday Agreement (B/GFA) of 10 April 1998. This affirmed the 'total and absolute commitment to exclusively democratic and peaceful means of resolving differences on political issues' and 'opposition to any use or threat of force … for any political purpose.'[209] The British and Irish governments, and most political parties (but not the DUP) in Northern Ireland signed the Agreement, which is also an international treaty signed by the UK and Ireland and lodged with the UN in New York. Its main provisions are:

- A new Northern Ireland Assembly, Executive and consultative Civic Forum (Strand 1); a North-South Ministerial Council (Strand 2); and a British-Irish Council (Strand 3);
- So as to ensure co-operation between unionists and nationalists, both sides had to be represented in the Executive, and key decisions of the Assembly could only be taken if supported by members from both sides;
- Confirmation that Northern Ireland remained part of the UK. However, it also required the UK government to organize a 'border poll' if it appeared

[207] KD Ewing and CA Gearty, *Freedom under Thatcher: Civil Liberties in Modern Britain* (Oxford: Clarendon Press, 1990) 209–254.

[208] Held under the Northern Ireland (Border Poll) Order 1973.

[209] 'An Agreement reached at the multi-party talks on Northern Ireland' (Cm. 3883, 1998) para 4.

likely that a majority would support a change of status. The UK government committed to respecting the result of that poll;

- Amendment of Articles 2 and 3 of the Constitution of Ireland (to delete Ireland's claim to the territory of all of Ireland, including Northern Ireland);
- A process for decommissioning weapons and accelerated release of paramilitary prisoners;
- The creation of a Northern Ireland Human Rights Commission and Equality Commission;
- An independent commission to make recommendations for future policing arrangements in Northern Ireland, and a review of criminal justice.

The cross-border institutions established in Strand 2 made steps towards a more unified Ireland, but on the other hand, the deletion of territorial claims to Northern Ireland from the Irish Constitution made clear the UK's sovereignty. The Agreement also stressed the importance of the 'principle of consent', for example in Article 1(ii):

> it is for the people of the island of Ireland alone … to exercise their right of self-determination on the basis of consent, freely and concurrently given, North and South, to bring about a united Ireland, if that is their wish, accepting that this right must be achieved and exercised with and subject to the agreement and consent of a majority of the people of Northern Ireland.

The B/GFA has been crucial to the peace process and relations between the UK and Ireland. It includes many provisions concerning EU and ECHR law. Indeed, the B/GFA Preamble notes the 'close co-operation between (the) countries as friendly neighbours and as partners in the European Union'. In a UK parliamentary hearing on Brexit and its impact, the former Irish Taoiseach John Bruton, claimed that the relationship between Britain and Ireland had been transformed by EU membership, giving rise to a more equal balanced partnership.[210]

However, the UK's Brexit vote means that the UK is no longer an EU partner and also deprives the British and Irish governments of a regular, neutral venue, the European Council, for Ireland and UK ministers to meet and to strengthen Anglo-Irish relations and discuss Northern Ireland. The impact of Brexit on Northern Ireland will be considered shortly.

The B/GFA was followed up by the Northern Ireland Act 1998 (UK legislation), adopted after referendums in both Northern Ireland and the Republic of Ireland had approved the B/GFA on a turnout of 81 per cent in Northern Ireland, in which 71.1 per cent voted Yes and 28.9 per cent No. The Northern Ireland Act also repealed the remaining parts of the Government of Ireland Act 1920, as well as the Northern Ireland Constitution Act 1973 (which imposed direct rule). A key provision in the Northern Ireland Act (s1(2)) is that which

[210] Available at www.parliament.uk/globalassets/documents/lords-committees/eu-select/Brexit-UK-Irish-Evidence-Volume.pdf

enables the Secretary of State for Northern Ireland to call for a referendum: 'if at any time it appears likely to him that a majority of those voting would express a wish that Northern Ireland should cease to be part of the United Kingdom and form part of a united Ireland.'

The Northern Ireland Act transferred many legislative functions from Westminster to the new Northern Ireland Assembly (elected under a single transferable vote system of proportional representation) and executive functions to Northern Ireland's First Minister and deputy First Minister. It also made provision for a 'complex scheme of power sharing between the main parties' – a species of devolution known as consociationalism.[211] Unlike in the Scottish, Welsh and Westminster Parliaments, Northern Ireland Assembly members do not take an oath of allegiance to the Crown, although they have to give an undertaking against paramilitarism. Three categories of legislative powers were established under the devolution settlement in the Northern Ireland Act 1998: *reserved, excepted and transferred*. As with the devolution systems in Scotland and Wales, Westminster remains sovereign, with the ability to legislate for all areas of Northern Ireland law. However, under the Sewel Convention, the UK Parliament does not normally legislate on devolved areas without first obtaining the consent of the Northern Ireland Assembly – which refused its consent for the EU (Withdrawal Agreement) Bill in 2020. Northern Ireland devolution, similarly to the systems in Scotland and Wales, is funded by a mixture of a 'block grant' from Westminster, moderated by the non-statutory Barnett formula, and locally raised revenue.

A dispute between the DUP and Sinn Féin (the parties with the largest vote from unionist and nationalist communities) led to the 2017 collapse of the power-sharing Executive and the suspension of the Northern Ireland Assembly. Both finally recommenced in January 2020 – so for most of the Brexit process, Northern Ireland had no effective Assembly. Sectarian discord had appeared to be diminishing in Northern Ireland – in a 2018 survey,[212] 50 per cent of the population considered itself neither unionist nor nationalist. However, governance in Ireland has been put under strain by Brexit. Also, since Sinn Féin gained most votes for the Assembly elections in May 2022, and since the Brexit Northern Ireland Protocol has been in operation, the DUP has refused to co-operate, and the Assembly was once again suspended.

2.10.3 Northern Ireland, the EU, and Brexit

Both the UK and Ireland joined the EEC (as it then was) in 1973. Under the terms of the EU Single Market, customs checks and other barriers to free

[211] See AW Bradley and KD Ewing, *Constitutional and Administrative Law* (London: Longman, 13th ed., 2003) 46–47; Arend Lijphart, 'The Northern Ireland Problem: Cases, Theories and Solutions' (1975) 5 British J'l of Political Science 1, 83–106.

[212] Northern Ireland political attitudes survey, available at www.ark.ac.uk/nilt/2018/Political_Attitudes/UNINATID.html

movement were eliminated, allowing the free movement of goods, persons, services and capital between the UK and Ireland.

However, on 23 June 2016, a majority of the UK electorate voted to leave the EU. But voters in Northern Ireland supported Remain by 56–44 per cent. (The DUP campaigned for 'Leave' and Sinn Féin 'Remain'.) Northern Ireland is the smallest jurisdiction of the UK, with 1.81 million (1.5 per cent UK citizens) but Brexit is arguably of more consequence here than the rest of the UK. Northern Ireland is one of the poorest UK regions, but will now no longer benefit from EU funding for Peace programmes (some €2.4 billion from 2014 to 2020[213]). Furthermore, Northern Ireland is the only part of the UK to share a land border with another EU member State (Ireland) and this border has enormous symbolic and practical importance. After the 1998 B/GFA, the border had been demilitarized, and checkpoints dismantled, so that people and goods could cross freely. But following Brexit, there are crucial questions as to how an open border can be continued, with the two countries on each side no longer both part of the EU. There are also fears for the future of peace, given that the open border facilitated not only trade and free movement, but also become an emblem of reconciliation. Nonetheless, there was little discussion by the Leave campaign of the border issue prior to the referendum, despite the matter being raised by several commentators. It was difficult to see how a 'hard' border across Ireland could be avoided, given that the UK had insisted that leaving the EU also entailed leaving the EU Single Market and Customs Union, thus necessitating mechanisms to ensure that goods crossing into Ireland from Northern Ireland complied with EU rules. This matter therefore became a particular challenge of the EU withdrawal negotiations. The UK's 'hard Brexit' approach had created a problem that had not previously existed and appeared almost impossible to resolve.

2.10.3.1 The Withdrawal Agreement and Protocol

In 2018, the UK and EU concluded a draft Withdrawal Agreement with a Protocol on Ireland/Northern Ireland.[214] This Protocol set out the provisions of the now notorious *'backstop'*, which provided a safeguard so that, until and unless a comprehensive trade agreement was concluded, the UK and Northern Ireland would continue in the EU Customs Union. In addition, Northern Ireland (but not the rest of the UK) would continue to apply EU agricultural and product standards. This 'backstop' arrangement, because it would have maintained the same customs rules and standards in both Northern Ireland and the Republic, would have ruled out any need for a hard border or checks on goods passing from the north to south of Ireland

213 Special EU Programmes Body (PEACE IV Programme (2014–2020)).

214 *Draft Agreement on the withdrawal of the United Kingdom of Great Britain and Northern Ireland from the European Union and the European Atomic Energy Community*, 14 November 2018, TF50 (2018) 55.

or vice versa. However, the backstop was particularly loathed by hard-line Brexiteers, because it was seen as undermining UK sovereignty and the ECJ would have overseen its compliance. So, the 2018 Withdrawal Agreement was repeatedly rejected by the UK Parliament (including by large numbers of conservative MPs).

In contrast, the *revised* Protocol to the Withdrawal Agreement, concluded in late 2019,[215] by Prime Minister Johnson, killed off the 'backstop', agreeing instead an arrangement with the EU that installed an economic border between Great Britain and Northern Ireland, although in theory, Northern Ireland continues to be part of UK customs territory. The 2019 Protocol also relates to Northern Ireland only, whereas the backstop would have retained all of the UK within the EU Customs Union. This was seen as a grand victory for Brexiteers. It has not made unionists in Northern Ireland so happy, and Northern Ireland has been unsettled since. The only possible way to avoid checks on goods crossing from Northern Ireland into Ireland is for the north to apply EU rules. Therefore, in practice, there are customs checks and controls on goods crossing from the Great Britain into Northern Ireland, so as to ensure the correct tariffs are applied.

The UK Parliament approved both the Withdrawal Agreement and the new Protocol in January 2020. However, the Scottish Parliament, Welsh Assembly and Northern Ireland Assembly vigorously rejected the Agreement. Those refusals of legislative consent, being based on convention only, were considered (at least by the UK Government) as not legally binding on the UK Parliament and so implementation of the Agreement went ahead. So, the UK Government, which presents itself as unionist and sovereigntist, concluded an Agreement that inserted an economic border within the UK.

2.10.3.2 The Northern Ireland Protocol Bill 2022

Nonetheless, and inconsistently, the UK Government had been attempting to change the Northern Ireland Protocol since 2020, arguing that it created internal trade barriers between Great Britain and Northern Ireland. This is at the very least disingenuous, as it was the Johnson government that negotiated this Agreement, deliberately discarding the previous 'backstop', and Johnson himself presented it as an 'oven ready' deal,[216] a key plank of his general election manifesto in 2019.

To be sure, the Protocol had always been hated by the DUP who held disproportionate influence while they supported the conservatives in the minority UK government from 2017 to 2019. Indeed, dissatisfied Ulster Unionists

[215] *Agreement on the withdrawal of the United Kingdom of Great Britain and Northern Ireland from the European Union and the European Atomic Energy Community*, 2019/C 384 OJ C 384, 12 November 2019.

[216] B Johnson, 'A Deal Is Oven Ready. Let's Get Brexit Done and Take This Country Forward', *Daily Telegraph*, 5 November 2019.

brought a challenge to the legality of the Protocol.[217] But the Protocol had the support of the majority of the Northern Ireland Assembly,[218] and the EU has rejected UK criticism of its conduct over the Protocol.

Notwithstanding, in June 2022, the UK Government introduced the Northern Ireland Protocol Bill[219] into the House of Commons. Although Johnson described it as a 'relatively trivial set of adjustments,'[220] this was an understatement – or misrepresentation even – as this Bill unilaterally overrode a large amount of the Protocol so as to remove the impact of EU law in Northern Ireland, and, in so doing, very likely violated international law.

2.10.3.2.1 Breaking International Law?

This was not the first time the UK unilaterally attempted to change its obligations under the Protocol. In September 2020, Brandon Lewis, then Secretary of State for Northern Ireland, admitted that clauses in the 2020 Internal Market Bill would breach the UK's international commitments under the Withdrawal Agreement in a 'very specific and limited way.'[221] Following this, the EU threatened legal action, and both the UK Advocate General and Treasury Solicitor (the most senior government legal official) resigned, and thereafter the clause was removed.

In June 2022, vice-president of the European Commission, Maroš Šefčovič, made it clear that the EU would not renegotiate the Protocol, and the EU Commission commenced legal action for breach of the Protocol against the UK. In addition to legal action, there was also the prospect of a trade war with the EU, bringing great economic damage.

What sort of mindset leads from a description of the Northern Ireland Protocol as an 'oven-ready' 'best deal ever' to a unilateral (and very possibly unlawful) attempt to repudiate and override it? Since Brexit, the issue of Ireland's partition, and Northern Ireland's membership of the UK, has returned to the political agenda. Some (but not all) opinion polls have indicated a small majority in favour of Irish unity, and in March 2017, Sinn Féin Assembly leader, Michelle O'Neill, called for an 'Irish unity referendum … as soon as possible'.[222]

2.10.3.3 The 'Windsor Framework' 2023

However, on 27 February 2023, the UK Government and EU agreed the 'Windsor Framework' which modifies aspects of the Northern Ireland Protocol. This Framework has the potential to alleviate some of the most contentious

[217] In *Allister and others* v. *Prime Minister and others* [2022] NICA 15, it was unsuccessfully argued that the Protocol violated the B/GFA, Northern Ireland Act 1998, and the 1800 Act of Union.

[218] 'Majority of Northern Ireland MLAs Condemn Plan to Alter Brexit Protocol', *The Guardian*, 13 June 2022.

[219] See further www.gov.uk/government/collections/northern-ireland-protocol-bill

[220] 'Britain defies EU with "relatively trivial" Northern Ireland law', *Reuters*, 13 June 2022.

[221] https://hansard.parliament.uk/commons/2020-09-08/debates/2F32EBC3-6692-402C-93E6-76B4CF1BC6E3/NorthernIrelandProtocolUKLegalObligations

[222] McAdam, 'Unionists Anger at Sinn Fein's Call for Irish Border', Belfast Telegraph, 14 March 2017. See also C Harvey and M Bassett, The EU And Irish Unity; Planning and Preparing for Constitutional Change in Ireland (Queen's Policy Engagement, 10 October 2019).

aspects of the Protocol and so improve relations between the UK Government and EU.

The Framework comprises a complex bundle of documents and agreements issued by both the UK and EU. A UK Government Command paper[223] describes it as 'an international law agreement' between the UK and EU and states that the amended Protocol would be governed by the Vienna Convention on the law of treaties. At the centre of the Framework is a draft Joint Committee decision[224] which amends the Protocol. However, an important part of the Framework is a political declaration by both parties[225] confirming that the UK Government will not proceed with the Northern Ireland Protocol Bill and the EU Commission will halt its legal proceedings relating to the Protocol against the UK.

The Windsor Framework aims to provide a more workable solution so that, while Northern Ireland remains in the EU Single Market and Customs Union, many of the burdensome checks applying to goods arriving from mainland Britain under the original Northern Ireland Protocol are cut back. The Framework uses a 'green' (Northern Ireland) and 'red' (Ireland/EU) lane system to separate goods moving only from Great Britain to Northern Ireland from those continuing into the EU. Those not destined for the EU will have lighter border controls, although Northern Ireland retailers must qualify as trusted traders to benefit from reduced checks. In this way, it is hoped that problems operating the Protocol, such as with travel of persons (and their pets!) and issues regarding supply of medicines from Great Britain to Northern Ireland, will be alleviated. Nonetheless, goods using the red lane moving into Ireland and the EU will still undergo full checks and must satisfy the required paperwork.

Post Brexit, even under the new Windsor Framework, many EU laws will still apply in Northern Ireland. However, because the UK is no longer an EU member State, there exists no official mechanism whereby Northern Ireland representatives can participate in the EU law-making process. This gives rise to a democratic deficit, which the Windsor Framework attempts to address. It therefore creates a new 'Stormont brake', giving the Northern Ireland Assembly (and ultimately the UK Government) power to decide whether changes to EU rules within the scope of the Protocol apply. The brake operates similarly to the 'petition of concern' under the Belfast/Good Friday Agreement (the special mechanisms for cross-party consent). It can be triggered by 30 MLAs from two political parties but only in exceptional circumstances. Any dispute about use

[223] HM Government, *The Windsor Framework: A New Way Forward*, CP 806 (February 2023).

[224] Available at https://assets.publishing.service.gov.uk/government/uploads/system/uploads/attachment_data/file/1139421/Draft_Decision_of_the_Withdrawal_Agreement_Joint_Committee_on_laying_down_arrangements_relating_to_the_Windsor_Framework.pdf

[225] Available here: https://assets.publishing.service.gov.uk/government/uploads/system/uploads/attachment_data/file/1139420/Political_Declaration_by_the_European_Commission_and_the_Government_of_the_United_Kingdom.pdf#page=5

of the brake should be resolved through an independent arbiter rather than the European Court of Justice (ECJ).

The Windsor framework also commits to developing existing UK–EU structures, including a new specialist committee for goods to ensure its implementation. Nonetheless, application of EU law in Northern Ireland will remain subject to EU oversight. This means retaining the ultimate jurisdiction of the ECJ, a court hated by more extreme UK Eurosceptics. But given that the ECJ is the ultimate jurisdiction for EU law, its eradication from the Framework was never going to be possible.

The Windsor Framework is a complex arrangement, and its implementation will be complex. Some aspects of it will require consent from 27 EU member States, and/or the European Parliament. The EU-UK Withdrawal Agreement Joint Committee must formally adopt measures that implement some parts of it. UK legislation would be needed to give effect to the Stormont brake. Although it seems that a vote on the Framework is not legally required, Prime Minister Rishi Sunak nonetheless stated that the UK Parliament would have the chance to vote on the framework 'at the appropriate time'.[226] However, it is unlikely that Parliament will have any chance to amend the Framework agreement, and most UK implementation will be by secondary legislation. The growth of secondary legislation in Brexit instruments is surely problematic but given that UK Conservative MPs have continuously voted against providing Parliament increased powers to inspect international agreements, this would be a self-inflicted wound.

Overall, the Windsor Framework does not radically alter the Northern Ireland Protocol. Nonetheless, it mitigates some practical problems caused by it, most particularly by streamlining the movement of products between Great Britain and Northern Ireland. The Protocol, as originally agreed, also played its part in impeding power-sharing government in Northern Ireland, given the DUP had refused to participate, citing the Protocol as one of their main grievances. It is to be hoped that the Framework's changes, including the 'Stormont Brake', will redress that. Additionally, the Framework may facilitate some important further steps – hopefully ensuring that future UK participation in the EU Horizon Europe programme (which supports research and development programmes across Europe) will be possible.

When speaking of the deal to an audience in Belfast, Rishi Sunak stated that it would put Northern Ireland in a 'unique position in the entire world, European continent, in having privileged access not just to the UK home market, which is enormous, fifth biggest in the world, but also the European Union's single market. Nobody else has that.'[227] The irony of the fact that this was exactly what the UK had before Brexit appeared totally lost to Sunak.

[226] House of Commons Research Briefing, 'Northern Ireland Protocol: The Windsor Framework' (28 February 2023).

[227] See 'Windsor Framework: New Brexit Deal about People of Northern Ireland, says Sunak', *BBC News*, 28 February 2023.

To be sure, at time of writing, all is not plain sailing. Although the Framework will facilitate trade between Great Britain and Northern Ireland, an Irish Sea border still remains. And even the very title of the agreement – the 'Windsor' Framework raises questions. Was the Windsor element designed to attract unionists? But if so, surely the title would be less appealing to nationalists? Hardly a unifying approach, conducive to 'the fellow feeling' that Prime Minister Sunak referred to as defining 'This family of nations – this United Kingdom.'[228]

2.11 Conclusion

Leyland has argued that the evolution of Ireland – from part of the UK, to Free State with Dominion status, to an independent republic – 'demonstrates the capacity of the Westminster Parliament to limit on an irrevocable basis the legislative competence of its successors.'[229] This confirms what Dicey already made clear that parliamentary sovereignty may be surrendered, and a continuing theme of this book has been that parliamentary sovereignty is neither absolute nor inalienable.

However, just as significantly, this chapter has illustrated the often unmindful and indifferent nature of Britain's relationship with Ireland, and how it has been unwilling to learn from past mistakes. Brexit – the most recent instalment of UK relations with Ireland/Northern Ireland – evokes and reflects that relationship's history. The UK's ignorance of Ireland has been emphasized recently by commentators of all political persuasions. Former UK Conservative Cabinet Minister, Michael Portillo, said, 'The British are always dealing with Ireland I'm afraid in this ignorant, off-hand way … from a unionist point of view.' UK film producer, David Puttnam, remarked that, 'I was staggered at the display of pig-ignorance towards the fundamentals of Irish history, let alone sensitivity towards the reality of cross-border relationships.'[230] And *Times* columnist, David Aaronovitch, wrote an article about Ireland entitled, 'A nearby country of which we know nothing,' noting that 'A hundred years after the Anglo-Irish Treaty, there's a casual ignorance among the English about Ireland and its history.'[231] These comments are all too easily supported with evidence – ranging from admissions of ignorance such as those of former UK Secretary of State for Northern Ireland, Karen Bradley, and recent YouGov polls recording just how little Britons knew about Ireland, the Irish

[228] Gov UK, 'PM speech on the Windsor Framework: 27 February 2023.'

[229] P Leyland, 'Referendums, Popular Sovereignty and the Territorial Constitution', in R Rawlings, P Leyland, and AL Young (eds.), *Sovereignty and the Law* (Oxford: Oxford University Press, 2016) 150.

[230] R McGreevy, 'Portillo, "Ignorance of Ireland among the British Is Rather Shocking"', *Irish Times*, 14 June 2020; D Puttnam, 'Oscar-Winner Hits Out at Britain's "Pig-Ignorance towards Irish History"', *Irish Examiner*, 17 October 2021.

[231] D Aaronovitch, 'A Nearby Country of Which We Know Nothing', *The Times*, 22 January 2022.

border and B/GFA,[232] to the more consciously reckless, such as comments by another former Northern Ireland Secretary (and Brexiteer) Owen Paterson, suggesting the B/GFA had 'outlived its use.'[233] Insouciance and ignorance of Irish affairs, coupled with a willingness to interfere and condemn, are nothing new in this long history. Indeed, some might go further, and allege not a negligent ignorance, but a deliberate amnesia – a partial, politicised history – of the sort described by Sanghera in a chapter titled 'Selective amnesia' in his *Empireland: How Imperialism Has Shaped Modern Britain.*[234]

In contrast, however, the Irish may feel that they have acquired rather too much knowledge of the British, often through an acquaintance that involved betrayal – exemplified by occasions such as the failure to make good on protection for Catholics in the treaty of Limerick; or in the Acts of Union; the absence of solidarity within the Union during the Famine; the denial of Home Rule; the afront of Partition, and now Brexit – the latest episode in this sorry saga.

For some time, it was thought that 'Britain's European Question'[235] had supplanted 'Britain's Irish Question'. This is not so. Attempted dismissal of the 'European Question' by Brexit has only made the 'Irish Question' more of a problem than ever.

[232] 'Karen Bradley Admits Ignorance of Northern Ireland Politics', *The Guardian*, 7 September 2018. Also https://yougov.co.uk/topics/travel/survey-results/daily/2020/09/17/2212e/2

[233] 'Brexiteers branded "reckless" over NI peace process', *BBC News*, 20 February 2018.

[234] Also Feenan, http://dermotfeenan.com/index.php/2022/02/14/an-english-conceit-ignorance-forgetting-and-amnesia-regarding-ireland/

[235] See further E Meehan, 'Britain's Irish Question: Britain's European Question' (2000) 26 *Review of International Studies* 83.

3

Britain's Loss of its North American Colonies in the Eighteenth Century

3.1 Introduction

Colonial resistance to the British in America did not start in 1775 with armed combat in Lexington and Concord. A familiar history of the American revolution starts in the early 1760s, taking the end of the Seven Years War in 1763 as the beginning of the troubles that led to American independence. This war was fought over many arenas, in Europe, in America, and worldwide, and had left Britain victorious but also heavily indebted, with huge new tracts of land (acquired by victory over the French) in North America which needed protection. One way to raise money was to tax American colonists to recoup the debt perceived as securing their defence. No matter that colonists claimed they would rather raise the taxes themselves. In Britain, the taxes were seen as moderate, and a fair exchange for the colonies' defence. And this is where the trouble started, because the American colonies rejected the taxes as illegal, and this became a dispute that eventually led to the war of independence.

Brexiteers sometimes cite the American revolution as inspiration for Britain's separation from the European Union.[1] The suggestion is of independence, of liberty from an oppressor. However, a perhaps more apposite association between Brexit and American independence is that in both cases Britain insisted on asserting a sovereignty it could not clearly justify or explain. Therefore, this chapter, in line with the book's focus on the 'unsettlement' of British constitutional history, has a *constitutional*, rather than an economic, military, social, or personality driven focus.

Indeed, to explain American independence primarily in terms of war and economics[2] is to greatly underplay the causes of this revolution. And so, in a

[1] E.g. Michael Gove: 'The Brexit referendum is akin to our own Declaration of Independence.' See further: 'No, Brexit Was Not Britain's "Declaration of Independence". It Was the Exact Opposite', *The Washington Post*, 29 June 2019.

[2] E.g. Louis Hacker: 'The [revolutionary] struggle was not over high-sounding political and constitutional concepts [but] over colonial manufacturing, wild lands and furs, sugar, wine, tea, and currency....' L Hacker, *The Triumph of American Capitalism* (Simon and Schuster, 1940) x.

hugely influential interpretation, Bernard Bailyn[3] analysed pre-revolutionary pamphlets as evidence of an 'ideological-constitutional struggle' fought by American colonists who believed it was Great Britain's intention to tyrannize them in violation of their long held British rights. The ideas in these pamphlets owed much to an earlier British dissenting tradition converging around an ideology of republicanism, one that believed liberty was likely to be abused by those in power. Many Americans believed Parliament's actions were designed to 'enslave' them and subject them to arbitrary power. In seventeenth-century England, John Hampden had opposed 'Ship Money' for the same reason.

Nonetheless, 1763 is significant because, in this year, in Britain, conservative reformers took over government and British legislation taxing American colonies was adopted. However, even at the time, it was apparent that the assertion of a 'right' to tax the colonies led to greater costs for Britain than would be collected in tax revenues. For example, in 1775, a group of Bristol merchants wrote to King George exhorting him to grant American colonists freedom from British taxation rather than endanger valuable trade.[4] Similar allegations of economic damage committed by Britain on itself have been made in the Brexit context.[5] Historian Barbara Tuchman stressed the folly of Britain acting against its own self-interest. She highlighted a 'record of successive blunderings by an arrogant, ignorant, culture-bound group of British aristocrats, out of touch with the people and the problems with which they were dealing, in spite of information and advice freely available.'[6]

In sum, British legislation taxing American colonies asserted a sovereignty, a legal jurisdiction to impose that law, and enforce it coercively. American colonists denied that sovereignty. So, at the centre of the American revolution was a dispute about law, sovereignty, and the correct interpretation of the British Constitution.

3.1.1 A Constitutional Interpretation

An example of a robust constitutional interpretation is provided by the American scholar, Charles H McIlwain, who, in 1923, in *The American Revolution: A Constitutional Interpretation*, claimed that 'that the central problem of the American Revolution was the true constitution of the Empire.'[7] McIlwain

[3] Bernard Bailyn, *Ideological Origins of the American Revolution* (Cambridge, MA: The Belknap Press of Harvard University Press, 1967); also Gordon Wood, *The Creation of the American Republic* (Chapel Hill: UNC Press, 1968).

[4] 'Petition of Bristol Merchants in Favour of the Americans' (1775) 45 The Gentleman's Magazine 479.

[5] E.g.: 'UK Insurers Say No-Deal Brexit Would Be "Act of Economic Self-harm"', *The Guardian*, 25 February 2019.

[6] B Tuchman, *The March of Folly* (New York: Knopf, 1984) Part 4: 'The British Lose America', chapter 1.

[7] C McIlwain, *The American Revolution: A Constitutional Interpretation* (New York: Macmillan, 1923).

argued that the British Parliament had no authority over the colonies, which were the British King's, and not Parliament's, dominions. McIlwain contended that America had not consented to British parliamentary supremacy, which had been achieved by the Glorious Revolution of 1688. McIlwain claimed that parliamentary authority had not been definitely established before the English Civil War, and so Parliament's exercise of authority over America was illegal. In response, in 1929, Robert Schuyler rejected McIlwain's thesis, claiming there was evidence of Parliament legislating for the King's dominions from as early as the fourteenth century.[8]

However, I do not believe it is necessary to engage in a detailed analysis of medieval law to decide if either author was right. For one can clearly argue that the Constitution formed the basis of the disagreement between Britain and the colonies without claiming that Americans based their case on loyalty to the King only. Indeed, many others have claimed the American revolution was prompted by serious constitutional disagreements. Edmund and Helen Morgan, in *The Stamp Act Crisis: Prologue to Revolution*,[9] also approached the American revolution as a constitutional crisis. A similarly constitutional approach is taken by another American scholar, Jack Greene, who, in *The Constitutional Origins of the American Revolution*, argues that 'the American Revolution derived from a disagreement over the nature of the constitution of the British Empire.'[10] And legal scholar, John Phillip Reid,[11] published a ten-volume constitutional history of the American revolution. Both Greene and Reid differ from many historical interpretations by emphasizing the importance of *law* in the American colonies. Indeed, many key colonial figures in the conflict were lawyers, for example Richard Bland, James Otis, Daniel Dulany, John Dickinson, James Wilson, Thomas Jefferson, John Adams, and Alexander Hamilton. Benjamin Franklin, Samuel Adams, and others were well versed in the culture of legal thought. Indeed, Edmund Burke remarked that in no country was the law so generally studied as in America; and that most Americans able to read knew some law.[12]

Conflicting understandings of British constitutional law, sovereignty, and the constitutional status of the American colonies paved the way to revolution. In the mid-eighteenth century, there was an emphasis on the following legal issues: the vitality of a juristic conception of English government as limited government; the persistence of an old doctrine of the 'fundamental law'

[8] R Schuyler, *Parliament and the British Empire* (Columbia University Press, 1929).

[9] ES Morgan and HS Morgan, *The Stamp Act Crisis: Prologue to Revolution* (Chapel Hill: UNC press, 1953).

[10] Jack Greene, *The Constitutional Origins of the American Revolution* (Cambridge: Cambridge University Press, 2010) xii.

[11] See e.g. John Phillip Reid, *Constitutional History of the American Revolution: The Authority of Law* (Madison: University of Wisconsin Press, 1995); Reid, *The Ancient Constitution and the Origins of Anglo-American Liberty* (DeKalb: Northern Illinois University Press, 2005).

[12] P Stanlis (ed.), *Selected Writing and Speeches of Edmund Burke* (Anchor, 1963) 161.

of the ancient Constitution; the consensual and contractual nature of law in the English speaking world; the importance of the doctrine of usage; the relative weakness of 'imperial law' in colonies and converse strength of local law; and the indeterminacy of an imperial Constitution.[13] Greene rightly states that many of these issues have not been given the attention they deserve, possibly be due to perceived impermeable boundaries between history and law.

In this chapter, I suggest that there were real doubts as to the correct understanding of the British Constitution on *both* sides of the Atlantic. This made it very hard to sustain Britain's assertion of the absolute nature of its sovereignty, as it attempted to do in the 1766 Declaratory Act. Furthermore, what is also notable is the lack of attention given to this subject revolution by *British* lawyers, and legal scholars. This chapter seeks to redress this lack of interest. Brexit has thrust the issue of sovereignty, and the nature of the British Constitution, centre stage. It is not adequate to make vague and incoherent claims. The stakes are too high.

3.2 The Pre-revolutionary Relationship

3.2.1 What Was the Constitutional Status of the American Colonies?

John Adams, writing as *Novanglus*, commented, '*colonization* is *casus omissus* at common law',[14] that is, that there was no precedent for the status of the American colonies in English law. James Duane and Joseph Galloway, delegates to the First Continental Congress in Philadelphia in 1774, similarly declared a 'manifest defect in the Constitution of the British Empire with respect to the Government of the Colonies.'[15]

So how then to characterize Britain's control of its evolving empire in North America? What were the legal and constitutional arrangements? They were ill defined at best. British North America was settled in circumstances where direct control by Britain was not always possible, most obviously because of the vast distance between Britain and America. In such an environment, Britain lacked the coercive means to enforce domination directly, and instead private persons became representatives of the British State through Charters[16] (issued by royal prerogative, i.e. action by the Crown).

[13] Authors who made these points include John Adams *Novanglus*; James Wilson, *Considerations on the Nature and Extent of the Legislative Authority of the British Parliament* (1774); Thomas Jefferson, *A Summary View of the Rights of British America* (1774); as well as already cited works of Charles McIlwain, Jack Greene, John Phillip Reid and also David Ammerman, 'The British Constitution and the American Revolution: A Failure of Precedent' (1976) 17 Wm. & Mary L. Rev. 473.

[14] *The Works of John Adams*, 121. 'Novanglus' was the pseudonym used by Adams in a series of published letters forming a celebrated debate-by-letter with Daniel Leonard, who wrote as 'Massachusettensis'.

[15] 1 *Journals of the Continental Congress*, 1774–1789 (W. Ford ed., 1904) at 48.

[16] Referred to as 'letters patent' up to 1666.

Should we even use the term 'colony'? 'Plantation', 'dominion', 'colony' 'province' 'dependency', 'conquest', and 'possession' were all employed as descriptions of the North American territories at one time or another. Many in North America preferred the term 'colony' because of its connotation of greater independence than 'dominion', 'conquest' or 'dependency'. Colonies were seen as settlements of free people who had exercised the natural right to emigrate. It was argued that colonies had voluntarily engaged through their Charters to remain the King's subjects, but in return for the Crown's recognition of their rights as Englishmen, and with these Charters, colonies became a separate 'body politic'. However, many in Britain preferred the term 'plantation', and in the seventeenth century, 'plantation' referred to persons and not crops. A 'Council for Foreign Plantations' was established as part of the Privy Council in the seventeenth century, which developed into the Board of Trade, with responsibility for the colonies. 'Plantation', however, can have unfortunate connotations, being part of the language of bitter controversy over seventeenth-century Ireland. The term 'colony' will be used throughout this chapter.

Nonetheless, even as to its most basic element of characterization, the legal and constitutional nature of the relationship was murky.

3.2.1.1 Charters

From the early 1600s, colonists had been granted Charters from the Crown for settlement in North America. But the basis for their grant was unclear. Although land was sometimes described as 'terra nullius' and thus open to settlement, this was of course to ignore native American tribes already present.[17] No Act of Parliament authorized establishment of the colonies. This was unlike Spain, which established institutions of imperial control over its American colonies, through extending its fundamental law, *Las Siete Partidas*, to regulate new municipalities overseas.[18] Linda Colley commented that, 'if one were rash enough to plump for only one underlying cause [of the American revolution] it would have to be London's failure to establish the kind of strong institutions of imperial control in North America that the Spanish had been able to construct in their Latin American colonies.'[19]

English colonization of the Americas was not uniform and it changed over time. Excepting Jamaica, Nova Scotia and New York, which were seized by force, all the American colonies were founded by private individuals or groups for specific aims – whether for commercial gain, or religious or political independence. During the seventeenth century, a number of Charters were granted which essentially took one of three forms – corporate, proprietary, or royal. Although

[17] Roger Williams, founder of the Rhode Island colony, denied the right of Charles I to grant lands he did not properly own – see e.g. M Kammen, 'The Meaning of Colonization in American Revolutionary Thought' (1970) 31 J'l of the History of Ideas 337.

[18] Detailed organization of Spanish colonies was set out in the 1681 *Recopilacion de las Leyes de los Reynos*.

[19] L Colley, *Britons: Forging the Nation 1707–1837* (New Haven: Yale University Press, 1992) at 135.

these Charters set out the governing rules and basic organization for colonies, none detailed how authority was to be exercised, although they frequently stated that settlers (and their progeny) should be treated as 'natural born subjects of England' and enjoy 'all the privileges, franchises and laws of England.'[20]

The earliest Charters were *corporate* in form,[21] granted to companies as in Virginia and Massachusetts (both later revoked) devised for profitable investment,[22] and basically self-governing enterprises. A second form was the *proprietary* Charter. Such inheritable proprietary Charters were granted by the Crown to noblemen, such as to Lord Baltimore in Maryland, and the Penn family in Pennsylvania. These left the proprietor effectively in control, although in theory responsible to the monarch. Originally, they were often feudal in structure, but this lessened as colonial assemblies grew in power. A third type of Charter was that of the *Crown* (or royal or 'provincial') colony, whereby the Charter was held directly from the Crown rather than by corporations or proprietors. Indeed, by the American revolution, nine of the thirteen colonies[23] had been converted to Crown colonies. But whatever their status, all pre-revolutionary colonies operated under a Charter, had their own colonial legislature, and an executive of sorts – whether royal governor, proprietor, or corporate representative. Each colony also had a system of courts, with an appeal to the Privy Council in London.

The Board of Trade had been created in London in 1696, to fulfil the Crown's policy of greater supervisory authority. But the Crown's attempt for greater control was not particularly successful, especially as, after the Glorious Revolution, Parliament increasingly legislated to reduce the royal prerogative over Charters.

And so, the perception was often that colonists, rather than the Crown, were in control. McLean Andrews suggested that 'In reality these settlements were not colonies; they were private estates, the proprietors of which, both corporate and feudal, were endowed with wide powers and privileges conferred on them by royal charters.'[24] Yet, Charters offered little protection against British interference, as was later illustrated by Parliament's adoption in 1774 of the Massachusetts Government Act, in which clauses in the 1691 Massachusetts Charter (then still in force) were treated as non-existent.

3.2.1.2 The Law Applying in the American Colonies

Charters provided some structural framework, but obviously, there had to be more general law in application in the colonies. Yet once again, things were

[20] E.g. the 1606 Charter of Virginia, drafted by Sir Edward Coke.

[21] This was not unusual in England at that time, where many boroughs were corporate entities.

[22] See also the Charter for the East India Company discussed in Chapter 4.

[23] Rhode Island and Connecticut remained corporate, and Maryland and Pennsylvania proprietary in nature.

[24] C McLean Andrews, *The Colonial Background to the American Revolution* (Yale University Press, 1961) at 6.

not very clear. In 1701, an anonymous 'American' had written: 'no-one can tell what is law and what is not in the plantations'.[25] Supreme Court Justice Story opined in *Van Ness* v. *Pacard* in 1829 that English common law was generally thought to apply from the time of settlement. However, the grounds for this view were imprecise.[26] Charters required laws to be 'as near as possible' or 'not repugnant' to the laws of England, but this was hardly an exact standard. In any case, it was difficult for colonial lawyers to gain access to English law reports and treatises, which were largely imported from England. Blackstone's *Commentaries* was the first major English law treatise to be published in the colonies in the 1771–1772 Philadelphia reprint. However, where colonial law diverged significantly, English courts had provided no ultimate guidance as to the status of English law in the colonies. In *Somersett's case*,[27] on no less an issue than slavery, Lord Mansfield insisted that the common law did not override colonial law on the legality of slavery in the colonies.

The situation was also vague regarding Acts of the English, and (from 1707) British Parliament. In the seventeenth century, English Attorney General, William Jones, had stated that colonies would only be bound by new statutes if expressly named.[28] Colonies adopted legislation in their assemblies, which took on a greater law-making role as time progressed. The Privy Council in London also operated, not only as an ultimate appeal from colonial courts but, in theory, as a control on colonial legislation, with a power to approve or invalidate colonial legislation for non-compliance with English law. However, although after 1690, 8500 colonial acts were submitted for review, only 470 were disallowed.

Therefore, it seems that, up to the 1760s, the view that Parliament had generally allowed the colonies to govern themselves is reinforced. Even so prominent an opponent of the colonial case as the English judge, Lord Mansfield, wrote that 'government left private adventurers to do as they pleased'.[29]

3.2.1.3 The Claim to English Rights and the 'Fundamental Law' of the British Constitution

Aside from Charters, colonists also insisted on their entitlement to English rights, asserting that the earliest English settlers had brought to America their 'rights of Englishmen', and these had been handed on to subsequent generations as their constitutional heritage. The assertion by the town of Cambridge Massachusetts, that they had: 'a legal Claim to all the natural, inherent, constitutional Rights of Englishmen, notwithstanding their great Distance from

[25] Mary Sarah Bilder, 'English Settlement and Local Governance', in *The Cambridge History of Law in America*, Volume 1 (Cambridge: Cambridge University Press, 2008) at 82.

[26] *Van Ness* v. *Pacard*, [1829] 27 US 143–144; see P Reinsch, 'The English Common Law in the Early American Colonies', in *Select Essays in Anglo-American Legal History* (Boston: Little, Brown and Co., 1907) 367.

[27] *Somerset* v. *Stewart* [1772] 98 ER 499.

[28] Bilder, 'English Settlement', at 98.

[29] N Poser, *Lord Mansfield: Justice in the Age of Reason* (McGill University Press, 2015) at 303.

Great Britain'[30] is a good example. These rights were often elucidated in colonial documents such as William Penn's *English Liberties*. Colonists also looked to old English traditions and writings, such as Sir John Fortescue's *de Landibus legum Angliae*, as well as to Coke, Selden, Hampden, Pym, Sir John Davies, Nathaniel Bacon, and Matthew Hale, all of whom considered how English liberties and the rule of law could act as a restraint on the Crown. According to Hulsebosch, 'Coke's work helped create the Anglo-American idea of a Constitution: a national legal environment anterior to the positive law of kings, their courts, and legislatures. In this sense, he was a 'framer' of the English constitution'.[31] Colonists also argued for specific rights, such as their right to form their own assemblies derived from the basic right to representative government. Many Americans, including Thomas Jefferson and Daniel Dulaney,[32] asserted that a British subject's property could not be taken away (by taxation) without consent (i.e. representation in government) – a right that could be traced back to Magna Carta. As the colonies were not directly represented in Westminster, it followed that Parliament had no right to impose taxes on them, an argument captured by the expression 'No taxation without representation'. This appeal to Magna Carta was often expressed in visual form. For example, a print[33] published by Paul Revere as *A View of the Year 1765* portrays a Stamp Act dragon, assisted by two demons, seeking to snatch Magna Carta from a man representing Boston. Hanging from the 'Liberty tree' is John Huske, hanged in effigy in November 1765, in retaliation for his many efforts to get the Stamp Act passed.

Yet, such colonial contentions were not always accepted in Britain. According to twentieth-century British constitutional theorist, Arthur Berriedale-Keith, 'Imperial Government regarded unfavourably every attempt by the colonies to strengthen the constitutional position of their assemblies and to assert by law their right to English liberties.'[34]

Nonetheless, British claims of parliamentary sovereignty were by no means fully established, even in Britain, in the earlier eighteenth century. Indeed, many invoked the unwritten English Constitution, including English rights, as 'fundamental', rather than considering all Parliamentary legislation to be supreme. JW Gough, writing (in 1955) about the British Constitution, commented that

30 Vote of the Town of Cambridge, 14 October 1765, in *Boston Evening-Post*, 21 October 1765, at 2, col. 1.

31 D Hulsebosch, 'The Ancient Constitution and the Expanding Empire: Sir Edward Coke's British Jurisprudence' (2003) 21(3) Law and History Review 444.

32 Thomas Jefferson, *A Summary View of the Rights of British America* (1774); D Dulany, *Considerations on the Propriety of Imposing Taxes in the British Colonies* (1765) 31.

33 Paul Revere was a Boston silversmith, and hero of the American revolution. He also produced a famous engraving of the Boston massacre in 1770. Revere's midnight ride to Concord in April 1775, warning patriots of the advancing British troops, was immortalized in Longfellow's poem, 'The Midnight Ride of Paul Revere'.

34 Arthur Berriedale-Keith, *Constitutional History of the First British Empire* (Oxford: Clarendon Press, 1930) at 141.

'two or three centuries ago, everyone (or almost everyone) wrote and spoke as if fundamental law were one of its features.'[35] For many centuries, there had existed a tradition of the English fundamental law, dating from medieval times. To be sure, it was often expressed in vague terms, but its essence could be distilled to three main components:[36] namely, that the law was legally supreme; that the fundamental Constitution was unwritten; and that it was also at least on some occasions, judicially enforceable.

There were authoritative statements as to the supremacy of the unwritten law. In the earlier seventeenth century, Coke had argued that both the King's authority, and that of Parliament, were limited by the fundamental law. Coke also considered that that 'Magna Carta is such a Fellow, that he will have no Sovereign.'[37] Indeed, one of the charges in the trial of King Charles I was that he 'had a wicked design to subvert the ancient and fundamental laws and liberties of this nation.'[38] This fundamental law derived from sources such as custom, usage, reason and natural justice, even an imagined immemorial antiquity. In this way, English law was presented as equal to the natural law reasoning of the scholastics and Roman and canon lawyers.

As Gough comments, 'it took quite a long time to kill off the doctrine of the fundamental law.'[39] In 1610, in *Dr Bonham's case*, Coke had famously declared of statutes that, 'when against common right and reason, or repugnant, or impossible to be performed, the common law will control it, and adjudge such act to be void.'[40] And even in the eighteenth century, there still existed divergent views as to parliamentary sovereignty. In 1701, in *City of London* v. *Wood*, Lord Chief Justice Holt affirmed Coke's reasoning in *Dr Bonham's case*, and in 1744, in *Omychund* v. *Barker* the Attorney General had submitted (with reasoning accepted by the judges) that 'the common law, that works itself pure by rules drawn from the fountain of justice, is for this reason superior to an act of parliament.'[41] This doctrine continues to this day, exhibited in 'anti-positivist' theories such as Dworkin's legal principles, as well as being illustrated by judicial decisions such as *HS2* in which the UK Supreme Court held that 'the common law itself also recognises certain principles as fundamental to the rule of law.'[42] In the early eighteenth century, Parliament itself appeared inconsistent, or even unaware of the implications of legislative sovereignty. The Acts of Union of England with Scotland of 1706/1707 contained many clauses

[35] JW Gough, *Fundamental Law in English Constitutional History* (Oxford: Clarendon Press, 1955) at 2.
[36] Ibid.; also T Grey, 'Origins of the Unwritten Constitution: Fundamental Law in American Revolutionary Thought' (1978) 30 *Stanford LR* 843, 850.
[37] J Rushworth, *Historical Collections* (London, 1682) at 562.
[38] *Act erecting a High Court of Justice for the King's trial*, 6 January 1649.
[39] Gough, *Fundamental Law in English Constitutional History*, 55.
[40] 77 Eng. Rep. [K.B. 1610] 646, 652.
[41] 12 Mod. 669, 88 Eng. Rep. 1592 [1702]; 1 Atkyns 32, 33 [1744].
[42] R Dworkin, *Taking Rights Seriously* (Cambridge MA., Harvard University Press, 1977); *R (HS2 Action Alliance Ltd)* v. *Secretary of State for Transport* [2014] UKSC 3.

inconsistent with unbounded parliamentary sovereignty, not least the assertion that the treaty was 'completed between the two kingdoms without any alteration thereof or derogation thereto in any sort forever.'

All of these examples are cited to argue that the position on sovereignty in eighteenth-century Britain was ambivalent, and there existed plenty of examples of continued adherence to a doctrine of the fundamental law, which included important liberties that statute could not abrogate. This doctrine had been the usual currency of law for hundreds of years in England, and it is not surprising that colonists cited it as authoritative. They were not without support in England, where some eminent legal figures, such as Lord Camden, repudiated the doctrine of absolute parliamentary sovereignty.[43] It was only with the ascendancy of Benthamite reasoning on legislation from the later eighteenth century, and then the Diceyan dominance of British constitutional law, that parliamentary sovereignty really took hold.

3.2.1.4 Natural Law

Natural law also played its part in the constitutional struggle. Some commentators, such as McIlwain and Reid, downplay its part, claiming it only surfaced with the 1776 Declaration of Independence, with its opening paragraph reference to 'the Laws of Nature and of Nature's God.' But natural law was in currency well before that. When arguing that colonies were *casus omissus,* John Adams also cited natural law as a source: 'It stands upon no grounds, then, of law or policy, *but what are found in the law of nature*, and their express contracts in their charters.'[44]

Natural law doctrine, although traceable to ancient times, was considerably developed in the sixteenth, seventeenth, and eighteenth centuries by Grotius, von Pufendorf, Burlamaqui, and John Locke. Locke was probably the greatest influence on Americans, as well as a significant figure in English whig political theory. Locke's *Second Treatise on Civil Government*[45] was published anonymously in 1690 (in justification of the Glorious Revolution) and asserted inalienable natural rights, as well as limited government based on consent, secured by (usually hypothetical) 'social contracts'. These contracts were formed to establish a government for the better preservation of natural rights to life, liberty and property than could be protected in a state of nature. If government failed to respect natural rights, then people had the right to resist or dissolve the government. Locke maintained that by taxing their subjects without their consent, absolute monarchs violated their subjects' property rights.[46] Indeed, James Wilson (later signatory of the Declaration of Independence) in 1774 formulated his case on

[43] Camden's contributions in the debates on the Stamp act and Declaratory Act are considered below.

[44] *The Works of John Adams,* 121 (italics added).

[45] John Locke, *Two Treatises of Government*, P Laslett (ed.), (Cambridge: Cambridge University Press, 1960).

[46] *Second Treatise of Government.*

explicitly Lockean principles, asserting that all lawful government was founded on the consent of those subject to it.[47]

Embrace of natural law was not confined to scholastics, philosophers, and continental jurists. There were also many English common lawyers who characterized natural law as no arcane continental theory, but as a well-founded source for the common law. These common lawyers included Sir Francis Bacon, Sir Edward Coke, Sir Matthew Hale, William Blackstone, Lord Camden and Lord Mansfield. Speaking in Parliament in 1766, Lord Camden castigated the Declaratory Act as a 'contrary to the fundamental laws of this constitution, a constitution grounded on the eternal and immutable laws of nature.'[48] Natural law reasoning was clearly employed in famous English common law cases, including *Calvin's Case* and *Somersett's Case.*[49] Therefore, it is unsurprising that colonists relied on the argument that natural law had been 'engrafted into the British constitution', as part of English law.

However, even if a practice were admitted as contrary to natural law, it might still be enforced by positive law. Coke's holding in *Dr Bonham's case* suggested that courts might nullify measures in breach of natural law, but this position was not subsequently enforced. Legislation might be considered in breach of natural law and yet still stand. This seemed to be the position of Blackstone and Lord Mansfield. We can go back to classical times for another example – Roman law stated that slavery was contrary to natural law, but at the same time, acknowledged the reality of slavery, and its recognition in Roman law.[50]

Therefore, although natural law was argued in the colonists' cause, its claims were often blended into contentions about the rights of Englishmen and fundamental law. These sources were not always clearly distinguished. This coagulation of sources undermines any criticism that colonists kept changing their arguments and turned to natural law late in the day.

3.2.1.5 Calvin's Case

American colonists often also cited Calvin's case (or the Case of the Postnati).[51] This case determined the English common law of allegiance (the precursor of modern nationality) well into the nineteenth century. Calvin was a Scot born after James VI and I ascended to the English throne in 1603. He brought a case for recovery of inherited land in England. Prior to the accession of James, Scots were considered aliens in England, and unable to bring such cases. The Court of Exchequer Chamber held that Calvin, as a *postnatus* (i.e. born after James unified the Crowns) was not an alien in England, and thus able to sue and

[47] James Wilson, 'Considerations on the Nature and Extent of the Legislative Authority of the British Parliament', in RG McCloskey (ed.), *The Works of James Wilson* (Cambridge MA., Harvard University Press, 1967) 2.

[48] Reprinted in 16 Parl. Hist. Eng. [1813] 178. Discussed further below.

[49] *Calvin* v. *Smith* [1608]; *Somersett* v. *Stewart* [1772] 98 Eng. Rep. 499.

[50] See Digest. 1.1.4. [51] [1608] 77 Eng. Rep. 277.

recover the land. This was reasoned on the basis that allegiance was personal, to the King. Calvin therefore had the same rights as Englishmen, even if he lived in Scotland, which in the seventeenth century had its own separate Parliament.

Calvin's case appeared a useful precedent to those American partisans who claimed personal allegiance to the King, without subjugation to Parliament. However, Scotland was not a particularly apt example for British North America. Scotland was neither conquered nor colonized by the English, and had become associated with England only through the union of the Crowns from 1603, and later by the Acts of Union in 1706/1707. Only from then was Scotland subject to the authority of the Westminster Parliament, when 45 Scottish MPs were added to the House of Commons. Americans lacked representation in Westminster and had not been a separate State prior to settlement.

In any event, during the later seventeenth century, new doctrines appeared, especially those of John Locke, with different views on the nature of political obligation from the personal allegiance/subjecthood of *Calvin's case*. These theories argued that government was legitimated by consent of the governed, and, as such, a challenge to the allegiance based subjecthood of *Calvin's case*. However, notwithstanding Locke and the social contract, English law was not prone to radical change, and the principles of *Calvin's case* continued, although somewhat modified by the political theory of the social contract.[52]

3.2.2 The Growth of Parliament's Power

What is clear, is that in seventeenth-century England, great constitutional change occurred, and after 1688 power began to shift from the King to Parliament, to an eventual position where, by the nineteenth century, Parliament claimed omnicompetence and sovereignty. Parliamentary sovereignty may have made sense in England, justified by Whig theory as satisfying the need to control an overbearing and abusive Monarch, and to provide a definite sovereign after civil wars and times of conflicting authority.[53] But this reasoning was less compelling in the colonies, where parliamentary sovereignty might not work for the common good, given they had no elected representatives in Westminster. Furthermore, Parliament was as capable of acting oppressively as had Stuart monarchs.

Prior to the 1760s, there was little parliamentary legislation claiming authority over the colonies. Although, in 1649, the English Interregnum House of

[52] The survival of *Calvin's case* as a precedent is perhaps explicable because Locke's theory could be used to justify the Glorious Revolution, without accepting that this event, as a revolution, had reduced Britain to a state of nature, and terminated all political obligation (Locke, *Second Treatise*, paras. 131, 132, 134, 143, 150).

[53] Locke, *Second Treatise*, was an important source for Whig theory, and Hobbes *Leviathan*, on the need for certain authority.

Commons had asserted authority over all 'Dominions and territories',[54] after this, Westminster interfered little with the colonies, with the exception of the Navigation Acts,[55] which effectively subordinated the economy of the colonies,[56] prohibiting them from trading, other than with Britain. Otherwise, most pre-eighteenth-century transaction between Britain and the colonies was by royal prerogative rather than parliamentary legislation, and a practice of parliamentary restraint had arisen regarding internal colonial matters. The British Government exercised powers that 'by necessity of case could not be exercised by colonials, such as the post office, naturalization, war and peace, foreign affairs, intercolonial and foreign commerce',[57] and American governments in practice were left with near exclusive jurisdiction over all local matters, including tax. Thus, the idea that colonies were more new settlements than conquered territories gained in support.

As a result, many colonists protested that Parliament's jurisdiction was limited to Britain. John Adams, in the *Novanglus,* denied that America had acquiesced in Parliament's authority, although did acknowledge that Americans had conceded parliamentary authority in imperial matters, that is, external trade, but not over internal affairs.[58] In Britain, both William Pitt the Elder and Lord Camden denied that Parliament had any right to tax the colonies. Edmund Burke, in 1774, even observed that prior to the Declaratory Act, 'the legislative rights of this country were not entire, but had certain restrictions and limitations.'[59] Edmund Burke was of course a notable politician, and distinguished orator and political theorist. Pitt, who later became the Earl of Chatham, was several times Prime Minister; Camden was both Lord Chancellor and Lord Chief Justice (well-known and popular after his decision regarding Wilkes in *Entick* v. *Carrington*).

In summary, on the one hand, then is a denial by Americans of parliamentary sovereignty over them. On the other hand, the dominant but not ubiquitous reaction in Britain was a denial that any matter lay beyond the power of Parliament.

54 'An Act Declaring and Constituting the People of England to be Commonwealth and Free State', 19 May 1649.

55 Of 1660, 1662, 1663, 1673, and William III's Great Navigation Act of 1696 (7 & 8 Will. 3 c. 22) s8 of which declared 'null and void' in the colonies any laws or usages repugnant to the Navigation Acts.

56 The 1696 Great Navigation Act also instituted Admiralty (i.e. jury-less) courts in the colonies, and writs of assistance for enforcement, both to become highly controversial. William III's strengthening of the Navigation Acts was partly in response to the perceived threat from the Scottish Parliament's 1695 statute creating the Darien trading company – a project which proved disastrous and was one of the contributing factors to the Union of England & Scotland in 1707.

57 Andrew McLaughlin, *The Foundations of American Constitutionalism* (New York: New York University Press, 1932) 133 et seq.

58 *Works of John Adams, IV*, 49–50.

59 Burke, *Speech on American Taxation*, in *Writings II*, 1–80.

3.2.3 Sovereignty

3.2.3.1 Indivisible Sovereignty

The dominant approach in Britain viewed sovereignty as indivisible. Blackstone's view was that, in all polities, there had to be 'supreme, absolute uncontrolled authority in which rights of sovereignty resided.'[60] The British Empire, including the American colonies, formed one single State, with one people, one Constitution and one King. Notably, Blackstone's *Commentaries* were first published in 1765 in the middle of the Stamp Act discord. This view asserted that, by the eighteenth century, Parliament had the legal authority to adopt any legislation for the colonies, and there was no bright line between legislation on external matters (i.e. trade) and internal matters (i.e. tax). By this view, any authority resting in colonial institutions was merely a matter of privileges which could be removed.

However, another view rejected parliamentary omnicompetence over the colonies, claiming instead supreme and final sovereignty was located in colonial legislatures, indeed often denying that Britain and the colonies formed a single State. John Adams argued that 'our provincial legislatures are the only supreme authorities in our colonies.'[61]

3.2.3.2 'Uncontrolled' Sovereignty?

In any case, Blackstone appeared somewhat inconsistent. For notwithstanding his assertion that Parliament was 'absolute and without control', he also denied that any positive (human) laws contrary to natural law could be valid.[62] Blackstone's position seemed to be that although Parliament's authority could be limited by natural law, such limitations could not, however, be applied as legal rules. Charles Francis Sheridan, Irish government official, and brother of the politician and playwright, saw America as salutary example of the destructive consequences of Blackstone's parliamentary sovereignty. In particular, Sheridan attacked Blackstone's advocacy of the 'uncontrolled, absolute, despotic power of Parliament'.[63] Sheridan highlighted the conflicting nature of Blackstone's arguments, for example, contrasting Blackstone's claim of parliamentary omnicompetence with his contention that no Parliament could destroy natural rights. Sheridan also compared Blackstone's argument that, if Parliament abused its power, then there was no remedy, with Blackstone's description of the available means of vindicating abused rights, from law courts to armed rebellion. Sheridan himself advocated the older concept of a

[60] Blackstone, *Commentaries on the Laws of England*, i (18th ed., London, 1829), 48–52.

[61] *Works of John Adams*, IV, 105.

[62] Blackstone, *Commentaries on the Laws of England*, 41; also J Goldsworthy, 'After the Revolution', in *The Sovereignty of Parliament* (Oxford: Oxford University Press, 2010) at 181.

[63] CF Sheridan, *Observations of the Doctrine Laid Down by Sir William Blackstone, Respecting the Extent of the Power of the British Parliament, Particularly in relation to Ireland* (Dublin: Hodges, Figgis, & Company, Grafton Street., 1779) 3–4.

Constitution of customary rights. Blackstone's approach was also rejected in the colonies, where Parliament was regarded as constrained by certain antecedent laws and rights. James Otis argued, in the *Writs of Assistance* case, that Acts against the Constitution were void.

3.2.4 What Then Was the Legal/Constitutional Status of the Colonies?

In conclusion, the precise legal status of colonies in relation to Britain was unsettled in the mid-eighteenth century. Although the dominant approach in Britain was that the authority of the British Parliament extended over North American colonies, this view was certainly not universally accepted by colonists. This section has attempted to give a sense of the major colonial claims. We can summarize the key arguments as follows:

First, in *Novanglus,* John Adams famously wrote that there was no explicit legal standing for American colonization as part of the British empire.

Second, many colonists (including Samuel and John Adams) argued that Great Britain and the colonies were distinct political entities, and although they acknowledged that they were connected through a common King, they denied any connection through Parliament, where Americans had no representation.

Third, colonists, including John Adams and Thomas Jefferson, insisted that the first settlers had brought English law and rights with them, rights which they traced back to Magna Carta, and which the ancient English Constitution provided that no Parliament could usurp. These included the right to no taxation without their consent.

Fourth, Americans denied that Parliament had any authority over internal colonial matters, even if Parliament had sometimes (but rarely) legislated on matters of external trade. This point was made, inter alia, by Benjamin Franklin, John Adams, and James Wilson.

Fifth, natural law was relied on to rebut Parliament's power. Thomas Jefferson, in the 1774 *A Summary View of the Rights of British America*, as in the later *Declaration of Independence*, set out a list of grievances, with natural law as the ultimate source of the claims. As with Adams and Wilson, Jefferson's account blended natural law and British constitutional rights.

Finally, Americans denied that Britain and the colonies formed a single State. James Wilson, in the 1774 *Considerations on the Nature and Extent of the Legislative Authority of the British Parliament,* argued that different parts of the British empire were distinct and independent, although linked by a common sovereign. According to John Adams, colonial legislatures, not Westminster, were supreme. If, however, the British Empire were not a unitary State, it was, nonetheless, according to Benjamin Franklin, 'all united in allegiance to one Prince and one common law.'[64] This seems rather like federalism, although

[64] Benjamin Franklin, 'Marginalia to an Inquiry', in L Labaree (ed.), *Franklin Papers*, (New Haven: Yale University Press, 1960 -) XVI, 246.

without the deliberate act of constitutional law-making separating states from the federal centre. Bilder suggests a 'dual authority', whereby legitimation derived from both the Crown and colonial legislatures.[65] Greene contends that the British Empire was 'predominantly federal in practice.'[66] But such a view seems too modern and deliberate to account for the messy, unconsidered way in which Britain's relationship with North America developed.

In any case, to use the term, 'dual authority' is misleading, because there was a separate legislature for every colony and little unity among them. In the face of growing French encroachment in the mid-eighteenth century, some colonials argued the need for a colonial confederation or union to provide greater protection against the French. In 1754, Benjamin Franklin, in the grandly named 'Albany Plan of Union', suggested a supra-colonial confederation and coined the motto 'Join or Die'. However, plans for a colonial confederation came to nothing and the failure of the Albany Congress even enabled the British Government to assume that joint colonial opposition to tax was unlikely. If anything, it was coercive British conduct, from the 1760s on, that began to unite Americans.

Putting all of this together, we can see that there existed no one generally accepted theory of the status of the American colonies in British law. There was never a conscious attempt to draft a Constitution for the British Empire, nor even a specific law on the status of the colonies, as there had been in Spain. Things evolved, as a matter of practice. And thus, the relationship between Britain and American colonies continued, without regularization. According to Morgan,

> During the first six decades of the 18th century, Britain had allowed her children to grow in their own way … the happy result of this power was that by 1760 the British Empire was the strongest and most prosperous power and British subjects the freest inhabitants in the western world. A less propitious result was that the rights of the colonists in relation to the mother country had never come up for close examination and hence no one knew exactly what they were.[67]

3.3 Britain's Loss of the American Colonies: Law and Politics

3.3.1 Introduction

This section discusses key events in more detail, principally those of greatest constitutional relevance.

After the Seven Years War, relations between Britain and the American colonies deteriorated. This was the most ruinously expensive war ever fought by Great Britain, although it led to a large gain in territory, much of it in

[65] Bilder, 'English Settlement', at 103. [66] Greene, *Constitutional Origins*, at 102.
[67] Morgan, *The Stamp Act Crisis*, 6.

North America. Britain wanted colonial support to help pay this large debt and defend the new territory – this meant taxes and a standing army (of at least 10,000 soldiers) in the colonies. Both were anathema in colonial America. Furthermore, these more coercive British measures required parliamentary legislation, rather than authorization by royal prerogative (i.e. action by the Crown). This was notably intrusive, and, from 1764, Parliament adopted a series of legislation, such as the Stamp Act 1765, to generate revenue from the colonies. But many colonists rejected Parliament's authority, arguing it had no power to remove a British subject's property (by taxes) without consent (i.e. representative government). Although the Stamp Act was repealed, Parliament continued to assert its sovereignty, most acutely by enacting that it had the power to legislate 'in all cases whatsoever' for the colonies, in the Declaratory Act of 1766. So at base, the issue of parliamentary sovereignty was a major component, perhaps *the* major component, of the American revolution.

Although undeniably distant, the colonies were of great importance to Britain, primarily for providing raw materials for British manufacture (without being allowed to challenge Britain's own manufacturing industries). The prevailing economic doctrine was *mercantilism*, or protectionism, which valued trading but protected British manufacturing. A subservient colonial role had been secured by a sequence of Navigation Acts, from the seventeenth century on, which prohibited colonies from trading with other States. The main purpose of these laws, at least up to 1764, was to regulate trade, rather than produce revenue. However, these laws had been undermined by smuggling, as well as by Britain's failure to enforce the law (i.e. the Molasses Act, which imposed duties on sugar).

Bailyn traced a growing fear of British tyranny and oppression in the colonies. However, British government in the mid eighteenth century appeared to lack sufficient cohesion to impose any coherent design on the colonies, other than a growing concern for financial solvency from 1763 on. One faction after another took office, often bumbling and haphazard, with no continuation in colonial policy.[68] Political appointment, and indeed even election as an MP, depended largely on patronage and connections, with MPs often securing seats in 'pocket' or 'rotten' boroughs. Many large and highly populated cities, such as Manchester, were totally unrepresented. Until 1768, there was no department in overall charge of the colonies, with the Board of Trade and Plantations instead supervising. In 1763, George Grenville (former financier and lawyer) took office as Prime Minister, and he was responsible for the initial legislation to exact funds from the colonies.

This then was the political environment in which Great Britain tried to increase its colonial revenue. A forerunner of subsequent battles had already

[68] See e.g. L Namier, *England in the Age of the American Revolution* (New York: Macmillan, 1930).

emerged with the *Writs of Assistance* case[69] in 1761. Britain had tried to enforce customs laws in the colonies by using 'writs of assistance', that is, a special type of search warrant of tremendous breadth,[70] authorizing officials to look for contraband in merchants' property. But a group of Boston merchants, represented by James Otis,[71] challenged the legality of this writ, arguing inter alia, that it contravened fundamental principles of law (including Magna Carta), and natural rights, and thus the statute was void. However, the challenge failed, and the Court, led by Chief Justice Thomas Hutchinson,[72] upheld the validity of the writ. Notwithstanding, colonial opposition to these writs continued, evolving into a battle cry for American resistance to Britain.[73]

3.3.1.1 The American Revenue Acts

Britain's decision to tax America became an acute issue after the Seven Years War. With the exception of customs duties, which regulated trade for the benefit of Great Britain, Americans were not subject to taxation from Britain and so a gradual assumption had arisen that Britain had no right to impose such a tax. All 29 Parliamentary statutes regarding commerce in America from 1660 until 1764 had as their purpose the regulation of trade, not raising revenue.[74] However, from 1764, Parliament adopted a series of Acts taxing the colonies, collectively known as the Revenue Acts. These were: the Sugar Act (1764), the Currency Act (1764), the Stamp Act (1765), the Townshend Acts (1767), and the Tea Act (1773). Nonetheless, these Acts were ultimately self-defeating – they did not raise much or any revenue, and they antagonized the colonies.

3.3.2 The Stamp Act 1765[75]

Already, in 1763, Grenville had introduced the Sugar Act, seeking to restore the ailing British economy by collecting the tax on sugar, or molasses, more efficiently, and so reduce smuggling. This was followed by the 1764 Currency Act, which banned colonies from printing paper money. However, although there were objections, opposition was relatively limited, due to a lack of

69 See generally MH Smith, *The Writs of Assistance Case* (University of California Press, 1978).

70 Importantly, overbroad search warrants had been found contrary to the rule of law in England in the 1760s (in *Entick* v. *Carrington* [1765] 95 Eng. Rep. 807. See the judgement of Lord Camden).

71 Otis was a prominent Massachusetts lawyer and activist in defence of the colonies' cause. Already somewhat unstable, Otis was injured by a Crown officer in 1769, and became insane after this.

72 Thomas Hutchinson, a crown loyalist, was the last civilian royal governor of Massachusetts, sometimes perceived as a tragic figure – e.g. B Bailyn, *The Ordeal of Thomas Hutchinson* (Cambridge MA.; Harvard University Press, 1976).

73 E.g. Otis' pamphlet, 'The Rights of the British Colonies Asserted and Proved' (1764).

74 Per Edmund Burke, 'American Taxation Speech', in *Writings* II, 18–19.

75 5 Geo. 3, c. 12 (1765).

organization and the unwillingness of colonial legislatures to take a stand against Parliament. James Otis even wrote at this time, 'We all think ourselves happy under Great Britain. We love, esteem and reverence our mother country, and adore our king.'[76]

The colonies did not think themselves happy for long. The Stamp Act was a major source of grievance to Americans, as well as being the legal measure that activated a great deal of debate about Britain's sovereignty over the colonies. As such it merits some detailed consideration.[77]

This legislation imposed the first direct tax (in contrast to the Sugar Act, which was viewed as a trade measure) on America, and it cleared Parliament with very little debate or opposition. It clearly, as its Preamble stated, aimed at 'defraying the expences of defending, protecting, and securing, the British colonies and plantations in America.' Stamp Acts were no strangers to domestic British legislation and had generated revenue for the Crown (and continue to do so on the sale of houses in England). Enforcement is almost automatic, as, without the required stamp a document is invalid. The 1765 Act was a complex statute that imposed a tax on all printed documents in the colonies. All such materials – which included legal documents such as bills of sale, wills, contracts, as well as newspapers, pamphlets, posters, calendars, licences for retailing wine and spirits, and even playing cards and dice – had to carry an embossed revenue stamp originally produced in London. Although the tax was lower than equivalent taxes in Britain, it was much more visible to the average American than sugar duties, and the stamp could only be paid for in hard to obtain British silver and gold. It hit lawyers and students (who needed many documents that now attracted a stamp tax) especially hard, and so was seen as deterring the growth of the professions in the colonies. As with the 1763 Sugar Act, those accused of violating the Act could be prosecuted, without juries, in Admiralty Courts, which could be located anywhere in the British Empire.

The Stamp Act affected virtually everyone in every colony, and there was impassioned resistance with many demonstrations organized by the 'Sons of Liberty'.[78] An informal alliance of objectors was formed by committees of correspondence across America and petitions were lodged by colonial assemblies. In August 1765, a Boston mob went on the rampage, attacking homes of several officials, including that of Lieutenant-Governor Thomas Hutchinson. There was much intimidation of tax collectors, so it became almost impossible to enforce the tax, and a considerable amount of stamped paper was destroyed. The most effective form of protest in the colonies was 'non importation', namely a boycott of all imported British goods. By the end of 1765, there was

[76] James Otis, *The Rights of the British Colonies, Asserted and Proved* (Boston: Edes and Gill, 1764) 51.

[77] See, generally, E Morgan and H Morgan, *The Stamp Act Crisis* (Chapel Hill: UNC Press, 1953).

[78] This name had been used before 1765, but after the Stamp Act was adopted by a more organized group, including in its members Samuel Adams and James Otis.

a huge loss of British trade, outweighing any revenue that might have been brought in by the Act. In 1765, a Stamp Act Congress was convened in New York City, indicating ability of colonists to organise together. This was seen as a forerunner to later Congresses, especially the Second Continental Congress which preceded the Declaration of American independence.

Resistance also took place outside America. British manufacturers and merchants who found their exports damaged by the boycott put pressure on Parliament, and petitions were sent from 24 British cities and towns. A letter from London traders stated that, 'if this cussed act is not repealed, we shall be great sufferers, and our manufacturers thrown on our parishes for want of support.'[79]

Colonists argued it was a violation of their rights to be taxed without their consent. Some argued that the colonies should be represented in Parliament – an argument supported at one stage by both Otis and Franklin.[80] Colonists rejected the argument that all British subjects had *virtual* representation in Parliament, even if they could not vote for members of Parliament (as indeed was the case for the majority of British residents who also lacked the suffrage). Thomas Whately (Treasury Secretary and author of the Stamp Act in Britain) noted that those excluded from the franchise in Britain included 'all monied Property' and the very wealthy City of London merchants, inhabitants of some very large cities such as Manchester, and also the East India Company, which had sovereign power in India but no vote in Britain.[81] However, the colonial lawyer, Daniel Dulaney contested this notion of virtual representation, arguing that relations between Americans and British MPs were 'a knot too infirm to be relied on' for proper representation, 'virtual' or otherwise.[82] In any case, many in America rejected the idea of any representation in the British Parliament, finding English society too corrupt to merit greater connection. John Adams, for example, wrote that England had reached the same stage as the Roman republic: 'a venal city, ripe for destruction.'[83]

Originally then, opposition was about colonial tax without representation. However, opposition soon broadened into a more general dispute over sovereignty. For claiming the right to tax is an unassailable assertion of sovereignty. Indeed, in the course of the Bill's passage, Grenville changed his approach from asserting American colonies were 'virtually' represented, to claiming that Parliament had the right to pass law and tax the colonists as the supreme legislator of the British Empire.[84]

79 *The Newport Mercury*, 18 November 1765.

80 Berriedale-Keith, *Constitutional History of the First British Empire*, at 348.

81 Thomas Whately, *The Regulations Lately Made Concerning the Colonies and the Taxes Imposed upon Them, Considered* (London, 1765) 103.

82 Daniel Dulaney, *Considerations on the Propriety of Imposing Taxes in the British Colonies, for the Purpose of Raising a Revenue, by Act of Parliament* (1765).

83 John Adams, *Novanglus*, 13 February 1775, *Papers of John Adams* II at 265–267.

84 PDG Thomas, *British Politics and the Stamp Act Crisis* (Oxford: Clarendon Press, 1975) 86.

However, some worried about dire economic effects of loss of trade with America and agitated for the Stamp Act's repeal. William Pitt the elder argued in parliamentary debates that, 'It is my opinion that this Kingdom has no right to lay a tax upon the colonies.'[85] Whatever its defence, the Stamp Act was counter-productive and became an explicit and significant element of the list of grievances set out in the Indictment of George III within the Declaration of Independence.

3.3.3 Repeal of the Stamp Act

On 10 July 1765, Grenville was replaced as Prime Minister by Lord Rockingham, whose decision to repeal the Stamp Act owes as much to complaints of British merchants who feared loss of trade, as to an understanding of American grievances. Rockingham's political secretary was Edmund Burke (himself an MP) and together they helped London merchants organize a committee of correspondence agitating for repeal of the Stamp Act.

Rockingham also invited Benjamin Franklin to give evidence to Parliament about colonial policy. Franklin was then in Britain, lobbying MPs against the Stamp Act, often writing anonymously as 'A Virginian' or 'FB' and 'Pacificus'. Franklin distinguished 'internal' from 'external' taxation, taking the view that Parliament could not levy taxes on the colonies without their representation.[86] Franklin had produced a cartoon, *Magna Britannia: Her Colonies reduced* which he distributed to the House of Commons on the eve of the Stamp Act debate (Figure 3.1).[87] This cartoon showed the dejected figure of Britannia, dismembered because of the Stamp Act, surrounded by her amputated limbs – marked Virginia, Pennsylvania, New York, and New England. There is a lifeless tree stump at the right; in the distance are merchant ships by the shore, with brooms on their mast heads indicating they are for sale. A pennant wrapped across the globe and Britannia bears the words DATE OBOLUM BELISARIO ('give a penny to Belisarius'), a classical reference which expressed the lesson that even the rich and famous may be reduced to penury.

Some in Britain were sympathetic to the colonial position that there were limits on Parliament's sovereignty. Lord Camden, Chief Justice of the Court of Common Pleas, who gave judgment in the famous case of *Entick* v. *Carrington*, stated that there were some things Parliament 'cannot do'. For example, he said, it could not act contrary to the fundamental laws of nature, nor contrary to the fundamental laws of this Constitution', thus distinguishing ordinary law from fundamental law.[88] Lord Camden also cited examples where Parliament had allowed unrepresented communities to tax themselves. Wales was not taxed

[85] *Parliamentary History* XVI, 99. [86] *Cobbett's Parliamentary History*, 156.
[87] Benjamin Franklin, *Writings*, IV, 290–291.
[88] Speech by Lord Camden (10 February 1766), reprinted in 16 *Parl. Hist. Eng.* 178 (1813).

Figure 3.1 Benjamin Franklin – Magna Britannia: Her colonies Reduc'd

until it had representation in Parliament.[89] Some radicals went further and opposed the doctrine of parliamentary sovereignty altogether. For example, Obadiah Hulme declared in *An Historical Essay on the English Constitution*: 'There is not a more dangerous doctrine can be adopted in our state, than to admit that the legislative authority hath any right to alter, the first principles of our constitution, by acts of parliament.'[90]

However, many in the UK took a robust view of Parliament's powers. Charles Yorke, then Attorney-General, in a speech in the House of Commons in 1766, asserted that: 'Dominions of the Crown wherever they lie are bound by Act of Parliament of Great Britain'. This, Yorke insisted, was a central maxim of Britain's 'mighty Empire', and he also added that 'the universality of the legislative power is the vital principle of the whole Empire'.[91] Lord Mansfield, speaking in the later debate over the repeal of the Stamp Act in the House of Lords, claimed that Parliament represented 'the whole British Empire' with 'authority to bind every part and every subject without the least distinction' in both matters of tax as well as legislation.[92] Therefore, for both Yorke and Mansfield, the colonies' claim to exemption from tax was a challenge to Britain's sovereignty. To allow the distinction made by the colonists, and by Pitt, that tax should be distinguished from other legislation, implied a slippery slope.

89 *Cobbett's Parliamentary History*, 170.

90 Obadiah Hulme, *An Historical Essay on the English Constitution* (London, 1771) at 141.

91 Charles Yorke, speech, 2 February 1766, in Simmons and Thomas (eds.), *Proceedings and Debates*, 2: 137.

92 Lord Mansfield, speech, 3 February 1766, in Simmons and Thomas (eds.), *Proceedings and Debates*, 2: 128–130.

However, due to widespread opposition, the Stamp Act was repealed almost one year after it gained royal assent, on 18 March 1766. According to Morgan, after the Act was repealed, the church bells of London rang out all day and rejoicing spread all over England, as there had been a severe economic depression in Britain, and in the minds of many the Stamp Act was to blame.[93]

An engraving was issued to celebrate this: 'The Repeal or the Funeral Procession of Miss America-Stamp 1766', which sold many copies.[94]

This was not an American cartoon. It was commissioned by the Rockingham ministry, as a means of ridiculing their opponents by elaborate caricature. Edmund Burke was tasked with engaging the artist Benjamin Wilson, a friend of Franklin, to execute the work. *The Repeal*, published on the day the repeal was voted by Parliament, was extraordinarily popular. The main figures are those who counselled most strongly against repeal. A funeral procession forms in the foreground, headed to a tomb inscribed, 'Within this Family Vault lie ... the Remains of Hearth mon[ey] Ship mon[ey] ...' and other unpopular measures. In the procession are Lord Mansfield and Sir Fletcher Norton, who carry flags on which are parodies of stamps, as well as the numbers of those voting against repeal in the Lords and Commons (71 and 102). George Grenville, former First Minister and originator of the tax, carries the coffin labelled 'Miss Ame. Stamp. B. 1765 died 1766.'

3.3.4 The Declaratory Act 1766

Yet, Britain was nonetheless in an awkward situation. It lacked sufficient military force to compel compliance with the Stamp Act, yet backing down, by repealing the Act, appeared to offer dangerous concessions to America. The solution to squaring this vicious circle was to be found in repealing the Stamp Act, but enacting new legislation, the Declaratory Act, that would declare the British Parliament's sovereignty in all matters in all of its domains. This was an obfuscation. For if Parliament had supreme legislative power, then surely this included taxation of the colonies, and in particular stamp duties?

The Stamp Act was repealed in March 1766. At the same time, the Declaratory Act 1766 (or American Colonies Act)[95] modelled on the 1719 Declaratory Act[96] over Ireland, was adopted. The Declaratory Act affirmed the right of Parliament to legislate for the colonies 'in all cases whatsoever'. It also declared that any colonial proceedings that questioned Parliament's right to legislate for America were 'utterly null and void.' But, although most parliamentarians voted it through, not everyone in Britain supported it, and eminent lawyers such as Lord Camden spoke against this 'absolutely illegal' bill, which he described as:

[93] Morgan, *The Stamp Act Crisis*, at 280.

[94] RT Haines Halsey, 'Impolitical Prints' (1939) 43 Bulletin of the New York Public Library.

[95] 6 Geo 3 c.12. [96] 6 Geo I c.5.

> contrary to the fundamental laws of nature, contrary to the fundamental laws of this constitution … so true are the words of that consummate reasoner and politician Mr. Locke. 'The supreme power cannot take from any man any part of his property without his own consent'.[97]

Nonetheless, it was clearly hoped that the Declaratory Act would settle the question of Parliament's authority over the colonies. That this was unclear in the 1760s is illustrated by Burke's (later 1774) comment, in his famous speech on America, that prior to the Declaratory Act, 'the legislative rights of this country were not entire, but had certain restrictions and limitations.' However, Burke continued, he believed that the Declaratory Act established 'a real, consistent, well-grounded authority in Parliament.'[98] But surely the very fact that Parliament thought it necessary to adopt the Declaratory Act suggests that its sovereignty was in doubt?

The Declaratory Act thereafter became a keystone of Parliament's right to legislate over America. Virtual representation and Charters were no longer argued as grounds for colonial taxation. And thus, Britain changed its constitutional position.[99] The Declaratory Act also rendered colonial opposition to Britain illegal, and the questioning of parliamentary sovereignty a violation of law. Shelburne (when Secretary of State for Britain's 'Southern Department'[100]) argued that anyone questioning the Declaratory Act by writing, preaching, or speaking against it, should be tried for treason.[101] Shelburne adopted an undoubtedly severe approach. However, his approach reveals the problem of how the Declaratory Act was to be enforced. As a 'Declaratory' Act, it was short, and specified no penalties for its non-obeisance, other than the nullity of colonial Acts that conflicted with it. And yet, positivist theories of law, such as Austin's, suggest that it is the essence of law that it impose sanctions for non-compliance. Otherwise, how may law be distinguished from morality or religion? And indeed, Acts asserting parliamentary sovereignty continue to face problems to this day.

Reaction to the Declaratory Act in the colonies was unfavourable but somewhat muted. It did not attract the same aggressive opposition as had the Stamp Act. Perhaps, colonists believed Parliament would not take action on the basis of it.[102] However, others, including John Dickinson and Thomas Jefferson were

97 'On the declaratory Bill of the Sovereignty of Great-Britain over the Colonies', House of Lords, January 1766. *Cobbett's Parliamentary History,* XVI, cols. 168–169. Camden's speech was reprinted in the colonies.

98 I, 241; Edmund Burke, *Selected Writings and Speeches on America*, Thomas H D Mahoney (ed.), (Indianapolis, 1963) 112–115.

99 If the criticism is made that the colonists changed their arguments to suit events, then it seems this accusation must also be made of the British.

100 Until 1768, the Southern department's remit included the American colonies. After 1768 a separate department for the colonies was established. The Southern department became the Foreign Office in 1782.

101 Shelburne to Chatham [ante 13 February 1767], *Chatham Papers*, 30/8, LVI, 86–90.

102 E.g. Ireland had not been taxed by Parliament since the 1719 Declaratory Act.

greatly opposed to the Declaratory Act.[103] Thomas Paine was yet more critical of the Declaratory Act, writing in 1782: '… If then the stamp act was an usurpation of the Americans' most precious and sacred rights, the declaratory act left them no rights at all; and contained the full grown seeds of the most despotic government ever exercised in the world'.[104]

One hears little of the Declaratory Act nowadays. Indeed, the 1776 American Declaration of Independence and Britain's recognition of US independence in 1783 appeared to render it obsolete. Yet in fact the Declaratory Act continued in force, applying to remaining British colonies across the Atlantic, and was only repealed in 1964. However, with the exception of the Taxation of Colonies Act 1778, Parliament no longer legislated to impose direct taxation on any of its colonies, preferring instead to ask colonial governments themselves to contribute towards defence of the Empire.

However, the notion of a 'Sovereignty Act' is still a current issue. Thus Parliament adopted the EU Act 2011 (repealed by Brexit), which not only required a referendum prior to any further major transfer of power to the EU, but also stated that EU law had force in the UK only by virtue of parliamentary statute. The EU Act 2011 was often perceived as unsatisfactory, merely restating a theoretical position on parliamentary sovereignty, without addressing its interaction with the conflicting supremacy of EU law. In 2016, David Cameron, while Prime Minister, suggested there was 'a good case' for a new sovereignty law.[105] However, the weaknesses of this approach had already been demonstrated by the inconsequential nature of the EU Act 2011's guarantee of sovereignty. The matter is inherently circular: an apparently sovereign Parliament cannot make itself sovereign by declaring itself so. In any case, history is best not forgotten. Declaring parliamentary sovereignty by way of the Declaratory Act did not end conflict with the colonies. It exacerbated it.

3.3.5 The Townshend Acts 1767

After the miscalculation of the Stamp Act – so blatant as to require that Act's repeal – one might have expected caution from the British government. Yet, policy was not reconsidered, partly because some in government believed the colonies were led by 'wicked and designing men',[106] but also because the British

[103] *An Essay on the Constitutional Power of Great Britain*, 1774; *Writings of Thomas Jefferson*, P Ford (ed.), (New York: GP Putnam, 1892) 469.

[104] Thomas Paine, *Letter to Abbe Raynal*, 1782.

[105] *BBC News*, 'David Cameron: There's "a Good Case" for New Sovereignty Law', 18 January 2016.

[106] House of Lords resolutions stated that 'wicked and designing men' in the colonies were 'evidently manifesting a design … to set up a new and unconstitutional authority independent of the crown of England.' Hansard, *Parliamentary History*, 479.

political scene was highly fractured. 'Tesselated' or 'checkered' government existed.[107]

Shortly after repeal of the Stamp Act, Rockingham was replaced by Pitt (now Earl of Chatham and in the Lords since August 1766) as First Minister. Pitt had argued forcefully for repeal of the Stamp Act, and given a speech in defence of the Colonies,[108] and one might perhaps have expected an era of better relations between Britain and America. However, Pitt was unwell, possibly suffering from depression,[109] and frequently absent, and this left no-one to restrain the erratic 'brilliant, irresponsible Townshend.'[110]

While Chancellor of the Exchequer, Townshend introduced legislation collectively known as the 'Townshend Acts.' These aimed to raise revenue from the colonies (in fact raising only £40,000). These Acts imposed duties on imported goods in the American colonies,[111] reorganized the Board of Customs Commissioners in Boston,[112] and introducing other measures, such as The Indemnity Act 1767, which made British East India Company tea competitive with tea consumed in the colonies, by shifting the burden of tax onto the colonies. The intention of all this legislation was to raise revenue, not only to pay for maintaining troops in the colonies,[113] but also to fund administration of justice and civil government, so as to appoint colonial governors and judges loyal to the Crown. However, these measures appeared both provocative and punitive, although they were framed as import duties, as trade measures, rather than direct internal taxes. A year later, in 1768, after Townshend himself died, the Vice Admiralty Court Act was adopted. This significantly, ensured that smugglers could be prosecuted in America, but in *British* naval courts (without a jury) rather than colonial courts. Thomas Jefferson specifically mentioned the establishment of new offices and courts in the Declaration of Independence, as part of a list of grievances against the King: 'He has erected a multitude of New Offices, and sent hither swarms of Officers to harrass our people, and eat out their substance.'

[107] Burke referred to the Chatham administration as 'so checkered and speckled … a cabinet so variously inlaid, such a piece of diversified mosaic, such a tessellated pavement without cement' (Burke, 'Speech on American Taxation', 19 April 1774).

[108] Pitt, *In Defence of the Colonies*, 14 January 1766; see also HWV Temperley, Debates on the Declaratory Act and the Repeal of the Stamp Act, 1766' (1912) 3 *The American Historical Review* 563.

[109] E.g. P Thomas, 'The Great Commoner': The Elder William Pitt as Parliamentarian' (2003) 22 *Parliamentary History* 145.

[110] Tuchman, *The March of Folly*, at 169. See also Lewis Namier and John Brooke, *Charles Townshend* (London: St Martin's Press, 1964).

[111] The Revenue Act 1767. This also endowed customs officials with wide enforcement powers, including 'writs of assistance', whose legality had already been challenged by James Otis.

[112] The Commissioners of Customs Act 1767.

[113] See e.g. the Quartering Act 1765 (or American Mutiny Act), which required colonies to provide supplies to British army regiments stationed in America.

3.3.6 John Dickinson and Other Reactions

Colonial indignation over the Townshend Acts was further agitated by John Dickinson's anonymous publication of the series of *Letters from a Farmer in Pennsylvania to the inhabitants of the British colonies,*[114] which commenced in December 1767. Dickinson was a Philadelphia lawyer and would later become a delegate to the Continental Congress. These letters were published in newspapers throughout America – only Thomas Paine's *Common Sense* proved more popular. They set out the colonies' case very clearly, employing arguments already held by many colonists.

Dickinson argued that *any* tax imposed on the colonies was unlawful, because there were no colonial representatives in Parliament. No difference existed between the Stamp Act, and the supposedly indirect Townshend duties. Dickinson's letters therefore mark a point when the distinction between internal and external taxation became less important for colonists. The *Letters* also protested the proliferation of new offices and the dangers of standing armies.

Then, in February 1768, the *Massachusetts Circular Letter* was issued. It was drafted mainly by Samuel Adams, then clerk of the Lower House of the Massachusetts Assembly and urged the colonies to resist the Townshend Acts. Some colonies followed suit, publishing their own Circular Letters, or adopting resolutions.

Britain's response to the Massachusetts Assembly letter came from Lord Hillsborough, Secretary of State for the newly created American colonial department.[115] *Hillsborough's Circular Letter* of 21 April 1768 ordered the Massachusetts Assembly to accept the duties or face being suspended or closed down. The Massachusetts Assembly, however, defied Hillsborough's order, so Governor Bernard dissolved it, which led to mass rioting in Boston. In response, Parliament proposed that Boston rebels be tried under an obsolete sixteenth-century law – 'An Act for the Trial of Treason Committed out of the King's Dominion.'[116] The legislatures of Maryland, North Carolina, South Carolina, Rhode Island, Georgia, New York, and Virginia were also subsequently suspended.

Attempting to enforce colonial obedience to Britain by shutting down colonial assemblies was an extraordinarily severe step. The colonies had no representation in Westminster, and now they lacked functioning colonial legislatures. Indeed, *The London Magazine* in August 1768 compared the British government's measures to those of the Stuarts in the seventeenth century. In any case, this reaction created a colonial unity which had been previously lacking.

114 RTH Halsey (ed.), *Letters from a Farmer in Pennsylvania* (New York: Outlook Co., 1903).

115 This was created in 1768 especially to deal with unrest in America, but also oversaw all of Britain's other colonies.

116 35th Henry VIII.

As tensions grew, the Customs Board in Boston requested military protection from Britain, which arrived in 1768. By sending troops, Britain appeared to admit that the only way to control the colonies was by force. Customs officials seized the ship *Liberty*, owned by John Hancock, on charges of smuggling. Hancock was successfully defended by John Adams, on the basis that the prosecution violated Magna Carta. The arrival of British troops in Boston eventually resulted in the Boston Massacre of 1770, when soldiers fired upon a group of citizens. In January 1769, Lord North became Prime Minister and would continue in office for most of the American revolution, forever to be remembered, and mostly remembered only, for that event. Then, on 5 March 1770, Parliament began to debate the repeal of the Townshend Act taxes. The American boycott had taken its toll, and the British economy had suffered yet again. All the taxes were eventually repealed, except for the tax on tea – and roughly three years of peace in North America ensued.

3.3.7 Tea

It was the 1773 Tea Act, which imposed duties on imported tea, that provided the catalyst for escalating the dispute between colonists and Britain to the next stage. The British East India Company, a private company, was on the point of bankruptcy. The 1773 Tea Act not only granted the East India Company a monopoly of tea sales in America, but also allowed it to ship its tea directly to the colonies without routing it through England. This meant the East India Company could undercut colonial merchants, who saw themselves ruined by East India tea. And so, problems with one part of the British Empire (the East India Company) led to the demise and independence of another (America).[117]

The Tea Act was a failure. It did not resolve the issue of Parliament's authority over America and instead provoked a crisis. Colonists in New York and Philadelphia refused to unload British East India Company tea and returned the ships to England. In other colonial ports, tea shipments were unloaded and left on the quay to rot. However, the most memorable event occurred in Boston, where Bostonians, led by the Sons of Liberty, refused to unload cargos of East India tea, and on 16 December 1773, a group dressed as Native Americans boarded the ships and dumped their cargo into Boston Harbor, in what became known as the 'Boston Tea Party'.

3.3.8 The Coercive or 'Intolerable' Acts 1774

The Tea Party was seen in Britain as an act of treason, a deliberate insult to the king and his ministry. However, Ammerman suggests that 'What makes

[117] Interestingly, there was more overlap – Charles Yorke, Attorney General and drafter of the Declaratory Act 1766, was counsel to the East India Company from 1751. Edmund Burke was later to be prime investigator into East India Company corruption.

the Boston Tea Party so significant was not the event itself but the response of the British Government.'[118] Parliament imposed the severe punishments of the 'Coercive' or 'Intolerable' Acts of 1774. This was yet another series of Acts, aimed this time at re-establishing order in Massachusetts and penalizing Boston for the tea party. The 'Coercive' Acts comprised the following statutes. The *Boston Port Act* mandated closure of the port of Boston until an indemnity was paid to the East India Company. The *Administration of Justice Act* made British officials immune from prosecution in Massachusetts, and also abolished the right of trial by jury there for colonial defendants (so even George Washington referred to it as 'the Murder Act'). The *Massachusetts Government Act* virtually revoked the colony's Charter and provided for unrivalled royal control. Additionally, most elective offices in Massachusetts were to be filled with royal appointees, not elected officials. The *Quartering Act* required colonists to house troops on demand. These measures were later joined by a separate *Quebec Act*, which extended Canada's boundaries to areas which American colonies claimed, and established freedom of worship for Catholics, and so was denigrated by (protestant) colonists as favouring Catholics.

Many Americans had become convinced, as Jefferson subsequently wrote, that there existed 'a deliberate and systematic plan of reducing us to slavery.'[119] However, it is just as likely that Britain's conduct was haphazard, negligent and poorly thought out. On 19 April 1774, in a debate on an Opposition motion for repeal of tea duty, Edmund Burke delivered his famous *Speech on American Taxation*. This was part of his enormous outpouring on America, which also included his *Speech on Conciliation* (1775), and *A Letter to the Sheriffs of Bristol* (1777) – all, however, unsuccessful in their attempts to persuade the King, Cabinet, Parliament, and the British public of the folly of Britain's treatment of the American colonies. Burke's maiden speech in the House of Commons in 1766 had forcefully urged repeal of the Stamp Act. From May 1771 until the outbreak of war, Burke acted as agent in London for the New York Colonial Assembly, a position that endowed him with a good grasp of colonial affairs.[120]

In his *Speech on American Taxation*, Burke analysed British legislation for America since the Navigation Acts, concluding with his criticism of 'the distempered vigour and insane alacrity with which you are rushing to your ruin'.[121] Burke's overall position was that, although parliamentary sovereignty included the right to tax, this right need not be applied. In this way, Burke found it

118 D Ammerman, 'The Tea Crisis and Its Consequences', in J Greene and J Pole (eds.), *A Companion to the American Revolution* (Wiley-Blackwell, 2003) at 197. However, not all colonists approved the actions of the Boston Tea Party – Washington disapproved of the destruction of the tea and Franklin insisted the East India company be reimbursed for the loss.

119 Thomas Jefferson, *Draft of Instructions to the Virginia Delegates in the Continental Congress*, July 1774.

120 In this, he joined some other notable colonial agents, such as Benjamin Franklin, who was agent for Philadelphia.

121 Burke, 'Speech on American Taxation', in *Writings II*, 1–80.

possible to accommodate both the British claims and the colonial ones, urging, 'Let the Coercive Acts be repealed, let the Americans tax themselves.' But his warning was rejected. In any event, as soon as the Coercive Acts were adopted, George III prorogued Parliament, in September 1774, partly to ensure the success of this colonial policy – so there was no further chance for debate.

It was exactly one year after the date of Burke's speech, on 19 April 1775, that the clashes at Lexington and Concord occurred, marking the outset of hostilities.

3.3.9 The First Continental Congress

The first Congress was formed in response to the imposition of the Coercive Acts. It met in Philadelphia for two months from September 1774, with 56 delegates from all colonies but Georgia.[122] Delegates included John Adams and Samuel Adams of Massachusetts, George Washington of Virginia, and future US Supreme Court Chief Justice John Jay of New York. The purpose was to collectively send a list of grievances to the British government, demonstrating the unified strength of the colonies.

This was a difficult task, as the delegates did not share a common approach. More conservatively inclined delegates, such as Joseph Galloway, John Dickinson and John Jay, although they desired repeal of the Coercive Acts, were more conciliatory. Early on, the Congress addressed the Pennsylvania delegate, Joseph Galloway's *Grand Plan of Union of Great Britain and the Colonies*, which argued for reconciliation with Britain.[123] Galloway's plan would have required power sharing with the British Parliament, amounting to a reorganization of the British Empire along almost federal lines, (not unlike Franklin's 1754 'Albany plan'). However, before the Galloway Plan could be endorsed, the much more radical 'Suffolk resolves' (drafted in Suffolk County, Massachusetts) were presented by Paul Revere, and adopted by a narrow vote of the Congress. These proposed, inter alia, the establishment of a free state of Massachusetts until the Coercive Acts were repealed, a boycott on trade with Britain, and the arming of local militia in Massachusetts.[124]

The Congress managed to agree *The Declaration of Rights and Grievances*, on 14 October 1774.[125] This was sent to King George, rather than to Parliament, to demonstrate their loyalty to the Crown. The Declaration disputed much of Parliament's authority – including the legality of the Coercive Acts. But there was

122 Georgia was fighting a Native-American uprising, dependent on British military supplies, so did not join at this point.

123 Indeed, Galloway's loyalist leanings led him to flee to Britain. See J Boyd, *Anglo-American Union: Joseph Galloway's Plans to Preserve the British Empire, 1774–1788* (Philadelphia: University of Pennsylvania Press, 1941).

124 D Knox, 'The Suffolk Resolves: A Neglected Catalyst of the American Revolution', (thesis, Angelo State University, 2015).

125 Also known as the 'Declaration and Resolves of the First Continental Congress'.

still disagreement over whether Parliament had a right to regulate trade. Some delegates denied only Parliament's authority to tax them, while others repudiated any parliamentary authority over the colonies whatsoever. And so, the matter was not ultimately resolved. The Congress also formed a *Continental Association*, a non-importation, non-consumption, and non-exportation agreement. These directed the colonies to cease importing British goods from 1 December 1774, if the Coercive Acts were not repealed. After proclaiming these measures, the First Continental Congress dissolved on 26 October 1774.

John Adams (in his 1804 *Autobiography*) stressed the continuities between the Declaration of Rights and the Declaration of Independence.[126] However, there was a crucial difference between the two Declarations. While the Declaration of Rights was still aiming to maintain the colonies' relationship with the British Empire, the Declaration of Independence of course broke with it. Ammerman described the Congress as 'a last, and grand, effort to propose a constitutional remedy to the Anglo-American dispute.'[127]

3.3.10 Britain's Response: Pitt, Burke, and the First Shot in Lexington

So, something happened between late 1774 and the Declaration of Independence in 1776 to propel the colonists on to independence. And that something had much to do with Britain's response.

To be sure, some in Britain were sympathetic to the colonies. Fox warned that the colonies could only be governed by 'affection and interest.'[128] Speeches by William Pitt and Edmund Burke, widely reprinted in colonial newspapers and pamphlets, provided strong arguments against the Government's position. Pitt, Lord Chatham since 1766, introduced a Bill for conciliation, but was defeated at first reading. A little later, Edmund Burke presented the *Speech on Conciliation with the Colonies*. This was Burke's best-known discussion of the American crisis, and Burke urged Parliament to see the conflict from the American perspective. Americans had grown used to conducting their own affairs, governing and taxing themselves. For Britain to start taxing them was unprecedented and near revolutionary. Burke counselled that 'Magnanimity in politics is not seldom the truest wisdom; and a great empire and little minds go ill together.'[129] The issue of sovereignty could best be settled by not raising it.

But the British Government thought differently. It decided that the issue of sovereignty could best be resolved by a forceful display of it. The British Government was in no mood to suspend the Coercive Acts, let alone repeal them. William Legge, Secretary of State for the Colonial Department, for one,

[126] LH Butterfield, LC Faber, WD Garrett, *Diary and Autobiography of John Adams* (Cambridge MA.: Harvard University Press, 1961) 3:310.

[127] D Ammerman, 'The British Constitution and the American Revolution: A Failure of Precedent' (1976) 17 Wm. & Mary L. Rev. 473, at 491.

[128] Cited in Greene, *Constitutional Origins of the American Revolution*, at 174.

[129] Both extracts, Burke, 'Speech on Conciliation', 22 March 1775.

wrote[130] that he was unaware of any mechanism in British law for 'suspending' Acts of Parliament.[131] The British Government saw treason in the Continental Congress, and General Gage (who had replaced Hutchinson as Governor of Massachusetts) was ordered to use troops to enforce the Massachusetts Government Act. In April 1775, General Gage sent a British force out from Boston with the aim of destroying a cache of arms in Concord. This did not go according to plan. A skirmish occurred in Lexington on the way, and the British Redcoats had to be rescued at Concord, which did the British army's reputation no good whatever. And so, the first step in the American war of Independence occurred.

3.3.11 The Second Constitutional Congress

News of the conflict in Lexington and Concord came shortly before the Second Continental Congress convened in Philadelphia[132] in May 1775. It was composed mainly of the same delegates as the first, but now also included Thomas Jefferson and Benjamin Franklin. Notwithstanding that armed conflict had now broken out between the British and Americans, at the start of the Congress, at least, the majority of delegates were not seeking independence from Britain.[133] In July, Congress approved the *Olive Branch petition*,[134] promoted by Pennsylvania delegate, John Dickinson, which was a direct appeal to the king, requesting a peaceful solution to the conflict. However, the king refused to receive the petition and declared the colonies 'in open and avowed rebellion' after the Battle of Bunker Hill in 1775 (in which the British suffered severe losses) and also declared the Second Continental Congress an illegal assembly.

The issues the delegates faced had changed from those of the first Congress. The second Congress now had to function as a unified form of government to organize and direct the colonies. On 6 July 1775, Congress approved a *Declaration of Causes* outlining the rationale and necessity of taking up arms in the thirteen colonies. A continental army was created and George Washington commissioned by the Congress as its supreme commander. Supplies for the army had to be funded, so the Congress authorized the printing of money

130 Reproduced in BF Stevens, *Facsimiles of Manuscripts, 1773–1783* (25 vols., London, 1889–1898) XXIV, 2025, 202.

131 Clear confirmation of such a mechanism would have to await application of EU law in the UK in the *Factortame* case (*R* v. *Secretary of State for Transport, ex parte: Factortame Ltd and others* [1991] A.C. 603).

132 The Second Congress met in different sessions until March 1781, when the Articles of Confederation were ratified.

133 Indeed, 'until early 1776 Washington and his officers continued to toast the health of George III.' D Ammerman, 'The Crisis of Independence', in J Greene and J Pole (eds.), *A Companion to the American Revolution* (Hoboken NJ: Wiley-Blackwell, 2003) at 207.

134 John Adams described it as a 'Measure of Imbecility' since the First Continental Congress had already unsuccessfully petitioned King George.

(although paper money depreciated rapidly in value). A standing committee was also appointed so relations could be established with foreign powers. The Congress therefore became a governing institution, with functions such as appointing ambassadors, treaty making (most importantly the 1778 Treaty of Alliance with France), raising armies, obtaining loans from Europe, and disbursing funds. Lacking the authority to impose taxes, the Congress requested funding from the colonies, which, however, was often ignored. John Adams became the leader of the faction demanding full independence, a group that included Samuel Adams, Thomas Jefferson, George Washington, and Benjamin Franklin. However, up to early February 1776, colonies in favour of independence were still in a minority.

3.3.12 British Reaction: The King's Proclamation and the Prohibitory Act

In Britain, in 1775, there was little doubt that the conflict could be won. The emphasis was on reaffirming sovereignty, and the King was committed to a forceful resolution of the dispute. After the clashes in Lexington and Concord, Lord Mansfield (then Chief Justice of the King's Bench Division) made his strongest speech in the House of Lords, advising vigorous action against the colonies, regardless of any impact this might have on commerce, employing the memorable phrase, 'If we do not kill them, they will kill you.'[135] It would only be several years later, after the defeat of the British in Yorktown in 1781, that effective opposition in Parliament would form.

Britain adopted further measures which could only convince the colonists that they faced two stark choices: complete submission or independence. The *King's Proclamation for Suppressing Rebellion and Sedition* appeared in August 1775. The British government also brought seditious libel charges against vocal support for the colonies in Britain. For example, newspapers had printed an advertisement by the English clergyman and politician, John Horne, who sought to raise £100 in support of 'beloved American fellow subjects'. All the newspapers, along with John Horne himself, were tried and found guilty by Lord Mansfield. Horne himself was tried in the Court of King's Bench on 4 July 1776 (somewhat ironically) and sentenced to one year imprisonment and £1200 in fines and costs.[136]

On 22 December 1775, Parliament (by a large majority) adopted the *Prohibitory Act*, which completely terminated British trade with all thirteen American colonies, and stated that all American ships 'shall be forfeited to his Majesty, as if the same were the ships and effects of open enemies.'[137] This

[135] Poser, *Lord Mansfield*, at 310–311. [136] Poser, *Lord Mansfield*, 312.

[137] 16 Geo. III, c. 5. Lord Mansfield's advice on suitable treatment for the crew of the captured American ship, *The Yankee*, was that American officers should be neither set free, nor put on trial (Letter from Lord George Germain to Lord Mansfield (6 August, 1776), TNA CO 5/43/342). This advice has been described as 'eerily reminiscent' of US government policy at Guantanamo over 200 years later. (Poser *Lord Mansfield*, 316.)

amounted to a virtual declaration of war against the colonies by Parliament. John Adams' views of the Prohibitory Act were expressed in a letter to Horatio Gates: 'It is a compleat Dismemberment of the British Empire. It throws thirteen Colonies out of the Royal Protection, levels all Distinctions and makes us independent in Spight of all our supplications and Entreaties'.[138]

A political cartoon appeared in the *Westminster Magazine*, published in London, on 1 May 1775. In it, King George and Lord Mansfield ride in an open carriage pulled by two horses labelled 'pride' and 'obstinacy'. Their carriage tramples two documents – Magna Carta and the Constitution – and they are about to drive the carriage into an abyss representing war with the American colonies.

Both the King's *Proclamation* and the *Prohibitory Act* had an immense impact on the Second Congress, emasculating the position of those asking for reconciliation. In response to the *Prohibitory Act*, the Second Continental Congress adopted the *Privateering Resolution* on 23 March 1776, declaring that 'all ships and other vessels … belonging to any inhabitant or inhabitants of Great Britain, taken on the high seas … shall be deemed and adjudged to be lawful prize.'[139]

A further insult to the colonies was the enlisting of Hessian and other foreign mercenaries to increase the British army in America. This was seen as the King using foreign mercenaries to kill his own subjects and converted many to independence. In February 1776, a cartoon appeared in Soho, representing British policies towards the American colonies, of *The Wise Men of Gotham and Their Goose*.[140] This image portrays Lord Bute,[141] with sword raised, was about to cut the head off the goose 'who laid each day an egg of gold'. While the government prepares to slaughter the American colonies, at the top of the image, a picture of a lion represents the British people, who are soundly asleep, oblivious to what is going on elsewhere. In the foreground a small dog urinates on a map of the British colonies.[142]

3.3.13 Common Sense

A further highly significant development was the publication in January 1776 (published anonymously, because then treasonable in Britain[143]) of Thomas

[138] in B Knollenberg, 'The Correspondence of John Adams and Horatio Gates' (1941) 67 Proceedings of the Massachusetts Historical Society.

[139] *Journal of the Continental Congress*, 23 March 1776, IV: 477–480.

[140] B Tucker, 'Symbols of the Revolution', in D Moore (ed.), *Liberty's Impact: The World Views 1776* (Providence, Rhode Island: Brown University 1975–1976) 49.

[141] Lord Bute was a Scot, and former First Minister. Although no longer in political office, many blamed him for the American war, seeing him as a corrupt influence on British government, hence his appearance in many political cartoons of the day.

[142] See, more generally, M Wynne-Jones, *The Cartoon History of the American Revolution* (New York: Putnam's, 1975).

[143] Paine was later, in 1793, placed on trial in absentia in Britain for publishing *The Rights of Man*, convicted and outlawed.

Paine's *Common Sense*, a short pamphlet which set out his arguments in favour of American independence.[144] 'Without the pen of the author of *Common Sense*, the sword of Washington would have been raised in vain', wrote John Adams (who in fact grew to dislike Paine[145]). *Common Sense*, written in plain, everyday language – in Paine's own words, 'simple facts, plain arguments, and common sense' – had a huge impact on both the American public and the second Congress. Very quickly over 500,000 copies were sold, with profits from sale donated to Washington's continental army.

Paine argued that reconciliation was impossible. Instead, Americans should be pursuing independence from Britain and the creation of a new democratic republic. Paine contended that only a republican form of government, with elected officials, assured a community of interest between the governor and governed. Paine argued that America was unique: 'We have it in our power to begin the world over again.... The birthday of a new world is at hand.'

Paine was highly critical of Britain, arguing that the British government had failed to use its collective common sense to deal fairly with Americans. Paine clearly blamed the King for the conflict and oppression in America – something many colonists had been reluctant to do. He denounced the monarchy, in striking and dehumanizing terms – describing George III as 'the royal brute of England', who has 'sunk himself beneath the rank of animals, and contemptibly crawl[s] through the world like a worm.' Paine insisted that England's problems stemmed from its long history of monarchy and hereditary succession, and also took aim at the British Constitution, which he excoriated as 'a rotten constitution of government.' Instead, Paine urged that the world shall know that, '... in America THE LAW IS KING.'[146] And, lest colonials think too fondly of their rights as Englishmen, Paine reminded colonists that America was composed of many different peoples, and was not an English nation: 'Europe, and not England, is the parent country of America. This new world hath been the asylum for the persecuted lovers of civil and religious liberty from *every part* of Europe.'

Therefore, the publication of *Common Sense* played a major role in framing and shifting attitudes in North America.

3.3.14 The Declaration of Independence

In June 1776, Congress set up a committee including Thomas Jefferson, John Adams and Benjamin Franklin, to draft a formal statement of the colonies' intentions. This committee was to produce the *Declaration of Independence*.

[144] T Paine, *Common Sense* (Philadelphia, 1776); see also E Foner, *Tom Paine and Revolutionary America* (New York: Oxford University Press, 1976).

[145] Jill Lepore, 'The Age of Paine', in *The Story of America* (Princeton NJ: Princeton University Press, 2013) at 63.

[146] All references are from Paine, *Common Sense*.

The *Declaration* was in the end largely written by Jefferson[147] and famously adopted by the Congress (after amendments) on 4 July 1776. Jefferson, although young, was already a well-known patriot after publication of *A Summary View of the Rights of British America*. In drafting the *Declaration* he drew on the Virginia Bill of Rights, and his own draft of the Virginia Constitution, and, indeed, the wording of the Declaration sometimes almost paraphrases the Virginia Bill of Rights.

The *Declaration* comprises five sections: the Introduction, the Preamble, the main Body (in two sections) and the Conclusion. The Introduction stated that independence from Britain had become 'necessary' for the colonies. The Body of the *Declaration* outlined a list of grievances – notably against the *King*, rather than Parliament – a list of instances in which King George had violated his contract of government with the American colonies. This might be compared with the 1688 Bill of Rights which lists abuses of power by James II.[148] The Preamble includes the *Declaration's* most famous passage: 'We hold these truths to be self-evident; that all men are created equal; that they are endowed by their Creator with certain inalienable rights; that among these are life, liberty and the pursuit of happiness; that to secure these rights, governments are instituted among men, deriving their just powers from the consent of the governed.' Therefore, the Preamble evokes the language of natural law and rights, a theory that asserts that rights are preconstitutional, prepolitical, and precede positive law.

The British government commissioned partisans to refute the colonists' complaints in the *Declaration*.[149] But in America, the Declaration of Independence was read aloud to the public across the colonies. After one such reading on 9 July, the American army destroyed the statue of King George III at the foot of Broadway in New York City.

In 1776, the *Declaration* was predominantly viewed as a justification and proclamation of independence. But the *Declaration* was notable for the wording it used in particular areas, especially the Preamble – one of natural law and natural rights. Was this a departure from arguments that colonists had employed over the past decades, which asserted their rights as Englishmen? Writers such as McIlwain and Reid believed this natural law language indicated a new direction. But Thomas Jefferson, who, after all, drafted much of the Preamble, did not take this view. Writing retrospectively in 1825, Jefferson argued that presenting 'new arguments, never before thought of', were 'not among the document's purposes.' Instead, the aim was 'to place before

[147] Although the draft was amended by Adams and Franklin, e.g. removing passages blaming King George for the transatlantic slave trade, or blaming British people rather than their government.

[148] 1688 Chapter 2, 1 Will and Mar Sess. 2.

[149] John Lind was commissioned by Lord North to write *An Answer to the Declaration* in autumn 1776. Thomas Hutchinson, now in England, produced *Strictures upon the Declaration of the Congress at Philadelphia*.

mankind the common sense of the subject, in terms so plain and firm as to command their assent, and to justify ourselves in the independent stand we are compelled to take.' Jefferson concluded that 'its authority rests … on the harmonizing sentiments of the day, whether expressed in conversation, in letters, printed essays, or in the elementary books of public right, as Aristotle, Cicero, Locke, Sidney.'[150]

In contrast, John Phillip Reid contested Jefferson's assessment. According to Reid: 'Except for a few lines in the Preamble, that contemporaries recognized as rhetoric and few in a slave-owning nation took seriously, there is no expression of natural rights in the Declaration of Independence.' Instead, 'The vast bulk of that document is an indictment of the British government, and almost every count in the indictment cites a constitutional right.'[151] For Reid, it was the British Constitution, and not natural rights philosophy that provided the theoretical motivations behind the *Declaration*.

And yet could it not be both? We have seen that both natural law and 'reason' were argued as sources of the common law in England by eminent lawyers such as Coke. It was the aim of Americans to make the case for the colonists in legal terms based on the British Constitution. Their argument was a constitutional one,[152] flowing out of the English fundamental law tradition, and rights of Englishmen, with the aim to show that legislation such as the Stamp Act was unlawful according to English law itself. But this did not rule out natural law as an important source of those rights.

Whatever the theory underlying the *Declaration*, the British government refused to accept its arguments. It would not compromise on parliamentary sovereignty.

3.3.15 Conclusions

This chapter, given that it focusses on British legal and constitutional history, says little of the ensuing war of independence and its military history. But it was not a happy story for Britain. The British Government was poorly prepared to subdue a continent, its military forces in no state of readiness. In 1778, the French having recognized the new USA, entered an alliance with them, which helped alter the balance of the war. A peace offer was made by the British in 1778 and commissioners were sent to negotiate with the newly founded

150 In M Peterson (ed.), *Thomas Jefferson, Writings* (Library of America, 1984) at 1500.

151 JP Reid, 'In an Inherited Way: English Constitutional Rights, the Stamp Act Debates, and the Coming of the American Revolution' (1976) 49 Southern California Law Review, 1126; and also JP Reid, 'The Irrelevance of the Declaration', in H Hartog (ed.), *Law in the American Revolution and the Revolution in Law* (New York: New York University Press, 1981).

152 This they had in common with Scottish Nationalists. Neil MacCormick remarked that 'A rigorous constitutionalism has always characterized the SNP's approach to its central policy objective of re-establishing Scotland's position as an independent state'. See N MacCormick, 'Is There a Constitutional Path to Scottish Independence?' (2000) 53 Parliamentary Affairs, 734.

United States. Parliament adopted legislation repealing the Massachusetts Government Act, eschewing the imposition of any taxation of the colonies (save for regulating commerce) and authorizing the commissioners to suspend the operation of any statute passed since 1763.[153] The King also appeared willing to agree that no colonial constitution should be modified by Parliament save on petition from that colony; that no standing army would be imposed on the colonies in peacetime save with their consent; and that the Declaratory Act could be repealed, and instead a Declaration agreed with the colonies as to the constitutional relations between the different parts of the British empire.

In Berriedale-Keith's view, 'It must be admitted that the mere offer of such terms is the severest condemnation of the attitude of the Imperial Government in 1774. It proves beyond doubt that the measures of that year were based on no fundamental principle essential to the Empire.'[154] Berriedale-Keith's comment is extraordinary, coming from a constitutional lawyer, who was elsewhere swift to condemn colonial approaches to Parliament.[155] In any event, the Conciliation Plan was rejected. Generous though some of its terms might have appeared, they did not recognize independence for the US, and also demanded payment by the colonies of war debt.

To King George it was unimaginable that Britain might be defeated. However lose they did. In October 1781, Lord Cornwallis was defeated at Yorktown, Virginia, and surrendered (while, according to legend, the band played 'The World turned Upside Down'[156]). Lord North's majority finally crumbled.

In March 1782, a parliamentary Bill authorizing the Crown to make peace was at last passed. At the same time, a motion of no confidence was passed in the North administration that had spent £100M only to lose the 13 American colonies (Indeed, there was a certain irony that a Britain committed to an austerity in the aftermath of the hugely expensive Seven Years War had become embroiled in one of the most expensive wars in British history.) Lord North then resigned, and a new administration was formed, including Fox, Burke, Camden, and Shelburne. Formal negotiations commenced with Franklin, Adams, Laurens, and John Jay, and the Treaty of Paris took effect in January 1783.

The mood in Britain was sombre. Adam Smith had believed that the *Declaration of Independence* presented Britain with few positive options – it was neither in Britain's advantage to use violence in America, nor to lose the

153 18 Geo III c.11; 18 Geo III c.12; 18 Geo III c.13.

154 Berriedale-Keith, *Constitutional History of the First British Empire*, at 385.

155 Berriedale-Keith declines further comment on the ground that the Conciliation Commission 'pursued a policy very close to that of British policy toward Ireland from 1916–22', and so 'too close to permit any wholesale censure of eighteenth century politics' (Ibid., 385).

156 See e.g. A Schrader, '"The World Turned Upside Down": A Yorktown March, or Music to Surrender By' (1998) 16 *American Music* 180–216. Also, it appears at this time that the King drafted, but did not however deliver, an abdication speech, see A Burns, 'The Abdication Speech of George III', available at https://georgianpapers.com/2017/01/22/abdication-speech-george-iii/

colonies and give up its Empire.[157] Lord Camden's response was to state that he was 'truly ashamed to be an Englishman', but also anxiety that Britain would be unable to escape 'the same ministers, the same folly, the same ignorance.'[158]

Britain was feared to be in a state of decline. In the event, this was not the case. The British Empire survived, or reinvented itself, in the nineteenth century, aided by its huge acquisition of empire in India. That resurrection is a matter for another chapter. But was this resurrection of the British Empire a serendipity aided by extraordinary outside events? Had the French Revolution and Napoleonic wars not occurred, would Britain have been in a position to achieve such dominance? This is, of course, unknowable. In any case, although it might be thought that the loss of the American colonies had exposed a complete failure of imperial governance, one might note that, thereafter, there was little, if any change in governance of British colonies. The introduction of 'responsible government' and Dominion status would have to wait until well into the nineteenth century.

3.4 Conclusion

We have now had a chance to examine some British reactions to the colonists' actions. Two, in particular are noteworthy. First, the Declaratory Act 1766 affirmed Parliament's right to legislate for colonies 'in all cases whatsoever'. This Act was supposed to settle the question of Parliament's authority over colonies. That this was unclear in the 1760s is surely illustrated by the statement in Burke's 1774 *speech on American taxation*, that prior to the Declaratory Act, 'the legislative rights of this country were not entire, but had certain restrictions and limitations.' Therefore, surely the fact that Parliament thought the Declaratory Act necessary suggests that its sovereignty was in doubt?

Second, there is the fact that, in the middle of the American war of independence, the British proposed a conciliation plan, which would have made all sorts of concessions, including repeal of the Declaratory Act, banning taxation of colonies, suspending operation of any post 1763 statute, and allowing that no colonial Constitution be modified by Parliament save on petition from that colony. As Berriedale-Keith asserts, this proposal proves that Britain's earlier measures were based on no fundamental principle essential to the Empire (and that parliamentary sovereignty was not nearly as well established as Britain had insisted).

The foregoing discussion illustrates that, in the decade before the American revolution, there existed real disagreement over the nature of the British

157 Adam Smith, 'Thoughts on the State of the Contest in America' [1778], in E Mossner and I Simpson Ross (eds.), *The Correspondence of Adam Smith* (Oxford: Clarendon Press, 2nd ed., 1987).

158 Camden to Stewart, 29 March, 30 April 1778 (Centre for Kentish Studies, Maidstone UK) U 840 C173/29, 31.

Constitution. In eighteenth-century Britain, the Constitution was evolving – towards a point where parliamentary sovereignty would become a supreme principle – but it had not yet been fully established, nor had it completely overridden older constitutional ideas that colonists emphasized. Custom, and compliance with natural or 'fundamental' law, were also important factors in establishing constitutional legitimacy.

But why was there disagreement between the colonists and British over the correct interpretation of the British Constitution? After all, all parties were British subjects, generally reading the same provisions of law.[159] Was there some extra-constitutional factor, that is, an economic or social explanation for the discord, as claimed by earlier generations of historians? Social and economic factors of course played their part, but we can contain the dispute within a legal/constitutional paradigm, by considering the following three factors.

3.4.1 Form and Substance of the British Constitution

First, Britain then lacked, as it still does, a codified Constitution. Instead, the Constitution comprised a collation of legislation, caselaw, conventions, customs, and practices. However, the absence of a written Constitution did mean that (as is broadly the case in Britain now) it was unclear which laws could be classed as 'constitutional', and the extent to which unwritten practices, customs and conventions might affect constitutional meaning. Therefore, provisions said to make up the Constitution could be subject to many competing interpretations, and there existed no institution – no Supreme or Constitutional Court – to give a definitive interpretation in case of doubt. So, what was actually constitutional in eighteenth-century Britain was difficult to determine.

3.4.2 Where Was the Ultimate Locus of Sovereignty?

Second, did sovereignty lie with the King-in-Parliament, or might it sometimes be found in a higher body of 'fundamental' law? Much constitutional change had taken place in seventeenth-century England, in the course of the Civil War, Commonwealth and Glorious Revolution. But events in the eighteenth century, most particularly clashes in colonial America, but also other factors (such as the Acts of Union of Scotland & England; arguments of radicals such as John Wilkes[160]; and the coming of the French Revolution) also had their impact. The post 1688 constitutional settlement instituted the pre-eminence of Parliament in law-making. Legislation was thereafter to be adopted by the King-in-Parliament.

159 For an enlightening account, see M Zuckert, 'Natural Rights and Imperial Constitutionalism: The American Revolution and the Development of the American Amalgam' (2005) 22 Social Philosophy and Policy 27–55.

160 The British weekly pamphlet, *The Crisis* (1775–1776) in its discussion of American affairs, displayed radical views, and fierce attacks on George III, even before Paine's *Common Sense.*

Yet 'the old idea of ... a fixed Constitution standing above ... still remained a respectable idea in England in the 1760s.'[161] But just when did the doctrine of parliamentary sovereignty overtake this older view? Was it really established at the time of the 1766 Declaratory Act? The speeches of Lord Camden, and of Burke and Pitt in Parliament suggest not. If not, then the divergence between Britain and America is more intelligible.

3.4.3 The Constitution of the British Empire

The *third* issue is that of how the British Constitution might apply in the colonies. Not everyone accepted that the British Constitution was itself unitary in nature. According to McIlwain,

> It was ... the most far-reaching of the constitutional arguments of Englishmen in the colonies just before the American Revolution that this unitary interpretation of the British constitution was fundamentally false. The true constitution of Britain was not unitary, but federal.[162]

Did the Constitution apply in the colonies in the same way as in mainland Britain, or was there a separate set of constitutional principles for the 'British Empire'? The Bill of Rights and post 1688 constitutional settlement contained no explicit provisions on the status of polities outside of Britain. John Adams, as we know, described the British Empire as a 'new case' in political history.

But in Britain, the view was different. The dominant view in Britain perceived the colonies as a subservient, subordinate extension of the British State, subject to the full authority of the Parliament. This perspective was evident in the Declaratory Act. In this way, the British Empire was understood as a single State, composed of a single people, one Constitution, and one King, and, if the colonies refused to obey Parliament, they were no longer viewed as subjects but as rebels. This response also answered the second question above – British authority was conflated with parliamentary authority, national sovereignty with parliamentary sovereignty.

However, according to an alternative, 'American' theory of Empire, the only *legal* link to Britain was through the King. It was only the existence of a shared monarch that connected the American colonies legally to Britain and, indeed, to each other. So, just as the King-in-Parliament could legislate and impose tax in Britain, so the King-in-the-Massachusetts-legislature could legislate and impose tax in Massachusetts. This approach suggested that colonial assemblies were comparable to the Westminster Parliament. The case of the union of the crowns of Scotland and England was used to support this argument – a monarch could reign over two countries, each with their separate

[161] J Greene, *Constitutional Origins of the American Revolution*, at 178.

[162] C McIlwain, 'The Historical Background of Federal Government', in R Pound (ed.), *Federalism as a Democratic Process* (New Brunswick NJ: Rutgers University Press, 1942) 35.

parliaments. By this argument, Britain might regulate colonial trade – as an 'external' measure (and the Navigation Acts might be justified by 'long usage and acquiescence') – but not impose internal taxation. The implication of this argument was that ultimate constitutional authority, or sovereignty, rested in each of the colonies, which were separate political entities.

3.4.3.1 Local Law in the Colonies

Furthermore, Greene argues we should recognise the distinct nature of local colonial law, in which custom and consensus was authoritative. This indicates an approach to sovereignty that understood it not as the command of the sovereign but instead as determined through vigorous local practice. Greene's argument is that British law was 'anaemic', and difficult to impose without the support of local communities who increasingly interpreted British law as a series of arbitrary measures intended to undermine their constitutional rights. This resistance to Britain, did not, however, lead to a collapse of law in general, because local law retained its full vigour. Public uprisings were perceived as challenging unconstitutional parliamentary statutes, and thus a lawful resistance to illegitimate power.[163]

Although Greene does not make this connection, his approach has much in common with that of Eugen Ehrlich,[164] an early anthropologist, of law. Ehrlich worked in Bukowina at the turn of the twentieth century (a region in modern day Romania, but then part of the Austro-Hungarian empire). His focus was on what he saw as the 'living law' applicable to his community, rather than the official law imposed by the Austro-Hungarian administration, which he found largely irrelevant. Ehrlich's conception of law was in sharp contrast to the legal formalism prevalent in the late nineteenth and early twentieth centuries.[165] The context of Ehrlich's work in the multi-cultural, fragmented, Austrian Empire raises interesting issues of legal pluralism, and I believe his argument works just as well in the diverse, indeterminate circumstances of the first British Empire.

3.4.3.2 The Eighteenth-Century Constitution of the British Empire?

However, this analysis prompts a further question. Even if there were local law operating in the colonies, was there nonetheless a distinct British 'imperial' Constitution (i.e. one distinguishable from the British Constitution)?

Greene's overall suggestion is that the eighteenth-century British Empire comprised three different types of Constitution.[166] First, there existed an (unwritten) British Constitution for the central State, including Wales and Scotland.

[163] Greene, *Constitutional Origins*, especially 'Prologue' and chapter 4.

[164] E Ehrlich, *Gesetz und Lebendes Recht* (Berlin: Duncker and Humblot, 1986 reprint).

[165] Ehrlich's work suffered from Kelsen's critique that 'legal' be used only for norms derivable from one unifying Basic Norm. Ehrlich was, however, later reinstated, e.g. by Gunther Teubner 'Global Bukowina: Legal Pluralism in the World-Society', in G Teubner (ed.), *Global Law without a State* (Brookfield Vt: Dartmouth, 1996).

[166] Greene, *Constitutional Origins*, chapters 1 and 4.

Second, there existed separate provincial Constitutions for Ireland and each of the American colonies, and some other imperial territories. The relationship between these first two was unclear and inexplicit. But Greene also proposes, thirdly, that there also existed an as yet undefined, even unacknowledged 'Imperial Constitution of the British Empire' – according to which authority was divided and unsettled in an ambiguous way between Britain and overseas territories. The innovation comes in describing this as an 'imperial Constitution'. There was no acknowledgement of this imperial Constitution in Britain, where arguments of the logic of undivided sovereignty continued to be used by most of those in power. If some Americans were looking beyond traditional and orthodox theories of sovereignty to try to explain and understand the situation, very few in positions of power in Britain were doing so.

3.4.4 The Rest Is History

Edmund Burke also sought to distinguish the British Constitution from the Constitution of the British Empire. Burke's account set out complementary functions for colonial assemblies and for Parliament. He suggested that:

> The Parliament of Great Britain sits at the head of her extensive empire in two capacities: one of the local legislature of this island, providing for all things at home.... The other, and I think her nobler capacity, is what I call her *imperial character*, in which ... she superintends all the several inferior legislatures, and guides, and controls them all without annihilating any. As all these provincial legislatures are only co-ordinate to each other, they ought all to be subordinate to her.... She is never to intrude into the place of the others, whilst they are equal to the common ends of their institution. But in order to enable parliament to answer all these ends of provident and beneficent superintendence, her powers must be boundless.[167]

At first reading, this suggests complete sovereignty for Westminster. But things were not that simple. For Burke, the Stamp Act, and other taxes, had violated this 'imperial character', the 'nobler capacity' to which he referred. In his *Speech on Conciliation*, Burke argued that Britain was bound by the 'immutable condition, the eternal law, of extensive and detached empire', which requires that authority be lightly asserted.[168] In an earlier publication, *Observations on a Late State of the Nation*,[169] Burke attacked William Knox's[170] concept of sovereignty, which according to Burke, asserted a false homogeneity and equality

[167] Burke, 'Speech on American Taxation', in P Stanlis (ed.), *Selected Writings and Speeches* (Gateway editions, 1997).

[168] Burke, 'Speech on Moving Resolutions for Conciliation with the Colonies', in *Selected Writings* at 137.

[169] Burke's essay 'Observations on a Late Publication entitled "The Present State of the Nation", in *Selected Writings* 6–56.

[170] Knox criticized the repeal of the Stamp Act (L Bellot, *William Knox: The Life and Thought of an Eighteenth-Century Imperialist* (University of Texas Press, 2011)).

across all politically relevant social entities. Rather, for Burke, diversity existed, and different peoples had their own traditions, belief-systems, character, and expectations. Uniformity was the enemy: 'In large bodies, the circulation of power must be less vigorous at the extremities. Nature has said it. The Turk cannot govern Egypt and Arabia and Kurdistan as he governs Thrace.' And so, for Burke: 'The old building stands well enough, though part Gothic, part Grecian, and part Chinese, until an attempt is made to square it into uniformity. Then it may come down upon our heads altogether, in much uniformity of ruin; and great will be the fall thereof.'[171]

But Burke's counsel was ignored, and the rest is history. The American revolution might have signalled independence for the US in 1776, but, on the other side of the Atlantic, it heralded a dissolution, the first break up of Britain. The historian, Linda Colley, explains how the American colonies were perceived in Britain as much more than distant possessions, rather – as 'our people, our brethren', and that American resistance and independence were thus 'a kind of ultimate amputation from the British body politic that has arguably never completely healed over.'[172]

This chapter does not argue that things would have been better if Britain had worked out a more coherent concept of sovereignty in the eighteenth century and applied it consistently to North America. However, there exists a dishonesty in claiming the sovereignty to impose coercion when that sovereignty cannot be explained and justified. In the absence of coherence, what then existed was an assertion of power and brute force that was often to prevail in the British Empire.

In conclusion then, the argument in this chapter is based on two contentions. First, that great ambiguity existed as to the constitutional status of the American colonies. Second, that there also existed ambiguity over the status of parliamentary sovereignty in Britain in the mid-eighteenth century. Britain lost the American colonies because it insisted on asserted a sovereignty of legislation over America that it could not justify.

[171] Burke, *Observations*.

[172] L Colley, *Acts of Union and Disunion* (London: Profile Books, 2014) at 111. This amputation was of course expressed literally as bodily dismemberment in Franklin's 1766 cartoon 'Magna Britannia Reduc'd'. See also, Neal Ascherson, 'The Long Brexit Ordeal Will Finish Off the Break-up of Britain', *The Guardian*, 27 October 2019.

4

The Constitutional Status of the British Empire and Commonwealth

4.1 The First British Empire

4.1.1 Introduction

Throughout the stages of the British Empire and later Commonwealth, its governance varied and followed no uniform model. Not all its instantiations were examples of direct rule from the centre or metropole (i.e. London). Many of Britain's overseas territories exhibited a degree of autonomy, or self-government, and we shall come onto that.

When did Britain first lay down the roots of its empire? Before distant places were colonized, Ireland and Wales were subdued, colonized or amalgamated with England. Frederick Madden, editor of the copious eight volume *Select Documents on the Constitutional History of the British Empire and Commonwealth*,[1] traced the origins of Britain's empire to the twelfth century, locating precedents that would influence later practice. In medieval times, solutions were found to the problem of governing territory from a distance. Devices such as the royal Charter, issued under the royal prerogative, granted privileges to medieval towns, or communal bodies. Charters were then used later, in the context of Empire, to authorize companies, such as the East India Company, or Massachusetts Bay Company, to pursue ventures abroad. One of the first English uses of the term 'Empire' is found in the 1533 Act in Restraint of Appeals (24 Henry VIII, c. 12) which forbade all appeals to the Church of Rome, and notably declared in its Preamble that 'this realm of England is an empire, entire of itself', thus stressing England's complete independence from any other jurisdiction.

Writers have distinguished first, second, third and even fourth British Empires,[2] suggesting that the Empire was distinct in character at different stages of its history. In this chapter we will commence with the traditionally understood 'first British Empire' that came to being in the seventeenth

[1] F Madden with D Fieldhouse (eds.), *Select Documents on the Constitutional History of the British Empire and Commonwealth* (Westport, CT: Greenwood Press, 1985 et seq.).

[2] E.g. John Darwin, *Unfinished Empire: The Global Expansion of Britain* (Allen Lane, 2012).

century, finding greater fruition in the eighteenth century.[3] In the seventeenth century, the British Empire was inchoate. It took time for the settlements in North America to develop, for the East India Company to grow into its vast eighteenth-century form, and for the metropole to develop systems of governance to administer the colonies and overseas trade. Whenever it began, this first Empire was at its height in the mid-eighteenth century, but disintegrated with the loss of the American colonies. A second Empire, more focussed in the east, then rose to take its place. According to Marshall,

> Throughout its long usage there has been a rough consensus as to what is meant by the term 'first British Empire' … It was an Atlantic Empire, based on North America and the West Indies. The spread of British dominion into Asia, Africa, and Australasia was one of the indications that the first Empire was giving way to a second one.[4]

4.1.2 Scope

It is common to describe the British Empire of the seventeenth and eighteenth centuries as an 'Atlantic' one, centred in North America and the Caribbean. (India is not included, or at least is considered separately – as it will be in this chapter.) As a result, its historiography tends to have been heavily influenced by US academics, and many of their arguments were considered in the last chapter. In the seventeenth and eighteenth centuries, many English, and later British, settled in North America, building on original settlements in Virginia and New England. This first British Empire was commercial in orientation, and the Crown played an important role in earlier settlements (many colonies had notably royal names – e.g. Carolina and Georgia), bestowing trading monopolies on corporations. The Navigation Acts underpinned the system, ensuring that trade between Britain and the colonies was carried only on English, and then British, ships. The West Indies were also colonized in the seventeenth century – with settlements in Barbados, the Leeward Islands, and Jamaica. In the east, the British East India Company was granted a monopoly of English trade east of the Cape of Good Hope from 1600, with trading settlements on the coast of India. This Empire expanded as a result of war. New York was surrendered by the Dutch in the seventeenth century but the main gains came from the French. As a result of defeats of the French in the Seven Years War, Britain gained much of Canada, the Floridas – effectively removing the French from North America – as well as more West Indian islands. The French presence in India was also

[3] See e.g. A Berriedale-Keith, *Constitutional History of the first British Empire* (Oxford: Clarendon Press, 1930); *Cambridge History of the British Empire*, vol. 1 *The Old Empire from the Beginnings to 1783*, vol. 1 (Cambridge University Press, 1929). Also, *The Oxford History of the British Empire* (*OHBE*), *The Origins of Empire* ed. N Canny; and vol. II, *The Eighteenth Century* ed. PJ Marshall; B Bailyn, 'The First British Empire: From Cambridge to Oxford' (2000) 57 William and Mary Quarterly 647–660.

[4] PJ Marshall, 'The First British Empire', in *OHBE*, vol. V, *Historiography*, ed. R Winks.

greatly weakened, enabling Britain to expand there. The Empire's population also greatly expanded – from about 265,000 in British North America at the beginning of the eighteenth century, to 2,300,000 by 1770.[5]

The First Empire was also heavily dependent on slaves, who were largely engaged in crop cultivation (i.e. sugar, cotton, tobacco, and rum). It is estimated that about 3.4m were transported as slaves by the British slave trade from West Africa to North America between 1662 and 1807 (when the slave trade was abolished in Britain).[6] Slaves were sold and the proceeds used to buy crops which were shipped back to Britain where they were in great demand. These crops were in turn sold to buy British manufactured goods which then were sold in West Africa to purchase slaves. And so the process continued.

4.1.3 Governance

4.1.3.1 Introductory

What form did governance of the first British Empire take? There was no codified Constitution for Great Britain, let alone any written document that set out a clear division of powers between Britain and her colonies. Nor was there any central authority with the overall task of setting a comprehensive colonial policy. So, we have to piece together the elements of governance, from components both in the metropole and in the colonies. And the view was often quite different in the centre and in the periphery.

Much of the metropolitan governance of Empire was carried out by officials of the Crown – Secretaries of State, or administrative bodies such as the Board of Trade, and it is in their records that one must search for traces of how this first British Empire was governed. Edmund Burke was, however, dismissive of characterizing imperial governance according to such bureaucratic practices:

> Do not dream that your Letters of office, and your instructions, and your suspending clauses are the things that hold together the great contexture of this mysterious whole. These things do not make your government … It is the spirit of the English constitution which, infused through the mighty mass, pervades, feeds, unites, invigorates, vivifies every part of the empire, even down to the minutest member.[7]

Burke refers to imperial governance as 'a mysterious whole', warning that 'the spirit of the English [sic] Constitution' not official paperwork, kept the Empire together. Indeed, perhaps such a shared belief was necessary to retain British North America in the Empire. When Americans lost their faith in that spirit, North America became lost to Britain. However, references to a 'mysterious whole' and to the 'spirit' of (an already unwritten, and less than transparent)

[5] Figures from PJ Marshall, 'Introduction', *OHBE*, vol. II. [6] Ibid.

[7] E Burke, 'Speech on Conciliation with America', 22 March 1775, in *The Writings and Speeches of Edmund Burke* (Oxford: Oxford University Press, 1981) 136.

Constitution are cryptic and ultimately unenlightening. And the role played by bureaucracy, by documents, by officials, in the British Empire should not be underplayed. It could not have functioned without them, even if they presented an overwhelming, somewhat incoherent, paper trail.

Overall, as described by Steele, 'Until 1760 effective administrative power remained diffuse, flexible, and limited.'[8] Perhaps this makes sense if one interprets the first Empire as a trading organization, defined by commercial regulations. But to understand further how this actually functioned, it is helpful to consider governance of the British Empire from both the metropolitan and colonial perspective.

4.1.3.2 Metropole

Imperial governance was taking shape during the first British Empire, but which British institutions were most involved in its development? Berriedale-Keith, perhaps the earliest formally to describe the constitutional governance of the first British Empire, considered the following metropolitan institutions important: the Crown; the Privy Council; the Secretary of State; the Board of Trade; the Treasury Board; the Commissioners of Customs; the Admiralty and War Office; the Imperial (Westminster) Parliament.[9] But as already stated, there was no overall policy, and no central constitutional document setting out imperial law and policy, so imperial governance developed in a fragmented way.

4.1.3.2.1 The Crown and Associated Bodies

The formal foundation for Empire was the authority of the Crown. It was the Crown rather than Parliament which was recognized as having supreme authority in the earlier British Empire, a point constantly made by American colonists in the eighteenth century. And so, persons and managerial offices deriving their authority from the Crown, such as the Secretary of State, Board of Trade, and Privy Council, supervised the governance of colonies. This continued to be the case even when Parliament asserted its ultimate sovereignty more intrusively against American colonies in the 1760s.

The Board of Trade was a significant body with a notable role[10] (indeed John Locke was one of its members) and many managerial functions in the colonies. These included drawing up instructions for royal governors, hearing petitions and appeals from the colonies and reviewing colonial legislation. But it lacked any legislative powers. The Board was a royally appointed body, answerable to

[8] Ian K Steele, 'The Anointed, the Appointed, and the Elected: Governance of the British Empire, 1689–1784', in OHBE, vol. II, at 105.

[9] Berriedale-Keith, *Constitutional History of the First British Empire*, 'Table of Contents'.

[10] See AK Siddique, 'Governance through Documents: The Board of Trade, its Archive, and the Imperial Constitution of the Eighteenth-Century British Atlantic World' (2020) 59 Jl of British Studies 264–290; K MacMillan, *The Atlantic Imperial Constitution* (New York: Palgrave Macmillan, 2011).

the Privy Council, and invested with the task of 'promoting the Trade of this our Kingdom' and 'Inspecting and Improving Our Plantations in America.'[11] By its practices, even in the absence of a written Constitution, imperial standards could be established and enforced by the Board's activities.

The King's ministers were also important. Earlier, the Secretary of State for the Southern Department had extensive responsibilities for both eighteenth-century Empire and Europe. In 1768, the post of a dedicated Colonial Secretary was created, with the specific task of dealing with the troublesome American colonies, a task at which all such secretaries seem to have failed. This post was formally renamed Secretary of State for War and the Colonies in 1801. Other Government departments also played an influential part – for example, the Treasury's role could be critical, given that it collected both British and colonial customs duties and excise taxes. Other officials with a significant role were the law officers of the Crown, namely, the Attorney General and Solicitor General, who were frequently called on to provide opinions on tricky legal issues from various parts of the Empire.[12]

4.1.3.2.2 Courts

Courts played a potentially significant role. Berriedale-Keith alluded to 'the glory of English jurisprudence' and contended that English common law was the root of the laws of the Empire.[13] Charters set out that settlers had the right to English law, and in *Calvin's Case,* Coke had famously held the King's subjects outside England had access to the common law.[14] Nonetheless, the protection of English law overseas was not so clear, as eighteenth-century disputes with American colonists had illustrated. There were of course high-profile legal decisions. Some caselaw related to whether territories were conquered or settled, and if so, how this might affect the power of the Crown to make law for them.[15] Other British litigation of note included the 1750 case of *Penn* v. *Baltimore,* which concerned the boundaries of Pennsylvania and Maryland, and *Somersett's case*, in which Lord Mansfield declared that slavery was an institution so odious and contrary to natural law that in the absence of such legislation in England, the slave relation was of no effect there.[16]

However, as Hulsebosch notes, 'Jurists in the first British Empire never developed a coherent body of imperial law or liberties. The empire remained a byzantine network of territories, jurisdictions, institutions, and peoples, which

[11] The National Archives (TNA), CO 391/9, 15 May 1696.

[12] E Cavanagh, 'The Imperial Constitution of the Law Officers of the Crown 1719–1774' (2019) 47(4) Jl of Imperial and C'wealth History 619–651; WS Holdsworth, 'The Early History of the Attorney and Solicitor General' (1918–1919) 13 Ill. LR 602.

[13] A Berriedale Keith, *The Constitution, Administration and Laws of the Empire* (London: W. Collins Sons & co., 1924) 8.

[14] *Calvin's Case* [1608] 77 ER 377.

[15] *Craw* v. *Ramsey* [1681] 1073 KB; *Blankard* v. *Galdy* 87 Eng Rep; *Rex* v. *Vaughan* [1769] 98 Eng Rep; *Campbell* v. *Hall* [1774] Cowper, 204.

[16] 1 Ves. Sen. 444 [1750]; 98 Eng. Rep. 499 [1771].

hindered the emergence of a unified imperial law.'[17] There was no unitary law for the first British Empire. With the exception of a couple of decisions, Berriedale-Keith's 'glory of English jurisprudence' failed to shine.

4.1.3.2.3 Parliament

Parliament was supportive of royal power in the earlier British Empire, adopting legislation which increased the power of the Crown in the colonies. This included the Navigation Acts, which strengthened the enforcement of Imperial trade regulations. However, by mid-eighteenth century, the British Parliament was truly flexing its muscles, shifting from its earlier approach of 'salutary neglect.' As well as the 1765 Stamp Act and 1766 Declaratory Act for North America, Parliament also passed the 1773 Regulating Act in an attempt to impose more control on the East India Company. Such legislation highlighted the question of how to interpret the constitutional status of the Empire. The resistance of Britain's North American colonies, which led to war and the breakup of the first British Empire, was followed by change in Ireland, when in 1783 Parliament renounced its sovereignty over the Irish Parliament (23 Geo III c 28). Parliament also formally declared that it would not impose any tax or duty on any of its colonies in America in the Taxation of Colonies Act 1778 (18 Geo III c12). However, Britain officially accepted no colony as its equal, and this did not change until the 1926 Balfour Declaration and 1931 Statute of Westminster. The term 'imperial' is used in this book, indicating occasions when Parliament legislated not only for the UK, but also for its overseas territories.

However, there existed clear practical limits to Parliament's powers. These included the strength of local legislatures in North America; the power of private bodies (e.g. the East India Company); as well as the weak and diffuse nature of colonial administration; and not to forget the failure of the British military to prevail in the American war of independence.

4.1.3.3 Governance in the Colonies

There was considerable use of royal Charters,[18] which authorized private parties to settle, manage and profit from overseas territories, and gave their recipients considerable independence and power. They also made grants of land in many of the Atlantic Charters, even although the Crown's claim to territory in North America was by no means clear. The language of Charters also set out basic principles of colonial government, permitting colonists to use English law to administer and manage the territory. In this way, earlier colonists tended to have a concept of the English Constitution as providing

[17] D Hulsebosch, 'The Ancient Constitution and the Expanding Empire: Sir Edward Coke's British Jurisprudence' 21(3) (2003) Law and History Review 479.

[18] Ken MacMillan, 'Imperial Constitutions: Sovereignty and Law in the British Atlantic', in *Britain's Oceanic Empire: Atlantic and Indian Ocean Worlds, c. 1550–1850*, HV Bowen, E Mancke, and JG Reid (eds.), (Cambridge: Cambridge University Press, 2012) 69–97, at 74–81.

customary rights and liberties that could not be violated by the sovereign.[19] Many colonial Charters included a proviso that laws should not be 'contrary to the Laws and Statutes of this our Realm of England.' Although Charters permitted colonies substantial autonomy from the metropole, it was also made clear that sovereignty lay with the King, whose imperial role was usually described in the Charter's Preamble.

By the late seventeenth century, most colonial government was using a three-fold structure, of Governor, Council, and Assembly. Governors were royal appointments, exercising delegated powers of the Crown in the colonies. However, colonies were required to submit new laws to the Privy Council in London for approval (in an arrangement similar to Poynings' Law, which required all Irish Parliament draft Bills be submitted to the Privy Council).[20] Colonial Assemblies tended to be locally elected bodies with some sort of role in legislation (often merely consultative) and local taxation. Members of Assemblies were elected by wealthier local property owners, and increasingly saw themselves as an alternative site of legitimacy challenging the role of the Westminster Parliament to pass laws for them.

4.1.4 Identity/Ideology

It is not clear that there existed any common identity in the earlier British Empire, although it has been suggested that Protestantism (including a perception of Catholic France as a deadly rival), liberty, Britain's maritime and commercial nature, and even the dissemination of civilization, were perceived as unifying factors.[21]

Protestantism was a motivating force in seventeenth- and eighteenth-century Britain.[22] However, even if Britain was assuredly anti-Catholic (and this would ignore the great majority of Catholic Irish) there existed no unified Protestantism. The Anglican Church in England was very different from the Scottish Presbyterian Kirk, and dissatisfaction with lack of church reform in England had led many Puritans to emigrate from England to North America in the early seventeenth century. England could not claim to be the leader of Protestant Europe and had not proved to be its saviour in the Thirty Years War.

Liberty has also been suggested as significant in defining an imperial identity for Britain. Yet, it was not so clear in what exactly this British liberty consisted. There was a tendency to cite English common law as guaranteeing English liberties, and Henry Care, seventeenth-century Protestant polemicist, declared,

[19] Jack Greene, *Peripheries and Center: Constitutional Development in the Extended Polities of the British Empire and the United States, 1607–1788* (Athens: University of Georgia Press, 1986).

[20] However, colonial assemblies could get round this issue by passing temporary laws which expired before the time for imperial review.

[21] E.g. D Armitage, *Ideological Origins of the British Empire* (Cambridge: Cambridge University Press, 2000) although Armitage was himself sceptical of some of these claims.

[22] L Colley, *Britons* (New Haven Ct.: Yale University Press, 1992) 18.

> The Constitution of our English Government (the best in the World) is no Arbitrary *Tyranny* … in France and other Nations the meer Will of the Prince is Law; his Word takes off any Man's Head, imposes Taxes, seizes any Man's Estate, when, how, and as often as he lists … [But] in *England*, the Law is both the *Measure and the Bond* of every Subjects Duty and Allegiance, each man having a fixed Fundamental Right born with him, as to *Freedom of his Person*, and *Property in his Estate*, which he cannot be deprived of, but either by his consent, or some Crime, for which the Law has Impos'd such a Penalty or Forfeiture.[23]

This book was undoubted Whig propaganda, but it became popular in the American colonies and did much to raise the profile of Magna Carta in English law. But for all the positive and progressive rhetoric, liberty had its conservative sense too, illustrated by some British reactions to the American and French revolutions. Although Burke declared that, 'Without freedom [the Empire] would not be the British Empire,'[24] many (including Burke) argued that revolution destroyed liberty and ended in tyranny.

Thirdly, Britain was perceived to be not only Protestant and free, but also crucially a *maritime* nation. Hugo Grotius might have argued in *Mare Liberum* (1609) that the seas should be open to all, but the image of Britannia ruling the waves became ever more popular. The British merchant fleet became the largest in the world by the later eighteenth century. Maritime power was closely linked to freedom and also commerce – another ingredient in the alchemy of Britain's imperial identity. Many saw trade with the colonies as responsible for the growth in Britain's wealth. As expressed by the Marquis of Halifax in 1667, 'Wee are a very little spot in the Map of the World, and made a great figure onely by trade, which is the Creature of Liberty.'[25] Adam Smith wrote in *The Wealth of Nations*, that, already, by 1600, England was 'a great trading country' with a 'mercantile capital [that] was very great'.[26] The proliferation of trading companies in the early days of Empire, such as the Muscovy Company, East India Company, Virginia Company, Royal African Company, and South Sea Company are testimony to the importance of trade, the establishment of new markets being a crucial feature of Empire.

Finally, for many, the British Empire was not only built on the above features but also seen as a force for civilization, to bestow colonies with English superiority and benevolence – a perception that was to grow larger in the nineteenth-century Empire.

However, most obviously incompatible with this civilizing project, this empire of liberty, were the brutal and exploitative elements which supported its profits. Many peoples of the first British Empire came from Africa, as

[23] Henry Care, *English Liberties: Or, the Freeborn Subject's Inheritance* (London: Printed by G. Larkin, for Benjamin Harris, 1680) 1–2.

[24] Burke, 'Speech on the Declaratory Act', 3 February 1766. Also Burke, *Reflections on the Revolution in France* (Oxford: Oxford World's Classics, reissue edition 2009).

[25] George Savile, Marquis of Halifax, *Rough Draught of a New Model at Sea* (London, 1694).

[26] Adam Smith, *An Inquiry into the Nature and Causes of the Wealth of Nations* (1776).

enslaved persons, and slavery became more and more important in the North American colonies and West Indies as the eighteenth century progressed. Until the growth of the anti-slavery movement in the 1780s, there was little opposition in Britain to slavery in the colonies. Nor of course, were native Americans given much, if any, consideration by the British.

4.1.5 Loss of the First British Empire and the Transition to the Second

Britain‘s loss of its North American colonies has been described in the last chapter. This might have been thought a catastrophe from which the British Empire could not recover. But this was not the case. Shortly after, the French Revolution occurred, inflicting severe military and economic loss on France (Britain's traditional rival) and many other European countries. Britain had also undergone an industrial revolution, making it highly competitive economically. But a reordering of Britain's Empire was also taking place, one that would lead to its apex in the nineteenth century. Vincent Harlow wrote of a permutation in the geographic focus of the British Empire, using the phrase 'the swing to the east.'[27]

But if there was a geographical reordering of Empire after the loss of the thirteen colonies, was there also a realization in the metropole that imperial governance needed to change? Certainly not immediately. Parliament gave up its right to tax colonies in 1778, but there were few other major changes in governance. The West Indies did not gain greater autonomy, but in fact became Crown colonies, a system which accorded greater direct rule to the Crown. There was no wholesale attempt to reform Imperial rule. In fact, as India became more clearly a part of the British Empire, rule there was autocratic, not autonomous and representative. It was not until well into the nineteenth century that 'responsible government' and autonomy were developed in what were to become the Dominions.

By the start of the nineteenth century, despite of the loss of the American colonies, many people lived under British rule, the great majority of them now in India. And it is to India that we now turn.

4.2 The British in India

4.2.1 From 1600 to the Mid-Eighteenth Century

The British Empire in India evolved from the actions of the British East India Company (EIC). From the seventeenth century, the Company had founded trading settlements (later known as Presidencies) in Surat, Bombay, Madras, and Calcutta. At this stage, India as a State did not exist – it was a land mass divided into territories, much of it controlled by the Mughal Empire.

[27] V Harlow, *The Founding of the Second British Empire, 1763–1793* (London: Longmans, Green & Co., 1952); PJ Marshall, 'Britain without America – A Second Empire?', in *OHBE*, vol. II.

These EIC settlements arose from a desire to strengthen trade between Asia and England. There was a constant demand in Europe for Asian commodities such as spices and textiles, whose trade could prove extremely profitable. But such commerce was a long term and risky business. Permanent trading posts were needed to secure the trade. So expensive and risky was the business that only large enterprises, with secure resources, could take on the venture. And this is how the British East India Company came into being. It was a private trading Company, but by the eighteenth century it had gained both territorial and political power in India, after victories at Plassey in 1757 and Buxar in 1764, when it gained the revenue (or *Diwani*) of wealthy Bengal. The British Government then had to determine its own relationship with the Company – and we consider that later in this section, but first we consider the Company's origins.

4.2.1.1 Founding of the East India Company and Earlier Governance

As Dalrymple comments, 'British relations with India actually began not with diplomacy and the meeting of envoys, but with a trade mission.'[28] In 1600, a group of merchants and adventurers, fired up by Dutch successes in Asia,[29] were granted a royal Charter,[30] giving them a 15 year (renewable) monopoly on trade to the East (on condition the trade was profitable to the realm). However, as Ferdinand Mount remarked, 'The charter … had a chilling arrogance about it, which was to cast a long shadow. The Company was to enjoy a monopoly on trade with all parts of Asia "not in the possession of a Christian Prince". The Queen gave the Company full powers to fine, ban and even lock up "interlopers" and anyone who presumed to interfere with its rights and privileges.'[31]

The EIC was set up as a joint stock company.[32] Thus it was not a family concern, or guild of traders, but an association of subscribers or investors – much wider in its composition and capital raising potential – who pooled their resources. It was managed from London and relied for finance largely on investments from the London business community. In this way, ownership (by subscribers or stockholders) of the EIC was distinct from its management. Indeed, much of the commentary on the EIC focusses on its nature as a large company, and (more recently) analogizes its position with the early twenty-first-century financial crisis, as a concern that was 'too big to fail'.[33]

However, in deriving its authority from a royal Charter, the EIC was not unlike many other establishments which established settler colonies across

[28] W Dalrymple, *The Anarchy: The Relentless Rise of the East India Company* (London: Bloomsbury, 2019) xxvi.

[29] The Dutch formed their own, very successful, East India Company, although by the eighteenth century, the British EIC far outstripped it.

[30] *Charter granted by Queen Elizabeth, to the Governor and Company of Merchants of London, Trading into the East-Indies*, 31 December, in the 43rd year of Her Reign. Anno Domini, 1600.

[31] Ferdinand Mount, 'Umbrageousness' (2017) 39(17) *London Review of Books*.

[32] The joint stock company, unlike the Charter, only dated from Elizabethan times.

[33] N Robins, *The Corporation that Changed the World: How the East India Company Shaped the Modern Multinational* (London: Pluto Press, 2012).

the Atlantic. The EIC was, like many of those entities, granted authority of law-making, establishing courts, building fortifications, coining money, declaring war, and conducting diplomacy. And, as time passed, the EIC's jurisdictional authority grew, and it became responsible for an ever greater array of civil and governance functions (as well as commercial ones). In return, the British Government might expect considerable loans on favourable terms, or gifts, from the Company. The EIC's headquarters were in Leadenhall street, London (now the Lloyd's building). The Company was to elect annually one Governor and 24 directors, which together made up its 'Court' and managed the Company's funds. The Company cultivated its authority with symbols of grandeur and solemnity – referring to itself as 'the honourable company', establishing diplomatic relations through embassies, and producing its own coins, medals and flags. The large quantity of EIC documents – reports, commissions, letters – are testimony to its bureaucratic governance in the seventeenth and eighteenth centuries. Nonetheless, the EIC also relied strongly on what we would now term 'outsourced labour', not least for sustaining a military force, and it was this powerful indigenous army that enabled the EIC to be so successful in its territorial conquests. However, the EIC was not exactly a private company as we understand one today. Its Charter required it to act not only in the interests of private shareholders but also for the good of the realm. So, this made its nature and mission more complex and composite.

What emerges from this brief description of the Company's organization is its hybrid structure. As Stern remarked: 'Company authority was constituted by the same sort of complex and overlapping forms of authority familiar in the rest of the British world overseas'.[34]

By the eighteenth century, the EIC had become well established, and by far the largest of Britain's overseas chartered trading companies. The EIC's initial interest was (as its name suggests) the East Indies (roughly present-day Indonesia) where it hoped to obtain spices. But there they found too much competition from the Dutch and Portuguese and so moved to India, where there were superb textiles to be traded. The EIC originally acted in partnership with Indian agents, intermixing with locals, very often adopting indigenous practices. As time passed, the EIC became more dominant, partly as a result of the declining fortunes of the Mughal empire. Later, the Company would (illegally) trade opium from India for tea in China, fighting opium wars with China to preserve its trade, as well as taking the port of Hong Kong. This tea in turn made its way around the globe, both to Britain and America. It was EIC tea that was thrown overboard into Boston harbour, thus setting off the American war of independence.

[34] Philip Stern, 'Company, State, and Empire: Governance and Regulatory Frameworks in Asia', in HV Bowen, E Mancke, and JG Reid (eds.), *Britain's Oceanic Empire: Atlantic and Indian Ocean Worlds, c.1550–1850* (Cambridge: Cambridge University Press, 2012) 141.

4.2.2 Plassey and the Acquisition of the *Diwani*

Marshall observed: 'The history of the British in Asia during the eighteenth century seems to fall into two clearly demarcated phases. A long period of stability ended in mid-century, when the British shifted from apparently peaceful trade to wars and conquests in India'.[35]

These wars and conquests were highly profitable for the EIC, which most famously, under Robert Clive, was victorious at Plassey in 1757, and then defeated the Mughal emperor, Shah Alam II, at Buxar in 1764. A settlement was agreed under the Treaty of Allahabad of 1765, by which Shah Alam gave the EIC the *Diwani* of Bengal, Bihar and Orissa (i.e. the right to tax collection). Under this 'treaty' (the terms of which Clive apparently dictated to Shah Alam) the Company took jurisdiction over roughly 20 million persons in Bengal, a tax revenue of £3 million, and Shah Alam issued a *Firman* (the Persian term for decree) authorizing the EIC to collect and administer the revenue. With this settlement, British influence extended almost as far as Delhi, giving the EIC a dominant position in India, and turning them into the effective rulers in Bengal. Although the Diwani was theoretically held in vassalage from the Mughal, the EIC was in control. Indeed, the grant of the Diwani is very often seen as the acquisition of sovereignty by the British in India. Robert Clive apparently remarked to William Pitt the elder: 'So large a sovereignty may possibly be an object too extensive for a mercantile company; and it is to be feared they are not of themselves able, without the nation's assistance, to maintain so wide a dominion.'[36] However, it would be a few years until Parliament absorbed the import of this statement.

Clive introduced a system of dual administration in Bengal, which continued up to 1772. This system acknowledged that the EIC derived its power in India both from its Crown Charters and from the Mughal Firman. Under this dual system, the British were responsible for revenue collection and military affairs in Bengal, while civil administration remained largely with the Nawab of Bengal. In this way, the fiction of Mughal sovereignty was continued, but the system separated EIC power from responsibility for administration of the province. From this point, things moved quickly, and within less than half a century, most of the subcontinent was subdued. The EIC rapidly increased its army to 260,000 men by 1803, mostly locally recruited sepoys. However, the story is not an edifying one. Bengal was a hugely rich area, but Company officials quickly proceeded to plunder and exploit it, in the process doing nothing to mitigate one of Bengal's very worst famines, which killed millions of people.

[35] PJ Marshall, 'The British in Asia: Trade to Dominion, 1700–1765', in *OHBE*, vol. II at 491.

[36] WS Taylor and JH Pringle (eds.), *The Correspondence of William Pitt, Earl of Chatham*, 4 vols. (London: John Murray, 1838–1840) I, 389–90.

4.2.3 The East India Company in Crisis in the 1760s and 1770s

Notwithstanding the huge revenue from the *Diwani*, the EIC was quickly in debt, and the Company faced collapse. In its both its headquarters in London and offices in India there was corruption, and the EIC was often brutal in conduct in India. Much Bengal wealth went straight into the pockets of EIC men, and those who became spectacularly wealthy in this way were derided in Britain as 'nabobs'.[37] In particular, Robert Clive, victor of Plassey, and sometime Governor of Bengal, profited hugely from the drain on Bengal's wealth. It was quite common for 'nabobs' who made fortunes in India to return to Britain and become MPs (often using Britain's corrupt electoral system to get elected to 'pocket' or 'rotten' boroughs) thus creating the perception of a corrupt and powerful EIC clique in Parliament. However, Robert Clive was reviled for corrupt practices and subjected to a parliamentary inquiry and fierce attack by General John Burgoyne in 1773.[38] Clive survived the inquiry but committed suicide shortly after, in 1774.

By the 1760s, the EIC encountered hostile attention at Westminster, and Parliament sought greater authority over colonial governance. The British Government was jealous of the huge Bengal revenues and keen to proclaim its sovereignty overseas. But the sovereignty issue proved hard to settle and, after bitter negotiations, in 1767 the EIC agreed to an annual payment of £400,000 to the Treasury, in return for the right to continue governing Bengal. However, matters could not rest because the EIC very quickly fell into worse financial straits, and it owed money to the Crown. Several parliamentary inquiries ensued, including a 'Secret Committee', which concluded nine (critical) reports on EIC affairs.[39]

4.2.3.1 The East India Company Loan and Regulating Act 1773

In July 1772, EIC directors applied for a very large loan from the Bank of England. The Bank was reluctant, yet the EIC really was too big to fail, and it got the bailout – but at a cost. In 1773, Parliament passed two laws – the East India Company Loan Act (13 Geo. III c64) and the East India Company Regulating Act (13 Geo III c63) – which together loaned money to the Company in exchange for recognition of Britain's ultimate authority over EIC territories and closer government supervision of EIC affairs.

The Regulating Act established a much more centralized government in India by creating the post of Governor-General of Bengal, who, balanced by a Supreme Council in Bengal of four members (appointed by the Crown and EIC) was

[37] This word derives from the Indian 'nawab', who were the Indian rulers in provinces such as Bengal.

[38] See further, Maya Jasanoff, *Edge of Empire: Conquest and Collection in the East 1750–1850* (Harper Perennial, 2006) 39–41; Dalrymple, in *The Anarchy*, describes Clive as an 'unstable sociopath'.

[39] In *Reports from Committees of the House of Commons*, III and IV.

to have overall authority over the Company's territories. The Act introduced a Supreme Court in Calcutta, so as to more effectively inculcate British law in India. It also provided for ministers in London to review all EIC despatches from India and further regulations prohibited EIC officials from involvement in private trade or receiving bribes or gifts from Indians. However, the Regulating Act did not assert formal direct Crown rule over territories in India[40] and Lord North in fact considered it only a first step in formal government supervision over the EIC. But the American war of independence intervened, leaving little time for consideration of Indian affairs. The Tea Act 1773 (13 Geo 3 c44), which was so resisted in the American colonies, was adopted in an effort to aid the EIC's troubled finances, granting the EIC a monopoly on tea sales in America. However, this impacted colonial merchants and inspired resistance including the Boston tea party. In any case, the Regulating Act proved unsatisfactory. There was almost continual conflict between the Supreme Council and Governor General, and the Supreme Court's jurisdiction was also unclear, failing to provide a clear demarcation between the application of English and Bengal law.

4.2.3.2 The 1784 India Act

By the 1780s, highly critical parliamentary reports appeared, and it became clear government must intervene far more directly in Company affairs. And of course, Britain had lost the North American colonies and had to come to terms with that. In 1784, William Pitt the younger noted the significance of India 'had increased in proportion to the losses sustained by the dismemberment of other great possessions.' At the same time, there was a growing public perception that abuses and mismanagement in the East might corrupt British politics and harm Britain. Pitt summarized the complexities of the situation in India: 'In it were involved the prosperity and strength of this country; the happiness of the natives of those valuable territories in India which belonged to England; *and finally the constitution of England* itself.'[41]

But the first attempt at more effective legislation had failed. In 1783, the King refused to accept the new British coalition government, finding them politically uncongenial, and threatened to abdicate.[42] Although he did subsequently grudgingly accept them, he was bitterly opposed to Fox's India Bill of 1783 (in which Burke had an important hand) which would have rendered the EIC accountable to Parliament. In promoting this Bill in December 1783, Burke declared that: '*Magna Charta* is a charter to restrain power and destroy monopoly. The East India charter is a charter to establish monopoly and create

[40] HV Bowen, 'A Question of Sovereignty? The Bengal Land Revenue Issue, 1765–67' (1988) 16 JICH 171.

[41] William Cobbett, *Parliamentary History of England*, XXIV, col. 1086. Italics added.

[42] John Cannon, *The Fox-North Coalition: Crisis of the Constitution, 1782–4* (Cambridge: Cambridge University Press, 1969) 99.

power.'[43] Although the House of Commons voted for the Bill, the King ensured that the House of Lords rejected it. When this happened, he then forced the coalition out of office, and called for Pitt to form an administration. This is not the first time we have seen the King frustrating a significant reform – his refusal to countenance Catholic Emancipation to accompany the 1800 Act of Union with Ireland arguably tainted that Union from the start. For whatever reason, the King prevented the EIC coming under greater parliamentary control. This led to great bitterness from those politicians ejected from office, and Burke's fierce conduct towards Warren Hastings has sometimes been attributed to the aggravation caused by this constitutional incident.

Pitt did, however, manage to get his 1784 India Act (24 Geo III c25) adopted by Parliament. This created a new committee of six government-appointed Commissioners, known as the Board of Control, to monitor, revise and direct the Company's policies, and thus strengthened government power over the EIC. However, it did not go as far as Fox's proposed India Bill, nor did it settle the issue of EIC sovereignty.

4.2.4 The Impeachment of Warren Hastings

In addition to the 1784 India Act's introduction of a Board of Control over EIC activities, a high profile impeachment also ensued, placing the EIC, and its governance, in the spotlight. Warren Hastings, EIC employee and first Governor-General of Bengal until 1785, was impeached in Parliament in 1787. Dalrymple remarks that 'it was the nearest the British ever got to putting the EIC on trial. They did so with one of their greatest orators at the helm.... Edmund Burke.'[44] Burke had already portrayed EIC misrule in India as a tyranny destructive of both Indian economy and society.[45] There is some irony in this, as Burke had in the past lauded both the EIC and Clive's gains, with the words 'I think there is something of a divine providence in it'.[46] But now Burke's manner was very different.

Warren Hastings' tenure as Governor-General of Bengal had been contentious. Hastings had attempted to reform the EIC system, but without great success. He had tried to restore features of Mughal rule, rather than imposing British law, and criticized the introduction of the new Calcutta Supreme Court. Indeed Hastings had corresponded with Lord Mansfield, defending Hindu and Moslem laws, which he considered 'as comprehensive and as well defined, as that of most states in Europe'.[47] Although Dalrymple acknowledges

[43] E Burke, 'Speech on Fox's India Bill', in *The Writings and Speeches of Edmund Burke*, vol. 5 (Oxford: Clarendon Press, 1991) 384.

[44] Dalrymple, *The Anarchy*, 308; PJ Marshall, *The Impeachment of Warren Hastings* (Oxford: Oxford University Press, 1965).

[45] Burke, 'Speech on Fox's India Bill'.

[46] Paul Langford (ed.), *The Writings and Speeches of Edmund Burke* (Oxford University Press, 1981) at 5.2.

[47] Hastings to Lord Mansfield, 21 March 1774, in GR Gleig (ed.), *Memoirs of Warren Hastings*, vol. I (London: Richard Bentley, 1841) 404.

that Hastings 'was certainly no angel,' he also argues that he 'was nevertheless by far the most responsible and sympathetic of all the officials the Company had yet sent to India…. He took concrete measures to make sure there was no repetition of the terrible famine of 1770.'[48]

Nevertheless, Hastings was portrayed as presiding over an exploitative system, condoning bribery and oppression. He was charged with high crimes and misdemeanours, originally on twenty articles of impeachment, and the actual trial, in Westminster Hall, lasted from 1788 to 1795, making it the longest impeachment in parliamentary history. Impeachment has more recently become obsolete in the British Parliament, unlike in the American Congress, but previously (especially in the seventeenth century) Parliament used it to control Crown officials.[49] Burke himself led the prosecution, denouncing the EIC, and accusing Hastings of being 'captain-general of iniquity', a 'spider of Hell' and a 'ravenous vulture devouring the carcases of the dead'. Burke also accused Hastings of 'geographical morality … as if when you have crossed the equatorial line all the virtues die'.[50]

Yet, despite the passion and forcefulness of Burke's moral outrage, Hastings was acquitted of all charges in April 1795. Much of the trial had appeared extreme and melodramatic in nature. However, the very fact of impeachment illustrated that the EIC was answerable to Parliament and that its abuses had not gone unnoticed. It would not be free from State oversight, a process which would come to fruition with the complete takeover of the Company in 1858. And as Dalrymple comments, Burke 'correctly identified what remains today one of the great anxieties of modern liberal democracies: the ability of a ruthless corporation corruptly to buy a legislature.'[51]

Hastings' replacement as Governor-General was Lord Cornwallis, the general in charge of the British army which finally surrendered to Washington, losing the American colonies – illustrating perhaps the interconnectedness of Britain's imperial administration.

4.2.5 Sovereignty in India

British India, whether under the EIC or the Raj, was never a completely determined sovereign entity. New territories were acquired but the sovereignty of their former rulers not always completely eradicated, as with the Nawab of Bengal at the time of the grant of the Diwani. The 1757 legal Opinion issued by

[48] W Dalrymple, *The Anarchy* 312–313. Dalrymple suggests that in fact Sir Philip Francis, strong critic of Hastings, and former Council member under the Regulating Act, who aided Hasting's prosecution, was more to blame.

[49] From 1620 to 1649, there were over 100 impeachments in the House of Commons.

[50] 'Burke on the Impeachment of Warren Hastings', in AB Keith (ed.), *Speeches and Documents on Indian Policy*, vol. I (London: Oxford University Press, 1922) 114.

[51] W Dalrymple, 'The East India Company: The Original Corporate Raiders', *The Guardian*, 4 March 2015.

the English Solicitor and Attorney-Generals (the *Pratt–Yorke Opinion*[52]) had advised that territories received by grant or cession from local rulers were EIC property (subject to royal sovereignty over British subjects) but that conquered lands would revert to the Crown. However, this failed to settle the matter. Clive himself had described the acquisition of the Diwani in this way:

> We may be regarded as the spring which concealed under the shadow of the Nabob's name, secretly gives motion to this vast machine of government without offering violence to the original constitution.... The Nabob holds in his hands, as he always did, the whole civil administration, the distribution of justice, the disposal of offices, and all those sovereign rights which constitute the essence of his dignity...[53]

Clive's reference to the 'sovereign rights' of the 'Nabob' (sic) illustrates the ambiguity of the situation.[54] The EIC issued coins in Bengal, but in the name of Mughal Emperor Shah Alam II. A valid conclusion seems to be that, 'EIC rule in Bengal appeared to occupy hazy middle ground between Mughal and British sovereignty. It existed as kind of masked sovereignty, the iron fist of the sepoy army in the velvet glove of *nawabi* administrative routines ... an inherently unstable predicament.'[55]

4.2.6 The East India Company to 1858

This next period brought change over two areas. First, the British government gained much greater control over EIC affairs in India. The 1813 Charter Act (53 Geo. III c155) extended the EIC Charter for 20 years but asserted 'the Crown's undoubted sovereignty over all of the Company's territories.' This was the first-time sovereignty of the British State over territory in India had been expressed in statutory form. Nonetheless, the EIC still governed India and some Indian rulers were still in place, so there was a system of indirect British rule there. Second, EIC territory was progressively expanded, by means of conquest and treaty – especially under the leadership of Governors-General Wellesley and the Marquess of Hastings. The defeat of Tipu Sultan of Mysore in 1799 was often seen as a turning point, opening up India to the dominance of the British, and one should not underestimate the bloodshed and turmoil

[52] 16 August 1757, GBPP 1757–1773 XXVI, 7. Also known as the 'Camden-Yorke opinion'. The Opinion was later used in disputes over whether settlers could purchase land directly from indigenous peoples in North America.

[53] Clive to the Board of Directors of the EIC, 27 January 1764, in G Forrest, *The Life of Lord Clive* (London: Frank Cassell & Co., 1918) 296.

[54] For continuing salience of Mughal sovereignty, see S Sen, *A Distant Sovereignty: National Imperialism and the Origins of British India* (London: Routledge, 2002) xi–xvii. A different view was taken by William Bolts, *Considerations on Indian Affairs* (London: J Almon, 1772) 49.

[55] R Travers, 'Constitutions, Contact Zones and Imperial Ricochets: Sovereignty and Law in British Asia', in HV Bowen, E Mancke, and JG Reid (eds.), *Britain's Oceanic Empire: Atlantic and Indian Ocean Worlds, c.1550–1850* (Cambridge: Cambridge University Press, 2012) 113.

that accompanied these conquests. However, by 1856 all the Indian subcontinent and a good deal of Burma were either under direct EIC or allied rule. A number of princely States, governed, at least in theory, by Indian rulers, but in friendly relations with Britain, continued under the Raj (and were granted their own constitutional body, the Chamber of Princes, in 1920). However, their existence further complicated the issue of sovereignty in India, evincing a 'residuary sovereignty' of the princes that 'was their own, not granted to them by the British'.[56]

Crown-Company relations had become easier since the 1780s, and the Government now had greater control over policy for India. The EIC lost all its trading monopolies by 1833 and yet it continued to administer India, and so a private company was in charge of Britain's Empire there. Yet it did not go uncontrolled, as the next section demonstrates.

4.2.6.1 Codification

By the 1830s, law in India was a cumbersome, convoluted coagulation, comprising different legal sources – a mixture of Acts of Parliament (which established some basic constitutional structures); Hindu and Moslem laws; many (often conflicting) regional rules; and some natural law principles of justice thrown in for good measure – leaving much scope for individual judicial discretion of judges.

The 1833 Government of India Act introduced a central pan-India legislative Council to adopt laws for all India. It also started the process of legal codification. Thomas Babington Macaulay was highly active in this area, opining that the purpose of codification was to create 'one great and entire work symmetrical in all its parts and pervaded by one spirit,'[57] an ambition influenced by the utilitarian Jeremy Bentham. Macaulay and three EIC officials were appointed to the first Indian Law Commission in 1834, and Macaulay enthusiastically described codification as 'a work which especially belongs to a government like that of India – to an enlightened and paternal despotism.'[58] And so India underwent an intense period of codification from the 1833 Government of India Act for much of the nineteenth century. However, Macaulay's attempts to apply a uniform jurisdiction to all, including British subjects, met with resistance. And Macaulay himself was no stranger to racist and discriminatory notions – his sense of British cultural superiority was notoriously illustrated by his 1835 'Minute on Indian Education',[59] which urged instruction in English, rather than Persian or Sanskrit.

[56] Sen, 'Unfinished Conquest: Residual Sovereignty and the Legal Foundations of the British Empire in India' (2012) 9(2) Law, Culture and the Humanities 227–242.

[57] 2 January 1837, in CD Dharker, *Lord Macaulay's Legislative Minutes* (G Cumberledge: Oxford University Press, 1946).

[58] *Hansard,* 3rd ser., vol. 19, 531.

[59] TB Macaulay, 'Minute of 2 February 1835', in *Macaulay, Prose and Poetry*, GM Young (ed.), (Cambridge MA.: Harvard University Press, 1957).

Therefore, from the late eighteenth century, the profile of Britain's Indian Empire was reconfigured to reflect increasing metropolitan control. Nonetheless, as Bowen observes, this change 'did not belong to any grand Imperial design or project. Rather, it emerged from pragmatic responses to very serious shortcomings within the EIC.'[60]

4.2.7 Government of the Raj

In May 1857, the infamous Indian mutiny started (also known in India as the first war of Independence). The EIC's own sepoy army rebelled against its oppressive rule, and particularly its treatment of their religion. Although the EIC regained command and suppressed the insurgency, it did so brutally, in what Dalrymple describes as 'probably the most bloody episode in the entire history of British colonialism.'[61] This brutality threw into focus the dangers of leaving the administration of Britain's empire to a private corporation. Therefore, with the Government of India Act 1858 (21 & 22 Vict. c. 106), the British State formally took over, removing the EIC from power, and establishing direct rule by the British Crown. The EIC itself was finally extinguished in 1874 (Act of 36 Vict. c17). India by then comprised 300 million people, three-fourths of the British Empire's population.[62] The era of the British Raj, and a new chapter of Indian constitutional history, of direct imperial rule of India by Britain, had begun. But the Indian mutiny had consequences – and the British mindset and demeanour on India became yet more distrustful, and racist in outlook.

4.2.7.1 The Government of India Act 1858

Palmerston introduced the Bill in the House of Commons in 1857, stating that,

> India, with all its vast and important interests, should be placed under the direct authority of the Crown, to be governed in the name of the Crown by the responsible Ministers of the Crown sitting in Parliament, and responsible to Parliament and the public for every part of their public conduct, instead of being, as now, mainly, administered by a set of gentlemen who … are yet a totally irresponsible body, whose views and acts are seldom known to the public.[63]

The Government of India Act was duly passed, and its terms promulgated in an 1858 Proclamation to India. Rule over India moved from EIC Directors in London to the British Secretary of State for India, advised by a Council of India,

[60] HV Bowen, 'British India, 1765–1813: The Metropolitan Context', in *OHBE*, vol. II, 548–549; also CA Bayly, *Imperial Meridian: The British Empire and the World* (London: Longman, 1989), 100–32.

[61] W Dalrymple, 'The East India Company'.

[62] Robin J Moore, 'Imperial India, 1858–1914', in A Porter (ed.), *OHBE*, volume III: *The Nineteenth Century* (Oxford: Oxford University Press, 1999) 442.

[63] Viscount Palmerston, HC Deb 12 February 1858, vol. 148, cc1276–359.

mostly appointed by the Crown. The Governor-General, now termed Viceroy, was also directly appointed by the Crown, as were provincial Governors in India.

4.2.7.2 Statutes from 1861

It was now more straightforward to impose British policy in India and, from 1858 to 1947, Parliament adopted 196 statutes concerning India. The 1861 Indian High Courts Act (24 & 25 Vict. c.104) empowered the Crown to set up High Courts in Calcutta, Madras and Bombay, all of whose judges were Crown appointed. The 1861 Indian Councils Act (24 & 25 Vict. c.67) established an Executive Council, which acted as a Cabinet for India. Each British Indian province (eleven in all) was to have its own Governor, in turn assisted by provincial legislative Councils of appointed officials. A few Indians belonging to the local elite were appointed on Councils but with no legislative powers. The 1909 Indian Councils Act (9 Edw. 7 ch. 4) considerably increased the number of Indians on these legislative Councils. Agrarian laws were passed to protect those who worked on the land, often modelled on statutes for Ireland. In 1876 the Royal Titles Act (39 & 40 Vict., c. 10) was passed, formally endowing Queen Victoria with the title of Empress of India, although she never in fact visited India.

4.2.7.3 'The Jewel in the Crown'

India became viewed as, in the familiar phrase, the brightest jewel in the imperial Crown. Indeed, Lord Curzon remarked in 1901 that, 'As long as we rule India we are the greatest power in the world. If we lose it, we shall drop straightaway to a third rate power.'[64] There was a substantial Indian army and civil service (criticized by nationalist leader Jawaharlal Nehru as 'neither Indian, nor civil, nor a service'[65]) both paid for out of Indian taxes, so it might be said that Indians were paying for their own subjugation. About 2/3 of the Indian continent was under direct British rule, described by Cell as a 'huge, multi-layered bureaucracy, comparable in size to those of the Tsarist Russian or Chinese empires.'[66] British India was administered by a Secretary of State in London, responsible to Parliament, and a Viceroy in Delhi (British Indian capital from 1911) whose administration was split up into provinces, each with its own Governor. However, the British themselves were a small group and in any case, not all of India was formally 'British'. About one-third of the Indian Empire was in the Princely States, which were nominally autonomous and varied in size, but included large provinces such as Hyderabad. Before the Mutiny, the EIC had annexed States for 'misgovernment' or 'lapse'.[67] During the Raj, annexation was discontinued, although Indian Princes were 'attached' to the Crown.

[64] Quoted in WM Roger Louis and J Brown (eds.), *OHBE, The Twentieth Century*, 5.

[65] Jawaharlal Nehru, *Glimpses of World History: Being Further Letters to His Daughter* (London: Lindsay Drummond Ltd., 1949) 94.

[66] J Cell, 'Colonial Rule' in *OHBE* vol. V, 236.

[67] This was depicted in Satyajit Ray's film, *The Chess Players* (1977), in which the kingdom of Awadh is taken over by the EIC.

The India National Congress was founded in 1885, and the Muslim League in 1906. Gradually, Indians took a part in both Indian and imperial politics. During the 1890s, two Indian MPs were elected to the Westminster Parliament. One, Dadabhai Naoroji, was a founder of the Indian National Congress and highly critical of British rule, publishing *Poverty and Un-British Rule in India,* which argued that India's wealth was being 'drained' by Britain.[68]

4.2.7.4 Jurists and Legal Reform

It is noteworthy how many high-profile Victorian theorists, especially jurists, were active in India. Codification continued during the Raj,[69] with the Mutiny an impetus to legal reconstruction. Macaulay's Penal Code, implemented after the Mutiny, was short and succinct, and prioritized security of the imperial regime. (It was also somewhat eclectic, drawing on the Code Napoleon and Louisiana Code.) Crimes against key State symbols such as counterfeiting coins or stamps could be punished by life imprisonment. A separate Indian Code of Criminal Procedure, issued in 1861, affirmed a distinct status for 'European-born British subjects', granting them special privileges, such as trial by British judges, right to jury trial (with a majority European jury), and restricted sentences. However, in 1881, Courtney Ilbert, Law member of the Viceroy's Council, introduced a Bill 'to remove from the Code, at once and completely, every judicial disqualification which is based merely on race distinctions.'[70] This was met with fury by British subjects, and, although the Ilbert Bill was eventually enacted, it was severely weakened by compromise. Codes were also adopted for most other areas, including civil and commercial law. The empire's data collecting capacities were also hugely increased, partly in an attempt to increase knowledge in Britain about India. The use of fingerprint evidence was trialled in British India.[71] And, from the first census of 1872, the British had codified the existent Indian caste system and catalogued all Indians by caste, religion, tribe, race and language and into various classes such as 'criminal tribes' and 'martial races'.[72]

A narrative emerged contending that Britain had provided administrative order out of the chaos caused by former rulers of India. Conquest was presented as a matter of imposing a rule of law rather than military power.[73] Codification

[68] D Naoroji, *Poverty and Un-British Rule in India* (London: Swan, Sonnenschein & Co., 1901).

[69] C Ilbert, 'Indian Codification' (1889) 5 *LQR*.

[70] 'Statement of Objects and Reasons', January 30, 1883, in *Extra Supplement to the Gazette of India,* July–December 1883.

[71] Chandak Sengoopta, *Imprint of the Raj: How Fingerprinting Was Born in Colonial India* (London: Macmillan, 2003).

[72] E.g. AM Bingley, *The Caste Handbooks for the Indian Army* (Calcutta: Superintendent Government Printing, India, 1918). Also, The Criminal Tribes Act (Act XXVII of 1871) which classified 13 million Indians as 'criminal' by 1913. See also CA Bayly, *Empire and Information: Intelligence Gathering and Social Communication in India, 1780–1870* (Cambridge: Cambridge University Press, 1996).

[73] E.g. in William Hunter Wilson, *England's Work in India* (London: Smith Elder & Co, 1881).

and consolidation of law was considered a vital means of bringing order out of disorder. Sir James Fitzjames Stephen, prominent jurist and judge (and cousin of AV Dicey), complained that, until 1857, law in India was a matter of 'its confusion and utter want of principle and unity'.[74] His monograph, *Liberty, Equality, Fraternity* (1873) was much inspired by his time in India, and Fitzjames Stephen himself was somewhat contradictorily both liberal and authoritarian. Early officials had been more willing to leave in place ancient Indian laws, but after the Mutiny, both Fitzjames Stephen and Henry Sumner Maine advocated the imposition of a new imperial legal system. Both believed law reflected the nature and character of a society, and that promulgating a new law in India could instil a new morality there, achieving good government through adoption of good laws.[75] In particular, Fitzjames Stephen was responsible for the codification of the Contract Acts, Evidence Acts and revised Code of Criminal procedures, although much of his work had to be done swiftly and there was agreement that remedial work would be necessary.

John Stuart Mill, whose famous work *On Liberty* is frequently contrasted with Stephen's *Liberty, Equality, Fraternity,* and cited as a bulwark of liberal philosophy, was employed in London from 1823 to 1858, by the EIC. Indeed, when the 1858 Government of India Act, which transferred the EIC's responsibility to the Crown, was debated in Parliament, Mill had the task of defending the EIC's interests.[76] Mill's arguments did not win the day, and the EIC was dissolved. But generally, Mill presented the EIC, and the British in India, as a force for good (if a paternalistic one), a view which seems in conflict with his other writings. In particular, *On Liberty* argues for toleration and self-determination, famously expressing the view that no one can 'rightfully be compelled to do or forbear because it will be better for him to do so.'[77] Perhaps the disjunction can be explained because Mill applied his principles of liberty only to 'civilized' peoples, and did not believe Indians to be sufficiently civilized. In his evidence to the Lords Select Committee in 1852, Mill said, 'I do not think that India has yet attained such a degree of civilization and improvement to be ripe for anything like a representative system.'[78] Such an approach was common in Victorian England, which preferred to see its imperial mission as one of benign civilization, in contrast to the plunder and exploitation of the EIC.

[74] Sir James Fitzjames Stephen, *A History of the Criminal Law of England* (London: Macmillan, 1883) 302.

[75] HS Maine, *Village Communities in the East and West* (3rd ed., London: J. Murray, 1876) 300. Indeed, many of the Indian Law Codes were later exported to other parts of the British Empire, e.g. to east and central Africa.

[76] Mill, *Memorandum on the Improvements in the Administration of India during the Last Thirty Years* (London: WH Allen, 1858). Indeed, Mill's father, James Mill, had himself become famous as an authority on India, publishing *The History of British India* (London: Baldwin, Cradock, and Joy, 1817) which described India as a land of chaos and disorder, before himself gaining employment with the EIC in Leadenhall street.

[77] JS Mill, *On Liberty*, D Spitz (ed.), (New York: WW Norton, 1975) 10.

[78] JS Mill, 'Evidence to the Lords Select Committee, 21/22 June 1852', in F Madden with D Fieldhouse (eds.), *Select Documents on the Constitutional History of the British Empire*, vol. V, 57.

All this juristic activity suggests some coherent plan, a vision of order and 'civilization' for India. Such a deliberate organization may well seem in itself reprehensible, the top down paternalistic imposition of one State's perceptions and practices on another – especially given the country deemed in need of 'civilizing' had its own near 4000-year-old culture. However, also pertinent is the critique from those (such as Jon Wilson[79]) who suggest British rule was not coherent and orderly, but dependent on domination. And in some areas, such as the hugely important area of personal law, the British failed. Although the issue of codifying the (Hindu and Muslim) personal (i.e. religious, family, inheritance and customary) laws had been mooted, it was rejected as too difficult to achieve. In such areas, for the most part the British policy was one of non-intervention, with the exception of the abolition of *sati* (widow immolation) in 1829.

In later life, Mill became more pessimistic about British rule in India, partly because of increasing violence in colonial rule,[80] and more unconfident about Britain's ability to carry out its mission. Indeed, the Indian lawyer (later High Court justice), Syed Mahmood, wrote a piece whose title asked if the British regime in India 'owes its origin to conquest and its maintenance to physical force'.[81] And Fitzjames Stephen wrote that the Raj was 'founded not on consent but on conquest', to him indicating the superiority of 'the conquering race'.[82] By this way of thinking, physical force maintained the Raj.

4.2.8 1914 to Independence

During the First World War, about 2 million Indians fought for Britain, and expectations were raised for greater Indian autonomy within the British Empire. In 1917, the Secretary of State for India issued the 'Montagu declaration' proclaiming Britain's constitutional objectives to be 'the gradual development of self-governing institutions with a view to the progressive realization of responsible government in India as part of the British Empire'.[83] Notable was his use of 'responsible government', which already existed in Canada, Australia and New Zealand, and took the form of a colonial executive responsible to a representative legislature. India was also given League of Nations membership after the Great War. In 1919, however, the Imperial Legislative Council in Delhi adopted the Indian Anarchical and Revolutionary Crimes

[79] Jon Wilson, *India Conquered: Britain's Raj and the Chaos of Empire* (London: Simon & Schuster, 2016).

[80] JS Mill, *The Collected Works of John Stuart Mill, Volume XVI: The Later Letters of John Stuart Mill 1849–1873 Part III.*

[81] S Mahmood, 'British rule in India' (1879) 135 Calcutta Review. Mahmood concluded that India had not been conquered, although condemned British arrogance. But Mahmood was later dismissed from his position of High Court judge, probably as a result of discrimination against him.

[82] *The Times*, 1 March 1883.

[83] L James, *Raj: The Making and Unmaking of British India* (London: Little, Brown, 1997) 458.

Act which continued emergency wartime legislation, limiting civil and political rights. This seemed more like a policy of repression than a move to responsible government. Moreover, Lord Birkenhead, Secretary of State for India in the 1920s, stated that it was 'frankly inconceivable that India would ever be fit for Dominion self-government.'[84]

However, on 13 April 1919, the Amritsar, or Jallianwala Bagh, Massacre occurred, when British troops, led by General Dyer, fired on an unarmed crowd in a park in Amritsar, the holy city of the Sikhs in Punjab, killing several hundred people, including women and children, and injuring many more. This was followed by floggings and martial law and marked a turning point, an exemplar of British colonial injustice and brutality. Mohandas Gandhi, the British educated barrister who had supported the British during the Great War (and spent 20 years in South Africa confronting the white minority government there), now became convinced of the need for Indian independence, and took over leadership of the Indian National Congress, beginning a campaign of non-violent mass civil disobedience, *or satyagraha.*

4.2.8.1 The Government of India 1919 and the Dyarchy

The Preamble to the 1919 Government of India Act of December (9 & 10 Geo. 5 c. 101) echoed the 1917 Montagu Declaration in stating that it was Parliament's policy to move to responsible government in India. This Act introduced a highly complex system of *dyarchy*,[85] or power-sharing, between British officials and a limited number of elected Indians in provincial legislative Councils. Central government remained completely under British control but provincial government was responsible to the legislature for 'transferred' matters, such as education. However, even within provincial government, many areas were classified as 'reserved' and remained in British control – including the army, currency, police, justice, press controls, irrigation, and land revenues – undermining the innovative devolutionary provisions of the dyarchy. Also the franchise, even if it now included some Indians, was very small, and British officials also had a *de facto* veto over Indian legislation. Gallagher and Seal condemned dyarchy as 'worthy of Solomon on a bad day'.[86]

The dyarchy was not a success, and the 1930 Simon Commission[87] report (under the joint chairmanship of Sir John Simon and a younger Clement Attlee, and which, although investigating the constitutional system of India did not contain one Indian) recommended its replacement by responsible

[84] D Judd, *The Lion and the Tiger: The Rise and Fall of the British Raj* (Oxford: Oxford University Press, 2004) 147.

[85] See further, KT Shah and GJ Bahadurji, *A Commentary on the Government of India Act* (Bombay: N M Tripathia, 1924). Also, L Curtis, *Dyarchy* (Oxford: Clarendon Press, 1920).

[86] J Gallagher and A Seal, 'Britain and India between the Wars' (1981) 15(3) Modern Asian Studies 387–414, 395.

[87] *Report of the Indian statutory commission* (Government of India Central Publication Branch, 1930).

government at provincial if not national level. In contrast, the 1928 report compiled by Motilal Nehru, father of Jawaharlal, had proposed complete self-government and Dominion status for India. (Since the 1926 Imperial Conference, Dominion status had been defined as self-government within the Empire-Commonwealth.) From 1930 to 1932, a series of 'Round Table' conferences on future governance of India was convened by the British Government in London (notably not in India). Although several Indian parties attended, the process was initially boycotted by the Indian National Congress, and its leader Mahatma Gandhi. The recommendations of the final conference influenced the 1936 Government of India Act.

4.2.8.2 The Government of India Act 1935

The 1919 Act was replaced by the 1935 Government of India Act (26 Geo. 5. Ch. 2), an extremely long, complex statute. The Raj kept control of central government but this legislation increased the franchise and established elected provincial legislatures. By 1937, the Indian National Congress formed administrations in seven out of eleven provinces, sharing power in others. Many, however, including Winston Churchill, were resolutely opposed to the 1935 legislation – indeed, it was these Indian reforms, not appeasement of Germany, that led to Churchill's resignation in the later 1930s – and Churchill was later to state that 'he regarded the Hindu–Muslim feud as the bulwark of British rule in India'.[88] It has also been suggested that the 1935 Act was an exercise of an existing policy of 'divide and rule',[89] furthering Hindu-Muslim antagonism, which would come to a climax with the departure of the British and partition of India and Pakistan in 1947.

Notwithstanding the reforms of the 1935 Act, the Viceroy, Lord Linlithgow, declared the outbreak of the Second World War without consulting any Indian nationalist leader. In 1943, another famine occurred in Bengal, and nearly 4 million died. These disastrous Indian famines, of which there had been quite a few, are sometimes referred to as a 'British colonial holocaust.'[90] Yet Indian support was vital militarily for the British during the war, and Britain had even made an offer to India in 1942, of full Dominion status or the option to secede from the Empire, in return for co-operation.[91]

4.2.8.3 Independence

At the end of World War II, the incoming British Labour government decided to grant full independence to India, and negotiated with representatives from the two main parties, the Muslim League, led by Jinnah, and the National Party, led

[88] L James, *Raj: The Making and Unmaking of British India* (London: Little, Brown, 1997) 542.

[89] See further, on 'divide and rule', Shashi Tharoor, *Inglorious Empire: What the British Did to India* (London: Hurst, 2017) *passim*.

[90] For example, referenced in Ferriter's review of S Tharoor, *Inglorious Empire* in *The Irish Times*, Sat, 4 March 2017.

[91] RJ Moore, *Churchill, Cripps, and India, 1939–1945* (Oxford: Oxford University Press, 1979).

by Nehru. These parties were opposed to each other, and the former demanded a Muslim homeland, to be called Pakistan, made up of the provinces of the Raj with majority Muslim populations. Louis Mountbatten was appointed British Viceroy in March 1947.[92] An early 'Plan Balkan' was produced, which would have fragmented India and established a weak union. This plan proved unacceptable. Crucial for Congress was that any solution maintained an Indian State as a continuing entity. Mountbatten then made a unilateral declaration that India would become independent on 15 August 1947. This required that the UK Parliament swiftly adopt the Indian Independence Act, in July 1947 (10 & 11 Geo. 6, c. 30). Under this statute, India and Pakistan became independent States. Nehru made his famous 'Tryst with destiny' speech: 'At the stroke of the midnight hour, when the world sleeps, India will awake to life and freedom.'[93]

The partition created a disjointed Pakistan, which was split into west and east Pakistan (later to become Bangladesh) as well as leaving many Muslims in India, and non-Muslim Indians in Pakistan. It had proved near impossible, even taking religion as the only basis, to make any division that did not leave large minorities on the wrong sides of the border. Boundary Commissions had been established for Punjab and Bengal, chaired by Cyril Radcliffe, a British lawyer, who was no expert in Indian affairs – with only 6 weeks to set the boundaries. The human cost of partition was immense, with about one million killed in the violence, and millions more forced to leave their homes and migrate across what was now an international border, in the largest mass migration ever. The bloodshed proved especially fierce in the Punjab, with its northern Muslim majority, and southern Sikh dominated area which looked to India. Both India and Pakistan subsequently became republics and members of the Commonwealth. Indian independence wholly changed the nature of the British Empire, as well as inspiring nationalists in other parts of the Empire to seek independence.

4.2.9 Conclusion

India has sometimes been described as an empire within an empire, so significant and distinctive that *The Cambridge History of the British Empire* devoted two of its volumes to India, and the prolific jurist AB Keith published a monograph *The Constitutional History of India*[94] distinct from his other works on the constitutional history of the British Empire. In the early twentieth century, India's territorial scope was 'greater than the Roman Empire' and had a population of 294,361,056 (India being roughly five times the size of the entire

[92] Actually born a German aristocrat, Prince Louis of Battenberg, during the First World War his father dropped his German royal titles and anglicized his name to Mountbatten.

[93] MJ Akbar, *Nehru: The Making of India* (London: Viking, 1988) 420.

[94] HH Dodwell (ed.), *Cambridge History of the British empire*, vol. IV: *British India, 1498–1857* and vol. V: *The Indian Empire 1858–1918*; AB Keith, *Constitutional History of India* (1926; repr. New York: Barnes & Noble & Methuen & Co. Ltd, 1969).

French colonial empire).[95] The length of this section reflects that importance. Yet British India, whether under the Raj, and certainly the EIC, frequently operated as what Acemoglu and Robinson describe in *Why Nations Fail* as an 'extractive' institution, namely one which a group exploits wealth and resources for their own benefit.[96] This suggests the British exploited India as much, or more than they developed it. The historian, Jon Wilson, argues that British administrators were driven by 'irrational passions' rather than 'calculated plans'.[97] For Wilson, there was no system or grand vision. The experience of British India was more often turbulent and violent than a carefully planned civilizing order. It provides a warning against imperial nostalgia for empire as a force for civilization and the rule of law.

4.3 Empire in the Nineteenth and Earlier Twentieth Centuries

4.3.1 Introduction

By the early nineteenth century, Britain was established as a 'Great Power' and leading State. Roughly speaking, in the nineteenth century, the British Empire consisted of three components, each in different stages of political and economic development. These were first, the 'white' settler colonies, diminished by the loss of America, but increasing to encompass more of Canada, as well as Australia, New Zealand and parts of South Africa. Secondly, there was the Indian empire, which had enlarged greatly since 1757. Third, there was the dependent empire – which consisted of other territories, either conquered or acquired through wartime gains – which continued to expand. Britain had become a wealthy, industrial economy – and part of the motivation for its imperial expansion was the search for new markets to feed this growth. The speedy development of all sorts of communications – whether transport, post or telegraph – as well as advances in corporate and banking structures, supported this growth and stimulated migration within the empire. But in turn, empire influenced Britain itself in many ways – culturally, socially, institutionally, and constitutionally.

In contrast to the eighteenth and twentieth centuries, the nineteenth century after 1815 saw little significant international combat, and, with the exception of the Crimean war, no conflict between Britain and another European Great Power. For most of the nineteenth century, no European State seemed powerful enough to challenge Britain's Royal Navy. Nonetheless, it was a period in which rivalries with other Great Powers often defined British imperial and foreign policy – as in the 'Great Game' in central Asia, where Britain was always worried about the possibility of Russian incursions into India. And there were

[95] David C Potter, *India's Political Administrators, 1919–1983* (Oxford: Clarendon Press, 1986).

[96] D Acemoglu, J Robinson, *Why Nations Fail: The Origins of Power, Prosperity, and Poverty* (New York: Random House, 2012).

[97] Jon Wilson, *India Conquered: Britain's Raj and the Chaos of Empire* (London: Simon & Schuster, 2016) 'Preface'.

also insurgencies and rebellions, such as the 1857 Indian Mutiny, and 1865 Morant Bay rebellion in Jamaica.

4.3.1.1 Territories

A brief audit illustrates the great increase in the extent, wealth and population of the British Empire during the nineteenth and early twentieth centuries. Although Britain had lost its thirteen North American colonies, its other colonies on that continent expanded west to the Pacific as Canada came into being. Britain's Caribbean colonies expanded with war gains from the French, Spanish, and Dutch, although the West Indies declined in its importance for Britain during the nineteenth century. The six colonies of Australia were federated in 1901, and New Zealand and South Africa colonized. In each case, this was at the expense of those countries' indigenous peoples. By 1911, the Empire's white population (mostly in 'settler' colonies) had grown from c550,000 (in 1815) to 18.9m. By the mid-nineteenth century, India was of central importance to the empire and British territories in India were consolidated and taken over by the Crown. Britain acquired other territories in Asia, such as Hong Kong, Singapore, Malaya, Burma, and some of Borneo. The British presence in Africa hugely increased in the nineteenth century, from its earlier small trading posts on the periphery, established for the slave trade, to all parts of the continent – 2.8m square miles by 1911.[98]

Britain also made its presence felt in the 'informal empire', namely, territories that were not British colonies, but in which Britain nonetheless exercised a commanding political and economic influence (Figure 4.1).

4.3.2 Institutions of Government

Many believe that at the centre of the British Empire was power. This may well be so, and it may have ultimately been impossible for so large a conglomeration of territories to be sustained by anything other than power. However, as Burroughs acknowledges, 'power had to be converted into systems of authority, exercised by agents through bureaucratic structures.'[99] We have already examined how some of these systems of authority functioned at the time of the first British Empire, and in India. Now it is time to see how the British managed their Empire at its height.

By the 1890s, the British Empire included about one quarter of worldwide territory and one fifth of the world's population. According to John Darwin, this encompassed 'an extraordinary range of constitutional, diplomatic, political, commercial and cultural relationships.'[100] Darwin lists at least ten diverse species of management: '*colonies of rule* (including the huge 'sub-empire' of

[98] All figures in this paragraph have been taken from A Porter 'Introduction', supra.

[99] P Burroughs, 'Imperial Institutions and the Government of Empire', in *OHBE* vol. III, 171.

[100] John Darwin, *The Empire Project: The Rise and Fall of the British World-System, 1830–1970* (Cambridge: Cambridge University Press, 2009) 1.

Figure 4.1 Imperialism Octopus. 'The Devilfish in Egyptian Waters.' An American cartoon from 1882 depicting John Bull (England) as the octopus of imperialism grabbing land on every continent.

India), *settlement colonies* (mostly self-governing by the late nineteenth century), *protectorates*, *condominia* (like the Sudan), *mandates* (after 1920), *naval and military fortresses* (like Gibraltar and Malta), *'occupations'* (like Egypt and Cyprus), *treaty-ports and 'concessions'* (Shanghai was the most famous), *'informal' colonies of commercial pre-eminence* (like Argentina), *'spheres of interference'* (a useful term coined by Sellar and Yeatman[101]) like Iran, Afghanistan and the Persian Gulf, and (not least) a rebellious province at home.' Darwin suggests the lack of any agreed term for governance of the empire may have led to 'Pax Britannia' as a convenient umbrella term.[102]

Unlike some other empires (such as the French and Spanish) the British never aspired to govern their empire solely from the centre, in a uniform way. Much was left to those on site, thousands of miles from London, and a diverse range of colonial governance developed to manage this. Often, British authority over territory was reactive and ad hoc in nature, with institutional governance lagging behind the conquest of territory. Lord Milner lamented the Empire's 'total

[101] WA Sellar and RJ Yeatman, *1066 and All That* (London: Methuen, 1930) 105.

[102] Darwin, *The Empire Project*. Although one might question how much peace there actually was in the British Empire.

want of any permanent binding force, or rational system.'[103] Mohr insightfully remarks that 'the Empire-Commonwealth was popularly perceived as an institution based on unwritten conventions with an absolute minimum of written law,'[104] an organic organization that had evolved out of a group of nations with a common history. However, Mohr also notes that there was, in fact, a fair amount of 'Imperial law' around. Most self-governing Dominions had been established by UK statutes which also included their Constitutions.[105] The 1865 Colonial Laws Validity Act and 1931 Statute of Westminster set the relationship between the Empire/Commonwealth and UK on a statutory basis. Moreover, there were also 'imperial statutes' that applied throughout the Empire, governing matters such as citizenship, nationality maritime law, territorial boundaries, and the military.

4.3.2.1 Central/Metropolitan Organs of Governance

In any imperial, supranational, federal or union system, where a central authority exercises a degree of control over dependencies or sub-State jurisdictions, there should be some institutional machinery to define and police the separation of powers between each. However, there was no single institution, no one central department, that governed the Empire from the metropolis. Instead, various government departments controlled different territories and aspects of empire, and their powers and capabilities changed as the century wore on. Courts – both Privy Council, and colonial courts – were also involved in the process, with a power of judicial review to invalidate colonial legislation (but not UK legislation, which was protected from judicial review by the doctrine of parliamentary sovereignty).

Earlier in the nineteenth century, most British government, including colonial government, was of a personal nature, with ministers such as Palmerston often taking individual charge of policy, and drafting foreign dispatches. There was no institutionalized civil service in the sense that would later develop, and most officials and clerks had been appointed under a system of patronage. However, as the century passed, things gradually changed.

Indian governance was overseen from London, first by the EIC in their headquarters in Leadenhall street, and then from 1858 by the India Office, a British Government department. These structures were considered in the last section. Most other colonial matters were in 1801 consolidated in the Secretary of State for War and the Colonies (later separated into distinct War and Colonial Offices) and from that date, the Colonial Office had a significant role

[103] Cecil Headlam (ed.), *The Milner Papers*, vol. 2 (London: Cassell & Co., 1933) 288. Lord Alfred Milner was a British colonial administrator, whose 'Round Table' movement was influential.

[104] Thomas Mohr, 'The United Kingdom and Imperial federation, 1900 to 1939: A Precedent for British Legal Relations with the EU?' (2016) 4(2) Comparative Legal History, 131–161, at 153.

[105] E.g. British North America Act 1867; New Zealand Constitution Act 1852; Commonwealth of Australia Constitution Act 1900; South Africa Act 1909; and the Irish Free State Constitution Act 1922.

in administration. It oversaw large swathes of Empire, both those under direct British rule (Crown colonies) and settler colonies with more self-government. With certain exceptions [such as Earl Grey (1846–1852), a very young Gladstone (1834–1835), and Joseph Chamberlain (1895–1903)] it proved difficult to attract able politicians, and so colonial matters were often managed by permanent officials, such as James Stephen (father of James Fitzjames Stephen and nicknamed 'Mr Mothercountry') who was first legal advisor, and then Permanent Under-Secretary from 1836 to 1847,[106] and played a highly important role in the Colonial Office. Stephen had to draft important despatches, as well as drafts of Acts of Parliament which applied in the colonies, and additionally scrutinize every law that Colonial assemblies forwarded to London for review. James Stephen's pivotal role has been captured by the statement that:

> It is typical of the British way of doing things that one of the vehicles of this important political process should have been a conscientious, overworked and underpaid professional man operating with discretion a technical legal discipline in a government office and not some grandiose constitutional body debating matters of high policy.[107]

But Stephen was only one of a small handful of men. And, according to Helen Taft Manning, 'To say that Stephen knew more about colonial government than anyone else is not to say that he knew very much' – because Colonial Office administrators had little control over what actually went occurred on the ground, thousands of miles away. Further, the Colonial Office might have had large responsibilities, but it was a very small department by contemporary standards. Its earlier nineteenth-century exterior was described as a 'commonplace brick house at the end of Downing Street whose inner family ruled the empire', and it was both dilapidated and overcrowded.[108] Its work was also hampered by obsolete procedures. However, as the century progressed, Colonial Office governance evolved. For Crown colonies (i.e. the dependent empire), Orders-in-Council (executive legislation) were increasingly adopted. In contrast, the Colonial Office was more deferential to the local governance of settler colonies, particularly after the adoption of the (imperial) Colonial Laws Validity Act in 1865. By 1907, a Dominions Division was established distinct from those divisions supervising Crown Colonies.

Aside from the India and Colonial Offices, the Foreign Office dealt with foreign policy matters – for example, declarations of war, peace and security,

[106] DM Young, *The Colonial Office in the Early Nineteenth Century* (London: Longmans, 1961); JW Cell, *British Colonial Administration in the Mid-Nineteenth Century* (New Haven: Yale University Press, 1970); K McBride, *Mr Mothercountry: The Man Who Made the Rule of Law* (Oxford: Oxford University Press, 2016).

[107] HH Marshall, review of DB Swinfen, 'Imperial Control of Colonial Legislation 1813–1865' (1971) 20 Int Compt Law Q 599.

[108] Helen Taft Manning, 'Who Ran the British Empire 1830–1850?' (1965) 5(1) Journal of British Studies, 88–121.

treaty negotiations, diplomacy, affairs of jurisdiction and extraterritorial rights, and the supervision of Protectorates. To the Foreign Office resources must be added those of the Admiralty and War Office, which were in charge of strategic planning and delivery of defence of Britain and her overseas possessions.

4.3.2.1.1 Colonial Office Review of Legislation[109]

All colonial legislatures were constitutionally subordinate to the Crown, which had been able to veto, ratify or amend colonial legislation since the earliest days of Empire. The review procedure had been exercised in the seventeenth and eighteenth centuries by the Board of Trade of the Privy Council, but, by the nineteenth century was largely exercised by the Colonial Office, although officially decisions were taken by the King, by Order in Council. Parliament was rarely involved in the process.

James Stephen, along with Sir Frederic Rogers, legal advisors at the Colonial Office, played key roles in review. By 1840, after 27 years at the Colonial Office, Stephen estimated that he had been asked for an opinion on roughly 21,000 colonial laws. In theory at least, this should have concerned review of colonial legislation prior to its coming into effect (rather than judicial review, which tends to be *ex post facto*). However, most colonial legislation was already in operation before reaching the Colonial Office, because it had usually taken effect on receiving the colonial Governor's assent. James Stephen was particularly critical of those legislatures (such as in Van Diemen's land) which passed legislation for so short a period that they had already expired by the time the review process could start – a situation which rendered the British Government's control of the colonial legislature nominal only. But in general, it seems that Colonial Office review aimed to avoid conflict with the colonies, after the sobering example of the American revolution. Disallowance was seen as an extreme remedy. Swinfen's study of this subject tends to support an interpretation of the Empire as becoming more decentralized, emphasizing locality rather than unity. Nonetheless, there are notable examples of insistence on legal uniformity throughout the Empire, as with colonial marriage law, nationality law and the status of aliens.[110]

4.3.2.1.2 The Repugnancy Principle and the Colonial Laws Validity Act 1865

But what were the laws and standards by which colonial legislation was to be assessed? Unfortunately, this was not very clear. In 1774, in *Campbell v. Hall*, building on Coke's earlier jurisprudence, Lord Mansfield distinguished

[109] An excellent analysis is David B Swinfen, *Imperial Control of Colonial Legislation 1813–1865* (Oxford: Clarendon Press, 1970) 123.

[110] Imperial statutes applying outside the UK include British Nationality and Status of Aliens Act 1914; Colonial Courts of Admiralty Act 1890; Merchant Shipping Act 1894; Maritime Conventions Act 1911; Extradition Act 1870; Fugitive Offenders Act 1881; Colonial Prisoners Removal Acts 1869; 1884 Naval Deserters Act 1847; Naval Discipline Act 1866; The British Settlements Act 1887; and Colonial Boundaries Act 1895.

applicable rules for conquered colonies (in which the previous legal system should be retained until replaced by the Crown) on the one hand, and settler colonies (in which English law was brought by the settlers and applied) on the other.[111] Many colonial Charters specifically provided that their legislatures should not enact laws repugnant to the laws of England, on pain of the law being null and void. However, many questions remained. For example, was a colonial law 'repugnant' if it merely varied from English law?

By the late 1820s and 1830s, several Commissions of Inquiry into colonial legal systems revealed imperial constitutional law to be incoherent and unsystematic, including the repugnancy principle. The Westminster statute, the Colonial Laws Validity Act of 1865 (28 & 29 Vic., c. 63.) was an attempt to define the legal relationship between Britain and her colonies. Section 2 provided that colonial legislation would have full effect in the colony unless it violated any Westminster statute 'made applicable to such Colony by … express Words or necessary Intendment.' Thus, ultimate sovereignty was maintained by Westminster although the colonies exercised self-government for most matters. The Act does not mention English common law, thus limiting repugnancy to conflict with UK statute law only. This statute originated in the actions of a South Australian judge, Benjamin Boothby, who maintained that colonial statutes must conform not only to Westminster statute law but also to English common law. This grew into such a severe problem that steps were taken to remove Boothby from office.[112] According to RTE Latham, 'The only great statute of imperial constitutional law passed in the nineteenth century … was occasioned not by any desire to clarify or amend, but the necessity of upsetting the eccentric decision of a colonial judge.'[113] While the Colonial Laws Validity Act was originally considered liberating, by the twentieth century it appeared restrictive and the 1931 Statute of Westminster, which repealed it, is discussed in a subsequent section.

In conclusion, it seems that the Colonial Office did not seek to use the review process so as to secure uniformity of law throughout the British Empire.

4.3.2.1.3 Appeals to the Judicial Committee of the Privy Council (JCPC)

The JCPC was originally the highest court of appeal for the British Empire (and today still functions in the same way for some overseas jurisdictions – namely, some Commonwealth countries, UK overseas territories, Crown dependencies, and military sovereign bases).[114] In the past, the JCPC had an extremely

[111] *Campbell* v. *Hall* [1774] 1 Cowp. 204 (KB).

[112] A Castles, 'The Reception and Status of English Law in Australia' (1963) 2 Adelaide L. Rev. 24–25; Alpheus Todd, *Parliamentary Government in the British Colonies* (2nd ed., 1893), 846–856.

[113] RTE Latham, 'The Law and the Commonwealth', in WK Hancock (ed.), *Survey of British Commonwealth Affairs* (London: Oxford University Press, 1937) 512.

[114] Five judges now usually sit for Commonwealth appeals, and three for other matters. They are usually UK Supreme Court Justices.

wide jurisdiction, hearing appeals from all over the Empire, and applying many different laws. According to Viscount Haldane, describing his experience as a judge on the Privy Council,

> We sit there to administer Buddhist law, or Hindu law, or Mohammedan law, one after the other. We administer Roman-Dutch law from South Africa or from Ceylon, or French law from Quebec, or the common law of England from Ontario, or curious mixtures of law which prevail in various colonies, sometimes Italian law, sometimes Roman law. We sit there and do our best.[115]

'Doing our best' meant attempting a unity for the common law. Until 1966, the JCPC was required to issue one single judgement and dissents were not permitted.[116]

The JCPC is a descendant of the medieval *curia regis*, which primarily advised the Crown but also acted as a legislator and court. Its overseas jurisdiction grew as the British Empire grew. By the 1830s, its organization became regularized and the Privy Council Acts of 1833 and 1844 separated the JCPC from the Privy Council, changing the JCPC from an irregular committee, whose members included non-lawyers, to an official permanent court of senior judges (sometimes including colonial judges). Under the Privy Council Act 1833, it could hear appeals from the highest court of any Dominion, Colony, Protectorate or Mandated Territory under British administration, and also from any British court in those countries, in any area of law, if considered to be in the interest of justice, and it could interpret the Constitution of any country under British administration. It also could hear cases brought by one part of the Empire against another.[117] Indeed, its jurisdiction was as varied as that of the European Court of Justice today. For the next 100 years, the bulk of its cases came from India, Canada and Australia. When the colonies became Commonwealth nations, or completely independent, JCPC jurisdiction ceased altogether for many of them, and its role as a constitutional court is no longer significant, although some important cases arise from its few remaining jurisdictions. It is now housed in the same building as the UK Supreme Court, but until the earlier twentieth century had offices in Downing Street, opposite the Foreign and Commonwealth Office.

The JCPC decided a vast variety of cases and a general review of its case-law is far too colossal to be contemplated here[118] – although inevitably some

115 Viscount Haldane, 'The Work for the Empire of the Judicial Committee of the Privy Council' (1922) 1 *CLJ* 146.

116 Judicial Committee (Dissenting Opinions) Order, 1966 (S.I. 1966, No. 1100).

117 E.g. the boundary dispute between Canada and Newfoundland (still then distinct from Canada) in Labrador reported at (1927) 43 TLR 289.

118 RH Sir I Richardson, 'The Privy Council as the final Court for the British Empire' (discussing a range of JCPC cases, including the extraordinary case of *Srimati Bibhabati Devi* v. *Kumar Ramendra Narayan Roy* [1946] AC 508 (PC), concerning whether a claimant was the second son of the Raja of Bhowal, and had survived attempted cremation after being taken for dead) University of Wellington RP, Richardson Paper 91.

of its decisions provoked bitterness in the Empire. Mohr remarks that while all national courts have on occasion issued unpopular decisions, these rarely prompt demands for their abolition, unlike the Privy Council, which shared a vulnerability with contemporary supranational courts.[119]

Nonetheless, the JCPC found a considerable number of colonial laws constitutionally invalid from 1829 to 1971 and played an especially important role in constitutional development in Canada and Australia. One important (and more progressive) JCPC case is *Edwards* v. *Attorney-General of Canada*. Henrietta Muir Edwards contested the prohibition on women sitting in the Canadian Senate. Canadian courts had justified this exclusion on the basis that women did not qualify as 'persons' under s24 British North America Act 1867, and indeed English domestic courts had also denied women the status of 'persons'. This line of reasoning was brought to an end in 1930, by the JCPC, which held in *Edwards* that women were 'persons' and so could hold office in the Canadian Senate, observing that the exclusion of women from all public offices was a relic of more barbarous days. Lord Sankey also famously commented that the 1867 Act 'planted in Canada a living tree capable of growth and expansion within its natural limits,' and that it was for the JCPC '… to give it a large and liberal interpretation so that the Dominion … may be mistress in her own house.'[120]

Some looked to the JCPC as protector of oppressed groups within the Empire. But in South Africa, after the 1948 election when apartheid became formalized, the right of appeal to the JCPC was eradicated. And the white minority government of Ian Smith (in what was then Rhodesia) unilaterally declared independence from Britain, abolishing appeals to the JCPC. The famous JCPC decision in *Madzimbamuto* v. *Landner-Burke*[121] related to this unilateral declaration of independence, and the JCPC held that the Queen-in-Parliament continued to be the lawful sovereign. This decision, however, was unenforceable in Rhodesia, where the courts implemented the laws of the Smith regime instead.

Both India and Pakistan abolished appeals to the JCPC on gaining independence. However, prior to that, the JCPC delivered some potentially repressive decisions regarding India. One significant case affirmed the power of the Governor-General to create special tribunals in emergency situations.[122] Negative reactions to this decision were not aided by the perception that the JCPC was dominated by English judges. In clear contrast, the JCPC did not adjudge cases from the UK. Lord Chancellor Haldane stated: 'Though the Privy Council is considered good enough for the colonies, it is not allowed in Great Britain and Ireland to be good enough for us'.[123]

[119] T Mohr, 'A British Empire Court: A Brief Appraisal of the History of the Judicial Committee of the Privy Council', UCD Working Papers in Law, No. 30/2010 at 16.

[120] *Edwards* v. *Attorney-General for Canada* [1930] AC 124 (PC) at 128 and 138.

[121] [1969] 1 AC 645 (PC) (Rhodesia). [122] *Bhagat Singh* v. *Emperior* [1931] 58 IA 169 (PC 1931).

[123] Hansard, House of Commons, vol. 83, col. 101, 14 May 1900.

4.3.2.2 Governance in the Colonies

A great deal of British authority and control depended on cooperation with the local population, and enforcement by those in place. Benton and Ford use the term 'middle power' to describe the legal authorities who enforced order throughout the British Empire in the earlier nineteenth century.[124] This middle power included the judges, magistrates, and commissioners who applied a form of legal governance of the colonies. Benton and Ford argue that it was through the jurisprudence of this middle power that not only imperial law, but also international law, began to take shape, and that, at its centre lay 'a fairly consistent set of constitutional minima – comprised chiefly of the rudiments of procedural fairness and jurisdictional hierarchy'. What is particularly interesting is Benton and Ford's focus on law, for they write that 'Law was everywhere', supplying 'the text and the subtext of numerous colonial controversies, including debates over colonial legislative powers and crown prerogatives' and that law 'installed empire as the ghost in the machine of global governance'.[125] However, the law they describe 'was not gathered up in the tomes of jurists or even Privy Council cases, the usual fixtures of constitutional law.' Instead, a 'vernacular constitution' was created, and, 'By and large, imperial commentary was an endemic and eclectic genre … the stuff of long dispatches and arcane complaints … in the pages of untidy commission reports, obscure manuals of colonial administration, and hagiographies of law-minded governors.'[126]

4.3.3 'Settler' Colonies

The existence of a large number of settler colonies distinguished the British Empire from other empires. This involved the migration of British settlers to overseas lands, with the intention of remaining there. Settlement had started with the 'plantation' of areas of Ireland, and America, and continued with Canada, Australia, New Zealand, South Africa, (then) Southern Rhodesia, and Kenya.

4.3.3.1 'Responsible Government'

In 1837–1838, following rebellion in Upper and Lower Canada, the British Government decided to reorganize government there, and asked Lord Durham, from 1838 Governor-General of Canada, to investigate the causes of the disturbances. Durham belonged to a British political circle known as the Colonial Reformers who argued that the British overseas should be self-governing as far as possible (which they believed would ensure their loyalty.) Durham produced his famous *Report on the Affairs of British North America* in

[124] As they acknowledge, the term 'middle power' comes from Governor Thomas Maitland, who used it to restructure the legal system in Ceylon, to fill mid-level posts with respected British officials to boost authority. L Benton and L Ford, *Rage for Order* (Cambridge MA: Harvard University Press, 2016) 8, 16.

[125] Benton and Ford, *Rage for Order*, 18, 6, 17, 5, and 1.

[126] Ibid., 3.

1839,[127] which ushered in responsible government. The term denotes a government drawn from and accountable to a locally elected legislature, rather than directly to the Crown or local Governor. Responsible government applied in Britain itself and it was this type of governance that Britain increasingly established in settler colonies during the nineteenth century.

4.3.3.2 Which Colonies?

4.3.3.2.1 Canada

Lord Durham had recommended that Upper (Ontario) and Lower Canada (Quebec) be combined into one single province with responsible government. This was done by imperial Act of Union of 1840. In March 1867, the imperial British North America Act (renamed the Constitution Act 1867, in 1982) established a federal Canada, dividing authority between a Federal Government and Parliament in Ottawa and initially four provinces (New Brunswick, Nova Scotia, Ontario, and Quebec). All Canada was under the overarching sovereignty of the British monarch, represented by the Governor-General. Manitoba, British Columbia, Prince Edward's Island, Saskatchewan and Alberta subsequently joined what was to be named the Dominion of Canada, after 1907. Although the 1867 British North America Act provided a Constitution for Canada, it contained no constitutional amendment procedure operable within Canada alone, and so such amendments had to be adopted by further statutes of the Westminster Parliament.

4.3.3.2.2 Australia

Initially, it was convicts who were brought to Botany Bay, on the east coast of Australia, from 1788. However, from the early nineteenth century, voluntary settlers arrived. At first, much of Australia was ruled more directly from London, but, following Lord Durham's report, responsible government was introduced. The 1850 imperial Australian Colonies Government Act established a number of colonies, with their Constitutions ensuring responsible government. Although once again, the Westminster Parliament was the ultimate sovereign, colonial legislatures were omnicompetent within their sphere of authority. Australia become a federation in 1900, when the Commonwealth of Australia Constitution Act was adopted by Westminster. This established a federal government composed of the six states, overseen by a Governor-General representing the British monarch. But native Aboriginals and their claims were largely ignored.

4.3.3.2.3 New Zealand

Increasing numbers of British settlers were arriving in New Zealand by the 1830s. Lieutenant-Governor William Hobson, British consul in New Zealand,

[127] CP Lucas (ed.), *Lord Durham's Report on the Affairs of British North America* (Oxford: Clarendon Press, 1912).

signed the 1840 treaty of Waitangi with Maori chiefs. This treaty established British sovereignty over New Zealand (at least in its English language version), annexing its islands to Britain, while at the same time assuring Maoris of British protection of their status, rights and lands. But in the Maori language version, it seems British sovereignty was not so clear, and there was conflict between Maoris and settlers. The British did not apply Maori law, and the English Laws Act 1858 declared English law to apply from 14 January 1840, prior to the Treaty of Waitangi. In 1852, Westminster passed the New Zealand Constitution Act, which established New Zealand government with a Governor, Executive Council and bi-cameral Assembly with an elected lower house. The New Zealand Constitution Amendment Act, 1857 allowed the New Zealand General Assembly to amend all but a few sections of the 1852 Constitution Act. Since then, New Zealand has been considered to possess an uncodified Constitution. In 1900, New Zealand determined to remain an independent colony and not to join the Australian federation. By 1907, it formally took the description of Dominion.

4.3.3.2.4 South Africa

By 1815, Britain had gained the Cape of Good Hope as a colony and annexed the neighbouring Natal in 1843. However, not only were there indigenous Africans in the region but also Boers (farmers), who were descendants of Dutch seventeenth-century settlers. By the 1830s, the Boers had established independent republics in the Orange Free State and Transvaal. But Britain was continually in conflict with the Boers, and there were two Boer wars from 1880 to1881 and 1899 to 1902. Eventually, Britain prevailed in the second Boer war, and by the *1902 Treaty of Vereeniging* the Boers had to yield their two republics. In 1910, the Union of South Africa came into being, establishing a unitary State comprised of the four provinces of the Cape, Natal, Orange Free State, and Transvaal, rather than a federation as in Canada – notwithstanding that the Boers and British were as distinct as French- and English-speaking Canadians. Indigenous Africans were excluded from all political activity, including the right to vote, and power became entrenched in the white, Transvaal-dominated minority for the subsequent 80 years.

4.3.3.3 Dominion Status[128]

In the early twentieth century, there was no formal definition of Dominion status, although the term derives from the Latin word 'dominion' which means property, ownership, or territory subject to a ruler. The problem was that the term had been generally and imprecisely used to describe all Britain's overseas territorial possessions, but then came to assume a more specific meaning by the early twentieth century, when it was applied to Britain's settler

[128] For a very good analysis: PC Oliver, '"Dominion Status": History, Framework and Context' (2019) 17(4) *I•CON* 1173–1191.

colonies with responsible government. 'Dominion' when used with a capital 'D' became the preferred term for Britain's self-governing settler empire (although Australia was a 'commonwealth' and South Africa, from 1910, a 'union') distinguishing it from 'dominions' more generally, which connoted the British Empire as a whole.

In 1917, an Imperial War Cabinet came into being, which included the Dominions, and that same year an Imperial War Conference resolution referenced the 'full recognition of the Dominions as autonomous nations of an Imperial Commonwealth.'[129] However, this Imperial Cabinet did not continue after the end of the war. And, in 1917, General Smuts of South Africa complained that 'in actual theory the status of the Dominions is of a subject character.'[130] Smuts had a point. The imperial Parliament in Westminster could still legislate for Dominions without any need for their consent. Britain concluded treaties on behalf of the whole empire, without any Dominion participation, as it did with Turkey in the 1924 Treaty of Lausanne. And appeals continued from the Dominions to the JCPC in London. Further, all colonial Constitutions made provision for disallowance of colonial legislation by the Crown.[131]

Yet, at the Versailles conference after the First World War, Britain requested that the Dominions represent themselves, and Dominions also became members of the League of Nations in their own right. In 1923, Canada negotiated a treaty with the US in her own right – the Halibut Fishery Treaty. All this seemed highly significant: Dominions were colonies 'at a stage of growing up'.[132] Dominion status was evolving, although the formal legal position had yet to be altered. Clause 2 of the 1926 Balfour Declaration[133] formally defined Dominion status in the following terms: 'They are autonomous Communities within the British Empire, equal in status, in no way subordinate one to another in any aspect of their domestic or external affairs, though united by a common allegiance to the Crown, and freely associated as members of the British Commonwealth of Nations'.

This Declaration was the product of the Imperial Conference Committee of Prime Ministers and Heads of Delegation (which was the sixth such Imperial Conference). The Committee report however also stated that it believed 'nothing would be gained by attempting to lay down a Constitution for the British Empire' because 'Its widely scattered parts have very different

129 WH Long and SE Baldwin, *Extracts from Minutes of Proceedings Laid before the Conference* (1917) at 5.

130 KC Wheare, *The Statute of Westminster and Dominion Status* (Oxford: Oxford University Press, 1938) 23.

131 See e.g. in Canada, sections 55 and 57 of the 1867 British North America Act.

132 FR Scott, 'The End of Dominion status' (1944) 38(1) American Journal of International Law, 34–49 at 34, 35.

133 This should not be confused with the 1917 Balfour Declaration which declared British support for a national home for Jewish people in Palestine.

characteristics, very different histories, and are at very different stages of evolution; while, considered as a whole, it defies classification and bears no real resemblance to any other political organisation which now exists or has ever yet been tried'.[134]

These are telling remarks, indicative of the somewhat casual attitude taken to law, and a preference for more flexible arrangements.

4.3.3.4 The Statute of Westminster 1931

The question then became – could the Balfour Declaration be converted into a statute? This was achieved in 1931, when Parliament adopted the Statute of Westminster. Section 1 of which formally applied the title of 'Dominion' rather than colony to Canada, Newfoundland, New Zealand, Australia, South Africa and the Irish Free State. This Act repealed the 1865 Colonial Laws Validity Act, and section 4 renounced the Imperial Parliament's right to legislate for the Dominions unless they had explicitly requested it, thus ceding its authority to them. It also permitted the Dominions to amend or repeal any imperial law extending to them. Although the Act was directed to the six Dominions existing in 1931, it was only formally ratified by Australia in 1942, and by New Zealand in 1947. South Africa re-enacted it in its own Union Parliament in 1934 in the Status of the Union Act.

The Statute of Westminster was censured by some contemporaries as putting Imperial relations in 'constitutional strait jacket'.[135] But, in contrast, it was also interpreted as only a rule of construction, a self-denying ordinance, which did not reduce parliamentary sovereignty, and had no ability to bind future imperial legislation.[136] Indeed, in *British Coal Corp v. The King*, Lord Sankey stated (*obiter*) that 'the Imperial Parliament could, as a matter of abstract law, repeal or disregard section 4 of the *Statute*.'[137]

But if this view (i.e. that parliamentary sovereignty could not be extinguished because Parliament could always repeal the Statute of Westminster) is supposed to represent an orthodox Diceyan approach, then it is disingenuous. For Dicey believed that Parliament could abdicate its sovereignty altogether – by transferring its sovereignty over territory to another body. Dicey wrote that

> the impossibility of placing a limit on the exercise of sovereignty does not in any way prohibit … the abdication of sovereignty…. To argue or imply that because sovereignty is not limitable (which is true) that it cannot be surrendered (which is palpably untrue) involves the confusion of two distinct ideas…. A sovereign may transfer sovereign authority to another sovereign or body of persons.[138]

134 *Report on Inter-Imperial Relations*, Cmd. 2768.

135 HL Debates 26 November 1931, vol. 83, cols 185–187, 195–196, 202.

136 See further for consideration, De Smith, 'The Constitution and the Common Market' (1971) 34 MLR at 612.

137 [1935] AC 500, 520 (PC).

138 Dicey, *Law of the Constitution*, 69 at n 30.

Surely this is what Parliament did – it abdicated its sovereignty with s 4 Statute of Westminster? Yet some writers have criticized Dicey for this. Winterton argued that Dicey 'sacrificed consistency and logic' in declaring that Parliament could abdicate sovereignty. Wade also criticized this position, seeing it as inconsistent with the theory of the 'continuing' sovereignty of Westminster (namely the view that Parliament may legislate on any subject but may not bind future Parliaments).[139] In contrast, Lord Denning, in practical vein commented, 'Freedom once given cannot be taken away. Legal theory must give way to practical politics'[140] and this is what has since happened.

4.3.3.5 Seeing the Light?

It might seem that the Dominions achieved what American colonies had pursued 150 years earlier. As the last chapter explored, the eighteenth-century American colonies disputed Parliament's sovereignty to impose legislation on them. In the eighteenth century, the issue could not be resolved peacefully with Britain, and the American colonies became independent. Britain had been intransigent, and many came to regret such an attitude. James Stephen of the Colonial Office remarked that:

> I am convinced that in the numerous concerns of this kingdom the error of acting upon a policy which is purely occasional and transitional and which does not attempt the anticipation of events ... has been the source of our greatest national misfortunes. It lost us the United States. It has rendered Ireland what we now see it to be.[141]

Oliver illuminatingly compares statements made by Americans in the 1770s with those made at the Commonwealth conference in 1926. For example, he compares James Madison's statement that, 'The colonies [are] coordinate members with each other and with Great Britain of an empire united by a common executive sovereign, but not united by a common legislative sovereign,' with the Balfour Declaration above ('They are autonomous Communities within the British Empire, equal in status, in no way subordinate one to another in any aspect of their domestic or external affairs, though united by a common allegiance to the Crown').[142] This achievement had taken time. According to US Constitutional scholar, McIlwain,

> It required the utter collapse of the old colonial system in the thirteen North American colonies ... the repeated assaults of men like Buller and Wakefield and Lord Durham upon a succession of stubborn and doctrinaire Colonial

139 G Winterton, 'The British Grundnorm: Parliamentary Supremacy Re-Examined' (1976) 92 LQR 600; Wade, 'The Basis of Legal Sovereignty' (1955) CLJ 172. HLA Hart explored the 'continuing' theory of sovereignty in *The Concept of Law* (Oxford: Clarendon) 145.

140 *Blackburn* v. *Attorney General* [1971] 1 WLR, 1037, 1040.

141 Stephen to Howick, 28 December 1837 (Durham University, Grey papers) 124.

142 PC Oliver, 'Dominion Status', 1179–1180.

> Secretaries ... before the light finally broke in and hopeful solutions of the perplexing problem of dominion rule could be found.[143]

4.3.4 Other Territories

4.3.4.1 Crown Colonies

Crown colonies came under the direct authority of the British Crown, as opposed to having responsible government. They tended to be conquered overseas territories, such as those in the West Indies, Mauritius, and India. Crown colony government was considered appropriate 'only when a colonial society was so backward, or so divided by race, nationality, religion, wealth or servitude, that no group capable of working the old representative system was likely to provide good government in the interests of the population as a whole.'[144]

Crown colonies were diverse, numerous and reflected many legal traditions. There also tended to be greater authoritarian government in Crown colonies, empowering the Governor with extremely wide powers of control.

4.3.4.2 Protectorates

Protectorates are States or territories under the control of a more powerful State, a relationship usually agreed by treaty. The stronger State normally agrees to protect the other from external aggression (and sometimes internal rebellion), while allowing it to continue regulating its internal affairs. However, the relationship does not extend to the formal annexation, or declaration of sovereignty, over the weaker State, and protectorates maintain their status as independent States, and usually continue governing their domestic affairs. Although the concept is somewhat opaque, it is by no means new, having been greatly practised by the Romans. Since then, it has been used to ensure a sphere of influence or control over certain routes, frontiers and trading posts, and Britain tended to insert a protected country as a buffer between its possessions and strong neighbours (particularly Russia) as in the far northwest of India. British Protectorates were especially prevalent in Asia, Africa and the Pacific, usually under Foreign Office supervision, rather than the Colonial Office. Other European countries also took up the protectorate model, and they were to be found in Tunis, Egypt, Abyssinia (as it then was), Zanzibar, and many other places. Uncertainty over the exact status of Protectorates became a subject of great interest at the 1884 Berlin conference, when great power competition provoked further thought on the matter.

143 C McIlwain, *The American Revolution: A Constitutional Interpretation* (New York: Macmillan, 1923) 57.

144 J Manning Ward, *Colonial Self-Government: The British Experience 1759–1856* (London: Macmillan, 1976) 83.

4.3.4.3 Extraterritoriality and Jurisdiction

Further exploration reveals how protected status evolved, as it became intertwined with the expansion of British extraterritorial powers. Gradually the British had begun to assert jurisdiction over non-British territories, often with the justification (or pretext) of protecting British subjects from perceived 'barbarous' indigenous laws. For example, in the 1830s, Governor George Maclean assumed jurisdiction over disputes on the Gold Coast, on the basis of avoiding 'uncivilised' indigenous laws, an action subsequently approved by a British parliamentary committee.[145] And so a 'civilising mission' became a justification for Britain's expansion of extraterritorial authority.

From the 1840s, Parliament legislated to support enforcement of extraterritorial jurisdiction. The Foreign Jurisdiction Act of 1843 covered activities of British nationals in such diverse countries as the Ottoman empire, Japan, China, and later Siam (1856) and Zanzibar (1866). British jurisdiction was extended more and more on grounds of 'necessity', rather than with the consent of those officially ruling the territory. In 1890, Parliament adopted the Foreign Jurisdiction Act, which was premised on the assumed consent of foreigners to British extraterritorial jurisdiction.[146] The device of the chartered company was also revived as a semi-official agency. For example, Cecil Rhodes' British South Africa Company was granted a Charter in 1889, to protect Britain's strategic interest in the Cape, constrain the Afrikaner republics, and occupy and administer (at its own expense) land that would become the Rhodesias. Elsewhere, more official consular jurisdictions were established, which engendered the Niger Coast Protectorate in 1893, and the Gambia and Sierra Leone Protectorates in 1895. As a result of all this activity, the distinction between Protectorates and actual colonies became less meaningful, as Protectorates became managed like colonies, and sometimes even reclassified as such.

The assumption of greater political control over these foreign territories was fortified by Joseph Chamberlain (at the Colonial Office from 1895), who believed that the State should take a more interventionist role in developing the Empire, including, if necessary, taking over sovereignty from those local rulers deemed incapable of modernization. Indeed, the radical liberal economist, JA Hobson, later termed this aggressive expansionism the '"[e]arth hunger" of the new imperialism'.[147] Nonetheless, this expansion of British Protectorates did not go unresisted. There was a revolt in Sierra Leone in 1897–1898 against

145 Report of the Select Committee on the West Coast of Africa, *British Parliamentary Papers* 1842, Paper no. 551.

146 W Ross Johnston, *Sovereignty and Protection: A Study of British Jurisdictional Imperialism in the Late Nineteenth Century* (Durham, NC: Duke University Press, 1973) 11; C Newbury, '"Treaty, Grant, Usage and Sufferance": The Origins of British Colonial Protectorates', in GA Wood and PS O'Connor (eds.), *W. P. Morrell: A Tribute* (Dunedin: University of Otago Press, 1973) 75–80.

147 JA Hobson, *Imperialism* (London: James Nisbet, 1902) 11.

a 'hut tax', and pushback from British humanitarians and also officials in the Colonial Office, who urged the importance of securing consent to Britain's expanding jurisdiction in Africa. There was also a move after 1900 to indirect rule as a more suitable means of imperial management.[148]

4.3.4.4 The Scramble for Africa

The Scramble for Africa lasted from about 1880 to 1900, and in this period, Africa was rapidly colonized by European powers. Until the nineteenth century, Africa had been basically uncolonized by Europeans, with the exception of some coastal areas, South Africa, and the area north of the Sahara, which had been controlled by Ottoman Turks. The British formerly considered West Africa important for trade, not colonization. However, as the nineteenth century progressed, Europeans realized that Africa contained a wealth of resources such as gold, silver, and timber, which could be exploited. Nineteenth-century international lawyer, John Westlake, wrote that:

> The inflow of the white race cannot be stopped where there is land to cultivate, or to be mined, commerce to be developed, sport to enjoy, curiosity to be satisfied.... Accordingly international law has to treat natives as uncivilised. It regulates, for the mutual benefit of civilised states, the claims which they make to sovereignty over the region and leaves the treatment of the nations to the conscience of the state to which the sovereignty is awarded, rather than sanction their interest being made an excuse the more for war between civilised claimants, devastating the region and the cause of suffering to the natives themselves.[149]

Curiosity in Africa was aroused by the exploits of missionaries and explorers. British born (but naturalized American) Henry Morton Stanley, who had crossed the African continent and located the missing Dr Livingstone, was a well-known explorer. However, Stanley is perhaps best known for his work as envoy of King Leopold II of Belgium, for whom he had obtained treaties in the Congo. But in the event, the Congo became a personal kingdom for King Leopold, who benefited greatly from partitions authorized by the Berlin conference, and the Congo lost half of its population under his brutal rule.

Most of Britain's interest in Africa was sparked, not by an intrinsic interest in Africa so much as to prevent its control by other European powers, although this combined with a desire to exploit Africa's natural resources for Britain's industries. Indeed, most European powers participated in the Berlin conference because the land grab and scramble for Africa was impairing European peace and stability.

148 A Pagden, 'Fellow Citizens and Imperial Subjects: Conquest and Sovereignty in Europe's Overseas Empires' (2005) 44 History and Theory 43.

149 L Oppenheim (ed.), *The Collected Papers of John Westlake on Public International Law* (Cambridge: Cambridge University Press, 1914) 138, 145.

4.3.4.4.1 The Conference of Berlin[150]

In 1884–1885, thirteen European States, the USA, and the Ottoman Empire gathered in Berlin, capital of the newly united State of Germany, in a conference convened by German Chancellor Otto von Bismarck, to agree the rules for African colonization and partition – basically, to divide up Africa among themselves. There were no Africans present. (Indeed, the request of the Sultan of Zanzibar to be included was ridiculed by the British.) On the wall of the Reich Chancellery, where the conference was held, was a gigantic map of Africa, over 5 m (16.4 ft) high. The Berlin conference has been compared to the 1493 Papal Bull of Demarcation, which divided the known world between Spain and Portugal[151] (although the latter was a unilateral act, condemned by other European countries).

Bismarck declared that the purpose of the conference was to 'civilize' Africa by opening it up to European trade. A more specific aim was to determine the legal conditions for territorial acquisitions in Africa to be effective in international law.[152] The conference conclusions were formalized in the General Act of the Conference, ratified by all parties but the US. Chapter I of the General Act established freedom of trade in certain areas and Chapters IV and V provided that navigation of the Congo and Niger rivers was to be free to all. Chapter II prohibited the slave trade and all the signatory powers were enjoined to eradicate it. Religious freedom was endorsed, although this only really covered Christianity, and to a degree Islam. African religions were not protected. Chapter VI (Articles 34 & 35) established conditions for effective occupation, providing no territory could be formally claimed prior to direct rule by colonial powers. The Act reaffirmed the principle of the 'sphere of influence', whereby, if a claim were properly notified to other signatory States and uncontested by them, then it could be transformed into a sovereign right. In this way, Italy annexed Tripoli from 1911 to 1912. However, the conference documents omitted any reference to the requirement of consent from African parties before their territory could be transferred.[153]

In fact, the conference failed to achieve its stated goals, and the Congo did not become a free trade area, but an exclusive possession of Leopold, not a model of civilization, but genocide. The doctrine of 'effective occupation' was not satisfactorily elucidated, and the issue of sovereignty and title over African territories was unsettled. Although some attempt at clarification of the status of

150 A Anghie, 'Berlin West Africa Conference (1884–85)', in *Max Planck Encyclopedias of International Law* (Oxford: Oxford University Press, online).

151 GN Uzoigwe, 'Reflections on the Berlin West Africa Conference' (1984–1985) 12 Journal of the Historical Society of Nigeria 9, 10.

152 CA Alexandrowicz, *The European-African Confrontation: A Study in Treaty Making* (Leiden: AW Sijthoff, 1973).

153 See John Mugambwa, 'Treaties or Scraps of Paper? A Second Look at the Legal Character of the Nineteenth Century British/African Colonial Agreements' (1987) 20(1) Comparative and International Law Jl of Southern Africa 79–93 at 82.

Protectorates was made at the Berlin Conference, its conclusions were vague, and competition between the great powers continued in Africa. In turn, this prompted Britain into more interventionist actions to forestall its competitors' claims on territories.

The Scramble for Africa accelerated, and by 1902, 90 per cent of Africa was under European control – all of Africa with the exception of Liberia and Abyssinia (present-day Ethiopia). And significantly, Africa became partitioned into areas administered by the British, French, German, and Belgians, rather than divided according to tribal, linguistic, historical or geographical boundaries – a division that was to have consequences in the twentieth century.

4.3.5 A Constitution for Empire?

4.3.5.1 Imperial Governance as Part of the British Constitution in the Nineteenth and Early Twentieth Centuries

Since the Second World War, and especially since the 1990s, theories of transnational constitutionalism have gained in strength. There has been a tendency to perceive this growth as the development of a new post-war legal order. But to do so is to neglect a possible earlier nineteenth-century transnational constitutionalism, one engendered by empires. In his long 'Introduction' to the 8th edition of *The Law of the Constitution*, Dicey included a lengthy description of constitutional structures of the Empire, describing its status as 'Imperial Constitution' as a central feature of the British Constitution. Dicey was also deeply engaged with the Irish question, and fervently unionist in his opposition to Home Rule and federalism. As Dicey expressed it, '[i]mperialism is to all who share it a form of passionate feeling', 'a political religion'.[154] This section highlights Dicey's views in particular, because of the great influence he has had on British constitutional law. As Oliver Comments: '[a]s any teacher of first year constitutional law will know, once Dicey's doctrine is in place in the minds of law students it is very difficult to dislodge it.'[155]

By the later nineteenth century, the British Empire was receiving attention from mainstream British constitutional scholarship (although imperial aspects of this thought have been somewhat overlooked[156]). Sir William Anson in 1888 published his *Law and Custom of the Constitution*, with seventy pages on the Empire.[157] Frederic Maitland's *Constitutional History of England* emphasized

[154] AV Dicey, *Lectures on the Relation between Law and Public Opinion in England during the Nineteenth Century* (2nd ed., London: Macmillan & Co., 1914) 45.

[155] P Oliver, *The Constitution of Independence* (Oxford: Oxford University Press, 2005) 350.

[156] For a very useful discussion, see Dylan Lino, 'Albert Venn Dicey and the Constitutional Theory of Empire' (2016) 36(4) OJLS 751–780. Also letters between Dicey and AB Keith focus mainly on imperial constitutional questions: RF Shinn and RA Cosgrove (eds.), *Constitutional Reflections: The Correspondence of Dicey and Berriedale Keith* (Lanham MD.: University Press of America, 1996).

[157] W Anson, *The Law and Custom of the Constitution* (Oxford: Clarendon Press, 1886–1892) vol. 1, 30; vol. 2, 219–272.

Parliament's rule over 'the whole of that huge collection of lands which it is convenient to call the British Empire.'[158] Thomas Holland, best known for his post-Austinian *Elements of Jurisprudence*, included 'the relations between the mother-country and its colonies and dependencies'[159] in his account of the boundaries of constitutional law. Indeed, there were few scholars who did not include Empire within the scope of their constitutional definitions, but James Bryce excluded Empire on the grounds that parliamentary representation in Westminster was essential for inclusion in the British Constitutional system.[160]

Dicey himself wrote that, '[t]he maintenance of the British Empire makes it possible, at a cost which is relatively small … to secure peace, good order, and personal freedom throughout a large part of the world'.[161] This was connected with a growing belief in the importance of 'civilization' for global advancement,[162] and the supposition that legal progress was linked to civilizational progress. In 1898, Dicey wrote that 'the spirit of legalism … is the main point on which the Anglo-Saxon race has reached a stage of civilisation to which other nations have hardly attained.'[163]

4.3.5.2 A Flexible Constitution for the Empire

Dicey also believed the British Constitution's flexibility to be one of the reasons for Britain's success in its imperial governance. The distinction between flexible (uncodified) and rigid (codified) constitutions was originally made by James Bryce,[164] but was adopted by Dicey, who believed that the British Constitution's flexibility could be contrasted with the greater rigidity of federalism, which Dicey believed led to weak government and was inappropriate for imperial rule.[165]

For Dicey, the Westminster Parliament was 'the absolute sovereign of the British Empire', whose enactments were 'binding on every Court throughout the British dominions'.[166] However, there are two important rejoinders to Dicey here. First, the evidence for such an absolute sovereignty applying throughout the British Empire is wanting, and the Empire was far more incoherent in its constitutional governance than Dicey's account allowed. This claim will be examined in further detail in Section 4.3.7. Second, if we accept Dicey's account of absolute parliamentary sovereignty throughout the British

158 FW Maitland, *The Constitutional History of England* (Cambridge: Cambridge University Press, 1908) 330. Delivered as lectures 2 decades earlier.

159 TE Holland, *The Elements of Jurisprudence* (Oxford: Clarendon Press, 1880) 249.

160 J Bryce, *Studies in History and Jurisprudence* (Oxford: Clarendon Press, 1901) 194.

161 Dicey, *Law and Public Opinion*, 454.

162 See D Bell, 'Empire and Imperialism', in GS Jones and G Claeys (eds.), *The Cambridge History of Nineteenth Century Political Thought* (Cambridge: Cambridge University Press, 2011) 867.

163 AV Dicey, 'England and America' (1898) 82 *Atl Mo* 441, 444.

164 James Bryce, 'Flexible and Rigid Constitutions', in *Studies in History and Jurisprudence* (Oxford: Clarendon Press, 1901).

165 Dicey, *Law of the Constitution*, 1st ed., 114; 8th ed., lxiii–xci.

166 Dicey, *Law of the Constitution*, 1st ed., 355.

Empire then such sovereignty, because it brought the danger of (legal) absolute and unconstrained law-making – risked abusive management of the Empire, and thus threats to its stability. We turn to this point immediately.

4.3.5.3 Limits on the Imperial Constitution

Although the orthodox Diceyan interpretation of parliamentary sovereignty admitted no (entrenched) legal limits, it acknowledged some (non-legal) practical, or moral, limits.

One such limitation is provided by representation in Parliament itself, which then sets practical limits on the legislation a government may adopt – as MPs are less likely to vote for something against their constituents' interests. But colonies had no representation in Westminster. But in Dicey's view, colonial representation in Westminster would have extended the notion of representative government beyond any meaningful application. There had to be a community of interest among the electors, which necessitated its territorial limitation, and he believed the Empire was simply too large to be effectively represented in Westminster.[167] Dicey, and others, also acknowledged that public opinion, and the possibility of rebellion, could act as a constraint on Parliament. But the threat of rebellion was a rather blunt and dangerous form of constraint – and as the American example had shown, could lead to war and independence.

In theory, a constraint on parliamentary sovereignty was the Crown's ability to veto parliamentary legislation, although a constitutional convention was now thought to mandate royal assent to any legislation passed in Britain itself. However, the veto could still be used to enjoin colonial legislation. Why this was so, if the British Constitution governed the whole Empire, was not clear, and Dicey was not himself clear on this matter. But such a veto could arouse colonial resentment, and a policy of non-intervention (which became akin to a constitutional convention) had arisen with regard to at least those colonies with responsible government.

In summary, a lack of legal restraints created a real risk of parliamentary misrule, particularly of the dependent empire, where there were no identifiable conventions requiring non-intervention.

4.3.5.4 The Rule of Law

However, parliamentary sovereignty was only one key principle of the British Constitution identified by Dicey. The rule of law also had its part to play. Dicey's account of the rule of law remained a point of reference for many discussions, although his interpretation is now often regarded as too evocative of outdated laissez-faire attitudes. According to Dicey, the rule of law had three main requirements: government through ordinary laws rather than discretion; formal equality before the law; and the slow accretion of individual

[167] See Dicey, 'Comparative Constitutionalism', 224. Also, D Bell, 'John Stuart Mill on Colonies' (2010) 38 *Pol Theory* 14.

rights through gradual, common-law development. Dicey's account accorded with his belief in English law as a product of civilizational development, something worthy of export, that could be contrasted with 'the fanciful caprice of the torments inflicted by Oriental despotism.'[168] David Sugarman notes how British legal textbooks, such as Dicey's *Law of the Constitution*, neatly organized English law and its supposed liberal principles for ready application in the colonies, and Niall Ferguson refers to the export of the rule of law, liberty and the common law as one of Britain's most valuable exports overseas.[169]

But imperial rule was not always about respect for the rule of law – indeed, Dicey's rule of law has been described as sometimes no more than an exercise in 'wishful thinking'.[170] Dicey had proudly stated that, unlike the law of some European States, the British Constitution made no formal provision for military rule during emergencies, which he cited as 'unmistakable proof of the permanent supremacy of law under our constitution'. However, Dicey also wrote that martial law was 'most assuredly recognised in the most ample manner by the law of England.'[171] These statements are hard to reconcile. But then, Dicey was not always consistent.

Incidents of rebellion in the British Empire reveal a less than scrupulous adherence to the rule of law. British soldiers had crushed violent uprisings in India, Ceylon and Cape Colony. There had also been notable deviations from the rule of law in Ireland. By 1913, Dicey considered 'recourse to the use of arms' permissible in Ireland once 'all possibility of legal resistance is exhausted'.[172] This hardly seems to uphold the rule of law as defined by Dicey elsewhere. Indeed, recognition of martial law in Jamaica and in the Boer wars uncomfortably undermined the rule of law, as a broader examination of the Morant Bay rebellion now illustrates.

4.3.5.4.1 The Morant Bay Rebellion

The 1865 Morant Bay rebellion in Jamaica was met with the imposition of martial law, great brutality, and the killing of over 400 black Jamaicans by then Governor Edward Eyre. The Jamaican politician, George Gordon, identified as a key antagonist, had been summarily executed. This incident had become notorious in Britain, where a 'Jamaica committee' was formed, guided by prominent liberals, radicals, and anti-slavery activists, including John Stuart Mill, John Bright and James Fitzjames Stephen. (On the other hand, Eyre was praised as a hero by Disraeli, Thomas Carlyle, and John Ruskin.) Eyre's actions in Jamaica were presented as a threat to the British Constitution, as exemplifying an arbitrary exercise of prerogative power, and martial law was

[168] Dicey, *Law of the Constitution* 168, 171.

[169] D Sugarman, 'The Legal Boundaries of Liberty: Dicey, Liberalism and Legal Science' (1983) 46 *MLR*, 107; N Ferguson, *Empire: How Britain Made the Modern World* (London: Penguin, 2003) xxiii–xxiv.

[170] M Taggart, 'Ruled by Law?' (2006) 69 MLR 1006, 1025.

[171] Dicey, *Law of the Constitution*, 269.

[172] AV Dicey, *A Fool's Paradise* (London: John Murray, 1913) 127.

attacked as illegal and unconstitutional.[173] But a further question was this: could a duofold system exist, with one model of legality for Britain and another, more pliant one, for the Empire?

A Royal Commission produced a report critical of the length and severity of the imposition of martial law in Jamaica. Fitzjames Stephen and Edward James QC provided a legal opinion for the Jamaica committee, concluding that Eyre had acted unlawfully and could be prosecuted in England. Although Eyre was dismissed, he was never successfully prosecuted, and received a pension. A famous civil case, *Phillips* v. *Eyre*, was brought against Eyre in England, but this failed, partly on account of the Act of Indemnity adopted by the Jamaica Legislature (in which Eyre himself played a dominant role as Governor) to protect him. Although the English Court found retrospective laws of questionable policy, it ruled they could be upheld if the statute evinced a clear intention to legislate with retrospective effect.[174] This finding was criticized by the *Law Times* as validating martial law as the unfettered law of war.[175]

According to Kostal, 'martial law was understood broadly as the "laws and usages of war"' and he argues there is little doubt that 'in the suppression of rebels and their communities the British military often had recourse to terror' – in other places, such as South Africa and Burma.[176] Other than the Jamaica controversy, however, there was little concern about the use of martial law in the Empire.

4.3.5.4.2 Abolition of the Slave Trade and Slavery

One other subject looms large in its relevance to humanitarian and rule of law concerns. Undoubtedly, the issue of slavery is too large, too fundamental for human freedom and dignity, to be considered under a sub-heading of the rule of law. But, in setting a marker for human rights, and a limit on how one group of humans may treat another, it places crucial constraints on how government and parliament may proceed. The slave trade is bound up with the history of Britain's Empire. Up to the late eighteenth century, Britain had played a key role in developing an overseas slave trade, and in the eighteenth century shipped more slaves to the Americas than any other State. Ports such as Bristol and Liverpool rapidly expanded as a result of the trade in goods.

Yet, paradoxically, Britain was also one of the earlier countries to end the slave trade and then slavery, and the growth of a humanitarian movement in Britain played an important role in this history of the British Empire. After the Seven Years War, a growing number of slaves were brought into to Britain, and legal questions arose as to their status – did they remain slaves in Britain,

173 See e.g. C Townsend, 'Martial Law: Legal and Administrative Problems of Civil Emergency in Britain and the Empire, 1800–1940' (1982) 25 Historical Journal 167.

174 *Phillips* v. *Eyre* [1870] LR 6 QB 1.

175 *Law Times* (2 July 1870) 160.

176 Rande W Kostal, *A Jurisprudence of Power: Victorian Empire and the Rule of Law* (Oxford: Oxford University Press, 2008) 455.

which had no slave law? In *Somersett* v. *Steuart*, in 1772, Lord Mansfield had determined that a slave could not be taken out of England against his will, but did not address a wider question as to whether slavery was legal in the Empire. Mansfield had also famously stated that slavery was alien to the common law and 'so odious that nothing can be suffered to support it but positive law.'[177] This was evocative of a British Constitution enforcing liberty, but hard to reconcile with practice in Britain's colonies, where slavery was enforced by law. However after American independence, concerns for Britain's moral reputation rose, as did the idea that colonization should be exercised for the benefit of the governed, which evolved into the doctrine of 'trusteeship'.

By the 1780s, in Britain, slavery could not be defended on moral or Christian grounds, nor was it reconcilable with a British Constitution that claimed to privilege liberty, and an imperial movement that stressed benevolent government. In 1787, the Society for Effecting the Abolition of Slave Trade was established. It was supported by the 'Clapham sect' (which was to include James Stephen in the Colonial Office) and William Wilberforce MP led the campaign for abolishing the slave trade in the House of Commons. However, the French revolution and war against France led to a more repressive atmosphere in Britain, and a powerful group of planters, merchants, manufacturers and ship owners mounted resistance to abolition in Parliament. It was only in 1807 that legislation – the Act for the Abolition of the Slave Trade (47 Geo. III, Sess. 1, c. 36) – was finally passed. As a result, it became illegal to transport slaves on British ships. However, other nations took over the slave trade, and there was no general abolition treaty. British ships could also avoid the legislation by operating under Spanish or Portuguese flags.

There had been an assumption that ending the slave trade would lead to the abolition of slavery but this did not happen. Indeed, support for slavery could be found in unexpected places – even the young Gladstone had defended slavery in the House of Commons.[178] So, in time, the Antislavery Society was formed. Abolitionist campaigns increased. The 1833 Slavery Abolition Act (3 & 4 Will. IV c. 73) – drafted by James Stephen[179] – abolished slavery itself. The Act emancipated all slaves in the British Empire except those held by the East India Company (which was subject to separate obligations to phase out indigenous slavery). It also contained provisions compensating slave owners for the loss of slaves, for which the government took out a loan (the £20 million fund was 40 per cent of the government's then total annual expenditure) only paid off in full in 2015.[180] But slaves received no compensation and also were forced to work as apprentices for a further six years, and it was only in August 1840

177 *Somersett* v. *Steuart* [1772] 98 ER 499.

178 Swinfen, *Imperial Control of Colonial Legislation*, 124.

179 Stephen was rebuked by the Duke of Wellington for this – see Swinfen, ibid., 123.

180 Britain raised the present-day equivalent of £17bn in compensation for slaveholders, which was the largest state sponsored payout until the bank bailouts in 2008 [per N El Enany, *(B) ordering Britain* (Manchester University Press, 2020)].

that full emancipation was achieved. Indeed, relations with Jamaica grew so bad that its Constitution was suspended and Crown colony rule (removing the representative institutions in which plantation owners had such influence) put in place. Strict control had to be maintained over West Indian employment law to prevent a regress to the pre-abolition situation, as Legislatures dominated by plantation interests adopted a multitude of laws to perpetuate their previous position.[181]

4.3.6 'Greater Britain' and Imperial Federation

4.3.6.1 'Greater Britain'

By the second half of the nineteenth century, talk of a 'Greater Britain' was becoming common. This involved consideration of a possible union between Britain and some, or maybe all, of its colonies.[182] Part of the impetus was a loss of Victorian self-confidence, and anxiety over the competition of other states, especially Russia and Germany. A larger polity of a Greater Britain was thought to provide strength against that challenge.

Support for Greater Britain coalesced around a group of Victorian intellectuals. The well-known historian JA Froude chose to designate his projected polity of Greater Britain 'Oceana', in a conscious bow to the earlier writer, James Harrington's republican, utopian vision.[183] However, this diverse group understood the term in differing ways. Some used the term to denote the entire British Empire, but, for others, Greater Britain included only the settler colonies, affirming certain concepts of race and identity. For example, Dilke, the politician and radical thinker, in his 1868 travelogue *Greater Britain*, argued the term should be restricted to the 'English-speaking, white-inhabited, and self-governed lands.'[184] The historian JR Seeley used the term in his 1883 work *The Expansion of England* to draw a sharp distinction between the colonial empire and Indian empire, which he saw as opposites.[185] These imperialist distinctions are also relevant to concepts of British identity. Many late Victorians conceived of Britishness as sustained in its global spread throughout settler colonies, a community of what Pocock describes as 'neoBritains'.[186] In this way, it was argued that British identity developed in reaction to a perceived alien and deviant 'Other.'[187]

181 A situation analogous to that which occurred in southern state legislatures in post–civil war America.

182 See D Bell, *The Idea of Greater Britain: Empire and the Future of World Order, 1860–1900* (Princeton NJ: Princeton University Press, 2007).

183 JA Froude, *Oceana, or England and Her Colonies* (London: Longmans, Green & Co, 1886).

184 Sir Charles Dilke, *Greater Britain*, 2 vols. (London: Macmillan, 1868).

185 JR Seeley, *The Expansion of England* (London: Macmillan, 1883) 11.

186 JGA Pocock, *The Discovery of Islands* (Cambridge: Cambridge University Press, 2005) 181–191 and 20.

187 Most influentially, Edward Said, *Culture and Imperialism* (London: Chatto & Windus, 1993).

4.3.6.2 A Federal Empire?

Others aspired to unite Britain and its colonies in some grand federal polity,[188] especially after the US example illustrated it was possible to create a successful federal State.

Federalism gained some academic recognition in 1832, with the publication of John Austin's *Province of Jurisprudence Determined.*[189] In this work Austin discussed federalism, remarking that in federalist States, sovereignty was divided and not supreme, but did not dwell on perceived weaknesses of federalism, in contrast to Dicey, half a century later. Bagehot, in the 1867 *The English Constitution*, was critical of the American system, finding that the states had too much power, which diminished the federal government's ability to redress the issue of slavery.[190] But Bagehot did not specifically address federalism. Dicey was sceptical that federalism could work in the UK, believing it would require a written Constitution, judicial review, the restriction of parliamentary sovereignty, and would also weaken British government and divide loyalties. In contrast, Bryce's treatment of federalism was much more positive, and in his 1888 work, *The American Commonwealth*, Bryce provided a detailed analysis of the American system.

Adherents of Greater Britain and imperial federation sought greater unity of Britain's empire, but their membership did not always overlap. Seeley and Froude supported imperial federation, along with James Bryce, Lord Rosebery, LT Hobhouse, JA Hobson, Alfred Tennyson, Joseph Chamberlain, WT Stead, Cecil Rhodes and others. However, Dilke was not a supporter of federation, and nor were AV Dicey, EA Freeman, Herbert Spencer, John Morley, John Bright, Gladstone, and Salisbury – all of whom considered that altering imperial constitutional structures would debilitate colonial accord. In 1885, EA Freeman argued that the federal and the imperial were irreconcilable, for, in the Empire:

> There is no voluntary union of independent states, keeping some powers to themselves and granting other powers to a central authority of their own creation. There is instead a number of dependant bodies, to which a central authority older than themselves has been graciously pleased to grant certain powers. The state of things is not a federation but … subjection.[191]

Federalists themselves differed as to what measures might be needed.[192] Some looked to a military alliance, others to a customs and free trade union (indeed, many references were made to the German *Zollverein*). The most

[188] Generally, J Kendle, *Federal Britain* (New York: Routledge, 1997).

[189] J Austin, *The Province of Jurisprudence Determined* (London: W&N, 1954) 245–253.

[190] Walter Bagehot, *The English Constitution* (London: Champman & Hall, 1867) 315.

[191] EA Freeman, 'Imperial Federation' (April 1885) 51 Macmillan's Magazine 430–445.

[192] G Martin, 'Empire Federalism and Imperial Parliamentary Union, 1820–1870' (1973) 16(1) The Historical Journal 65–92; Frederick Young, 'Schemes and Suggestions for Imperial Federation' (1886) 1(3) *IF*, 71–72.

demanding proposals were for a 'supraparliamentary federalism' with a new federal assembly with members from both Britain and the colonies, comparable to the US federal Congress. An alternative was parliamentary federalism, whereby the colonies would be able to send their own representatives to Westminster. The least ambitious suggestion was for an Advisory Council, a federation operating outside the UK Parliament, and not legally binding.

The federalist movement of the later nineteenth century did not meet with any great success. Neither of the two then principal party leaders – Salisbury and Gladstone – supported it, nor was there great interest from the general public or colonies. However, partly as a result of the impetus created by the federalist movement, a series of Imperial Conferences was launched from 1887,[193] mostly held in London. At the 1897 Imperial conference, Joseph Chamberlain had proposed a 'Council of the Empire' which was rejected. At the 1911 Imperial conference, Sir Joseph Ward, then Prime Minister of New Zealand, proposed a federal system with an Imperial Parliament focussing on defence and foreign policy, and an 'Imperial Council' with two votes each for the UK and every Dominion member.[194] This also failed, partly because it was resisted by Prime Minister Asquith as allowing Britain to be outvoted on the Imperial Council. The focus then shifted to achieving greater autonomy for some parts of the empire by voluntary co-operation. Subsequent developments, including the 1926 Balfour Declaration and 1931 Statute of Westminster strengthened this autonomy, eventually leading to independence and the development of the British Commonwealth of Nations.

Nonetheless, federalist solutions continued to be promoted, partly as a result of the Round Table movement. This had been set up in 1909 by members of Milner's 'kindergarten' (one of whose members, Lionel Curtis, has already been discussed in the context of India and Ireland) influential in establishing the Union of South Africa. It aspired to closer union of the Empire to counter growing competition from Germany, Japan and the US, aiming to give the Dominions a greater say in policy formulation.

However, opponents of federal proposals argued it was unworkable. The objections included: that distances were too great across the Empire for it to be manageable (despite improvements in communications, reliable air travel was unavailable until well into the twentieth century); that federalising defence and foreign policy would require an imperial or federal tax raising power; and that creation of an additional federal Parliament would also require a federal Council or Executive, as the British Government as it then stood, could not be responsible to two separate Parliaments. And so, nothing came of 'imperial federalism'.

193 J Kendle, *The Colonial and Imperial Conferences, 1887–1911* (London: Longmans, 1967).

194 TNA, CO 886/5B, 2nd meeting, 25 May 1911.

4.3.7 Incoherence of Empire

John Darwin argues that:

> There are good grounds for thinking that the British empire of rule, let alone its self-governing or 'informal' outriders, had no logic at all. The result was a pile of possessions whose purpose or meaning was long since forgotten, half-opened packets of quickly waning appeal, and new acquisitions made on the spur of the moment.[195]

For Darwin, the imperial system had 'emerged by default not from design'. It was 'an empire of hybrid components, conflicting traditions and unsettled boundaries between different races and peoples', its governance secured by 'a series of compromises'.[196] There had been no master plan, and the expansion of the British Empire had been driven by a 'chaotic pluralism'. Yet, nonetheless, Darwin identified a diffuse and nebulous 'system' of the British Empire. This system had not been imposed by the imperial Government, but nonetheless emerged, an immense realm of acquisitions and concerns.[197] Benton and Ford, in describing a 'Rage for Order', identify a fundamental *disorder* – the disorderliness of this ordering.

4.3.7.1 Incoherence and Pluralism

This book focusses on Law and on the Constitution, and seeks an account of Empire through that lens. But the constitutional law of the British Empire lacks a sharp definition and focus. Even in the heyday of the British Empire, its constitutional structures were not regularly evangelized as an impressive global structure of law. As Benton and Ford remark, two phenomena, or 'constitutional experiments' – the working out of the US federal Constitution, and the State system declared in the 1815 Congress of Vienna – overshadowed nineteenth-century attempts to build a constitutional order for the British Empire.[198]

One reason for neglect of any constitutional order of the British Empire is very likely to be its challenging lack of uniformity and consistency. Dicey posited a constitutional law of the British Empire, in which the British Parliament understood as a unified, single, sovereign entity, had sovereignty over all British territories, implying some sort of organized system. But this does not correspond to what actually existed, which was messy and lacking in uniformity. In analysing the British Empire in this way, I share of approach of Dilley and Wilson who write,

> the history of the British empire was always one in which mutually disruptive sovereignties and a maelstrom of political projects clashed, coalesced and

[195] John Darwin, *The Empire Project*, 2.

[196] Darwin, *The Empire Project*, 23; John Darwin, *Unfinished Empire: The Global Expansion of Britain* (London: Bloomsbury, 2013) xiv–xv.

[197] Darwin, *The Empire Project*, 3, 10. [198] Benton and Ford, *Rage for Order*, 13.

> contradicted one another. 'The empire' was an unstable field of difference and contestation, not a unit of common action.[199]

Others have taken a similar approach, and wondered if there was a coherent, unitary British Empire. Helen Taft Manning famously asked 'Who ran the British Empire?' but Ged Martin suggests we should instead ask, 'Was there a British Empire at all?' and whether 'the dozens of constituent territories, large and small, could be fitted into more than the most superficial pattern under the heading of 'Empire'. For Martin, this involves the following inquiries: 'Was there any real and effective measure of central control over the units which could justify the rhetoric of imperialism? Were there features common to the member territories which make it reasonable to generalize about an Empire?' Answering 'No' to these questions suggests that the Empire 'was a loose and accidental association of units embodying in their disorganization the worst features of the feudal and federal systems.' And so, Martin sees Empire as 'a very inadequate term', identifying it as less monolithic structure and rather 'a bundle of relationships between a strong power and a diversity of weaker territories.'[200]

Dilley and Wilson also contend that, although sovereignty may have been at the core of the language of Empire, in reality there existed a plurality of incompatible and incoherent claims to sovereignty – which meant that 'the empire could never be a single power, space, or set of networks',[201] nor even, in Darwin's term, a single 'project.' For Benton and Ford, 'the imperial constitution emerges as a fluid vernacular' – leading them to describe Britain as a weak hegemon in the complex and fragile global order emerging in the early nineteenth century.[202]

4.3.7.2 Sovereignty in the Empire

These accounts chime with the project of this book. For, in highlighting a plethora of plural and incompatible sovereignties, they confront the problems of identifying any uniform constitutional structure to the British Empire. It may be that power underlay the Empire, but that power could not be derived from a unified, coherent account of legal and political sovereignty. And power by itself lacks legitimacy – it must be validated by something else, some normative grounding – which is where sovereignty becomes relevant. Yet, the claims of sovereignty made by the Empire were mutually self-contradictory, as the next section illustrates.

[199] Andrew Dilley and Jon Wilson, *The Incoherence of Empire. Or, the Pitfalls of Ignoring Sovereignty* (2019), available at https://aura.abdn.ac.uk/bitstream/handle/2164/13025/Dilley_and_Wilson_Incoherence_of_Empire_Sept_2019.pdf?sequence=3

[200] Helen Taft Manning, 'Who Ran the British Empire?'; Ged Martin, 'Was There a British Empire?' 562–569.

[201] Dilley and Wilson, 'The Incoherence of Empire', 3.

[202] Benton and Ford, *Rage for Order*, 3, 4.

4.3.7.2.1 Diverse Conceptions of Sovereignty

First, we can say that Britain exercised a monarchical sovereignty, which was expanded as England (and then Britain) developed an Empire overseas. The monarch's claim to ultimate authority relied on 'divers sundry old authentic histories and chronicles' to trace its continuity back to before the Norman conquest'.[203] This authority was asserted overseas, often by violence, over people and territories across the world.

A second, rival claim to sovereignty was that of popular sovereignty, derived from the will of the people that granted the monarch its authority, and thus could be identified as the ultimate source of authority and legitimacy. As this book has discussed elsewhere, the doctrine of popular sovereignty has not figured greatly in English history, other than during the civil war era in the mid-seventeenth century, although it has flourished in Scotland, in the United States, with the Declaration of Independence, and possibly in Ireland.

A third archetype is that of parliamentary sovereignty, a conception of sovereignty particularly absolute in Britain, which also loomed large in the British Empire – in Parliament's asserted sovereignty over North America from 1763, and in the claims for the Imperial Parliament to legislate for the Empire in the nineteenth century. This third archetype was often at odds with the first two, as the American war of independence illustrated.

A fourth archetype is a pluralistic understanding of sovereignty, whereby sovereignty is divided, shared, indeterminate – and may be illustrated by legal devices such as the Mandate, or Protectorate, and other fuzzy concepts, where sovereignty had no one single source. Benton and Ford describe 'plural state systems infused by British legal influence', whereby the British exercised a 'legal force in the world'[204] and their identification of 'middle power' at work in British colonies, not always in line with the metropole, enlarges on how this legal force operated.

All four paradigms of sovereignty were argued for, sometimes successfully asserted, and sometimes the situation deliberately left vague, during the British Empire. Neither the archetypes themselves, nor the modes of acquisition of territory, should be considered exclusive and they sometimes overlapped. Within one territory, different groups might make different sovereignty claims within the same time period – as in America, where absolute parliamentary sovereignty was denied by the colonists, but different and distinct claims were made regarding the King's sovereignty and popular sovereignty.

As a result of these diverse, sometimes incompatible conceptions of sovereignty, the British Empire lacked institutional coherence and certainty as to its legal basis. Benton & Ford describe the diverse and diffuse nature of imperial power thus:

[203] David Armitage, *The Ideological Origins of the British Empire* (Cambridge: Cambridge University Press, 2004) 34.

[204] *Rage for Order*, 181, 196.

> it could consist of the capacity to intervene and settle conflicts among other polities. It could exist in the influence of British standards and expectations with regard to the protection of property and disciplining of subjects. It could result from incremental interventions in response to acts of arbitrary justice. It could flow from attempts to enforce British bans in areas not under British rule.[205]

Nonetheless, defining the empire in terms of incoherent and discordant conceptions of sovereignty should not be seen as neglecting the violence inflicted by it. Indeed, because there was no single motivation for empire, and instances of it varied across time and place, force was often all the more necessary to ensure its endurance. The perpetuation of distinct law and sovereignty regimes often resulted in differing rights and privileges for subjects across the Empire, as many found out, to their cost – including Americans, Jamaicans and Indians. Difference and discrimination bred resentment, which bred rebellion, which in turn was often brutally suppressed by the British. And any justification, or legitimating basis, for this exertion of force was often incoherent and vague.

4.4 End of Empire

4.4.1 Background

Britain was still an imperial force, even after the Second World War. Nonetheless, the territories of the Empire, as it stood in the first half of the twentieth century, were far from homogeneous.[206] The British Empire had two principal faces: the self-governing empire of the Dominions (autonomous and for all practical purposes independent after the 1931 Statute of Westminster) and the dependent empire (exemplified by the autocratic, 'enlightened' despotism in India, and then by large expanses of Africa). Both were important.

After the First World War, 'Mandates' were also established under Article 22 of the League of Nations Covenant. These were set up mainly for former German colonies in Africa and certain regions formerly within the Ottoman Empire. Although these territories were not annexed, Britain was responsible for their administration. In this way, a British Middle Eastern Empire emerged, as these Mandates included Iraq (formerly Mesopotamia) which became independent by 1930, Palestine, whose mandate was ended in 1948, and Transjordan, whose mandate ended in 1946. The establishment of such Mandates furthered the notion of 'trusteeship' as a justification for colonialism, namely, the belief that colonial societies were held in trust by their controllers, until sufficiently developed to rule themselves. After the Second World War, the African Mandates were converted to UN trust territories, under

[205] Ibid., 24.

[206] See especially AW Brian Simpson, *Human Rights and the End of Empire* (Oxford: Oxford University Press, 2004) chapter 6: 'The Burdens of Empire'; JM Brown and WR Louis (eds.), *OHBE*, vol. IV. *The Twentieth Century* (Oxford: Oxford University Press, 1999).

Articles 75–91 UN Charter, and by the 1950s, the UN was an important venue in which to protest colonialism.[207]

A further category of empire territories was that of 'Condominia', which were jointly administered by Britain and other States.[208] There also existed territories whose status was simply unclear, such as the Gambia, of which Simpson writes:

> The learned Sir Kenneth Roberts-Wray, in whose *Commonwealth and Colonial Law* one can pursue the Byzantine complexities of the subject, stated gloomily: 'Extensive research would be necessary before one could hope to produce a precise and reliable appreciation of the constitutional status of the whole country.'[209]

4.4.1.1 Decolonization and Independence

India became independent in 1947, splitting into India and Pakistan, with ensuing bloodshed, and then Pakistan itself split, with part of it forming Bangladesh. Sri Lanka (formerly Ceylon) became independent in 1948. Burma also became independent and, unlike India and Pakistan, left the Commonwealth in 1948.

According to John Darwin, 'before 1939 it was usual to suppose that even if the pattern of rule in the colonial world was modified, ultimate European control would continue indefinitely almost everywhere.'[210] However, much had changed since earlier in the century, and there had been a strong growth in ante-colonial feeling, as well as the seismic shifts caused by the war. Nonetheless, Churchill famously accused the postwar Labour government of undignified haste in divesting itself of empire: 'The steady and remorseless process of divesting ourselves of what has been gained by so many generations of toil, administration and sacrifice continues. 'Scuttle' is the only word that can be applied'.[211]

However, it was in 1959–1961, under the conservative administration of Harold Macmillan as Prime Minister and Iain Macleod as Colonial Secretary, that the decolonization process reached its peak. Macmillan first used the famous phrase 'winds of change' in South Africa in 1960.[212] The speed of decolonization has sometimes been described as a 'domino effect', whereby each act

[207] E.g. M Mazower, *No Enchanted Palace: The End of Empire and the Ideological Origins of the United Nations* (Princeton NJ: Princeton University Press, 2009).

[208] E.g. the New Hebrides, jointly administered by Britain and France.

[209] Simpson, *Human Rights and the End of Empire*, at 280, citing K Roberts-Wray, *Commonwealth and Colonial Law* (London: Stevens, 1966) at 786.

[210] J Darwin, *Britain and Decolonisation: The Retreat from Empire in the Post-war World* (London: Macmillan, 1988) 8.

[211] Parliamentary Debates (Commons), Fifth Series, CDXXXI, 20 December 1946, cols. 2343 and 2350.

[212] The use of this phrase signalled that Britain would not impede the independence of its African territories. Richard Lamb, *The Macmillan Years, 1957–1963: The Emerging Truth* (London: John Murray, 1995).

of independence prompted other colonies to urge independence. And so, in the 20 years after 1945, the population under British rule outside of the UK reduced from 700 million to five million (three million of which were in Hong Kong).[213] At time of writing, in addition to the four nations of the British isles, the only overseas remnants of the British Empire are three Crown dependencies and fourteen British Overseas Territories (mostly tax havens).[214] However, perhaps what is surprising is that, although membership of the UN has grown – largely as a result of decolonization, from its founding in 1945 with 51 members, to now 193 states – international borders have not changed greatly. Jansen and Osterhammel record that 40 per cent of today's international borders were drawn by Britain or France.[215]

According to John Gallagher's memorable phrase: 'the sun never set' on the British Empire's crises.[216] There were a number of hot and troubled spots – for example, in India, Burma, Malaya, Palestine, Suez, and Kenya. The Suez crisis originated in the overthrow of the Egyptian monarchy in 1952 by Colonel Nasser, who declared a republic and nationalized the Suez Canal. Nasser also gained some military support from the USSR. Britain in return prepared to invade Egypt, along with France and Israel, to retain control of the Suez Canal, in 1956. But they lacked support from the US (partly irritated by the failure to consult them), and so were forced to withdraw, enduring also a public condemnation in the UN. This was a humiliation for Britain and France. Suez is still considered by many as a psychological trauma for Britain.

Given the swiftness of decolonization, but also the great variety of governance in the many territories that were decolonized, a salient question is – how we should define decolonization? Should decolonization simply be considered to be the transfer of sovereignty, that is, a political-constitutional-legal event? Yet constitutional status does not necessarily provide an unequivocal account of the relations between States. For example, Egypt was declared independent in 1922 but occupied until 1956. On the other hand, the Dominions of Canada, Australia and New Zealand were granted constitutional autonomy and equality by the statute of Westminster in 1931, without any declaration of their independent status. In neither case could we say that the decolonization had been completed. This has led to the suggestion that decolonization was

213 Wm. Roger Louis, 'The Dissolution of the British Empire', in *OHBE*, vol. 4.

214 The overseas territories are Anguilla, Bermuda, the British Antarctic Territory, the British Indian Ocean Territory, the British Virgin Islands, the Cayman Islands, the Sovereign Base Areas of Akrotiri and Dhekelia on Cyprus, the Falkland Islands, Gibraltar, Montserrat, the Pitcairn Islands, St Helena Ascension Island and Tristan da Cunha, South Georgia and the South Sandwich Islands, Turks and Caicos Islands. The Crown dependencies are Jersey, Guernsey, and the Isle of Man. The reference to tax havens is from D Dorling and S Tomlinson, *Rule Britannia: Brexit and the End of Empire* (London: Biteback, 2019) 50–51.

215 Jan C Jansen and Jürgen Osterhammel, *Decolonization: A Short History* (Princeton: Princeton University Press, 2017).

216 J Gallagher, 'Nationalisms and the Crisis of Empire, 1919–1922' (1981) 15(3) Modern Asian Studies 355.

often no more than a mere formality (i.e. the attempt to ensure a continuing Westminster model of government[217]), a tactic to preserve imperial influence by other means than formal constitutional status. Yet this assertion is also unsatisfactory, as the end of formal empire often did change constitutional structures considerably and reduce British influence.

However, as Darwin notes, there is a larger explanation of decolonization that locates it in 'the *virtually* simultaneous collapse of all the European colonial empires' and thus 'is a warning against any explanatory scheme that lays too much weight upon purely British circumstances'.[218] This account suggests that the decolonization of the British Empire was not exceptional – it was part of a larger global phenomenon affecting other European empires.

4.4.1.2 The Commonwealth

The institutional successor to the British Empire was the Commonwealth. Within this organization, former colonies could associate as independent States. As Roger Louis remarks, 'Until 1947 the Commonwealth had resembled a white man's club consisting of Britain and the old Dominions of Australia, New Zealand, Canada, South Africa, and Ireland.' However, things changed when India gained independence in 1947, and remained in the Commonwealth, breaking the dead hand of the white man's grip.[219] India after independence was a republic, so its Commonwealth membership was a compromise that required India to recognize the King as the head of the Commonwealth. Other republics followed, and in 1994, South Africa rejoined, on the ending of apartheid. The Commonwealth provided assistance, economic, cultural and educational, especially to smaller States.[220] The Commonwealth now comprises 54 States (any country may now join, there is no requirement to have been part of the British Empire) and contains about one third of the world's population (about 2.4 billion people) and takes up about 15 per cent of the world's territory.[221]

4.4.2 How Particular Countries Gained Legal Independence

4.4.2.1 Autochthony

The British Empire never had a clear constitutional basis. Its territories lacked independence and full sovereignty, but there was no master document, or Constitution for the Empire. Yash Ghai asked: 'why do the new leaders so rapidly,

217 See further YP Ghai, 'Constitutions and the Political Order in East Africa' (1972) 21(3) ICLQ 403–434.

218 J Darwin, 'Decolonisation and the end of Empire', in R Winks, W Roger Louis, (eds.), *The Oxford History of the British Empire: Volume 5 Historiography* (Oxford: OUP, 1999), 541.

219 Wm Roger Louis, 'Introduction', in *OHBE*, vol. IV, *The Twentieth Century*.

220 See further Philip Murphy, *The Empire's New Clothes: The Myth of the Commonwealth* (London: Hurst & Co, 2018).

221 See further *The Commonwealth, About Us* (official Commonwealth website) at https://thecommonwealth.org/about-us

and sometimes so extensively, change the constitution?'[222] An answer is that for many, it was perceived insufficient on independence, to be *merely* autonomous, in control of legislation and policy. Very often a further factor was required. KC Wheare named this further factor *autochthony*.[223] Autochthony demonstrated that the newly independent State's Constitution was entirely separate from Britain, self-sufficient and sprung from their own soil. This severed the national Constitution from any external legal power, such as that exerted by Britain in granting independence through an Act of Westminster legislation.

Autochthony also has a wider sense of a document rooted in native traditions. But it is the procedural sense, of a constitution/legal system that does not derive its validity from any British legislation, with which we are here concerned. According to Kelsen, the *Grundnorm* of the former imperial system would remain at the pinnacle of a newly independent State's legal system, despite a formal transfer of power.[224] One way to achieve such autochthony is through revolution, as in the case of the USA. American independence was not granted by Great Britain but through the 1776 Declaration of Independence. Revolution breaks any chain of legal causation. However, the decolonization of the British Empire in the twentieth century was not achieved though armed struggle, but lawfully, through grants of independence. The problem was that these acts were traceable back to Britain and so did not appear to allow the newly independent State completely to own its Constitution. Hence the attempt to assert a complete constitutional independence in another way. Wheare argued that, for a Constitution to be autochthonous, 'The essential point … is that such action as is taken must not be taken under the authority of an act of parliament of the United Kingdom.' So:

> a specially elected or selected constituent assembly might prepare and pass the constitution and provided it did not do so under powers conferred by an act of the legislature which had received the royal assent, and did not submit the constitution for the royal assent, then it could claim that the constitution was enacted on its own authority. Or a constitution, prepared by the houses of a parliament or by a constituent assembly, could be submitted for the approval of the people and could come into effect subject to that approval.[225]

According to the Wheare line of thought, some action must be taken to break the legal chain that leads to the legal system of the parent country. Examples

[222] YP Ghai, 'Constitutions and the Political Order in East Africa' (1972) 21(3) ICLQ 403–434.

[223] KC Wheare, *The Constitutional Structure of the Commonwealth* (New York: Oxford University Press, 1960) chapter 4. The word autochthony is derived from the Greek αυτοχθονία – 'sprung from that land itself' (OED).

[224] H Kelsen, *General Theory of Law and State*, A Wedberg (trans.) (Cambridge MA: Harvard University Press, 1949) 110.

[225] K Wheare, *The Constitutional Structure of the Commonwealth* (New York: Oxford University Press, 1960) chapter 4.

of such action may be found in the redrafting of the Irish Constitution in 1937, and in India in 1949/50.

4.4.2.2 Ireland

Ireland's independence was recognized under the (UK) Irish Free State (Agreement) Act 1922. At the same time, however, the Dáil Eireann passed the Constitution of the Irish Free State (Saorstat Eireann) Act. Yet, according to the British view, because the Dáil Eireann had not been authorized by the Irish Free State (Agreement) Act, it had no power to enact a Constitution, and so Westminster passed its own Irish Free State Constitution Act (13 Geo. V (sess. 2), c. 1.) Therefore, the Irish and British took completely different views of the Irish Free State Constitution. Whereas, in 1934, the Irish Free State Supreme Court, in *The State (Ryan)* v. *Lennon*, held that the Constitution was 'set up by the Third Dáil Eireann sitting as a Constituent Assembly',[226] in 1935, the JCPC held in *Moore v. Attorney-General for the Irish Free State*, that: 'the Constitution of the Irish Free State derived its validity from the Act of the Imperial Parliament, the Irish Free State Constitution Act, 1922.'[227]

Ireland moved towards constitutional autochthony from 1932 to 1937, when many amendments were made to the Free State Constitution, to remove from the Irish State what were seen to be remnants symbolic of British rule. However, it was only in 1937 that any doubts as to the autochthony of the Irish Constitution were completely removed, by the enactment of a new Constitution for Eire to replace the 1922 one. In this case, the Constitution was 'home grown' both in practice and in theory, as it was not enacted by the Dáil, but approved by a referendum, whose approval constituted the enactment of the Constitution.[228] This deliberately did not follow the amendment procedure in the 1922 Constitution and so caused a break in constitutional history, thus terminating the chain of validity with the UK. This undoubtedly produced an autochthonous institution, and, as Ireland was still in the Commonwealth at the time this occurred, illustrated to other Commonwealth States how they could break with the legal/constitutional past other than by a revolution, and without leaving the Commonwealth.

4.4.2.3 India

India formally achieved independence by the (UK) Indian Independence Act, 1947. However, an earlier (1946) executive decision determined that the 1935 Government of India Act should continue in force while a Constituent Assembly drew up a new Constitution for India. The Preamble to the 1950 Indian Constitution reads: 'We, the people of India, having solemnly resolved to constitute India into a sovereign democratic republic … in our constituent assembly … do hereby adopt, enact, and give to ourselves this Constitution,'

[226] [1935] IR 170; Per Kennedy CJ at p 203. [227] [1935] A.C. 484.
[228] The Plebiscite (Draft Constitution) Act, 1937 (No. 16 of 1937).

thus locating the source of validity of the Indian Constitution in the Indian people. However, unlike in the case of Eire, there was no popular referendum to enact the Indian Constitution. Instead, the people acted through the Constituent Assembly.

Yet, the UK Independence Act 1947 had also specified that this new Constitution should be approved by the Governor General of India (in the name of the British Crown). But the Constituent Assembly did not do this, and in not doing this, and in repealing British statutes, it managed to achieve autochthony in a different way than Eire. Article 395 of the Indian Constitution repealed both the Indian Independence Act, and the 1935 Government of India Act, thus executing a symbolic denial of the Imperial Parliament's grant of Indian independence. In this way, India could claim to have produced an autochthonous Constitution.

4.4.2.4 Canada, Australia, and New Zealand

Why is autochthony in fact an issue? The problem is that, if a country owes its independence to an Act of the UK Parliament, then, according to classic understandings of the doctrine of parliamentary sovereignty (such as Dicey and Wade), Westminster could repeal that independence by passing a later statute.

Peter Oliver considers the situation of how Canada, Australia and New Zealand (CANZ) obtained their constitutional independence from Britain.[229] He contrasts their situation with their 'tearaway siblings', such as Ireland, which took matters into their own hands to achieve constitutional autochthony. Instead, these Dominions achieved their independence through a UK Act of Parliament, in conjunction with some local statutes. But did this procedure overshadow their independence? Oliver makes an important distinction between 'constitutional', 'political', and 'international' independence. According to Oliver, the 1926 Balfour Declaration and 1931 (UK) Statute of Westminster provided these Dominions with practical independence, so they achieved political (i.e. regardless of strict law) and international (i.e. in the eyes of foreign States) independence earlier in the twentieth century. However, constitutional independence was acquired only in the 1980s, at a time when all three adopted domestic constitutional legislation. There was no revolution or armed conflict in these Dominions, nor did the way in which they achieved independence suggest a break in the chain of legal continuity with Britain. So, were they truly autochthonous? There were some local attempts to explain how independence had been achieved. In New Zealand, it was contended that there had been a 'disguised revolution' following arguments used by Wade[230]

[229] Peter C Oliver, 'Introduction', in *The Constitution of Independence* (Oxford: Oxford University Press, 2005).

[230] HWR Wade, 'The Basis of Legal Sovereignty' [1955] CLJ 172, 191F: 'When sovereignty is relinquished in an atmosphere of harmony, the naked fact of revolution is not so easy to discern beneath its elaborate legal dress.'

(an explanation Wade also used regarding the EU). The trouble was that the situation in New Zealand did not seem to be revolutionary, but in compliance with existing UK law. In Australia, extra-legal explanations were proffered, with the suggestion that, following the Australia Acts 1986, the Constitution was based in popular sovereignty. Canada finally 'patriated' its Constitution in 1982, after requesting a final UK statute which ended Westminster's law-making powers for Canada and provided a law amending power in the Canadian Constitution itself. In all three, there may be room for doubt as to their truly autochthonous status.

Oliver, however, provides his own, persuasive explanation, adopting a different view of sovereignty from the orthodox absolutists, relying at least partly on Hart's theory of 'self-embracing sovereignty'.[231] This theory contends that Westminster's powers include the capacity to impose limits on itself (an argument also used of the ECA 1972 which limited Parliament's powers on joining the EEC). This understanding also owes much to the related 'new' approach to sovereignty adopted from the 1930s by Ivor Jennings and other scholars.[232] For example, Hart described a situation whereby:

> The legal system in the former colony has now a 'local root' in that the rule of recognition specifying the ultimate criteria of legal validity no longer refers to enactments of the legislature of another territory. The new rule rests simply on the fact that it is accepted and used as such a rule in the judicial and other official operations of a local system whose rules are generally obeyed.[233]

According to Hart, this development might take place in a number of ways (for example, the imperial legislature might renounce legislative power over the former colony, or the break be achieved by a violent revolution). Although the orthodox theory of parliamentary sovereignty might not accept that Parliament could irrevocably divest itself of its powers, the courts of Commonwealth States might take a very different view.[234] Oliver also regrets the overpowering influence of Dicey, noting that the persistence of Diceyan orthodoxy explains perhaps why both the Balfour Declaration and Statute of Westminster were not seen as clearly delivering independence or sovereignty to the Dominions. Oliver, however, also comments that, 'The dominant account was always based more on dogma than authority.'[235]

Oliver's conclusion is that a new constitutional order can materialize quite independently from the existing one, because: 'An amending formula can

[231] HLA Hart, *The Concept of Law 148–150* (2nd ed., Oxford: Clarendon Press, 1994).

[232] E.g. I Jennings, *The Law and the Constitution* (London: University of London Press, 1959) chapter 4; G Marshall, *Parliamentary Sovereignty and the Commonwealth* (Oxford: Clarendon Press, 1957).

[233] HLA Hart, *The Concept of Law* (Oxford: Clarendon Press, 1961) 116–117.

[234] E.g. *Harris* v. *Donges* (1952), 2 SALR (AD) 418.

[235] Oliver notes, at 9, *The Constitution of Independence* that Dicey himself referred to it as 'dogma'.

both validate a new amending formula and terminate itself, and accordingly the Westminster Parliament can both validate a new Constitution, including new or enhanced amendment procedures, and terminate its role for that Constitution.'[236] In this way, Oliver maintains, a former Imperial legal system may split into many independent legal systems.

4.4.2.5 Decolonization, Independence, and Parliamentary Sovereignty

In this way, it can be argued that an independent legal system exists, without even a formal deliberate break in continuity as was achieved in the case of Ireland or India. Such reasoning is also of relevance to supranational theories of law, such as the EU, because self embracing theories of sovereignty provide that Parliament may modify its powers so as to transfer power to the EU, thereby ceding some hierarchical supremacy.

In the twentieth century, a new, and less Diceyan generation of British constitutional lawyers turned their attention to the constitutional laws of the British Empire and Commonwealth. Some, such as Jennings, were active in developing a 'new theory' of parliamentary sovereignty, which used many Commonwealth authorities to argue that Parliament could impose 'manner and form' limitations and redefine itself. De Smith described the legislation by which British dependencies achieved independence in the following way:

> the Jamaica Independence Act 1962 provides that as from independence day no Act of the United Kingdom Parliament shall extend to Jamaica as part of its law. Why should this not mean what it says?.... To assert, in the name of inalienable parliamentary sovereignty, that Parliament can nevertheless repeal or disregard the independence Act and make laws for Jamaica as if it were still a colony, is to fly in the face of international law and comity, public policy and common sense. Once a legal theory becomes ridiculous, it ought to be abandoned. It is plain that the United Kingdom Parliament has irrevocably renounced its formerly absolute power to change the law of most if not all of the independent Commonwealth countries.[237]

4.4.3 End of Empire

Earlier in the twentieth century, it had been thought that Empire might save Britain from economic disaster, as territories could be exploited to sustain Britain and provide cheap products. By the 1950s, however, it became clear that this was not going to happen. Britain had been impoverished by the war and was highly dependent on America for financial aid and defence. Prime Minister Harold Macmillan was convinced that the Empire was too expensive and troublesome to maintain, and Britain turned instead to Europe, and an

[236] Oliver, 'Introduction', at 13 and chapter 12.
[237] AS de Smith, 'The Constitution and the Common Market' (1971) 34 MLR 587. 613.

EEC bid, for economic deliverance. Thomas Hobbes referred to 'the deceased Roman Empire' and we might now refer to a deceased British empire.[238]

Some commentaries suggested there was some deliberate grand design for decolonization, usually involving the idea that colonial territories were to be administered in trust until those countries could take care of their own affairs. In fact, there was no such deliberate plan for dissolution.[239] However, the myth fulfilled a self-serving purpose, explaining the Empire as a beneficial organization, to be concluded by peaceful, orderly transfers of power. By this interpretation, the end of Empire did not reveal a loss in Britain's status as a world power, but instead was rationalized as the fulfilment of Britain's contribution to world civilization. But in reality, the British were not in control of events and decolonization accelerated rapidly for fear of disturbances that would occur if it were not achieved.

In contrast, a very different approach may also be identified – one that saw the end of colonialism not as planned and deliberate but as inevitable. In 1917, Lenin published *Imperialism: The Highest Stage of Capitalism* predicting the downfall of empires (as a prologue to the destruction of capitalism itself).[240]

Further, domestic attitudes underwent a shift in their approach to the Empire in the twentieth century, with some perceiving empire as shameful, or at the very least disconcerting and unnecessary Early in the twentieth century, the anti-imperialist, JA Hobson, had attacked the Empire at the time of the Boer war (even at the same time as Colonial secretary Joseph Chamberlain extolled the Empire's benefits in his patriotic vision). Hobson argued that imperial expansion was very largely motivated by the search for profit,[241] and his work influenced much anti-imperialist thought, including that of Lenin and Rosa Luxemburg. The writers of the Bloomsbury group also had an influential anti-imperialist slant.[242]

Some anti-colonialists expressed their opposition to Empire in terms of a people's right to self-determination. However, the Universal Declaration of 1948 contained no explicit right to self-determination, although the right is to be found in the UN 1966 Covenants.[243]

4.4.4 Post Imperial Nostalgia

As Brian Simpson remarked, 'Everyone knew in their heart of hearts that there was something very peculiar in a small off-shore European island running the

[238] Hobbes, *Leviathan* (1651) pt. 4, ch. 47.

[239] See further for exploration of this, John Darwin, 'Decolonization and the End of Empire'.

[240] V Lenin, *Imperialism: The Highest Stage of Capitalism* (New York: AMS Press, 1970).

[241] E.g. JA Hobson, *Imperialism: A Study* (3rd ed., London: Allen & Unwin, 1938).

[242] The hugely prolific Leonard Woolf criticized imperialism in many works, including *Mandates and Empire* (League of Nations Union, 1920), and *Imperialism and Civilisation* (London: Hogarth Press, 1928).

[243] A Walworth, *Wilson and the Peacemakers: American Diplomacy at the Paris Peace Conference, 1919* (New York: Norton, 1986) 468–518; A Cassese, *The Self-Determination of Peoples: A Legal Appraisal* (Cambridge: Cambridge University Press, 1995).

affairs of so large a part of the globe.' And thus, it was necessary for the Empire to have some sort of ideological justification, that, in Simpson's words could, 'render this state of affairs tolerable'.[244] Such attempts at justification have been considered at various points in this chapter and mostly found wanting.

Simpson identified this justification as trusteeship in the twentieth century. He linked it with the common law and the complacent assertion of benevolent colonial rule, also believed to advance liberty and other desirable values. But such justifications had been around for some time. In 1850, Lord Palmerston had declared in Parliament that, 'I hold that the real policy of England … is to be the champion of justice and right … giving the weight of her moral sanction and support wherever she thinks that justice is, and whenever she thinks that wrong has been done.'[245] Nearly a century later, the British Overseas Information Services produced a document in 1946 that also stressed Britain's role in promulgating justice and liberty:

> Britain is free. One of her main contributions to civilisation has been its emphasis on personal freedom, and we have succeeded – where some others have failed – in reconciling liberty and order…. We wish to see this concept of individual liberty adopted throughout the world.[246]

In contrast, Bernard Porter argued in *The Absent-Minded Imperialists*[247] that the British Empire was of little concern to most British people, and had left virtually no remnants in British society. Although it might sometimes have seemed this way, such an analysis is surely mistaken. For, however one interprets the Empire, it played an unavoidable role in the definition of Britain over a couple of centuries, and some attitudes revealed by Brexit, illustrate an inability to come to terms with its demise. The high circulation *Daily Mail* vociferously asserted 'The Power, the Supremacy and the Greatness of the British Empire' (formerly printed on its banner-head). And remnants of the Empire have been surfacing in the twenty-first century, sometimes in a psychological form. For example, in March 2020, a *YouGov* poll found that a third of Britons believed the Empire to have been a force for good rather than harm in the colonies, and over one quarter desired its return, and that, overall the UK was 'more nostalgic for empire than other ex-colonial powers'.[248] However, identities are surely diverse in early twenty-first-century Britain. For some, usually younger Britons, the shift has been away from the Empire towards Europe and the EU. For others, Britain's EEC membership terminated the possibility of furthering and expanding its Commonwealth ties, as well as ending Britain's

244 AW Brian Simpson, *Human Rights and the End of Empire*, chapter 6: 'The Burdens of Empire'.

245 Lord Palmerston, 'Speech to the House of Commons', 1 March 1848, Hansard vol. 97 col 122.

246 CAB 124/1007, no. 62 (*BDEE*, Series A, vol. ii, Doc. 68 of 17 August 1946).

247 Bernard Porter, *The Absent-Minded Imperialists* (Oxford: Oxford University Press, 2004).

248 Robert Booth, 'UK More Nostalgic for Empire than Other Ex-colonial Powers', *The Guardian*, 11 March 2020.

independence. Perhaps it was not so surprising then that the post Brexit policy of some Brexiteers was only half-jokingly tagged 'Empire 2.0'. However, there is no evidence whatever that a Brexit Britain could make up lost EU trade through the Commonwealth.

4.4.4.1 Negative Legacies of Empire

Moreover, clearly not everyone enjoyed the benefits of the British Empire, nor its legacy. If some regret the passing of the British Empire, for others it has become an uncomfortable subject. An exhibition on the British Empire, *Artist and Empire; Facing Britain's imperial past* was held at the Tate Britain from 2015 to 2016. Alison Smith, in her introduction to this exhibition, referred to 'the abiding sense of embarrassment or distaste with which many Britons regarded their overseas affairs'.[249] The British historian Catherine Hall warned that society should not discard 'uncomfortable memories of colonialism', but instead make sure to do some 'memory work' on the legacy of Empire.[250] Frantz Fanon's *The Wretched of the Earth*[251] is one of the best known works of postcolonial scholarship, which argued that former colonial subjects could not shed their former colonial dependency by independence alone, but that it was necessary to purge, by violence, newly independent States of all settlers and imperial presence.

The British did not hesitate to use military force where necessary, nor hesitate to discriminate against some of their subjects. There have also been violent conflicts in some former colonies, sometimes the product of arbitrarily drawn States, mixing divers and incompatible peoples, as in parts of Africa. These undermine the claims made for Britain's ability to export liberty and justice overseas. This chapter has already discussed the brutal suppression by the British of the Morant Bay revolt and the Amritsar Massacre. And if Britain abolished both the slave trade and slavery by legislation, it had also supported the slave trade for two centuries, and grown rich on the profits of slavery.

There are many illustrations of ways in which Britain has been far from welcoming to its imperial subjects. And not only unwelcoming but also confusing, opaque, and riddled with a morass of complicated and untransparent immigration laws and policies. From the 1960s to 1980s, as decolonization increased, and the British Empire came to a swift end, Britain quickly adopted a series of Immigration Acts, controlling the entry of citizens from its former colonies. In 1962, the Commonwealth Immigrants Act was adopted to control non-white Commonwealth immigration, and from then on, most Commonwealth citizens were required to have a Ministry of Labour employment voucher in order

[249] A Smith, *Artist and Empire: Facing Britain's Imperial Past* (London: Tate Publishing, 2015).

[250] See e.g. C Hall, *Civilizing Subjects: Metropole and Colony in the English Imagination, 1830–1867* (Cambridge: Polity Press, 2002).

[251] Frantz Fanon, *The Wretched of the Earth*, originally published in French as *Les Damnés de la Terre* (Paris: François Maspéro, 1961).

to enter the UK, even if they had British passports. The 1971 Immigration Act permitted only those citizens of the UK and Colonies and Commonwealth citizens who had a parent or grandparent born in the UK to reside in Britain. Especially key was the 1981 British Nationality Act, which excluded certain categories of 'citizens' from entry into Britain. The struggles of the 'Windrush' generation in the twenty-first century are testimony to the effects of this string of immigration laws and policy, only exacerbated when the 2014 Immigration Act promulgated the notion of the 'hostile environment'. Concern over free movement of persons and migration was a key element of Brexit debates, but was only yet another instance of an attitude to immigration that had existed for decades.

4.4.5 Conclusion

This chapter has tried to illustrate how Britain's Empire developed, from small beginnings, in a haphazard way, with no overall master plan, or legal status. All of this undermines any claims for a coherent concept of sovereignty of the Westminster Parliament over Empire, as for instance claimed by Dicey. Seeley's famous phrase, that it had developed 'in a fit of absence of mind' captures its erratic and careless development. Nonetheless, this casual organization grew to become a great source of pride and national identity for many people, even if the Empire was also responsible for great suffering and acts of discrimination.

It seems impossible to suppress the realities, the memories and the legacies of this Empire. Paul Gilroy referred to a 'post-colonial melancholia', and a cultural disorientation that accompanies the collapse of imperial certainties'.[252] For some, the Brexit vote represented 'the last vestiges of empire working their way out of the British psyche',[253] a somewhat melancholic longing for what was perceived as a more majestic past. Some would dispute such a diagnosis, seeing Brexit as a new beginning. For others the 'more majestic past' is something regrettable and best forgotten.

[252] P Gilroy, *After Empire: Melancholia or Convivial Culture?* (London: Routledge, 2004) 117, 131.

[253] D Dorling and S Tomlinson, *Rule Britannia: Brexit and the End of Empire* (London: Biteback, 2019) 3.

5

Britain and Europe

5.1 Introduction

It is about 8,000 years since Britain was severed from continental Europe (probably by a giant tsunami wave). Yet in those subsequent years, although Britain has been an island, it has maintained all sorts of links with the continent, and seen the movement of people and goods from Europe into Britain, and vice versa. People and ideas flowed in with Roman, Anglo-Saxon, Viking and Norman occupations. Indeed, in reviewing the 2018 British Library exhibition, 'Anglo-Saxon kingdoms', Jonathan Jones commented that 'This vast and engrossing survey of Saxon art and manuscripts reveals a place that was not very English at all. One minute it looks Scandinavian, the next Celtic – but mostly it seems, well, European.'[1] The hero of the famous Anglo-Saxon literary work, *Beowulf*, is Scandinavian. After the Norman conquest of England, English kings ruled much of France until the fifteenth century. Magna Carta, so often lauded as a unique fountainhead of English liberties, was in fact only one of several such arrangements, whereby nobles had managed to constrain royal feudal powers across Europe. The British monarchy has always had European connections – and in modern times, the Crown was held by a Dutch king, William of Orange, after the Glorious revolution, and only a few decades later by the German speaking House of Hanover. Victoria continued the German links by marrying a Prince of Saxe Coburg, with whom she spoke German, and their progeny peopled the thrones of Europe. Even Queen Elizabeth I, with seemingly less visible European connections, described herself as a 'prince of Europe', and was proficient in six European languages.[2]

However, by the seventeenth century, Britain was on its way to developing an Atlantic empire. Although Spain and Portugal had initially taken the lead in developing American empires, by the seventeenth and eighteenth centuries these countries were flailing. Britain's navy was used not only to help develop its empire but also to counter challenges from European powers, which by the

[1] Jones, www.theguardian.com/artanddesign/2018/oct/21/anglo-saxon-kingdoms-review-barbaric-splendour-and-fierce-vision

[2] See Will Hutton and Andrew Adonis, *Saving Britain* (London: Abacus, 2018).

eighteenth century focussed on the French. Thus, Britain looked two ways – both to the riches of its global empire, but also to the prevention of any dominant power in Europe. However, in the twentieth century, two world wars, fought at tremendous cost in Britain, reduced Britain's economic resources by 1945.

5.1.1 The Narrative of British Exceptionalism

One familiar narrative looks to British exceptionalism, asserting that Britain is different from other continental European powers. This account focusses on Britain's separate, island status, but also asserts a distinct British history, a whiggish narrative of the organic evolution of institutions of liberty, of the common law, the unwritten Constitution, trial by jury, habeas corpus, the rule of law, a free press, and the weakening of the royal prerogative by the supremacy of Parliament. The Whig historical narrative highlights the hard fight against the Crown's prerogatives – a commitment to liberty that was seen as elevating Britain above continental European powers, who often manifested despotic rule.[3] This separate history was seen as protecting Britain from political instability, monarchical despotism and bloodshed – a history traced in the historical work of HAL Fisher, GM Trevelyan, Arthur Bryant, Winston Churchill,[4] and Henrietta Marshall's *Our Island Story*.[5]

This last is a children's book, first published in 1905, which told the tale of Britain from the departure of the Roman legions to the death of Queen Victoria. Indeed, it is both a children's story book and a patriotic tale, with its emphasis on the valiant island people, the small country, which nonetheless expanded to form a global empire, ruling beneficently and wisely over many races in far off lands. And so, although designed as a children's tale, the book nonetheless carries a message of Britain's constitutional development and overseas exploits that illustrates it as exceptional, distinct from the rest of Europe. This was a familiar nineteenth-century narrative, especially for those promoting the 'Greater Britain' movement. For example, Seeley wrote that 'Greater Britain' was 'a real enlargement of the English [*sic*] state' carrying across the seas 'not merely the English race, but the authority of the English Government.'[6] But the more general narrative of British exceptionalism was also a message that many eurosceptics would take to heart.

[3] This idea of liberty was admired by Voltaire and Montesquieu. See I Buruma, *Anglomania: A European Love Affair* (New York: Vintage Books, 2000).

[4] HAL Fisher, *History of Europe* (London: Eyre & Spottiswoode, 1935); GM Trevelyan, *History of England* (London: Longmans, 1926); A Bryant, *Freedom's Own Island: A History of Britain and the British People* (London: Collins, 1986); W Churchill, *A History of the English-Speaking Peoples* (London: Cassell, 1956).

[5] HE Marshall, *Our Island Story* (London: TC & EC Jack, 1905) – republished in 2005 by the Think Tank *Civitas*.

[6] JR Seeley, *The Expansion of England* (London: Macmillan, 1885) at 38. But, in contrast, see T Sasson, J Vernon, M Ogborn, P Satia, and C Hall, 'Britain and the World: A New Field?' (2018) 57 Jl of British Studies 677.

This exceptionalist narrative focussed on Britain's global legacy, its status as a world, rather than a European, nation and power. For example, although Disraeli pursued a role for Britain in keeping the balance of power in Europe, he also stated in 1866 that 'England has outgrown the continent of Europe ... she is really more an Asiatic power than a European',[7] stressing the role of Britain's Indian empire in maintaining Britain's wealth and prestige. Britain's imperial role as crucial for the development of English/British history is also explored by the influential historian JGA Pocock. Pocock published an article in 1975 – 'British History: A Plea for a New Subject' – in which he urged a *British* history that was the product of a broader 'Atlantic archipelago' and decried Britain's apparent willingness 'to declare that neither empire nor commonwealth ever meant much in their consciousness, and that they were at heart Europeans all the time'.[8] This was written when Britain had newly joined the EEC (as it then was) and Pocock (originally from New Zealand) also criticized a perceived abandonment of British sovereignty for economic motives. A later article by Pocock in the *London Review of Books* argued that UK accession to the EEC 'entailed a rejection by that kingdom's peoples of the former global capacity of their culture; it was a confession of defeat, and at the same time a rejection of the other nations of that culture'.[9]

5.1.2 Britain and Europe

But other works consider British history to be more embedded in a European framework, emphasizing Britain's links with Europe. Norman Davies, in *The Isles*,[10] firmly locates Britain's history in Europe, attempting to balance a perceived bias to Anglocentric history.

More recently, Cambridge historian Brendan Simms has criticised the separatist approach of 'our island story', arguing that this approach fails to account for the centrality of Europe in Britain's domestic and foreign policy.[11] Although Simms himself takes a whiggish approach, noting continuity over a long period, he interprets the history very differently from Marshall. Many, including Simms, have repeated Churchill's remark that 'Europe is where the weather came from', and Simms also includes Burke's response to those who believed that being an island was sufficient security against the chaos from the French Revolution – 'They talk as if England were not in Europe.'[12] Simms, and others, highlight how British foreign policy habitually aimed to prevent the dominance of continental Europe by a single power, illustrated by for

[7] Disraeli, 'Speech on re-election in Beaconsfield', *The Times*, 14 July 1866.

[8] JGA Pocock, 'British History: A Plea for a New Subject' (1975) 47 J Mod Hist 601.

[9] JGA Pocock, 'Deconstructing Europe' 13(24) LRB, 19 December 1991.

[10] Norman Davies, *The Isles: A History* (Oxford: Oxford University Press, 1999).

[11] B. Simms, *Britain's Europe: A Thousand Years of Conflict and Cooperation* (London: Allen Lane, 2016). Yet somewhat surprisingly, Simms also favoured Brexit (arguing it would enable the EU to progress to a more united Europe unhampered by British doubts).

[12] *Cobbett's Parliamentary History of England*, XXX, col 112 (London, 15 December 1792).

example coalition building to oppose the Spain of King Phillip II or Napoleon's France from becoming dominant powers. In turn, these European challenges impacted on the growth of the British State. A strong motivation for the 1707 Union between Scotland and England was the desire to prevent France invading England through Scotland; the Irish and British Parliaments were united in 1801 to strengthen against Napoleonic invasion.

In any case, to make a different point, many would deny that exceptionalism is uniquely British. For example, the German concept of the 'Sonderweg' or special way, seeks to explain how and why Germany took a separate and special path. The French postwar concept of the 'troisième force' sought to place France apart from other European States, as ranking with superpowers the USA and USSR.

5.1.3 A Complicated Intertwining Relationship

Perhaps the motif emerging from this very brief survey of Britain's relations with Europe is that of tension – of sometimes competing narratives – between an exceptionalist, isolated Britain and a Britain firmly rooted in Europe. Churchill captured some of this in his famous 'three great circles' speech in Llandudno in 1948, in which he stated that,

> The first circle for us is naturally the British Commonwealth and empire. Then there is the English-speaking world in which we, Canada, and the other British Dominions and the United States play so important a part. And finally there is United Europe. These three majestic circles are coexistent and if they are linked together there is no force or combination which could overthrow them or even challenge them … we have the opportunity of joining them all together. [In doing so] we hold the key to opening a safe and happy future to humanity, and will gain for ourselves gratitude and fame.[13]

Yet now, over 70 years later, Britain appears to have a place in none of these circles.

In any case, Timothy Garton Ash reminds us that this issue is far more complicated than the simple question 'Is Britain European?' would suggest. For a start, what do we mean by 'Europe' or by 'Britain'? These are loaded, contested concepts, with a variety of possible meanings. 'Europe' is broader than the EU, just as 'Britain' is broader than England. Garton Ash's conclusion (as true now as when Garton Ash wrote this article over 20 years ago) is that 'The answer to the question 'Is Britain European?' has to be 'yes, but not only.' Britain's European identity can only ever be a partial one, for Britain has always been and will remain – so long as there is a Britain – a country of multiple, overlapping identities'.[14]

[13] Churchill, 'Speech at Llandudno, 9 October 1948', reprinted in R Churchill (ed.), *Europe Unite – Speeches: 1947 and 1948 by Winston S. Churchill* (London: Cassell, 1950), 417–418.

[14] Timothy Garton-Ash, 'Is Britain European?' *Prospect*, 22 February 2001.

5.2 Britain and the ECHR

5.2.1 Introduction

When many contemporaries, especially lawyers, refer to 'Europe', they have in mind either the EU or the European Convention on Human Rights (ECHR), so synonymous have these legal institutions become with the idea of Europe. This link is not accidental, but perceived as linked to the losses of sovereignty that both institutions are seen to inflict on their member States. However, even if this is true of the EU (and I would argue that it was not), it is an unfair criticism of the ECHR, which is completely separate and independent of the EU.

Earlier generations of British jurists had shunned what they saw as 'continental' Bills of Rights.[15] However, Britain signed the 1950 ECHR, and played a major part in its drafting. The significant British involvement in the Convention's genesis is today stressed by those arguing that the UK should not depart from an institution it helped to create. However, as Lord Irvine (the Labour Lord Chancellor who steered the Human Rights Act through Parliament in 1998) highlighted in a House of Lords debate in 2011:

> In fact it is the Conservative Party, not Labour, that can make the strongest claim to credit for the European convention. Its main proponents were Churchill, Macmillan and John Foster, with some Liberal and Labour support. Its principal author was David Maxwell-Fyfe, the future Conservative Chancellor, Viscount Kilmuir. The convention was substantially the work of British jurists within a tradition going back to the Petition of Right of 1628 and our own Bill of Rights of 1689.[16]

Britain's important role in the formation of the ECHR was a product of post-war situation. The UN was founded in 1945, and the UN Universal Declaration of Human Rights adopted in December 1948. The next step was for the UN to adopt a legally binding Charter of Rights. However, it soon became apparent that such an international Charter could not be readily agreed and adopted by States. Indeed, it was only in 1966 that two UN Human Rights Covenants would be open for signature. In part, this lack of progress was due to a growing suspicion of Soviet communism, which divided western countries from the USSR and its satellites. As a result, some decided to press ahead with a regional, European Charter instead.[17]

However, it was not only increasing disillusion with the UN and fear of Soviet communism that prompted the move to a European Human Rights

[15] E.g. AV Dicey, *Introduction to the Law of the Constitution* (9th ed., London: Macmillan, 1952): 'There is in the English constitution an absence of those declarations or definitions of rights so dear to foreign constitutionalists' (197) and 'The Habeas Corpus Acts declare in principle and define no rights, but they are for practical purposes worth a hundred constitutional articles guaranteeing individual liberty' (199).

[16] Lord Irvine of Lairg, House of Lords, 19 May 2011, Hansard, vol. 727. Also J Norman and P Oborne, *Churchill's Legacy: The Conservative Case for the Human Rights Act* (London: Liberty, 2009).

[17] These negotiations are considered in detail in AWB Simpson, *Human Rights and the End of Empire* (Oxford: Oxford University Press, 2004).

Charter. There had also been an impetus towards a federated Europe, coming from a number of western European organizations, who drew on their experience of occupation during the second world war, and sought as a result to take action against the risk of future abuses by the State. In 1947, the United Europe movement was formed, co-ordinated by British former Minister Duncan Sandys, with Winston Churchill (then in opposition) at its head. Churchill had famously called for 'a kind of United States of Europe'[18] (although it is unlikely that Churchill actually favoured a federal Europe that included Britain). In May 1948, a high-profile Congress of Europe was held at The Hague, with many important European politicians participating. The European Movement committed to greater European unity resulted from this Congress, and the Congress adopted two resolutions: one requiring a European Parliamentary Assembly, the other a European Charter of Human Rights. This in turn led to the founding of the Council of Europe in May 1949, whose institutions were an intergovernmental Committee of Ministers, which took decisions by unanimity, and a consultative Parliamentary Assembly. It was thus an organization based on the cooperation of States, which did not involve the loss of State sovereignty.

By early 1949, the European Movement was working on its plans for human rights protection. The British Conservative MP, David Maxwell-Fyfe[19] (later to become both Home Secretary, and as Viscount Kilmuir, Lord Chancellor) was its most prominent figure, and had been a UK prosecutor at the Nuremberg trials of Nazi war criminals, where he had cross-examined Hermann Göring. A barrister, John Harcourt Barrington (on Fyfe's prosecution team at Nuremberg) also did much of the work. Professors Arthur Goodhart and Hersch Lauterpacht were also involved, although their level of participation is unclear. (It was Hersch Lauterpacht, Whewell Professor of International Law at Cambridge University, whose 1945 book first proposed an international bill of rights, involving a 'radical innovation in international practice and a surrender … of the sovereign rights of the state.'[20]) Fyfe's experiences at Nuremberg had a lasting effect – establishing him as an ardent European, and instilling a commitment to human rights as a means of avoiding future atrocities (although later, in domestic political office, he would oppose ending capital punishment and decriminalising homosexual acts). As a result, he became deeply involved in drafting the European Convention.

A juridical section was set up by the Council of Europe, with the aim of developing the human rights proposals. Pierre-Henri Teitgen, law professor

[18] Churchill used the phrase on many occasions, perhaps most notably at the University of Zurich, 19 September 1946: Churchill, *Complete Speeches*, vol. 7, 19/09/1946, 7379–82.

[19] For further on Fyfe, see Neil Duxbury, *Lord Kilmuir: A Vignette* (London: Bloomsbury, 2015).

[20] H Lauterpacht, *An International Bill of the Rights of Man* (New York: Columbia University Press, 1945) 81. Lauterpacht had lost nearly his entire family in the Holocaust. See AWB Simpson, 'Hersch Lauterpacht and the Age of Human Rights' (2004) 120 *LQR* 49–80.

and Minister for Justice in post war France (formerly a resistance hero) chaired the section and Fyfe was co-rapporteur with Fernand Dehousse, the Belgian politician and jurist. Along with Teitgen, Fyfe and Barrington played a significant role in producing the draft Rights Convention, which set out a list of rights, with provision for their enforcement by a Commission which could receive individual petitions, along with a Court. The draft Convention was presented to the Council of Europe Assembly on 19 August 1949, which (after some wrangling) approved the draft and it was referred to the Council's Committee of Ministers.

Maxwell-Fyfe urged that: 'we cannot let the matter rest at a declaration of moral principles and pious aspirations, excellent though the latter may be. There must be a binding convention, and we have given you a practical and workable method of bringing this about'.[21]

Indeed, Fyfe's statement was somewhat surprising, coming as it did from a mid-twentieth-century British Conservative politician committed to parliamentary sovereignty. However, a row took place in the Cabinet over whether the UK should even commit to the Convention,[22] and the British Government determined to eliminate, or at least contain, the role of the Court and right of individual petition. Notably, the UK was then in a position to influence the form the Convention finally took because, although weakened by war, Britain was still a powerful European State and colonial power. It would have been difficult for any Convention to take effect without the UK agreeing to its terms. As a result, the draft Convention was amended to render the Court's jurisdiction optional; to allow derogation by States from specific provisions 'in time of war or other public emergency threatening the life of the nation'; and to insert a 'colonial clause' so the Convention would only apply to dependencies if the relevant State so declared.

The Convention was signed in the Palazzo Barberini in Rome on 4 November 1950. At the signing ceremony, the President of the Assembly, Paul-Henri Spaak, made the memorable remark that it was 'not a very good Convention, but it is a lovely Palace',[23] reflecting perhaps the view that the need for compromise had watered down the ECHR. The Convention itself entered into force on 3 September 1953, after receiving sufficient ratifications, and the Commission of Human Rights was set up in 1954. The Court was only established in 1959, after the required eight States had accepted its optional jurisdiction, with a British judge, Lord McNair, as its first President. France, also concerned at the Convention's implications for national sovereignty, did not ratify the Convention until 1974, and thus Pierre-Henri Teitgen, one of the ECHR's

[21] 'First Session of the Consultative Assembly at Strasbourg 1949' (*Travaux Préparatoires* (Martinus Nijhoff, 1975)).

[22] AWB Simpson, 'Britain and the European Convention' (2001) 34(3) Cornell International LJ 550.

[23] Cited in J Christophersen and M Madsen, *The European Court of Human Rights between Law and Politics* (Oxford: Oxford University Press, 2011) 29.

drafters, was not appointed to the Court until 1976.[24] A first Protocol to the Convention was swiftly drafted, including provisions on the right to property, and on elections and education which had proved controversial during the earlier drafting process for the Convention itself.

The ECHR contains civil and political rights – the right to life, to liberty and to a fair trial, to freedom of expression and association, respect for private and family life, freedom from torture, slavery and inhuman and degrading treatment, and freedom from retrospective legislation, and in its Protocols some other rights, including the rights to vote, to property and abolition of the death penalty. Many such rights were criticized by Karl Marx in 1843 as privileging the bourgeois 'preservation of their property and their egoistic selves.'[25] Others might criticise the ECHR as a product of the Cold War that omitted the social and economic rights the USSR had prioritized (although not necessarily enforced). To be sure, the ECHR does not contain many of the socio-economic rights which are to be found in the Universal Declaration on Human Rights, such as the right to work. Nonetheless, many ECHR rights are also found in the 1789 French Declaration of the Rights of Man and of the Citizen, a revolutionary document (criticized as too radical by Burke, Bentham and Dicey). In contrast to Spaak, Maxwell-Fyfe's own characterization of the ECHR was positive, noting that:

> Some may say that it is of doubtful value that the democratic nations should reinforce individual liberty among themselves and leave the totalitarian states untouched. We do not accept this pessimistic view. We consider that our light will be a beacon to those at the moment in totalitarian darkness and will give them a hope of return to freedom.[26]

The UK was the first State to ratify the ECHR, on 8 March 1951, although did not opt to accept the Court's jurisdiction nor the right of individual petition. (Notably, according to former UK Law Lord, Lord Hoffmann, the UK's motivation was mainly to set a good example for others, and it did not expect to be found in violation itself.[27]) The UK also agreed to apply the Convention in 42 Commonwealth territories. However, the British assumption that extending the ECHR to much of its empire would have little effect on it (based on the belief that the Convention was drafted by the British, that Britain conformed to human rights, and that the right of individual petition had not yet been accepted) was quickly disproved once the Convention came into effect. From 1955 to 1959, there was a dispute over the British

[24] See M Madsen, 'From Cold War Instrument to Supreme European Court' (2007) 32(1) Law & Social Inquiry 137 at 145.

[25] Karl Marx, 'On the Jewish Question', in RC Tucker (ed.), *The Marx-Engels Reader* (New York: WW Norton & Co., 1978).

[26] Cited in B Haller, *An Assembly for Europe: The Council of Europe's Parliamentary Assembly, 1949–1989* (Council of Europe, 2006) 69.

[27] L Hoffmann, 'Human Rights and the House of Lords' (1999) 62 MLR 159, 166.

colony of Cyprus, involving Greece (which wanted to annex Cyprus) and Turkey (which objected to this). Both Greece and Turkey were members of the ECHR, and Greece brought an action against the UK claiming it had violated the ECHR, because there had been rebellion in Cyprus, which Britain had attempted to crush using emergency powers. A subsequent case brought by Greece claimed the UK had been complicit in widespread torture.[28] The dispute was resolved by a political settlement in 1959, and the UK reluctantly complied with the Convention investigations. Although Britain no longer had most of its colonies by 1966, when it adopted the right of individual petition, the practical consequences of agreeing to the Convention became more evident as time passed.

5.2.2 A 'European Bill of Rights?'

In 2008, the year in which the Court delivered its 10,000th judgement, Michael O'Boyle, then Deputy Registrar at the European Court (ECtHR), described the emergence of the authority of the Court as 'one of the most remarkable phenomena in the history of international law, perhaps in the history of all law'.[29] But how did the ECtHR evolve to this position from its (certainly modest) earlier role in the mid years of the twentieth century? As Bates suggests, the Convention as drafted in 1950 was the result of a compromise between those who viewed it as an 'interstate pact' that would function as an early warning system to guard against a return to totalitarianism in Europe, and others who viewed it as a potential European Bill of Rights for a new, post-war Europe.[30] Therefore, even at the early stage of drafting there were those who aspired for the ECHR to be a Bill of Rights for Europe – and this vision was cultivated at the Court from the 1950s on. It is this latter vision that has prevailed. Yet these developments took time, and in its earlier years, during which the Convention had little impact, the Court was seen as a 'sleeping beauty'. Only a few UK lawyers (such as Anthony Lester and Brian Simpson) then expressed any great interest in the Court.

The approach taken by the British judge, Sir Gerald Fitzmaurice, sheds some light on those earlier years. Fitzmaurice joined the Court in 1974, from the International Court of Justice at The Hague (and subsequently resigned two years early, in 1980). Fitzmaurice dissented in most cases. These dissents deliberately and energetically expressed Fitzmaurice's total opposition to the direction which the ECHR was taking. Most famously, or perhaps infamously, Fitzmaurice held that the 'five techniques' (used by the British against IRA

[28] Application 176/56 of 7 May 1956 and 299/57 of 4 September 1957.

[29] Michael O'Boyle, 'On Reforming the Operation of the European Court of Human Rights' (2008) 13 *EHRLR* 1.

[30] E Bates, *The Evolution of the European Convention on Human Rights* (Oxford: Oxford University Press, 2010) chapters 3–5.

suspects and found by the European Commission of Human Rights to amount to torture) did not even amount to 'degrading' treatment.[31]

However, the 1970s were the turning point for the Court, a decade in which it decided a succession of high profile, path-breaking cases, such as *Golder* v. *UK*, *Engel* v. *Netherlands*, *Tyrer* v. *UK*, *Marckx* v. *Belgium*, *Handyside* v. *UK*.[32] It was in these cases that the Court introduced many of its most important principles, such as the margin of appreciation; the notion that the ECHR is 'a living instrument'; and the doctrine that the ECHR can create 'positive obligations'. It is also worth remembering that it was the (now defunct) European Commission of Human Rights that often played an important role in developing the ECHR. Other developments ensued as the ECHR evolved, and further Protocols were ratified, most notably Protocol 11 which entered into force in 1998 and transformed the Court into a permanent, full-time Court, making its jurisdiction compulsory, and abolishing the Commission of Human Rights. More recently, by the early twenty-first century, after accession of post-Communist States had taken ECHR membership up to 47 States and about 830 million people, the Court became a victim of its own success, with an overwhelming amount of applications clogging up its machinery and making it difficult to deliver timely judgements. Many cases came from newer member States, and from Russia in particular. Protocol 14 was then drafted with the aim of reducing the Court's workload, and by 2019 the backlog of pending applications had been considerably reduced.

Nonetheless, the Court has received bad publicity for certain judgements – for example, *Hirst*, in which it held that the UK could not impose a blanket ban on giving prisoners the right to vote.[33] Another illustration of resentment against the Court in the UK was the reaction to the Court's judgement in *McCann* v. *UK* (in which UK security service agents shot dead three IRA suspects in Gibraltar[34]). However, until relatively recently, the UK implemented ECtHR judgements, and there was no serious thought of withdrawing from the ECHR. And one might add that the UK is not alone in its opposition to some of the Court's judgements – the 2004 *Caroline von Hannover* judgement[35] was received in Germany with similar opprobrium.

And it must be stressed that the ECHR has undoubtedly brought important and profound benefits. Looking only at the impact of the Court's judgements in the UK, for example: the police cannot permanently retain the DNA of innocent people; nor stop and search individuals without reason; nor detain them indefinitely without charge; prisoners have a right to private legal

31 *Ireland* v. *United Kingdom* [1978] ECHR 1. These five interrogation techniques were prolonged wall-standing, hooding, subjection to noise, deprivation of sleep, and deprivation of food and drink.

32 *Golder* v. *UK* [1975] 1 EHRR 524; *Engel* v. *Netherlands* [1976] 1 EHRR 647; *Tyrer* v. *UK* [1978] ECHR 2; *Marckx* v. *Belgium* [1979] 2 EHRR 330; *Handyside* v. *UK* [1976] ECHR 5.

33 *Hirst* v. *UK (No 2)* [2005] ECHR 681.

34 *McCann* v. *UK* [1996] 21 EHRR 97.

35 *Von Hannover* v. *Germany* [2005] 40 EHRR 1.

correspondence; certain severe interrogation techniques are prohibited as inhuman and degrading; homosexuality is no longer a crime; and homosexuals may participate in the military without discrimination.[36] According to Lord Bingham: 'Most of the supposed weaknesses of the Convention scheme are attributable to misunderstanding of it, and critics must ultimately answer two questions.... Which of the [Convention's] rights would you discard? Would you rather live in a country in which these rights were not protected by law?'[37]

5.2.3 The Human Rights Act 1998 and the Commission for a British Bill of Rights

The year 1998 was a significant year for human rights in Britain. For in that year, not only did it become mandatory for member States to accept the jurisdiction of the ECtHR, but the new Labour Government implemented (most of) the ECHR into domestic law by means of the Human Rights Act (HRA). This Act, which entered into force in 2000, imposed a duty on all public authorities (aside from Parliament itself) to act compatibly with most European Convention rights. As a result, ECHR rights could be litigated in British domestic courts, instead of cases having to be pursued in Strasbourg, an expensive process that could take years.

Section 3 HRA requires UK courts to interpret British laws compatibly with Convention rights as far as possible.[38] However, if British courts find an irresolvable conflict between a domestic statute and the UK's human rights obligations under the HRA, they cannot invalidate the statute, but only instead, under s4HRA, issue a 'declaration of incompatibility'. It is then up to the UK Parliament to decide whether and how to change the law. In this way, the HRA therefore does not violate Westminster parliamentary sovereignty. Furthermore, the Act also provides that, although UK courts are obliged by section 2 HRA to 'take into account' judgements of the European Court, they are not bound by them. As a result, British courts have become more willing to depart from ECtHR precedents when they consider it necessary, especially if the Strasbourg caselaw is seen as inconsistent with fundamental domestic law. Such approaches were illustrated in *Horncastle, Pinnock,* and more recently in *R (Hallam)* v. *Secretary of State for Justice.*[39]

[36] *S & Marper* v. *UK* [2008] ECHR 1581 (DNA); *Gillan and Quinton* v. *UK* [2010] ECHR 28 (stop and search); *A and Others* v. *UK* [2009] 49 EHRR 29 (no indefinite detention); *Golder* v. *UK* [1975] 1 EHRR 524 (right to solicitor in prison); *Ireland* v. *UK* [1978] ECHR 1 (prohibition of 'five techniques'); *Dudgeon v UK* [1981] 4 EHRR 149 (prohibition of homosexuality violated private life); *Smith and Grady* v. *UK* [1999] 29 EHRR 493 (no discrimination against homosexuals in military).

[37] T Bingham, *The Rule of Law* (London: Allen Lane, 2010) at 84.

[38] This provision has been criticized for empowering the judiciary to amend legislation by interpretation – see Chapter 10.

[39] *R* v. *Horncastle* [2009] UKSC 14, paras. 10–11 and 108 (Lord Phillips); *Manchester City Council* v. *Pinnock* [2010] UKSC 45, para. 48 (Lord Neuberger); *R (Hallam)* v. *Secretary of State for Justice* [2019] UKSC 2.

Nonetheless, there has been hostility to the HRA in Britain – much of it from the tabloid press.[40] One might speculate on why there has been such opposition. For some, it may have been antagonism to a statute seen as European, not British, and thus alienating, 'especially among those for whom "Europe" is a dirty word.'[41] Interestingly, however, the Human Rights Act also attracted criticism from some of the very politicians who had introduced it in the first place,[42] thus illustrating the capacity of 'European' law to serve as a whipping boy of all persuasions.

In 2011, the UK Coalition government launched a Commission tasked with considering the creation of a Bill of Rights for the UK,[43] although this failed to agree, producing a divided report,[44] and no legislation was forthcoming. Indeed, two Conservative Commission members argued for UK withdrawal from the ECHR altogether,[45] although two other members opposed any change, declaring that 'for some of our colleagues a UK bill of rights is a means towards withdrawal from the European convention', and that 'We believe that such a path would be catastrophic for the UK, for Europe and for the protection of human rights around the world.'[46]

Moreover, the ECtHR was itself becoming concerned about 'seriously misleading' British press reports.[47] In 2012, Sir Nicolas Bratza, UK judge and President of the European Court, described,

> The vitriolic – and I am afraid to say, xenophobic, fury directed against the judges of my Court [and] the scale and tone of the current hostility directed towards the Court, and the Convention system as a whole, by the press, by members of the Westminster Parliament and by senior members of the Government.... The withdrawal of the United Kingdom from the Convention would do untold damage to the system itself. It would also, in my view, do immeasurable harm to the standing of the United Kingdom within the wider community of Europe in which it plays such an important part.[48]

Elsewhere, Bratza noted that: 'the Strasbourg Court is not a "foreign" court', but an international court in a system in which the United Kingdom has from

[40] See e.g. D Mead, '"You Couldn't Make It Up": Some Narratives of the Media's Coverage of Human Rights', in K Ziegler, E Wicks, and L Hodson (eds.), *The UK and European Human Rights: A Strained Relationship?* (Oxford: Hart, 2015).

[41] Lord Lester, 'A Personal Explanatory Note', in *A UK Bill of Rights: The Choice Before Us*, vol. 1, at 233.

[42] For example, by Jack Straw (Home Secretary when the HRA was adopted).

[43] Commission on a Bill of Rights: *A UK Bill of Rights? The Choice Before Us*, vol. I (2012).

[44] see M Elliott, 'A Damp Squib in the Long Grass: The Report of the Commission on a Bill of Rights' (2013) 2 EHRLR 137.

[45] Lord Faulks QC and Jonathan Fisher QC, 'Unfinished Business', in *A UK Bill of Rights*, 182.

[46] Baroness Helena Kennedy QC and Professor Phillipe Sands QC, 'In Defence of Rights', in *A UK Bill of Rights*, 221.

[47] 'Why Is the European Court of Human Rights Hated by the UK Right?' Jon Henley, *The Guardian*, 22 December 2013.

[48] N Bratza, 'The Relationship between UK Courts and Strasbourg' (2011) 5 EHRLR, 505–506.

the outset played, and continues to play, an important role and in which a United Kingdom judge sits in all cases against his or her country'.[49]

5.2.4 Continued Attacks on the ECHR and HRA in the UK

However, in spite of the divided Commission report, the HRA was not to be let alone. In October 2014, the Conservative party published further proposals for changing UK human rights laws.[50] This document argued that Strasbourg judgments finding the UK in breach of the Convention should be treated as advisory only, and also referred to the ECHR's illegitimate 'mission creep'. Failing any accord with Strasbourg over this approach, it stated that 'the UK would be left with no alternative but to withdraw from the Convention'. These proposals were critically received, even by conservatives, partly for inaccuracies.[51] Such plans were put on hold during Brexit, but, in December 2021, Justice Secretary Dominic Raab launched a consultation[52] on a new Bill of Rights to replace the HRA, and in June 2022 introduced a Bill of Rights Bill into the House of Commons to repeal and replace the HRA, even although responses to consultation were overwhelmingly in favour of keeping the HRA. The new Bill introduced a permissions stage to 'deter spurious human rights claims'; removed the obligation 'to take account' of Strasbourg judgements, as well as disabling UK courts from delivering rights-compatible interpretations (as under s3 HRA); and also provided for a new interpretation of Article 8 ECHR (on the right to family and private life) that would allow the government to 'deport more foreign offenders'.[53] However, by summer 2023, Dominic Raab was no longer in office, and these plans to repeal the HRA appeared to have been suspended, or even abandoned.

These constant reform plans illustrate a distrust and dislike of Strasbourg as an international court, although very few cases (with the exception of *Hirst*) have been cited in support of this. In 2005, the ECtHR held in *Hirst* that the UK government's blanket ban on prisoner voting was incompatible with the ECHR.[54] *Hirst* quite clearly did not require the enfranchisement of all convicted prisoners. However, the UK did not change its laws on prisoner voting.[55] This was in breach of the UK's obligation under Article 46(1)ECHR to abide by judgments of the ECtHR, and would seem to undermine the rule of law. Over ten years later, the whole prisoner voting saga ended with somewhat of a whimper

[49] Cited in Kennedy and Sands, 'In Defence of Rights', 224.

[50] 'Protecting Human Rights in the UK: The Conservatives' Proposals for Changing Britain's Human Rights Laws' (2014).

[51] E.g. by former Attorney General Dominic Grieve QC MP, 'Why Human Rights Should Matter to Conservatives', lecture UCL, 3 December 2014.

[52] *Human Rights Act Reform: A Modern Bill of Rights* (Ministry of Justice, 2021). This followed a 2020 Independent Human Rights Act Review, www.gov.uk/guidance/independent-human-rights-act-review, which did not recommend repealing the HRA.

[53] See further Chapter 10.

[54] *Hirst* v. *the United Kingdom (No 2)* [2005] ECHR 681.

[55] In parliamentary debate, then UK Prime Minister, David Cameron, said the thought of giving prisoners the right to vote made him 'physically ill' (HC Deb 3 November 2010, vol. 517, col 921).

when Strasbourg accepted as compliant the British resolution of the matter, which provided that a small number of prisoners would in future be allowed to vote.[56]

Some high-profile judicial figures have also been critical of the ECtHR in the UK.[57] Former UK Supreme Court Justice, Lord Sumption, delivered a sceptical view of human rights in the 2019 Reith Lectures,[58] where he argued that the ECHR had been extended beyond original intentions – a contention similar to Judge Fitzmaurice's arguments in the 1970s. This criticism also chimes with the US-style 'originalist' argument; namely that a text should be interpreted as the people who drafted it would have done. However, whatever the modalities of originalist interpretation in the US, the European Court has made clear that it does not apply to the ECHR, holding that, 'the Convention is a living instrument which must be interpreted in the light of present-day conditions.'[59]

To be sure, the UK is not the only government that has attacked judgements of the European Court in recent years. For example, Russia introduced legislation to ensure its constitutional supremacy over the ECHR, and in 2022 was expelled by the Council of Europe and left the ECHR altogether.[60] Nonetheless, UK hostility to the ECHR has been sustained by the euroscepticism that fuelled Brexit – for example, by accounts of foreign judges frustrating deportations, such as that of Abu Qatada to Jordan.[61] Yet, the Strasburg judgement in the Abu Qatada case simply followed the approach of the UK Court of Appeal. So, this was hardly a case of the Strasbourg Court 'mov[ing] the goalposts by establishing new, unprecedented legal grounds upon which [deportation was] blocked'[62] as alleged by Theresa May when Home Secretary. And in June 2022, UK Attorney-General and Tory leadership candidate, Suella Braverman, declared the intention of removing Britain from the ECHR if elected leader.

Indeed, the fallout from UK withdrawal from the ECHR would be severe. The only other State than Russia to have withdrawn from the ECHR was Greece, and that was when it was ruled by a military junta in the 1960s. If the UK were to withdraw, it would be alone with Belarus and Russia outside the greater European area of 47 ECHR States. However, this would be an example that some other countries would be only too willing to follow. As Council of Europe Commissioner for Human Rights stated: 'Many are in fact eager to exploit any backsliding in Westminster's commitment to the Convention

56 Council of Europe Committee of Ministers final resolution, CM/ResDH (2018) 467.
57 E.g. Lord Judge 'Constitutional Change – Unfinished Business', UCL 3 December 2013; LJ Laws, 'The Common Law and Europe', 27 November 2013.
58 Lord J Sumption, *Trials of the State: Law and the Decline of Politics* (London: Profile Books, 2019).
59 *Tyrer* v. *UK* [1978] ECHR 2.
60 'Russia ceases to be a Party to the European Convention on Human Rights on 16 September 2022', *Council of Europe Newsroom*, 23 March 2022
61 E.g. 'Abu Qatada: Get This Creature Out of Our Country', *Daily Mail*, 18 January 2012; see *Othman (Abu Qatada)* v. *UK* [2012] 55 EHRR 1.
62 HC Deb 8 July 2013, vol. 566, col 23 (Theresa May MP).

system to justify measures reducing their own citizens' and residents' ability to obtain justice through the Convention system.'[63]

And such a withdrawal becomes easier for the UK after Brexit. It is relatively straightforward to withdraw from the ECHR by giving the required 6-month notice, but EU membership rendered this impossible, since all EU countries are required to be ECHR members. Indeed, Conor Gearty, writing after the Brexit referendum in 2016, in the Preface to *On Fantasy Island: Britain, Europe and Human Rights*, cautioned that: 'Now that the larger European entanglement has been successfully seen off, the time has come for finishing the unfinished business of human rights destruction.'[64]

One may conclude, along with Adam Wagner, that withdrawing from the ECHR would be an 'act of epic historical selfishness'.[65]

5.3 UK and EEC Membership

5.3.1 Formation of the EEC and Post-War History

And what of the other significant European Institution – the EU? What has been the nature of Britain's relationship with it?

If anything could discredit the notion of the sovereign State it was the horrors of the Nazi era's glorification of the nation State. After the Second World War there were concerted efforts to find realistic ways to limit State sovereignty, through some European initiative. The momentum for a shared European human rights mechanism has already been discussed. This section considers other directions (mostly economic) in European integration.

When the first step towards the future EU was taken, its immediate impetus was a French desire to contain Germany's now resurgent coal and steel industries in the Ruhr and Saar. Putting French and German coal and steel under a common structure could contain Germany but also serve a long-term interest: the development of European political institutions, and hopefully economic prosperity. So, the new European Coal and Steel Community (ECSC) was set up by the Treaty of Paris in 1951. It regulated a common market in coal and steel, abolishing internal customs duties, and restrictions on imports and exports in these commodities. Jean Monnet, the French diplomat and entrepreneur, was the first President of the ECSC High Authority (the main – supranational – institution of the ECSC).

The next attempted step towards European integration was more obviously federal in nature. The 1950s were a time of insecurity caused by world events.

[63] 'Non-implementation of the Court's judgments: our shared responsibility', 23/08/2016, at www.coe.int/en/web/commissioner/-/non-implementation-of-the-court-s-judgments-our-shared-responsibility

[64] C Gearty, *On Fantasy Island: Britain, Europe and Human Rights* (Oxford: Oxford University Press, 2016).

[65] A Wagner, 'After Brexit They Will Come for Human Rights – and This Time the Public Debate Must Be Won', *Prospect*, 9 June 2019.

Communist threats were posed in the 1950s and early 1960s by the Korean war, the coup in Czechoslovakia and the Berlin blockade. It seemed as if western Europe might need its own security community to deal with these threats. And so, the French foreign minister, René Pleven, proposed the pooling of common resources into a European Defence Community, which would also include a European army. The Italian politician and federalist, Alberto Spinelli, then called for a European Political Community treaty. But these initiatives foundered when the French Assemblée Nationale, and newly elected President de Gaulle, declined to ratify these draft defence and political community treaties, seeing them as a threat to the State. Britain had never in any case wished to join, preferring to deal with security through NATO.

However, this was not an end to the integration initiative. An earlier plan of 1953, proposed by the Dutch foreign minister, Beyen, suggested integration of a different sort, in the economic field only, by abolishing barriers to trade, which did not appear such a threat to national sovereignty. As Benjamin Franklin said in another context, 'No nation was ever ruined by trade.' The Belgian Prime Minister, Spaak, drafted a report in 1956 which was to lead to the treaties of Rome (a separate treaty on atomic energy being added to appease the French) of 1957, approved by the same six countries as had signed the ECSC treaty. These came into force on 1 January 1958, and the European Economic Community (EEC), the predecessor of today's EU, came into being with six member states – France, West Germany, Belgium, Italy, Luxembourg, and the Netherlands.

5.3.2 Early British Non-Involvement in European Integration

And where was Britain in all this? When the ministers of the six ECSC States met to discuss economic integration in 1955, Britain had also been invited to attend. Britain however sent only a relatively junior official from the Department of Trade, who after remaining silent during the meeting, stated at the end:

> The future treaty you are discussing has no chance of being agreed; if it was agreed it has no chance of being ratified; and if it were ratified, it would have no chance of being applied. And if it was applied, it would be totally unacceptable to Britain. You speak of agriculture which we don't like, of power over customs, which we take exception to, and institutions, which frighten us. Monsieur le president, messieurs, au revoir et bonne chance.[66]

This hostile response is partially explained by the British exceptionalism doctrine, discussed earlier, and also because much British foreign policy had been formed in response to some 'Other'. In earlier years, the 'Other' had

[66] Richard Weight, *Patriots: National Identity in Britain 1940–2000* (London: Macmillan, 2002) 265, cited in Fintan O'Toole, *Heroic Failure: Brexit and the Politics of Pain* (London: Apollo, 2018) 5–6.

been Catholic, or French, or German. For eurosceptics, it was very often simply 'European' – so Britain was disinclined to join this European initiative. Britain's attitude was also strongly affected by its Second World War experiences, and Britain tended to see herself as a major world power, along with the USA and USSR, and as different from European allies – in having been neither aggressor, nor conquered, nor collaborator during the war. Britain therefore took the decision to stand apart from moves to European economic integration in the 1950s, looking instead to trade with the Commonwealth, and was initially negative about the ECSC and EEC. There was a strong view in the Labour party that Europe was propelled by right of centre Christian Democratic parties, and that European integration was a capitalist cause. Nor were Conservatives more favourable. Macmillan's initial reaction to European integration was to see it as a threat to Britain, which might even give rise to a trade war.[67]

In particular, Britain found both the EEC's common agricultural policy and common external tariff unacceptable, as impositions on government planning which would also have interfered with Britain's preferential tariffs with Commonwealth countries. So instead, Britain promoted a Free Trade Area, which attracted other European States – Sweden, Norway, Denmark, Austria, Switzerland, and Portugal – which together with Britain, formed the EFTA, or the European Free Trade Area, in 1960. In any event, Britain's hostility to European economic integration soured relations between Britain and the EEC, perhaps partly explaining Britain's initial lack of success in attempting to join.

5.3.3 British Economic Decline

However, several factors combined to ensure that British views changed regarding the advantages of EEC membership. By the later 1950s, Britain was no longer the major world power she had once been – her defeat in the Suez crisis of 1956, when Britain had tried and failed, along with France and Israel, to regain control of the Suez canal in response to its nationalization by Egypt, had illustrated this. Britain could also no longer rely on a vast empire to provide her with economic resources. Britain's Commonwealth trade was growing weaker, and British economic growth flailing. Whereas in 1956, about 40 per cent of British trade was with the Commonwealth, and only 25 per cent with the EEC and EFTA, by 1964 this had shifted to 30 per cent trade with the Commonwealth and 32 per cent with Europe.[68] EEC States were performing better economically than Britain, and provided valuable markets for British trade.[69] Additionally, Britain had no independent missile defence programme,

[67] See John Darwin, *The Empire Project* (Cambridge: Cambridge University Press, 2009) 586.

[68] Lee Burke, 'Britain and the EEC' (1967) 130(3) World Affairs 163–176.

[69] See further, A Lamfalussy, *The UK and the Six* (Homewood Ill: Irwin Inc., 1963).

relying instead on the US Polaris system. This weakened arguments against reliance on international or supranational programmes.

5.3.4 Britain's Failed Membership Bids

In 1961, the decision was made by Harold Macmillan's Conservative government to open talks with 'the Six' on British membership of the EEC. This application, however, was vetoed in 1963 by General de Gaulle, who opined that Britain was insufficiently European and 'In short, the nature, the structure, the very situation that are England's differ profoundly from those of the continentals.'[70]

De Gaulle's was not the only opposition to British membership. Although Parliament had approved Britain's application, there were still fears over what EEC membership might mean in practice for Britain. Some saw it as a threat to Commonwealth interests, involving the abolition of imperial tariff preferences (necessary to fall in line with the EEC common external tariff). This would in particular be harmful to New Zealand, which then depended very greatly on the UK market for meat, butter and cheese. Harold Macmillan, who instigated the 1961 membership application, nonetheless recognized that 'it was ... asking a great deal of the Conservative Party, so long and so intimately linked with the ideal of Empire, to accept the changed situation'. And later, after negotiations commenced, Macmillan wrote in his diary that 'There are ... many very anxious Conservatives. It is getting terribly like 1846'[71] (i.e. the year in which the Conservative Party split after repeal of the Corn Laws). EEC membership was also seen as threatening Britain's 'special relationship' with the US – a feature that played heavily in De Gaulle's rejection of Britain's application. Opposition to membership was also found within the Labour party. Hugh Gaitskell (by then Labour party leader) gave a speech to the party conference in October 1962, expressing opposition to EEC membership. His concerns included loss of sovereignty, arguing that: 'It means the end of Britain as an independent nation state ... the end of a thousand years of history.... And it does mean the end of the Commonwealth.'[72]

Nonetheless, despite de Gaulle's rejection and some British opposition, the impetus for EEC membership increased in Britain. Only five MPs had voted against applying for membership in 1961 (and no member of the House of Lords had then voted against). Britain's economy was faring worse and worse, and EEC membership appeared increasingly attractive. Moreover, fears of the EEC developing into a political union that annihilated its member States' identity had receded after the 'Empty Chair crisis' prompted by General de Gaulle's

[70] De Gaulle, Western European Assembly, General Affairs Committee, Press conference, 14 January 1963.

[71] H Macmillan, *At the End of the Day, 1961–1963* (London: Macmillan, 1973), 5 and 19.

[72] Speech by Hugh Gaitskell (3 October 1962) in *Britain and the Common Market* (London: Labour Party, 1962) at 7.

refusal of engagement in EEC business. This crisis (caused by de Gaulle's fear of a loss of national sovereignty) was resolved by the 1966 'Luxembourg Accords' – an affirmation that each member State could exercise a national veto where its vital national interests were at stake. Moreover, political control was shifting in Europe – opening up to the left in Italy, and to social democratic government in West Germany – both more attractive to the Labour government now back in office in Britain from 1964.

However, a second British membership application was also vetoed in 1967 by de Gaulle who accused Britain of a 'deep-seated hostility' towards European integration.[73] After that, Britain did not give up on EEC membership, but internal opposition continued. Although Gaitskell died (suddenly) shortly after the 1962 conference, many other Labour party members continued with a similar anti-EEC message – including Barbara Castle, Tony Benn and Denis Healey. Likewise, within the Conservative party, euroscepticism (or 'anti-marketeerism' as it was then called) continued, propelled by its most vocal proponent, Enoch Powell, who in 1971, at the party conference, delivered an impassioned speech against EEC membership. Nonetheless, the conference voted by 2,474 to 324 for British entry.

5.3.5 Britain Joins the EEC in 1973

Generally, the EEC had made good progress in its first ten years, and its economic and commercial achievement was substantial. According to the figures in the 1971 British Government White Paper[74] (issued just before the debate in Parliament prior to Britain's entry) the EEC's abolition of tariffs encouraged intra-Community trade, which by 1969, had increased by 50 per cent. In all, EEC countries had a rate of GNP twice that of Britain in 1971. Such impressive economic progress would have been unlikely without the EEC membership of the six original member States.

Britain had continued to take refuge in the much less ambitious EFTA. But it did eventually join the EEC, along with Ireland and Denmark, under the enthusiastically committed Heath Government in 1973, on, it has to be said, somewhat unfavourable terms, with a large budget contribution. These new memberships brought new interests and attitudes to the EEC. However, as long as the EEC could be regarded as in essence an economic and trading community, then most were uninclined to challenge EEC membership. In particular, the Conservatives were the more pro-European of the two major British parties, and it was not until the later 1970s that euroscepticism would really start to blossom within it.

[73] http://news.bbc.co.uk/onthisday/hi/dates/stories/november/27/newsid_4187000/4187714.stm, 27 November 1967: 'De Gaulle says "non" to Britain – again'. (Although it seems the other five EEC States were not opposed.)

[74] *The United Kingdom and the European Communities* Cmnd 4715 (London, July 1971).

5.3.6 The European Communities Act 1972[75]

As the UK does not have a codified Constitution, it could not become a member of the EEC by means of a constitutional amendment such as Article 24 of the German *Grundgesetz*. UK membership was introduced instead by Act of Parliament, the European Communities Act (ECA) of 1972, which also, given that the UK takes a dualist approach to international law (such that treaties do not immediately take effect within the domestic legal system) gave domestic effect to EEC law. Otherwise, as Lord Denning made clear, 'Even though the Treaty of Rome has been signed, it has no effect, so far as these courts are concerned, until it is made an Act of Parliament.'[76]

Therefore, under the ECA 1972, Parliament voluntarily gave effect to the UK's obligations under the EEC (now EU) Treaties in national law. The ECA defines the legal relationship between these two otherwise distinct and separate spheres of law, and without it EU law could not become part of national law (the ECA is a 'conduit pipe', according to the UK Supreme Court in *Miller*[77]). To be sure, incorporating 'the new legal order' of EEC Law into national law provided a challenge for legislative drafters. Yet, as JDB Mitchell commented in 1972, accommodating a 'new legal order' should not have been an unfamiliar task for the UK: 'Constitutionally they did it for themselves in 1707, and in recent years have constantly participated in such a creation for the new independent members of the Commonwealth.'[78]

Section 2(1) ECA stated that 'enforceable' provisions of EEC law (i.e. those directly applicable or direct effective, such as EEC Regulations and some EEC Treaty provisions) were automatically incorporated and binding in national law without the need for further legislation (as would usually be the case, given the UK is a dualist State). Therefore, when an EEC Regulation entered into force, it automatically became part of UK law that same day, as it did in other EEC member States. Section 2(1) applied to EEC law both immediately and as it developed in the future either by Treaty revision or by interpretation by the European Court of Justice (ECJ).

Section 2(4) ECA provided that all UK statutes, whether already enacted or yet to be enacted, 'shall be construed and have effect subject to' enforceable EEC law. Notably, s2(4) did not state that Parliament could not enact legislation in conflict with EEC obligations, nor expressly give supremacy to EEC law. Nonetheless, through s2(4), EEC law achieved supremacy (as required by the ECJ in *Costa*[79]) over national law, including the power to bind future Parliaments. Significantly, this might seem to conflict with the classic Diceyan

[75] Now repealed by s1 EU (Withdrawal) Act 2018.

[76] *McWhirter* v. *Attorney-General* [1972] CMLR 882 at 886.

[77] *Miller* v. *Secretary of State for Exiting the EU* [2017] UKSC 5, at para. 65.

[78] JDB Mitchell, S Kuipers, and B Gall, 'Constitutional Aspects of the Treaty and Legislation relating to British Membership' (1972) 9 CMLR 137.

[79] See further below on *Costa*.

doctrine that an earlier Act of Parliament cannot bind a later one – and we shall explore this issue further below.

Interestingly, although sovereignty was raised in debates in Parliament prior to Britain's membership, it was not seen as presenting an insurmountable obstacle to that membership. According to Lord Hailsham, Lord Chancellor in 1971:

> It has always been my conviction … that the issue of sovereignty was a non-runner … basically the foundation of the Communities is contract.… The Treaty is a contract to use the sovereignty of each member for limited purposes in concert with the others and to create institutions to enable this to be done without derogation of national independence.[80]

And Edward Heath, the Prime Minister who took the UK into the EEC, stated in 1971: 'I would put it very simply. If sovereignty exists to be used and to be of value, it must be effective.… In joining we are making a commitment which involves our sovereignty, but we are also gaining an opportunity … to influence its decisions in the future'.[81]

Geoffrey Rippon QC was the Conservative MP, and Cabinet minister, with the responsibility for negotiating Britain's entry into the EEC. In February 1972, he steered the ECA (which he helped draft) through Parliament. He put great emphasis on the fact that the ECA, which provided for the supremacy of EEC law over conflicting domestic law, was *itself* an exercise of parliamentary sovereignty.

> As the then Prime Minister, now Leader of the Opposition, explained: Accession to the Treaties would involve the passing of United Kingdom legislation.[82] This would be an exercise, of course, of Parliamentary sovereignty, and it is important to realise that Community law, existing and future, would derive its force as law in this country from that legislation passed by Parliament … restraints of this kind on our legislative freedom are by no means unprecedented. We had accepted them for example, in accepting the Charter of the United Nations, the North Atlantic Treaty, in our membership of the General Agreement on Tariffs and Trade and again in EFTA …
>
> The House as a whole may therefore be reassured that there is no question of this Bill making a thousand years of British law subservient to the Code Napoléon …
>
> By accepting the directly applicable law in Clause 2(1) and accepting the jurisprudence of the European Court in Clause 3(1) the Bill provides the necessary precedence. In relation to statute law, this means that the directly applicable provisions ought to prevail over future Acts of Parliament in so far as they might be inconsistent with them …

80 HL Deb 27 July 1971, vol. 323 cc195–256.

81 HC Deb 28 October 1971, vol. 823 cc2076–2170, 2210.

82 Rippon referred to Command 3301: *Legal and Constitutional Implications of United Kingdom Membership of the European Comm*unities, presented to Parliament 8 May,1967, on the occasion of the UK's second application to join the EEC in 1967.

> Of course nothing in this Bill abridges the ultimate sovereignty of Parliament. As Lord Gardiner said in another place when he was Lord Chancellor, The United Kingdom legislation would be an exercise of Parliamentary sovereignty and Community law existing and future would derive its force as law in this country from it.[83]

However, a further taste of the 1972 parliamentary debate is provided by some contrasting views. For example, Sir Derek Walker-Smith, Conservative MP for Hertfordshire East, argued:

> Our parliamentary institutions are the product of a slow unfolding over the generations. Here where we sit today parliamentary democracy had its genesis, cradled in the care and fostered by the faith of our forefathers. The Six, by contrast, are mainly young in nationhood and younger still in parliamentary institutions.... Our sacrifice would be greater because of our long and deep attachment to parliamentary institutions.[84]

And in that same debate on the ECA, Mr. Charles Fletcher-Cooke MP, a lawyer and Conservative MP, asked a prescient question:

> The real question is what the courts will do if a situation arises in which subsequent legislation of this Parliament appears to conflict with the regulations of the Council or decisions of the European Court. I find in this Bill no guidance to the courts on that important point.... The courts should be given this guidance because the problem has vexed the courts of the existing Member States.[85]

In fact, an answer to Fletcher-Cooke's question would have to wait until the *Factortame* litigation in 1990, which is discussed below.

5.3.7 The 1975 Referendum on EEC Membership

In 1975, with now a different (Labour) government in office, Britain held a referendum on the question: 'Do you think the UK should stay in the European Community (Common Market)?' By spring 1975, the new Prime Minister, Harold Wilson, had been able to achieve renegotiation of some issues concerning Britain's membership, including a budgetary correction mechanism and market access for New Zealand dairy products. Although these reforms did not require treaty change, they were generally met favourably by the public.[86] Wilson then put them to the public, in the 1975 referendum on Britain's EEC membership – a campaign that seems to have

[83] HC Deb 15 February 1972, vol. 831 cc264-377, Second Reading.
[84] Ibid. [85] Ibid.
[86] 'The 1974–75 UK Renegotiation of EEC Membership and Referendum', HC Briefing Paper, No. 7253, 13 July 2015.

been conducted with greater civility than the 2016 referendum (although the 'Get Britain Out' campaign repeatedly warned that accession to the Common Market marked a 'new Munich'[87]). Saunders notes how pro-Europeans in 1975 made much of the EEC's role in keeping the peace and containing aggressive nationalism – creating posters with messages such as 'Forty million people died in two European wars this century. Better lose a little sovereignty than a son or daughter.'[88] A study carried out at the time by the European Parliament entitled *The Effects on the United Kingdom of Membership of the European Communities*,[89] considered the impact of Community membership on parliamentary sovereignty. Interestingly, this study highlighted the great amount of delegated legislation (i.e. orders made by government ministers, without a great deal of parliamentary scrutiny) already applying in Britain, noting that far more delegated legislation applied in Britain than EEC legislation. The capacity of delegated legislation to reduce parliamentary sovereignty remains of concern today (particularly given the volume of delegated legislation required in the Brexit context by the EU Withdrawal Act 2018).

Many however, were ambivalent about the referendum, such as Oxford historian, AJP Taylor:

> There is no British opinion about 'going into Europe' intellectual or otherwise. No one understands it. No one cares about it, for or against, except perhaps for a few politicians who have taken up the affair as a means of professional advancement. Maybe it is the most decisive moment in British history since the Norman conquest or the loss of America. No one takes any notice all the same.[90]

Nonetheless, Britain's EEC membership was endorsed by a large majority in 1975, by a vote of 67.23 to 32.77 per cent, on a national turnout of 64 per cent. The 'Yes' vote included nearly all of the UK's sixty-eight administrative regions, with only Shetland and Western Isles voting 'No'. However, the Labour party later split, partly over this issue, with its pro-Europe wing forming the Social Democratic Party. On the other hand, the Conservative party remained generally in favour of EEC membership, until increasing eurosceptic attitudes became a problem. Margaret Thatcher, Conservative party leader from 1975, campaigned to remain in the EEC, as illustrated in Figure 5.1.

[87] See further Robert Saunders, *Yes to Europe: The 1975 Referendum and Seventies Britain* (Cambridge: Cambridge University Press, 2018).

[88] *Yes to Europe*, 25–27. Interestingly, many of those campaigning to remain in the EEC thought that Britain could play a leading role in Europe, thus exhibiting as much 'post-imperial nostalgia' as those eurosceptics who harked back to the greatness of Britain's empire.

[89] EP Directorate-General for Research Documentation, Doc. PE 37.460/rev. (March 1975).

[90] AJP Taylor, *Encounter*, June 1971, 3–17.

Figure 5.1 Margaret Thatcher campaigning to remain in the EEC during the Referendum in 1975

5.4 The UK and EU Pre Brexit

5.4.1 The Supremacy of EU (EEC) Law

It is now time to examine the issue of the supremacy of EU law in more detail, given that the sovereignty issue has dogged Britain's relationship with Europe. Notably, the 1957 EEC Treaty contained no provision for the supremacy of EEC law over that of its member States. The fundamental principle of supremacy of EEC/EU law over conflicting national law is a creation of the European Court of Justice (ECJ), dating from the early years of its existence. A key stage in the history of the EU was the case of *Van Gend en Loos*, decided by the ECJ in 1963.[91] This case established that provisions of EEC law were not just tools of international law, but had direct effect, meaning that they could be relied upon by individual litigants in their national courts. However, if such directly effective provisions of EEC law could be pleaded in domestic courts, then they might conflict with incompatible national law. How should domestic courts deal with such a situation? Detailed consideration came when the ECJ considered the issue a little later in *Costa* v *ENEL*. According to the Court,

> By creating a Community of unlimited duration … the member States have limited their sovereign rights, albeit within limited fields, and have thus created a body of law which binds both their nationals and themselves.
>
> [the] terms and spirit of the Treaty … make it impossible for the States, as a corollary, to accord precedence to a unilateral and subsequent measure over a legal system accepted by them on the basis of reciprocity…. The executive force

[91] Case 26/62 *Van Gend en Loos* [1963] ECR 1.

> of Community law cannot vary from one State to another in deference to subsequent domestic laws, without jeopardizing the objectives of the Treaty …[92]

This argument, based on the necessity of ensuring the uniformity and effectiveness of Community law, has been frequently used by the ECJ over the years. History shows us that the ECJ's technique was not unique. Comparisons may be made with the US Supreme Court's success in maintaining ultimate control over federal and state legal systems in the early nineteenth century. In both systems, judges promoted strong central values which were in conflict with State sovereignty. In *Martin* v. *Hunter's Lessee* US Supreme Court Justice Story upheld the jurisdiction of federal courts over state courts, insisting that this could be derived from the need for uniformity and harmony of decisions, otherwise: '… the laws, the treaties and the constitution of the United States would be different in different states, and might perhaps, never have precisely the same construction, obligation or efficacy in two states.'[93] These arguments resurfaced, 150 years later, in *Costa*.

Over the next ten years or so after *Costa*, the European Court expanded its declaration of the supremacy of EEC law. Regardless of its status (i.e. whether treaty provision, EEC legislation or agreement with a non-EEC State) a directly effective EEC law provision was held to prevail over national law. Even a fundamental constitutional provision could not be invoked to challenge the supremacy of EEC law.[94] Perhaps the surprising fact is that member States, including the UK in *Factortame*, rather quietly accepted the European Court's extensive interpretation of the treaties. The fervent reaction of later British eurosceptics should not lead us to believe that such responses were the norm in the EEC's earlier days. True, de Gaulle had deadened the progress of the EEC by insisting on the maintenance of a member State veto through the Luxembourg Accords. But member States were certainly not threatening to nullify the effects of the European Court's judgment.

5.4.2 Supremacy of EU Law in the UK

Nonetheless, many EEC States did experience problems with the supremacy of EEC law.[95] However, it took almost two decades before the clash between enforceable EEC law and parliamentary sovereignty arose head on in the UK. This came about in the first *Factortame* case in 1990, and concerned the conflict between EEC law and an incompatible but subsequently enacted UK statute.[96] The case concerned the EEC Common Fisheries Policy, which allocated

[92] Case 6/64 *Flaminio Costa* v. *ENEL* [1964] ECR 585 at 597.

[93] *Martin* v. *Hunter's Lessee* 14 US (1 Wheat) 304 [1816].

[94] E.g. Case 11/70 *Internationale Handelsgesellschaft gmbH* [1970] ECR 1125.

[95] E.g. *Cohn-Bendit* [1970] CMLR 395 (France); *Solange 1* [1974] 2 CMLR 540 (Germany); *Frontini* [1974] 372 (Italy).

[96] *R* v. *Secretary of State for Transport, ex parte Factortame* [1990] ECR 1 2433.

fishing quotas to member States. However, on exhaustion of the Spanish quota, Spanish fishing concerns had turned to Britain, where, by setting up as English companies, they were able to fish out of the British quota. The British government passed the 1988 Merchant Shipping Act, stipulating residency and nationality requirements for company licence holding to prevent this invasion of the British quota. However, such requirements violated the EEC Treaty, namely non-discrimination on grounds of nationality, as well as freedom to supply services and freedom of establishment. The ECJ ruled that parliamentary sovereignty could not prevent English courts from providing relief, even if that meant they would have to set aside the application of an English statute (a state of affairs unknown in twentieth-century English law.[97]) In this way, EEC law provided UK courts with powers denied them perhaps since the seventeenth century. Yet, on return of the case from Luxembourg to the House of Lords, little space was given to explaining how EEC law could require setting aside a provision of statute law. Lord Bridge held that:

> whatever limitation of its sovereignty Parliament accepted when it enacted the European Communities Act 1972 was entirely voluntary. Under the terms of the 1972 Act it has always been clear that it was the duty of a United Kingdom court, when delivering final judgment, to override any rule of national law found to be in conflict with any directly enforceable rule of Community law.... Thus there is nothing in any way novel in according supremacy to rules of Community law in those areas to which they apply and to insist that, in the protection of rights under Community law, national courts must not be inhibited by rules of national law from granting interim relief in appropriate cases is no more than a logical recognition of that supremacy.[98]

Lord Bridge's ruling set out the legal situation but did not go into any great detail as to how a fundamental principle of the British Constitution had been modified. The crucial issue after *Factortame* was to explain how, in order to give effect to the supremacy of EEC/EU law, the ECA could override later UK statutes – because this capacity seemed to violate a fundamental tenet of parliamentary sovereignty (the 'implied repeal' rule, whereby a later statute automatically overrides an earlier one).

5.4.3 Elucidating Lord Bridge's Holding in *Factortame*

Prior to *Factortame*, the idea that the judiciary might disapply an Act of Parliament seemed unthinkable. Lord Donaldson MR stated in the early stages of the *Factortame* litigation, 'Any attempt to interfere with primary legislation would be unconstitutional.'[99] The English courts' recognition of their ability

[97] Although in *Dr Bonham's case* [1610] 77 Eng. Rep at 652, Coke declared that English common law could 'controul acts of Parliament. and sometimes adjudge them to be utterly void'.

[98] Lord Bridge, *Factortame*, [1990] 3 CMLR 375, at 380.

[99] *Factortame* [1989] 2 CMLR 353 (CA) at 397.

do so, and their subsequent disapplication of the Merchant Shipping Act in *Factortame* thus represented a major shift in the constitutional order of the UK. However, in his judgment following the ECJ ruling, Lord Bridge had suggested that there was 'nothing in any way novel' in this. This section therefore examines several attempts to explain how EEC/EU law could be given effect over conflicting national law under s2(4) ECA.[100]

5.4.3.1 The Construction/Interpretation View

S2(4) ECA was central to the supremacy of EU law, in requiring that any British 'enactment passed or to be passed' should be subordinated to conflicting directly effective EU law. Nonetheless, English courts initially understood s2(4) as a rule of interpretation: that Parliament was presumed not to intend to override EU law, unless it had stated clearly and expressly that it intended to do so. Lord Denning held in *McCarthy's* v. *Smith*, 'Unless there is such an intentional and express repudiation of the treaty it is our duty to give priority to the treaty.' In *Garland* v. *British Rail Engineering*, Lord Diplock stated:

> it is a principle of construction of United Kingdom statutes ... that the words of a statute passed after the treaty has been signed and dealing with the subject matter of the international obligation ... are to be construed, if they are reasonably capable of bearing such a meaning, as intended to carry out the obligation and not to be inconsistent with it.[101]

All very well – but such an interpretation was not always possible. In that case, the second limb of s2(4) ('have effect') appeared to *require* the courts to give effect to EEC law and not national legislation. This mandated they hold inconsistent provisions inoperable. But could we put this in even stronger terms, and say that s2(4) actually *entrenched* the supremacy of EEC law?

5.4.3.2 Revolutionary

Indeed, not all constitutional theorists accepted that there was, in the words of Lord Bridge in *Factortame*, 'nothing in any way novel in according supremacy to rules of Community law in those areas to which they apply.' In contrast, constitutional theorist, William Wade, found such an approach 'revolutionary'. Wade suggested that the basic rule of a system (such as parliamentary sovereignty) could only be altered by revolution, because he believed the source for parliamentary sovereignty was extra-legal and therefore an official recognition that this had changed would be revolutionary. No kings had been beheaded, but the constitutional changes wrought by EU membership nonetheless constituted 'a quiet revolution'. Wade remarked that Lord Bridge 'takes it for granted that Parliament can "accept" a limitation of its sovereignty which

[100] The following section is indebted, to a certain extent, to a schema followed by Paul Craig, in 'Sovereignty of the United Kingdom Parliament after *Factortame*' (1991) 11 YBEL 221 (and also his Oxford lectures on UK Constitutional law).

[101] *McCarthys* v. *Smith* [1979] 3 All ER 325; *Garland British Rail Engineering Ltd* [1983] 2 AC 751.

will be effective both for the present and for the future. It is a statement which could hardly be clearer: Parliament can bind its successors. If that is not revolutionary, constitutional lawyers are Dutchmen.'[102]

Wade's view was not shared by everyone. Some, such as Neil MacCormick, argued that Parliament was capable of redefining what was to count as valid law by inserting new criteria into existing rules – a sort of variant on the 'new view' (or 'manner and form') theory of parliamentary sovereignty[103] – and that is what the 1972 Act did.[104] And Sir John Laws commented that:

> Sir William Wade regards this development as 'revolutionary', because in his view it represents an exception to the rule that Parliament cannot bind its successors. But I do not think that is right. It is elementary that Parliament possesses the power to repeal the European Communities Act in whole or in part (I leave aside the political realities); and the most that can be said, in my view, is that the House of Lords' acknowledgement of the force of European law means that the rule of construction implanted by section 2(4) cannot be abrogated by an implied repeal. Express words would be required. That, however, is hardly revolutionary: there are a number of areas where a particular statutory construction is only likely to be accepted by the courts if it is vouchsafed by express provision [as where a statute is said to exact taxes, impose criminal liability or to have retroactive effect].[105]

5.4.3.3 The Common Law 'Constitutional Statutes' Theory

Laws' own views on the ability of EU law to override statute was elucidated in his (obiter) pronouncement in the *Thoburn* case, where he stated that there existed a hierarchy of statutes, comprising both 'ordinary' and 'constitutional' statutes. Examples of the latter included Magna Carta, the Bill of Rights 1688, the Human Rights Act 1998, and the ECA 1972. Laws explained that 'a constitutional statute is one which (a) conditions the legal relationship between citizen and state in some general, overarching manner, or (b) enlarges or diminishes the scope of what we would now regard as fundamental constitutional rights.'[106] The crucial point was that whereas ordinary statutes could be impliedly repealed, constitutional statutes could not:

> There are now classes or types of legislative provision which cannot be repealed by mere implication ... there are certain circumstances in which the legislature may only enact what it desires to enact if it does so by express, or at any rate specific, provision. The courts have in effect so held in the field of European law itself, in the *Factortame* case.[107]

102 HWR Wade 'Sovereignty – Revolution or Evolution?' (1996) 112 *LQR* 573, 574. Also Wade's earlier work, 'The Basis of Legal Sovereignty' (1955) Cambridge LJ 172.

103 E.g. I Jennings, *The Law and the Constitution* (London, 1959); RFV Heuston, *Essays in Constitutional Law* (London: Stevens, 1961); and Chapter 6.

104 N MacCormick, 'A Very British Revolution', in *Questioning Sovereignty* (Oxford: Oxford University Press, 1999).

105 Sir John Laws, 'Law and Democracy' [1995] Public Law at 89.

106 *Thoburn* v. *Sunderland City Council* [2002] EWHC 195 Admin, per LJ Laws at para 62.

107 *Thoburn*, at para 60.

LJ Laws' holding was a departure from the orthodox view of parliamentary sovereignty. Dicey, for example, had claimed that the Acts of Union of Scotland and England were no more fundamental than the Dentists Act. But the constitutional statutes doctrine supports the *Factortame* holding. According to orthodox doctrine, the 1988 Merchant Shipping Act should have impliedly repealed relevant provisions of the 1972 Act. Yet in *Factortame,* the House of Lords gave priority to EU law, incorporated via the 1972 Act, over the 1988 Act. The constitutional statutes doctrine has since received the approval of the UK Supreme Court, most notably in *Miller I*, where the majority noted the 'constitutional character' of the ECA 1972 and that EU law is protected from implied repeal because of the Act.[108]

5.4.3.4 The Principled View

Craig argues that the doctrine of parliamentary sovereignty must rest on some principled justification, that it must cohere with some 'broader constitutional map'.[109] Thus, parliamentary sovereignty in the UK is not *a*contextual: those who advocated it in its earlier days supported it with reasoned arguments. Blackstone argued for the sovereignty of Parliament as a check against government. Dicey partly justified arguments for it on the basis that the elected Parliament (even if not by universal franchise) represented the will of the people, and should be able to implement that will. As an accurate description of the constitutional legal order at that time these arguments were probably inaccurate, but they are significant as an attempt to provide a principled, normative support for a constitutional system. According to Craig, arguments used by Lord Bridge in *Factortame* furnished such principled arguments as to why the UK should be bound by EEC law while it remained within the EU: namely, that the UK had voluntarily contracted to pool its sovereignty and that the efficiency of EU law rested on its uniform enforcement by all member States.

5.4.4 Affirming National Sovereignty

In any case, the nature of the relationship of parliamentary sovereignty to EU law apparently remained insufficiently clear for some ministers to urge further clarification post-*Factortame.* And so, s18 EU Act 2011 (now repealed) stipulated that EU law had effect in the UK only because Parliament, by enacting the 1972 Act, had allowed it to.[110] This however failed to satisfy those intent on stressing parliamentary sovereignty and in early 2016, David Cameron stated that he desired to 'put beyond doubt' the sovereignty of the House of Commons

108 *Miller* [2017] UKSC 5; also *HS2 Action Alliance Ltd* [2014] UKSC 3, paras. 207, 208; *R (Privacy International)* [2019] UKSC 22; and *H* v. *Lord Advocate* [2012] UKSC 24, para. 30.

109 Craig, 'Sovereignty of the United Kingdom Parliament after *Factortame*', 254 et seq.

110 David Allen Green suggested this provision would be better called the 'Circular Logic Act' (The Fragility of Parliamentary Sovereignty', *Financial Times*, 3 May 2016). Also M Dougan, 'The UK's European Union Act 2011: "Who Won the Bloody War Anyway?"' (2012) 37 ELR 3.

and Downing Street, and announced that proposals enabling British courts to uphold British sovereignty would soon be introduced.[111] It is difficult to see how the EU could function without the supremacy principle, derived as it was on the need for uniformity across the EU as reasoned by the ECJ in *Costa*. The German Constitutional Court (which had been suggested as a possible model) has never in practice disapplied EU law. In any case, proposals for a Sovereignty Act were never put forward in any concrete form, and were overtaken by Brexit.

Also, in 2014, in an extra-judicial lecture, Lord Neuberger, then President of the UK Supreme Court, had remarked that the 'German Constitution enables a German court to say that German law sometimes trumps EU law. This is an option which is much more rarely, if at all, open to a UK court as we have no constitution to invoke.'[112] This statement appeared to suggest national legal sovereignty could override EU law in a way other than a trivial restatement of a theoretical parliamentary sovereignty, but that it would take a different kind of Constitution, a written one, like that in Germany, for this to work. But Brexit has since happened, and in any case, perhaps the more recent statements of Lord Neuberger himself in *HS2* (to the effect that there are limits to the capacity of EU law to override fundamental principles of the UK Constitution) have now overtaken this?[113]

5.4.5 Going beyond Sovereignty?

According to the ECJ, EEC law rests at the pinnacle of the legal order, but according to most member States, their own Constitutions, or principles such as parliamentary sovereignty, occupy that position. Thus, there is a clash of two constitutional visions, and there appears no ultimately authoritative manner (in law at least) for resolving conflicts: a situation which leads to a lack of legal certainty.

However, an alternative approach is furnished by the idea of 'post-sovereignty'. This contends that sovereignty has been transformed and is no longer the dominant mode of political organization. Post-sovereign approaches argue States share their powers with supra-State, sub-State, and trans-State systems. Neil MacCormick's work has been influential in this area,[114] and his view was that the inexorable linkage of law with sovereignty and the State was but the passing phenomena of a few centuries – a passing by no means regrettable.

111 'EU Deal: Cameron Vows to Put Commons Sovereignty "Beyond Doubt"', *The Guardian*, 3 February 2016.

112 Lord Neuberger, 'The British and Europe', Cambridge Freshfields Annual Law Lecture, 12 February 2014.

113 *HS2* [2014] UKSC 3, paras. 207 and 208; in *Pham* [2015] UKSC 19, Lord Mance developed this, holding that 'a domestic court must ultimately decide for itself what is consistent with its own domestic constitutional arrangements including under the 1972 Act' (para. 90). See further Chapter 6.

114 E.g. Neil MacCormick, *Questioning Sovereignty* (Oxford: Oxford University Press, 1999).

MacCormick's *Questioning Sovereignty* suggested that we are now 'beyond sovereignty',[115] arguing that sovereignty need not be single and indivisible, contrary to what orthodox theorists such as Dicey stipulated. Indeed, MacCormick believed that an organization such as the EU could be seen as comprising multiple, overlapping sovereignties – an 'interlocking of legal systems, with mutual recognition of each other's validity, but with different grounds for that recognition.'[116]

For all that, perhaps the 2016 phenomena of Brexit (and Trump, and some other regimes) might appear to challenge this vision of post-sovereignty? Perhaps the most common constitutional idea to feature in Brexit debates was the notion of sovereignty – 'taking back control' – an apparent yearning for a sovereignty that could not be reconciled with continuing EU membership, and a desire for a clearly national constitutional architecture.

5.4.6 National/External and Pooled Sovereignty

Yet, at this point it should be stressed that Britain's national sovereignty was never in fact disturbed by EU membership, and the only aspect of parliamentary sovereignty to have been affected by EU membership was the implied repeal rule, which was in any case under attack.

National (or external) sovereignty is a nation's right to be recognized as a State, and exercise jurisdiction within its borders. It connotes legal freedom of action regarding other States in the international community, subject to international law obligations. It is that power which the UK exercised in joining the EEC in 1973 and exercised again in leaving the EU in 2020. The UK's national/external sovereignty was unaffected by its EU membership and is unchanged by EU withdrawal.

National sovereignty and parliamentary sovereignty are not identical, although often confused (especially in the Brexit context). National sovereignty is larger and more fundamental than parliamentary sovereignty. A country may be sovereign and recognized as independent by the international community, yet lack a sovereign Parliament (because the national Constitution is seen as fundamental, and parliamentary statutes that violate the Constitution may be struck down). National sovereignty could also, however, be described as a matter of degree. Treaties might appear to constrain sovereignty in practice, given that all treaties involve some voluntary restriction on a State's freedom of action (which States have accepted). However, rather than limiting sovereignty, participation in treaties could be described as a characteristic of sovereignty[117] – a situation in which some States have voluntarily chosen to pool

[115] Indeed, MacCormick wrote an article entitled, 'Beyond the Sovereign State' (1993) 56 MLR 1.

[116] *Questioning Sovereignty*, chapters 6 and 7.

[117] E.g. Lord Lloyd, Hansard, HL Debs 27 July 1971, vol. 323, cc 367–368, 'This view has been reiterated on many occasions in many weighty judgments both of international and State courts, including the Supreme Court of the United States.'

some of their national sovereignty for the benefits this brings. In the debates on Britain's EEC entry in 1973, as already noted, Lord Hailsham stated: 'The Treaty is a contract to use the sovereignty of each member for limited purposes in concert with the others.'

However, some Brexiteers argued that domestic legislation rather than EU law should govern withdrawal of the UK from the EU.[118] Such an approach suggests a *strong* parliamentary sovereignty, governing all things, including Britain's relations with other States, and the unilateral ability to ignore treaty obligations. A similar approach was evident in the 2020 UK Internal Market Bill, whose provisions violated the UK-EU Withdrawal Agreement.[119] These provisions were justified by Attorney-General Suella Braverman, who argued Parliament has the authority to pass primary legislation in breach of UK treaty obligations.[120] However, such an approach is unlawful in international law (it violates the *pacta sunt servanda* principle in Article 26 Vienna Convention on the Law of Treaties) and harmful to Britain's reputation, raising issues of trust. This approach also conflates parliamentary sovereignty with national/external sovereignty, suggesting that the UK can use its domestic law to govern its relationships with other States and international organizations. That is not how national sovereignty functions in the international arena. States observe treaties and join international organizations because they know that in ceding some freedom in certain areas, they gain a greater benefit from pooling sovereignty or accepting certain obligations.

5.4.7 The 'Death' of Parliamentary Sovereignty

One final point must be made here – even although Brexit has repealed the ECA, it is impossible to return to the pre 1972 situation. The Parliament of 1972 succeeded in limiting future Parliaments by means of the ECA. There is no reason why this should not occur again. Nick Barber identified 'the quiet death of parliamentary sovereignty', because *Factortame* demonstrated that 'it is no longer the case that "whatever the Queen-in-Parliament enacts as a statute is law": the courts can sometimes set aside these statutes',[121] adding

118 E.g. John Redwood MP who said 'a lot of us don't think there is any need to trigger Article 50 any time at all.' 'EU's Article 50 could become first Brexit stand-off', *Financial Times*, 24 June 2016.

119 Northern Ireland Secretary, Brandon Lewis, actually made the 'confession' that the legislation would breach international law in a 'specific and limited way'. 'Northern Ireland Secretary admits new bill will "break international law"', *BBC news*, 8 September 2020. Notably both the Scottish Advocate-General (Government legal advisor on Scottish affairs) and Treasury Solicitor (Head of the Government Legal Service) resigned in protest at the Government's approach.

120 UK Internal Market Bill: Northern Ireland, 24 September 2020, Hansard Volume 680, col 1124. And the issue seems to have been raised again by the Northern Ireland Protocol Bill, introduced into Parliament in 2022.

121 N Barber, 'The Afterlife of Parliamentary Sovereignty' (2011) 9(1) International Journal of Constitutional Law 151.

that 'Parliament could give the courts the power to strike down statutes that conflicted with human rights, or it could, if it wished, place legal limits on its capacity to legislate in devolved matters.'[122] Having achieved this in the case of EU law, there is no reason of principle why Parliament should not limit itself with regard to other matters.

5.5 The UK, EU, and Brexit

5.5.1 Introduction

It is sometimes forgotten that, prior to Brexit, the UK government had already, in 1975, obtained a renegotiation of the terms of the UK's EU membership. However, since the 1975 referendum, the EU had considerably expanded its powers into fields other than the purely economic. For example, the 1992 Maastricht Treaty introduced new competences in Justice and Home Affairs (JHA), Common Foreign and Security Policy, and the legal structures for Economic and Monetary Union. The EU had also expanded its membership to 28 States.

The 'Bruges Group' of anti-European Conservatives was formed in 1989. In the eyes of some, and of eurosceptics to be sure, the EU had stealthily progressed well beyond its initial characterization as a 'Common Market'. As Britain had willingly and knowingly signed up to new competences and 'ever closer union' in successive EU treaties, such statements were disingenuous at best. In any case, Britain had already secured a slew of opt-outs and special arrangements from many of these policies (i.e. Britain did not participate in EMU); Britain was not a member of the Schengen area (i.e. States which had abolished most border controls); and Britain also did not participate in many JHA measures.

Nonetheless, in 2015, David Cameron put forward proposals to European Council President Donald Tusk, requesting reform in four key areas: economic governance, sovereignty, competitiveness and immigration.[123] On 19 February 2016, the UK and the other 27 member States reached an agreement on a new settlement for the UK within the EU. In summary, the deal provided for: an 'emergency brake' on migrants' in-work benefits for four years if there were 'exceptional' levels of migration; child benefit sent overseas by EU migrants in Britain to be indexed to the cost of living in their home country; the possibility of the UK enacting 'an emergency safeguard' to protect the City of London, to ensure British business did not face discrimination for being outside the eurozone; and a proposal for a 'red card' to allow 55 per cent of national parliaments to object to draft EU legislation. This agreement did not require treaty

[122] Ibid., 153, 154.

[123] 'PM's Letter to President of the European Council Donald Tusk' (10 November 2015) www.gov.uk/ government/publications/eu-reform-pms-letter-to-president-of-the-european-council-donald-tusk.

amendments,[124] with the exception of agreement to amend the EU treaties (at the next IGC) to insert a specific provision that 'references to ever-closer union do not apply to the United Kingdom.'[125]

Reactions to the deal within Britain were mixed – eurosceptics tended to deride it as worthless, whereas business and pro-Europeans were more welcoming. When David Cameron announced this renegotiation deal at the European Council, he stated: 'When it comes to Europe, mine is a hard-headed assessment of what is in our national interest.'[126] However, this new deal was subject to the EU membership referendum held in Britain on 23 June 2016 and would only have come into force in the event of a Remain vote.

5.5.2 Brexit and Its Consequences

And so the UK's EU renegotiation was overtaken by the UK referendum on continued EU membership – a referendum many have accused David Cameron of holding to settle feuds in the Conservative party, rather than to serve Britain's national interests.[127] This was no repetition of the 1975 Referendum – as Saunders remarks, when Cameron 'sought to replicate his predecessor's success, the device blew up in his hands.'[128]

The UK has been the first, and so far only, State to leave the EU. On 23 June 2016, a Referendum on EU membership was held, and the UK overall voted to leave the EU, by a majority of 51.9–48.1 per cent.[129] The EU Referendum was held under the parameters of the EU Referendum Act 2015. Notably, there was no requirement in the Act that the UK Government implement its results. It was an advisory rather than a mandatory referendum. However, the UK government stated in a policy paper, in February 2016, that it was under a 'democratic duty to give effect to the electorate's decision.'[130] Neither the referendum legislation, nor the vote itself, provided any guidance as to what the UK's future relationship might be with the EU. The question put to the electorate was in binary form: 'Should the United Kingdom remain a member of the European Union or leave the European Union?'[131] The electorate voted only to leave the EU. They did not agree to any particular exit agreement.

[124] In this way, it was like Wilson's 1975 EEC reforms.

[125] *European Council conclusions*, Brussels, 19 February 2016, EUCO 1/16.

[126] Katya Adler, 'EU Deal: A Hard-Headed Calculation to Avoid Brexit', BBC News, 20 February 2016.

[127] According to Ipsos Mori polling, the EU was not thought to be a major issue by the British public only months before the referendum – 'British people hardly ever thought about the EU before Brexit, now it dominates their lives', *The Conversation*, 9 October 2019.

[128] Saunders, *Yes to Europe*, at 2.

[129] Electoral Commission, UK Referendum results: www.electoralcommission.org.uk/find-information-by-subject/elections-and-referendums/past-elections-and-referendums/eu-referendum/electorate-and-count-information

[130] *The process for withdrawing from the European Union,* HM Government, 29 February 2016, at 7, para 2.1.

[131] S1(4) EU Referendum Act 2015.

The UK government started the official process for exit in March 2017. This followed the procedure under Article 50 TEU, which required the UK to formally notify the EU of its intention to leave, and to negotiate with the EU a Withdrawal Agreement. However, before that happened, a serious issue arose over the official notification to the EU of Britain's triggering of the Article 50 process. In the UK, treaty making and foreign affairs are usually managed by the executive, using the prerogative, sometimes with legislative participation. But leaving the EU, it was asserted, involved far more than an executive act of foreign relations. It would result in the repeal of the ECA, and the termination of all sorts of rights (free movement, workers' rights and so on) under EU law. This was claimed to infringe basic UK constitutional law if effected without parliamentary consent.

A lawsuit was brought by Gina Miller and others claiming that the 'constitutional requirements' (in the terminology of Article 50 TEU) required Parliament's authority for triggering Article 50. The UK had enabled its accession to the EEC to be ratified by the ECA 1972. Under UK constitutional law, a statute may only be repealed by another statute, and not by the exercise of prerogative power.[132] The claimants won the case at first instance.[133] But the three High Court judges who gave the ruling were headlined on the front page of the *Daily Mail* as 'enemies of the people'. The same article also described the lead claimant, Gina Miller, a British citizen, as 'foreign born'. Nonetheless, the Lord Chancellor[134] (then Liz Truss), who has a constitutional duty[135] to protect the independence of the judiciary, was very slow to defend the judiciary from these attacks. Lord Neuberger, President of the UK Supreme Court at that time, criticized (extra-judicially) Liz Truss' delayed response, remarking that undermining the judiciary undermined the rule of law, as judges were 'the ultimate guardians' of it.[136]

The High Court hearing was not the end of the *Miller* litigation. The government appealed the case to the UK Supreme Court and lost again. In *Miller* v. *Secretary of State for Exiting the EU*,[137] delivered in January 2017, the UK Supreme Court ruled that the government cannot use the royal prerogative to trigger Article 50, and so leave the EU, without Parliament's authority. Both *Miller* rulings acknowledge the crucial role of Parliament in protecting rights, as well as underlining that a UK statute may not be repealed by prerogative alone. The prerogative cannot be exercised in a manner which would 'turn a statute into what is in substance a dead letter' or 'cut across the object and purpose of an existing statute'.[138]

[132] *R* v. *Secretary of State for the Home Department, ex p Fire Brigades Union* [1995] 2 AC 513.
[133] *R (Miller)* v. *Secretary of State for Exiting the European Union* [2016] EWHC 2768 (Admin).
[134] The Lord Chancellor is also the Justice Minister in the UK and sits in the Cabinet.
[135] S2 Constitutional Reform Act 2005.
[136] BBC News, 'Attacks on Judiciary Undermine Law', www.bbc.com/news/uk-38986228
[137] *Miller* v. *Secretary of State for Exiting the EU* [2017] UKSC 5.
[138] *ex p Fire Brigades Union* [1995].

After the *Miller* decision, Parliament legislated to give its consent for Article 50 to be triggered and the Brexit process set in motion. It passed the EU (Notification of Withdrawal) Act 2017, an ultra-short piece of legislation, containing one very short substantive provision: 'The prime minister may notify, under Article 50(2) of the Treaty on European Union, the United Kingdom's intention to withdraw from the EU.'

Negotiations under Article 50 between the UK and the EU (often fraught and tortuous) eventually resulted in a Withdrawal treaty, focussing specifically on three elements, often known as the 'divorce' agreement. These were the UK's budgetary contributions, the rights of EU citizens, and the specific status of Northern Ireland. A Withdrawal Agreement[139] was concluded between the EU and the UK government on 17 October 2019, and entered into force on 1 February 2020, after the UK Parliament had adopted the EU (Withdrawal Agreement) Act 2020. From that date, the UK was no longer an EU member (although a transition period applied until 31 December 2020, during which most EU law continued to apply in the UK). In 2021, a further Trade and Cooperation Agreement (TCA) was concluded between the UK and EU, to govern the UK's future relationship with the EU.[140] The UK was very keen to ensure that there was no role for the ECJ in the governance and dispute settlement provisions of this treaty. Although this treaty provides that no tariffs or quotas will be imposed on trade in goods provided EU rules of origin are met, there are increased non-tariff barriers (such as technical, sanitary and phytosanitary barriers) to UK trade with the EU. UK citizens, service providers and companies no longer enjoy the freedom of movement they previously had in the EU. This Agreement is highly unusual in that it actually *raises* barriers to trade between the parties. This was inevitable once the UK decided to leave the EU Single Market and Customs Union.

5.5.3 Domestic Legislation for Brexit

Five major pieces of domestic legislation have been adopted by the UK Parliament in the Brexit process. The 2015 EU Referendum Act which set up the mechanisms for the referendum; the EU (Notification of Withdrawal) Act 2017, whereby Parliament gave consent to the triggering of Article 50 TEU; the EU Withdrawal Act (EUWA) 2018, which makes provision for the UK legal system after Brexit; the EU Withdrawal Agreement Act (WAA) 2020, which implements the 'divorce agreement' in the UK; and the EU (Future Relationship) Act (EUFRA) 2020. All raise rule of law issues, for example: legality,

[139] *Agreement on the withdrawal of the United Kingdom of Great Britain and Northern Ireland from the European Union and the European Atomic Energy Community*, 2019/C 384 OJ C 384, 12.11.2019.

[140] *UK–EU trade and cooperation (future relationship) agreement 2020.* https://eur-lex.europa.eu/legal-content/EN/TXT/HTML/?uri=CELEX:22021A0430(01)&from=EN

legal certainty, the availability of parliamentary and judicial scrutiny, as well as affecting human rights.

In particular, the EUWA 2018 and WAA 2020 change the constitutional landscape considerably. The EUWA provided the apparatus for the huge revision of the UK legal system necessary as a consequence of the UK's exit from the EU. This is 'a legal undertaking of a type and scale that is unique and unprecedented'[141] and, as a result, the EUWA is hugely complex, with the following main functions. First, s1 repeals the ECA 1972. Ss2–7 provide for legal continuity by converting EU law into national law as 'retained EU law', otherwise there would be huge gaps in the law, as it will take some time to replace the field once covered by EU law. s8 EUWA grants UK Government ministers huge law-making powers to amend or repeal retained EU law, even granting such powers by means of a 'Henry VIII' clause (namely a ministerial order which is able to overturn Acts of Parliament). Henry VIII was not a model legislator and such procedures have a highly undemocratic air – rather curious, surely, if an aim of Brexit was to regain democracy. Ss10–12 EUWA set out important and controversial provisions regarding devolution, and it should be noted that the EUWA was enacted without the consent of the Scottish Parliament,[142] a fact that appears to violate the Sewel Convention (now inserted in the Scotland Act 2016) that Westminster will not normally legislate with regard to devolved matters in Scotland without the consent of the Scottish Parliament.

Nonetheless, despite the general conversion of EU law into national law, s5(4) EUWA provides that the Charter of Fundamental Rights is not part of domestic law as from exit date. While the UK was an EU member, because of the supremacy of EU law, neither the EU Charter, nor rights provisions in EU treaties and legislation, could be repealed by the UK Parliament, and national courts were empowered to disapply domestic legislation incompatible with those EU rights, as in *Benkharbouche*.[143] Contrast this with the traditional British system of unbridled UK parliamentary sovereignty, where entrenchment is considered unachievable, and so ultimately it is not possible to protect against abuse of legislative power. Exclusion of the Charter also leaves open the question as to how there will exist 'equivalent rights' in Northern Ireland and Ireland after Brexit, as required by the Belfast/Good Friday Agreement.[144]

The EU (Future Relationship) Act [EUFRA] 2021 was introduced into Parliament on 30 December 2021 and passed the same day just before the transition period came to an end. This statute incorporated vast amounts of this very long Agreement into domestic law with no time to assess the implications.

[141] Per House of Lords Constitution Committee, *European Union (Withdrawal) Bill*, 29 January 2018, HL 69 2017–19, 3.

[142] E.g. Scottish Parliament Motion S5M-12223: www.parliament.scot/parliamentarybusiness/Bills/105997.aspx

[143] *Benkharbouche* v. *Secretary of State for Foreign and Commonwealth Affairs* [2017] UKSC 62.

[144] Chris McCrudden, 'The Good Friday Agreement, Brexit, and Rights', Royal Irish Academy Brexit Briefing, October 2017.

Section 29 EUFRA is truly remarkable, in providing that any change required to be made in UK domestic law to give effect to the Trade and Cooperation Agreement is deemed to have taken such effect. Yet the Agreement is so broad and vague overall that s29 seems to exclude Parliament from its law-making function. There are also more controversial 'Henry VIII' powers in s31 that allow ministers to make any law required to implement the TCA by regulations. Therefore, it would seem that the EUFRA gives the Executive a new range of powers to exercise with very little Parliamentary scrutiny.

5.5.4 Northern Ireland

Although Britain's post-war formal legal links with the EU have come to an official end, matters remain unsettled. One of the most difficult issues proved to be the question of Northern Ireland. The 1998 Belfast/Good Friday Agreement (B/GFA) ended many years of factional violence in Northern Ireland and introduced a new legal settlement of power sharing, actualizing a consociational, pluralist system very different to Dicey's constitutional model. Given that Brexit requires an external border across Ireland, demarcating an EU State (Ireland) from a non-EU state (Northern Ireland) it was imperative to find a resolution that would not reinstate a hard border across Ireland, reviving memories of the role that border played in the violent recent past.

Yet, it is truly surprising how little thought was given to Northern Ireland in the Brexit referendum. The UK Government insisted that Brexit meant the UK leaving the Customs Union and Single Market (in which case there must be a customs and regulatory border between the Republic and the North). Yet the UK also maintained there would be no hard border, no physical infrastructure, nor checks or controls – but this would only be possible if Northern Ireland remains in the Customs Union and Single Market. Yet, the UK Government had repeatedly promised that there would be no barrier between Northern Ireland and the rest of the UK. In this way, the UK Government pledged incompatible outcomes. It has been known for British commentators to describe the Irish border issue as a modern version of the 'Schleswig-Holstein question', which Lord Palmerston disparaged as understood only by three people, one gone mad, the other dead.[145] But this comparison underplays the huge significance of the Irish border issue. Nor should one forget that the issue of whether Schleswig-Holstein was a part of Denmark or Germany was finally settled by referendum, a mechanism which is provided to the people of Northern Ireland by law in the B/GFA, to determine whether they wish to become part of a united Ireland. Nor does the conundrum appear settled. There is also a certain irony to this predicament – in the 2016 EU Referendum, the majority in Northern Ireland voted to remain in the EU, but it was the DUP that urged a troublesome hard Brexit, and from 2021 was incensed by the inescapable result of that approach.

[145] Cited in Lytton Strachey, *Queen Victoria* (London: Chatto & Windus. 1921) 229.

The 2019 Withdrawal Agreement Protocol on Ireland and Northern Ireland effectively included Northern Ireland in the EU's Customs Union, although officially, Northern Ireland remains part of UK customs territory. According to the Protocol, any customs checks or controls occur between Northern Ireland and Great Britain. This in effect creates an internal border between Great Britain and Northern Ireland in the Irish Sea – a solution which has led to fractious dealings between the EU and UK. In June 2022, the UK Government introduced a Northern Ireland Protocol Bill to Westminster, which appeared to violate much of the existing Protocol, in breach of international law, and was widely criticized. However, the 2023 'Windsor Framework' may mitigate some of the more problematic elements of the Protocol. This is discussed further in the chapter on Ireland (Chapter 2).

5.6 Conclusion

Leaving the EU, Gavin Williamson (sometime Defence Secretary) told the *Daily Telegraph*, would restore Britain as 'a truly global player', determined once again to 'play the role on the world stage that the world expects us to play'.[146] Some Brexiteers advocated the notion of the CANZUK (a pact between Canada, Australia, New Zealand and the UK) – thus seeking to revive links with the former 'White settler' colonies of the British Empire. In 2016, journalist and historian Andrew Roberts argued that 'of all the many splendid opportunities provided by the British people's heroic Brexit vote, perhaps the greatest is the resuscitation of the idea of a CANZUK union.'[147] There has also been a call for a more unified 'Anglosphere',[148] referencing a shared history, language, culture and values, in a call that has been ongoing since the nineteenth-century movement for a 'Greater Britain'. Indeed, many Brexiteers castigated Britain's EU membership as a betrayal that, in the words of Boris Johnson, 'betrayed our relationships with Commonwealth countries such as Australia and New Zealand.'[149] The proximity of Europe is eschewed in favour of what are perceived to be closer ties of identity and kinship, however great the physical distance. But a very pertinent question is exactly what does Britain produce now that other (maybe Commonwealth) countries would be willing to purchase? Britain does very little trade with CANZ countries in contrast with the EU. And notably, during the EU referendum campaign, all CANZ leaders supported Britain remaining in the EU. Dorling and Tomlinson suggest

[146] C Hope, 'Britain to Become "True Global Player" Post-Brexit Says Defence Secretary', *Daily Telegraph*, 30 December 2018.

[147] A Roberts, 'CANZUK: After Brexit, Canada, Australia and New Zealand Can Unite', *Daily Telegraph*, 30 September 2016.

[148] See e.g. M Kenny and J Pearce, *Shadows of Empire: The Anglosphere in British politics* (Cambridge: Polity Press, 2018).

[149] B Johnson, 'The Aussies are just like us so let's stop kicking them out', *Daily Telegraph*, 25 August 2013.

that 'in the near future the EU referendum will become widely recognized and understood as part of the last vestiges of empire working their way out of the British psyche.'[150] For them Brexit is a manifestation of post-imperial angst, the last gasp of the British Empire.

As I have attempted to illustrate in this chapter, the notion of Britain as a leader in a global domain is nothing new. However, in the twenty-first century, it is unrealistic, fantasy even – Britain cannot revert to an empire to furnish it with economic powerhouse status in trade and raw materials. And in any case, the image of a post Brexit Britain is a very confused one. For in contrast to the world leader image, has been another interpretation current in euroscepticism: that of Britain as colonized, surrendered, in vassalage – to what O'Toole has termed a 'phoney oppressor'.[151]

The EU has done many worthy things, ensuring greater peace and prosperity over 60 years for citizens of its now twenty-eight States, and has publicly subscribed in its treaties to values such as the rule of law, human rights and democracy. However, it is not flawless. Even convinced Remainers would acknowledge that EU law has as many faults, and often the same faults, as national law. It can get bogged down in bureaucracy or worse – such as when the EU Commission resigned *en masse* in 1999 due to fraud and mismanagement, or in the harshness of the austerity imposed on some of its States during the 2008–2009 financial crisis. Some EU policies are easily criticized and caricatured – such as the CAP, for which almost no-one seems to have a good word. The EU is of course, a huge market, and while such a market brings economic benefits, it may also bring the dark side of neoliberal privilege, which may be too willing to let the weak collapse. Some benefit and others do not. As Fintan O'Toole remarks,

> Being angry about the European Union isn't a psychosis – it's a mark of sanity. Indeed, anyone who is not disillusioned with the EU is suffering from delusions.... There is a European technocratic elite ... that has lost its memory. It has forgotten that poverty, inequality, insecurity and a sense of powerlessness have drastic political repercussions. The EU was founded on a kind of constructive pessimism. Behind its drive towards inclusion and equality lay two powerful words: or else. It was an institution that knew that, if things are not held together by a reasonable expectation that life will get better for ordinary people, they will fall apart. In the best sense, the EU itself was a Project Fear.[152]

However, O'Toole continues, for all that Brexit counters [a] 'sense of powerlessness with a moment of real power. it's still self-harm'.[153] The loss of trade, especially in services, harms Britain deeply. And the freedom from 'red tape'

[150] D Dorling and S Tomlinson, *Rule Britannia: Brexit and the End of Empire* (London: Biteback Publishing, 2019) 3. Also Nadine El-Enany, 'Things Fall Apart: From Empire to Brexit Britain' at https://blogs.bath.ac.uk/iprblog/2017/05/02/things-fall-apart-from-empire-to-brexit-britain/

[151] See further, O'Toole, *Heroic Failure*, at 30.

[152] Ibid., 130–131. [153] Ibid., 131–132.

will remove protective social and environmental regulation, and ironically require more 'red tape'.[154] Further, 'taking back control' ignores the fact that so many transnational issues cannot be resolved through isolated self-regulation at State level. Even if the UK is no longer in the Single Market, it still has to observe many Single Market regulations if its products are to be recognized and marketable in the EU. 'Passporting' for banks and city firms has become a much used term, but passports are used to cross external borders and that is exactly what UK business has to do post Brexit, and without metaphorical passports, commerce will be very difficult. As a non-EU country, the UK is in a situation that poorer third countries have endured for many years. They have often been required under trading agreements to enact certain product standards to be allowed to export. They may have to grant foreign investors specific privileges. They possess sovereignty in name, but in reality are regulated from outside through economic pressures, even without the constraints (or benefits) of a formal system like the EU. This is why the Brexiteer's claims for sovereignty and red lines are ultimately futile.

Additionally, one might ask how can the UK 'take back control' as a sovereign state when its very own national identity is so fragmented? For the EU referendum result does not point to unity and the vote was extremely divided, with a small percentage separating Remainers and Leave voters. This division of Remain and Leave also took specific paths – separating young from old, urban from rural, educated from uneducated.

Indeed, the UK is a strange nation State, not least because it actually consists of four nations (England, Scotland, Wales, and the conflicted Northern Ireland, which is quite possibly not a nation) not just England, even though so eminent a writer as Dicey made the mistake of using the term 'English' Constitution when he was actually writing about the British Constitution.[155] Scotland and Northern Ireland both voted, by considerable margins, to remain in the EU. In both, independence from the UK is considered as a means to preserve EU membership. The UK government no longer appears able to engender policies and decisions acceptable to all of its nations' differing and multifarious views. Whose national sovereignty is at issue when the mantra of 'Taking Back Control' is repeated? In affirming Brexit and Britain's borders, Brexiteers show a reckless disregard for borders internal to the UK, including that most fateful of borders running through the island of Ireland.

Ultimately, this blunt and direct statement captures the reality: 'There is no end state in our relations with Europe. There is only millennia of collaboration, conquest, disputes, exchange, competition and alliance'.[156]

154 E.g. 'Brexit red tape knocks £17bn off UK trade with EU in just three months, watchdog finds', *The Independent*, 5 November 2021.

155 This conflation was also made in Walter Bagehot, *The English Constitution* (1867).

156 Dan Snow, 'Brexit Is Not an End to Britain's Liaison with Europe. It's Just a New Beginning', *The Guardian*, 1 January 2019.

Part II
Five Themes

6

Sovereignty

6.1 A General Introduction to Sovereignty

6.1.1 Sovereignty as a Contested Concept

What us the point of sovereignty today and why are we still talking about it? Is it a vestige of old, absolutist times, a focus for dictators, an anomaly even, when power is constrained by constitutionalism and human rights? Or might there still be some point, something intelligible, to this concept?

Sovereignty is the notion that there exists a final and absolute political authority within a territory. It is usually understood as having both an internal (i.e. supremacy *within* a particular community) and external (i.e. vis-a-vis other States) sense, and we will return to this bifurcation. Sovereignty has been a significant concept for the past 400 years or so, as one would expect of a doctrine concerning the ultimate location of power and authority. There exists a vast amount of scholarship on sovereignty,[1] yet its meaning has become fiercely contested, to the point where some deny it has any worthwhile role in our contemporary age.[2]

Although some might trace its roots to ancient classical thought (e.g. to Aristotle and Roman law) sovereignty, as we know it today, only really came to be articulated in the sixteenth century, and many locate the European wars of religion as the origin of our present understanding of the term.[3] In this context, sovereignty provided a useful apparatus for those who sought order out of the chaos wrought by devastating and brutal conflict.

Many ground the modern conception of sovereignty in the treaty of Westphalia of 1648, which ended the Thirty Years War (one of the most brutal wars

[1] Panu Minkkinen noted that the British Library catalogue, for the first decade of the twenty-first century alone, listed 330 monographs containing sovereignty in their title. P Minkkinen, *Sovereignty, Knowledge, Law* (Abingdon: Routledge, 2009) 6.

[2] Don Herzog, *Sovereignty RIP* (New Haven CT: Yale University Press, 2020); N MacCormick, *Questioning Sovereignty* (Oxford: Oxford University Press, 1999)

[3] E.g. Herzog, Sovereignty RIP, at 16. Also Dieter Grimm, *Sovereignty* (New York: Columbia University Press, 2015); but see Giorgio Agambem, for a more expansive view of the origins of sovereignty in ancient thought [*The Omnibus Homo Sacer* (Stanford CA: Stanford University Press, 2017)].

in history). This treaty initiated huge power shifts in Europe, inaugurating the modern State system founded on the notion of sovereignty.[4]

6.1.2 Modern Conceptions of Sovereignty

The first modern theory of State sovereignty is very often ascribed to Jean Bodin, who published *Les six livres de la République* in 1576, although it took some time until the work's significance became fully realized. Significantly, Bodin's sovereign may not be bound by anything or anyone: 'Majesty or Sovereignty ... is the most high, absolute, and perpetual power over the citizens and subjects in a Commonweale' and 'Sovereignty is not limited either in power, charge, or time certain.'[5]

Nearly a century later, in 1651, Thomas Hobbes published the *Leviathan*, providing an account of sovereignty similar to Bodin's. Like Bodin. Hobbes envisioned the sovereign as absolute – 'Power Unlimited, is absolute Sovereignty.'[6] However, unlike Bodin, Hobbes reasoned that the origins of the sovereign's power derived from a (fictional) contract among peoples, who willingly gave up some of their liberty in return for submission to, and protection by, the sovereign against the chaos of anarchy. This involved positing a state of nature outside any sovereign State, by no means an attractive condition but envisioned as 'a war of all against all', in which human life was 'solitary, poor, nasty, brutish, and short'.[7] And, according to Hobbes, effective protection could only come from a sovereign with absolute authority. Of relevance perhaps to Hobbes' vision is the fact that the Civil War had raged shortly before *Leviathan*'s publication, in which different royalist and parliamentarian factions had battled each other. The famous original cover of *The Leviathan* portrays a massive monarchical figure comprised of the multitude of subjects who had voluntarily submitted to absolute sovereignty to obtain peace and social order.

Hobbes provided one of the earliest examples of social contract theory, but he was not the only theorist of sovereignty to do so. He was followed by John Locke, who also posited a putative state of nature and social contract, whereby people consented to government by a compact among themselves, with government deriving legitimacy from their consent.[8] Locke's state of nature, however, was not warlike and brutish, but a place of absolute liberty, and its occupants exchanged it for government so as to protect their rights. But Locke's

[4] See e.g. V Gerhardt 'On the historical significance of the Peace of Westphalia: 12 theses' in *1648 – War and Peace in Europe I* (Council of Europe, 1998/99). Besson, however notes that 'this constitutes a historical simplification' [S Besson, 'Sovereignty', Max Planck Encyclopedia of International Law (Oxford: Oxford University Press, 2011) at 14].

[5] Jean Bodin, *The Six Bookes of a Commonweale*, K Douglas McRae (ed.), (Cambridge MA: Harvard University Press, 1962), 84, 85.

[6] Hobbes, *Leviathan* (1651) 115. [7] *Leviathan*, 9.

[8] Locke, *Second Treatise of Government* (England, 1689).

sovereign, unlike Hobbes', was not absolute and could be held accountable for violating the contract and infringing individual rights.

Jean-Jacques Rousseau also theorised in terms of a social contract, binding the people of a community together. But in Rousseau's theory, sovereignty lies with the 'general will of the people' – that is, it is a popular sovereignty, not located in a monarch or ruler. From the eighteenth century on, the idea of popular sovereignty was to become more prevalent (although popular sovereignty also has older roots[9]) and to find expression in for example the newly independent USA, as well as revolutionary France, where the people were seen as ultimately sovereign, although governing through laws and institutions. In the modern era of democracy, popular sovereignty is the belief that a State's legitimacy derives from the will or consent of its people, who are the source of all political power.

In the UK, however, the idea of popular sovereignty did not take off (although enjoyed a brief spell of popularity at the time of the Civil War, under the Levellers, and was more widely held in Scotland, believed by some to date back to the medieval Declaration of Arbroath). In 1653, Oliver Cromwell's *Instrument of Government* declared legislative power resided in the Lord Protector 'and the people', but this did not survive the demise of Cromwell. Rather, *parliamentary sovereignty* has been the bedrock of the British Constitution, and UK politics have in recent times been based on representative democracy. England did not develop a tradition of popular sovereignty in constitutional terms, even if we sometimes talk of 'sovereignty of the electorate' in political terms. However, such political sovereignty only allowed the people to choose a government, it did not ground the British Constitution in the authority of people.

The absolutist version of sovereignty articulated by Hobbes found further expression in Blackstone, who wrote that, 'there is and must be … a supreme, irresistible, absolute, uncontrolled authority, in which the *jura summi imperii*, or the rights of sovereignty, reside.'[10] Shortly after Blackstone's *Commentaries* were published, the Declaratory Act of 1766 was passed, which asserted the British Parliament's authority to impose laws of any sort on the American colonies. The timing was surely not coincidental. And around the same time, in February 1766, Lord Chancellor Northington propounded an arresting (and notably similar to Blackstone) account of sovereignty, 'Every government can arbitrarily impose laws on all its subjects … there must be a supreme dominion in every State; whether monarchical, aristocratical, democratical, or mixed. And all the subjects of each State are bound by the laws made by government.'[11]

[9] See e.g. Marsiglio: *Defensor Pacis* (1324) I, chapters 9–15.

[10] William Blackstone, *Commentaries on the Laws of England*, 4 vols. (Oxford: Clarendon Press, 1765–1769) 1:48–49.

[11] House of Lords, *Proceedings and Debates*, 1754–1783, 2:129 (3 February 1766).

It was John Austin's positivist theory of sovereignty that was particularly influential in the nineteenth century, both within the UK, and throughout the British Empire, where it was widely disseminated. Indeed, Hart commented that Austin's doctrines 'dominated the teaching of Jurisprudence in England and the Commonwealth.'[12] Austin's *Province of Jurisprudence Determined* aimed to set out a 'map of the law', and to inculcate order and coherence into the analysis of English law. Austin identified the sovereign as a politically superior body, habitually obeyed by the bulk of the population and not itself obedient to any superior. The sovereign's powers were legally unlimited, and any supposed constraints, such as custom, constitutional convention, or international law, were dismissed by Austin as not law 'properly so called'. However, Austin's theory struggled to explain the status of the Common law and the role of the judiciary. In the nineteenth century, much English law was judge-made and did not seem to emanate from any sovereign, being often instead perceived as some sort of distillation of community wisdom. But according to Austin, the judge was merely the delegate of the sovereign, and judicial decisions were the sovereign's 'tacit commands'. But this seems to strain language – especially given that much judge-made law appears independent of any sovereign will. Overall, Austin's theory emphasises the role of *coercion* in law – laws are the sovereign's commands, backed up by sanctions in the event of non-compliance. This presents the legal system primarily as a power structure. Laws made by the sovereign do not require popular consent or justification. Rights are only emanations of coercively enforced duties. It makes no *legal* difference if a law is morally repugnant or socially harmful, providing it emanates from a sovereign competent to act. In contrast to natural law theories and some accounts of the Common law, morality plays no part in the identification of law. Laws are identified on a factual basis as emanations of a sovereign's will.

Although much of this chapter will focus on the absolutist concept of parliamentary sovereignty that developed in the UK, in direct line from Hobbes, Britain was not the only country to embrace such an absolutist view of sovereignty. The USA, although openly dividing sovereignty through the doctrine of federalism, and sourcing the federal Constitution in the popular sovereignty of the people, also illustrated strains of a more absolutist version. The notion of states' sovereignty challenged federalism. Early in the nineteenth century, certain US states adopted nullification ordinances, claiming the right to annul federal tariff laws in the name of state sovereignty. For example, it was declared that,

> South Carolina claims to be a sovereign State. She recognizes no tribunal upon earth as above her authority.... The States are as Sovereign now, as they were prior to their entering into the compact.... Sovereignty is a unit. It is one, indivisible,

[12] HLA Hart, 'John Austin', in AWB Simpson (ed.), *Biographical Dictionary of the Common Law* (London: Butterworths, 1984) 23.

> and unalienable. It is therefore an absurdity to imagine, that the Sovereignty of the States, is surrendered in part, and retained in part.[13]

The southern states claimed the right to secede from the Union, sparking the US Civil War. However, the end of the Civil War did not lead to confederate leaders abandoning their vision of sovereignty. So Jefferson Davis, former leader of the Confederacy, stated in Atlanta in 1871

> You went to war upon the same question for which your ancestors and theirs contended in the first revolution against the government of Great Britain – the right of communal independence, or State sovereignty. You secured it in that first war, and State sovereignty must again be restored or else the republic of America is a failure.[14]

And we cannot consign such visions to the distant past. In the US, state sovereignty continued to be embraced by opponents of the civil rights movement. For example, James Jackson Kilpatrick (the US journalist who encouraged the states' rights based 'Massive resistance strategy' to the *Brown* v. *Board of Education* decision) made the familiar (and surely wrong) claim that 'sovereignty, like chastity, cannot be surrendered in part.'[15]

6.2 Problematizing Sovereignty

Geoffrey Marshall noted that 'sovereign legislative power, as expounded by Hobbes, Austin, and Dicey, has never enjoyed universal acceptance or acclaim'[16] and Harold Laski went as far as to argue that 'It would be of lasting benefit if the whole concept of sovereignty were surrendered' on the grounds that 'it is at least possible that it has deleterious moral consequences.'[17]

In the second half of the twentieth century, however, the landscape in which sovereignty developed began to look different. There was a shift to supranational institutions, but also demands for more self-government from sub-State nations. There developed a proliferation of international, regional and subregional institutions, to which States formally relinquished varying measures of decisional authority. At the same time private power increased, as supersize transnational corporations and massive accumulations of private wealth became increasingly isolated from State oversight.

This period saw new definitions of sovereignty, reconceived for example as 'post-sovereignty', 'late sovereignty', 'divisible sovereignty', 'mixed sovereignty',

13 The Report, Ordinance, and Addresses of the Convention of the People of South Carolina (Columbia, 1832), 14, 21, 22.

14 Papers of Davis, 13:31 (1871); also J Davis, *The Rise and Fall of the Confederate Government*, 2 vols. (New York: D. Appleton and Co., 1881).

15 JJ Kilpatrick, *The Sovereign States: Notes of a Citizen of Virginia* (Chicago: Henry Regnery, 1957) 10, 14.

16 Geoffrey Marshall, *Constitutional Theory* (Oxford: Clarendon Law series, 1980) at 35.

17 Harold Laski, *A Grammar of Politics* (London: Allen and Unwin, 1925) 44–45.

'perforated sovereignties', and other conceptions.[18] Notwithstanding, sovereignty has shown itself well able to endure and even fight back, both as a mantra in political debates (such as the Brexit formula of 'Take Back Control') and in more scholarly writings. Many writers have declared sovereignty obsolete, but it is still with us.

6.2.1 Sovereignty RIP?

One contemporary writer who believes sovereignty to be redundant is Don Herzog, who wants 'to denounce the concept's role in our politics and law as obsolete, confused, and pernicious.'[19] For Herzog, while the concept may once have had value, those days are long gone. Herzog concedes that sovereignty had an important role in conceptualizing order after the chaos of the sixteenth- and seventeenth-century religious wars. But the price paid was a conception that insisted sovereignty must be unlimited, undivided, and unaccountable to any higher authority. While such features may once have been plausible, they no longer are, and every one of them has been disproved. State authority has been limited by constitutionalism, federalism has shown that sovereignty may be divided, and sovereignty has been rendered accountable under the rule of law. The classic theory of sovereignty does not expound a timeless objective truth of politics. It was a contingent, time relevant intervention that sought to remedy the problems of early modern Europe. And yet, rues Herzog, we are still plagued by a 'zombie sovereignty' that will not go away.

Historical examples illustrate the errors and failings of absolute sovereignty. King Charles I claimed 'an absolute Right and power in Us, to adjourn, as well as prorogue or dissolve' Parliament,[20] but he learned, as Boris Johnson has more recently, that such an absolute right and power did not exist. Even in the seventeenth and eighteenth centuries, claims to absolute sovereignty were strongly opposed. John Locke, for example, worried that absolutism provided no security for the people against absolute despotism. And Grotius maintained that sovereignty could be divided: 'Though the sovereign Power be but one, and of itself undivided … yet it sometimes happens, that it is divided.'[21]

Our American case study illustrated the perils of insisting on an absolute sovereignty, and also that sovereignty can be divided and limited. John Adams wrote to Thomas Jefferson that,

> The fundamental article of my political creed … is, that despotism, or unlimited sovereignty, or absolute power, is the same in a majority of a popular assembly,

[18] E.g. MacCormick, *Questioning Sovereignty*; Neil Walker (ed.), *Sovereignty in Transition* (Oxford: Hart Publishing, 2003).

[19] Herzog, *Sovereignty RIP*, at ix.

[20] See *By the King: A Proclamation for Suppressing of False Rumours Touching Parliament* (London, 1629).

[21] Hugo Grotius, *On War and Peace* (1625) 1:305–306.

> an aristocratical council, an oligarchical junto, and a single emperor. Equally arbitrary, cruel, bloody, and in every respect diabolical.[22]

Unsurprisingly, when Americans drafted their federal Constitution, they limited the sovereign through constitutionalism and federalism.

Such opinions were not only found in America. Jeremy Bentham contested Blackstone's adage that there must exist in all governments 'a supreme, irresistible, absolute, uncontrolled authority,' countering that such a pronouncement 'would be saying that there is no such thing as government in the German Empire; nor in the Dutch Provinces; nor in the Swiss Cantons; nor was of old in the Achaean league.'[23] (But Bentham's insights were not taken up by later positivists such as John Austin, who instead insisted that, 'the power of a sovereign is incapable of legal limitation.'[24]) Henry Sumner Maine also endorsed the possibility of divisible sovereignty, and in his 1861 treatise, *Ancient Law* (described by AWB Simpson as 'the only legal best seller' of the century[25]) rejected the theories of sovereignty expounded by Hobbes, Locke and Austin, which he argued ignored wide-ranging historical and social antecedents. Instead, Maine wrote that '[t]he powers of sovereigns are a bundle or collection of powers, and they may be separated one from another.'[26] In 1862, Maine became a member of Britain's colonial administration in India, where his ideas on sovereignty acquired practical significance. Furthermore, we may note that examples of divided sovereignty, whether federal, or international, have not led to anarchy.

Herzog's language is strong and robust – 'sovereignty stinks', and 'admiration for its historic role is no reason to keep the putrescent corpse around'.[27] And yet, even if Herzog has demonstrated that the classic idea of sovereignty is easily demolished, what conclusions should we draw? For surely, all these ill effects and despotism would have occurred even in the absence of sovereignty – Charles I would still have abused his prerogative, the US southern states would still have fought over the issue of slavery. Abuse of power can occur in the absence of any coherent definition of sovereignty. Is there any chance that sovereignty might be redefined as a resource that might be limited, divided and used, for positive purposes?

6.2.2 Resuscitation by Popular Sovereignty?

Is the concept saved by recourse to popular sovereignty? Jürgen Habermas comments that 'the source of all legitimacy lies in the democratic law-making

[22] John Adams to Thomas Jefferson, 13 November 1815, in *The Works of John Adams*, 10 vols. (Boston, 1850–1856) 10:174.

[23] J Bentham, *A Comment on the Commentaries and A Fragment on Government*, JH Burns and HLA Hart (eds.), (London: Athlone, 1977) 488–489.

[24] John Austin, *The Province of Jurisprudence Determined* (London: John Murray, 1832) 294–295.

[25] Simpson, quoted in Raymond Cocks, *Sir Henry Maine: A Study in Victorian Jurisprudence* (Cambridge: Cambridge University Press, 1988) 1.

[26] Henry Sumner Maine, *International Law* (London: John Murray, 1888) 58.

[27] Herzog, *Sovereignty RIP*, 291.

process and this in turn calls on the principle of popular sovereignty.'[28] This seems attractive, but may give rise to new problems. For it seems that popular sovereignty, if understood as meaning that the people govern themselves, is practically unrealizable.

A basic problem derives from the difficulties of popular self-government. Modern government is complex and it is impossible to conduct State business through endless referendums. There is no such thing as the objective general will of the people. Rules are needed, to enable and implement it. Popular self-government can only function if already defined and managed by pre-existing constitutional rules. Indeed, popular sovereignty presupposes such constitutional rules – and risks anarchy without them. And doubtlessly, such rules need further elaboration and definition to deal with the many, varied ways in which politics develop. People require representative bodies to be set up, and so delegate to others the business of government. The French Constitution of 1791 stated that 'The French Constitutions is representative, its representatives are the legislative body and the king.' But there is still the question of what the legislative body is to represent? How do they know what the popular will is? Not everyone shares the same ideas. Because of this difficulty in identifying the popular will, some argue the people must have a strong, homogenous political identity, often of an ethnic sort as identified by Carl Schmitt. This brings a host of other problems that will be discussed below.

However, it might be argued that the above arguments are overstated, as political legitimacy may be ultimately derived from sovereignty of the people, even if the people do not determine every little detail of government, but instead use what Abbé Sieyès termed their '*pouvoir constituant*' – their 'constituent power' – to lay down the basic rules for constitutional ordering. Some Constitutions declare that sovereignty 'belongs to the People'. The German Basic Law states in the Preamble that the Constitution has been adopted by the people exercising their constituent power. Does this not illustrate that the people are indeed sovereign?

Yet, the German Basic Law was adopted in May 1949 by a Parliamentary Council, a representative body of parliamentarians and jurists, not by the German people acting collectively. The US federal Constitution refers to 'We the People', yet was drafted by a Constitutional Convention and then ratified by the individual states. These do not appear as examples of the people constituting themselves by their own actions. Although this leaves room to derive the ultimate legitimacy of the State from an assertion of popular sovereignty, it is a very distant, dormant and abstract sovereignty – what John Austin termed a 'sleeping electorate', 'a despot hard to wake'.[29] This discussion about popular sovereignty will be further explored in the chapter on democracy and referendums.

[28] J Habermas, *Between Facts and Norms* (Cambridge MA: MIT Press, 1996) 89.

[29] Austin, *The Province of Jurisprudence Determined* (1832).

6.2.3 The Rescue of Sovereignty in the Twentieth/Twenty-First Centuries?

Even if it seemed that the idea of the absolute State was in retreat, Brexit (and Trump, and some other phenomena) with its stress on sovereignty and 'taking back control', challenges this vision of post-sovereignty. But there are earlier precedents.

In 1922, Carl Schmitt made the well-known statement, 'Sovereign is he who decides on the state of exception', meaning that all law and order is ultimately based on human actions, and not norms.[30] Schmitt's version of sovereignty has much in common with the classic, absolutist theory, whereby the sovereign stands outside of the law and is not controlled by it. That is why they can always suspend it, and this makes phrases such as 'the sovereignty of law' meaningless. Schmitt directed most of his work against liberal theories of law and justice, formulating his theory under the unstable conditions of Weimar Germany, and rise to power of the Nazi party. However, the Schmittian analysis has also undergone a renascence in the context of the 'war on terror', and post 9/11 emergency measures. The 'state of emergency', or exception, a favoured subject for Schmitt,[31] involves the suspension of law and other constitutional guarantees, and subjection of law to politics – a reversal of liberal law's order in which rules are thought to govern, or at least structure, politics. The whole Nazi period in Germany might be described as one long state of exception.

Schmitt's theory rests on a singular, atavistic theory of politics – one that interprets politics as a sphere of human activity rent by an inexorable division between 'friend' and 'foe', as identified by the sovereign.[32] In such a situation, Schmitt believed political actions should be based on the active decisions of a strong leader and not on reason, discussion and justification. This decisionism leaves no room for liberal concepts such as the social contract or rule of law. Law is thus reasoned as subject to politics, which in the final instance is a matter of raw power.

Notably also, Schmitt's theory rests on a particular notion of democracy quite distinct from any found in liberalism. For Schmitt, political strength depends on extensive homogeneity in society, which in turn relies on ethnic and/or national bonds. In Schmitt's words, 'democracy requires, therefore, first homogeneity and second – if the need arises – elimination or eradication of heterogeneity'.[33] This links democracy to the dangerous ties of ethnicity and cultural homogeneity which have sparked so many conflicts in the twentieth century and denied cultural, legal and political entitlements to minorities. It has ramifications for multicultural and pluralist societies in which ethnic homogeneity is unlikely, and also for the possibility of commitment to, and

30 C Schmitt, *Political Theology: Four Chapters on the Theory of Sovereignty* (1922) G Schwab (trans.) (Cambridge MA: MIT Press, 1986).

31 See e.g. Schmitt, *Political Theology*.

32 C Schmitt, *The Concept of the Political* (Chicago: University of Chicago Press, 1996).

33 C Schmitt, *The Crisis of Parliamentary Democracy* (Cambridge MA: MIT Press, 1988) at 9.

governance by, transnational organizations such as the EU. In contrast, theorists such as Habermas believe that in such pluralistic situations, attachments to shared values can achieve societal integration. Habermas suggested the concept of 'constitutional patriotism' to a republican constitution, in distinct contrast to what he (Habermas) refers to as 'the *pre-political* crutches of nationality and community of fate',[34] thus illustrating a very different concept of the political to that of Schmitt. Indeed, Schmitt's theory appears particularly unsuited to describe the contemporary fragmented, pluralistic, legal landscape. Most nation states are not (and perhaps never were) unified and homogenous in this way. Does this mean there are no democracies? There is something rather curious about suggesting that only a unified, homogenous demos is capable of giving rise to democratic politics.

Nonetheless, there are traces of this view in Dieter Grimm's (former Justice of the German Constitutional Court) theorizing on sovereignty. Although distinguishing himself from a Schmittian type of ethno-cultural homogeneity, Grimm nonetheless ties sovereignty closely to collective identity, community and loyalty. Grimm argued that 'supranational organizations have not attained sovereignty'.[35] For Grimm, sovereignty made little sense without the concept of Statehood, and State sovereignty provides the only realistic public realm in which democracy can flourish.[36] Grimm's argument rests on the premise that, unlike the State, supranational communities cannot provide a shared sense of identity, common interests nor democratic institutions. Certainly, recent developments, such as Brexit and the election of populist candidates and political parties inimical to intergovernmental institutions, suggest that many people are unwilling or unable to acquire meaningful transnational loyalties or empathize with those beyond their national community. Undoubtedly, unprogressive, nationalist parties have relished State sovereignty as a reactionary and racist tool with which to bash immigrants, refugees, human rights, and international institutions.

6.3 External Dimensions of Sovereignty

6.3.1 'External' Sovereignty

So far, we have been largely concerned with internal sovereignty. However, the issue of external sovereignty, and the international relations of States, became more important[37] with the development of public international law. External

34 J Habermas, 'Yet Again German Identity', in H James and M Stone (eds.), *When the Wall Came Down* (London: Routledge, 1992) 86, italics added.

35 D Grimm, *Sovereignty: The Origin and Future of a Political and Legal Concept* (New York: Columbia University Press, 2015) 128. See also Dieter Grimm, 'Does Europe Need a Constitution?' (1995) 1 ELJ 282; J Habermas, 'Comment on the Paper by Dieter Grimm, "Does Europe Need a Constitution?"' (1995) 1 *ELJ* 303.

36 Grimm, *Sovereignty*, at 96.

37 The term 'external sovereignty' was not used systematically until the eighteenth century; see e.g. E de Vattel, *The Law of Nations* (1758).

sovereignty is a State's ability to be recognized as an independent and equal in status to other States by the international community. Although earlier theorists of international law, such as Grotius, had looked to natural law as the ultimate foundation of authority, by the nineteenth century naturalism was on the wane. International law developed in the nineteenth century as a consolidated legal order, and positivism became 'a determining influence',[38] emphasizing law as the will of States (however moral or immoral that will might be) most particularly those within the European system.

After the First World War, the League of Nations was founded, coming into effect in 1920, with as many as 58 members at its peak in 1935. Its main objects were the maintenance of peace through collective security and disarmament. But the League lacked the ability to impose sanctions, relying on its member States to enforce its measures, which they often did not do, and was also hampered by the principle that any State could exercise a veto.[39] However, the Permanent Court of International Justice (PCIJ), attached to the League, was set up, and in action from 1922, delivering twenty-seven advisory opinions. Two of its opinions, the *Lotus* and the *Wimbledon,* are famous for affirming external sovereignty. In its 1927 *Lotus* case the PCIJ held:

> [i]nternational law governs relations between independent States. The rules of law binding upon States therefore emanate from their own free will as expressed in conventions or by usages generally accepted as expressing principles of law.[40]

After the Second World War, the League of Nations was replaced by the UN. Like the League, this international organization was established to prevent further war, but unlike the League, the UN's institutional and legal framework was more robust. The UN Charter affirms, but also in some ways restricts, the sovereignty of its member States. Thus, Article 2(1) UN Charter declares that 'The Organization is based on the principle of the sovereign equality of all its Members', but other subsections of Article 2 impose obligations on States, such as that in Article 2(3) which requires that all members 'shall refrain in their international relations from the threat or use of force.' Thus, while the Charter asserts its members' sovereignty, it also appears to constrain some of their freedom of action. The UN Charter does not define sovereignty – but notably, its Preamble refers to: 'We the Peoples of the United Nations ...' stressing the importance of peoples, even if it is the States themselves that are sovereign.

[38] Hans J Morgenthau, 'Positivism, Functionalism, and International Law' (1940) 34(2) Am. J. Int'l L. at 263.

[39] Julius Stone, 'The Rule of Unanimity: The Practice of the Council and Assembly of the League of Nations' (1933) 14 Brit. YB Int'l L. 18.

[40] *SS Lotus (Fr.* v. *Turk.)* 1927 PCIJ (ser. A) No. 10, at 18; also *SS Wimbledon (UK et al.* v. *Germany),* 1923 PCIJ (ser. A) No. 1.

6.3.2 'Questioning Sovereignty'

In the latter part of the twentieth century, other international organizations were established, the EU and ECHR notable among them. And, with these developments, international law gained new subjects in addition to States. Individuals became the subjects of human rights treaties such as the ECHR (as did companies and other organizations) and able to bring actions against States. International law developed into spheres previously the preserve of domestic law, such as environmental and migration law. It also became established that certain fundamental principles (also known as *Ius Cogens*) – such as those against slavery or genocide – would be binding on States and part of international law, whether States had explicitly assented to them or not. The concept of universal jurisdiction – namely that certain crimes may be charged and prosecuted in courts of any State, regardless of where they were committed – was also affirmed. For some, it might seem that international law can now interfere with State sovereignty.

Neil MacCormick's theory is relevant here, and his particular concern is the role of sovereignty in an age where the State is often no longer unitary, and has sometimes been displaced by transnational and subnational institutions.[41] MacCormick's argument was that we are now 'beyond sovereignty', and that this requires a revolution in the 'political imagination', captured by the idea of 'post sovereignty'. MacCormick memorably wrote that 'sovereignty and sovereign states, and the inexorable linkage of law with sovereignty and the State, have been but the passing phenomena of a few centuries, that their passing is by no means regrettable, and current developments in Europe exhibit the possibility of going beyond all that.'[42] This was echoed by William Twining, who suggested that the Westphalian State legal order should be viewed as the exception – existing for a mere two centuries or so in the North, an anomaly in a broader historical mass of legal experience.[43]

Legal Pluralism has become popular in some quarters,[44] and a widespread view among theorists is that there exists, at least within the EU, a constitutional pluralism of orders,[45] consisting of State legal orders but also of the EU itself, in which no order may be identified as ultimately controlling the legal space overall, whatever that legal order's insiders such as judges and lawyers, may claim from an internal point of view. However, as MacCormick wrote, 'The diffusionist (pluralist) picture is a happy one from many points of view, but its proponents must show that the Hobbesian problems (about societal

[41] N MacCormick, *Questioning Sovereignty* (Oxford: OUP, 1999).

[42] N MacCormick, 'Beyond the Sovereign State' (1993) 56 MLR at 1.

[43] W Twining, 'Normative and Legal Pluralism: A Global Perspective' (2010) 20 Duke Jo. of Comp. and Int. Law 47.

[44] E.g. S Roberts, 'After Government? On Representing Law without the State' (2005) 68 MLR.

[45] E.g. MacCormick, *Questioning Sovereignty*; N Walker, 'The Idea of Constitutional Pluralism' (2002) 65 MLR 317; M Kumm, 'The Jurisprudence of Constitutional Conflict' (2005) 11 ELJ 262.

insecurity) can be handled even without strong central authorities, last resort sovereigns for all purposes'.[46] This reveals a problem for postsovereignty (and pluralism) relating to a lack of settlement as to which institutions should have the final say, or ultimate authority. Sovereignty has proved to be an effective element of organization and identity and to occupy a normative role that is hard to replace. But this does not mean that sovereignty must be absolute and illimitable.

In any case, to view transnational and pluralist developments in terms of an abandonment of sovereignty is a mistake. For States have voluntarily accepted limits on their sovereignty (through a free exercise of that same sovereignty) by signing treaties to behave in a certain way, to protect the human dignity of their peoples. Sharing sovereignty, through treaties and agreements, through combination and pooling of influence, can advance the interest and prosperity of States in ways that could not be achieved if they acted alone. Here, we might say that sovereignty is being used as a *resource*, which can be limited so it can be best used. This of course does not please those who see sovereignty in monistic and illimitable ways, but nor does it amount to the extinction of sovereignty.

6.3.3 The Formative Role of Empire

So far, this chapter has distinguished external and internal sovereignty, noting that a particular concept of sovereignty emerged with the appearance of the modern State. However, what also needs to be addressed is how the accretion of empires – the control of vast territories overseas – interacted with State sovereignty. Sovereignty played an important role in the governance of empires, but not necessarily one identical with the absolute sovereignty of the Westphalian State.

Lauren Benton suggests that European imperial expansion be understood 'as an assemblage of variegated legal spaces,'[47] often tortuous in their nature, where power could be separated from formal rule. Benton's work, *A Search for Sovereignty*, challenges the more conventional, Westphalian narrative of sovereignty as the consolidation of territory. The traditional approach usually assumes that, while empires trailed behind States in consolidating territorial authority, they nonetheless progressed towards a more complete and coherent rationalization of space. Benton however argues that a closer look at empires reveals anomalies and lumpy, fragmented spaces. Empires constantly had to deal with legal and geographic variations, which included irregular territories such as penal colonies, trading enclaves, missions, garrisons and roughly aligned jurisdictions.[48] Such sites experienced ambivalent and erratic legal

[46] MacCormick, *Questioning Sovereignty*, 78.

[47] Lauren Benton, *A Search for Sovereignty: Law and Geography in European Empires, 1400–1900* (Cambridge: Cambridge University Press, 2016) 33.

[48] Ibid., at 2, 282.

relations with the metropole. In particular, Benton explores places of quasi-sovereignty (i.e. where authority was divided between colonial power and semi-autonomous colonized). Examples include the Indian princely States (territories that never came under the direct control of the British government); Basutoland (now Lesotho) in southern Africa, which fought the Boers, was placed under British 'protection' and then relinquished to British rule in South Africa as a British High Commission territory; and native Americans, whom the US treated in line with a policy of 'measured separatism' which included the reservation system.[49] Benton argues that imperial law provided 'a new jurisprudence', one that might be seen 'as a hybrid of municipal law and international law that could encompass divided sovereignty.' Within the colonial sphere, sovereignty was conceived of as a bundle of capacities and authorities to be divided and gradually applied over separate territories. Empires were not always neatly ringfenced, and there existed within them many gaps in authoritative sovereign rule. But Benton's conclusion is that these territories were not just anomalies in an overall, even, regular empire, but actually exemplified the essence of European overseas settlements, which were uneven, erratic and legally varied. Thus, Benton challenges more orthodox theories of sovereignty which understand it as emanating from a central authority, uniform in nature.

6.3.4 Sovereignty and the Imperialism of International Law

Antony Anghie's work is also salient to our investigation of sovereignty, and like Benton, he highlights the irregularities and erratic nature of colonial rule. Anghie argues that imperialism has been central to the way in which sovereignty had been constructed. However, instead of centring sovereignty around the Westphalian paradigm, Anghie's focus is on how an 'international legal order' was created from a plurality of diverse doctrines and mechanisms, in order to manage, suppress and exploit the peoples of overseas European empires, so that international law has been complicit in colonialism.[50] Sovereignty plays an important part in Anghie's argument, although his conception is very different to classic ideas of sovereignty. According to Anghie, 'Europe is the subject of sovereignty and non-Europe the object of it,' because the essential requirements for admission to the society of international law withheld legal personality to those territories deemed insufficiently civilized by the predominant imperial European culture.[51] However, this created some tricky legal problems which were never really satisfactorily settled. For example, imperial powers

[49] Ibid., 294, 269.

[50] Antony Anghie, *Sovereignty, Imperialism and the Making of International Law* (Cambridge: Cambridge University Press, 2005) at 36. Anghie cites prominent nineteenth-century treatises, including: Lassa Oppenheim, *International Law* (London: Longman, 1905); John Westlake, *Chapters on the Principles of International Law* (Cambridge: Cambridge University Press, 1894); Henry Wheaton, *Elements of International Law* (Boston: Little, Brown & Co., 1866).

[51] Anghie, *Sovereignty, Imperialism and the Making of International Law*, at 102.

often relied on 'unequal treaties' – which in essence allowed European powers to do as they pleased. Take the treaty in which the Wyanasa Chiefs apparently stated:

> We ... most earnestly beseech Her Most Gracious Majesty the Queen of Great Britain and Ireland, Empress of India, Defender of the Faith, &c., to take our country, ourselves and our people, to observe the following conditions:
>
> I. That we give over all our country within the above described limits, all sovereign rights, and all and every other claim absolutely, and without any reservation whatever, to Her Most Gracious Majesty ... and heirs and successors, for all time coming.[52]

Yet, if the peoples with whom imperial powers traded were denied sovereignty, and considered insufficiently civilized to merit legal personality, then how could such treaties be binding, that is, satisfy conditions of international law as voluntarily concluded pacts between two sovereign parties? Fears over disputes of title led to the Congress of Berlin which oversaw the 'scramble for Africa' (from which all African people were excluded) but did nothing to improve the situation of non-Europeans. According to Anghie: 'The ambivalent status of the non-European entity, outside the scope of law and yet within it, lacking in international personality and yet necessarily possessing it if any sense was to be made of the many treaties which European States relied on, was never satisfactorily defined or resolved.'[53]

6.4 Conclusions

This brief consideration reveals sovereignty as a concept that is anything but simple. Its interpretation varies according to context and its salience and vitality may be traced to historical circumstances that demanded a strong ruler. It has an external and internal dimension. It may operate differently overseas in the context of empire – highly relevant given the UK's history. Some believe it to be redundant but it is hard to extinguish.

Where does this lead us? Even if the absolutist concept now appears unworkable, must we now deny any value to the concept of sovereignty at all?

At the very least, the conclusion must be that absolute, illimitable sovereignty no longer makes sense as a legal concept operable within the State. On the other hand, sovereignty retains an intelligible, salient aspect, if understood as a means of identifying a legitimate political community claiming autonomy for itself as a collective. In this way, sovereignty can be understood as not absolute, but as a power, a relational capacity that can be used for the common good, as for example when the UK enters into treaties.

[52] Cited in MF Lindley, *The Acquisition and Government of Backward Territory in International Law: Being a Treatise on the Law and Practice Relating to Colonial Expansion* (London: Longman, Greens & Co.,1926) at 186.

[53] Anghie, *Sovereignty, Imperialism and the Making of International Law*, at 81.

6.5 Sovereignty in the UK: An Introduction

Armed with these observations, what sense then, can we make of sovereignty as it is understood in modern Britain? In short, it is confused and confusing but not dead. Sovereignty was a key factor in Brexit, and the phrase 'take back control' was a mantra of Leave campaigners. Accordingly, the *Foreword* to a Brexit Government White Paper stated, 'At the heart of that historic decision was sovereignty. A strong, independent country needs control of its own laws. That, more than anything else, was what drove the referendum result: a desire to take back control.'[54] This may or may not have been so, but the sense of sovereignty revealed was incoherent.

The remainder of this chapter seeks to identify and unpick these confusions. Discussion in the earlier part of this chapter revealed at least three different understandings of sovereignty, and it is now time to revisit these.

6.5.1 External Sovereignty

We may start with *external sovereignty* (also frequently described as 'national' sovereignty) which is a nation's right to be recognized as a State by the international community, and exercise jurisdiction within its borders. Article 2 of the UN Charter recognizes the 'sovereign equality', 'territorial integrity' and 'political independence' of all its member States. External sovereignty and parliamentary sovereignty are not identical, although were frequently confused in the Brexit context. A country may be sovereign and recognized as independent by the international community, yet lack a sovereign Parliament. External sovereignty connotes legal freedom of action regarding other States in the international community, subject to international law obligations. It is that power which the UK exercised in joining the EEC in 1973, and again exercised in leaving the EU.

Such sovereignty has also however been viewed as constricted by international law and, *a fortiori*, EU law, given that all treaties involve some restriction on a State's freedom of action. However, such arguments are misplaced, given that treaty obligations are voluntarily accepted and entered into as an exercise of the ratifying State's sovereign rights. Therefore, rather than limiting sovereignty, treaty participation is an expression of sovereignty. British EU membership was achieved through Britain's sovereign capacity to contract treaties, and membership was a manifestation of that sovereignty.

However, it is sometimes argued that domestic law rather than EU, or international law, could govern international matters.[55] Such views suggest *parliamentary* sovereignty governs all matters, including Britain's relations with

[54] *Legislating for the United Kingdom's withdrawal from the European Union*, Cm 9446 (March 2017) at 7.

[55] John Redwood, MP was reported in the *Financial Times* suggesting 'a lot of us don't think there is any need to trigger Article 50 any time at all.'

other States.[56] Yet, such an approach violates international law and harms Britain's reputation, raising issues of trust. This approach also conflates parliamentary sovereignty with external sovereignty, suggesting that the UK can use Parliament and domestic law to govern its relationships with other States and international organizations, because of some misplaced idea of parliamentary sovereignty. That is not how national sovereignty functions in the international arena. States observe treaties and join international organizations because they know that in ceding some freedom in certain areas, they gain a greater benefit from pooling sovereignty or accepting certain obligations. While international law and membership of international organizations does not of itself, limit the powers of Parliament,[57] nor can Parliament alter international law, and if Parliament legislates contrary to any of its treaty obligations then the UK is violating international law.

Therefore, to summarize: the UK always possessed a national, external sovereignty, which remained untouched throughout its EU membership, and was unchanged by EU withdrawal.

6.5.2 Internal Sovereignty

The other two major types of sovereignty are *internal* in nature, relating to a State's domestic affairs. There is the conception of *parliamentary sovereignty,* said to have particular resonance in the UK where the Westminster Parliament has been recognized as a body with unlimited legislative power, exercised through a representative democracy. Yet parliamentary sovereignty may seem at odds with *popular sovereignty* as exercised in a referendum. Popular sovereignty also has other implications, such as in Scotland, where an indigenous Scottish tradition claims that sovereignty resides in the Scottish people, in spite of alternative claims of Diceyan parliamentary sovereignty.

Confusion over these types of sovereignty sometimes rendered Brexit debates incoherent just when clarity was crucial. I do not argue that there exists just one essential interpretation of sovereignty. But I do argue that the weight of justification for highly important acts of union or disunion, such as Brexit, cannot be borne by incoherent and confused assertions of sovereignty. Very often, what the muddled assertion of retaking sovereignty and control ultimately appeared to boil down to was an (unsubstantiated) claim for a unified English/Westminster/governmental sovereignty to the exclusion of other parties. Such excluded parties included international organizations, courts, constituent nations and territories of the UK (e.g. Scotland, Northern Ireland, Wales, Gibraltar) and certain

[56] This approach was pursued in earlier drafts of the 2020 UK Internal Market Bill, which ignored, and indeed, knowingly violated, obligations under the treaty the UK had already concluded with the EU.

[57] E.g. *International Tin Council case* [*JH Rayner (Mincing Lane) Ltd* v. *Department of Trade and Industry* [1990] 2 AC 418].

persons (i.e. EU citizens denied a vote in the EU referendum, and UK nationals in the EU).

However, Brexit is by no means the only instance of a British confusion over sovereignty. This point can be well illustrated with examples from Britain's past and Britain's Empire. The core of the argument to come is that Britain developed its constitutional law, most particularly its understanding of sovereignty, all too casually, often leaving it very unclear what the law was. But at the same time, Britain sometimes chose to assert an absolute sovereignty for which there was too little support. However, this exclusive, unified sovereignty claim is incoherent and not born out by history, although history is often wrongly prayed in its aid. This claim is incoherent because it conflates different conceptions of sovereignty, namely: Britain's external sovereignty (which was never threatened by EU membership or membership of other international organizations), parliamentary sovereignty (a complex and contested notion, which the British government itself misrepresents and mangles), and popular sovereignty (which is insufficiently developed in UK constitutional law to ground an argument that it has replaced parliamentary sovereignty as a mandate for action, i.e. through referendums).

6.5.3 Parliamentary Sovereignty

Nonetheless, sovereignty has a particular connotation in the UK, where due to the idiosyncrasies of the UK's uncodified Constitution, the sovereignty of the Westminster Parliament has come to be recognized as fundamental, mandating a Parliament with unlimited legislative power, whose laws may not be invalidated by any other institution such as the judiciary. If the concept of absolute sovereignty proves generally unsustainable, then, *a fortiori*, UK parliamentary sovereignty reveals itself as an outmoded, incoherent concept.

According to the nineteenth-century jurist and constitutional doyen, AV Dicey, 'The one fundamental dogma of English constitutional law is the absolute legislative sovereignty or despotism of the King in Parliament.' Dicey's account has two key facets, namely, that the Crown-in-Parliament:

> 'has, under the English constitution, the right to make or unmake any law whatsoever; and, further, that no person or body is recognized … as having the right to override or set aside the legislation of Parliament'.[58]

This contrasts with the position in many other States, where legality of legislation may be reviewed by a Constitutional Court or equivalent institution.

Blackstone asserted that there had to be a 'supreme, absolute uncontrolled authority in which rights of sovereignty resided.'[59] But such an approach meant

[58] AV Dicey, *An Introduction to the Study of the Law of the Constitution* (10th ed., London: Macmillan, 1959), 27.

[59] Blackstone, *Commentaries* I, 48–52.

that no legislation, however special and valued, could be entrenched, or protected against subsequent parliamentary legislation, because to do so would limit Parliament's sovereignty, its future freedom of action. So, for example, Dicey famously wrote that: 'neither the Act of Union with Scotland, nor the Dentists Act, 1878 has more claim than the other to be considered a supreme law.'[60]

6.6 Critical Challenges to Parliamentary Sovereignty

That was the theory. But, in practice, the doctrine of parliamentary sovereignty is (and has been) incoherent and contested. I look at a variety of historical, constitutional and territorial challenges to illustrate just how contested it has been. I spend some time on this because it is important to counter the arguments of those who insist on the continued merits of this outmoded, harmful doctrine.

6.6.1 The Historical Challenge

As Loughlin and Tierney comment:

> The legal doctrine of parliamentary sovereignty is such a fundamental tenet of constitutional belief that we commonly assume it to be of ancient provenance. In reality, it is a late-nineteenth century creation. Its author, Albert Venn Dicey, presented it as the central element of a work that sought to shift the basis of British constitutional thought.[61]

Historically, parliamentary sovereignty does not have a long pedigree. Even if some, such as Goldsworthy, claim to find early its realizations in the Middle Ages, the English Parliament was a very different institution then – more court than assembly, and with jurisdiction only for England, and not Scotland, for example. Parliamentary sovereignty, as a recognizable phenomenon, dates only as far back as the Glorious Revolution, possibly even only the eighteenth (or even nineteenth) century. Although the doctrine gained in support after the 1688 Glorious Revolution, it was notably not mentioned in the Bill of Rights of 1688, nor the Acts of Union of 1706/7.

In 1610, in *Dr Bonham's case*, Sir Edward Coke declared the right of common law courts to adjudge an Act of Parliament void, if 'against common right and reason, or repugnant'.[62] Later cases, such as *Day* v. *Savadge* and *Sheffield* v. *Ratcliffe*[63] approved Coke's holding. Coke also stated during the parliamentary debate on the Petition of Right in 1628 that '"sovereign power" is no parliamentary word.... Magna Carta is such a fellow that he will have no sovereign.'[64]

[60] Dicey, *An Introduction to the Study of the Law of the Constitution*, at 145.

[61] Martin Loughlin and Stephen Tierney, 'The Shibboleth of Sovereignty' (2018) 81 MLR 989.

[62] [1610] 8 Co.R ep. 114, 118; also Coke in *The Prince's Case* [1606] 8 Co. Rep. 481.

[63] *Day* v. *Savadge* [1614] Hob. 85; *Sheffield* v. *Ratcliffe* [1615] Hob. 334.

[64] John Rushworth, *Historical Collections of Private Passages of State, Weighty Matters in Law* (1721) 566.

Admittedly, Coke did, in the extra-judicial *Institutes*, describe Parliament as 'transcendent and absolute,' but his remark is easily misconstrued, for Coke's comment related to the unlimited range of matters over which Parliament might legislate,[65] and does not claim that there was no external control over Parliament. Some Parliaments (i.e. the US Federal Congress) are limited in their subject matter, which is specifically limited by the Constitution. This was not so with the British Parliament. Dicey claimed that Coke's doctrine in *Dr Bonham's case* was obsolete, yet it has never been over-ruled.[66] FW Maitland remarked that: 'It is always difficult to pin Coke to a theory, but he does seem to claim distinctly that common law is above the statute.'[67]

Given that the doctrine of parliamentary sovereignty is not stated in any legislation, one must look elsewhere for its sources. Yet, Dicey simply 'announced that it was the law that Parliament was omnicompetent, explained what this meant, and never devoted so much as a line to fulfilling the promise he made to demonstrate that this was so.'[68] Indeed, there is confusion over the sources of parliamentary sovereignty. Some such as Goldsworthy, argue it has theoretical roots in English writers from the thirteenth century, and is the product of a political consensus,[69] while others interpret parliamentary sovereignty as a 'common law construct.'[70] According to Wade, 'the decision of this question is not determined by any rule of law which can be laid down or altered by any authority outside the courts.'[71] However, there is hardly a burgeoning caselaw on the subject. The earlier cases usually cited in support of the Diceyan theory are not numerous and include: *Edinburgh & Dalkeith Ry.* v. *Wauchope*; *Vauxhall Estates Ltd.* v. *Liverpool Corporation;* and *Pickin* v. *British Railways Board*.[72] To these we can add dicta of Lord Bingham in *Jackson*,[73] and elements of the Supreme Court holdings in *Miller 1* and *Miller 2*.[74]

65 Coke, 4 *Inst.* 36, cited by Chijoke Dike, 'The Case against Parliamentary Sovereignty', (1976) Public Law.

66 Dicey, *An Introduction to the Study of the Law of the Constitution*, 61–62; Indeed, it was endorsed by Lord Denning: 'Misuse of Power' (1981) 55 ALJ 720 at 723.

67 FW Maitland, *The Constitutional History of England* (Cambridge: Cambridge University Press, 1908) 300.

68 AWB Simpson, *Oxford Essays in Jurisprudence* (2nd ed., Oxford: Clarendon Press, 1973) at 96.

69 Jeffrey Goldsworthy, *The Sovereignty of Parliament. History and Philosophy* (Oxford: Clarendon Press, 1999).

70 E.g. Lord Steyn, '[T]he supremacy of Parliament … is a construct of the common law. The judges created this principle' (*Jackson* v. *Attorney-General* [2005] UKHL 56, at 102).

71 Wade, 'The Basis of Legal Sovereignty', at 188.

72 *Edinburgh & Dalkeith Ry.* v. *Wauchope* [1842] 1 Bell App.Cas. 252; *Vauxhall Estates Ltd.* v. *Liverpool Corporation* [1932] 1 KB 733; *Pickin* v. *British Railways Board* [1974] A.C. 765.

73 Lord Bingham stated in *Jackson* that 'The bedrock of the British constitution is, and in 1911 was, the supremacy of the Crown in Parliament' (at para. 9). But this should be read in the light of comments by other judges, suggesting that parliamentary sovereignty could be less than absolute.

74 In *Miller/Cherry*, the Supreme Court held 'that laws enacted by the Crown in Parliament are the supreme form of law in our legal system, with which everyone, including the Government, must comply' [*Miller/Cherry* [2019] UKSC 41, at para. 41].

Dicey also wrote that parliamentary sovereignty was a matter of logic, and that limited sovereignty was a 'contradiction in terms'.[75] But why must sovereignty be understood only as unlimited and indivisible? Divisible sovereignty was well understood by the Framers of the US Federal Constitution. Dicey's answer was because sovereignty was always understood this way in England. But, even if true, that can only be contingent, distinct from Dicey's claim for logical truth.

In any case, Dicey's theory is not watertight historically. Although, by the eighteenth century, the British Constitution was evolving, parliamentary sovereignty had not then completely overridden older ideas, of an unwritten English Constitution, spoken of as 'fundamental', instead of Parliamentary legislation being supreme.[76] The main tenets of the theory of the fundamental law were that: the law was legally supreme; that the fundamental Constitution was unwritten; and that it was also at least sometimes, judicially enforceable.[77] The fundamental law was composed of sources other than legislation, such as custom, usage, reason and natural justice, even an imagined immemorial antiquity. And therefore, English law could claim parity with natural law reasoning. In 1744, in *Omychund* v. *Barker* the Attorney General argued (with reasoning accepted by the court) that 'the common law, that works itself pure by rules drawn from the fountain of justice, is for this reason superior to an act of parliament.'[78] Eminent legal figures, such as Lord Camden, a renowned eighteenth-century English judge, repudiated the doctrine of absolute parliamentary sovereignty, arguing, in the House of Lords, that Britain did not have unlimited authority over the North American colonies, and that the 1766 Declaratory Act was 'absolutely illegal, contrary to the fundamental laws of nature … and fundamental laws of this constitution.'[79]

These examples are cited as illustrations that the position on sovereignty in eighteenth-century Britain was ambivalent, and that there was continued adherence to a doctrine of the fundamental law, which included important liberties that statute could not abrogate.

Blackstone himself was contradictory, writing both that Parliament was 'uncontrollable' and that it was subject to 'common reason'.[80] According to CK Allen, such inconsistency 'shows clearly that in 1765 English jurisprudence had not reached a clear conclusion on this point.'[81] Allott argued that the doctrine of absolute parliamentary sovereignty, able to override any rights and liberties:

[75] Dicey, *Introduction to the Law of the Constitution*, chapter 1, 24, fn 48.

[76] JW Gough, *Fundamental Law in English Constitutional History* (Oxford: Clarendon Press, 1955) at 2.

[77] Ibid. [78] 1 Atkyns 32, 33.

[79] Speech by Lord Camden (10 February 1766), reprinted in 16 PARL. HIST. ENG. (1813) 178.

[80] Blackstone, *Commentaries* I, 160–161, 91.

[81] Sir Carleton Kemp Allen, *Law in the Making* (Oxford: Oxford University Press, 1961) 435.

> fl[ies] in the face of one thousand years of talk about 'fundamental law' by Kings, judges, political men, and commentators ... if there is one thread which runs through the whole turbulent story of British constitutional development it is the belief that we are the servants of fundamental constitutional rules which were there before us and will be there after we have gone.[82]

It was only later, especially with the Diceyan dominance of British constitutional law, that parliamentary sovereignty really took hold. But even Dicey himself was inconsistent, in 1913 advocating a referendum, or even armed rebellion, to defeat Asquith's Home Rule legislation for Ireland[83] – a suggestion undermining both parliamentary sovereignty and the rule of law. Therefore, the doctrine of parliamentary sovereignty was compromised even by its greatest exponent. Dicey also vigorously opposed Votes for Women, expressed concern over the expansion of the franchise for the working man, and opposed the removal of the veto of the unelected House of Lords, thus apparently undermining any democratic legitimacy his theory of untrammelled parliamentary sovereignty might have possessed.

Why then have lawyers and legislators taken Dicey so seriously? According to Walker, English law:

> by dint of sheer repetition, academic preaching of the absolutist theory of sovereignty has ... diverted the attention of bench and bar away from the more limited and balanced principle developed by common lawyers during the seventeenth century ... [namely] one of Parliamentary *supremacy,* not sovereignty.[84]

However, the 'fundamental law' has not been completely forgotten. This doctrine survives, exhibited in 'anti-positivist' theories such as Dworkin's legal principles,[85] as well as surfacing in judicial decisions such as *HS2* in which the UK Supreme Court held that 'the common law itself also recognizes certain principles as fundamental to the rule of law' which may take priority over other laws, including statutes – even fundamental laws such as the European Communities Act 1972 itself.[86]

6.6.2 Constitutional Challenges

6.6.2.1 The Separation of Powers Challenge: Parliamentary Sovereignty Is Not Executive Sovereignty

It is often forgotten that parliamentary sovereignty is in fact really only *legislative* sovereignty. However, because the UK has a fused system, in which the

[82] P Allot, 'The Courts and Parliament: Who, Whom?' [1979] 38 CLJ 79 at 114.

[83] See also *A Fool's Paradise* (1913), in which Dicey suggested recourse to violence if the Home Rule Bill was enacted even if 'the British electorate sanction the monstrous iniquity.'

[84] G Walker, 'Dicey's Dubious Dogma of Parliamentary Sovereignty' [1985] 59 ALJ 276 at 279–280.

[85] R Dworkin, *Taking Rights Seriously* (Cambridge MA: Harvard University Press, 1977).

[86] *R (HS2 Action Alliance Ltd)* v. *Secretary of State for Transport* [2014] UKSC 3; Also *Pham* [2015] UKSC 19.

Government is nested in and drawn from Parliament, the Government is usually able to control parliamentary time (this was particularly so in the Brexit process). Without Government support, it is very difficult for backbenchers to get legislation through Parliament. The EU Withdrawal Act 2018, a Government bill, transferred massive powers from Parliament to the Government by introducing extensive ministerial powers to amend or repeal EU legislation, very often with inadequate parliamentary scrutiny, some through 'Henry VIII' clauses[87] – which allow ministers to *repeal* statute law.[88] Because of Government domination, it is sometimes hard for Parliament to assert itself. Indeed, the Government can pose more of a threat to parliamentary sovereignty than the judiciary or EU. Examples of Government abuse of Parliament include being found in contempt of Parliament for refusing to supply the Attorney General's full advice on Brexit,[89] and ignoring Parliament's role in triggering Article 50, until litigation in *Miller 1* forced it to obtain Parliament's consent to do so. The Supreme Court held in *Miller 1* that the Government may not use the prerogative to stultify an Act of Parliament (in this case the ECA 1972), for to do so would be exactly what the 1688 Bill of Rights forbids – to dispense with laws by regal authority.[90]

Perhaps the most striking example of Government overreach was provided by Boris Johnson's prorogation (suspension) of Parliament in autumn 2019 for 5 weeks, a step taken so MPs could not prevent an October 31 'No deal' Brexit. During that time, Parliament could not sit. No legislation could be adopted, nor could Parliament call the Government to account for any actions it was taking. In the usual course of events, prorogation is unremarkable, a break between parliamentary sessions. However, use of prorogation to suspend Parliament altogether for the Government's own political purposes, is profoundly undemocratic – with echoes of Charles I, who also prorogued Parliament, and from March 1629–1640 governed without it altogether. This did not go well for Charles (leading ultimately to Civil War, his demise, and a permanent reduction in the King's powers). Notably, the first Article of the 1688 Bill of Rights declares: 'That the pretended power of suspending of laws or the execution of laws by regall authority without consent of Parlyament is illegall.' Since then, the authority of the monarch has been reduced, while parliamentary (as opposed to monarchical) sovereignty has increased. Johnson's prorogation was challenged in the UK Supreme Court,[91] which unanimously found the prorogation unlawful, in a judgement of huge constitutional moment, upholding parliamentary sovereignty against an overbearing Executive. The Court articulated the legal test as the following:

87 So called because The 1539 Statute of Proclamations gave Henry VIII the power to pass laws directly, bypassing Parliament.

88 Ss 8 and 9 EU Withdrawal Act 2018.

89 'Theresa May government in contempt of parliament over failure to publish full Brexit legal advice', *The Independent*, 4 December 2018.

90 *R (Miller)* v. *Secretary of State for Exiting the European Union* [2017] UKSC 5.

91 *R (Miller/Cherry)* v. *The Prime Minister* [2019] UKSC 41.

> a decision to prorogue Parliament ... will be unlawful *if the prorogation has the effect of frustrating* or *preventing*, without reasonable justification, the ability of Parliament to carry out its constitutional functions as a legislature and as the body responsible for the supervision of the executive. In such a situation, the court will intervene if the effect is sufficiently serious to justify such an exceptional course.[92]

This ruling was surely devastating in its clarity and unanimous condemnation of unlawful behaviour. However, it was not accepted by everyone, not least Boris Johnson, who described the ruling as 'wrong'.[93] And, in 2022, the Johnson government adopted the Dissolution and Calling of Parliaments Act, which repealed the Fixed Term Parliaments Act 2011, and reverted to dissolutions by prerogative, as well as including an ouster clause to prevent government decisions taken by royal prerogative from being referred for review to the courts.[94]

These examples suggest an Executive sometimes unwilling to acknowledge its accountability to Parliament, and Parliament's independence from, and supremacy over it. They also question whether 'Taking Back Control' was seen as a means to Government rather than Parliamentary empowerment.

6.6.2.2 The Rule of Law Challenge

As Geoffrey Marshall remarked, the classic doctrine of parliamentary sovereignty gives rise to a paradox (because it holds that the one thing a supposedly omnicompetent Parliament cannot do is to bind its successors).[95] But aside from this, it also has the unfortunate consequence that Parliament cannot apparently impose any limitations on itself that might restrict a future Parliament's power – using entrenchment, for example. Although, since the UK Human Rights Act 1998, courts have been able to issue declarations of incompatibility under s4 of that Act when a UK statute is clearly and unambiguously incompatible with human rights, nonetheless, the choice is with Parliament as to whether it will amend that statute, or leave it in force.

Dicey sought to mitigate this potential despotism of parliamentary sovereignty by declaring the rule of law to be another guiding principle of the Constitution. According to Dicey, the rule of law required: government through ordinary laws rather than discretion; formal equality before the law; and the slow accretion of individual rights through gradual, common-law development.[96] Although Dicey's rule of law was rather narrow, in theory at least it should mediate

[92] Ibid., at para. 50.

[93] 'Boris Johnson Tells Parliament "the court was wrong"', *BBC News*, 25 September 2019.

[94] See R Kelly, 'Dissolution and Calling of Parliaments Bill 2021–22', RP, House of Commons, 4 March 2022.

[95] Geoffrey Marshall, *Parliamentary Sovereignty and the Commonwealth* (Oxford: Oxford University Press, 1957) 13.

[96] AV Dicey, *The Law of the Constitution* (9th ed., 1952) 188, 193.

parliamentary sovereignty by ensuring that legislation is interpreted to respect the principles and values of the common law.

Dicey however wrote that, 'Parliamentary sovereignty ... was an instrument well adapted for the establishment of democratic despotism.'[97] And so it has been noted that there exists a tension between parliamentary sovereignty and the rule of law in Dicey's account. For if Parliament is truly omnicompetent, no law can restrain it. Yet Dicey also argued that the rule of law and parliamentary sovereignty were not in conflict, but mutually reinforcing, sustained, if not explicitly, by constitutional conventions. But on this, Dicey's argument was unclear, controversial, and unsatisfactory.[98] This is unsurprising, because absolute, illimitable parliamentary sovereignty is simply incompatible with the rule of law. Indeed, Dicey's rule of law has been described as sometimes no more than an exercise in 'wishful thinking'.[99]

In any case, by the twentieth century, Dicey was endorsing neither parliamentary sovereignty, nor the rule of law, at least with regard to Ireland. As noted, Dicey opposed the Liberal Government using parliamentary sovereignty to enact home rule for Ireland.[100] Dicey instead urged a referendum on the issue and a Referendum Act which itself would itemise a number of laws which could not be altered by Parliament without a referendum. But such a measure, if effective, would have undermined parliamentary sovereignty, and instilled new fundamental principles into the Constitution by way of entrenchment – the very consequences Dicey had himself predicted for Home Rule. But surely use of a referendum undermines the very parliamentary sovereignty that Dicey had been so keen to insist on as a cardinal principle of the British Constitution? However, by 1913, Dicey had gone even further, arguing that armed resistance to home rule by Ulster could be both a right and a duty.[101] In so pledging himself to rebellion was not Dicey undermining representative democracy and the rule of law?

So, at the heart of Dicey's constitutional theory lies an inescapable tension between the rule of law and parliamentary sovereignty – a tension or contradiction that Dicey never managed to eradicate, and indeed sought to escape from, by abandoning both principles in certain cases. Why then should we cleave to such a conflicted and inconsistent theorist?

Dicey aside, the courts may be doing a better job in asserting the constraints of the rule of law against parliamentary sovereignty. Lord Bingham specifically

[97] Dicey, *England's Case against Home Rule* (1886) 23.

[98] Heuston refers to Dicey's chapter 13 on 'Relations between Parliamentary Sovereignty and the Rule of Law' as 'a curiously tortuous chapter' [RFV Heuston, 'Sovereignty', in AG Guest (ed.), *Oxford Essays in Jurisprudence* (Oxford: Oxford University Press, 1968) at 199].

[99] M Taggart, 'Ruled by Law?' (2006) 69 MLR 1006, 1025.

[100] Dicey, 'Ought the Referendum to Be Introduced into England?' (April 1890) *Contemporary Review*.

[101] Dicey to Strachey, 16 September 1909, *Strachey Papers* (St Loe Strachey was editor of the Unionist *Spectator*).

included within the rule of law the need to 'afford adequate protection of fundamental human rights'.[102] British courts possess no power of 'hard judicial review' to strike down legislation, however unconstitutional that legislation may seem. Nonetheless, courts may have other means to mitigate unbridled parliamentary sovereignty. Most such examples concern legislation which excludes access to the courts. In the 1969 *Anisminic* case, the judicial House of Lords famously made clear that Parliament cannot insert ouster clauses (even those using clear and unambiguous words) into legislation so as to exclude any scrutiny by the courts. In the *Jackson* case Lord Steyn stated (obiter):

> The classic account given by Dicey of the doctrine of the supremacy of Parliament, pure and absolute as it was, can now be seen to be out of place in the modern United Kingdom.... In exceptional circumstances involving an attempt to abolish judicial review of the ordinary role of the courts, the.... Supreme Court may have to consider whether this is a constitutional fundamental which even a sovereign Parliament acting at the behest of a complaisant House of Commons cannot abolish.[103]

In the *Unison* case (in which the Supreme Court nullified a ministerial order that would have introduced high fees for employment tribunals) Lord Reed (now the Court's President) affirmed that, 'The constitutional right of access to the courts is inherent in the rule of law.'[104] Although the Courts have never set aside an Act of Parliament (outside of EU law), obiter statements suggest that such a truly exceptional statute might not be legally enforced.

6.6.2.3 The Manner and Form Challenge

Marshall suggested that 'for the English lawyer or political theorist, sovereignty may be purged of its dangerous absolutism. He can believe both in an ultimate Sovereign and in the possibility of restraint imposed by law upon the way in which legal power is used.'[105] This is the 'new view' of Parliamentary sovereignty,[106] and, as Marshall described it, 'On this view a sovereign legislature may validly reformulate what shall count as legislation for particular purposes.'[107] But, as Marshall admitted, the 'new view' did not have unanimous support.

The term 'manner and form' is also sometimes used to describe the new theory. It derives from s5 of the Colonial Laws Validity Act, 1865 which

[102] Lord Bingham 'The Rule of Law' [2007] 66 CLJ 67.

[103] *Anisminic* [1969] 2 AC 147. *Jackson* at 302–03, para. 103.

[104] *R (UNISON)* v. *Lord Chancellor* [2017] UKSC 51.

[105] Geoffrey Marshall, *Constitutional Theory* (Oxford: Clarendon Press, 1980) at 42.

[106] 'New view' is a bit of a misnomer, as it dates back almost 90 years. Arguments in its favour are to be found in Sir Ivor Jennings, *The Law and the Constitution* (London: University of London Press, 1959); DV Cowen, *Parliamentary Sovereignty and the Entrenched Sections of the South Africa Act* (Johannesburg: Juta, 1951); RFV Heuston, *Essays in Constitutional Law* (London: Stevens, 1961); G Marshall, *Parliamentary Sovereignty and the Commonwealth* (Oxford: Clarendon Press, 1957).

[107] Marshall, *Constitutional Theory*, at 43.

authorized colonial legislatures to amend their Constitutions as long as the amendments were 'in such manner and form as may from time to time be required by any Act of Parliament … for the time being in force in the said colony'. Cases from the Commonwealth also provide support for the new view. For example, the 1932 case of *AG for New South Wales* v. *Trethowan* concerned an Act of the New South Wales Parliament providing that the Parliament's Upper House could not be abolished except by a Bill approved in a referendum. However, in 1930, a Bill to abolish the Upper House was approved by both Houses but not put to a referendum. The Privy Council upheld an injunction granted by the High Court of Australia preventing the later Bill becoming law, on the basis that the Colonial Laws Validity Act 1865 required all colonial legislatures to legislate in accordance with stipulated manner and form. In 1952, in *Harris* v. *Minister of the Interior* the South African Supreme Court refused to accept the validity of legislation establishing apartheid because it did not comply with the procedure stipulated in the earlier South Africa Act 1909, s152 of which provided that black citizens could not be removed from the electoral register except by a Bill passed by a majority of two-thirds of both Houses of the South African Parliament.[108] *Bribery Commissioner* v. *Ranasinghe*, an appeal from (then) Ceylon, is also cited in support of the theory. The Ceylon Supreme Court's holding was affirmed by the Privy Council, which cited *Trethowan's* case as supporting their conclusion that 'where a legislative power is given subject to certain manner and form that power does not exist unless and until the manner and form is complied with.'[109] Some (e.g. Wade[110]) have suggested that the 'new theory' applies only to subordinate legislatures, and not the UK Parliament. However, in *Ranasinghe,* Lord Pearce of the Privy Council seemed to suggest that all legislatures could be made subject to procedural rules entrenching parts of the law from simple majority repeal.[111]

More recently, the *Jackson* case illustrates how Parliament may place procedural limits on itself. In 2004, the Hunting Act, which banned fox hunting, was adopted by Parliament. Because it had been continually opposed by the House of Lords, it was passed using the Parliament Act 1949, which prevented the House of Lords from permanently vetoing a Bill. The claimant, Jackson, argued that the Hunting Act 2004 was invalid as the 1949 Parliament Act (passed using the procedure in the Parliament Act 1911[112]) was itself illegal. Wade's argument,

[108] *AG for New South Wales* v. *Trethowan* [1932] AC 526; *Harris* v. *Minister of the Interior* [1952] (2) SA 429.

[109] *Bribery Commissioner* v. *Ranasinghe* [1965] AC 172, at 198.

[110] 'The Basis of Legal Sovereignty', 181–182. But Han-Ru Zhou, 'Revisiting the "Manner and Form" Theory of Parliamentary Sovereignty' (2013) 129 LQR 610, argues no logical reason prevents manner and form conditions being applied in the UK context.

[111] *Ranasinghe* at 198.

[112] The 1911 Parliament Act provided for legislation by Crown and House of Commons alone, should the House of Lords veto a Bill for two sessions.

that the 1911 Parliament Act was a form of delegated legislation, and so could not be used to adopt the 1949 Parliament Act, was relied on by the claimants. The House of Lords rejected Jackson's claims, finding both Parliament Acts to be valid legislation and not delegated in form. Wade's argument was therefore not accepted. The result confirms that the Parliament Acts of 1911 and 1949 managed to redefine the requirements for valid legislation. Some judges went further. Lady Hale suggested that, if Parliament could redefine legislative procedure to make it easier to legislate (i.e. by removing the House of Lords' veto), then it would also be possible to make legislation harder, by for instance requiring, 'a particular parliamentary majority or a popular referendum for particular types of measure'. This suggestion aligns with what Jennings and other supporters of the 'manner and form' limitation had contended. Lord Steyn also stressed that 'pure and absolute' parliamentary sovereignty was 'out of place in the modern United Kingdom'.[113]

The new theory is therefore backed up by caselaw suggesting that Parliament may reformulate what is to count as legislation. This is important because, although there is no evidence yet that judges have abandoned parliamentary sovereignty – the Supreme Court in *Miller/Cherry* perceived it as a foundation of the British Constitution – there is clear evidence that Parliament may impose procedural limitations on itself. This indicates the possibility of entrenchment of a procedural sort, such as allowing repeal of certain statutes only by a supermajority in Parliament, or only after holding a referendum. Indeed, this latter was the formula used by the EU Act 2011 (now repealed), which required a referendum before any statute incorporating further EU treaty changes into UK law could be adopted. It might also be argued that the ECA 1972, by binding future Parliaments to comply with EU law, imposed at the very least, a manner and form limitation – this will be discussed in a further section below.

Therefore, all of the above suggests that manner and form limitations can and do apply within UK constitutional law and operate to constrain parliamentary sovereignty. In this sense, Marshall was correct, and parliamentary sovereignty has been 'purged of its dangerous absolutism'.

6.6.3 Territorial Challenges

Heuston argued that the doctrine of parliamentary sovereignty is, 'almost entirely the work of Oxford men'[114] – a list which includes Thomas Hobbes, Blackstone, Sir William Anson and AV Dicey. But outside of the Oxford location, parliamentary sovereignty is territorially challenged. These sections will be short because this they have already been given extensive treatment in the case analyses.

[113] *Jackson*, at 319, para. 163 for Lady Hale and 302–303, para. 103 for Lord Steyn.

[114] RFV Heuston, *Essays in Constitutional Law* (London: Stevens and Son, 1979) 1.

6.6.3.1 Dislocated Sovereignty in the British Isles

First, other nations of the UK are less inclined to recognize the supposed orthodoxy of parliamentary sovereignty. For example, in the 1953 Scottish case of *MacCormick* v. *Lord Advocate*, Lord Cooper stated: 'The principle of the unlimited sovereignty of parliament is a distinctively English principle which has no counterpart in Scottish constitutional law ….'

> I have difficulty seeing why it should have been supposed that the new parliament of Great Britain must inherit all the peculiar characteristics of the English parliament but none of the Scottish parliament, as if all that happened in 1707 was that Scottish representatives were admitted to the parliament of England.[115]

Nonetheless, under present devolution legislation, Westminster retains ultimate sovereignty – s28(7) Scotland Act 1998, for example, relates to Acts of the Scottish Parliament, but declares that, 'This section does not affect the power of the Parliament of the United Kingdom to make laws for Scotland.' S28(8) Scotland Act, however, which translated the Sewel convention into legislation, states that 'it is recognised that the Parliament of the United Kingdom will not normally legislate with regard to devolved matters without the consent of the Scottish Parliament.' Such constitutional conventions might be valuable constitutional glue, intended to ensure Britain's Constitution functions for the benefit of all. The problem is that such conventions are not legally enforceable,[116] and if they are ignored (as recently with three Brexit bills adopted without devolved consent[117]) there is no legal recourse.

However, those embracing absolute parliamentary sovereignty ignore history at their peril. Many Scots of different political persuasions stand by an indigenous Scottish tradition of popular sovereignty claimed to date back to the Declaration of Arbroath in 1320. They hold that, before the 1707 Act of Union, sovereignty resided in Scottish people – and still does so, in spite of claims of Diceyan parliamentary sovereignty. When the English and Scottish Parliaments united in 1707, it is denied that the new Parliament of Great Britain was no more than the former English Parliament with a new name. It was a Union of two Parliaments. Therefore, it is not logical to contend that the English doctrine of parliamentary sovereignty should prevail, and Scottish notions of sovereignty of the people should be ignored.

6.6.3.2 The Loss of the American Colonies

The American War of Independence at base was caused by arguments about legal sovereignty. From 1763 to 1776, the first British Empire confronted a crisis

[115] *MacCormick* v. *Lord Advocate* [1953] SC 396 at 411.

[116] Even although the Sewel Convention was given statutory form in the Scotland Act 2016, it was still declared by the Supreme Court in *Miller 1* not to be legally enforceable.

[117] The EU Withdrawal Act 2018 refused legislative consent by the Scottish Parliament; the EU (Withdrawal Agreement) Act 2020, refused legislative consent by Scotland, Wales and Northern Ireland; and the EU (Future Relationship Act) 2020, refused legislative consent by the Scottish Parliament.

over the authority of the British Parliament to control colonial America. In Great Britain many saw 'Empire' as a unitary State, with sovereignty vested only in Parliament. This view was reflected in the 1765 Stamp Act and 1766 Declaratory Act which asserted Parliament's authority to 'bind the colonies.... and peoples of America ... in all cases whatsoever' – an assertion of sovereignty and control, if ever there was one. However, many Americans rejected the Declaratory Act[118] along with parliamentary sovereignty, viewing Parliament's authority as circumscribed by custom and law, and relied on an older notion of the fundamental Constitution. And given the fact that even in Britain, in the eighteenth century, that concept still carried weight, this was not unreasonable. According to the 'American' theory of Empire, it was a shared monarch that connected the colonies legally to Britain. The earlier Union of crowns of Scotland and England was used to support this argument – to illustrate that a monarch could reign over two countries, each with separate parliaments. But the British Government would not accept this view. Britain and its colonies went to war – a war that Britain lost.

However, what is interesting is that, in the middle of the American War of Independence, the British proposed a Conciliation Plan (which was rejected by Americans), whereby Britain was willing to make concessions – such as banning taxation of the North American colonies, suspending operation of offending parliamentary legislation and repealing the Declaratory Act. According to Berriedale-Keith, this 'proves beyond doubt that the measures of that year were based on no fundamental principle essential to the Empire.'[119]

6.6.3.3 Empire

Many late nineteenth-century textbooks suggested that parliamentary sovereignty applied throughout the British Empire.[120] Yet, the reality of Britain's Empire undermines that. For the Empire was diverse and incoherent in legal form. Insouciance, or 'a fit of absence of mind,' as the Victorian historian Seeley described the development of the British Empire, left things hazy.[121] Indeed, an anti-formalist attitude prevailed, presenting itself as eschewing law, and conceiving the Empire as a family, managed by informal assurances, customs, and conventions.[122] There was little unitary law and no attempt to

[118] See Jack P Greene, *Peripheries and Center: Constitutional Development in the Extended Polities of the British Empire and the United States* (New York: Norton, 1990).

[119] A Berriedale-Keith, *Constitutional History of the First British Empire* (Oxford: Clarendon Press, 1930) 385.

[120] E.g. Dicey, *Law of the Constitution*, 8th ed.

[121] 'We seem, as it were, to have conquered and peopled half the world in a fit of absence of mind ...' John Robert Seeley, *The Expansion of England* (London: Macmillan, 1884 ed., 8, 179).

[122] See further, Thomas Mohr, 'The United Kingdom and Imperial Federation, 1900 to 1939: A Precedent for British Legal Relations with the EU?' (2016) 4(2) Comparative Legal History 131–161, at 153.

establish a uniform legal code. The Empire included 'an extraordinary range of constitutional, diplomatic, political, commercial and cultural relationships.'[123]

Further, the colonies were not represented in Westminster. The situation could not be compared to, for example, the EU Parliament where British citizens had directly elected MEPs, in a Parliament with a co-say or veto on legislation. The colonies had no say in Westminster, and their own legislatures, their own officials, largely determined the law. Much of the British Empire lent itself to a more pluralistic type of sovereignty – one that was divided, shared and indeterminate. Legal devices, such as the mandate, the Protectorate, and other fuzzy concepts, typified a divided sovereignty with no single source.[124] Indeed, in 1864, Maine, who was by then working as Law Member in the Council of the Viceroy of India, wrote an influential minute on the sovereignty of Kathiawar, where he defined sovereignty as:

> a term which, in International Law, indicates a well ascertained assemblage of separate powers or privileges. The rights which form part of the aggregate are specifically named by publicists, who distinguish them as the right to make war and peace, the right to administer civil and criminal justice, the right to legislate, and so forth. A sovereign who possesses the whole of this aggregate of rights is called an independent sovereign, but there is not, nor has there ever been, anything in International Law to prevent some of these rights being lodged with one possessor and some with another. Sovereignty has always been regarded as divisible.[125]

In this way, the Kathiawar States, according to Maine, could be both sovereign and non-sovereign. Maine's work was well known by many significant colonial administrators, such as Ibbetson, Tupper and AC Lyall in India, and Lugard in Nigeria, so his ideas, especially of 'indirect rule', inspired many of their actions, so his influence was hardly purely academic.

Westminster also had a complicated relationship with 'settler colonies', such as Canada and Australia, which rested on conventions of non-interference by Britain in their affairs, Self-government was given a legal form in the 1931 Statute of Westminster. Indeed, for those embracing the Diceyan view of absolute parliamentary sovereignty, the Statute of Westminster had uncomfortable consequences. As Marshall remarked, 'Anyone who accepts the traditional notion of sovereignty is … also committed to saying that Section 2 of the Statute of Westminster … do not mean what they say when they provide

123 John Darwin, *The Empire Project: The Rise and Fall of the British World-System, 1830–1970* (Cambridge: Cambridge University Press, 2009) 1.

124 According to Alexandrowicz: 'The Protectorate means a split of sovereignty and its purpose is to vest in the Protector rights of external sovereignty while leaving rights of internal sovereignty in the protected entity.' [CH Alexandrowicz, *The European-African Confrontation: A Study in Treaty Making* (Leiden: AW Sijthoff, 1973) 62].

125 Minute by Henry Sumner Maine, 22 March 1864, in A Sever (ed.), *Documents and Speeches on the Indian Princely States*, vol. 1 (Delhi: BR Publishing, 1985). Kathiawar is the collective name for small princely States in the peninsular region of western India.

that Commonwealth Parliaments shall have power to repeal any British Act of Parliament in its application to them ...'[126] According to the orthodox theory, whatever the UK Parliament can do, a subsequent Parliament can undo, and so the Statute of Westminster could be repealed. However, in *Blackburn* v. *Attorney-General*, Lord Denning acknowledged that 'freedom once given cannot be taken away', and Parliament has consistently complied with section 4.[127]

This short review suggests that the issue of sovereignty within the British Empire was often deliberately undefined, so that it might be wielded when desired and found useful. It was likely that *power* underlay the Empire. According to SN Dhyani, a law professor at Rajasthan University in Jaipur,

> during the heydays of British imperialism and absolute power no theory of law could fit in so eminently as Austin's Analytical positivism which meant despotism, status quo, police state, anti-people government and alien laws and judicial system – all rolled into one.[128]

Indeed, as Dicey himself acknowledged, 'Under all the formality, the antiquarianism, the shams of the British constitution', 'there lies an element of power which has been the true source of its life and growth'. Dicey claimed that sovereignty was 'at bottom, nothing else but unlimited power' and the 'pliability' contained in the English formulation was 'essential to the maintenance by England of the British Empire'.[129] However, power by itself lacks legitimacy – it must be validated by something else – which is where sovereignty becomes relevant, in providing that grounding, in furnishing both coercion and compliance, force and legal obligation. Yet the claims of sovereignty made by the Empire were often mutually contradictory, and incoherent.

6.6.4 The EU Challenge

Finally, it might be argued that EU membership posed the biggest challenge to parliamentary sovereignty. It is oversimplistic to view EU law as another form of territorial challenge, because, during Britain's EU membership, EU law was *part of* national law, not an external system. This challenge has already been examined in another chapter. However, it is so important that it cannot be omitted. For, as Barber writes, 'Whatever the precise content of Parliamentary sovereignty was, it ceased to be a feature of the UK's Constitution in 1991.'[130]

The supremacy of EU law, meaning its priority over conflicting member State laws, is a fundamental principle of the EU's legal system. This principle

[126] Marshall, *Constitutional Theory*, 62–63.

[127] *Blackburn* v. *Attorney-General* [1971] 2 All ER 1380; but see L Sankey, *British Coal Corporation* v. *The King* [1935] AC 520.

[128] SN Dhyani, *Jurisprudence: A Study of Indian Legal Theory* (New Delhi: Metropolitan Book Co., 2nd ed., 1985) 19–20.

[129] Dicey, *England's Case*, 168.

[130] NW Barber, 'The Afterlife of Parliamentary Sovereignty' (2011) 9(1) International Jl of Constitutional Law, at 144.

was clarified by the ECJ in *Costa* v. *ENEL*.[131] The most evident challenge posed by EU membership to parliamentary sovereignty lay in explaining the capacity of the European Communities Act (ECA) 1972 to override later UK statutes. This capacity appeared to infringe the rule against 'Implied repeal', which requires that a later statute takes priority over an earlier in the event of conflict. Under the ECA 1972, the UK Parliament gave effect to the UK's EEC obligations in national law, deliberately according priority to EEC law in certain circumstances. It is the ECA that defines the legal relationship between the two otherwise separate spheres of EU and UK law. Section 2(4) ECA provided that all statutes must be read and given effect to consistently with EU law. In *Factortame*[132] the House of Lords accepted the supremacy of EU law and disapplied the Merchant Shipping Act 1988 (which directly conflicted with (then) EEC law) – an outcome which was seen as challenging traditional notions of parliamentary sovereignty.

For William Wade, *Factortame* could only be explained in terms of a revolution: 'While Britain remains in the Community we are in a regime in which Parliament has bound its successors successfully, and which is nothing if not revolutionary.'[133] Yet, Wade did not believe that the ECA 1972 provided a precedent for further possibilities of parliamentary self-limitation. It is unclear why this should be so and others certainly did not share Wade's interpretation. Nick Barber, while not describing this as a revolution, does refers to 'the quiet death of parliamentary sovereignty', because *Factortame* made clear that 'it is no longer the case that "whatever the Queen-in-Parliament enacts as a statute is law": the courts can sometimes set aside these statutes.'[134]

Yet, Barber noted that parliamentary sovereignty seemed to have such a pull that some constitutional jurists wrote as if it still existed. But he believed them to be wrong, arguing that, 'Even if the 1972 act were repealed, this would not resurrect the old rule of Parliamentary sovereignty.' This is because 'The old rule did not permit Parliament to place effective substantive limits on its successors. After *Factortame*, there is now authority for the proposition that Parliament can impose such limitations; the old absolutism of sovereignty is no longer viable.' Barber also wrote that 'The old rule of sovereignty no longer prevents Parliament from placing limits of substance, as well as form, on itself. Parliament could give the courts the power to strike down statutes that conflicted with human rights, or it could, if it wished, place legal limits on its capacity to legislate in devolved matters.'[135] This is similar to the view expressed by Vernon Bogdanor in *The New British Constitution*,[136] who argued that, far from being a mere manner and form entrenchment, the 1972 Act imposed a substantive limitation on the powers of Parliament. Bogdanor also stated that

[131] Case 6/64 *Costa* v. *ENEL* [1964] ECR 58. [132] *ex p Factortame (No 2)* [1991] 1 AC 603.

[133] HWR Wade, 'Sovereignty – Revolution or Evolution?' (1996)112 LQR at 573. See also Wade, 'The Basis of Legal Sovereignty' [1955] CLJ 172.

[134] Barber, 'The Afterlife of Parliamentary Sovereignty', at 151. [135] Ibid., 153, 154.

[136] V Bogdanor, *The New British Constitution* (Oxford: Hart, 2009).

'this interpretation of what the sovereignty of Parliament means is of course quite different from the pristine version put forward by Dicey', adding that, 'This interpretation of the ECA raises an awkward question. If Parliament could voluntarily limit its sovereignty in the ECA, why might it not also do so with respect to other statutes – the Human Rights Act, or the devolution legislation?'[137]

This seems to me persuasive. Limits were placed on parliamentary sovereignty by the ECA, so that future UK legislation should comply with, and be interpreted according to the UK's obligations under EU law. But, having achieved this in the case of EU law, there is no reason of principle why Parliament should not limit itself with regard to other matters after that. [A separate but related argument draws on HLA Hart's distinction between 'continuing' and self-embracing' sovereignty. Although, according to the 'continuing' theory, no Parliament has the power to bind its successor, Hart argued that the continuing or 'orthodox' Diceyan concept of sovereignty was 'only one arrangement among others, equally conceivable.'[138] Self-embracing sovereignty allows Parliament to place restrictions on its future actions, understanding this as an act of sovereignty in itself.]

But note that Parliament's capacity to self limit is not such a tremendous matter as some, such as Wade, would make out. First, the implied repeal rule was already subject to inroads from domestic law prior to EU membership – as there already existed situations where a statute would only be given effect if phrased in express words (where it exacts taxes, imposes criminal liability or has retroactive effect). Second, the 'manner and form' theory had already convincingly demonstrated that procedural limits could be placed on absolute parliamentary sovereignty. The impact of EU law on parliamentary sovereignty accelerated a process that had already commenced. Third, there is a very real sense in which the UK never lost any sovereignty when it was a member of the EU. This is because the UK always retained its external sovereignty, as a State, and that Parliament could always repeal the ECA 1972 and leave the EU – which of course, it ultimately did, with Brexit.

Confusion over sovereignty was nonetheless exemplified by the UK Government Brexit *White Paper* which stated: 'Whilst Parliament has remained sovereign throughout our membership of the EU, it has not always felt like that.'[139] This admission, that Parliament had been sovereign during the UK's EU membership, is at odds with the Government's *Foreword* to the 'Great Repeal Bill' White Paper, where it cited regaining sovereignty as the motivation for Brexit.

[137] V Bogdanor, 'Imprisoned by a Doctrine: The Modern Defence of Parliamentary Sovereignty' (2012) 32(1) *OJLS* 190.

[138] HLA Hart, *The Concept of Law* (2nd ed., Oxford: Clarendon Press, 1994) 148–150 – although we should note that Hart himself did not present self-embracing sovereignty as a valid interpretation of the UK Constitution. Ibid., at 145.

[139] HM Government, *The United Kingdom's exit from and new partnership with the European Union* CM 9417 (February 2017), chapter 2 'Taking Control of Our Own Laws', 13.

This illustrated the muddled and convoluted thinking at the heart of Brexit. This is because the Government conflated external and parliamentary sovereignty and was less than transparent about the existing arguments as to the status of parliamentary sovereignty. Not only does this statement reveal confusion, but its reference to something as nebulous as feelings divulges the lack of solid ground on which the sovereignty claim rests. But this illustrates the obfuscation over sovereignty.

6.6.5 Conclusion

So to summarize the challenges to parliamentary sovereignty:

1. *The historical challenge*: the historical sources for parliamentary sovereignty are not of ancient lineage. Most of the case was made by Dicey, who did not supply much historical evidence, and was himself sometimes contradictory.
2. *The constitutional challenge*: parliamentary sovereignty is not the same thing as executive sovereignty but is often confused with it, and recent events demonstrate increasing attempts by the UK Government to claim sovereignty. In fact, if anything, parliamentary sovereignty was developed to counter the abuses of an overbearing executive in the seventeenth century.

Parliamentary sovereignty has always been in tension with the rule of law. There is no reason why parliamentary sovereignty should always prevail over the rule of law and UK judges have increasingly emphasized the importance of the rule of law as a constraint on parliamentary sovereignty.

The new theory, or manner and form theory, that asserts that Parliament may impose its own procedural limits on parliamentary legislation, is supported by both Commonwealth and UK caselaw and by wording of some UK statutes.

3. *The territorial challenge*: The British Parliament's assertion of absolute sovereignty over the American colonies was rejected as an unfounded injustice. Furthermore, in spite of claims made for imperial parliamentary sovereignty, the British Empire was in fact very diverse, underpinned by many types of sovereignty which cannot all be cramped into a straitjacket of parliamentary sovereignty. Scotland draws on historical traditions of popular sovereignty distinct from parliamentary sovereignty.
4. *The EU challenge:* At the very least, the implied repeal rule did not apply while Britain was a member of the EU, and parliamentary sovereignty was compromised to at least that extent, if not more. The application of the ECA illustrated that Parliament may by legislation limit its sovereignty and the courts will observe this. There is no reason why this should not apply in other (non-EU) cases.
5. Lastly, it is worth stressing that parliamentary sovereignty should not be confused with external sovereignty, although it often is. Britain retained its

> external sovereignty throughout its membership of the EU. Parliamentary sovereignty should also not be confused with popular sovereignty, which is as yet undeveloped as a legal doctrine in the UK.

Barber wrote that:

> It would probably be best if constitutional scholars ceased discussing sovereignty as an ongoing rule of the Constitution, however interpreted or reinterpreted. Attention could more profitably be directed to the questions that often hide behind such discussion, questions relating to the position and vitality of Parliament within the Constitution, the United Kingdom's relationship with Europe, the future of devolution, and so on.[140]

I agree. But this has not happened. Instead, Dicey's concept of sovereignty has been conflated with sovereignty generally, with pernicious effects. Why does this matter? Because the stakes are high.

The UK no longer has an empire. It has also left the EU. But it has lessons to learn from the past, from its history of belonging to, or managing, larger territorial organizations. The UK is still a conglomerate or union State of four nations. If the UK is to function effectively as single State, then its constitutional structures should acknowledge this variety. Yet, at present, they do not. The UK has a Constitution that is supposedly flexible, full of synergies, conventions, to suit every situation. Except that they fail to do so. Because most of this flexible Constitution is political, not legally enforceable, and when it suits, Britain retreats into a hard minimal legal shell – an eccentric legal understanding of parliamentary sovereignty as impermeable, indivisible and unshareable. This concept of sovereignty makes federalism or effective home rule impossible. And because the UK has a fused system with an Executive drawn from Parliament, this system of sovereignty empowers the Government. Yet this eccentric understanding of parliamentary sovereignty fails to survive sustained examination.

There is it seems, nothing that a government with a parliamentary majority may not do. It can abolish human rights legislation, reduce civil liberties (especially at time of coronavirus) and constrict the opportunities for judicial review. But we should recognize that there is not necessarily a sound legal basis for many of these actions, and that much of the doctrine of parliamentary sovereignty rests on a foundation of sand, and has relied on power and force.

However, to point out the contradictions of the Diceyan case is not to deny that there is some value in acknowledging parliamentary ***supremacy***. In a democratic age, legislation by elected representatives should be accorded greater value than most other institutional acts, such as executive orders – something recognized in the *Miller/Cherry* case. But there is no principled reason why

[140] Barber, 'The Afterlife of Parliamentary Sovereignty', 154.

parliamentary legislation should always prevail over human rights, rule of law concerns, nor any reason why Parliament should not be able to impose procedural limits on its future actions.

To conclude: there is no reason why 'zombie' parliamentary sovereignty should enjoy an afterlife. However, national sovereignty, understood as something divisible, as a resource that may be pooled, may certainly be put to good use.

7

Unions and Disunions

7.1 Unions Generally

7.1.1 Introduction

This chapter is concerned with unions. But what do we mean by unions? The United Kingdom considers itself to be a union, but it is only one of the many different sorts of union that may exist. This introduction looks a little more closely at unions in general, as well as comparing them to other types of State organization, such as empires and unitary States.

The term 'union' has no specific legal meaning, nor indeed any single generally accepted meaning. Unions may, but need not, involve an amalgamation of previously distinct elements. A quick look at the literature reveals a is distinction often made between 'personal' unions and 'real' unions.[1] 'Personal' union is a term first recorded by Göttingen law professor Johann Pütter,[2] although such unions were in existence before the eighteenth century. With personal unions, two or more States combine under the same monarch, although it is usual for their laws and borders to remain distinct. The person of the sovereign would normally be the only connection between the States. Examples of personal unions are the union of Scotland and England as separate kingdoms from 1603 to 1707, and of Hanover with Great Britain from 1714 to 1837 (United Kingdom from 1801) as well as independent Commonwealth States which currently share the British Crown. We could also add the many personal unions England formed with other European countries in the past[3] – proof, if such were needed, that England has always had close European connections.

It is very hard to discern a precise legal meaning for 'real union'. However, the constituent States of real unions are linked by some further element than the monarch alone. They may share government institutions, or certain

[1] James Crawford, *Modes of the Creation of States in International Law* (2nd ed., Oxford: Oxford University Press, 2006).

[2] Johann Stephan Pütter, *Elementa iuris publici germanici* (Göttingen: Bossiegel, 1760).

[3] I.e. with Denmark in the earlier part of the eleventh century (North Sea Empire); with French territories, such as Normandy, Anjou, Aquitaine in the middle ages; Spain from 1556 to 1558; the Principality of Orange (1689–1702).

combined institutional arrangements, sometimes even constituting a single international personality. The example of Austria-Hungary after the *Ausgleich* of 1867 is sometimes given.

Then there are 'political' unions. This is another rather vague term, but generally it denotes States which are constituted out of smaller States, and the new State – the union – is recognised internationally as a single political entity. In political unions, the constituent (former) States share a central government. Political unions may take a number of forms, such as incorporating unions, federal unions, and mixed unions. They involve a greater intensity of association than real or personal unions. The UK after 1707 became such a political union, although not everyone agrees that it was an 'incorporating' union.

The fact is that unions take a variety of forms and it is not always clear what species of legal entity one is dealing with. Unions need not require a unitary State. Indeed, as we shall see, many choose to define the UK as a 'union State' rather than a unitary State. Unions may exist along a spectrum of State connectivity, from an affiliation of separate States, through to their complete fusion. The manifold unions that have existed over time illustrate this – from confederations, through the European Union, the Norway-Sweden union in the nineteenth century, the United States, to the unitary 'England and Wales' and former Czechoslovakia. All are unions of some sort and all are discussed and compared to the UK Union later in this chapter.

Unions may comprise a number of distinct territories or 'nations' within one juridical State (as with the UK or Canada) but may also involve groups of distinct States joining together without forming a single State, as with the EU. Murray Forsyth, in *Unions of States*, focusses on unions that are not a complete fusion but States which establish close and long-lasting links with each other, by means of international treaty. Other terms may also be used for this relationship, such as confederacy, confederation, system of States, community, perpetual league, république fédérative, *Staatenbund*, and *Eidgenossenchaft*. As Murray Forsyth contends, these are unions of States that 'occupy a half-way house between interstate and intrastate relations.'[4]

7.1.1.1 Jellinek

However, surprisingly few legal scholars have investigated the concept of unions generally. One to do so was the nineteenth-century Austrian legal scholar, Georg Jellinek – and perhaps his situation as a law professor working in Austria-Hungary, which was composite in nature, had something to do with this. Jellinek set out a typology of unions in his 1882 work *Die Lehre der staatlichen Verbindungen,* surveying the different kinds of entities created between States. Jellinek stressed that the federal State was not treaty-based, and in this way resembled the modern nation State, being in Jellinek's mind the product of

[4] M Forsyth, *Unions of States: The Theory and Practice of Confederation* (Leicester: Leicester University Press, 1981).

historical forces rather than a legal contract. Nonetheless, the federal State was still a connection between *states*, even if the constituent member states were non-sovereign in nature.

In fact, it was part of Jellinek's purpose to stress that, throughout history, the unitary nation State was the exception, and not the norm.[5] No doubt the sovereign State, with its fixed territorial boundaries, and its claim to a monopoly of legitimate coercion within that territory, became a model in the nineteenth century.[6] But Jellinek also proffered many examples of federal or non-unitary States, such as Switzerland, the USA, Austria-Hungary, Norway-Sweden, as well as the 'entire Orient', as more characteristic of the nature of States within the international order.

Also worth mentioning in this context is the work of jurist Eugen Ehrlich, a near contemporary of Jellinek. Ehrlich developed the concept of 'living law', by which he meant the law as daily applied in a far flung part of the Austrian empire, as opposed to formal imperial law – thus highlighting the legal pluralism of the Austrian empire, and, more generally, the variegated nature of law within unions. The title of one much-cited article, 'Global Bukowina', once again put Ehrlich's concept to use in the context of the late twentieth century.[7]

7.1.1.2 Composite States

The sovereign State is but the creature of a couple of centuries. History reveals a predominance of 'multiple kingdoms' or 'composite States' – phenomena explored by historians such as HG Koenigsberger and JH Elliott. (These might also be categorized as 'personal unions'.) Within the composite State, there existed a legal pluralism in that distinct polities shared a common monarch but retained their political and legal independence. Koenigsberger[8] argued that in the early modern period, most States were composite in nature, with countries joined by marriage or inheritance. Constituent parts of composite States antedated the union and retained their own laws and rights. Koenigsberger noted that the concept of *dominium politicum et regale*[9] (whereby monarchs needed consent to rule, usually given by the local representative assembly) was well suited to composite monarchies, with each constituent part keeping its own laws, as had England and Scotland in the seventeenth century. Koenigsberger

5 *Die Lehre von der Staatenverbindungen* (Berlin, 1882) 4.

6 See Max Weber, 'Politics as a Vocation' for a definition of the State as holding a monopoly of violence within a territory (in *Essays in Sociology*, transl. HH Gerth and C Wright Mills (Oxford: Oxford University Press, 1946)).

7 See further E Ehrlich, *Fundamental Principles of the Sociology of Law* (W. Moll trans., 1936, New Brunswick: Transaction Publishers, 2001). Also G Teubner, 'Global Bukowina: Legal Pluralism in the World-Society', in G Teubner (ed.), *Global Law without a State* (Aldershot: Dartmouth, 1996).

8 HG Koenigsberger, 'Composite States, Representative Institutions and the American Revolution' (1998) 62(148) Historical Research 135–153.

9 HG Koenigsberger, 'Monarchies and Parliaments in Early Modern Europe: Dominium Regale or Dominium Politicum et Regale' (1978) 5(2) Theory and Society 191–217.

argued that things became problematic in the eighteenth century, for Britain at least, when the Westminster Parliament was developing the concept of absolute parliamentary sovereignty and seeking to impose this on the American colonies. *Dominium politicum et regale* could no longer function in such conditions, where a unitary absolute parliamentary sovereignty was mandated. Thus, Americans were left with a choice of accepting absolute parliamentary supremacy or opting for independence. A Bodinian style of absolute sovereignty could not function in a composite State adapted to *dominium politicum et regale.*

John Elliott[10] also explored how the composite monarchy, which had flourished for so long, began to wane. Composite Statehood had been an attractive notion for distinct entities that wished to maintain their own laws and self-government, at a time when it was in any case difficult for the monarch to control far flung lands. However composite Statehood was also brittle, especially if the monarch was unable to foster a sense of loyalty in all territories. Religious divisions, external threats and wars threatened the composite State, strengthening the case for a concentration of power – or, as Olivares expressed it – 'many kingdoms but one law.'[11] For Britain, frequently at war with France (which had become a centralized and unified State), stronger union and consolidation appeared attractive. The movement towards unitary States in Europe accelerated, and, in Britain was also justified as a means to protect the result of the Glorious Revolution and the Protestant settlement.

7.1.1.3 Unions, Composite States, and Empires

The analysis so far also prompts the question of how unions and composite States differ from empires? For while it amassed an empire, Great Britain (and subsequently the UK) was also a composite monarchy, and for some time shared a King with Hanover. Indeed, the American colonies sometimes cited the Britain-Hanover union as a comparator. Both unions and empires could be multicultural, multi-ethnic, and diverse. All can be the product of colonization and conquest. Indeed, some authors suggest that England's first empire was an internal colonization – of the rest of the British Isles – and that the later British Empire, as well as the modern UK, were the inheritors of that venture.[12] However, contemporary definitions of empire tend to define it as a composite polity in which the centre dominates and exploits the periphery.[13] By this account, empires are not organized around the political equality of their various territories, but rather on dominance of the periphery by the centre. This is not necessarily the case with composite States, as we have seen.

[10] JH Elliott, 'A Europe of Composite Monarchies' (1992) 137 Past and Present 48–71.

[11] JH Elliott, *The Count-Duke of Olivares* (New Haven CT: Yale University Press, 1989) at 197.

[12] Niall Ferguson, *Empire: How Britain Made the Modern World* (London: Allen Lane, 2004).

[13] E.g. M Doyle, *Empires* (Ithaca, NY: Cornell University Press, 1986) at 12. K Kumar, 'Nation-States as Empires, Empires as Nation-States: Two Principles, One Practice?' (2010) 2 Theory and Society 119.

In the present era, when States are often ineffective if acting alone, and when unitary sovereignty is challenged both from above, by supra national organizations such as the EU, and from below, by sub-State entities and nations, then unions, composite States and empires are attracting interest as objects of study, due to their multicultural and multinational composition. According to Keating, 'The nation-state, an import from western Europe selectively encouraged by the victors of 1919, was a failure. There are more promising traditions within the history of the western part of Europe as well as in the central empires themselves.'[14] But for unions to thrive, there needs to a clear sense of their rationale and purpose, a sense which is unfortunately lacking in the present UK, as the ensuing discussion will illustrate.

7.2 The UK Union

7.2.1 Introduction

The United Kingdom lacks any single definition as to what constitutes the Union between England, Scotland, Wales and Northern Ireland. There is no codification or statute setting this out. Colin Kidd has suggested that, as recently as 60 years ago, the Union was seen as so unproblematic that few bothered to study it, especially since the external threat of the Second World war had strengthened the bonds of togetherness in the UK. The more apparent divisions were those of class, rather than nationality.[15] Perhaps this was once so, but changed circumstances now require investigation of the Union. In the absence of any clear definition, one falls back on an historical account of how the UK Union came together, through a series of individual acts of union between the nations of the UK. Much of this has been considered elsewhere in this book, so the account here will be brief.

Wales was absorbed into England in the sixteenth century, and in 1706–1707 the personal union of 1603 between England and Scotland was augmented by a political union between these countries, and subsequently joined by Ireland in 1800, when Great Britain became the UK. From 1714 to 1837, Great Britain (subsequently the UK) was in a personal union with Hanover, which was dissolved in 1837 (because Queen Victoria, as woman, was unable to inherit the electorship of Hanover). In 1922, the Irish Free State was formed, and as a result, only the six counties of Northern Ireland remained in the UK Union. Devolution to Scotland, Wales and Northern Ireland in 1998 has left the UK Union somewhat asymmetric in nature, with difference in legal systems, religion, language, education and local government between the different nations and parts of the UK. Additionally, there are at least 6,000 islands surrounding

14 Michael Keating, *Plurinational Democracy: Stateless Nations in a Post-Sovereignty Era* (Oxford: Oxford University Press, 2001) chapter 1.

15 Colin Kidd, *Union and Unionisms: Political Thought in Scotland, 1500–2000* (Cambridge: Cambridge University Press, 2008).

Britain, some of which – such as the Isle of Man and the Channel Islands – are not within the UK as such. In conclusion, the UK is comprised of not one union but three – between England and Wales, Scotland and England & Wales, and between Great Britain and (now) Northern Ireland – all three different in nature. As Linda Colley writes: 'the UK, as it exists now, is substantially the result of luck, accident and above all multiple wars. Each of the acts of Union … occurred in wartime or amidst anticipation of war.'[16]

7.2.2 A 'Union State'?

While the nations and territories[17] of the UK make up one State, there exists no agreement as to what type of State the UK is. In the past, it was often described as a unitary State, but this term is now often rejected, in favour of terms such as 'union State', 'State of unions', or 'composite State'. All of this needs unpacking.

If 'nation State' is used as a term to designate a polity in which the State and nation coincide, then this seems unsuited to the UK, which comprises different nations. However, if nation State is used to describe a territory with a shared identity, citizenship, common culture and sense of solidarity, then this might have some purchase in the UK, although it is becoming more tenuous, as we shall explore.

The term 'union State' has come to be preferred to 'unitary State' as a description of the UK. The latter term implies a unified State, with a unitary political centre, shared governing institutions and legal and administrative standardization – an overall, undifferentiated polity. In contrast, the term 'union State' became popularized after its use by the Norwegian political scientist, Stein Rokkan, to denote a State where the centre does not directly control in every part of the territory.[18] The UK is not unitary in nature, and a plurality and diversity of arrangements exist over its composite parts. For example, Scots law, and the Scottish Church were unaffected by the 1707 Union. So 'union State' appears preferable to describe it.

Georg Jellinek, residing in the composite, almost undefinable territory of Austria-Hungary, advocated a more nuanced account of jurisdiction than the rather blunt division of States and non-States, and employed the doctrine of 'State fragments'.[19] He argued that State fragments constituted an 'inbetween' level, namely entities 'that are not States themselves, but present the rudiments of a State'. Indeed, Jellinek gave as examples of 'State fragments' both the historic principalities of the Habsburg Empire, and Australia and Canada, which

[16] L Colley, *Acts of Union and Disunion* (London: Profile, 2014) 147–148.

[17] England, Wales, and Scotland are all recognized as 'nations'. Northern Ireland is a complex and divided community that many would deny is a nation.

[18] S Rokkan and D Urwin, 'Centre and Peripheries in Western Europe', in S Rokkan and D Urwin (eds.), *The Politics of Territorial Identity: Studies in European Regionalism* (London: SAGE Publications, 1982).

[19] Georg Jellinek, *Ueber Staatsfragmente* (Heidelberg: Gustav Koester, 1896) 8.

had State organs without being completely independent States in their own right.[20] 'State fragments' may be nations in their own right (like Scotland and Wales), or provinces or territories within a larger State.

7.2.3 Defining the UK Union

The UK Union has been, perceived differently over space and time. Keating has characterized the Union in terms of 'family resemblance', in that it cannot be reduced to one thing which all its parts have in common.[21] Indeed, strictly speaking, the Union is not singular but plural – three separate unions, the 'State of unions' referred to by James Mitchell.[22]

Whereas the England & Wales union is an incorporating one, constitutionally at least, with Welsh identity taking shape through Welsh culture and language rather than a separate Welsh legal system; the Anglo-Scottish union left key areas within a sphere of Scottish autonomy; and the union with Northern Ireland is different again, having most recently incorporated a form of governance – consociationalism – not to be found elsewhere in the UK. So an understanding of the Union in one part of the UK may not work for its other nations.

The Union has also been understood differently throughout history. Kidd suggests that a 'banal unionism' existed in Scotland until the mid-twentieth century, whereby 'the nature or reasons for one's loyalty to the British state were never quite spelled out.'[23] However, the term 'unionism' has a particular political sense in the UK, affirming the political sovereignty of Westminster, if recognizing some cultural diversity within the union. In Northern Ireland it denotes adherence to the party political beliefs of the DUP and other unionist parties, who wish to maintain the union of Northern Ireland with the UK. And, in the past, in Scotland, unionism had a very specific meaning – it was the doctrine of the Conservative & Unionist party, centred on the vexed issue of the Union with Ireland of 1800, and not even on the Anglo-Scottish Union.[24]

In these circumstances, one wonders what meaning there might be today for the Union and for Britishness. Whereas Britishness developed in the past as a reaction to external threats and often took shape as a specific Protestant identity,[25] today, its meaning may be more bland, as a concept without ethnic undercurrents, of somewhat synthetic manufacture. But can the Union, and Britishness more generally, be conceived in some sort of overarching way, acceptable to all – to achieve some sort of 'overlapping consensus' to use Rawlsian language? The problem is that attempts to find a meaningful

[20] *Ueber Staatsfragmente*, 25, for discussion of Canada.

[21] Michael Keating, Written evidence (UDE0010) House of Lords Constitution Committee, *The Union and Devolution* (10th Report of Session 2015–16, HL Paper 149).

[22] James Mitchell, *Devolution in the UK* (Manchester: Manchester University Press, 2009).

[23] Kidd, *Union and Unionisms*, 23. [24] Ibid., 11.

[25] L Colley, *Britons: Forging the Nation 1707–1837* (New Haven CT: Yale University Press, 1992).

dimension to the Union have not been particularly successful. Reflections on the past – on a shared history and heritage, including the Empire and royalty – may not provide a particularly compelling rationale for the Union today. Other conceptions look to the Union as a fabric for shared solidarity, shared risk and financial arrangements. That account also seems to have less purchase today – as we shall consider.

7.2.4 Key Elements of the UK Union

If it is hard to define the Union, then we can at least aim to be a little more concrete in setting out certain of its perceived key elements. In the 2016 House of Lords Constitution committee report, *The Union and Devolution*, these were given fairly extensive consideration.[26] The report considered five distinct elements, which provide a useful template for analysis here.

First, the UK is an *economic union*. This comprises a single market with a single currency and single fiscal and macroeconomic framework.[27] It will be remembered that access to the English market was an important element of the Anglo-Scottish union in 1707. The UK's economic union has provided the UK's nations with a larger and more diverse market than each would have had separately. The economic union also provides each nation with some protection against economic shocks. The continuing salience of the economic union was illustrated by the spirited debates over whether the economic union – especially the common currency – could remain if Scotland became independent.

Another important element is the UK's *social union*.[28] In its 2009 report on Scottish Devolution, the Calman Commission described the social union in the following way:

> the UK has created a system of welfare for all its citizens, which is both comprehensive and substantially uniform.... A basic feature of the welfare state is that, in general, its cost is borne out of general taxation and its services and support are supplied on the basis of need. This implies a relatively high degree of ... social solidarity.[29]

Notably however, any social union had failed in the nineteenth century, during the Irish Famine, with the perception that Britain had neglected to support

[26] *The Union and Devolution* (10th Report of Session 2015–16, HL Paper 149) especially chapter 2, 'What Is the Union?'

[27] Although the single fiscal framework has become more diluted since Scotland and Wales gained greater fiscal autonomy.

[28] As pointed out in *The Union and Devolution*, the term 'social union' has different senses – whereas the Scottish Government tended to emphasize its cultural aspects in the 2014 independence campaign, others have used it to denote a welfare union, and the latter use will be followed here.

[29] Calman Commission, *Serving Scotland Better: Scotland and the United Kingdom in the 21st Century*, Cm 7738 (Scotland Office, 2009) 35.

Irish sufferers. And devolution has reshaped this social union, given that the 2016 Scotland Act devolved many areas of social security to Scotland.

The UK also comprises a *political union*. This is grounded in the Westminster Parliament, in which all nations and regions of the UK are represented,[30] as well as by its external embodiment in the UK's international recognition as a single State. To this may be added a common UK citizenship and common civil and political rights. One again, however, the situation is complicated. Scotland, Wales and Northern Ireland have had their own Parliaments or Assemblies since Devolution, arranged on different principles to Westminster and devolved parliamentary laws have sometimes deviated from Westminster in adopting proportional representation, so there have developed distinctive national political identities. National governments have met through the intra-UK Joint Ministerial Committee (JMC), which has not functioned well, especially in Brexit matters. The Civil Service is less unified than it used to be.

The extent to which the political union translates into a *legal or constitutional union* is highly debateable. There are three separate legal jurisdictions across the UK (Scotland, Northern Ireland and England and Wales, although Wales has recently asserted itself legally.[31]) Although there exists a common framework formed by UK parliamentary legislation concerning all four nations, with the UK Supreme Court as court of final resort, and the British Constitution is itself a reserved matter, there is nonetheless divergence, especially for Scotland, which since the 1707 union retained its separate legal system.[32] Much impetus was provided by Lord Cooper's dicta in *MacCormick* v. *Lord Advocate* which appeared to depart from the English Diceyan stress on parliamentary sovereignty.

There also exists a *security and defence union*. Key institutions here are the armed forces and security services. Defence is a retained competence of the UK Government, and there exists a single UK immigration policy and single borders (even if the Northern Ireland Brexit Protocol has complicated this situation). Yet, a common defence may not always be a unifying factor. There is Scottish resentment at the location of trident nuclear submarines in Scotland, and a difference of opinions between the Scottish and UK governments over immigration since Brexit.

Finally there is a *cultural union* formed by a shared language, history, and common institutions such as the BBC and monarchy, as well as Britain's past empire, and common experience of fighting two world wars. This cultural union is less tangible than the other forms of union but might be captured by the expression of Britain's 'soft power', illustrated in matters such as Britain's

[30] Although elected Sinn Fein MPs for Northern Ireland do not take their seats in Westminster.

[31] 'Welsh Byelaws' case: *AG* v. *National Assembly for Wales Commission* [2012] UKSC 53.

[32] Per TB Smith: 'The Scottish legal system has its basis upon philosophical principles and is deductive; the English system, which is inductive, is a product of empiricism and precedent' TB Smith, 'Severalty of Administration of Justice in the United Kingdom' (1949) 56 *JR* at 167.

reputation for universities, the arts, as well as the predominance of English as first second language in the world.

Do all the above give rise to a coherent sense of a British identity? Linda Colley explored this in *Acts of Union and Disunion*, produced at the time of the 2014 Scottish independence referendum. For Colley, an important part of Britishness has been the stories people tell themselves,[33] including that of 'our island story', suggesting a country alone, detached, isolated from other continental landmasses. And yet for much of its history, Britain was a composite monarchy sharing rulers with other European States. The narrative of liberty, traced back to Magna Carta as an element of Britain's 'liberty-drenched ancient past', was exported with Britain's imperial exploits, although often deployed to maintain the political status quo, so that by 1900, Britain had one of the smallest electoral franchises in Europe. In other work,[34] Colley also drew upon stories of a Protestant people, the importance of trade and empire, and the bonding in face of a common enemy especially during world wars, as significant in the development of a British identity.

Whatever the cohesion, shared history, institutions, and cultural connections achieved by these stories, such common identities are on the wane, as British society has become more diverse and heterogeneous. And disunion threatens – most immediately in Scotland, since most of Ireland already left the UK in the earlier twentieth century, although Irish re-unification also looms and Welsh nationalism is ever present. It is hard not to conclude from reading Colley that it is *fear* – of a common enemy, of some other – that provided cohesion for Britain.

7.2.5 Values and Principles

In *The Union and Devolution*, the House of Lords Constitution Committee also enquired of its witnesses what they considered to be the basic principles and values of the Union, and indeed, whether it was even possible to identify such principles. While some believed it essential to set down the basic principles of the UK's Union, others disagreed, citing the fact that the Union was in many respects a *series* of unions, whose meaning varied in different parts of the country, making it hard to reach agreement other than at a very abstract level.[35] Closely related to the desire for a statement of principles of Union is the issue of *clarity*. For example, the Silk Commission argued that clarity is important because 'voters should understand where decisions are made and the settlement should be straightforward to operate'.[36] At present such clarity does not exist and citizens are confused, both by the complexity of the devolution settlements, as well as by their asymmetry.

33 Colley, *Acts of Union and Disunion* (London: Profile, 2014) 9.

34 Colley, *Britons*, generally.

35 *The Union and Devolution*, evidence of Professors Ailsa Henderson and Nicola McEwen.

36 Silk Commission, *Empowerment and Responsibility: Financial Powers to Strengthen Wales* (November 2012) at 28.

As a result, the Lords Constitution Committee itself argued there was a good case for setting out general principles that underpin the Union and Devolution. This would ensure that Devolution could proceed in a coherent, principled manner rather than in the reactive ad hoc manner in which it had done to date.

7.2.5.1 Equity

This principle was suggested as key by the Silk Commission but not included in the Lords report. This is puzzling, as equity between Union territories appears essential for a flourishing Union and Devolution settlement. To be sure, Devolution has not created uniformity. But a lack of uniformity need not mean an inequality of rights, nor inequity of treatment. Nevertheless, the variegated, asymmetric Devolution settlement raises the issue of how to reconcile a multiplicity of governing models with the principle of equity.

Two examples of perceived inequity of treatment across nations of the UK illustrate the problem. Regarding Brexit, Scotland and Northern Ireland's vote to remain in the EU was ignored, in the face of an overall majority vote to leave in the UK. (Indeed, if taking a UK wide approach, a majority English vote will almost always outweigh contrary votes in the other UK nations because of the size of the English population.) Second, the Barnett Formula,[37] which calculates funding for devolved nations, is resented in England as favouring the devolveds and seen as inequitable for that reason. Such perceptions become a source of grievance, weakening the Union.

How then to promote equity? It cannot be straightforwardly legislated. But perhaps the inclusion of a 'harm principle' within common UK policy making might ensure that UK policy makers were required to consider (and make provision for?) the effect of common policies in all nations of the UK.[38]

7.2.5.2 Solidarity

Solidarity can be fostered by sharing resources and a redistribution of funds according to needs through the social union, which in turn enables greater social cohesion, and a sense of unity, mutual responsibility and common purpose. However, it seems that the sense of solidarity is breaking down. Of course, if constituent parts of the Union feel that there is inequity in the operation of Devolution, solidarity is harder to achieve. For example, if Scots feel they have been ignored or overridden on vital constitutional issues such as Britain's removal from the EU, or if the English feel that the Barnett formula requires an unfair transfer of resources from England to devolved nations, then solidarity may be at risk.

[37] The Barnett Formula introduced in 1979 calculates devolved budgets on the basis of the previous year's budget, adjusted according to increases or decreases in comparable spending per person in England.

[38] See further, House of Lords, *The Union and Devolution*, evidence of Professor Ailsa Henderson.

7.2.5.3 Diversity

Although the concept of Union implies some commonality, the constitutional settlement of the UK is nonetheless diverse in nature, a feature that existed long before Devolution. Indeed, as we have seen, the British Empire allowed a certain amount of diversity in its component parts, rather than imposing a uniform law on all outposts of empire. However, in contrast to diversity, there stands the doctrine of Westminster parliamentary sovereignty, which when imposed, undermines the capacity for diversity and overrides it where necessary. In fact, these two separate principles combine to form a contradiction, which has never been fully resolved in UK law, but which threatens to damage the Union.

7.2.5.4 Subsidiarity

Subsidiarity is related to diversity and federalism. In brief, the subsidiarity principle requires that power should be exercised at the lowest level compatible with good government. Once again, there is some conflict with parliamentary sovereignty, which is ultimately reserved to Westminster under all Devolution settlements, and which may act as a competing principle of organization. However, absolute parliamentary sovereignty may appear increasingly incongruous in a devolved multinational UK, in which devolved institutions such as the Scottish and Welsh Parliaments, have confirmed permanent status over a wide range of powers.

7.2.5.5 Consent

Another important principle is that the UK Union is a *voluntary* union. This can be distinguished from Spain, whose Constitution guarantees that State's territorial integrity, or from the US, where the right of the southern states to secede and form the confederacy was denied and discredited in the Civil War. According to the 1954 Report of the Royal Commission on Scottish Affairs 'Scotland is a nation and voluntarily entered into Union with England as a partner and not as a dependency.'[39] The principle of consent is also evident in provision for a referendum on Irish re-unification in s1 Northern Ireland Act 1998. In both the Northern Ireland Act 1998 and the 2012 Edinburgh Agreement (which was based on s30 Scotland Act 1998 and facilitated the 2014 Scottish independence referendum) the UK Government acknowledged that it would respect a vote to reunify Ireland or for Scottish independence. Nonetheless, since Brexit, the UK Government has refused to agree to another 30 order as the basis for a second Scottish independence referendum – which would seem to undermine the perception that the UK Union is consensual and voluntary. The Bingham Rule of Law centre declared the first principle of its Charter of Union: 'the United Kingdom is a voluntary union of the UK nations and parts expressed through informed and democratic processes.'

[39] Report of the Royal Commission on Scottish Affairs Cmnd. 9212 (HMSO, 1954) at 12.

7.2.6 Maintaining the Union

7.2.6.1 The Problem with the Union

The Union is becoming a controversial topic. Immediately after the Second World War, the sense of 'Britishness' may have been high, but things have changed since. The Thatcher years, and then the 'austerity' policies from 2010, tend to have vanquished a feeling that 'we're all in it together'.[40] From the mid-twentieth century, Scottish nationalism became more of a factor to be reckoned with, and the onset of the 'troubles' in Northern Ireland also forced a reassessment of the Union. In the last decade or so, there has been a profusion of inquiries, commissions and other investigations into the Union and its constitutional arrangements. Such inquiries have included: the 2007 Calman Commission on Scotland; the 2014 Smith Commission after the 'No' vote on Scottish independence; and in Wales the 2002–2004 Richard Commission, the 2007–2010 Holtham Commission, and the 2011–2014 Silk Commission. The House of Commons Political and Constitutional Reform Select Committee launched its report *A New Magna Carta* in 2014, which enquired if the UK should have a written Constitution. The Liberal Democrats' Home Rule and Community Rule Commission advocated 'home rule all round' in a new federal union. The House of Lords Constitution Committee produced its 2016 report *The Union and Devolution*. The Bingham Centre published a draft Charter for the Union, as well as the Report, *A Constitutional Crossroads: Ways Forward for the United Kingdom* in 2015. The Constitution Reform Group, chaired by the Marquess of Salisbury, introduced Act of Union Bills into the House of Lords in 2018 and 2021. All of this activity underpins the feeling that there is something dysfunctional about the Union, in need of repair.

Nairn, in *The Break-Up of Britain*, likened the present-day UK to the struggling Austro-Hungarian Empire of the late nineteenth century. The Austrian author Robert Musil used the term 'Kakania' in the trilogy *The Man Without Qualities* to evoke the spiritual decay of the Habsburg monarchy. Nairn, in turn, has used the term 'Ukania' to suggest a collapsing authority of the British State. The Austro-Hungarian union suffered a lack of coherence because of its many component national identities, to which its inhabitants felt more strongly bonded than to the centre. It therefore proved almost impossible to maintain a loyalty to a transcendent, institutional identity. Nairn, in his adaptation of Musil's term, suggested the same is true of the UK.[41]

7.2.6.2 A Charter of Union?

If the UK Union is to survive, then it might seem that longer-term solutions are needed than the piecemeal ad hoc Devolution that has taken place to date. One way to mitigate the prospect of disintegration is to improve the quality of

[40] See P Hennessey, *The Kingdom to Come* (London: Haus Publishing, 2015) 27.

[41] T Nairn, *The Break-up of Britain: Crisis and Neonationalism* (London: Verso, 1981).

governance of the Union, especially given that, as Colley argues, 'many of the old sustaining stories – shibboleths – Protestantism, empire and sagas of the sea – are played out.'[42]

In its 2015 report, *A Constitutional Crossroads*, the Bingham Centre for the Rule of Law proposed a written Constitution for the UK, resting on principles of 'union constitutionalism' to underpin the Devolution Acts. These were larger in number than those of the House of Lords Constitution Committee, although not particularly British in nature: consent; respect for democracy; respect for the rule of law; shared commitment to personal liberty and human rights; social solidarity; common security and defence; common economic framework; autonomy; subsidiarity; accountability; and comity, trust and fair dealing.[43] The Bingham Centre drafted a *Charter of the Union* to set down the powers and principles governing the relationship between the four nations of the Union.

The Constitution Reform Group proposed its second Act of Union Bill in 2021. Its stated aim was to 'to affirm that the peoples of [our] nations and parts have chosen to continue to pool their sovereignty for specified purposes, and to provide universal citizenship with social and economic rights'. This Bill was based around the existing Devolution settlements, but includes new proposals, such as for an English Parliament; a strengthened Scottish Parliament; abolition of the House of Lords and its replacement by a new Chamber with members elected from the UK's national Parliaments; increased regional Devolution; financial reform and replacement of the Barnett Formula; renaming of the Bank of England as the Bank of the UK with board members drawn from across the UK. The Bill treats each of the four nations as self-governing territories but makes clear that each retains the right to secede by referendum. Nonetheless, the Act of Union Bill also contains a clause preserving Westminster Parliamentary sovereignty. This means that its proposed system would be unlike federalism, and the UK Parliament would retain the right to repeal this very Bill itself, were it to become law. This surely undermines the commitment to the self-determination and sovereignty of the nations.

Has the time come for a codified Constitution as a means to enable a Charter of the Union? Times have changed, and as Lord Neuberger (former President of the UK Supreme Court) noted in an extra-judicial speech, a codified Constitution may help focus minds.[44] However, perhaps the problem with all the suggestions in this section is that any wholescale reform of the British Constitution is unattractive to many Unionists, most of whom believe that the British Constitution has functioned quite adequately to date; and on the other hand, insufficient for nationalists, many of whom are unwilling to contemplate

[42] Colley, *Acts of Union and Disunion*, 152.

[43] Bingham Centre, *A Constitutional Crossroads*, 20–21.

[44] Lord Neuberger, 'The UK Constitutional Settlement and the Role of the UK Supreme Court', Legal Wales conference, 10 October 2014.

any perceived halfway measures to independence in any case. There may be a sizeable group of people in the middle who believe constitutional reform necessary to save the Union, but their number may not outweigh those on both sides who reject such changes.

7.2.6.3 The House of Lords as a Federal Chamber?

It is, however, worth scrutinizing one strongly advocated element of constitutional reform. That is the suggestion that the House of Lords be redesigned as a second Chamber to represent the nations and regions of the UK. This is based on the idea that such a Chamber could create a greater sense of territorial agency in UK governance. House of Lords reform has been on the agenda in British politics for more than a century, although never fully satisfactorily resolved, and at present, although the House of Lords may sometimes function effectively as a revising Chamber, it is often seen as lacking in legitimacy. However, if the Lords were reconstituted, with powers to restrain perceived excesses of the English dominated House of Commons then this might be some sort of solution. Nonetheless, there are problems with such reform. Should a reformed House of Lords represent electorates of different parts of the UK, as in the US Senate, or the governments or parliaments of the devolved nations and England (whether further devolved or not), as in the German *Bundesrat* (or the EU Council of Ministers)? If the Second Chamber were to operate effectively as a mechanism to remedy the perceived injustices of an English, and UK Government, dominated House of Commons, it would need power to override legislation, where felt to be detrimental to other parts of the Union. This would presumably require repeal of the 1911 and 1949 Parliament Acts, which removed the veto power of the House of Lords. It would also require that any representation of England (with about 85 per cent UK population) in a revised second Chamber could not automatically override the wishes of other devolved nations.

But perhaps the main problem would be that such a suggestion – indeed all proposals for new Acts of Union, could come too late for convinced nationalists who will brook no further union of parliaments.

7.2.6.4 What Doesn't Work

It should go without saying that, if policymakers wish to stabilize the Union, they should consider the consequences for the Union of any intended course of action. This relates to the notion of a harm principle discussed earlier.

The lack of any formal voice for the devolved nations in the Brexit withdrawal negotiations (with the exception of the DUP from 2017 to 2019) and the resentment this caused, reveals the failings of Devolution. It also reveals radically different views of the nature of the British Constitution. From the perspective of the UK Government, the British Constitution is unitary in nature, with foreign affairs reserved to the UK Government, including EU membership. This approach sees the devolveds as lacking legal rights in this area, at most to be consulted as matter of courtesy. However, an alternative approach views the UK as a union State rather than a unitary State. It interprets the UK as a union founded on treaties and reliant on ongoing consent. This alternative interpretation also recognizes that the UK has been transformed by external memberships (such as the EU and Council of Europe) and internally by arrangements such as Devolution, and also a desire for a more principled constitutional development than parliamentary sovereignty allows.

If only the former view of the Constitution is unilaterally imposed, we risk constitutional crisis. Yet improved governance will not, of itself, be enough to keep the Union together. Hearts and minds must be reached, and a strong case for the Union made. This requires a constructive framework for fostering a positive sense of the Union. This was not the case during the 2014 Scottish independence referendum, where the opportunity to do so was missed. Perhaps, this was because the three Unionist parties found it difficult to secure agreement on anything other than opposition to independence, and as a result, presented a somewhat negative argument founded on 'Project Fear'. Indeed, sometimes politicians not only fail to make a positive case for the Union but do exactly the reverse. This was illustrated, for example, by David Cameron's comments about the need for 'English votes for English laws' in the immediate aftermath of the Scottish independence referendum, ignoring and undermining Scotland and the narrowness of the vote, or in Boris Johnson's comments that 'devolution had been a disaster'.[45] Instead of building solidarity and mutual respect, such actions tend to incite opposing nationalisms, in this case, English and Scottish.

7.2.6.5 Hearts and Minds?

Finally, something must be said about how the Union is sustained by emotional attachments. This is hard to put in words. However Peter Hennessey wrote, at the time of the Scottish independence referendum, 'For me the Union is a matter as much of emotional geography as it is political or physical' continuing that 'Had Scotland separated in 2014, for me it would have been like a bereavement.'[46] This is sometimes expressed as a matter of 'hearts and minds'. However one expresses this, emotional attachment to the Union, and a sense of identity with it, is fundamental to its continuance. The fewer who feel this affinity, the weaker the Union becomes.

7.3 Comparison with Other Unions

7.3.1 Roads Not Taken

Before we compare other unions to the UK, it is worth remembering some potential paths to union that were not taken in Britain. For example, there was much talk in the later nineteenth century of a Greater Britain, along with

[45] 'Boris Johnson "called Scottish devolution a disaster"' *BBC News*, 17 November 2020.

[46] P Hennessey, *The Kingdom to Come* (London: Haus Publishing, 2015) at vi.

the urging of an Imperial Federalism, establishment of an Imperial Parliament and Grand Council of the Empire (potentially including colonial representation at Westminster). This never happened, and the Empire took a different route, including Dominion self-government, with looser imperial connections. A federal UK was also under discussion around the same time. Thus, FS Oliver, a Scottish liberal imperial unionist, fearing disintegration as a potential consequence of Irish home rule, suggested both the reconstitution of the UK on a federal basis, and an imperial union. Oliver wrote the monograph, *Alexander Hamilton: An Essay on American Union* (1906), spelling out what he took to be parallels between the British Empire, and the situation that had faced Hamilton, namely, 'how may we convert a voluntary league of states, terminable upon a breath, into a firm union'.[47] Oliver thought that the solution lay in the construction of an imperial union. But of course, nothing came of the movement for a Greater Britain, nor or a federal UK. The Empire came to an end. Will the same happen to the UK Union?

We now explore some other unions. Space dictates a limited survey, but the examples cited are chosen for their relevance to the UK Union.

7.3.2 Austria-Hungary

Austria-Hungary from 1867 to 1918 provides a good example of a complex composite State, with some parallels to offer the British Union. In the earlier modern period, Austria's Habsburg dynasty had been a major European imperial power, although its influence had lessened by the nineteenth century. Hungary was fully part of this empire, having come under Habsburg rule in 1699, when 150 years of at least partial Ottoman control ended. The *Pragmatic Sanction*, which provided for imperial succession, was adopted from 1713, and acknowledged the distinct existence of Hungary, under an overarching Habsburg union. Rather like the British Empire, however, there had never been a centralized imperial Constitution for the Austrian Reich. Indeed, as Wheatley remarks,[48] until the 1848 revolutions, the Austrian Empire's constitutional law and history were not even within the university syllabus. Within a half century, this changed dramatically, and universities became powerhouses of Public law, with standard works promulgated by figures such as Georg Jellinek, Eugen Ehrlich, Hans Kelsen, Hersch Lauterpacht, and Alfred Verdross.

However, Hungary sought greater autonomy in the nineteenth century. Austria was defeated in battle both by the French (1859) as well as by Prussia at Koniggratz in 1866, an event which concluded Austria's dominance of the

[47] FS Oliver, *Alexander Hamilton: An Essay on American Union* (London: Thomas Nelson & Sons, 1906) at 476.

[48] Natasha Wheatley, *The Temporal Life of States: Central Europe and the Transformation of Modern Sovereignty*, PhD thesis. (now published as Natasha Wheatley, *The Temporal Life of States: Central Europe and the Transformation of Modern Sovereignty* (Princeton NJ: Princeton University Press, 2023).

Holy Roman Empire. Austria then needed to retain its multinational empire in the face of centrifugal forces. It was in these circumstances that the legal and political settlement – named the *Ausgleich* in German and *Kiegyezés* in Hungarian (in English the 'Compromise') – of the dual monarchy of 1867 came about.

7.3.2.1 The 'Compromise': Its Nature

The 'Compromise' of 1867 consisted of a legal agreement between the Hungarian Parliament and Habsburg monarchy, and a separate law issued by the Austrian Parliament. There was no common imperial Parliament,[49] and the Austrian and Hungarian governments were responsible to their respective Parliaments. The Austro-Hungarian union, or 'dual monarchy', whereby Austria and Hungary were coequal partners, provided internal autonomy while limited imperial common affairs (foreign affairs, war, and finances for war and foreign affairs) were managed by three Joint Ministries appointed by the Crown. They were not responsible to any unified common imperial forum but instead to separate Delegations deputized by the Austrian and the Hungarian Parliaments, which met alternately in Vienna and Budapest. However, the Compromise agreement made no conclusive provision on other potential matters of joint interest, such as state debt, customs, and interstate commerce. These were regulated instead by a separate Commercial Compromise, renewable every 10 years.

7.3.2.2 Issues

7.3.2.2.1 Unique and Unprecedented

It was recognized at the time that this was a unique and unprecedented legal phenomenon. Even the dual sovereignty of federalism, as found in the USA, did not match this. The *Ausgleich* was mysterious. Louis Eisenmann, in his classic 1904 study, *Le compromis austro-hongrois*, described it as 'A regime woven of contradictions, with its unity which is a duality, with its parity which means inequality, its constitutionalism which implies absolutism.'[50] British historian, RW Seton-Watson, descried the dualist theory as 'almost as theological as the doctrine of the Trinity',[51] noting that, while in foreign relations there might be unity, in internal matters, at least in Hungary, unity was disavowed.

One explanation for the mystery of the *Ausgleich* lies in the fact that it was crafted out of two very different agreements – one between the Monarch and the Hungarian Parliament, and the other between the Monarch and the

[49] Indeed, § 28 of the Hungarian Law XII of 1867 expressly declared any form of central Parliament unacceptable to Hungary.

[50] Louis Eisenmann, *Le Compromis Austro-Hongrois de 1867: Étude sur le Dualisme* (Paris: societe nouvelle de libraire et d'edition, 1904) 639.

[51] RW Seton-Watson, 'The Austro-Hungarian Ausgleich of 1867' (1939) 19 Slavonic and East European Review 134.

Austrian Parliament. There was no legal agreement between Austria and Hungary. The relationship between these two laws of the two parliaments was unclear – the statutes were not virtually identical, as in the case of the Acts of Union of the English and Scottish Parliaments and the Acts of Union of the Irish and British Parliaments. These two laws were also drafted in German and in Magyar – and this caused problems. For example, the Austrian statute used the term '*gemeinsam*' for the shared areas of war and foreign affairs – which might be translated as 'common', but also as 'unified' or 'unitary'.[52] This interpretation was rejected in Hungary where the relevant term '*együttes*', signified two separate sovereign States working together but not on the basis of a unified polity and policy. And so they could reject the existence of any common Reich.

7.3.2.2.2 Sovereignty

One significant conclusion of the 1878 Congress of Berlin was that Austria-Hungary take over the administration of Bosnia-Herzegovina. This was to prove a cause of resentment, as the aggravation of the Balkan situation was a major cause of the First World War. However, for the more limited purposes of this chapter, it was significant that this mandate over Bosnia was assigned to emperor Franz Joseph, as if he reigned over a unitary State. But things were much more complex. Austria-Hungary was known as a 'dual monarchy' or 'dual State'. But how could there be a 'dual monarchy' when there was only one monarch – namely Franz Joseph? However, Hungary judged Franz Joseph as two separate juridical persons – namely, the emperor of Austria and the king of Hungary, each with distinct rights. Furthermore, what is a dual State? Hungarian legal scholars, such as Ernő Nagy, described the relationship of Austria to Hungary as that of two sovereign States.[53] While some aspects of these two distinct sovereignties were exercised in common, distinctness was more apparent in other areas. Citizens of Austria were not recognized as citizens of Hungary nor vice versa, and Hungarian scholar, Heinrich Marczali, argued that Austrians citizens were 'foreigners' under Hungarian constitutional law, at least as far as some activities were concerned.[54]

7.3.2.2.3 International Law

The complex nature of dual monarchy sovereignty also evokes the relationship between international law and constitutional law (already encountered in the chapter on Sovereignty[55]). For, if both Austria and Hungary possessed legal

[52] Edmund Bernatzik, *Die österreichischen Verfassungsgesetze* (Wien: Manz, 1911) 452.

[53] Ernst [Ernő] Nagy, 'Ungarn: A. Staatsrecht', in Mischler and Ulbrich (eds.), *Österreichisches Staatswörterbuch* (Wien: Alfred Hölder, 1909) 587.

[54] Marczali, *Ungarisches Verfassungsrecht* (JCB Mohr, 1911) 39.

[55] This was a feature of the British Empire, with a sometimes permeable boundary between constitutional, imperial and international law. E.g. Benton, 'From International Law to Imperial Constitutions: The Problem of Quasi-Sovereignty, 1870–1900' (2008) 26(3) Law and History Review 595.

sovereignty and their citizens could be aliens, at least for some purposes, in the other part of the realm, then was their relationship not better characterized by international law rather than constitutional law? And did this mean that Hungary, as a sovereign State, had legal personality in international law? So claimed some Hungarian commentators, such as Gyula Andrássy, Prime Minister of Hungary at the time of the *Ausgleich*, who contended that the 1867 *Ausgleich* had an international character.[56] However, not everyone agreed, especially Austrian legal scholars. In his 1910 treatise, Austrian historian Harold Steinacker argued that the *Ausgleich* involved external unity and internal duality, that the empire was suspended somewhere between constitutional and international law and concluded that the actual legal nature of the empire was insoluble.[57] The Austrian jurist Hermann Bidermann put it this way:

> it is not a simple, unified but rather a *plural*, compound polity. Everything else is doubtful or at least contested, in particular: how many states does it consist of? what are they called? what is their legal relationship to one another? do they together form a state-of-states or a federal state [*Staatenstaat oder einen Bundesstaat*]? or is their union is to be considered merely as a state confederation [*Staatenbund*], so that together they don't form a state at all, but rather merely hang together in international law?[58]

Wheatley uses the engaging metaphor of 'two sets of Russian dolls joined at the hip' and captures the perplexing issue of the empire's legal status in her discussion entitled: *The Arithmetic of Witches: Translating A Common Empire.*[59]

7.3.2.2.4 Comparisons with the British Constitution

Was it possible for Austria-Hungary to be two distinct sovereign States and yet maintain a common foreign policy under the emperor? And yet its continuation depended on these two almost irreconcilable contentions. The mysteries and contradictions of the *Ausgleich* recall a central quandary of the British Constitution and UK Union. On the one hand, a diversity and self-governance of component parts has been recognized, whether of devolved nations or Dominions of the empire. In contrast, Westminster parliamentary sovereignty has been held to apply, undermining diversity. But can a legally workable union continue under irreconcilable constitutional circumstances? Reflection on Austria-Hungary thus provides a valuable comparison for the British empire and UK Union.[60]

[56] J Andrássy, *Ungarns Ausgleich mit Österreich vom Jahre 1867*, (Leipzig, Duncker & Humblot, 1897) 171–172.

[57] H Steinacker, *Zur Frage nach der rechtlichen Natur der österreichisch-ungarischen Gesamtmonarchie* (Wien: Fromme, 1910) 8.

[58] Bidermann, *Die Rechtliche Natur der österreichisch-ungarischen Monarchie* (Wien: Fromme, 1877) 4.

[59] Wheatley, *The Temporal Life of States.* I learned much from this wonderful work, and this section follows some arguments she made.

[60] E.g. A Kiralfy, 'Independent Legal Systems under Common Dynastic Rule: England and Hungary' (1990) 11(1) Jl of Legal History 118.

7.3.2.3 The Collapse of an Impossible System?

Archduke Franz Ferdinand, heir to the Habsburg monarchy, favoured amending the *Ausgleich,* and set up a 'brains trust', which recommended replacing the *Ausgleich* with a centralized federal arrangement, with much greater autonomy for specific regions. Another similar proposal for a 'United States of Great Austria' was made in 1906 by the Romanian lawyer and politician Aurel Popovici. These suggestions were closely contemporaneous to those for a 'Greater Britain'. However, Franz Ferdinand was assassinated in Sarajevo in 1914, an event that triggered the outbreak of the First World War, and also put an end to any plans to carry out his revision programme. Other reflections on Austria-Hungary highlight its unwieldy, unmanageable nature. Many scholars, such as AJP Taylor, and Jacques Droz,[61] were highly critical of the *Ausgleich* and, according to Seton Watson, 'The history of the forty-nine years following 1867 is the history of the gradual crumbling and collapse of an impossible system.'[62]

The Austro-Hungarian empire collapsed after the First World War, and self-determination and nationalism were given a boost of a different sort by the Treaty of Versailles. This ushered in an era of nation States in Europe, which was to prove no more peaceful than what preceded it.

7.3.2.4 Analogies with Ireland and Scotland

The salience of Austria-Hungary to the UK was recognized during its existence. It also provided inspiration for Irish and Scottish nationalists seeking greater autonomy within the UK Union. Indeed, even Gladstone cited the Hungarian analogy in promoting the Second Irish Home Rule Bill in Westminster.

7.3.2.4.1 Ireland

WB Yeats described Ireland as 'the Hungary of the West' in his poem *How Ferencz Renyi Kept Silent.* Members of the 'Young Ireland' group identified the parallels for Ireland in Hungary's search for political freedom, as did Arthur Griffith, who founded Sinn Féin. Griffith had argued that the Act of Union of Great Britain and Ireland in 1800 was illegal and that, as a result, the Anglo-Irish dual monarchy under Grattan's Parliament and the 'Constitution of 1782' had endured, in theory, if not in actuality. In this way, he argued, the Irish Constitution, just like the earlier 1848 Hungarian Constitution, still lived, and had not been subsumed in a greater empire. Writing almost contemporaneously with Griffith, the Austrian jurist Hans von Frisch, wrote,

> The formation of large states through the thorough incorporation of smaller states … is a relatively simple and uninteresting process. How different though, if the individual life-guarantees of the incorporated entities did not completely

[61] AJP Taylor, *The Habsburg Monarchy, 1809–1918* (Chicago: University of Chicago Press, 1976), 78; J Droz, *L'Europe centrale* (Paris: Payot, 1960), 161–165.

[62] Seton-Watson, 'The Austro-Hungarian Ausgleich of 1867'.

> end with the incorporation, if the parts united in the integral state continue to exist much more as corporations subordinated under the new state.[63]

Such a reflection carried much of interest for Scottish and Irish writers seeking to demonstrate how their nation's sovereignty had not in fact been completely overridden by Acts of Union, but could instead be characterized as a State-entity in its own right.

Griffith's account of nineteenth-century Hungarian history may have been somewhat tendentious and selective, but its real weight lay in his advocating that Ireland adopt a disruptive parliamentary policy in Westminster similar to that previously pursued by Hungary, which became known as the *Sinn Féin Policy*. In 1904, Griffith expanded on these ideas in a series of articles in the *United Irishman*, which were subsequently published as *The Resurrection of Hungary* (which sold 5,000 copies within its first 24 hours) – a work described as 'one of the seminal documents of modern Irish history'.[64] Griffith himself was not a monarchist, but he did accept that many Irish would find continuation of the monarchy acceptable, if Ireland could be independent from and equal in status to Great Britain. In this way, he offered a different path from both the existing parliamentarism he regarded as ineffective, and the alternative route of political violence.

7.3.2.4.2 Scotland

In the run up to the 2014 independence referendum for Scotland, the Scottish Constitutional Commission[65] issued a discussion paper on 'Secure Autonomy' for Scotland. This paper attempted to reconcile the existence of the UK Union with the right of the people of Scotland to determine the form of government best suited to their needs. Both devolution and federalism were rejected as not offering any realistic solution, given the doctrine of parliamentary sovereignty. Instead, the Commission paper sought an Autonomy Act for Scotland and a solution quite similar to the 'Compromise' of the Dual Monarchy in 1867.

The argument for secure autonomy was made on the basis that, whereas the doctrine of parliamentary sovereignty dictates that Parliament may not bind its successors, and so no devolution scheme may be safely regarded as permanent, Parliament can *renounce* its sovereignty. It advocated that the UK Parliament legislate a Scotland (Autonomy) Act, of a comparable form to post-colonial Independence Acts, whose effect would be to enact an irreversible renunciation of Westminster's sovereignty over Scotland. The discussion

[63] H von Frisch, 'Die Stellung der Kronländer im Gefüge der österreichischen Verfassung: Eine Rundfrage' (Wien: Österreichische Zeitschrift für öffentliches Recht, Sonderheft: Länderautonomie, 1916) 31.

[64] Donal McCartney, 'The Political Use of History in the Work of Arthur Griffith' (1973) Journal of Contemporary History at 9.

[65] The Constitutional Commission was founded in 2005 by John Drummond (former Convenor of the Independence Convention) and Canon Kenyon Wright (former Convenor of the Scottish Constitutional Convention).

paper also suggested that, with Scotland's consent, certain essential functions could be shared with the UK Government and Parliament (mostly those necessary to sustain the UK as one single State for international law) such as foreign affairs, defence, royal succession and the currency, and perhaps also a customs union and single market, as well as free movement. All other matters would be for Scotland to determine. In this way, the authors of the paper claimed that there would be a new Union, which would be equal and consensual, not the 'incorporating union' of 1707. They cited historical examples of such a union, in which the Austro-Hungarian example featured prominently. As with Griffith's suggestion a century earlier for Ireland, the argument for Scottish Secure Autonomy was presented as one attractive to moderate supporters of independence, and maybe to those who would still wish to be able to call themselves British, while maintaining self-determination for Scotland.

Nonetheless, the example of Austria-Hungary illustrates the problems of a compromise of a dual monarchy, not least, unresolved debates over sovereignty, as well as the need for workable amendment procedures and joint arbitration mechanisms (which also proved problematic in the Brexit context). But at the very least, the Scottish paper and Griffith's early twentieth-century arguments illustrate how the singular example of Austria-Hungary has continued to be a relevant example for twenty-first-century nations seeking greater autonomy within a union.

7.3.3 The Holy Roman Empire

Although the formerly feudal monarchies of England, Spain, and France gradually transformed into more unified States in the modern period, this was not the case with the Holy Roman Empire, which continued as a loose association of States until the early nineteenth century, when it was dissolved by Napoleon. James Bryce strikingly claimed that Francis II's forced 1806 abdication had extinguished 'the oldest political institution in the world.'[66] We might also add, one of the very largest, for in its latter days it was geographically Europe's second largest polity, surpassed in size only by Russia. And yet, it has been too easily forgotten.

The Holy Roman Empire was a multi-ethnic, but mainly Germanic, compound of territories in central Europe that developed during the Early Middle Ages and continued until its dissolution. The Empire came into being in 800, when Pope Leo III crowned Charlemagne Emperor of the Romans (over an area the *Economist* describes as 'eerily similar' to the original EEC – West Germany, France, Belgium, the Netherlands, Luxembourg, and Italy[67]). Over time, the Empire had evolved into a decentralized, elective monarchy composed of

[66] James Bryce, *The Holy Roman Empire* (London: Macmillan, 1864) 1.

[67] 'European Disunion Done Right', *The Economist*, 22 December 2012. Indeed, *The Economist* named its European column after Charlemagne.

hundreds of sub-units: kingdoms, principalities, duchies, counties, prince-bishoprics, Free Imperial Cities, and other domains, whose rulers governed their land independently from the Emperor. The Emperor never directly governed the whole Empire. There was no imperial foreign policy, and there existed no formal organization and no clearly defined territory.

A select few princes known as Electors would elect the Emperor, although the office of Emperor was frequently hereditary, as when the Habsburgs ruled almost continuously from 1452 until 1806. The Empire had no formal Constitution, only some basic laws, among the most important Charles IV's Golden Bull of 1356,[68] and the 1532 *Constitutio Criminalis Carolina* (one of the most important criminal codes of early modern Europe). Yet even significant laws, such as the Golden Bull, were less an assertion of the sovereign's will (who in any case lacked coercive power) than a practice of constant human interaction and renegotiation.[69] The Imperial Diet was not a legislature by contemporary standards, but more a central gathering where issues were negotiated, which moved around until it finally settled in Regensburg.

The Empire was not a State in the modern sense but a confederation of States. It lacked an imperial capital, and, unlike the modern nation State, did not demand its inhabitants' exclusive loyalty, but instead permitted diverse communities within its borders. Integration throughout the Empire was accomplished by reciprocal validation of member status rather than administrative centralization – a practice that brings to mind the 'mutual recognition' doctrine of today's EU. Indeed, the Empire was not an empire in the sense of many modern imperialist theories, which interpret empire through the lens of European colonial power, as having a central government coercively imposing its orders on peripheral regions. However, the Holy Roman Empire had no core, nor even an official capital. Instead, power was devolved, multiple and plural. And yet, the Empire did provide a transnational form of governance, and in this sense, it could be seen as imperial, forming a distinct civilization.

7.3.3.1 Criticism and Re-evaluation

It became common to view the Empire with derision, as an archaic relic of the middle ages, a dysfunctional polity that hampered Germany's development into a modern nation-State. An early such example came in 1667, from Samuel von Pufendorf who described the Empire as 'a somehow irregular body, similar to a monster'.[70] Voltaire famously remarked that it was neither holy, nor Roman, nor an empire.[71] And, from across the Atlantic, even to a federalist

[68] The eighteenth-century jurist, Johann von Ludewig, wrote 2,500 pages of commentary on this Bull in *Vollständige Erläuterung der Güldenen Bulle* … (Frankfurt und Leipzig 1716).

[69] Barbara Stollberg-Rilinger, *Des Kaisers alte Kleider: Verfassungsgeschichte und Symbolsprache des Alten Reiches* (Munich: CH Beck, 2008).

[70] '*irregulare aliquod corpus et monstro simile*' (Samuel von Pufendorf, *De statu imperii Germanici* (1667) VI §9, 198).

[71] Voltaire, *Essay on the Customs and the Spirit of Nation* 1756, chapter 70 on Europe.

such as James Madison, seeking a workable decentralized structure, the Empire was 'a nerveless body; incapable of regulating its own members; insecure against external dangers and agitated with unceasing fermentations in its own bowels.'[72] And of course, much of the Thirty Years War, fought over religion (and one of the most violent, bloody wars in history) was fought mainly within Empire territory. So the Empire was by no means always a peaceful place to be.

However, in the past 50 years or so, there has been a reappraisal of the Empire, and a recognition of its ability to protect liberties, through the rule of law. For example, Peter Wilson's[73] work argues that the Empire provided effective structures to balance central authority and provincial autonomies; sustain corporate liberties; and arbitrate disputes among its members. Indeed, the successes of its decentralized nature ensured its lasting existence. The Emperor was never intended to exercise sovereignty in the modern Bodinian sense, but to support the Church, providing some sort of moral leadership by seeking consensus, and allowing different parts of the empire to co-exist. And even Pufendorf's 'monster' designation of the Empire was a veiled compliment.[74] For its 'monstrous' structure permitted freedom and diversity impossible in more absolutist States.

The more positive evaluation of the Empire has led to further comparisons between the Empire and the EU. Wilson, for example, has contrasted the 'essentialist definitions of identity' that developed in Europe after the Empire's demise, with 'the Empire's ability to accommodate different identities within a common framework'.[75] Wilson certainly does not suggest that the Empire provided a model for the EU[76] – indeed, the inequality and social standards that applied within the Empire's time would today be untenable. Yet this more sympathetic analysis of Empire suggests that something more ambiguous and complicated than the absolute sovereignty of the State may provide a more durable and attractive prospect for Europe today.

But this comparison also brings out another point. The Holy Roman Empire may seem alien to British eyes, but less so to Central European ones, where it flourished for hundreds of years. Likewise, the complicated structures and shared sovereignty of the EU perhaps appear less unpalatable to countries formerly part of the Empire.

7.3.4 The German Confederation (1815–1866)

Napoleon brought the Holy Roman Empire to an end. But after Napoleon's fall, the 1815 Congress of Vienna deliberately established the German Confederation

72 Alexander Hamilton and James Madison, *The Federalist*, No. 19.

73 Peter H Wilson, *The Holy Roman Empire: A Thousand Years of Europe's History* (London: Allen Lane, 2016).

74 At least according to The Economist, 'European Disunion Done Right'.

75 Wilson, *The Holy Roman Empire*, at 290, 292.

76 Others come closer to this, e.g. Peter Claus Hartmann, *Kulturgeschichte des Heiligen Römischen Reiches* (Wien: Böhlau, 2001).

(*Bund*) to replace the former Empire, support monarchical government (particularly those who feared a radical French style revolution) and provide a mutual defence system for its members. As with the Holy Roman Empire, the Confederation comprised a multitude of smallish but varied States, along with the two much larger European powers – Austria and Prussia. Indeed, until 1837, the British monarch was also a member of the Confederation, in their capacity of King of Hanover.

The German Confederation was constituted by the Federal Act of 1815 and the Vienna Final Act of 1820, which specified that, regarding external relations, it 'constitutes a collective Power, bound together in political unity'. However, whatever the nature of this unity, the Federation lacked exclusive competence, and its members maintained their own full international rights, which some made full use of. Most of the Federation's specified powers related to security and defence. There was little provision for economic integration, and it was for that reason that a majority of Federation members (excluding Austria) established their own *Zollverein*, or Customs Union in 1834 – a development that was to prove key for the economic prosperity and integration of Germany.

Generally, the Confederation was rather weak in design. Indeed, it has been commented that the Confederation 'had some marked similarities to the League of Nations, and, like that organisation, it left the internal affairs of the members unaffected by its existence.'[77] Dissatisfaction with the Confederation was expressed, in ways familiar to those pressing for completion of the EU Single Market. For example the *Duesseldorfer Zeitung*, in 1843 regretted that:

> … we have instead of one Germany, 38 German states, almost the same number of courts, as many representative bodies, 38 distinct legal codes and administrations, embassies and consulates. What an enormous saving it would be if all of that were taken care of by one central government …[78]

There existed only one central institution – the standing Diet or Assembly located in Frankfurt-am-Main, which operated a rather complex voting system (rather like that of the present day EU) so that neither Austria nor Prussia could outvote the other members. Just as in the case of the US Articles of Confederation, federal power was weak, and there was no centralized monetary system, nor regulation of interstate commerce. However, unlike the Diet of the Holy Roman Empire, the Federation Diet could promulgate its own legislation, which was directly effective in the EU sense, meaning that such laws did not have to be ratified by members, but were immediately binding when published. According to Christopher Clark, one such law concerned clandestine information collection.[79]

77 GW Keeton, 'The Zollverein and the Common Market' (1963) 16 Current Legal Problems 1 at 4.

78 WO Henderson, *The Rise of German Industrial Power, 1834–1914* (Berkeley and Los Angeles: University of California Press, 1975), 40.

79 C Clark, 'Germany 1815–1848', in J Breuilly (ed.), *Nineteenth-Century Germany* (London: Arnold, 2001).

Although Austria preferred a weak cooperative structure (many Austrian territories, such as Hungary, were non Germanic and outside the Confederation in any case) Prussia favoured a stronger confederation, geographically identified with Germany. It was a Prussian proposal – that the Confederation be reorganized – that sparked the war that would end the Confederation. In 1866, Austria was defeated at Königgratz, and Germany unified around Prussia, and the Confederation was dissolved by the Prague peace treaty.

7.3.5 The United Netherlands

The United Netherlands was a confederation up to 1795. An agreement had been secured at the treaty of Utrecht, in 1579, whereby a group of northern sovereign provinces of the Netherlands formed a loose confederation, a union of mutual support against the Hapsburgs. This republic of seven united provinces was officially recognized at the treaty of Westphalia in 1648. Thus, the Union of Utrecht became the constitutional basis of the United Netherlands (or Dutch Republic, as it was also known). Members of the Union were required to aid each other against external threats, and, although provinces retained the right to make international treaties, this was subject to consent of the generality. There existed a States-General which promulgated ordinances over a wide range of subjects, including war, shipping, religion and coinage. During this time, the Netherlands gradually broke away from Spain. Notably the province of Holland was much larger than the other provinces, making up over half of the population and wealth, and with predominant power.

The United Netherlands was also one of a number of unions and confederations – including those in ancient Greece, and the Holy Roman Empire – researched by the American federalists and criticized by them for their weak central government. In the *Federalist Papers* James Madison and Alexander Hamilton coruscated the United Netherlands: 'What are the characters which practice has stamped upon it? Imbecility in the government; discord among the provinces; foreign influence and indignities; a precarious existence in peace, and peculiar calamities from war.'[80] This criticism was surely somewhat unfair, because the seventeenth century produced the golden age of the Dutch republic, which became a premier trading nation with a colonial empire of considerable wealth, although it declined in the eighteenth century. In some ways, the United Netherlands provides an interesting comparison with Britain. Both countries were highly dependent on maritime trade, both possessed an overseas empire and both were generally Protestant. However, the United Netherlands was brought to an end by the French Revolution (with a short-lived Batavian Republic established in 1795 under French protection). Then, from 1815 to 1839, a new Union of the United Netherlands was formed, whereby the Southern Netherlands (today Belgium) was merged with the

[80] *Federalist Papers no. 20.*

northern provinces in a union ruled by a Protestant Dutch-speaking monarch. There were tensions between the two parts of the Netherlands and the remaining history will be considered in the section on Disunion.

7.3.6 Norway-Sweden

Sweden and Norway formed a personal union from 1814 to 1905. This union came into being at the end of the Napoleonic wars, partly engineered by the Great powers at the 1815 Congress of Vienna as a reward for Sweden's aid in those wars. The Norwegian people were not consulted on this new union and the Swedish people had very little say. It was not the first Scandic Union. The Kalmar union (1397–1523) had united Sweden and Norway with Denmark, and Denmark and Norway had been in union until the Treaty of Kiel in 1814, when Norway was transferred to Sweden. A formal Act of Union was confirmed by the parliaments of Norway and Sweden in 1815. Although the monarchy and foreign policy (matters of the royal prerogative) were common institutions of the union, Norway and Sweden had their own Constitutions, governments and parliaments, and separate legal, economic and cultural systems. There were two separate capitals – Christiania (Oslo) and Stockholm – although the Norwegian government divided its time between the two, so as to be closer to the Stockholm-based monarch. Therefore, this union was no incorporation of Norway into a greater Sweden, but a confederation of two States that shared a king.

The new union was officially called The United Kingdoms of Norway and Sweden. The Swedes and the Norwegians were not on particularly good terms, and although both were predominantly Protestant (so difference of religion was not an issue as with Britain and Ireland) there were other issues. As Jackson has written, 'With Sweden and Norway … flags, coats of arms, and royal titles all fed into a festering rancour with union.'[81] The renowned Norwegian explorer, Nansen, complained that Sweden had configured the coat of arms 'just as though Norway were actually a province of Sweden …'[82]

Another bone of contention for Norway was that their Constitution did not give them the power to manage their own foreign affairs, which included commercial matters, and was a much greater part of the Norwegian than Swedish economy.[83] Norway had self-government, but its foreign affairs was conducted by the Swedish foreign minister. In 1905, King Oscar formally denied Norway the right to separate consular representation, vetoing a measure which had been agreed to by a joint committee from the two nations. This was enough for the Norwegian Parliament to declare that the king had violated the Constitution, thereby dissolving the union, peacefully, if with some acrimony.

[81] Alvin Jackson, 'Union States, Civil Society and National Symbols in the Nineteenth Century: Comparing United Kingdoms' (2019) 58(2) Scandinavica at 68.

[82] F Nansen, *Norway and the Union with Sweden* (London: Macmillan, 1905) at 28 n1.

[83] R Berg, 'Norway's Foreign Politics during the Union with Sweden, 1814–1905: A Reconsideration' (2020) 31(1) Diplomacy & Statecraft 1–21.

7.3.7 The European Union

What does it mean to say that the EU is a 'Union'? It is not a Union in the same sense as the UK or US, as in those countries, there now exists only one State, previous distinct States being subsumed under the Union's Statehood. That has not happened with the EU – each of its member States preserves its external sovereignty in international law. However, as discussed at the outset of this chapter, 'Union' can have many senses. Although the EU is not a political union, as it does not form a single political entity, it displays certain aspects of that, i.e. centralized institutions such as a Parliament, Court, Commission and Council and exclusive competence to promulgate certain laws. It is much more unified economically than politically – and of course, its previous name was the European Economic Community, which was established by the 1957 Treaty of Rome. The EU includes a Customs Union, Single Market, and a common currency for many of its States, although it does not have a common economic or fiscal policy. Nonetheless, even the EEC went beyond a free trade area: in addition to free movement of goods, the Treaty of Rome provided for free movement of workers, enterprises, and capital. It also contained the provisions for common agricultural, competition and transport policies, and made some provision for social policy in the field of employment.

Since the 1992 Maastricht Treaty (TEU) came into force, the EU has formally been in existence. This treaty consolidated the Union, introducing a three pillar structure, composed of the EC (a title replacing the 'EEC', to account for the now broader range of Community affairs) a Common Foreign and Security Policy and Justice and Home Affairs – all three nonetheless to be served by a single institutional framework. However, it was not really a very unified construct, as some pillars were more intergovernmental in nature, thus allowing a smaller role for the Commission and ECJ. This, along with all the protocols, opt-outs and declarations, made it unwieldy in nature.

The legal nature of the EU remains controversial to this day, raising questions as to its identity, and whether the term 'Union' is any more meaningful than the 'Community' that preceded it. The EU is neither a State, nor a traditional international organization. It has certain 'State-like' characteristics, such as a wide exclusive legislative competence, institutions that function in ways comparable to State government, and a doctrine of the supremacy of EU law. Its treaties express a commitment to democracy, the rule of law and fundamental rights. However, it lacks other State-like traits, such as a common army, direct powers of taxation and general competence in welfare, health policy and education. EU citizenship is not free-standing but derivable only from member State citizenship. So the EU lacks the full sovereignty often seen as characteristic of the modern State. The EU also lacks external sovereignty in most areas of international relations, a key feature of the State in international law, and it may conclude treaties only for those matters within its field of competence. And it has no power to wage war or to make peace. Its system of governance is incomplete, and it lacks the legal means, administration, finances and coercive force of its member States – and so relies on them to support it in many instances (as did the US Confederation from 1781 to 1787).

In conclusion, the EU is polycentric in character – its power is fragmented and dispersed, and constantly transformed. As Philip Allott has written, the EU 'represents Europe seen darkly through a constitutional looking glass, full of distorted images of familiar constitutional forms.'[84] It seems to lack its own freestanding identity – a fact which is underlined by A4(2) TEU which stipulates that 'The Union shall respect the equality of member States before the Treaties as well as their national identities'.

There has been unease over the EU's *sui generis* approach, or its *Sonderweg*.[85] Attempts to enact a formal EU Constitution were rejected in 2005. In fact, even to mention that the EU might have a 'Constitutional' identity is to provoke ire from some quarters. Back in 2001, at a symposium entitled *Can Europe have a Constitution?*,[86] Miguel Poiares Maduro presented a paper with the title, 'Europe and the Constitution: what if this is as Good as it Gets?'[87] Many were urging for an EU Constitution, but Maduro's title was perhaps prescient, and at least for the UK and its relations with the EU, that indeed was as good as it got.

7.3.7.1 'Ever Closer Union?'

Prior to the Brexit referendum, the UK's Conservative Government sought to renegotiate the terms of the UK's EU membership. In particular, the UK took issue with the term 'ever closer union of the peoples of Europe' in the preamble to the EU Treaty. Then Prime Minister, David Cameron, expressed an objection to 'being dragged into a state called Europe',[88] which suggests that this wording inexorably compels all EU States towards a federal Europe. However, a closer look at this term undermines the stated aim of the Prime Minister in renegotiating it.

The expression has been present in EU law since the EEC's very earliest days. The EU treaties actually refer to 'ever closer union of the *peoples*' of Europe, not the governments. They also in this context employ the word 'union' with a small u, unlike those references to the EU in the Treaties which use a capital U. Additionally, the current treaty references to 'ever closer union' do not create

84 Philip Allott, 'The Crisis of European Constitutionalism' (1997) 34 CMLR 439, at 466.

85 JHH Weiler, 'Federalism without Constitutionalism: Europe's *Sonderweg*', in K Nicolaidis and R Howse (eds.), *The Federal Vision* (Oxford: Oxford University Press, 2001).

86 An edition of the King's College Law Journal for 2001 was given over to this. See e.g. S Douglas-Scott 'Constituting Europe: In Defence of Public Reason' (2001) 12 King's Law Journal 75.

87 M Poiares Maduro, 'Europe and the Constitution: What If This Is as Good as It Gets?', in JHH Weiler and M Wind (eds.), *European Constitutionalism beyond the State* (Cambridge: Cambridge University Press, 2003).

88 David Cameron made this statement when reporting to the House of Commons on the 2015 June European Council.

any specific EU competences, nor require that the EU continuously expand its powers, nor impose specific obligations on EU member States. Therefore it seems that the phrase 'ever closer union' does not imply the objective for the EU of a super-State or Federal Union. On the other hand, the TEU quite clearly obliges the EU to respect the history, culture and traditions of the peoples of Europe (Preamble and Article 3(3)TEU) and to respect the national identities of the member States, their fundamental structures, political and constitutional, as well as their essential State functions (Article 4(2)). So it is also arguable that national sovereignty is adequately protected from any encroachments that the phrase 'ever closer union' might wreak.

In conclusion, the EU, although possessing some State-like qualities, is at present a Union of separate States that retain their sovereignty in international law, and in a large chunk of their domestic law. It is not a Union in the same sense as the federal USA, nor the 'Union State' of the UK.

7.3.8 The United States of America

The USA declared its independence from Great Britain in 1776. Arrangements had been made for common governance of the newly formed USA by the second Continental Congress which met in Philadelphia in 1775, and which, of necessity, took over the essential powers previously exercised by the British Government, including raising money for the war effort, maintaining troops and enforcing trade regulations. But the weakness of these arrangements soon became apparent and so the Congress adopted the Articles of Confederation and Perpetual Union, which came into force between the thirteen states in 1781. Notably, the Articles of Confederation were drafted so as to ensure State sovereignty, with Article 2 declaring: 'Each state retains its sovereignty, freedom and independence, and every power, jurisdiction and right, which is not by this Confederation expressly delegated to the United States in Congress assembled'.

The Congress established by the Articles was constituted of members appointed by state legislatures, who acted according to their states' instructions and could be recalled at will (Article 5). But the really fundamental problem for the Confederation was that, although certain powers were allocated to the centre, it was a decentralized form of government, lacking essential powers and fundamentally weak. It could not regulate trade between the states, and, having no power to raise finances itself, was dependent on the states for funding. It also lacked the power to enforce sanctions against those states that ignored it. As a result, the Constitution drafted by the Philadelphia Convention in 1787 came to replace the Articles of Confederation.

The 1787 Constitution established a stronger federal government than the Confederation, with three branches – executive, legislative and judicial – along with a system of checks and balances so that no single branch would have too much power. The powers of the three major branches were set out in Articles 1–3 of the Constitution, and those powers not assigned to them were reserved to the states. The Constitution also required the states to give 'full faith and credit' to the laws, contracts, and judgements of other states. Congress was given new abilities to levy national taxes and control interstate commerce. Ten amendments were added as the Bill of Rights in 1791, and thereafter 17 more. Nonetheless, the 1787 Federal Constitution was clearly the result of a compromise – most particularly over slavery, states' rights and political representation. According to Kreitner, it was 'Neither a miracle in Philadelphia nor a solemn conclave of plain honest men – the Constitutional Convention was a series of intense hostage takings … with no satisfying resolution in sight.'[89]

There were disagreements over representation in the federal Congress. A compromise (proposed by the Connecticut delegation) narrowly passed – stipulating that each state be represented by two delegates in the Senate, but that in the House of Representatives there should be representation according to each state's population. However, this had the result that the less populous states enjoyed proportionately greater power in the Senate – a distinction that has only grown over time (today California has a population 67 times greater than that of Wyoming, the smallest state).

The issue of slavery was contentious from the very outset. The first problem was whether, and how, slave populations should be counted for a state's representation in the House of Representatives. The compromise was that each slave was to count as only three-fifths of the free population. An additional compromise prohibited Congress from banning the import of slaves until 1808. These compromises made it possible to secure agreement to the Constitution but left the controversial issue of slavery in place.

Therefore at base, the Constitution, and thus the US Union, was founded on compromise, on shaky foundations, repressing a conflict that finally erupted with the Civil War in 1861.

7.4 Disunion

So far, this chapter has discussed States coming together in some way to form unions. Now we consider the opposite process of disunion. This may occur in a number of ways. A union might dissolve into component parts, leaving nothing of the former union, as was the case with Austria-Hungary in 1919, or Czechoslovakia in 1992. In these cases, we are looking at *dissolution*, and will examine this further below. But most common is *secession*, whereby one part of a State removes itself from a larger entity. Notably, *decolonization* tended not to be seen as a case of secession or dissolution by the international legal order, although it became the most important way of creating a new State

[89] R Kreitner, *Break It up: Secession, Division, and the Secret History of America's Imperfect Union* (New York: Little Brown, 2020) 80.

in the second half of the twentieth century. However, according to the 1970 Declaration of Principles of International Law: 'the territory of a colony or other non-self-governing territory has, under the Charter, a status separate and distinct from the territory of the State administering it'.[90] UN membership grew from 51 member States in 1945 to 149 in 1984, largely due to decolonization. It has since increased to 193 members, due mainly to secession.[91]

7.4.1 Self-Determination

The principle of self-determination emerged at the time of the American Declaration of Independence and the French Revolution, both of which stressed that government should be responsible to the people.[92] Self-determination also featured strongly at the Paris Peace conference after the First World War, and was understood as the right of peoples to choose their government (although US President Woodrow Wilson avoided the term 'self-determination' in his fourteen-point Declaration to Congress in 1918). However, it proved virtually impossible to establish ethnically homogeneous States in territories which had previously been multi-ethnic empires (such as Austria-Hungary and the Ottoman empire). Further, those regions that had called for nation State status were themselves challenged by large minorities within their territory. Therefore, treaties on minority rights were adopted, limiting the sovereignty of the new post war States. Somewhat ironically, Hitler used the issue of minority rights to destabilize the peace settlement and push for annexation of the Sudetenland in 1938. After the Second World War, collective minority rights were seen as less pressing, and there was no explicit protection given to minority rights in either the Universal Declaration or the UN Charters of 1966.

7.4.1.1 The Right to Self-Determination in International Law

Self-determination denotes the legal right of people to decide their own destiny in the international order. This right is protected in the UN Charter and the International Covenant on Civil and Political Rights (ICCPR) as a right of 'all peoples.' So, for example, Art 1 ICCPR states: 'All peoples have the right of self-determination. By virtue of that right they freely determine their political status and freely pursue their economic, social and cultural development'.

However, it is not so easy to successfully assert a legal right to self-determination. In the years after the adoption of the UN Charter, self-determination was primarily associated with decolonization, and took the form

[90] These principles are embodied in UNGA Resolution 2625 (XXV).

[91] M Cohen (ed.), *Secession: International Law Perspectives* (Cambridge: Cambridge University Press, 2006) at 1.

[92] See e.g. *Antonio Cassese, Self-Determination of Peoples: A Legal Reappraisal* (Oxford: Oxford University Press, 1999).

of 'external self-determination' namely, a right to independent Statehood. But it was only applied for overseas (or 'saltwater') colonies, such as those of the former European empires in Africa and Asia. The UN General Assembly recognized the right of colonies to external self determination in its *1960 Declaration on the Granting of Independence to Colonial Countries and Peoples,* and the International Court of Justice (ICJ) then found the right to external self-determination in the colonial context had achieved the status of customary international law.[93]

However, there has been little support for a right to external self-determination beyond that colonial context. Even former colonies, having successfully invoked self-determination, rejected further claims to the right from within their own borders. In 2010, the ICJ, in its *Advisory Opinion* on the legality of Kosovo's secession from Serbia, avoided the issue of remedial secession, and instead restricted its *Opinion* to the narrower question of whether Kosovo's declaration of independence violated international law.[94] The ICJ found that international law does not prohibit declarations of independence. But by avoiding the issue of remedial secession, the ICJ did nothing to dispel doubts over the viability of non-colonial external self-determination claims. Indeed, Kosovo's secession has been disputed by many States.

Therefore, under international law, self-determination rarely equates with an *enforceable* right to secession and independence, and as currently understood it does not give rise to a right to Statehood outside of the colonial context. If a claim for self-determination is made by those within an existing State, the most that international law can guarantee is 'internal self-determination', which consists of human rights and democratic freedoms. Such an 'internal self-determination' was central to the League of Nations' resolution of the *Aaland Islands* issue.[95]

7.4.1.2 The Quebec Example

However, there may be some assistance regarding the right to self-determination from the Canadian Supreme Court. The Canadian province of Quebec has held two independence referendums, in 1980 and 1995. The 1995 referendum produced a very close result with 50 per cent voting to stay and 49 per cent to leave.

In 1998, the Canadian Supreme Court issued an *Advisory Opinion* at the request of the Canadian Government.[96] On the one hand, the Court found the Quebecois had no right to remedial secession. However, the Court also held that while Canadian law did not condone unilateral secession, the Constitution was 'not a straightjacket'. Canadian constitutional principles

[93] *Western Sahara, Advisory Opinion,* 1975 ICJ 12, at 110.

[94] *Advisory Opinion on Kosovo,* 2010 ICJ 403.

[95] *The Aaland Islands Question,* (1921) League of Nations Doc. B.7 21/68/106, at 27.

[96] *Reference re Secession of Quebec* [1998] 2 SCR 217, 2.

such as federalism, democracy, constitutionalism, the rule of law and respect for minorities could be used to outline the possibility of a negotiated secession. 'A clear majority vote in Quebec ... in favour of secession would confer *democratic legitimacy* which all of the other participants in Confederation would have to recognize'[97] – and this would require the remaining Canadian State to engage with Quebec in negotiations concerning separation. In this way, the Canadian Court distinguished the international right to self-determination from the constitutional principle of secession.

The Canadian Supreme Court's analysis of 'negotiated' self-determination has interesting implications. There has been a growing recognition that democracy must acknowledge the right to self-determination, and international law is now moving in the direction of 'a right to be heard', even if not to an enforceable right to secession.[98] This also conforms with the growing practice of recognizing self-determination not as a question of nationality or ethnicity but as a question of *democracy*.

7.4.2 Secession

Secession may occur in a number of ways. First, the seceding State may assert the right to self-determination – a right which, as discussed here, has rarely been successfully exercised outside of the colonial context. Secession may also occur constitutionally – as would have been the case if Scotland had voted by majority for independence in the 2014 referendum. Secession may also come about by war or revolution as with the American Declaration of Independence from Great Britain in 1776. Usually, with secession, the State from which the new State broke away will remain, as did Britain after 1776, but there will additionally be a new State. It has been said that secession is both revolutionary and conservative in nature. It is revolutionary, in that it challenges State sovereignty, but at the same time it is conservative, because the seceding State asserts a sovereignty of its own, creating a new State.[99]

Secession is usually justified either on the basis of a *free-standing* right to secede, or alternatively, as a right to *remedy* injustices caused by the larger State.[100] *Free-standing* theories proclaim the right either on a nationalist or democratic basis. Nationalist theories assert a moral value to a national, ethnic or culturally homogeneous group located in the territory seeking to secede. However, such an ethnic homogeneity is often lacking in today's multi-cultural society. Therefore, secession is more likely to be premised on democracy, voluntary membership and

[97] Ibid., at 150.

[98] Jan Klabbers, 'The Right to Be Taken Seriously: Self-Determination in International Law' (2006) HRQ 186.

[99] S Mancini, 'Secession and Self-Determination', in M Rosenfeld and A Sajo (eds.), *The Oxford Handbook of Comparative Constitutional Law* (Oxford: Oxford University Press, 2001) at 481.

[100] See further, S Mancini, 'Secession and Self-Determination', at 483–484, which this account largely follows.

popular consent, regardless of ethnic membership. In this case, it is grounded in the right to associate politically, with the will of the group being ascertained in a referendum. We can see such a basis at work in independence claims made for Scotland. Yet this account is not completely independent of territory and history. There must be a franchise for a referendum, and there may be arguments over whether certain groups outside a specific territory may be included – that is, Scots living outside of Scotland in the 2014 referendum, or British citizens resident outside of the UK in the Brexit referendum. So there is still a strong link to territory, or even history, culture, and nationality.

Remedial theories derive a right to secession from injustices suffered by the territory wishing to secede – for example, by the forced annexation of that territory, as of the Baltic States by the former USSR. As we have seen, the right to self-determination in international law has developed largely to recognize only remedial secession.

7.4.2.1 Within the United Kingdom

The UK Union is voluntary in nature. There is no legislation prohibiting secession by one part of the UK, nor any constitutional provision asserting and mandating constitutional integrity. The 1707 Articles of Union were voluntarily negotiated between Scotland and England and ratified in the Acts of Union. The voluntary grant of the 's30 order' by the UK Government in 2014 set the power of Scotland to hold an independence referendum beyond doubt. Section 1 of the Northern Ireland Act 1998 explicitly states that Northern Ireland's membership of the UK rests on the consent of the people of Northern Ireland. (There is no explicit provision for Wales, although it might be assumed that the same right exists in that case.)

The UK is no stranger to secession. The North American colonies were lost in the eighteenth century (described by Linda Colley as felt like an 'amputation'). The Irish Free State, formed in 1922, is perhaps the most obvious example of secession from the UK, whereby the UK lost some 20 per cent of its territory. But the intense period of self-reflection and self-doubt came later, after the end of the Second World War and the departure of India and move to decolonization of many of Britain's other colonies. Since the Scottish independence referendum of 2014, and EU referendum of 2016, disunion of the UK has become a matter for discussion.

7.4.2.2 Secession from the EU: Brexit

The UK has been the first, and so far only, State to leave the European Union. On 23 June 2016, a Referendum on EU membership was held, and the UK overall voted to leave the EU, by a majority of 51.9 to 48.1 per cent.[101] The UK

[101] See the Electoral Commission, UK Referendum results: www.electoralcommission.org.uk/find-information-by-subject/elections-and-referendums/past-elections-and-referendums/eu-referendum/electorate-and-count-information

Government then started the official process to exit the EU. This followed the procedure set out under Article 50 TEU, which required the UK to formally notify the EU of its intention to leave, and to negotiate with the EU a Withdrawal Agreement. Article 50 TEU controls exit from the EU and was inserted into the TEU by the Lisbon Treaty in 2009. Previously little discussed, it became a live issue with Brexit, and provides details as to how withdrawal negotiations are to be conducted. The Article 50 procedure governed the terms of separation, rather than setting out the details of any UK future relationship with the EU, which was determined in a further agreement.

However, the Article 50 withdrawal negotiations between Britain and the EU were often fractious, unproductive, and painful. During the withdrawal process, the UK got through three prime ministers and three Brexit secretaries.[102] For the EU, negotiations were conducted by Michel Barnier on behalf of the Commission throughout. Part of the problem was that, although Britain had voted to leave the EU, it was unclear what would follow on from that. Did a vote to leave the EU require the UK to leave every aspect of it, or might the UK remain in the EU Single Market and Customs Union (as many Leave campaigners had suggested during the Referendum campaign)? There was no clear answer to this and Theresa May's slogan 'Brexit means Brexit' (an empty slogan if ever there was one) did not help. Politics stepped in to fill the void, with those demanding a 'Hard Brexit' (i.e. leaving the Single Market and the Customs Union) dominant, although this created problems in Northern Ireland, where the prospect of a hard border between the two parts of Ireland, north and south, re-emerged, as a 'Hard Brexit' meant an external border between the EU (Ireland) and non-EU (Northern Ireland) running through the island of Ireland – and Northern Ireland remains unsettled, even after the Northern Ireland Protocol, negotiated as part of the Brexit Withdrawal agreement, came into effect.[103] Another reason why the process was often unclear, was that Article 50 was untested. (Although in 1985, Greenland, which is part of Denmark, withdrew from the (then) EEC, and Denmark remained.[104] As the EEC treaties then contained no provision for the withdrawal of a member State, the necessary arrangements had to be negotiated[105].)

Brexit Withdrawal negotiations eventually resulted in a treaty with the EU focussed on three elements (often known as the 'divorce' agreement). These were the UK's budgetary contributions, the rights of EU citizens, and the

102 The prime ministers were David Cameron (resigned 2016), Theresa May (resigned 2019), and Boris Johnson (2019-resigned 2022). The Brexit secretaries were David Davies (2016–2018), Dominic Raab (July–November 2018), and Stephen Barclay (2018–2020).

103 In 2023, a new 'Windsor Framework' was agreed for Northern Ireland. See further chapter on Ireland.

104 This took three years. See F Weiss, 'Greenland's Withdrawal from the European Communities' (1985) EL Rev 173.

105 *Status of Greenland: Commission Opinion*, COM (83) 66 final, 2 February 1983.

specific status of Northern Ireland. This Withdrawal Agreement was concluded in late 2019,[106] ratified by the UK Parliament, and the UK left the EU on 31 January 2020 (although continued to apply most EU law during a transitional period in 2020). In December 2020, a further treaty was concluded between the UK and EU.[107]

Perhaps, the most common constitutional idea to feature in Brexit debates has been sovereignty, often expressed as 'taking back control', expressing an apparent yearning for UK parliamentary sovereignty that could not be reconciled with continuing EU membership. However, such a notion of sovereignty fails to capture how pooling sovereignty in one area, for example by EU membership, may actually empower a State, which is one important reason why supranational approaches have been embraced. It also ignores the fact that many transnational issues cannot be resolved through isolated State regulation. The post-Brexit UK must still observe many Single Market regulations if its products are to be marketable in the EU. 'Passporting' for banks and city firms has become a much used term, but passports are used to cross borders and that is exactly what UK business has to do post Brexit, and without metaphorical passports, commerce is very difficult. As a non-EU country, the UK is placed in a situation that third countries have endured for many years. They have often been required under trading agreements to enact certain product standards to export to the EU. They possess sovereignty in name, but in reality are regulated from outside through economic pressures. This is why unions continue to offer advantages in the modern world.

7.4.2.3 Catalonia and Scotland

The potential secession of Scotland has already been discussed in the chapter on Scotland. But Catalonia provides a useful comparator for the UK Union that can shed light on the British constitutional settlement. Both Scotland and Catalonia are similarly sized[108] democratic European nations in which there exists substantial debate about whether to become independent States. JH Elliott, in *Scots and Catalans: Union and Disunion*, wonders whether both could be described as 'stateless nations'[109] (an expression that recalls Jellinek's 'State fragments').

The 1978 Spanish Constitution creates a division of powers between the national government and 17 autonomous communities, but section 2 of the Constitution states that: 'The Constitution is based on the indissoluble unity of the Spanish Nation, the common and indivisible homeland of all Spaniards'.

106 *Agreement on the withdrawal of the United Kingdom of Great Britain and Northern Ireland from the European Union and the European Atomic Energy Community*, OJ C 384, 12.11.2019.

107 *EU-UK Trade and Cooperation Agreement*, OJ L 444, 31 December 2020.

108 Although at 7.6m, Catalonia's population is a bit larger than that of Scotland.

109 JH Elliott, *Scots and Catalans: Union and Disunion*, (Yale University Press, 2018) at 5.

Further, Article 149, paragraph 32 declares that 'authorisation of popular consultations through the holding of referendums' is exclusively the competence of the Spanish State. The British Constitution contains nothing comparable to either of these provisions.

Notwithstanding these constitutional provisions, in 2017, an independence poll was held in Catalonia (although declared illegal by both the Spanish Government and Constitutional Court[110]) and 93 per cent of participants (on a 43 per cent turnout) voted for independence. Pro-independence Catalan MPs voted to unilaterally declare independence from Spain, but the Spanish Government assumed direct rule of Catalonia, sacked Puigdemont (the leader of the separatists in the Catalan Parliament) and his Cabinet, and called an immediate regional election, in which, although pro-independence parties won a small majority, the centre-right, pro-unionist Citizens party won the largest amount of seats. Direct rule was lifted in June 2018 when the new Catalan government was sworn in. Puigdemont and others fled into self-imposed exile abroad before they could be arrested. In October 2019, nine Catalan independence leaders were sentenced to between nine and thirteen years in prison by the Spanish Supreme Court.[111] The situation in Catalonia remains restless and unresolved.

Both Scotland and Catalonia are modern, democratic nations, with strong independence parties. However, unlike Scotland, Catalonia was never a sovereign State. And unlike Scotland, in which the Articles of the 1707 Treaty of Union guaranteed the independence of Scottish institutions such as Scots law, the Church, and the education system, Catalonia's traditional institutions were abolished in the eighteenth century, when the Spanish monarchy centralized Spain following the War of Spanish Succession.[112] Under Franco's rule, Catalan nationalism was repressed. The 1978 Spanish Constitution results from particular political circumstances – namely, the transition from the Franco dictatorship – but Madrid now insists that Catalonia cannot become independent without amendments to the Spanish Constitution, which requires a vote throughout all of Spain. In contrast, the British Constitution is permissive as far as secession goes and does not place specific constitutional hurdles in its way.

But can reliance on a constitutional path to independence continue in Scotland? Since Brexit, the impetus for a second independence referendum has grown in Scotland. This increase partly results from support from those preferring an independent Scotland in the EU to membership of a Brexited UK.

7.4.2.4 The United States: Potential Secession?

Disunion has threatened the USA on many occasions. As Kreitner comments: 'The founding of our country was especially disordered and vitriolic, even

[110] See further Spanish Constitutional Court Judgment No. 114/2017; and Spanish Constitutional Court Judgment, No. 124/2017.

[111] Known as *Causa Especial* 20907/2017.

[112] See e.g. JH Elliott, *The Revolt of the Catalans* (Cambridge: Cambridge University Press, 1963); R Herr, *Modern Spain: An Historical Essay* (Berkeley: University of California Press, 1971).

less thought through than the genesis of the similarly beleaguered European Union.'[113] Indeed, Kreitner's recent book, *Break It Up* pursues the arresting argument that, although this impulse to disunion found its bloodiest manifestation in the secession of the South in the nineteenth-century Civil War, most parts of the US have contemplated secession on some occasion. Indeed, a column in *The New Yorker* recently asked 'Is America a Myth?'[114]

The US Constitution itself was a factious document that deliberately left the most decisive issue – slavery – unresolved, making the Civil War inevitable. At the time of the revolutionary wars, the North American colonies were a group of separate and disunited territories, where loyalty to one's own colony (and subsequently, state) was more important than to any federal centre.[115] The history of the US from 1789 to 1861 was an ongoing wrangle between the federalist centre and advocates of states' rights, neither of which prevailed as ultimately sovereign. However, what is perhaps surprising for non-Americans is the extent to which disunion movements occurred outside of the South – as in 1842, when northern abolitionist William Lloyd Garrison urged the repeal of the Union, accusing the Constitution of being proslavery.

However, it is the South that is famous for its pursuit of states' rights and secession. In 1832, South Carolina drafted a Nullification Ordinance, in protest against a federal tariff law (perceived as affecting slaveholders' interests) asserting a right to self-determination and arguing that the Constitution was a compact of sovereign states. Although this dispute died down (President Andrew Jackson insisted that the Union was indestructible) other crises followed.

A notable propellant to disunity and the Civil War was the 'Compromise' of 1850, which admitted California into the Union as a non-slave state, but also included the 1850 Fugitive Slave law, which compelled Northerners to assist in catching runaway slaves, as well as banning jury trials. The Fugitive Slave law was viewed as a huge expansion of federal power, and as a result, Northern cities themselves adopted nullification doctrines, as well as personal liberty laws that accorded runaway slaves the right to jury trial and other procedural rights. It also sparked civil disobedience. Emerson, for one, resolved to disobey the Fugitive Slave law, declaring 'The Union is at an end as soon as an immoral law is enacted.'[116]

Nor was the federal Congress immune from these squabbles, which spilled over onto violence in the Capitol building. In 1856, South Carolinian Congressman, Preston Brooks, famously violently caned Massachusetts Senator, Charles Sumner, in revenge for an anti-slavery speech Sumner had given. But this was

113 Kreitner, *Break It Up*, at 6.

114 Robin Wright, 'Is America a Myth?' *The New Yorker*, 8 September 2020.

115 See Peter Onuf, 'Anarchy and the Crisis of the Union', in R Hoffman and PJ Albert (eds.), *To Form a more Perfect Union: The Critical Idea of the Constitution* (Charlottesville: University of Virginia Press, 1992).

116 'Address to Citizens of Concord 3 May, 1851', in *The Complete Works of Ralph Waldo Emerson*, vol. 11 (Boston: Houghton, Mifflin and Co, 1876).

only the most high-profile of around 70 physical attacks from 1830 to 1861, in Congress itself – most of which involved attacks by southerners against anti-slavery northerners. Joanne Freeman describes these attacks as a product of the 'emotional logic of dis-Union'.[117] Indeed, in 1836, the US Congress introduced the 'gag rule' forbidding consideration of any anti-slavery petitions – a means of silencing abolitionist agitation and surely a violation of freedom of expression.

Most notorious though, is the judgement in the *Dred Scott* case,[118] in which the US Supreme Court held that Scott, enslaved in Virginia but removed to slave-free Wisconsin, could not sue for his freedom since neither he, nor any slave, could be an American citizen. The Court also held, for good measure, that any law that sought to ban slavery in any US territory was unconstitutional. As a result, the US Federal Government ceased issuing passports to (free) black Americans. In retaliation, some states (such as Maine) declared the Supreme Court decision not binding, and many northern states adopted resolutions recognising the citizenship of free blacks.

In 1860, following the election of anti-slavery Abraham Lincoln as the US' first Republican President, South Carolina was the first state to announce its secession, in a notice declaring *The Union is dissolved!* In 1861 the Civil War began. The Confederacy was declared, with a separate Presidency under Jefferson Davis, with its capital in Richmond Virginia, and own currency. The war only came to an end after four years of destruction, loss of life and the assassination of President Abraham Lincoln. It was the confederacy's own divisions as much as anything else, that contributed to its defeat.

The US Constitution itself is silent on secession. President Andrew Johnson, Lincoln's successor, declared a blanket amnesty for ex-confederates in 1868, but the specific issue of secession was raised *Texas* v. *White*. At issue was whether Texas had successfully seceded from the Union during the Civil War. In a 5:3 majority judgement, Supreme Court Chief Justice Salmon Chase held that the Constitution did not allow secession and any acts of confederate states were null and void. Chase stated that the Federal Constitution was established 'to form a more perfect Union' and that 'The union between Texas and the other States was as complete, as perpetual, and as indissoluble as the union between the original States.'[119] *Texas* v. *White* has been criticised for its somewhat summary treatment of secession. Notably, in his 1862 essay, *The Contest in America*, John Stuart Mill acknowledged a right of secession, but, however, argued that secession could be morally wrong, if its object were for an ignoble purpose, such as slavery.[120]

117 J Freeman, *The Field of Blood: Violence in Congress and the Road to Civil War* (New York: Farrar, Straus and Giroux, 2018) 291.

118 *Dred Scott* v. *Sandford* 60 US 393 [1856].

119 *Texas* v. *White* 74 U.S. 700 [1869].

120 John Stuart Mill, *The Contest in America* (Boston: Little, Brown and Company, 1862).

After the War ended, the Reconstruction era (largely a failure) followed, along with three amendments – the 13th, 14th, and 15th – which considerably changed the nature of the Federal Constitution. However, a newish term – America's 'cold civil war' suggests that the issue of disunion has not gone away in today's US, where rival political visions clash with little room for compromise. In 2013, a Bill was adopted in the Oklahoma House of Representatives declaring the Obama era Affordable Care Act 'null in this state',[121] and many lawsuits were brought in individual states to overturn it. Attempts were made in Texas to secede during the Obama era and again after the inauguration of President Biden.[122] California was pursued by the Trump administration for refusing to cooperate with its immigration enforcement. In response, California appealed to 'dual sovereignty' a doctrine going back to Calhoun, although then used for very different purposes.[123] So there are still examples of disunity in today's America, which have only grown as differences between Red (Republican controlled) and Blue (Democrat controlled) states have increased. Further, these differences have sometimes been exacerbated by recent US Supreme Court caselaw such as the 2022 case of *Dobbs*,[124] where the Court overturned *Roe* v. *Wade*, holding that there was no federal constitutional right to abortion, and that this was a matter for individual states to determine – thus leading to a very sharp cleavage between those states where abortion continues to be permitted, and those where it is now illegal (the majority of states).

7.4.3 Dissolution

This next short section considers some examples where the breakup of a union leads to its dissolution, rather than only one part seceding. Three earlier examples have already been considered. After the First World War, the Austria-Hungarian empire dissolved and a new order was established by the Treaties of Trianon and Saint-Germain. Several successor States, including (a much smaller) Hungary, Czechoslovakia, and Yugoslavia were established. This new order was not a particularly happy one and new divisions it provoked helped lead to the Second World War.

In 1905, when the King vetoed a measure for a separate Norwegian consulate, the Norwegian Parliament declared the King had violated the Constitution, thereby dissolving the union.[125] The end of the union was peaceful and achieved by legal means. But its failure illustrates that even unions providing much

[121] See further, www.oklahoman.com/article/3765408/oklahoma-house-attempts-to-nullify-obamacare

[122] E.g. 'Texas Secession Bill Filed in House', *Austin American-Statesman*, 26 January 2021.

[123] See e.g. J Gerstein, 'Trump Administration Goes to War with States over Immigration', *Politico*, 2 October 2020.

[124] *Dobbs* v. *Jackson Women's Health* 597 US [2022].

[125] See 'The Dissolution of the Union of Norway and Sweden' (1907) 1(2) The American Jl of International Law, 440–444.

autonomy for each territory may fail if there is discord over remaining centralized policies (here, foreign policy).

The Kingdom of the United Netherlands collapsed in 1839 due to tensions between the Northern part (mainly Dutch speaking and Protestant) and the Southern part (Belgium today, mainly Catholic with dominant French speaking elites). It lacked a sense of common nationhood. The matter was finally settled by the treaty of London in 1839, which separated the two parts into two sovereign States. Nonetheless, this still left Belgium with a cleavage between Flemish speaking parts (the majority) and French speaking elites, that would have a lasting impact on Belgian politics to this day.

7.4.3.1 The End of the Cold War

The end of the Cold War brought dramatic changes and the breakup of the former Communist Warsaw Pact federations. Both the right to democracy and ethnic rights took on a central focus and sometimes conflicted. In particular, the collapse of the USSR and Yugoslavia revealed the problem of how, and if, to recognize new States. At the very least, new States were required, as a condition of recognition, to acknowledge and protect ethnic and cultural pluralism.

7.4.3.1.1 Czechoslovakia: 1918–1992

Czechoslovakia, like Yugoslavia, came into being in 1918 after the First World War, created out of territories formerly belonging to Austria-Hungary. Czech and Slovak peoples are culturally separate but the new Czechoslovakia was a unitary State, although with a clear border between the two parts, and Prague, the capital city, located in Czech territory. However, there were always internal divisions. The Czech part – at around 10m population – was roughly twice the size of the Slovak. Whereas the Czechs were largely Protestant, Slovakia was mainly Catholic.

In 1989, in the 'Velvet Revolution', Czechoslovakia's Communist government was overthrown. However, within a year of free elections, the country was pulling apart. And so the Czech and Slovak governments agreed to a separation into two distinct States. Notably, this was a dissolution, and the old State of Czechoslovakia vanished. What is interesting is that the propulsion towards independence came from politicians rather than the people. Although there was considerable support for independence from both sides, at 35 per cent this was well below majority support and a referendum on independence was never held. It did, however, take the form of a peaceful negotiated settlement. Assets and liabilities of Czechoslovakia were divided by a ratio of 2:1 (following the population division). It was agreed that citizens of each new State would have easy access to the other State. Although the economies of both countries suffered somewhat, the effect was less than expected, and softened perhaps by both parties' EU membership from 2004, which kept borders open and free movement between Czechia and Slovakia.

One might argue that the split in Czechoslovakia could be compared to issues with the UK Union. Czechoslovakia was an asymmetric federation, whereby one part (Czech) was larger and richer with the capital city, similar to England, and the other Slovakia, might be compared to Scotland. However, what is notable is that Czechoslovakia split because this was the will of its politicians, on both sides, whereas in Britain, nearly all of the propulsions to independence have come from Scotland. UK politicians in Westminster and Edinburgh have not been in agreement.

7.4.3.1.2 Yugoslavia

Yugoslavia (meaning land of the south Slavs) was also created after the First World War, when Austria-Hungary was dissolved and its former Croat, Slovenian, and Bosnian lands were joined with the Kingdom of Serbia. Yugoslavia was unified after the Second World War as a socialist federal republic (SFRY) under the former partisan Josep Tito.

But there had always been tensions between the different nationalities, ethnic and religious groups, and Serbia was by far the largest group. Yugoslavia was an artificial State that had grown from fragments of other States. Yugoslavia was also a federation, but unlike Czechoslovakia, highly decentralized. Unlike Czechoslovakia, Yugoslavia dissolved in a violent manner, after collapse of Communist party rule. Yugoslavia broke apart in a terrible violent war, riven by war crimes and ethnic cleansing, the worst fighting being in the multi-ethnic region of Bosnia and Herzegovina – somewhat ironically, in Sarajevo. International efforts at mediation largely failed.

Five States (Slovenia, Croatia, Bosnia and Herzegovina, Macedonia, and the Federal Republic of Yugoslavia – now Serbia) signed the Agreement on Succession Issues confirming that five sovereign equal successor States were formed on the dissolution of the former SFRY. Kosovo declared independence unilaterally in 2008, but only gained limited international recognition and is not a UN member.

7.4.3.1.3 Soviet Union: 1922–1991

The USSR, or Soviet Union, which was formally established in 1922, collapsed mainly as a result of economic failure, and the huge sums spent in the arms war with the USA. In 1991, former Soviet republics signed the Alma-Ata Protocol, and the Soviet Union was dissolved and replaced by the CIS (Commonwealth of Independent States).[126]

Dissolution of the USSR raised a difficult question – was Russia the continuator or successor State to the USSR – and this issue is discussed further below.

[126] *Agreement Establishing the Commonwealth of Independent States*, UN Doc A/46/71 (1992) 31 ILM 138.

7.4.4 Successor and Continuator States

What happens after a State is divided up? When a State is dissolved, the former country is extinguished and its sovereignty replaced by new successor States. This happened with the dissolution of Czechoslovakia, whereby both Czechia and Slovakia became the new successor States. On the other hand, some secessions do not involve dissolutions and in that case, there is what is known as a 'continuator' State. When Bangladesh separated from Pakistan, Pakistan retained recognition by the international community and was thus the continuing State. Bangladesh was the successor State. However, even where is a dissolution, the example of the USSR illustrates that one State (in this case Russia) may still be identified as the continuator State.[127] Russia declared itself the USSR's continuator State on the basis that it contained 77 per cent of former USSR territory and 51 per cent of its population. This now seems to have been generally accepted and Russia identified as continuator in international treaties and organizations and retains the seat on the UN Security Council.[128]

But supposing Scotland were to become independent after a 'yes' vote in a referendum? Would this mean the dissolution of the UK, given that the United Kingdom of Great Britain only came into being after the 1707 Acts of Union? Or would England, Wales and Northern Ireland retain UK Statehood (as 'rUK'), as the continuing State?

Much follows from this. If rUK were recognised as continuator State, it would retain the UK's existing treaty obligations and memberships of international organizations such as NATO and UN (including the permanent seat on its Security Council). It would also retain all UK public institutions (including the Bank of England, the BBC and the Westminster Parliament). During the first Scottish independence campaign, many commentators (including international law experts James Crawford and Alan Boyle) argued that Scotland would indeed be a 'successor' State[129]. The UK Government endorsed this position and drew on international precedents for support. For example, Russia was the continuator State after the breakup of the Soviet Union. Also Great Britain and Northern Ireland continued as the UK after the secession of the Irish Free State in 1922. Further, where only new States have been created on dissolution – such as when Czechoslovakia split – this is usually by mutual agreement. Nonetheless, in the run up to the first independence referendum, the Scottish Government was not completely clear on this matter, although the bulk of opinion favours viewing rUK as 'continuator'.

[127] E.g. by KG Buhler, *State Succession and Membership in International Organizations* (The Hague: Kluwer, 2001). Also R Mullerson, 'The Continuity and Succession of States, by Reference to the Former USSR and Yugoslavia' (1993) 42 ICLQ 475.

[128] *Decision by the Council of Heads of State of the Commonwealth of Independent States, 21 December 1991* [1992] 31 ILM, 151. However, Russia is often (i.e. Wikipedia) described as 'successor state' to the USSR.

[129] J Crawford and A Boyle, *Annex A Opinion: Referendum on the Independence of Scotland – International Law Aspects* (2012).

7.4.5 Conclusion: Why/How Does Disunion Occur?

Disunions occur in all sorts of circumstances. Nevertheless, we can draw some conclusions.

First, disunion very often occurs as the result of war, or serious economic shock. This was the case with the dissolution of Austria-Hungary after the First World War, and also one of the reasons why the USSR broke up, after severe economic challenges.

Second, imbalanced unions tend to be weak. This is often so where one territory is much larger than other parts of the union, and/or when there is asymmetry between different parts. There are lessons here for the UK. It is easy to identify unions where some territories are much larger in geographical size or population than other parts – that is, California and Texas compared to North Dakota or Wyoming in the US, Catalonia and Madrid in Spain, or the Czech Republic compared to Slovakia. But these examples differ from Britain in not comprising the majority of the union's population. England comprises 84 per cent of the UK population.[130] Such an imbalance makes it difficult to sustain equitable representation in matters that are shared (even where there is autonomy elsewhere) such as foreign policy, defence and common currency. This was evident in the case of Norway-Sweden, which ended over disputes as to Swedish control of foreign policy.

Third, a further propulsion towards breakup may be the behaviour of the central government, if it insists on concentrating power in the centre, refusing greater self-government for some of its nations or territories, or favouring one nation over another (as in the case of Austria-Hungary). Such behaviour often breeds resentment and leads to disunion.

On the other hand, disunion can also occur constitutionally, without revolution or bloodshed. This usually happens when the various parts accept that secession or dissolution will occur, and politicians agree to it. This happened in former Czechoslovakia, Norway-Sweden, and in Singapore-Malaysia, for example, where the Malaysian Parliament very swiftly adopted the necessary constitutional amendment to remove Singapore from the federation. Such lawful secessions also illustrate that it is not always necessary to hold a referendum. In the UK, there is no formal legal requirement for any referendum prior to secession of any part of the union, although the holding of referendums in 1979 (Scotland and Wales), 1997 (Scotland and Wales), 1998 (regarding the Greater London Authority) 1998 (Northern Ireland referendum on the Belfast/Good Friday Agreement) 2011(Wales) 2011 (UK AV referendum), 2014 (independence referendum in Scotland), 2016 (Brexit referendum), may now have set some sort of precedent, requiring referendums on issues of devolution or secession.

In 1869, the US Supreme Court denied that secession was possible. Over a century later, in 1998, the Canadian Supreme Court outlined the form that

[130] UK demographics profile: www.indexmundi.com/united_kingdom/demographics_profile.html

a democratic secession process could take. In the intervening period, many changes occurred to the way that federations and unions were conceived. We will examine federalism in the next chapter, but here we might note that political decentralization has been increasingly used to deter centrifugal movements and establish greater self-government for subnational groups. Unions may do better if they are more elastic and less constraining.

7.5 Conclusions

What conclusions then, concerning the UK Union, may we draw from this consideration of many types of union and disunion?

In 2016, an interesting and revelatory exchange took place in an evidence session in the House of Lords Constitution Committee. Lord Lester, questioning Oliver Letwin MP, remarked that:

> Should the Government not be worried that at the moment our system is fragile. We risk exiting from the European Union; we risk Scotland exiting from us; in Northern Ireland there is a state of near- paralysis of the political system; and the Government need the ability to produce a framework which is stable and enduring and based on principles?

In response Letwin replied:

> I do not think that the constitution of the UK is in some terrible state of crisis … I think it is the genius of it that it does change and that it accommodates, progressively, the various demands that are placed upon it
>
> So there is a fundamental fork in the road here. As I say, there is a group of serious, well- intentioned, intelligent commentators who believe in neatness and codes and are worried about the fact that there is no basic law or written constitution which sits here to guarantee something or other; and then there is British history, which operates in the opposite way. One has to choose which way one thinks is the better route. I am on the British history side and, more importantly, so are the Government.[131]

This exchange reveals a rift between those who believe in constitutional reform, in the need to provide a more stable and enduring framework, but are often condemned as unrealistic, overly academic or unduly Cartesian, seeking to wreck something that isn't broken; and, on the other hand, those who believe that the British Constitution can evolve to accommodate any situation and is superior to any formalised document – an attitude that displays the insouciance we have noted in other chapters – for example regarding the British Empire, which Victorian historian Seeley suggested had been developed in 'a fit of absence of mind'.[132]

[131] House of Lords report, *The Union and Devolution*, q 314.

[132] JR Seeley, *The Expansion of England* (London: Macmillan, 1883) at 8.

There has been too little progress from the devolution debates in the 1970s, in which Lord Wilberforce, then a Lord of Appeal, regretted what he termed the 'present state of constitutional anarchy', insisting that it was time 'that we in this country took our constitution seriously' instead of muddling through 'with a fuzzy kind of reliance upon convention'.[133] Since then, devolution has taken place, enshrined in primary legislation, and there has also been a series of commissions and inquiries, as detailed earlier in this chapter. And yet, for many, it is no clearer what the Union is for, and at the centre of the UK Union appears to lie a vacuum, a lack of concern or definition, over what exactly this Union might consist of.

Part of the problem is persistence in asserting a particular notion of parliamentary sovereignty – one that sees Parliament unconstrained by any greater power, and where, as Dicey insisted, the Act of Union with Scotland (or indeed any devolution legislation) has no greater authority than the Dentists Act 1878. This understanding of sovereignty led to the Brexit call for more UK control over British affairs – a call that may turn out very hollow in today's globalized world where there exist powerful transnational corporations. In such circumstances, unions may provide an important and powerful defence to globalization that dwarfs the State and lessens its capabilities. Yet if unions are to thrive, there must be a clearer sense of purpose and a less stark bifurcation from the nation State. But the current understanding of sovereignty makes that very difficult. Such an interpretation places an almost insurmountable barrier to resolution of issues threatening the Union today, particularly those of devolution and the need to accommodate the UK's different nationalities. It renders federalism impossible, and any recasting of the House of Lords as an effective Chamber of the nations and regions highly problematic. Moreover, as other chapters have argued, this extreme version of sovereignty is incoherent and contradictory, and yet it is still advanced even when the Union is at risk.

Hennessey refers to 'Wilson's law', namely, the notion of former Cabinet Secretary, Richard Wilson, 'that the British go into their big constitutional changes "as if under anaesthetic." Only later do they wake up and say, "Did we really mean to do it like that?"'[134] And George Orwell noted the habit of the British (or English, as he describes them) of 'sleepwalking' into disaster.[135] As this chapter illustrates, many unions have gone the way of history. Will the UK Union follow them into oblivion?

[133] Cited in 'Colin Kidd on how to balance 'England's' House of Commons' 36(8) London Review of Books, 17 April 2014.

[134] P Hennessey, *The Kingdom to Come* (London: Haus Publishing, 2015) 75.

[135] George Orwell, *The Lion and the Unicorn* (London: Secker & Warburg, 1941) 15.

8

Federalism, Devolution, and Differentiation

8.1 Introduction

In recent decades, the British Constitution has undergone a gradual reform process, capable of affecting sovereignty and lines of authority. This included: devolution in Scotland, Wales and Northern Ireland challenging the notion of a unitary UK; the weak entrenchment of the 1998 Human Rights Act, enhancing the judiciary's ability to shape a human rights culture; reform of the House of Lords; and of course, EU membership, from 1973 to 2020, which challenged Parliamentary supremacy. All of this rendered the Constitution (and Britain) less unitary and more heterogeneous, more willing to recognize centres of power elsewhere, without however bringing any coherence or consolidation of constitutional form.

This constitutional transformation was accompanied by the development of pluralism within law more generally, beyond the UK. For a brief period (from roughly the mid-seventeenth to mid-twentieth centuries) the 'Westphalian' order of sovereign States governed the order of things in western Europe. However, since earlier last century, and certainly by the end of the Second World War, the Westphalian order has been breaking down. Since 1945, there have been shifts to supra-national institutions, and international law has become more important. But there have been demands for self-government from sub-State nations as well. These also concern the nature and bounds of the political community and locus of ultimate authority. However, there has not always been a claim for full Statehood, but sometimes a push for greater self-government within the existing State. The theoretical underpinning for these movements is the idea of 'post-sovereignty', which maintains that sovereignty is no longer is the dominant mode of political organization. Post-sovereign approaches argue that States must share their powers with supra-State, sub-State, and trans-State systems.[1] Neil MacCormick's view was that 'sovereignty and sovereign states, and the inexorable linkage of law with sovereignty and

[1] A note on terminology: throughout this chapter I use the term 'State' to denote the single State, and 'sub-State' to denote its component parts, whether they be states (as in the US), Länder (as in Germany), provinces (as in Canada), or nations (as Scotland, Wales, and – possibly – Northern Ireland are recognized to be) or some other form of territory.

the state, have been but the passing phenomena of a few centuries, that their passing is by no means regrettable, and that current developments in Europe exhibit the possibility of going beyond all that.'[2]

So it might seem that the idea of the unitary State is in retreat. Yet Brexit challenged this vision of post-sovereignty. Indeed, Brexit brought huge changes to the UK's Constitution. Perhaps the most common constitutional idea to feature in the Brexit debates was the notion of sovereignty, of 'taking back control',[3] a desire for a clearly national constitutional architecture. However, this approach fails to capture the way in which pooling sovereignty in one area, as with EU membership, may actually empower a State. Indeed, Brexit may even imperil national sovereignty, as it risks shattering UK stability by threatening the peace settlement in Northern Ireland and possibly inciting a further independence referendum in Scotland. In these circumstances, Brexit heralds a period of uncertainty, during which many of the foundations of the UK constitutional settlement will be tested.

This chapter considers forms of governance that exist as alternatives to the unlimited absolute sovereignty of the unitary State. These include the many and varied forms of federalism. But this chapter also reviews other forms of differentiated governance – arrangements that make provision for diversity while stopping short of full-blown federalism. All these alternate forms are understood as having a normative justification – lying in the belief that dividing power and granting greater autonomy to territories within a State leads to greater freedom and better governance for all. Therefore, this chapter explores possible constitutional paths for the UK at a critical point. The underlying premise is that constitutional change is necessary, in large part due to the rifts caused by Brexit.

8.2 Federalism

We start with federalism. According to Palermo and Kössler, 'Federalism is at the heart of one of the most pressing challenges in the history of mankind: how to order public life, and how to limit, organize and regulate power in a way that guarantees freedom and efficiency, unit and plurality, autonomy and co-ordination.'[4] Federalism is widespread in the world today, existing as the main mode of governance in many countries – for example, in Australia, Belgium, Brazil, Canada, Germany, India, Malaysia, Mexico, Nigeria, Russia, Switzerland, and the US. However, although according to Daniel Elazar,

[2] N MacCormick, 'On Sovereignty and Post-Sovereignty', in N MacCormick (ed.), *Questioning Sovereignty: Law, State, and Nation in the European Commonwealth* (Oxford: Oxford University Press, 1999); also N MacCormick, 'Beyond the Sovereign State' (1993) 56 MLR 1.

[3] Indeed, the very domain name of the Vote Leave website was www.voteleavetakecontrol.org/why_vote_leave.html

[4] F Palermo and K Kössler, *Comparative Federalism: Constitutional Arrangements and Case Law* (Oxford: Hart Publishing, 2017) at 1.

in 1994, roughly 90 States had federalist arrangements, Ronald Watts identified only 23 thoroughgoing federal States in 1999 – suggesting these authors understand the term 'federalism' differently.[5] Indeed, the exact number of countries that are federalist is disputed.

8.2.1 Interpretations and Varieties of Federalism

As Halberstam has commented, 'Federalism' can be a charged and confusing word,[6] and indeed there exists no agreed criteria for what makes a legal order federal. For some, it is a means of decentralization, for others it may mean a strong central government.

Federalism, understood broadly, has a long history – and earlier variants were often closer to confederation (i.e. did not unify component parts into one State). However, federalism in its modern sense was born in the USA, in the late eighteenth century, and conceived as a means of dividing power to ensure greater liberty. A series of 85 *Federalist Papers* was published by Hamilton, Jay and Madison after the 1787 Philadelphia Convention and was very influential in making the case for federalism, and in convincing reluctant states to ratify the US Constitution.

Yet, according to Madison, in *Federalist Paper No. 39*, the 1789 US Constitution was 'in strictness neither a national nor a federal Constitution; but a composition of both.'[7] And indeed, the ratified version of the 1789 Constitution followed a more international approach in requiring each state to have equal representation in the Senate, but was more national in its stipulation that it was the product of 'We, the People' – which suggested a direct relationship between the people and the centre, rather than states as intermediaries. Nonetheless, the US Constitution applied to one State only, not many States, and, following its implementation, federalism began to be understood less as a confederal system. Switzerland, which had been a confederation of 19 independent cantons, became a federal State with the adoption of its 1848 Constitution, and was strongly influenced by the US example.

8.2.1.1 Distinguishing Federations from Confederations

This reflection on early US federalism prompts the question of how to distinguish the 'confederal' from the 'federal'. It is a salient distinction, connoting on the one hand, a looser alliance (confederation) with lesser implications for national sovereignty, and on the other hand, something more closely knit (federalism).

[5] D Elazar, *Federal Systems of the World* (2nd ed., London: Longman, 1994) XVI ff; RL Watts, *Comparing Federal Systems* (2nd ed., Kingston Ont: McGill-Queen's University Press, 1999).

[6] D Halberstam, 'Federalism: Theory, Policy, Law', in M Rosenfeld and A Sajó (eds.), *The Oxford Handbook of Comparative Constitutional Law* (Oxford: Oxford University Press, 2012) at 578.

[7] James Madison *The Federalist Papers No. 39* (New York: Penguin, 1961).

Confederations have existed since ancient times – for example, the ancient Greek Achaean league and Lycian confederation. Very simply, confederations are alliances of independent, sovereign States which have decided to transfer certain limited powers, such as defence. In contrast, in a federal system, there exists only the one sovereign State, in which power is divided between a nation-wide/federal government and regional or sub-State governments.

According to Palermo and Kössler, confederations must satisfy three conditions. They are governed by international rather than constitutional law; decision-making is taken unanimously, with each component State having a veto over confederation decisions; and the confederation lacks its own resources and is dependent on States for revenue.[8] This means that confederations often have difficulty in imposing uniform standards. Indeed, this was the experience of the US after independence from Great Britain and before the Federal Constitution came into effect. The US 'Articles of Confederation and Perpetual Union' (in force from 1781), established a Congress of the Confederation with very limited powers. Article 2 provided that 'each state retains its sovereignty, freedom and independence and every other power … which is not by this Confederation expressly delegated to the US, in Congress assembled.'

Confederation need not be a step to federalism. There exist loose associations of States – such as the Commonwealth of Nations (which evolved from the British Commonwealth) and Commonwealth of Independent States (a descendant of the USSR) – which are unlikely to develop into federations. And there is the example of the EU. Is the EU a federation, confederation, or *sui generis* entity?[9] It manifests both federal and confederal elements, but has not developed into a federal 'super-State' and, indeed, the 2005 attempt to develop an EU Constitution failed.

The federal/confederal distinction has long been acknowledged by German literature,[10] which employs the terms *Staatenbund* (confederation) and *Bundesstaat* (federation) – a distinction that grew in significance, especially as Germany progressed from looser forms of territorial affiliation to the federalism of the *Bundesrepublik* today. It also includes the term *Staatenstaat*, which is another form of federation, but distinguished from the *Bundesstaat* by its origins, which tended to be feudal in nature, involving more domination over constituent parts, such as with the Ottoman and Holy Roman Empires.

8.2.1.2 Further Clarifications

Further clarifications may be helpful. Federalism and Federation, both of which terms are used in this chapter, can be distinguished. Federation is a descriptive term, denoting a territorial entity operating a federal system, whereas

[8] Palermo and Kössler, *Comparative Federalism*, 35.

[9] The EU is discussed in Section 3.

[10] E.g. Georg Jellinek, *Allgemeine Staatslehre* (3rd ed., Berlin: Springer, 1921); G Jellinek, *Die Lehre von den Staatenverbindungen* (Berlin: A. Hölder, 1882).

federalism is a normative concept, requiring a multi-faceted administration with elements of shared and self-rule.[11]

There is also the question of what differentiates a federation from a union? There is a deal of overlap, and a State may be both. The US is a federation, operating a federal system, but it is also a union. The former Soviet Union was both. On the other hand, the UK is a union, but is not a federation. India is often treated as a federal State, although Article 1 of the Indian Constitution describes India as a 'Union of States' rather than a federal State. Additionally we might query how a federation differs from an empire? Both terms involve an aggregation of States, or territories. But whereas a federation is normally based on the free consent of its component parts, empire usually involves coercion of colonies or peripheral parts.[12]

And finally, it is also worth distinguishing devolution, which is the practice whereby a State's central government delegates greater autonomy and control to sub-State units. Unlike federalism, however, under devolution it is constitutionally possible for the central government to take back these powers. This is the case in the UK.

8.2.1.3 Defining Federalism

KC Wheare's significant work, *Federal Government,* in 1946 defined federalism as 'the method of dividing powers so that the general and regional governments are each, within a sphere, coordinate and independent.'[13] However, Wheare's account ignores the *cooperative* elements of federalism, whereby various levels of governance are not necessarily completely separate but may also compete and intermingle in a diverse synergy. And so Wheare's definition has been criticized[14] as somewhat narrow. In contrast, Morton Grodzins employed the memorable image of federalism as a 'marble cake', denoting an entity veined and intertwined all over, thus undermining the notion that federalism must involve mutually separate spheres.[15] And Daniel Elazar straightforwardly defined federalism as a combination of 'self-rule plus shared rule,' which extends the scope of federalism beyond US structures to other systems that might also include unions, confederation, federacy, associate statehood, condominium, and league,[16] although leaving the notion somewhat vague.

No one account of federalism is preferred in this chapter, which accepts that many different forms of federalism exist in the world today.

[11] Preston King, *Federalism and Federation* (Baltimore: Johns Hopkins Press, 1982).

[12] See further, O Beaud, 'Federation and Empire: About a Conceptual Distinction of Political Forms' (2018) 16(4) *I•CON*, 1199.

[13] KC Wheare, *Federal Government* (Oxford: Oxford University Press, 1946) 11.

[14] See e.g. D Elazar, *The American Partnership* (Chicago: Chicago University Press, 1962).

[15] Morton Grodzins, *The America System: A View from the States* (Chicago: Rand McNally & Company, 1966).

[16] D Elazar, *Exploring Federalism* (Tuscaloosa: University of Alabama Press, 1987).

8.2.1.4 The Varieties of Federalism

There exist a great variety of federal States today. They differ not only in their understanding of 'federalism', but also in the size and number of sub-State units. For example, the US is composed of 50 states below federal level, which vary greatly in size, from the largest – California (pop 40m) down to Wyoming (pop 500,000). In India, the state of Uttar Pradesh is 307 times larger than Sikkim. Belgium is one of the smallest federal States, with three regions, three cultural communities and significant linguistic differences. Some States operate symmetric federalism – for example, the US, in which all states possess equal representation in the US Senate. Asymmetry occurs, however, when some sub-States have different, or greater powers than others. So, in Canada, there exist differences between provinces, and Quebec has distinct arrangements.

A further distinction is often made between *dual* and *cooperative* federalism.[17] Wheare's theory captures the essence of dual federalism, which allocates powers between different levels of government, with each level autonomous regarding its powers. However, in practice there has been a lot more cooperation within federal orders. And so, in many instances, dual federalism (sometimes known as 'layer cake' federalism) has given way to cooperative (or 'marble cake' per Grodzins) federalism.

Within federalism, it is usual for some powers to be reserved to the national government and others to sub-State parts, while yet other powers may be shared. Funding and revenue raising differ across federal States. In Germany, both the Länder and federal government collect taxes, but the federal government also administers a specific programme to benefit poorer Länder financially. This was of particular significance at the time of reunification. In the US, although both the federal and state governments collect income taxes, there is some redistribution of revenue to states by the federal government. The allocation of powers and finance is explored further below.

8.2.2 Why Federalism?

8.2.2.1 Advantages

Federalism sees advantages in a plurality of governance levels. James Madison asserted his classic caution in the *Federalist Papers* that, 'we will not be governed by angels, or even enlightened statesmen'. Madison's conclusion was clear: 'Ambition must be made to counteract ambition.' This meant dividing power and splitting 'the atom of sovereignty'.[18] This required different levels of government, and federalism is often seen to bring the following advantages.

[17] E.g. Robert Schütze, *From Dual to Cooperative Federalism: The Changing Structure of European Law* (Oxford: Oxford University Press, 2009).

[18] J Madison, *The Federalist Papers No. 51.* Also *United States Term Limits, Inc.* v. *Thornton*, 514 U.S. 779 [1995] (per J Kennedy, 'The Framers Split the Atom of Sovereignty').

Diversity: Federal arrangements are particularly common in countries with strong national, ethnic, religious, or linguistic diversity – such as Belgium, India, Malaysia, or Nigeria. In such cases, policy conflict may be mitigated by allowing sub-State units greater autonomy.

Community: Smaller authorities can encourage citizens to participate in local public life. Such public engagement in turn fosters a greater sense of civic virtue. De Tocqueville argued that smaller communities can function as 'schools of democracy'.[19]

Expertise: Local officials are likely to have a better understanding of local conditions. EU law illustrates the value of local expertise in its adoption of EU Directives, which, while emanating from the EU, are implemented at local level, so as to address local conditions.

Abusive concentrations of power: The existence of many sites of authority can safeguard against an abusive concentration of power. Indeed, the German Constitution contains an 'eternity' clause for its federal political arrangements in Article 79(3). However, a greater range of governments, including a strong central level, also helps prevent the colonization of small communities by undesirable factions. Therefore it is quite common for fundamental rights to be protected at federal level, so as to ensure the protection of minorities against local majorities. Overall, Madison considered federalism, bicameralism and the Separation of Powers to be bulwarks against the threat of populism: 'a rage for … any other improper or wicked project, will be less apt to pervade the whole body of the Union, than a particular member of it.'[20]

Experimentation and risk: According to US Supreme Court Justice Brandeis, it was 'one of the happy incidents of the federal system that a single courageous state may, if its citizens choose, serve as a laboratory; and try novel social and economic experiments without risk to the rest of the country.'[21]

8.2.2.2 Disadvantages

Competition: However, competition is not always beneficial. It may cause a 'race to the bottom', as where distinct parts of a federal State compete by lowering corporate tax rates or workers' protections.

Inefficiency, unaccountability and cost: Diversity of jurisdictions can cause coordination problems and increase costs. For example, the US was unable to co-ordinate state-federal efforts sufficiently quickly during Hurricane Katrina in 2005, which destroyed vast swathes of Louisiana, Mississippi, and Alabama. This can also lead to Fritz Scharpf's 'joint decision trap,' which occurs when two or more levels of government have to cooperate, but the resulting decisions are not optimal.[22]

[19] A de Tocqueville, *Democracy in America* (New York: J. & H.G. Langley, 1840) 62.

[20] Madison, *The Federalist Papers No. 10.*

[21] Brandeis J in *New Ice Co* v. *Leibman* [1932] 285 US 262, 311 (dissenting).

[22] FW Scharpf, 'The Joint-Decision Trap: Lessons from German Federalism and European Integration' (1988) 66 Public Administration 239.

Inequality: In many federal States, services such as education or social services are provided at sub-State level, and there exists great discrepancy in provision. However, some federal States, such as Germany, have managed to mitigate this problem by redistributing funds from richer to poorer levels.

These advantages and disadvantages are sometimes confused – particularly given conflicting interpretations of federalism in the US. Many understand US federalism as closely allied to states' rights, which is generally perceived as a conservative theory, linked to pro-slavery Southern states which formed the confederacy in the nineteenth century and contested federal desegregation laws in the twentieth century. Indeed, if states have more power and the federal government less, the significance of state legislature elections increases – and in the US, Republicans have taken advantage of this, and now control thirty state legislatures,[23] while Democrats control only eighteen. In 1964, political scientist William Riker notably wrote that 'if in the United States one disapproves of racism, one should disapprove of federalism.'[24] However, another tradition in both American political culture and more generally, understands federalism as more progressive and beneficial, with authors such as Elazar[25] stressing that federalism not only strengthens unity where there is common purpose but also recognizes the value of separate and unique diversities.

But is either of these understandings of federalism to be preferred? The answer surely is that federalism is in itself neither progressive nor regressive, although can promote checks, balances and the avoidance of concentrations of power. But it can be pursued for better or worse causes. Federalism is not only about decentralization of power and states' rights, but also support for central power, and indeed, during the Great Depression, and President Franklin Roosevelt's strong federal New Deal program enjoyed strong backing.

Federalism is a system of dual sovereignty. In all systems, federalism requires a balancing act, a well-thought-out relationship between national/central and subnational governments. In the US, the Supremacy Clause (Article VI, Para. 2 US Constitution) generally makes federal law supreme over state law, but the Tenth Amendment reserves unenumerated rights 'to the States [...] or to the people.' The years since the drafting of these clauses witnessed a battle as to how US federalism should work, leading to actual physical conflict in the Civil War, and their understanding continues to be disputed.

Federalism may reduce some of the dangers of an abusive concentration of power, but its operation in practice will only be as satisfactory as the actual laws created at federal or state level. States cannot always be relied on to protect fundamental rights – one of the reasons why the US Civil War was fought over

[23] www.washingtonpost.com/opinions/2021/02/18/republicans-now-enjoy-unmatched-power-states-it-was-40-year-effort/?utm_source=link_newsv9&utm_campaign=item_394823&utm_medium=copy

[24] William H Riker, *Federalism: Origin, Operation, Significance* (Boston: Little, Brown and Company, 1964) 13.

[25] Elazar, *Exploring Federalism.*

slavery, and also why the Federal Bill of Rights began to be applied to the states by the US Supreme Court. In the absence of federal standards for fundamental rights, there is a danger of intense conflict between states – a conflict that may spill beyond state borders, when states seek to enforce their laws beyond their boundaries, as in the case of fugitive slaves in the nineteenth century, and over abortion provision in the present US. This presents not only a serious conflict of laws, but a real constitutional challenge.

8.2.3 Divided Sovereignty

It is generally accepted that sovereignty in federal States is divisible.[26] Therefore, each level of government is seen as possessing ultimate authority and sovereignty within its own sphere. According to de Tocqueville, in America, 'two sovereigns are necessarily in the presence of each other.'[27] Divided sovereignty also characterizes other federal States. For example, Article 3 Swiss Constitution provides, 'the Cantons are sovereign except to the extent that their sovereignty is limited by the federal government.' Germany's Constitutional Court recognized the principle of divided sovereignty.[28]

However, the possibility of divided sovereignty has hampered the development of federalism in the UK, where there is resistance to abandoning the theory of unlimited parliamentary sovereignty. This is discussed further below.

8.2.4 Division of Competences

In federal States, it is normal for legislative powers to be divided, and usually expressly enumerated, in a Constitution.

Exclusive competences are specifically allocated to a particular level of government. These may specify only the powers of the federal government, as in the US or EU, or take the form of two separate lists – that is, one for the federal government, and one for the provinces, as in Canada. In some jurisdictions, exclusive powers of the federal government are limited, as in the US, where they are listed in the Constitution to include common defence, regulating commerce, printing money, declaring war, raising and supporting armies and a navy, and ratifying treaties. In other systems, federal institutions have a greater number of exclusive powers. The Canadian federal government's powers also include marriage, divorce, gun policy and most of the criminal law. Indeed, the Canadian Constitution (British North American) Act 1867 was specifically drafted to avoid some of the constitutional problems over contested competences which had led to the US Civil War. So, it is far more precise than the US Constitution about the location of exclusive competences.

[26] See e.g. *The Federalist Papers No. 39*.

[27] A de Tocqueville, *Democracy in America*, vol. 1 (1835) (New York: Vintage, 1954) 172.

[28] 36 BVerfGE 342, 396f (*Renumeration Law of Lower Saxony*).

Concurrent competences may be exercised by either level of government, but if one level acts, then that will usually pre-empt the other level from acting.[29] Concurrent powers are detailed in some Constitutions, such as the Swiss, Indian and German.

Residual clauses assign by default all powers not expressly enumerated. For example, the 10th Amendment of the US Constitution, Article 30 German Constitution and Article 73 Russian Constitution vest these powers with sub-State units. On the other hand, in India, Canada and South Africa, residual powers vest at federal level. Indeed, Article 91 of the 1867 Canadian Constitution Act contains a specific residual provision that allocates to the federal government all powers not exclusively allocated to the provinces, in order to ensure 'peace, order and good government'.

8.2.4.1 Asserting Federal Competence

Nonetheless, it is not always straightforward to assign a legislative competence to a particular level of government. The problem is that enumerated powers are often drafted very broadly, and it may be tricky to determine if a particular action falls within their ambit.

A good example of a federal Constitutional provision drafted in a flexible and open way is the US Commerce clause (Article. 1, s8, cl3 Federal Constitution). This gives Congress the power to regulate 'commerce with foreign nations, among the several states, and with the Indian tribes'. Although this might appear, on its face, to deal only with trade, it has proved a hugely important source of powers for the federal government, and, as early as 1824, was given a broad interpretation by the US Supreme Court.[30] It was used in the 1960s as the basis of Civil Rights legislation, often because federal lawmakers felt that the states had failed to handle problems properly themselves. However, in the 1995 *Lopez* and 2000 *Morrison* cases,[31] the Supreme Court rejected the use of the Commerce clause as a base for Congress's attempt to ban guns near local schools, and to adopt a federal violence against Women Act – nullifying the federal legislation.

In Shelby County v. *Holder*[32] in 2013, the US Supreme Court struck down a critically important provision in the 1965 Federal Voting Rights Act[33] that required certain jurisdictions with a history of discrimination in voting to obtain federal 'preclearance' to pass any new electoral or voting laws. The

[29] See e.g. S Gardbaum, 'The Nature of Preemption' (1993–1994) 79 Cornell L. Rev. 767.

[30] Starting with *Gibbons* v. *Ogden* 22 U.S. (9 Wheat.) 1 [1824].

[31] *United States* v. *Alfonso D. Lopez, Jr.*, 514 U.S. 549 [1995]. *United States* v. *Morrison* [2000] 120 S Ct 1740 at 1751.

[32] 133 Sct [2013] 2612.

[33] This was legislated to reinforce the 15th Amendment to the US Constitution – which declares that 'The right of citizens of the United States to vote shall not be denied or abridged by the United States or by any state on account of race, color, or previous condition of servitude' – and was reauthorized by Congress in 2006.

Supreme Court found the federal provision requiring preclearance to be 'out of date', and also that it infringed the 'equal sovereignty' of the states and imposed 'federalism costs' (although did not explain what those costs were). As a result, voting soon became more difficult in many states such as Texas, where strict voter ID laws were immediately introduced which has been blocked under the preclearance system. In *West Virginia* v. *EPA* in 2022, the US Supreme Court greatly abridged the Environmental Protection Agency's ability to regulate power plants under the federal Clean Air Act. The implications of the *West Virginia* ruling could extend well beyond environmental policy, especially as it seemed to ignore the *Chevron* deference doctrine, whereby the Supreme Court had previously held that, if a statutory provision administered by a federal agency is ambiguous, then the courts should defer to that interpretation, providing it is reasonable.[34] These cases illustrate the crucial role courts have played in determining where power lies.

8.2.4.2 Implied Powers

The political theory underlying conferred powers is that of limited government. However, this has been complicated by the doctrine of implied powers, which originally developed in the US, where the 'necessary and proper clause' of the US Constitution (Article 1, s8, cl 18) grants Congress the power 'to make all laws which shall be necessary and proper for carrying into execution the foregoing powers….' Until quite recently, the US Supreme Court tended to uphold federal actions taken under the necessary and proper clause. In 1819, in *McCulloch* v. *Maryland*[35], the Court approved the federal government's power to use Article 1 s8 cl 18 to establish a federal bank. However, this approach has altered recently, and in *Printz* v. *US* in 1997, the Supreme Court declared that states retained a 'residual and inviolable sovereignty.'[36]

Such issues were raised in the US in the high profile legal challenges to 'Obamacare' – cases which were described by the *New York Times* as the most significant federalism cases since the New Deal.[37] The 2010 federal Patient Protection and Affordable Care Act ('Obamacare') was based on both the US Constitution's Commerce clause and 'Necessary and Proper' clause and required all individuals ('the individual mandate') not already covered by a health plan (or Medicare or Medicaid) to obtain one, or pay a penalty.[38] The Supreme Court held (5:4) that neither the Commerce clause nor the Necessary and

[34] *West Virginia* v. *EPA* 597 US [2022]; *Chevron USA, Inc.* v. *Natural Resources Defense Council, Inc.*, 468 U.S. 837 [1984].

[35] *McCulloch* v. *Maryland*, 17 U.S. (4 Wheat.) 316 [1819].

[36] *Printz* v. *United States*, 521 U.S. 898 [1997]. *Printz* concerned federal legislation requiring a national system for background checks on handgun purchases.

[37] A Liptak, 'Supreme Court Upholds Health Care Law, 5–4, in Victory for Obama' *New York Times*, June 28, 2012.

[38] It did this by offering individuals discounts (described as tax credits) on government-sponsored health insurance plans, and by expanding the Medicaid assistance program to cover more people who were too poor to finance their own health care.

Proper clause could be used as a basis for the individual mandate.[39] However, the legislation was not nullified because the majority held that its imposition of a penalty on individuals who did not obtain health insurance could be justified under Congress' tax raising powers and so was a valid exercise of Congressional authority. A separate jointly written dissent argued that the whole law should have been invalidated, and that the majority approach 'amounts to a vast judicial overreaching.'[40] And the attacks on 'Obamacare' continue. So the division between federal and state powers is very much a live issue in the US.

Other jurisdictions contain similar 'implied powers' clauses. Article 91 of the Canadian Constitution enables the Federal Parliament to legislate in all areas not specifically reserved to the provinces to guarantee 'peace order and good governance', although this clause has generally been more restrictively interpreted than the US 'necessary and proper' clause. Article 352 TFEU contains a provision similar to the 'necessary and proper' clause which is discussed below in the EU section.

8.2.4.3 Subsidiarity

The term 'Subsidiarity'[41] is not much used in the common law world, although it shares common ground with federalism in being an attempt to protect freedom by the fragmentation of power. Notably, the Tenth Amendment of the US Constitution provides that: 'The powers not delegated to the United States by the Constitution or prohibited by it to the States, are reserved to the States respectively, or to the people.' However, the Tenth Amendment does not express any preference for a particular distribution of power and there are no US structures which regulate the distribution of competence between the state and federal governments in a way similar to subsidiarity in the EU. Article 72(2) German Constitution (the so-called necessity clause) has been considered an example of the subsidiarity principle,[42] and, when the German Federal Constitution was drafted at Herrenchiemsee after the Second World War, the desire was to maintain the strength of the Länder vis-a-vis the federal government.[43]

8.2.5 Shared Rule: Participation of Sub-State Entities at National Level

It will be remembered that Daniel Elazar described Federalism as 'self-rule plus shared rule'. It is this element of shared rule that is often thought to be lacking

[39] *National Federation of Independent Businesses* v. *Sebelius* 567 US [2012].

[40] *National Federation of Independent Businesses,* at 2644–2650.

[41] Discussed below in the EU section.

[42] Article 72(2) provides: 'The Federation shall have the right to legislate on matters falling within … Article 74, if and to the extent that the establishment of equivalent living conditions throughout the federal territory or the maintenance of legal or economic unity renders federal regulation necessary in the national interest.'

[43] However, the German Constitutional Court for many years found Art 72(2) non-justiciable, until the 2002 *Geriatric Nursing* case. BVerfGE vol. 106, pp. 62ff.

in devolved States, such as the UK. Power is shared where sub-States participate in decisions concerning the whole State, although the areas and means of shared decision-making vary considerably. Some prominent examples are highlighted below.

8.2.5.1 Areas of Shared Decision-Making

8.2.5.1.1 Constitutional Amendments

This is perhaps the most significant example of shared rule and protects against unilateral amendments by one level of government alone. But there is no unanimous method of participation for sub-State units. In the US, Art V of the federal Constitution requires ratification of amendments by either by three-fourth state Legislatures, or conventions in three-fourth states. In Canada, prior to 1982, constitutional amendments had to be adopted by the UK Parliament. However, in 1982, the Canadian Constitution was 'repatriated' to Canada. Prior to then, it was not clear that Canadian provinces had to be consulted on amendments. This matter was litigated in the Canadian Supreme Court, which determined that, although provinces did not have a formal veto, by constitutional convention they could be granted a high level of protection, as in the case of Quebec.[44]

8.2.5.1.2 Territorial Changes

An alteration of a State's boundaries usually requires the consent of sub-State units, given that this concerns their territorial integrity and indeed, their possible existence. In the US, territorial alterations require the consent of affected state legislatures of, as well as that of Congress (Article IV, section 3). In Canada and Australia, territorial alterations must be by constitutional amendment. Likewise in South Africa.

8.2.5.2 Means of Shared Decision-Making

8.2.5.2.1 Second Chambers

An obvious and much used *means* of shared governance is that of a federal second Chamber, which provides sub-States with a voice in the legislature.[45] The US Constitution stipulates the Senate as Second Chamber, whereby senators are directly elected by citizens, with each state equally represented by two Senators. This was the result of the 'Connecticut compromise' at the 1787 Philadelphia Convention, which reconciled the interests of the largest and smallest states by allowing their equal representation in the Senate, but with House representation proportionate to each state's population.[46] However, in other systems,

[44] *Reference Re Resolution to amend the Constitution* [1981] 1 SCR 753.

[45] E.g. N Baldwin and D Shell, *Second Chambers* (London: Frank Cass & Co., 2011).

[46] See *Garcia* v. *San Antonio Transit Authority* 469 US 528, 550 f [1985], where the Supreme Court held that states 'were given a more direct influence in the Senate'.

such as Germany, Länder representation in the second Chamber (*Bundesrat*) varies according to territorial size and population. Although each EU State is represented by only one minister in the EU Council of Ministers, votes are weighted according to population.[47] However, the EU Council of Ministers is not part of the EU Parliament, whereas the arrangement in Germany is that the federal Parliament is comprised of both the *Bundestag* and *Bundesrat*. There also exist some hybrid second Chambers, such as in Russia and South Africa. Second Chambers can play an important role in constitutional amendments in federal systems. Specific majorities are usually required, as under Article 79 German Constitution.

In contrast to all of the above, in the UK, which is of course not a federal system, the House of Lords does not represent the specific interests of the nations and regions of the UK – although it has been suggested that it should be reformed to do so.[48]

8.2.5.2.2 Federal Courts

Federal court rulings can support uniformity in interpretation, strengthening centripetal tendencies. The US federal courts gives rulings that bind federal government and the states. However, whereas dual federal systems such as the US, will tend to have separate judiciaries for each level of government, more cooperative (or integrative) systems are more likely to have a single judiciary, as is the case in Canada.

However, federal courts can give rulings that are more or less protective of the federal government or of the states. The US Supreme Court provides a good example. Although until the late twentieth century, the Supreme Court tended to defer to Congress at the expense of state sovereignty, since the 1990s there has been a noticeable move in favour of states' rights. Back in 1995, *New York Times* Supreme Court reporter Linda Greenhouse wrote that 'it is only a slight exaggeration to say that … the Court [is] a single vote shy of reinstalling the Articles of Confederation.'[49] Since then, the process has accelerated, with many recent US Supreme Court decisions – such as on abortion access and voting rights – appearing to have returned power back to the states. The most notable significance of these decisions is their capacity to increase the distinction between red (Republican dominated) and blue (Democrat dominated) states. In *Dobbs* v. *Jackson Women's Health*,[50] the US Supreme Court overturned the 1973 *Roe* v. *Wade* and 1992 *Casey* precedents, holding that there is no federal constitutional right to an abortion. Although *Dobbs* was not decided on federalism grounds, the Supreme Court held that US states should make this decision – seen by many as a victory for states' rights, and there is

[47] See Article 16 TEU, Articles 237–243 TFEU.

[48] See the chapter on Union and disunion. Also, it is worth noting that the largest political party in Scotland, the SNP, does not nominate any members to the House of Lords.

[49] L Greenhouse, 'Focus on Federal Power', *NYT*, 24 May 1995. [50] 597 US [2022].

now some talk of a 'post-*Roe* federalism'.[51] However, in 2023, the US Supreme Court in *Moore v Harper* rejected the 'independent state legislature theory', which holds that state legislatures may not be constrained when setting rules for federal elections, even if they violate their state's Constitution.[52]

However, the Supreme Court has not been entirely consistent in deciding when to defer to the state democratic process, as cases such as *New York State Rifle & Pistol Association* v. *Bruen*[53] (in which court struck down a century-old New York law that placed strict limits on carrying guns outside the home) illustrate.

8.2.6 Federalism and Treaties

Foreign relations is generally regarded as the domain of federal central government, although sub-States often have involvement. In the UK, foreign policy is reserved to the UK Government but treaty involvement is topical, post-Brexit, because devolved UK nations have shown some interest in acquiring their own treaty-making capacity, for fear that the UK Government might infringe their trade regulating powers.

8.2.6.1 Sub-State Treaty Involvement

In 1923, the *Wimbledon* judgment of the Permanent Court of International Justice characterized the right to conclude international agreements as 'an attribute of State sovereignty.'[54] Nonetheless, sub-State, supranational, and extra-national bodies all now engage in treaty-making in their own right, and many States have accepted this. Ukraine and Belarus joined the UN Charter while part of the Soviet Union, as did India and the Philippines prior to independence (from the UK and US). The German and Austrian Länder, Swiss Cantons, Hong Kong, Bermuda, Jersey, the Cook Islands, New Caledonia, Puerto Rico, Tatarstan, Quebec, Wallonia, and Flanders (all sub-State actors) have also all concluded treaties.

Increasingly, States have formalized the treaty-making capacity of sub-State entities through national law. Since 1993, Belgium has authorized its constituent 'regions' to enter into treaties on matters within their exclusive competence (e.g. environmental resources).[55] Such a situation would not be possible in the UK without considerable further devolution legislation.

[51] See further, 'Fair-Weather Federalism: Strategic Uses of the 10th Amendment', Brennan Centre for Justice, 5 July 2022.

[52] *Moore v Harper* 600 US [2023]. See further, V Amar and A Amar, 'Eradicating Bush-League Arguments Root and Branch: The Article II Independent-State-Legislature Notion and Related Rubbish' (2021) 1 Supreme Court Review.

[53] 597 US [2022].

[54] *Case of the S.S. Wimbledon* (PCIJ), Ser. A., No. 1 (1923). But see M Koskenniemi, 'The Future of Statehood' (1991) 32 Harv. JIL 397; H Michelman and P Soldatos (eds.), *Federalism and International Relations, the Role of Subnational Units* (Oxford: Oxford University Press, 1990).

[55] Articles 115–140 Belgian Constitution.

Under the German Constitution, 'relations with other states are … conducted by the Federation' (Article 32(1)) but Länder specifically concerned must be consulted, and under the principle of federal loyalty (*Bundestreue*) the Federal Government is obliged to take into account the opinion of the Länder. German Länder participate in decision-making related to European integration under Article 23, which requires the consent of the *Bundesrat* for the transfer of sovereign powers to the EU. Länder also participate in the EU legislation process. The position is similar in Austria. Therefore, Länder are in a stronger position than Britain's devolved nations. And, while Article 1 US Constitution prohibits US states from treaty making, it does authorize them to enter into 'compacts' with foreign powers, provided they obtain approval of the US Congress. The UK itself has used an 'Instrument of Entrustment' to authorize overseas territories such as Bermuda, the British Virgin Islands, and Jersey to conclude certain treaties with the United States and Canada.[56]

Sub-State participation in multilateral agreements is less common because other States often refuse consent to the sub-State actor's participation. However, there are exceptions. For example, WTO Agreement Article XII authorizes any 'customs territory possessing full autonomy in the conduct of its external commercial relations' to accede on terms agreed to between it and the WTO.' Prior to their reversion to China from the UK and Portugal, both Hong Kong and Macau joined the WTO under Article XII.

In many federal States, the notion that central government can employ the cover of foreign treaties to invade sub-State competences has been very controversial. Although the US President has full power to make treaties, under Article II(2) US Constitution such treaties require the concurrence of two-thirds of the Senate present, and limits on federal treaty power require that it not encroach on constitutional autonomy of the states. The Canadian Constitution is not explicit on treaty-powers, but under Canadian constitutional law conduct of foreign affairs is a federal function. However, because provinces must implement treaties relating to their competences, they have tended to be involved in treaty negotiations to ensure later compliance and have a de facto veto over treaties concerning their jurisdiction. In some instances, provinces have even taken the lead in international negotiations. For example, the negotiation of an integrated Canadian-American energy plan was led largely by Alberta. So, Canada provides an interesting example for devolution in the UK, because, although there is no explicit constitutional provision for provinces in the treaty process, in practice they have gained a greater role than explicit terms might suggest. This demonstrates that widespread legislation is not always necessary for constitutional change.

[56] See I Sinclair and S Dickson, 'United Kingdom', in M Leigh and M. Blakeslee (eds.), 1995 *National Treaty Law and Practice* (Washington DC: American Society of International Law, 1995) at 244.

Therefore, even although UK devolved nations currently have no formal treaty-making powers, examples from other jurisdictions prompt questions of whether the UK may conclude treaties that intrude on devolved competences, and also whether devolveds may exercise power in the way that treaties are implemented.

8.2.7 Finance

Most federal systems set out the revenue-raising powers of both levels of government in their Constitutions. This covers all sorts of issues such as: who has the authority to impose tax; who is authorized to dictate public spending; which levels of government may borrow money; whether sub-State units may raise their own revenue, and if not, what arrangements exist for revenue transfers from the federal government. There is no uniform model for any of these decisions. The major areas of tax include personal income tax, corporation tax, sales and consumption tax, and customs and excise. Customs and excise is almost always a federal tax because of the need for an effective Customs Union and Internal Market. Corporation tax is usually imposed federally as corporations often tend to operate cross border and it is simpler to regulate at federal level. Personal income tax is more likely to be shared between governance levels as it relates to individual residence, although is sometimes exclusively federal, as in Austria and India. In most federations, the majority of revenue sources are allocated to the federal government even where taxes are imposed concurrently, because federal governments have more infrastructure for redistribution of wealth.

Sometimes federal government provides funding in areas exclusive to sub-State units. This has happened in the US since the depression of the 1930s. Sub-State governments have accepted federal assistance but if it has been made conditional, it has often been resented as interference with sub-State exclusive jurisdiction. The UK Internal Market Act 2020 somewhat controversially gave the UK government the power to fund devolved areas.

In the non-federal UK, devolved nations are funded through the non-statutory Barnett formula, which is considered further below.

8.2.8 Multinational Federalism

Even if federal States are internally divided along national lines, there may exist within those sub-States further minorities, sometimes known as 'internal minorities'[57] at risk of being marginalized. As a result, there may exist federal measures to reduce that risk – such as catalogues of fundamental rights, and specific power-sharing arrangements within sub-States such as

[57] E.g. S Choudhry, 'Does the World Need More Canada?' (2007) 5 International Journal of Constitutional Law 624.

consociationalism,[58] which is mainly characterized by proportional representation, veto rights and segmental autonomy for minority groups. Consociational governance has been used in Northern Ireland, Bosnia-Herzegovina, and Lebanon. It is a form of democracy but very different from majoritarian democracy. Consociational power sharing takes place in the Northern Ireland Assembly and Executive. Executive power-sharing includes the joint office of First Minister and Deputy First Minister, each holding equal powers, and a multi-party Executive. At legislative level, Northern Ireland Assembly decisions require cross-community support on certain designated issues.[59] Thus, Northern Ireland governance is built on the issue of *consent*.

8.2.9 The Pathology of Federations

The term 'pathology' is used by Watts. He notes that most federations are very effective and include many of the most long-standing constitutional governments – such as the US (1789), Switzerland (1848), Canada (1867), and Australia (1901). However, there have also been failed federal attempts, including the West Indies (1962) Yugoslavia (1991) USSR (1991), the splitting of Pakistan (1971) the expulsion of Singapore from Malaysia (1965), and civil war in Nigeria (1967–1970).

In such cases, the sources of stress are varied. Very sharp regional divergences and internal divisions certainly contributed in the case of the USSR and Yugoslavia. Institutional failures may also contribute – where, for example, there exists extreme diversity in the size and population of sub-State units, and in particular where one becomes over-dominant, such as Russia in the old USSR, or Jamaica in the West Indian federation, and institutional arrangements have not been recalibrated to take account of this. This is also exacerbated where the language of a major regional group is denied recognition.

8.2.9.1 Secession

Most Constitutions either explicitly prohibit, or do not explicitly grant, a right to secession. It is sometimes said this is because Constitutions are not 'suicide pacts.'[60] Only a few Constitutions have made explicit provision for secession, and even so, in most cases such terms have not been taken very seriously. The 1930s Soviet and Chinese Communist Constitutions included a right to secede, but no legal procedure to enforce that right. However, the EU treaties contain the specific Article 50 TEU, first used on the occasion of the UK's Brexit. This makes it one of the very few provisions setting out an explicit secession procedure, although the EU is of course not a federal State.

[58] E.g. A Lijphart, 'Consociational Democracy' (1969) 21(2) World Politics 207.

[59] See e.g. J McGarry and B O'Leary, *The Northern Ireland Conflict: Consociational Engagements* (Oxford: Oxford University Press, 2004); also Part IV Northern Ireland Act 1998.

[60] See e.g. C Sunstein, 'Constitutionalism and Secession' (1991) 58 University of Chicago LR 633.

8.2.10 Federalism All the Way?

A further question is whether *more* federalism is better. Normally, the focus of federalism is on only two levels of government – on State and sub-State levels. However, it has been argued that federalism should extend down to local government and beyond. For example, both the Brazilian and Indian Constitutions provide that federalising arrangements may apply to cities and regions.[61]

And of course, this issue extends in the other direction, to governance beyond the State at a regional or global level. In the eighteenth century, Kant's 'On Perpetual Peace'[62] considered the notion of world federation, although saw obstacles to its realization. More recently, David Held and others have asserted the possibility of global, hierarchically organized, multilevel rule.[63] The EU provides an example of multi-level governance – neither completely federal, nor confederal – that will be examined shortly. On the other hand, there is opposition to extending levels of governance beyond the State, particularly for those who assert that sovereignty is important and can only function at State level.

8.2.11 Federacies and Associated States

Finally, it is worth considering *federacies* (and associated States)[64] which are distinct from federations. Both have much in common with situations of asymmetrical devolution such as in the UK, in that they concern a relationship between a smaller territorial unit and a larger State. However, unlike devolution in the UK, the smaller unit retains internal autonomy.[65]

Federacies are usually small populations and are often islands. There are less than 20 of them in existence. Stepan, Linz and Yadav define a *federacy* in the following way:

[61] Articles 18, 30 Brazilian Constitution; and Art 243B Indian Constitution.

[62] I Kant, 'Perpetual Peace: A Philosophical Sketch', in H Reiss (ed.), *Kant's Political Writings* (Cambridge: Cambridge University Press, 1970).

[63] E.g. D Held, *Cosmopolitanism: Ideals and Realities* (Cambridge: Polity, 2010).

[64] According to Ronald Watts, examples of federacies are the Aaland Islands (Finland), Azores Islands (Portugal), Faroe Islands (Denmark), Greenland (Denmark), Guernsey (United Kingdom), Isle of Man (United Kingdom), Jammu and Kashmir (India), Jersey (United Kingdom), Madeira Islands (Portugal), Northern Marianas (United States), and Puerto Rico (United States). Examples of associated states are Bhutan (India), Cook Islands (New Zealand), Liechtenstein (Switzerland), Monaco (France), Netherlands Antilles (Netherlands), Nieue Island (New Zealand), and San Marino (Italy) (R Watts 'Foreword: States, Provinces, Lander, and Cantons: International Variety among Subnational Constitutions', 31 Rutgers L.J. 941 1999–2000).

[65] Dr Eve Hepburn and I addressed this issue in written evidence to the 2015 Scottish Parliament inquiry (Scottish Parliament Devolution (Further Powers) Committee Implementing the Smith Agreement: The UK Government's Draft Legislative Clauses). Our evidence, *The*

> a federacy is a political-administrative unit in an independent unitary state with exclusive power in certain areas, including some legislative power, constitutionally or quasi-constitutionally embedded, that cannot be changed unilaterally and whose inhabitants have full citizenship rights in the otherwise unitary state.[66]

In such arrangements, there is considerable *self-rule*, but much less *shared-rule* than in federal States such as Germany. So, for example, Denmark and Finland have both legislated Autonomy Acts that constitutionally protect the self-governing powers of some of their sub-State units, including Greenland, the Faroe Islands and the Åland Islands.[67] These sub-State units can veto any competence transfer away from them and thus escape the constitutional uncertainty of their powers being revoked, unlike in the case of devolved UK nations which endure a hierarchical relationship with the centre.

Associated States are similar to federacies, in that the smaller unit benefits from a high level of internal self-determination and its autonomy is constitutionally guaranteed. In the associated Statehood model, the sub-State unit has substantial autonomy over a range of competences (indeed, often more extensive than those of a federacy), whilst the larger power often assumes control for foreign policy and defence. However, in contrast to federacies, the relationship 'can be dissolved by either of the units acting alone on prearranged terms.'[68] As a result, their stability is less secure. Among their number are Monaco (associated with France), Liechtenstein (with Switzerland), and the relationships between the United States and the Marshall Islands, and New Zealand and the Cook Islands.

Federacies and associated States thus provide interesting examples concerning a sub-State entity's relationship with a unitary State and even with an international organization.

8.3 The EU and Federalism

The EU can be a difficult polity to fathom. Perhaps, for eurosceptics, this is part of its problem. If it appears too close in its structures to a sovereign State, then it is prone to censure as an unwanted 'superstate', undermining national

'Permanence' Issue: A Question of Symbolism or Power?, is available at: www.scottish.parliament.uk/S4_ScotlandBillCommittee/General%20Documents/Dr_E_Hepburn.pdf

[66] A Stepan, J Linz, and Y Yadav, *Crafting State-Nations: India and Other Multinational Democracies* (Baltimore: Johns Hopkins University Press, 2011).

[67] The Greenlandic Self Government Act (Act no. 473 of the Danish Parliament 12 June 2009); the Faroese Home Rule Act (Act 137 of the Danish Parliament 23 March 1948). The Self-Government (Autonomy) Act of the Åland Islands was enacted by the Parliament of Finland in 1991 (No. 1144/1991).

[68] RL Watts, *Comparing Federal Systems* (Kingston Ont: Queen's University Press, 1999) 8–9.

sovereignty. On the other hand, if its configuration is perceived as more diffuse, then it is dismissed as ineffective and unworkable. In fact, the EU has often been regarded as *sui generis*, as something more than an international organization but still not a State. There has certainly been no consensus of opinion among scholars as to its legal status.

Part of the problem is that, in spite of the 'post sovereignty' evolution, many (in Britain especially) continue to interpret governance as something irredeemably connected to national sovereignty and a strong central State, and have not appreciated what has been described as Europe's 'Sonderweg'.[69] However, to understand the EU properly, we need to consider its governance arrangements, and interrogate its relationship to federalism. This reveals that the EU's relations with the UK were far more nuanced, and delicately balanced, than eurosceptics ever allowed.

8.3.1 Is the EU a Federal Polity?

Lord Beloff, writing in the 1990s, in somewhat eurosceptic vein, suggested that 'the EEC was the basis for a federal system.'[70] To be sure, early European federalists, such as Spinelli, were clearly aware of the benefits of a federalist structure for Europe. However, the very word 'federal' – in an early draft of the Maastricht treaty – was enough to cause apoplexy in some quarters, so it has usually been avoided in the EU context. Yet, aside from mere avoidance of an issue unpalatable to some, there are two reasons why the EU's relation to federalism is a difficult question to answer. The first is that, as we have seen, the concept of federalism is itself complex and contested. The second is that of the complex multidimensional nature of the EU – trying to pigeonhole it within a single concept may simply not do it justice. So, it is helpful to carry out a short audit of the EU, considering which 'typical' features of federalism might apply to it, and what conclusions to draw from that.

8.3.1.1 The Division of Competences

As we have seen, federations tend to set out a formal division of competences between federal and sub-State components. The division of powers between the EU and its member States has been set out since the 2009 Treaty of Lisbon, and the Treaty on the Functioning of the EU (TFEU) now clarifies these competences into three main categories. First, exclusive competences (Article 3), which the EU alone is able to exercise, and which are limited in number, comprising only the Customs Union, common commercial policy towards third countries, competition rules necessary for the functioning of the Internal

[69] JHH Weiler, 'Federalism without Constitutionalism: Europe's *Sonderweg*', in K Nicolaidis and R Howse (eds.), *The Federal Vision: Legitimacy and Levels of Governance in the US and the EU* (Oxford: Oxford University Press, 2001) 54.

[70] Lord Beloff, *Britain and European Union: Dialogue of the Deaf* (London: Macmillan, 1996) at 35.

Market, certain aspects of the common fisheries policy, monetary policy for member States whose currency is the euro, and conclusion of certain international agreements. Second, and much more numerous, there are shared competences (Article 4) which both the EU and member States may exercise, but which the EU can exercise only if it conforms with the principle of subsidiarity. Thirdly, there are competences under Article 6, whereby the EU has no original legislative power and can only intervene to support, coordinate or complement the action of member States. Further, Article 5 TEU makes it clear that the EU may only 'only act within the limits of the competences conferred on it by the member States in the Treaties to attain the objectives set out therein.' It also specifies that 'Competences not conferred upon the Union in the treaties remain with the member States.'

Therefore, despite fears of intrusive 'Brussels bureaucrats', the EU is clearly limited in what it can do. Any action taken by the EU must have a legal basis (either in the EU treaties or EU secondary legislation) which must be clearly stated in the preamble to EU legislation. Moreover, attitudes towards competence have shifted over the years. In the post-Maastricht years, member States reacted to the perceived growth of EU competence by seeking to impose boundaries on actions the EU could take. This backlash took several forms, including the insertion of the subsidiarity principle into EU treaties. A warning also came from the German Constitutional Court, in its *Maastricht* judgment of 1993, which stressed the limited democratic authority of the EU to extend its powers.[71]

And then, in 2000 the ECJ annulled the Tobacco Advertising directive (which banned or heavily restricted the advertising of tobacco products in the EU), on the basis that the EU lacked the competence to adopt it[72] – the first time the Court had ever annulled an EU measure on this basis. Article 114 TFEU (Article 100a EC as it then was) confers on the EU the competence to enact 'measures for the harmonization' of national rules regarding the establishment and functioning of the internal market.' Although by no means identical with the US Commerce Clause, there is a similarity between these two provisions. Both Article 114 and the Commerce Clause regulate economic activity, but in wide and open-textured language. The ECJ accepted that the directive could not be an internal market measure, but must be a public health measure, in which case the EU did not have the jurisdiction to adopt it. The ECJ found, in terms echoing that of the US Supreme Court in *Morrison*, that '… If a mere finding of disparities between national rules and of the abstract risk of obstacles to the exercise of fundamental freedoms or of distortions of competition … were sufficient to justify the choice of [Article 100a] as a legal basis, judicial review of compliance with the proper legal basis might be rendered nugatory.'[73]

71 *Brunner* v. *European Union Treaty* [1994] 1 CMLR 57.

72 Case C-376/98 *Germany v Council and Parliament* and Case C-74/99 *R* v. *Secretary of State for Health, ex parte Imperial Tobacco* [2000] ECR I-8419.

73 Ibid., at paras 76 and 84.

Therefore, there exists EU caselaw concerning the division of powers between the EU and member States, that could be said to raise federal issues. Although the ECJ has sometimes been criticised for an expansive interpretation of EU powers, the *Tobacco* case indicated a willingness to set boundaries to EU expansion by way of caselaw.

8.3.1.2 Implied Powers

We may also draw comparisons between the 'necessary and proper' clause in the US Constitution and the 'implied powers' clause in EU law, which is now found in Article 352(1) TFEU and states:

> If action by the Union should prove necessary, within the framework of the policies defined in the Treaties, to attain one of the objectives set out in the Treaties, and the Treaties have not provided the necessary powers, the Council, acting unanimously on a proposal from the Commission and after obtaining the consent of the European Parliament, shall adopt the appropriate measures.

Article 352 is textually ambiguous, and the notion of an objective is hardly clear cut. In the early years of the EEC, Article 352 was little used. However, in 1976 it was used as a legal basis for the Equal Treatment Directive 76/207. From then on, its use increased, often being used for environmental legislation, in the absence of specific provisions in the treaty. It was also the basis for legislation for the increasingly popular idea of a 'people's Europe'. Indeed, it was not until 1996 that a judicial limit was placed on its use, when the ECJ held that it could not be used as a basis for the (then) EC to accede to the European Convention on Human Rights.[74]

One might question the harm of an over-expansive use by the EU of Article 352. After all, Article 352 requires member State unanimity (in contrast to the US 'necessary and proper' clause, which does not require unanimity in the Senate). The answer must be, however, that if Article 352 is used to exceed EU powers, it bypasses the democratic process for treaty amendment in Article 48 TEU (which requires treaty amendments to be ratified by member State parliaments). This upsets the balance between the EU and member States. So there might be some ground for fearing an EU 'competence creep' (namely, the idea that EU treaty provisions are broadly drafted and so enable competence to creep beyond enumerated limits).

8.3.1.3 The 'Balance of Competences' Review

However, lest there be fear that evolution of EU/member State division of competences illustrates a power grabbing exercise, one might note that the UK Government's 'Balance of Competences review' – comprised of 32 volumes, 3,000 pages of evidence, and more than 1500 independent sources – concluded

[74] *Opinion 2/94* [1996] ECRI-1759. This competence continues to be contested, e.g. *Opinion 2/13 re ECHR Accession* [2014] ECR.

there was no evidence that the EU had excessive competence, nor that its competences need be repatriated.[75] It noted that most EU competences are shared with member States, that the EU has few exclusive competences, and those that exist are mainly driven by practical reality, given neither the Customs Union nor EMU could function if there were multiple national policies. This Review was described as 'an audit of what the EU does and how it affects the UK',[76] although, regrettably, it was overshadowed by the renegotiation and EU referendum processes in 2016, and then generally ignored.

8.3.1.4 Subsidiarity

Although subsidiarity was the buzz word of the Maastricht Treaty negotiations, Pope Pius XI also played a part in developing subsidiarity, in the context of Catholic philosophy.[77] But Catholic thought is by no means the only source of the subsidiarity principle. The focus on the inappropriateness of State action when more localized steps are preferable is also a theme of modern liberal thought. The boundaries of State action are perennial themes in the writings of de Tocqueville and Mill, and Rousseau advocated for small States over larger ones.

In the EU context, subsidiarity is a means of determining the appropriate level of action and reconciling the conflicting needs of unity and diversity within the EU. It is closely related to the concepts of necessity, effectiveness, proportionality, or even good government. As set out in Article 5(3) TEU, subsidiarity (which applies only in areas of concurrent competence) permits EU institutions to act 'only if and insofar as the objectives of the proposed action cannot be sufficiently achieved by the member States, either at central level or at regional and local level, but can rather, by reason of the scale or effects of the proposed action, be better achieved at Union level.' However, its justiciability had proved very limited.

In summary, while subsidiarity may have a specific legal formulation in the context of the EU, which concerns the exercise of competence, it also has a more general meaning, relating to key questions of political authority, government and legitimacy of government which have been posed by political philosophers and theorists over the years. Indeed, as expressed by the French politician Jean Pierre Cot, 'only subsidiarity could manage to put Jacques Delors perfectly in tune with Mrs Thatcher'.[78]

[75] See e.g. FCO, *Review of the Balance of Competences between the United Kingdom and the European Union*, Cm 8415, July 2012.

[76] *Review of the Balance of Competences* 'Introduction'.

[77] In the papal encyclical, *Quadragesimo Anno* it was stated that:
'It is an injustice, a grave evil and a disturbance of right order for a larger and higher association to arrogate to itself functions which can be performed efficiently by smaller and lower societies.'

[78] Cited in John Peterson, 'Subsidiarity: A Definition to Suit Any Vision?' (1994) 47 Parliamentary Affairs 116.

8.3.1.5 Other Factors

There are further components of EU law which are indicative of some federal drift – for example: the doctrines of supremacy and direct effect,[79] which provide scope for strengthening the EU against its member States. The decision-making processes of the EU, which lend a role both to the member States acting in the Council, but also to peoples of Europe as represented in the EU Parliament, is also capable of looking federal. The EU now has a Charter of Fundamental Rights, applying to all EU law, and there are also treaty provisions such as Article 4(2)TEU, which requires the EU to respect the national identities of its member States, an indication of a federal concern with protecting the diversity of the parts.

However, other aspects of the EU seem less federal, given the amount of intergovernmental decision-making that they involve. Foreign and security policy, usually the preserve of the central government in federal systems, is such an example. Under EU Common Foreign and Security Policy Articles 23–46 TEU, decision-making is unanimous, and thus in the hands of the member States, although the EU Commission and Parliament play some role. Further, although, on the one hand, the EU now has a common currency, shared by some member States, on the other hand, the USA had a federal government and Constitution before it had a uniform dollar currency, so a uniform currency is perhaps not a must.

8.3.1.6 An Affective Dimension

However, it is not just institutional arrangements which are indicative of federalism. Dicey, for example, argued that a successful federal system required a singular sentiment among the inhabitants of the countries which it was to unite.[80] In perhaps an attempt to articulate such a singular sentiment, Article 2 TEU provides that: 'The Union is founded on the values of respect for human dignity, freedom, democracy, equality, the rule of law and respect for human rights, including the rights of persons belonging to minorities.' Notwithstanding, a constant argument has been that Europe lacks a *demos* and that there is little affective support for the EU.[81] Yet, affective support may also be lacking in individual States – there may be little support for Westminster in Scotland, or for Washington DC in much of the USA.

8.3.2 Differentiation in EU Law

8.3.2.1 A 'Multi-speed' EU

The EU is clearly not a federal super-State. Moreover, it also permits differentiated integration *between* its member States. There exists a 'multi-speed' EU, or

[79] Neither doctrine has a basis in the EU treaties. They are judicial creations of the ECJ.

[80] AV Dicey, *The Law of the Constitution*, vol. 1, JWF Allison (ed.), (*Oxford Edition of Dicey*, Oxford University Press, 2013) at 144.

[81] E.g. D Grimm, 'Does Europe Need a Constitution?' (1995) European Law Journal 282–302.

a variable geometry, whereby different parts of the EU can integrate at different rates. Examples of this are found in the Schengen free movement agreement, and the Eurozone, in both of which only some States participate, and also in the enhanced co-operation provisions in the EU treaties.[82] Moreover, EU treaties introduced opt-outs and protocols, enabling some countries, such as the UK, to follow a less intense path of integration.

8.3.2.2 EU Provisions Allowing Sub-State Participation

Nevertheless, the EU treaties suggest that only States can be EU members (Article 49 TEU: 'Any European State … may apply to become a member of the Union.') In traditional international law, the 'State' is a formal category, with legal personality, in a way that the sub-State or region usually is not.[83] The EU itself was founded as an entity of international law, set up by treaty, by sovereign States.

However, there exist provisions in EU treaties that permit sub-State entities to participate in certain EU institutions. The 1992 Maastricht Treaty first introduced measures with a clearly regional dimension, partly under pressure from regional actors, especially the German Länder. It was also then that the subsidiarity principle was formally introduced into EU law and provision made for regional government ministers to represent a member State in the Council.[84] A new institution, the Committee of the Regions, was created,[85] which some hoped would stimulate a 'Europe of the Regions' as a next step in European integration. However, 30 years later, the Committee of the Regions is still not acknowledged as an EU formal institution under Article 13 TEU.

There are other ways in which diverse parts of a State's territory may have different relationships with the EU – usually after special arrangements have been negotiated. Several examples came from Britain, including the Isle of Man and Channel Islands (which are not part of the UK nor were part of the EU, but possessions of the British Crown). Nonetheless, Protocol 3 UK Accession Treaty to the (then) EEC permitted trade for their goods without non-EU tariffs, although they were excluded from EU provisions governing free movement of people.[86] Another example is Gibraltar, a British overseas territory with its own Constitution and self-government, except for defence and foreign affairs for which the British Government is responsible. Although it was part

82 Such as Article. 20 TEU, Articles 326–334 TFEU – which enable a smaller group of EU States to adopt certain measures, such as cross border divorce, patents, and international property.

83 Montevideo Convention on Rights and Duties of States 1933, Article 1. As with the EU, under UN Charter Article 4, only 'States' can be admitted to UN membership.

84 The Treaty provides for participation of a 'representative of each member State at ministerial level, authorized to commit the government of that member State' – Article 16(2) TEU.

85 Now Arts 305–307 TFEU.

86 Their relationship with the EU is set out under Article 355(5)(c) TFEU, and Protocol 3, annexed to the Treaty of Accession 1972.

of the EU, Gibraltar was outside the Customs Union and VAT area, exempted from the CAP, and did not form part of Schengen. Nonetheless, it was required to leave the EU along with the UK after the Brexit referendum, despite having voted to remain.

A further example (although one could give many others[87]) of differentiated EU membership is provided by the no longer extant West Berlin. In 1955, the Federal Republic of Germany (FRG) had no governmental authority over Berlin and instead the Allied Control Authority, City Council and Senate were the governing bodies in Berlin. At the time of the Treaty of Rome in 1957, which set up the EEC, Berlin was not treated as a European territory for whose external relations the FRG was responsible under the EEC treaties.[88] Instead, the treaties were extended to West Berlin by special declaration annexed to the Treaty of Rome. The point of this excursus into the status of a now defunct territory is that a significant territory, such as West Berlin, closely linked to the FRG, and yet subject to government by different States' authorities altogether, could enjoy membership of the EEC up to 1990, in spite of (then) Article 237 EEC treaty, which declared 'Any European *State* may apply to become a member of the Community' (italics added). Therefore, it is clear that the EU by no means imposes a uniform governance on its members.

8.3.3 Conclusion: The *Sui Generis* Character of EU Law

In conclusion, what this brief investigation into the EU suggests is that relations between the EU and member States defy straightforward hierarchical relationships of EU centre to State periphery. The EU is not straightforwardly federal, and federalism is not an agreed goal for the EU. This problematizes Brexit as a zero-sum exercise of taking back control.

8.4 The UK: Federalism, Devolution, and the Union

8.4.1 The Status of the UK: A Rejection of Federalism?

Although composed of several sub-State territories, Britain is not a federal State. Even if, in the period immediately preceding the First World War there was a brief enthusiasm for 'home rule all round',[89] in fact federalism has never operated within the UK, where Dicey's attacks on federalism still remain influential. Dicey visited the US in 1870 and compared the fragmentation of sovereignty there with parliamentary sovereignty in the UK, perceiving federalism

[87] E.g. Cyprus (which joined the EU in 2004) is de facto partitioned in two parts, with the north, self-declared Turkish Republic of Northern Cyprus recognized only by Turkey. Despite joining the EU as a de facto divided island, the whole of Cyprus is EU territory, although EU legislation is suspended in Northern Cyprus.

[88] (former) EEC Treaty, Article 227(4).

[89] See JE Kendle, *Federal Britain: A History* (London: Routledge, 1997).

as too fragmentary and debilitating, for Britain.[90] He also argued that a federal scheme would necessitate a new written Constitution for Britain. Therefore, for Dicey, writing in 1886, federalism was not a solution, but a constitutional revolution. The 1973 (Kilbrandon) Report of the Royal Commission on the Constitution took a similar approach to federalism, stating that: 'a federal system of government would require a written Constitution, a special procedure for changing it and a constitutional court to interpret it,' and that 'the UK is not an appropriate place for federalism and now is not an appropriate time.'[91]

8.4.1.1 A 'Union State'?

The Union of Scotland and England was the founding act of the United Kingdom of Great Britain in 1707. Surprisingly, however, there has been little debate about what the 'Union' or 'Britain' is, or should be, even in the context of the first Scottish independence referendum. However, a salient question, already discussed in an earlier chapter, is whether it is correct to view the UK as a 'Union State' rather than unitary in nature. The term 'Union State' was used by Rokkan and Urwin to connote a polity distinct both from the unitary and the federal State.[92] Although the concept of union is widely used in political and constitutional studies to refer to the consolidation of existing units into one, it is not the same as a unitary State, a term which implies a constitutional order with a single, unrivalled, legal competence, and uniform laws for all parts of the State.

Britain might be described as a 'Union' State, as it lacks uniform laws for the whole of its territory, and there is a strong argument that it lacks an unequivocal, unitary sovereignty (although traditionalists might contest this point). There exist very different constitutional settlements in the different parts of the UK. Devolution is not symmetric, and this makes unity difficult. Further, since 1998, the UK's devolved nations have developed some progressive constitutional forms,[93] as well as more pro-EU inclinations that challenged the unitary constitutional approaches of the centre. Additionally, the Scottish and Welsh Parliaments are for all intents and purposes permanent[94] (which, if this is to be taken seriously, undermines the doctrine of an unlimited Westminster parliamentary sovereignty that could repeal those provisions).

[90] Dicey, *England's Case against Home Rule*, 54.

[91] Royal Commission on the Constitution 1969–1973 (Cmnd. 5460, 1973) at paragraphs 527, 539.

[92] S Rokkan and D Urwin, *Economy, Territory, Identity: Politics of West European Territories*, (London: SAGE Publications, 1983). Also N MacCormick, *Questioning Sovereignty* (Oxford: Oxford University Press, 1999); N Walker, 'Beyond the Unitary Conception of the United Kingdom Constitution?' (2000) Public Law 384.

[93] Such as proportional representation for elections to the Holyrood Parliament, and consociationalism in Northern Ireland.

[94] Section 1 Scotland Act 2016 states: 'The Scottish Parliament and the Scottish Government are a permanent part of the United Kingdom's constitutional arrangements.' The Wales Act 2017 established the National Assembly on a new constitutional basis, making it a permanent part of the UK Constitution.

8.4.2 A Devolved State

As well as being a Union State, the UK is a *devolved* State, raising all sorts of issues about the relationship of Britain's component parts to the centre.

The 1973 Kilbrandon report suggested that representative institutions be set up in Scotland and Wales. However, due to the addition of a last-minute threshold requirement, the 1979 devolution referendums in Scotland and Wales were lost. It took almost another 20 years, and the new Labour Government in 1997, for devolution to come to the UK. This resulted in the Scotland Act 1998, the Government of Wales Act 1998, and the Northern Ireland Act 1998 (which domestically implemented much of the 1998 Belfast/Good Friday Agreement).

Although initially, these devolution settlements were different in nature, subsequent amendments lessened this (although devolution has always operated somewhat differently in Northern Ireland). Over-simplifying matters, we might summarize the present situation in the following way. First, each devolved nation has a devolved parliament or assembly with legislative powers, and a devolved government. Second, these legislative powers are limited in nature, with certain matters reserved to the Westminster Parliament. Third, there exists no completely autonomous sphere of self-rule within the devolved nations, as UK sovereignty has been preserved in all matters to the UK Parliament. Nonetheless, the Sewel Convention was generally applied, according to which Westminster 'will not normally legislate with regard to devolved matters' without the consent of the devolved parliaments. However, since Brexit, the status of the Sewel convention has become questionable, and the lack of devolved parliamentary consent was ignored when major Brexit legislation was passed in Westminster.[95]

However, England, the largest of the four nations, lacks its own Parliament. This was seen as giving rise to the 'West Lothian Question', whereby MPs elected to Westminster from devolved territories could vote on matters in England (such as education) which were devolved competences in Scotland, Wales, and Northern Ireland, and so on which English MPs had no vote for those territories. Indeed, this forms part of the larger 'England Question', given that, because England is so much larger than the three devolveds, it is difficult to see how federalism could be applied to the whole UK in such unbalanced circumstances. The day after Scotland's 2014 independence vote, then Prime Minister Cameron announced that the question of English votes for English laws (EVEL) required a decisive answer and that any new powers for Scotland must be balanced by a reassessment of the influence and voting power of devolution MPs at Westminster. This, at one and the same time, seemed to downplay

[95] The EU Withdrawal Act 2018 was adopted without the legislative consent of Scotland; the EU Withdrawal Agreement Act 2020 adopted without the legislative consent of Scotland, Wales and Northern Ireland. Both the Scottish and Welsh Parliaments refused legislative consent to the Internal Market Act 2020. The Scottish Parliament refused consent to the 2020 EU Future Relationship Act.

the issue of greater autonomy for Scotland, and also concretized into the issue of EVEL, which became a Conservative party manifesto commitment at the 2015 General Election. A new procedure for EVEL was introduced in 2015, by means of changes to the standing orders of the House of Commons.[96] Notably, this was a highly complex procedural and not legislative change, giving English MPs a veto over legislation concerning England only, and was not a form of devolution to England.[97] And EVEL was quietly abandoned in July 2021.

8.4.2.1 Finance

A comparison with some federal States, such as Canada and Switzerland, reveals a lower level of sub-State tax autonomy in the UK. Although there exist some direct devolved revenue raising powers, the UK Government provides funding for the devolved administrations by the Block Grant. This apportions funds from the UK's combined Consolidated Fund (the aggregate tax revenue from all four nations). This means that each devolved nation draws on the total UK resources to support its public services rather than relying solely on revenue raised within its borders. Devolved governments have autonomy to choose how to spend the Block Grant according to their policy priorities. Changes to the allocation of funding through the Block Grant are calculated by the Barnett Formula, which reflect per capita changes in UK government spending on 'comparable' public services in England. The Barnett Formula was introduced in 1979 as a short term non-statutory measure, by Joel Barnett who was then Chief Secretary to the Treasury, but it is still with us today. Although most taxes in the UK are set by the central government in London, devolved governments also have some tax raising powers of their own and further tax raising powers were devolved (by the Scotland Acts 2012 and 2016, and Wales Acts 2014 and 2017), so that a total of 31 per cent total tax revenue is now devolved to Scotland, for example. This tax devolution means that the revenue from some taxes goes directly to the devolveds and their Block Grant funding is proportionately reduced.

However, the UK Government can circumvent the Barnett formula altogether – as it did, for example, with £1bn funding for Northern Ireland, delivered as part of the conservative-DUP confidence and supply agreement from 2017 to 2019.[98] Although the Scottish and Welsh governments objected to this, they had no legal means to challenge it. The UK Internal Market Act 2020 Part 6 also gives the UK government the power to spend money directly in devolved areas, through the UK Shared Prosperity Fund, even where it does not have policy competence over those areas, and without the consent of the relevant devolved ministers.

[96] See further, D Gover and M Kenny, 'Answering the West Lothian Question? A Critical Assessment of 'English Votes for English Laws' in the UK Parliament' (2018) 71 Parliamentary Affairs 760–782.

[97] There has been relatively little demand for English devolution. In 2004, North East England voters rejected elected regional assemblies in a referendum.

[98] See e.g. '£1 billion for Northern Ireland won't buy off the DUP on Brexit', *New Statesman*, 29 October 2018.

8.4.2.2 Intragovernmental Relations

Although certain matters such as foreign affairs are reserved to the UK Government, there exist Concordats to ensure effective co-operation between central and devolved governments.[99] Under these Concordats, UK government must consult devolved administrations over formulation of the UK position, involve devolved administrations in negotiations relating to devolved matters and formally notify devolved administrations once agreed. The problem is that the Concordats are not legally binding, so devolved nation positions are not ensured, and devolveds thus seem to be in a weak position when it comes to international treaties. This was especially evident during the Brexit withdrawal negotiations. A Joint Ministerial Committee (JMC) also exists as a forum to discuss matters such as foreign affairs, but provides devolveds with no legal rights. Thus, UK devolution leaves the UK's intragovernmental relations informal – as non-legally binding Concordats, Memorandums of Understanding and the less than successful JMC.

In 2021, the UK Supreme Court held that certain parts of a Bill, adopted by the Scottish Parliament to incorporate the UN Convention on the Rights of the Child into Scots law, exceeded the Scottish Parliament's powers.[100] This incident raises the issue of sub-State implementation of treaties. In the UK, observation and implementation of international human rights obligations generally fall within devolved competence. However, the situation is complicated by the fact that, in Scotland for example, some areas of human rights obligations fall within reserved areas (i.e. immigration, foreign affairs, employment law) whereas others – such as housing, education and health – are devolved, and still others, such as social security, fall within both devolved and reserved powers. The incorporation of the UNCRC Bill was described as 'arguably the most important law that the Scottish Parliament has considered' by the Scottish children's and young persons' Commissioner.[101] The Scottish Parliament therefore had to consider how to adopt this Bill consistently with its devolved powers. These challenges reveal the dilemmas that devolved administrations currently face in implementing and observing treaties.

8.4.2.3 Conclusions

US Supreme Court Justice, Sandra Day O'Connor stated that devolution in the UK, 'though cut from a different mould from our federalism, reflects many of the same values, and therefore many of the same opportunities.'[102] But have

[99] For an early example, see e.g. P Bowers, 'Concordats and Devolution Guidance Notes', HC RP, 2005, SN/PC/3767.

[100] *Reference by the Attorney General and the Advocate General for Scotland – UN Convention on the Rights of the Child (Incorporation) (Scotland) Bill, European Charter of Local Self-Government (Incorporation) (Scotland) Bill* [2021] UKSC 42.

[101] Bruce Adamson, quoted in 'Landmark for Children's Rights,' Scottish Government News, 16 March 2021, available at www.gov.scot/news/landmark-for-childrens-rights/

[102] Sandra Day O'Connor, 'Altered States: Federalism and Devolution at the "Real" Turn of the Millennium' (2001) 60 *CLJ* 493, 502.

those opportunities been realized in the UK? The last two decades have, according to Tierney, seen a 'gradual dispersal of powers' to devolved territories, although the UK is still not a federal State, despite Bogdanor's description of it as 'quasi-federal' in 2001.[103] O'Connor might have detected a similarity, but in the UK, federalism has usually been ruled out. Parliamentary sovereignty is seen as excluding the entrenched autonomy of self-rule for sub-State nations, as does the disproportionately large size of England.

8.4.3 The Problem of Brexit for Devolution

It has been claimed[104] that approximately 80 per cent of UK devolved policies fell within EU competences – for example, fisheries, agriculture, environmental policy and economic development. Although not always acknowledged, EU membership provided an external support system for UK devolution, facilitating relations within the UK and conciliation between the UK and Ireland. Indeed, EU membership insulated devolved nations from a unitary UK-wide approach, by, for example, distributing EU funds on a basis more beneficial to some parts of the UK than others – an approach unlikely to continue post-Brexit.

Brexit risks undermining this already brittle devolution settlement. In the referendum on the UK's EU membership, the UK as a whole voted to leave. However, 62 per cent of Scotland's voting electorate, and 56 per cent of those voting in Northern Ireland, voted to remain. Yet the devolved nations had no formal role in the Article 50 withdrawal proceedings, and thus no means of ensuring that their constitutional interests were protected. Although the SNP had argued in Westminster that a 'quadruple lock' mechanism should apply to the EU referendum, requiring majorities in all four UK nations for a decision to leave the EU, this approach was rejected by the UK government. The UK's departure from the EU caused a major change to the UK Constitution. But unlike with amendments to federal Constitutions, there was no requirement for devolved participation in or consent to this major constitutional change.

Brexit raises the question of how a purely UK Internal Market is to be sustained. Since 1973, the EU has controlled much of the UK's economic union, relocating the machinery that might be needed for a UK Internal Market to EU level. The 2020 UK Internal Market Act is intended to replace this EU regulation. This Act relies on two major principles (both familiar from EU and international trade law) – that of mutual recognition, and that of non-discrimination – to provide a basic framework for the UK Internal Market and to prevent trade barriers within it. Although devolved nations may set their own

[103] S Tierney 'Drifting towards Federalism?', in R Schütze and S Tierney (eds.), *The United Kingdom and the Federal Idea* (Oxford: Hart, 2018) at 101. V Bogdanor, *Devolution in the UK* (Oxford: Oxford University Press, 2001).

[104] E.g. J Hunt, 'Devolution and Differentiation: Regional Variation in EU Law' (2010) 30 Legal Studies 421–441.

regulations in devolved areas, the mutual recognition provision prevents them applying these to goods and services already marketed in other parts of the UK (this extends to goods imported under a trade deal with third countries). The non-discrimination principle prohibits devolved governments from enacting laws that discriminate against goods and services from other parts of the UK. Overall, devolved Governments have viewed the Act as weakening their ability to legislate in devolved areas[105] – and we may contrast this with the position discussed earlier relating to some federal sub-States, such as the German Lander, or even US states. where US Supreme Court's more recent interpretations of the US Commerce Clause has accorded more autonomy to states.

8.4.3.1 The Northern Ireland Protocol[106]

Further, although the UK government declared that the UK would leave the EU as one State, the Northern Ireland Protocol problematized that. Yet this problem was entirely of the UK Government's making, because of its insistence that Brexit meant the UK leaving the Customs Union and Single Market, (in which case there must be a customs and regulatory border between the Republic of Ireland and the UK). However, along with this insistence, the UK also maintained there would be no hard border, no physical infrastructure, nor checks or controls across Ireland. This would only have been possible if Northern Ireland remained in the Customs Union and Single Market. The UK Government therefore promised irreconcilable results.

This pressing and seemingly intractable problem was 'solved' by the Protocol attached to the Withdrawal Agreement agreed between the EU and Boris Johnson's government in 2019 (after Theresa May's earlier solution of the 'Backstop'[107] had been rejected). This (third) version of the Protocol basically transferred required post-Brexit regulatory processes to the Irish Sea. Therefore border checks became focused on trade between Britain and Northern Ireland, apparently distinguishing Northern Ireland from the rest of the UK – a solution found abhorrent by Unionists in Northern Ireland. Under the Protocol, Northern Ireland remains in the EU Single Market for goods, and also applies EU customs rules, although it is still officially part of the UK customs territory. As Northern Ireland remains in the EU Single Market, it must apply strict EU regulations on food standards and plant and animal health. This resulted in additional checks on certain produce entering from Britain.

UK Prime Minister, Boris Johnson, deliberately opted to put a border between Great Britain and Northern Ireland rather than take the alternative mooted

[105] *After Brexit: The UK Internal Market Act and Devolution* (Scottish Government, 8 March 2021).

[106] Revised Protocol on Ireland and Northern Ireland Included in the Withdrawal Agreement, 17 October 2019, TF50 64 (2019).

[107] The earlier 'backstop' was an insurance policy that guaranteed no hard Irish border after Brexit by keeping the UK inside a single EU-UK 'customs territory; until a trade deal could be struck.

option of keeping the UK in the EU Customs Union. This led to a very clear fragmentation of the UK's Internal Market, with Northern Ireland applying different rules. In this way, Brexit dogma, and the perceived need to maintain absolute UK sovereignty by leaving the EU altogether, were prioritized over the peace process in Northern Ireland, and (somewhat ironically) the UK's constitutional integrity. Unionists in Northern Ireland became very dissatisfied with the Protocol (sometimes described by them as the 'Betrayal Act') which they believed undermined the constitutional integrity of the Union, by placing a barrier between Great Britain and Northern Ireland. This led to some violent incidents.[108]

Boris Johnson described Brexit as 'the greatest single restoration of national sovereignty in Parliamentary history'.[109] Yet the UK, in signing both the Belfast/Good Friday Agreement of 1998 and the Northern Ireland Protocol, adopted international agreements that do not accord with this absolutist version of sovereignty. However, the 2023 'Windsor Framework' may at least mitigate some of the more problematic aspects of the Northern Ireland Protocol. Time will tell.

8.4.3.2 Scotland and the EU

Scotland made its own energetic effort to continue some sort of relationship with the EU post-Brexit. Shortly after the 2016 EU Referendum, the 'reverse Greenland' option was floated as a possibility for Scotland. In 1985, Greenland, which is part of Denmark, withdrew from the (then) EEC, although Denmark remained.[110] It was therefore suggested that the EU treaties might be amended, enabling Scotland to remain a member of the EU, even if England/'rUK' were to leave. However, this position was soon abandoned. Greenland is a federacy with greater autonomy than the UK's devolved nations, and the UK would need a different constitutional settlement to achieve this sort of autonomy. Nonetheless, the Greenland case at least illustrates that it is possible for only part of a State to secede from the EU.[111]

In December 2016, the Scottish Government published a White Paper, *Scotland's Place in Europe,* attempting to retain some sort of EU participation for Scotland, notwithstanding Brexit. This White Paper contemplated continued Single Market membership for Scotland, even in the absence of Single

[108] 'Northern Ireland riots: 41 police hurt in Unionist violence', *The Times*, 7 April 2021.

[109] Prime Minister's Statement, Hansard, Volume 666, col 571: 19 October 2019.

[110] This process took 3 years. See e.g. F Weiss, 'Greenland's Withdrawal from the European Communities' (1985) ELRev, 173.

[111] Article 29 of the Vienna Convention on the Law of Treaties provides: 'Unless a different intention appears from the treaty or is otherwise established, a treaty is binding upon each party in respect of its entire territory'. This implies it would be possible for a treaty to define which parts of a State's territory fall within its scope.

Market membership for 'rUK'.[112] However, the UK Government embraced a unitary, top down approach, taking control of all the Brexit negotiations, and insisting that the UK act as one, and leave the EU as one (while acknowledging that a special solution had to be found for Northern Ireland) and refused to consider the Scottish proposals. The UK Government also took the same approach to Gibraltar, which had voted overwhelmingly to remain in the EU in the 2016 referendum.

But would continued Scottish Single Market membership – possibly through the European Economic Area (EEA)[113] rather than the EU – have been achievable? The EEA is not part of the EU, although does apply many EU Single Market laws, but with different enforcement and adjudication mechanisms. However, the UK rejected EEA membership, and admittedly, including a sub-State such as Scotland in the EEA raises problems. First, there would have to be a change to EEA rules to allow in a sub-State. Scotland, although a nation in its own right, lacks the external legal competence to enter into treaties on their its behalf – unlike some other sub-State entities, such as the Belgian regions. Second, any UK devolved nations' application for EEA membership would depend on UK sponsorship, for which there is unlikely to be any political will in the UK government. Thirdly, there would need to be a wider-ranging devolution of powers to Scotland to enable it to comply with Single Market rules. Although the Scottish Paper also argued from analogy that, whatever solutions might be found for the Irish border should also be applied to relations between Scotland and 'rUK', the UK Government refused to contemplate this. In June 2022, the Scottish Government reinvigorated the independence process by referring an independence referendum Bill to the UK Supreme Court. However, the UK Supreme Court found that the Scottish Parliament lacked the competence to adopt such legislation. This is further discussed in the chapter on Scotland.

8.4.4 A Federal UK?

Brexit has therefore caused considerable problems for the devolution settlement. Might some of these issues be resolved if the UK were to move to a federal Constitution? We have seen how federal States allow greater autonomy to sub-States, for example in some cases making provision for their treaty making powers and requiring their consent to constitutional amendments. In the post-Brexit context, some of those troubled by the UK's constitutional

[112] Although *Scotland's Place in Europe* (www.gov.scot/Resource/0051/00512073.pdf.) started by recommending continued Single Market access for the whole UK.

[113] For further on the EEA see e.g. TI Harbo, 'The European Economic Area Agreement: A Case of Legal Pluralism' (2009) 78 Nordic Journal of International Law 201.

future, who fear the Union will shatter, but do not favour independence for the devolveds, have suggested a federal UK.

Although the UK Liberal-Democrat party has long favoured a federal UK, most other parties have not tended to do so. However, post Brexit, things might be changing. In 2016, the Constitution Reform Group (CRG), a group with cross-party membership (including former first ministers of Scotland, Wales and Northern Ireland) led by Conservative peer Lord Salisbury, argued for radical constitutional change in the UK[114] – an argument since renewed into the 2020s with a new Bill.[115] The CRG argued that Devolution should be 'turned upside down' to create a broadly federal system of government' for Britain, contending that the existing union should be replaced with fully devolved government in each part of the UK, each with autonomy over its own affairs, and with the right to secede, by means of a referendum. This would require transformation of the UK's current constitutional arrangements.[116]

However, the CRG's claim of 'a broadly federal system of government' is surely undermined by their Bill's preservation of parliamentary sovereignty. Clauses 29(5) and (6) of the 2021 Act of Union Bill state respectively that 'The UK Parliament continues to exercise the authority of the Sovereign Parliament of the United Kingdom' and that 'Nothing in this Act diminishes or otherwise affects the extent of that Sovereignty.' These clauses surely frustrate the Bill's commitment to devolved sovereignty. Further, the Bill, although reforming the House of Lords, does not transform it into a federal Second Chamber, thus missing the opportunity to make UK institutions more federal in nature. The CRG Bill also seems to lack any formalization of intragovernmental measures, with the 'Ministerial Council' proposed in clause 52 likely to perpetuate the weaknesses of the JMC. Therefore, the Bill looks likely to preserve a devolutionary system rather than instigate a federal one.

The two major obstacles to a federal UK appear to be the 'England problem' and parliamentary sovereignty. It has long been recognized that federalism may be destabilized by the disproportionate size of one federal unit – such as Russia within the former USSR, or England within the UK. Such an imbalance can affect the capacity of other territorial units to influence central government or to assert constitutionally assigned powers.

However, the main obstacle to UK federalism is the insistence on preserving unlimited parliamentary sovereignty. David Marquand described the UK's antipathy to federalism as a 'neurosis'.[117] Even if an insistence on parliamentary

[114] 'Brexit Vote Paves Way for Federal Union to Save UK, says all-party group', *The Guardian*, 10 July 2016.

[115] The 2021 CRG Bill is available at www.constitutionreformgroup.co.uk/download/act-of-union-bill-2021/.

[116] These proposals are also discussed in the chapter on Union and disunion.

[117] D Marquand, 'Federalism and the British: Anatomy of a Neurosis' (2006) 77 The Political Quarterly 175.

sovereignty had a resonance of sorts at the time Dicey was writing, continued insistence on it as a fundamental principle of the British Constitution distorts the situation today. In April 2021, Ciaran Martin (formerly the Constitution Director at the Cabinet Office who helped agree the framework for the 2014 Scottish independence referendum) in a lecture generally sympathetic to the case for a second Scottish independence referendum, ruled out the prospects for federalism in the UK. Martin's argument was that UK federalism would require 'abolition of ancient doctrine of parliamentary sovereignty' that had been 'the bedrock of English constitution for centuries.'[118] This book has already argued that the case for parliamentary sovereignty as an ancient principle of the English Constitution is less well supported than sometimes supposed. Martin also however argued that a referendum would be required to abolish parliamentary sovereignty and move to a written Constitution, and that it would be hard to find support for this in the UK. This might seem a stronger argument, although the constitutional status of referendums is by no means clear in the UK (and is considered in a subsequent chapter). To be sure, it is hard to imagine that many English voters would agree to a permanent limitation of parliamentary sovereignty. Those satisfied with Brexit are unlikely to desire a written Constitution or federal option, given that a desire for strong parliamentary sovereignty is likely to have motivated their euroscepticism in the first place. Advocates of Scottish or Welsh independence, or a united Ireland, may have little enthusiasm for an arrangement that would anchor them into the UK, even if it provided authoritative and legally enforceable constitutional procedures for protecting different national communities within the State. Such approaches, and distinct political identities, may militate against a comprehensive approach which would address issues of disputed authority and the challenges of Brexit.

However, between these two – between those who favour absolute parliamentary sovereignty, and those who seek an independent Scotland or a united Ireland – there may be a sizeable group, a majority even, who desire a different constitutional settlement for Britain. But can that group be animated into action?

8.4.5 Constitutional Amnesia

A further relevant factor is, as this book has already argued, British experience in former transfers of power – whether in the case of Irish independence, or in Britain's constitutional relationships with former colonies – which has been too quickly forgotten. David Williams linked British distaste with federalism and dissatisfaction with the UK's EU membership, and also noted that difficulty in defining concepts such as federalism, confederation,

[118] C Martin, *Resist, Reform or Re-Run*? Available at www.bsg.ox.ac.uk/sites/default/files/2021-04/Scotland_Referendum_final.pdf.

devolution and Home Rule, 'were all anticipated in the turbulent 1880s and especially in 1886.'[119]

Previous debates on sovereignty are worth revisiting. The lesson is that inflexibility over sovereignty may rest on a flimsy constitutional base and is liable to have unfortunate consequences. The American War of Independence was caused by a deep disagreement over the British Constitution, which led to war and Britain's loss of its colonies. When American colonists challenged the British Parliament's authority to impose the 1765 Stamp Act on them, they appealed to principles of English common law, and to an understanding of England's ancient Constitution. In this they were supported by figures in England such as Lord Camden, a renowned eighteenth-century English judge, who repudiated the doctrine of absolute parliamentary sovereignty. There existed no clear constitutional law for the British Empire, and constitutional law was, in any case, in a state of flux.

The nineteenth-century constitutional law of the British Empire really was no clearer than it had been for the American colonies in the eighteenth century. For the Empire included 'an extraordinary range of constitutional, diplomatic, political, commercial and cultural relationships.'[120] In the nineteenth and early twentieth centuries, Westminster passed the *Colonial Laws Validity Act* of 1865 (CLVA) as an attempt to settle issues of authority between colonial legislatures and Westminster. However, the sovereignty of the imperial Parliament in London, as imposed by the CLVA, was only one of many types of sovereignty that existed. For it was impossible for Westminster to produce sufficient legislation for nearly a quarter of the globe. Instead, most government and legislation was left to those *in situ* – often to the 'middle power' of judges, magistrates, and commissioners,[121] who applied their own form of legal governance of the colonies, creating a vernacular Constitution. Therefore, a good deal of the British Empire lent itself to a more pluralistic type of sovereignty – one that was divided, shared, indeterminate. There was no unitary law. There was no attempt to establish a uniform legal code. The British Commonwealth was popularly perceived as based on unwritten conventions with a minimum of written law, which contrasts with the positivist concept of the bureaucratic rule-governed State.[122]

8.4.5.1 Power

Indeed, it was likely that *power* underlay the British Empire, as it underlies claims for parliamentary sovereignty today. However, that power could not

119 Sir David Williams, 'Ireland 1880–2005: A Constitutional Perspective' (2007) 41 University of Richmond LR 356.

120 John Darwin, *The Empire Project: The Rise and Fall of the British World-System, 1830–1970* (Cambridge: Cambridge University Press, 2009) 1.

121 L Benton and L Ford, *Rage for Order* (Cambridge MA: Harvard University Press, 2016) 8, 16

122 See e.g. Weber, 'The Sociology of Law' (from *Max Weber on Economy and Society*, transl. Rheinstein, Cambridge MA: Harvard University Press: 1954); J Austin, *The Province of Jurisprudence Determined*, W Rumble (ed.), (Cambridge: Cambridge University Press, 1995).

and cannot be derived from a unified, coherent account of legal and political sovereignty. And power by itself lacks legitimacy – it must be validated by something else – which is where sovereignty becomes relevant, in providing that grounding. Yet the claims of UK sovereignty were often mutually self-contradictory.

The UK no longer has an empire. It has also left the EU. But it has lessons to learn from this history of belonging to, or managing, larger organizations as already argued in the chapter on Sovereignty. The UK is still a conglomerate or union State of four nations. If UK to function effectively, then its constitutional structures must acknowledge this variety. Yet, at present, they do not. There exists a Constitution that is supposedly flexible, full of synergies and conventions to suit every situation. Except that it does not. Because most of this flexible Constitution is *political*, and when it suits, Britain retreats into a hard minimal legal Constitution shell – a highly eccentric understanding of parliamentary sovereignty understood as impermeable, illimitable and unshareable, ignoring crucial elements of the political Constitution, such as constitutional conventions. Nonetheless, adherence to this flimsily reasoned concept of sovereignty makes federalism or effective home rule impossible, because it sees sovereignty as indivisible, and impossible to share between different levels of British government. And because Britain has a fused system with an executive drawn from Parliament, this system of sovereignty empowers the UK government. In these circumstances, the UK Government chooses to ignore the political Constitution (the various conventions, that operated as constitutional glue in the past) and insist on (thinly reasoned) legal sovereignty, backed up ultimately, by power.

8.5 Conclusion

8.5.1 The Sovereignty Issue

At present, the UK government exemplifies a 'robust unionism', understanding the UK as a unified, homogeneous State, without critical territorial differences, with a constitutional foundation of unlimited parliamentary sovereignty. Brexit has strengthened this attitude. For these reasons, federalism is ruled out – but there is no viable basis for this. For Dicey, federalism would not work in Britain, because it would require a new, codified British Constitution, which he believed impossible. But Dicey's account was not even accepted by all at the time of writing. Others, such as James Bryce, viewed federalism more favourably.[123] Indeed, former EU judge, David Edward, went so far as to describe Britain as the 'spiritual and intellectual home of federalism', given that American colonists drew on earlier Scottish thought in their constitutional design, that federal constitutions operated in Britain's former colonies of

[123] J Bryce, 'Flexible and Rigid Constitutions', in *Studies in History and Jurisprudence vol 1* (Oxford: Clarendon Press, 1901) 145–254.

Canada, Australia, and South Africa, and that, in the early nineteenth century, 'the only democratic federal constitution which did not owe its origins, directly or indirectly, to British constitutional thought was that of Switzerland.'[124]

Why should the Diceyan approach be taken so seriously? It does not have a long pedigree. There is no mention in the 1688 Bill of Rights, of a sovereign, illimitable Parliament. It was only with the ascendancy of Benthamite reasoning from the later eighteenth century, followed by the Diceyan dominance of British constitutional law, that Parliamentary sovereignty really took hold. Dicey wrote that parliamentary sovereignty was a matter of logic, and that 'limited sovereignty' was a 'contradiction in terms.' For him, this ruled out federalism. But why must sovereignty be understood only as unlimited and indivisible? Dicey's answer was that sovereignty was always understood in this way in England. But there is no overwhelming evidence for this, especially given the continued adherence to the doctrine of the old Constitution and the fundamental law. Yet, even if Dicey's claims regarding the English Constitution were accurate, they can only be contingent, distinct from Dicey's claim for logical truth. Other parts of the UK are less inclined to recognize the supposed orthodoxy of parliamentary sovereignty. For example, in the 1953 Scottish case of *MacCormick* v. *Lord Advocate,* Lord Cooper stated: 'The principle of the unlimited sovereignty of parliament is a distinctively English principle which has no counterpart in Scottish constitutional law....'[125]

The supremacy of EU law was always hard to accept for those cleaving to the absolutist theory of sovereignty. Yet, in *Factortame* the House of Lords accepted the supremacy of EU law and disapplied the Merchant Shipping Act 1988. In this context, Barber simply referred to 'the quiet death of parliamentary sovereignty' and surely Barber was right when he then argued that, 'Even if the 1972 act were repealed, this would not resurrect the old rule of Parliamentary sovereignty.'[126] For, after *Factortame,* there is clear authority for the proposition that Parliament can impose limitations on itself; the old absolutism of sovereignty is no longer viable. And therefore, if Parliament could voluntarily limit its sovereignty in the ECA, why might it not also do so in other statutes, such as for devolution legislation? A federal solution of shared sovereignty would be possible.

8.5.2 Alternatives

However, it is also said that federalism would not work in the UK because of the 'England problem', that no federal state can flourish with the discrepancy

[124] D Edward, 'The Community's Constitution – Rigid or Flexible? The Contemporary Relevance of the Constitutional Thinking of James Bryce', in D Curtin and T Heukels (eds.), *Institutional Dynamics of European Integration* (Dordrecht: Martinus Nijhoff, 1994).

[125] *MacCormick* v. *Lord Advocate* 1953 SC 396.

[126] NW Barber, 'The Afterlife of Parliamentary Sovereignty' (2011) 9(1) International Journal of Constitutional Law 144–154, at 144.

of population and size exhibited by the UK, and that in any case, the English simply do not want to divide England up into federal regions nor do they want an English Parliament.[127] This may be an issue, but surely there are alternatives. Indeed, self-government is not a cut and dried matter – that is, either of complete independence, unitary State, or federalism somewhere in between. If we step back, we can see that there exist possibilities across the spectrum, concepts such as 'Independence lite' or 'Devo max' that indicate a quest for greater sub-State autonomy without full independence. Federacies also offer instructive precedents. Such examples might have indicated paths for Britain's future constitutional development, but instead, there has been a tendency to perceive the UK's Constitution as singular.

8.5.2.1 Dominions

Peter Oliver has suggested that, in considering how the British constitutional tradition might adapt to federal models and so accommodate Scotland, Wales and Northern Ireland, we reconsider how that same tradition worked over 100 years ago, in the context of the Dominions of Canada and Australia (which were themselves federations).[128]

By the late nineteenth century, Canada, Australia, and New Zealand all had considerable autonomy and systems of 'responsible self-government.'[129] Gladstone considered Canada a possible constitutional model for Ireland in the context of the 1886 First Home Rule Bill. By the 1907 Colonial Conference, there were few imperial reserve powers applicable to Dominions, save for foreign affairs and defence, and, by the early twentieth century, the term 'Commonwealth' was applied to them rather than 'Empire'. The convention that the Imperial Parliament would not legislate for them without their consent was strongly observed, albeit dependent on the good faith of Westminster. Dicey insisted that the colonial model could not work for Ireland, because of the fractious relationship between Ireland and Great Britain. Others, such as James Bryce, were more convinced of the workability of the self-governing colonial model for Ireland. Irish Home Rule did not come about, although the Irish Free State was accorded Dominion status after the Anglo-Irish Agreement of 1922. But the self-governing colonies increased their autonomy, being independently represented at the 1919 Versailles Peace Conference, and joining the League of Nations in their own right. By 1923, it was understood that that they might sign their own treaties. The 1926 Balfour Declaration stated that 'Equality of status, so far as Britain and the Dominions are concerned, is

[127] E.g. Matthew Parris, 'Don't Wreck England Just to Foil Sturgeon', *The Times*, 30 January 2021, who writes 'Panicking Unionists pushing for a federation of four nations risk awakening English anger and Balkanising a nation'.

[128] Peter C Oliver, 'Parliamentary Sovereignty, Federalism and the Commonwealth', in R Schütze and S Tierney (eds.), *The United Kingdom and The Federal Idea* (Oxford: Hart, 2018) 49.

[129] See further KC Wheare, *The Constitutional Structure of the Commonwealth* (Oxford: Clarendon Press, 1960) 8.

thus the root principle governing our Inter-Imperial Relations.'[130] This Declaration in effect achieved what the American colonists had insisted on 150 years earlier – equality under one monarch. Five years later, the 1931 Statute of Westminster sought to achieve *legal* autonomy and equality for the Dominions. In particular, s4 of that Statute declared: 'No Act of Parliament of the United Kingdom passed after the commencement of this Act shall extend, or be deemed to extend, to a Dominion as part of the law of that Dominion, unless it is expressly declared in that Act that that Dominion has requested, and consented to, the enactment thereof'.

Although this Statute was interpreted in different ways, all in all, it was sufficient for the Dominions, with some citing 1931 as the date of their independence, although, in fact, formal independence legislation was not adopted in Canada and Australia until the 1980s. However, the Dominion model was not used for other parts of the British Empire, becoming 'increasingly deprecated in many quarters and in the 1950s was quickly dropped'[131] – probably seen as smacking of colonialism, and a disparaged imperial past. Nonetheless, the Dominion example demonstrates the possibility of self-government, autonomous from London, even in the absence of a formal declaration of independence. Many legal elements of this device might be adopted constitutionally, without use of a name rooted in Britain's colonial past. To be sure, such a situation depends on the observance of conventions, and good faith – qualities that may no longer be in great supply post-Brexit, given the ignoring of the Sewel Convention and the suggestion from Peter Hennessey that the 'good chaps' are no longer in charge of government.[132]

Nonetheless, the Dominions provide an illustration of self-governance, of a differentiated relationship short of independence, compatible with the British Constitution, requiring no alteration to the Constitution as it applies in England.

8.5.2.2 Federacies

Another possible alternative lies in the notion of Federacies and Associated States, which as we have seen, have much in common with the sort of asymmetrical devolution that exists in the UK, in that they concern a relationship between a smaller territorial unit and a larger state, in which the smaller unit shares the benefits of association with the larger polity (but, unlike UK Devolution, has internal autonomy). However, what distinguishes federacies from traditional federal models is that in federacies the autonomous institutions

130 Balfour Declaration, available at www.foundingdocs.gov.au/resources/transcripts/cth11_doc_1926.pdf

131 W David McIntyre, *British Decolonization 1946–1997* (London: Macmillan, 1998) 20.

132 See e.g. 'Good Chaps No More? Safeguarding the Constitution in Stressful Times' by Andrew Blick and Peter Hennessy, (2019) Constitution Society https://consoc.org.uk/wp-content/uploads/2019/11/FINAL-Blick-Hennessy-Good-Chaps-No-More.pdf

of a sub state territory in an otherwise unitary state may be made permanent, but without federalizing the rest of the country. In the present circumstances, it may not be so likely that the UK will undertake a more radical process of federal reform across the entire territory, and thus the federacy model is more appropriate to understand, for example, Scotland's evolving status in the UK.

8.5.2.3 Composite States

Alternatively, we might look at other examples of composite States that experienced centrifugal pressures. Within the composite State, there existed a legal pluralism in that distinct polities shared a common monarch but retained their political and legal independence. Austria-Hungary from 1867 to 1918 provides an example of a complex composite State, with parallels to offer the British Union. The Austro-Hungarian Union, or 'dual monarchy', whereby Austria and Hungary were coequal partners, provided internal autonomy with limited imperial common affairs. Although Austria-Hungary has been disparaged as an example of a decaying empire, its fate depended on many events, including the horror of the First World War, which led to its demise and dissolution. But as a legal model, the Austria-Hungary dual monarchy is still worth considering. Such an arrangement proved to be of interest to Scottish and Irish writers seeking to demonstrate how their nation's sovereignty could be respected within a large Union. In the 1900s, Arthur Griffith recommended a similar solution for Ireland-Great Britain. In 2012, prior to the 2014 independence referendum, a Scottish Constitutional Commission discussion paper on 'Secure Autonomy' for Scotland, argued that, whereas parliamentary sovereignty dictates that Parliament may not bind its successors, and so no devolution scheme may be safely regarded as permanent, Parliament can *renounce* its sovereignty. This paper argued that there could be a new Union, which would be equal and consensual, not the 'incorporating union' of 1707. They cited historical examples of such a union, in which the Austro-Hungarian example featured prominently. If there are regrettable associations with a bygone, dead Empire, nevertheless, key elements of the device might be recalibrated to construct an 'Autonomy Statute' for the UK's devolved nations today.

8.5.3 Conclusion: Reforming an 'Old Building'

There are many legal, constitutional and transnational forms and battles in our present age. The reality is not coherent but messy. The British Constitution is an old building and it is hard to renovate.

Churchill had the idea of three majestic overlapping circles (the US, the Commonwealth, and Europe), stating 'we are the only country that has a great part in every one of them.'[133] Had Britain been less distracted by maintaining

[133] WS Churchill, *Europe Unites: Speeches 1947 and 1948* (London: Cassell, 1950).

its global power in the 1950s, perhaps it might have played larger role in reconstruction of Europe, and helped to shape an EU closer to British interests and inclinations. Instead, the EU developed as a source of disunion for Britain, and of disagreement between different parts of the UK. The product has been Brexit and the constitutional challenges it now poses.

James Bryce, Oxford professor, politician and diplomat, employed the terms *centripetal* and *centrifugal* (used by Madison at the US 1787 Constitutional Convention) to capture the notion of two conflicting forces that operate on Constitutions.[134] Centripetal forces 'draw men or groups of men together into one organized community', and centrifugal forces, 'make men, or groups, break away and disperse'. Bryce emphasized the importance of deterring centrifugal forces from bringing down the system. Brexit may have centripetal or centrifugal effects. For many, Brexit is centripetal, emphasizing a robust unionism. There have undoubtedly been strong impulses towards recentralization and a reassertion of Westminster sovereignty, as powers are repatriated from the EU. English, Scottish, Irish and Welsh unionists may prefer the UK Union to that of the EU, discarding Leave or Remain affiliations. However, in such a situation, Scottish, Welsh and Irish nationalists are marginalized, without adequate legal support in Westminster. Yet, on the other hand, there exist countermanding centrifugal forces. There is the possibility of UK disintegration with Scottish independence and Irish reunification.

This chapter has explored some of the possibilities suggested by devolution, federalism, federacy and other structures. It attempts to build on the spirit of 'post sovereignty' while acknowledging that there are no easy answers. Brexit presents a challenge, not just to constitutional law and international relations, but also to the legal imagination. How to bring about realistic but difficult legal and constitutional futures? There is a need for trust, fair dealing and mutual respect between institutions.

It has been suggested that the British built up an Empire and then decolonized in a 'fit of absence of mind'.[135] The same may be true of Brexit, where Britain joined the EEC without any real enthusiasm, and has now left the EU – seemingly in a state of insouciance as to the consequences. A closer look at the solutions outlined above, however, suggests that there are other possibilities.

[134] J Bryce, 'The Action of Centripetal and Centrifugal Forces on Political Constitutions', in J Bryce, *Studies in History and Jurisprudence*, vol. 1 (Oxford: Clarendon Press, 1901). See further HAL Fisher, *James Bryce*, 2 vols (London: Macmillan, 1927).

[135] JR Seeley, *The Expansion of England* (London: Macmillan, 1883) 8.

9

Democracy and Referendums

Democracy is considered an essential element of government in much of the world today. This chapter considers whether democracy functions adequately in the UK. The EU Referendum is sometimes considered a prime example of both direct democracy and popular sovereignty, and this claim is considered. The chapter argues that the UK suffers from a democratic deficit and that the Brexit referendum did not remedy this. However, before the specifics of British democracy are considered, the chapter discusses democracy and referendums more generally.

9.1 Democracy

Mostly everyone writing about democracy agrees that it has no one single meaning. It is an essentially contested concept if ever there was one. It has been discussed for over twenty-five centuries, but, as Robert Dahl noted,[1] like fire or writing, democracy seems to have been invented, or discovered, more than once. Dahl was also careful to distinguish the ideal(s) of democracy from its actuality. Bernard Crick captured the elusive nature of democracy by naming it a 'most promiscuous word',[2] and further elaborated by delineating three distinct understandings of democracy, namely: 'democracy as a principle or doctrine of government; … democracy as a set of institutional arrangements or constitutional devices … democracy as a type of behaviour (say the antithesis of both deference and of unsociability). They do not always go together.'[3] This is an important insight – that democracy may be understood in different ways, ideal and actual, and importantly, is 'not just a set of institutional arrangements but a culture and a spirit, a way of doing politics.'[4]

Many writers distinguish earlier manifestations of democracy, in ancient times, from modern democratic political systems. The word democracy originates from the Greek 'demos' (people) and 'kratos' (to rule) but this is not

[1] Robert Dahl, *On Democracy* (2nd ed., New Haven CT: Yale University Press, 2015) 9.

[2] Bernard Crick, *Democracy: A Very Short Introduction* (Oxford: Oxford University Press, 2003) 11.

[3] Ibid., 'Introduction'.

[4] Tony Wright, 'Democracy in Britain: Retrospect and Prospect' (2017) 88(2) The Political Quarterly 7.

very helpful, as both 'people' and 'rule' are amenable to differing interpretations. Many systems have considered themselves democratic, without allowing all of their members the right to vote: the exclusion of slaves in pre-civil war America, or women in all systems until the twentieth century, being obvious examples. 'Rule' need not necessarily mean taking the decisions oneself, nor imply actual self-government, but may instead denote the selection of rulers, being in a position to influence their decisions, and, possibly, to control them. Greek city states, such as Athens, operated a form of democracy, with an assembly in which all citizens could participate. Officials were elected or selected from these assemblies.

The Roman Republic (after a struggle) allowed the people to participate in the assembly in the Roman forum. But neither Greece nor the Roman Republic developed a system of popular government that could function beyond a small group of people. This was especially pertinent for Rome, where the reach of the Republic extended far beyond Rome, and so many, even Roman citizens, were denied the opportunity to participate in government.

Although there were some instances of more popular rule in the middle ages (e.g. in Italian city states, from c1100 to 1300) these had little in common with modern democratic standards. Civil war and revolution spurred democratic thinking. In England, the Putney debates of 1647, which were held among elected representatives of Cromwell's New Model Army, encompassed discussion of the franchise, social justice, and the English Constitution. Thomas Rainsborough, the English soldier and republican, and supporter of the Levellers, famously argued for the connection between the right to vote and submission to government:

> For really I think that the poorest hee that is in England hath a life to live, as the greatest hee; ... and I do think that the poorest man in England is not at all bound in a strict sense to that Government that he hath not had a voice to put Himself under.[5]

Democracy was notably invoked by the American colonists, in their opposition to taxation without representation and also in the debates formulating of the US Constitution in Philadelphia in 1787. Americans drew on pamphlets and other literature from the seventeenth-century civil wars in Britain, as well as on ancient examples, and many had a proclivity for classical pseudonyms, such as the *Publius* of the *Federalist Papers*. But the eighteenth-century American notion of federalism was original, different from that of various ancient leagues and alliances. The aim of American federalism was to divide power, and regulate it by checks and balances, and so to prevent tyranny, and all this was closely related to an understanding and realization of democracy in the United States.

The newly formed United States was to be a 'republic' and it is relevant to ask how the term 'republic' relates to 'democracy'. They have a great deal in

[5] *Putney Debates Record Book 1647* (Worcester College, Oxford) *MS 65*.

common, and at the centre of the theory of republicanism lies the notion of government by the people. The term 'republic' derives from the Latin 'res' (thing/affair) 'publicus' (public). The Roman Republic operated rudimentary democratic practices, allowing for popular participation (by the later Republic through the tribunes of the peoples). The sixteenth and seventeenth centuries saw a revival of the tradition of Roman republicanism – for example, in Machiavelli's *Discourses* – and the belief in the duty of citizens to participate in public life and governance.[6] And of course Aristotle stressed the political good of an active citizenry.[7] Republicanism was a highly influential ideal in the American and French Revolutions, Indeed, it seems that the terms 'republic' and 'democracy' were used pretty much interchangeably in the eighteenth century.[8]

9.1.1 What Is Democracy?

But if 'democracy' is capable of many meanings, how should we understand it in the context of a contemporary liberal 'democratic' State, such as the UK or US? Democracy is clearly distinct from autocratic government – that is, government by one privileged person or group – but beyond that it is hard to reach a consensus. Although some accounts of democracy stress the importance of certain institutional or structural arrangements (e.g. assemblies elected by a universal franchise, separation of powers, checks, and balances), others look to ideals (i.e. liberty and equality).

A very different account was given by Joseph Schumpeter, who defined democracy as the selection of ruling elites by competitive struggle for the peoples' vote.[9] This 'realist' understanding of democracy may capture something of contemporary politics, but it omits the ideals of equality, pluralism, and self-government, so often seen as essential to democracy. Indeed, in the Schumpeterian vision, political participation is not integral to democracy, and the achievement of democracy becomes more like the packaging of a commercial product.

In contrast to Schumpeter, this chapter proceeds on the basis that, while it is very difficult to produce a definition of democracy with which all would agree, democracy nonetheless requires a combination of political ideals such as equality, inclusive citizenship, rule of law, rights, pluralism, and self-government. It also necessitates particular institutions capable of ensuring popular participation, fair and free elections, a real choice when electing officials, freedom of expression and information, and an independent judiciary. Democracy also

6 JGA Pocock, *The Machiavellian Moment: Florentine Political Thought and the Atlantic Republican Tradition* (Princeton NJ: Princeton University Press, 1975).

7 Aristotle, *Politics* (Jowett transl., Modern Library, 1943).

8 Dahl, *On Democracy*, chapter 2.

9 J Schumpeter, *Capitalism, Socialism and Democracy* (New York: Harper & Bros., 1942).

exists as a culture, spirit, and attitude – a willingness to participate in public affairs – among individuals. This may seem a tall order, and can probably only be imperfectly realized, but without the combination of, and (attempted) realization of, these different elements, democracy may dissipate into tyranny, autocracy, or populism.

9.1.2 Why Democracy?

But why should democracy be preferred to other forms of government? For example, Plato attacked democracy as the rule of the poor and ignorant over the educated and the knowledgeable – and instead, in *The Republic*, advocated 'Guardianship' by an educated and expert elite who would govern for the general good. Sometimes autocratic government may even bring some benefits. A modern update would be the technocratic governance by experts in the modern State (and international institutions) which is seen as resting on similar guardianship foundations. Sir John Laws cited the example of the Roman Emperors between Domitian and Commodus, who gained the approbation of Gibbon for their governance of the Roman empire, but admitted that 'any set of examples will be contentious.'[10] Friedrich Hayek argued that democracy is dispensable in certain circumstances, and that an authoritarian government which guaranteed the basic principles of a liberal market order, including property rights, may be preferable.[11] But in all these cases it is hard to say who should form the guardianship/expert/technocratic control. It is not enough for such groups to possess technical knowledge. Effective governance requires other qualities such as moral judgement and incorruptibility. And who is to ensure that everyone's interests will be protected by a non-representative governing elite? In 1861, John Stuart Mill pointedly argued that, as a result of the working class in England being denied the vote, no one advocated their interests.

Dahl defended democracy in other ways, arguing that democracies are better able to protect fundamental rights, and ensure greater self-determination. He also suggested that modern democracies are less likely to go to war with each other, and that countries with democratic governments tend to be more prosperous, although this last defence may rely on an affinity between democracy and a market economy – a connection many repudiate.

But perhaps the best we can provide is a negative account of democracy's virtue – 'an antidote against tyranny.'[12] Such a minimalist account does not guarantee good laws. In such circumstances, other constitutional principles – the rule of law, fundamental rights, and judicial review – become necessary supplements to democracy's worst tendencies. There is no space to provide a

[10] John Laws, *The Constitutional Balance* (London: Bloomsbury, 2021) 26.

[11] F Hayek, *The Principles of a Liberal Social Order* (1966) 31 Il Politico 601.

[12] Laws, *The Constitutional Balance*, 31. However, in a democracy, the majority may assert a tyranny of their own.

full defence of democracy here, but one might concur with Churchill's all too familiar quote that, 'No one pretends that democracy is perfect or all-wise. Indeed it has been said that democracy is the worst form of Government except for all those other forms that have been tried from time to time ....'[13]

9.1.3 The Scale of Democracy

John Gray has argued that the nation State 'has proved to be the upper limit of democratic accountability'[14] And the Brexit referendum was, among other things, an expression of distrust of the supranational EU's ability to act democratically.[15] But does this mean international organizations should be rejected as decision-making fora? No, for three reasons. First, many international institutions play a vital role in policy issues that cannot be resolved at individual State level – issues including international trade, the environment, and the migration crisis. It is hard to see how these matters could be resolved if States did not pool sovereignty internationally. Second, the same accusation – that non-elected officials have considerable policy making and implementation power – might also be made of many States.

Third, why should we accept that international organizations are incapable of functioning democratically? To be sure, many international institutions are remote from citizens, and operate complex and obscure processes. It is often difficult to draw a direct line from the individual voter through to many of the decision-making officials. In the case of the EU, power has sometimes been delegated to non-elected officials (i.e. in EU Commission and Council committees) and their power to negotiate justified on the basis of expertise, rather than democratic accountability.[16] Yet perhaps a different interpretation of democracy should apply to the post-national polity? The EU is not a State and should not be assessed as one. Many very different interpretations of the EU have been suggested: intergovernmental, regulatory, or multilevel governance, or even a *sui generis* institution. The purpose of this chapter is not to consider what theory of democracy should apply to international organizations but to acknowledge that one's preferred model of democracy may shape one's view of whether, for example the EU can be democratic, and simple notions of an electorate 'throwing out the scoundrels' may need some adaptation.

And this leads us to contemplate a related, but different issue – that of the composition of the *demos*, the body of people comprising the democratic polity. Modern democracy, as it emerged in the eighteenth century, surfaced contemporaneously with nationalism, meaning that the demos tended to be

[13] W Churchill, House of Commons, 11 November 1947.

[14] J Gray, 'Europe's Hubris', *The Guardian*, 18 October 2012.

[15] Although notably Article 2 TEU states that the EU is founded on the principle of democracy.

[16] See, for example, J Cohen and C Sabel, 'Directly-Deliberative Polyarchy' (2002) 3(4) European Law Journal.

derived from national identities. In these cases, the demos was often the same as the *ethnos* (i.e. the ethnic group, or group with a common national, cultural tradition). The twentieth-century German constitutional theorist, Carl Schmitt (sometimes known as the 'Crown Jurist of the Third Reich') famously identified demos with ethnos. On his theory, the people of a polity, the demos, or *Volk*, is seen as a concrete, identifiable, ethno-cultural feature. For Schmitt, the demos must possess a feeling of shared identity based on a common culture, history, ethnic origin, and so on. In Schmitt's words, 'democracy requires, therefore, first homogeneity and second – if the need arises – elimination or eradication of heterogeneity'.[17] On Schmitt's view, parliaments are democratic because they represent the *Volk*. Yet this is surely an unattractive view, ill-adept for States such as the multi-cultural UK, as it links democracy to the ties of ethnicity and cultural homogeneity which have sparked so many conflicts in the twentieth century and denied cultural, legal, and political entitlements to minorities. It also undermines the very point of supra-national institutions such as the EU, one of whose original functions was to preserve peace by supplanting harmful nationalist urges.

Views such as Schmitt's accord poorly with the pluralism necessary for democracy to flourish. States are very often ethnically diverse, and the criteria for inclusion or exclusion within the relevant demos tend to be contestable. If we take the example of the Brexit referendum, we can see the full force of this point. The relevant demos – the franchise – for the EU referendum was taken to be the same as that for UK general elections. EU citizens, of whom there were over 3 million long-term resident in the UK, were not permitted to vote. Nor were 16 and 17 year olds, or British nationals resident abroad for more over 10 years. And yet these were the very groups most likely to be impacted by a vote to leave the EU. In 2014, only those residents in Scotland, and not in the rest of the UK, were permitted to vote in the Scottish independence referendum – a fact deplored by some. It has been suggested that the franchise for a potential second Scottish referendum should be extended to include Scots resident in the UK. Yet, apart from risking the appearance of gerrymandering, such a move also appears regressive, and atavistic, a move to an ethnos-based franchise, however difficult it might be to identify ethnic Scots in the rest of the UK.

9.1.4 Representative Democracy and Direct Democracy

A crucial issue, which leads quite neatly to the later discussion on referendums, is the distinction between representative and direct democracy. Although a form of direct democracy likely applied in some locations in ancient Greece, direct decision-making is very difficult in larger polities, where millions of citizens cannot all run the government in person. So, it is necessary for them to exercise control through their representatives, the Parliament. Representative

[17] Carl Schmitt, *The Crisis of Parliamentary Democracy* (Berlin: Duncker & Humblot, 1923) 9.

democracy exists because the citizenry in general possess neither the time nor, in most cases, the knowledge, expertise and inclination, to deal directly with complex and detailed issues such as the economy, foreign policy, defence, health, education, and commerce.

Well-known, classic defences of representative government were made both by Edmund Burke and John Stuart Mill. In 1774, Edmund Burke gave an address to his electorate in Bristol, stating:

> It is his duty to sacrifice his repose, his pleasures, his satisfactions, to theirs; and above all, ever, and in all cases, to prefer their interest to his own. But his unbiased opinion, his mature judgment, his enlightened conscience, he ought not to sacrifice to you, to any man, or to any set of men living.... Your representative owes you, not his industry only, but his judgment; and he betrays, instead of serving you, if he sacrifices it to your opinion.[18]

For Burke, therefore, MPs were not delegates with a duty to act on their electors' views, but rather plenipotentiaries, possessing a full power of independent action. Mill provided a sustained defence of representative democracy in *Considerations on Representative Government*.[19] Mill argued that the optimum government took the form of a body of representatives elected by universal suffrage, and that this representative body should identify the electorate's policy needs through free and open discussion.

A modern-day refinement of direct democracy is deliberative, or participatory, democracy, which argues that representative democracy has failed modern society because it is too remote, involving the citizen only through their occasional choice of government officials. Instead, it argues that policies are legitimate if they result from collective deliberation conducted among rational, free, and well-informed individuals.[20] The belief is that through such deliberation people will come together to find a common cause. This also depends on the belief that the process itself forces individuals to articulate their reasons and also to think about what constitutes good reasons for others, what Arendt, following Kant, referred to as an 'enlarged mentality'.[21] Modern-day deliberative democracy advocates a plurality of modes of association: political parties, but also citizen initiatives, social

[18] Edmund Burke, 'Speech to the Electors at Bristol', *Works*, 2: 373, September 6, 1780.

[19] JS Mill, *Considerations on Representative Government* (first published 1861; Cambridge: Cambridge University Press, 2010).

[20] See e.g. John Rawls, *Political Liberalism* (New York: Columbia University Press, 1993); J Habermas, *The Theory of Communicative Action* (Cambridge: Polity Press, 1984); Joshua Cohen, 'Reflections on Deliberative Democracy', in T Christiano and JP Christman (eds.), *Contemporary Debates in Political Philosophy* (Oxford: Wiley-Blackwell, 2009); Benjamin Barber, *Strong Democracy: Participatory Politics for a New Age* (Berkeley: University of California Press, 1984); Iris Marion Young, *Inclusion and Democracy* (Oxford: Oxford University Press, 2002).

[21] See further S Benhabib, 'Judgment and the Moral Foundations of Politics in Arendt's Thought' (1988) 16(1) Political Theory 29–51.

movements and the like, and suggests that, through this multiple network of interlocking associations, a public conversation will emerge. This is an attractive addition because it suggests that democracy is about more than elections and formal politics.

However, one may have reservations about the *completeness* of deliberative democracy. Part of the problem is that many deliberative democrats believe democratic governance can be achieved by process alone.[22] Surely there must additionally be some factor around in which to ground the process. In addition to engaging participation at all levels, and spectrums, of society, it is also necessary to get the *structures* of government right (as is revealed in the debates shaping the development of the US federal Constitution). A whole bureaucracy is necessary – one that creates and implements the laws necessary for a democratic policy to flourish. Institutional design cannot be ignored.

9.1.5 The Death of Democracy

Finally, a lot has been written recently about the dangers of populism, and cautionary tales abound of how democracies can die. This topic was especially prevalent after the election of Donald Trump in the US. An example is provided by Steven Levitsky and Daniel Ziblatt's *How Democracies Die.* Although some democracies die 'at the hands of men with guns', Levitsky and Ziblatt emphasize that there are 'other ways to break a democracy', analysing how officials have enfeebled the formal and informal infrastructures of democracy. Formal structures – that is, institutions, constitutional principles and checks and balances – are weakened or destroyed by a variety of measures, many of them overt, such as the attempt by Trump and his supporters to overturn the 2020 presidential election, the assault on voting rights in US states,[23] and intimidation of the press. Other attacks are less obvious – such as undermining independence of the judiciary which has occurred in Poland and Hungary, by lowering the retirement age of judges, so they may be replaced with more compliant supporters. Levitsky and Ziblatt also consider democracy's more informal infrastructure, including the practices of mutual toleration and institutional forbearance. They define mutual toleration as the idea 'that as long as rivals play by constitutional rules, they accept that the other has an equal right to exist, compete for power and govern'; and forbearance, as 'patient self-control' and restraint, and recognition of the other party's situation as constitutionally and democratically valid.[24]

[22] See e.g. J Tully, *Strange Multiplicity: Constitutionalism in an Age of Diversity* (Cambridge: Cambridge University Press, 1995) for this view.

[23] David Smith, 'Is America Heading to a Place Where It Can No Longer Call Itself a Democracy?', *The Guardian*, 5 June 2021.

[24] Steven Levitsky and Daniel Ziblatt, *How Democracies Die* (New York: Crown Publishing, 2018) 102, 106.

The demise of mutual toleration and forbearance linked with growing populism is very dangerous. Crick suggests a definition:

> Populism has come to mean many things, but I see it as a style of politics and rhetoric that seeks to arouse a majority, or at least what their leaders passionately believe is a majority (like 'moral majority' today, who are plainly a minority), who are, have been, or think themselves to be outside the polity, scorned and despised by an educated establishment.[25]

Increasing inequality also presents a risk to democracy, and it has been all too easy to use money to undermine democracy by influencing electoral politics. This has been exacerbated by cases such as *Buckley* v. *Valeo* and *Citizens United* in the US, in which the US Supreme Court refused to place limits on political campaign spending, on grounds that to do so would violate the First Amendment.[26]

Democracy is an ongoing project. It must always be worked upon. People have to believe that democracy is worth fighting for. This requires a strong democratic culture, and also guarding against the ability of some to skew the terrain of democracy, or undermine it from within.

9.2 Referendums

Referendums are contentious. As Morel and Qvortrup remark, 'For some reason this particular political institution arouses much more passion and touches upon more raw emotions than, say, second chambers, constitutional courts or congressional committees.'[27] They also cite, as evidence of contrasting opinions, on the one hand, Bogdanor's comment that, 'arguments against referendums are also arguments against democracy', and, on the other, MacGinty's contention that:

> Simple majoritarian devices do little to help manage the complexity of conflict. Instead they validate the position of one side and reject that of another. Often, they do little other than delimit and quantify division.[28]

And Robert Dahl simply ignored referendums, not discussing them in his otherwise comprehensive, *On Democracy*.

Qvortrup provides a comprehensive history of referendums,[29] noting that they can be traced back to at least the sixteenth century (when they were used

25 Crick, *Democracy*, 77.

26 *Buckley* v. *Valeo*, 424 U.S. 1 [1976]; *Citizens United* v. *Federal Election Commission*, 558 U.S. 310 [2010].

27 Laurence Morel and Matt Qvortrup, 'Introduction', in L Morel and M Qvortrup (eds.), *The Routledge Handbook to Referendums and Direct Democracy* (London: Routledge, 2017).

28 Vernon Bogdanor, *The People and the Party System* (Cambridge: Cambridge University Press, 1981) 93; R MacGinty, 'Constitutional Referendums and Ethnonational Conflict: The Case of Northern Ireland' (2003) 9(2) Nationalism and Ethnic Politics 3.

29 Matt Qvortrup, 'The History of Referendums and Direct Democracy', in L Morel and M Qvortrup (eds.), *The Routledge Handbook to Referendums and Direct Democracy* (London: Routledge, 2017).

by the French king Francis I to lend legitimacy to acquisitions and transfers of territory). Indeed, most earlier examples of referendums concerned self-determination, and were supported by scholarly writings. Hugo Grotius, writing in the seventeenth century, observed in *De Jure Belli ac Pacis* that 'in the alienation of a part of sovereignty, it is required that the part which is alienated consent to the act [*ut etiam pars de que alienda agitur consentiat*].'[30] However, referendums only began to be used extensively in the nineteenth century, and later gained a bad reputation due to their use in Nazi Germany, when Hitler called a number of plebiscites, which included the vote to leave the League of Nations in 1933, to approve Hitler as *Reichskanzler* in 1934, to approve the National Socialist assembly in 1936, and to annexe Austria in 1938. Carl Schmitt contended that 'institutions of direct democracy' would always be 'in a position superior to the so-called indirect democracy of the parliamentary State.'[31] This contrasts with Attlee's view that:

> I could not consent to the introduction into our national life of a device so alien to our traditions as the referendum, which has only too often been the instrument of Nazism and Fascism. Hitler's practices in the field of referenda and plebiscites can hardly have endeared these expedients to the British heart.[32]

Nonetheless, use of referendums has grown since 1945, most particularly since the 1980s, and as Tierney notes, referendums 'are being deployed increasingly in the settlement of fundamental constitutional questions.'[33] European integration has been a source for the proliferation of referendums – such as the French and Danish votes on the Maastricht treaty, the two negative votes in France and the Netherlands on the EU Constitutional Treaty, the two Irish votes on the Lisbon treaty (the first a No, and the second a Yes) and the Greek referendum in response to the EU reaction to the financial crisis[34] – and of course the two UK referendums on EU membership. In recent times, there has also been an increasing tendency towards unilateral independence referendums, as in Kosovo in 2008, Catalonia in 2017, and Kurdistan in 2017. However, such unilateral referendums are risky and uncertain in effect as, under international law, they are only lawful where there exists no other democratic means of recourse.[35]

Given the increase in referendum use over the past 30 odd years, Tierney suggests that 'we need to locate the rise of the referendum within broader changes in contemporary democratic practice and critique.'[36] Such broader

[30] H Grotius, *The Rights of War and Peace* (1625) 570; Also S Pufendorf, *Of the Law of Nature and Nations: Eight Books* (1672).

[31] Schmitt, *The Crisis of Parliamentary Democracy*, 60.

[32] Attlee, House of Commons, *The Times*, 14 June 1945.

[33] Stephen Tierney, *Constitutional Referendums* (Oxford: Oxford University Press, 2012) 1.

[34] See further e.g. F Mendez, M Mendez, and V Triga, *Referendums and the EU: A Comparative Inquiry* (Cambridge: Cambridge University Press, 2014).

[35] See further *Reference re Secession of Quebec* [1998] 2 SCR. 217.

[36] Tierney, *Constitutional Referendums*, 8.

changes include the fall of communism (with the consequent breakup of many multinational States), European integration, and globalization, as well as a notable growth in public disaffection with politics, and loss of trust in politicians, which has rendered citizens more eager to take more key decisions themselves. Representative democracy has been seen as wanting. But are referendums the answer to this dissatisfaction?

9.2.1 The Legitimacy of Referendums

How legitimate is the referendum as an instrument of democracy? Referendums, or plebiscites,[37] are claimed to provide legitimacy on the basis that democracy requires public participation and it is the function of government to implement the will of the people. Closely related is the notion of popular sovereignty, which is the belief that a State's legitimacy derives from the will or consent of its people, who are source of all political power. This idea is found in French revolutionary discourse, and 'We the People' is the opening phrase of the 1787 US Constitution.

Referendums are advocated on the basis that they strengthen democracy by enabling all citizens to participate, rather than representative democracy, in which decisions are made on the peoples' behalf. In consequence, some argue that anything that frustrates the will of the people as expressed in a referendum is anti-democratic. Indeed, in Brexit, this argument was made with bells and whistles, urging that government had a direct democratic mandate from the people to start the process of withdrawal from the EU.

Yet there are problems with the legitimacy of plebiscitary democracy. *First*, history tells us that this theory of democracy – direct mandate from people to government – has been misused to legitimate executive domination. Napoleon III used a popular plebiscite to acquire autocratic power in 1851. In Latin America, plebiscites have enabled elected presidents to claim to embody the higher interests of the nation over competing political parties. And Carl Schmitt posited a direct link between the people's will and the Fuhrer. That was democracy for him. Donald Trump described his inauguration as 'the day the people became the rulers of this nation again'.[38] But what happens if you oppose a leader who makes that claim? Does that mean you oppose the people?

Second, there is no such thing as the objective general will of the people. Rules are needed, to enable and implement it. Only on that basis does the idea of popular self-government make sense. A referendum in a constitutional democracy is always a product of law. Legal safeguards are needed for the interpretation of

[37] It has been argued that 'plebiscite' has more negative connotations than 'referendum' (and was used in an undemocratic way by French Emperors as well as Hitler and Mussolini). However, the two terms are often used in interchangeably, and I follow that use in this chapter. See further R Rose, 'Referendum or Plebiscite: What's the Difference?' at https://ukandeu.ac.uk/referendum-or-plebiscite-whats-the-difference/

[38] See e.g. Trump: 'People Became the Rulers of This Nation Again', *BBC News*, 20 January 2017.

its constitutional significance, just as legal powers are needed to establish it. I will argue that, in the case of Brexit, those safeguards were lacking.

Third, the argument is made that most citizens are inadequately prepared for direct decision-making, because they lack sufficient knowledge of highly complicated matters. Referendums tend to simplify significant and complex subjects. This argument is related to Plato's elitist argument for guardians, and as such is a rather unattractive, exclusionary argument against referendums. However, this argument can be reformulated as suggesting that it is not that people lack understanding of relevant issues, but rather that referendums tend to present issues in binary black and white terms that fail to capture their complexity. Further, referendums can lock in certain policy outcomes in areas of enormous consequence, where opinions may rapidly fluctuate. And unlike other policies which may be reversed by a change of government, the referendum decision tends to remain frozen, and unchangeable.

Lastly, there is also the argument that referendums and plebiscites can threaten individual rights and oppress minorities, because they so often depend on a simple majority decision-making. The 'tyranny of the majority' is a real danger, and the people may be less tolerant than their elected representatives – capital punishment in the UK, supported by the general public, but not by MPs, provides such an example.

To be sure, none of the above arguments provide a knockdown case against the use of referendums. Indeed, referendums can perform a highly valuable role in democracies, most especially in cases of secession and union. However, it does suggest that referendums should be used with caution and operate through already established and well thought out constitutional procedures.

9.3 Democracy in Britain

According to Gamble, 'When democracy finally arrived in Britain, it was an add-on to the existing liberal constitutional order and its representative institutions, not a new kind of state.'[39] All of Britain's major institutions – the Crown, Parliament, the judiciary, the civil service, the military, the Church, the universities, the media – were established in pre-democratic times. David Marquand has described Britain's 'crablike progress towards democracy.'[40] Wright also notes how, 'In the First World War centenary commemorations, the fact that most of the men slaughtered on the Somme could not vote … went unremarked.[41] However, after the Fourth Reform Act of 1918 and extension of women's franchise in 1928, most adults in Britain had the vote.

[39] A Gamble, 'A Hundred Years of British Democracy', in A Gamble and T Wright (eds.), *Rethinking Democracy* (Oxford & London: Wiley, 2019) 152.

[40] D Marquand, *Britain since 1918: The Strange Career of British Democracy* (London: Weidenfeld and Nicolson, 2008) 5.

[41] T Wright, 'Democracy in Britain: Retrospect and Prospect', in A Gamble and T Wright (eds.), *Rethinking Democracy*, 191.

Democratic reform had been achieved in increments over the previous century, starting with the 1832 Reform Act. This so-called 'Great' Reform Act in fact had very little of the democratic about it. Although it organised constituencies on a more rational basis, abolishing rotten boroughs such as Old Sarum, whose seven voters returned two members of Parliament, and providing – for the first time in many cases – representation for the densely populated towns that had sprung up with the industrial revolution, it only increased the franchise from about 435,000 to 652,000.[42] The 1832 Act also abolished the right to vote of the very few women who then possessed it.[43] After the 1832 Act, there was still no Secret Ballot (only provided by the Ballot Act 1872) so those who could vote could be coerced or bribed into voting a particular way. Of greater importance was the Second Reform Act of 1867, although even after its reforms only about a third of adult males were entitled to vote, which, after the Third Reform Act of 1884 increased to about 40 per cent. Nonetheless, these two latter Reform Acts mobilised the electoral system into the era of mass politics, and the parties were forced to become more organized and to campaign nationally. Although neither Gladstone nor Disraeli were committed to a completely democratic franchise, nonetheless, as Saunders remarks, 'The constitution occupied an extraordinary place in the political culture of Victorian Britain,' with many prominent figures writing weighty constitutional treatises.[44]

Some commentators have linked nineteenth-century agitation for domestic constitutional reform with the politics of the British Empire. For example, Catherine Hall has argued that 'it was impossible to think about the "mother country" and its specificities without reference to the colonies'.[45] Rande Kostal's study of the controversy over the 1865 Jamaican 'rebellion', and Governor Eyre's response to it, argued that domestic franchise reform and the Jamaica controversy concerned the same issue, namely, that of legal accountability in a constitutional state.[46] Duncan Bell argues that, although both the Second and Third Reform Acts increased democracy, they also induced anxiety over the future of the empire among those arguing for imperial federation, partly due to worries that many of the new increased franchise would be less supportive

42 Figures in Crick, *Democracy*, chapter 5.

43 This is because the 1832 Act for the first time specified that the right to vote was restricted to 'male persons'.

44 R Saunders, 'The Politics of Reform and the Making of the Second Reform Act, 1848–1867' (2007) 50(3) The Historical Journal 571, at 573. Saunders notes Russell's *History of English government*; Gladstone's *The state in its relations with the church*; Disraeli's *Vindication of the English constitution*, de Tocqueville's *Democracy in America*, John Stuart Mill's *Considerations on representative government*, and Walter Bagehot's *English constitution*, in the period before the Second Reform Act.

45 Catherine Hall, 'The Nation Within and Without', in C Hall, K McClelland, and J Rendall, *Defining the Victorian Nation* (Cambridge: Cambridge University Press, 2000) 180. Also A Middleton, 'The Second Reform Act and the Politics of Empire' (2017) *Parliamentary History*.

46 RW Kostal, *A Jurisprudence of Power: Victorian Empire and the Rule of Law* (Oxford: Oxford University Press, 2005), 162–163.

of empire.[47] Certainly, connections between political reform and empire were drawn at the time. Many of the 'settler colonies' enjoyed a wider franchise and secret ballot. John Stuart Mill made reference to Australian examples in arguing the case for 'personal representation'.[48] But many references were also made to America and to France. Although empire was relevant, the internal threats to, and understanding of, the British State, were probably more important in reform debates.

There was some incremental improvement in the franchise in the half century from 1918 – such as extending the vote to all women at 21 in 1928, lowering the voting age to 18 in 1969, and abolishing anomalies including the university seats and additional votes for business in local elections. However, from 1997, the Blair Labour government implemented many constitutional reforms. These included House of Lords reform, removing all but 92 hereditary peers; the establishment of a new Supreme Court independent of the House of Lords; devolution establishing directly elected parliaments/assemblies in Scotland, Wales and Northern Ireland; Britain's first directly elected mayor in London; and the Human Rights Act, incorporating the European Convention on Human Rights in the UK. But some of this had an unfinished feel to it (i.e. House of Lords reform, which literally remained incomplete after the 1999 House of Lords Act); and some was deeply opposed or regretted by at least some Opposition MPs. These reforms were still characteristic of the ad hoc nature of British constitutional reform. Britain continued to lack a codified Constitution, and as a result, lacks some formal constitutional principles to structure and constrain constitutional reform.

9.3.1 How Well Does Britain Function as a Democracy?

But just how effectively has Britain performed as a democracy since 1918? In international surveys of democracy and good governance, Britain tends to be roughly midway down the first league, better than many, but below Scandinavian States. For example, *The Economist* Intelligence Unit[49] operates a Democracy Index, which in 2020 rated the UK as a full democracy – in a survey which only ranked 23 of 167 States as full democracies, and rated the US, France, Italy, and Japan as flawed democracies. However, Britain came behind Germany, Canada, Australia, New Zealand, Uruguay, and the Nordic countries. When one turns to social, rather than liberal democracy as a category, Britain fares less well. Stein Ringen, in his 2007 book, *What Democracy Is For*, presented a comparative analysis of social democracies, measuring both the quality of services delivered to citizens, as well as

[47] Duncan Bell, *The Idea of Greater Britain: Empire and the Future of World Order, 1860–1900* (Princeton, NJ: Princeton University Press, 2007) 2.

[48] Mill, *Personal Representation* (1867).

[49] *The Economist Intelligence Unit*, at www.eiu.com/n/

political institutions. Although Nordic States performed very well on this index, Britain and the US were far behind, and this index was produced before the financial crisis, the introduction of austerity, measures, and the election of Donald Trump.[50]

9.3.2 Democratic Deficits in British Democracy

One of the major criticisms made of the EU, often by eurosceptics, was that it contained a democratic deficit. However, there exist democratic deficits in British law and politics. As already stated, the basic constitutional order was well established in Britain before the coming of democracy with the enlargement of the franchise, and there still exist inequalities of wealth, race gender and power in Britain.

The British tradition has been one of 'strong government', based on a first past the post system, rather than pluralist power sharing. LS Amery, conservative politician and journalist, notably described Britain's political system as 'government of the people, for the people, with but not by the people.'[51] It features a powerful and predominant executive that dominates Parliament and insufficient constitutional checks and balances. The next sections detail nine distinct elements of this democratic deficit in Britain.

9.3.2.1 The First Past the Post Voting System

This is perhaps the source of the largest democratic deficit in Britain's political democracy, at least as far as Westminster politics is concerned. The first past the post voting system used in general elections means that the candidate with the most votes wins the election, even if the combined votes of other candidates is greater. Those who voted for other candidates are not represented, although in theory MPs are supposed to represent all their constituents. Indeed, Britain is one of the few democracies to persist with this system. But the result is that parties are able to obtain a majority of seats and form a government, even if (as is usually the case) they received only a minority of votes. The converse is also true – a party may obtain many votes and few or no MPs, such as was the case with UKIP, which in 2015 got 4 million votes but only one MP. This means that Britain's democracy – at least as far as UK-wide general elections are concerned – is not very representative, and, for those who do not vote for a winning candidate, there is little feeling of the equality that democracy is supposed to ensure. There have been several occasions when the system might have changed, but nothing came of it. The 1916/17 Speaker's conference had recommended proportional representation for larger constituencies but Lloyd

[50] S Ringen, *What Democracy Is For: On Freedom and Moral Government* (Princeton and Oxford: Princeton University Press, 2007).

[51] LS Amery, *Thoughts on the Constitution* (London and New York: Oxford University Press, 1947).

George's Liberal Coalition government did not implement this (although later regretted not having done so). The minority government of 1929–1931 introduced legislation to change the system, but fell before the legislation could be adopted. And the 2011 Alternative Vote Referendum failed to achieve a majority.

However, aside from general elections, different voting systems have applied in the UK, especially in the devolved nations of the UK, for the European Parliament, and for the Greater London Assembly. All of these systems rely on some form of proportional representation and are more representative of the electorate overall.

9.3.2.2 Ongoing Restrictions on the Right to Vote

The right to vote is at the heart of democracy – properly respected and exercised it ensures that every person is equally treated, but it is too easily subject to manipulation.

The 2019 Conservative party manifesto declared there will be 'updated and equal parliamentary boundaries, making sure that every vote counts the same.'[52] Here of course the devil lies in the detail, as constituencies with equal populations can be fashioned in many ways, with scope for gerrymandering, as in the US.[53] The manifesto also states, 'We will continue to support the First Past the Post system of voting, as it allows voters to kick out politicians who don't deliver, both locally and nationally.' This does not sit well with the previous commitment to ensure every vote counts the same, given many constituencies constantly elect MPs for the same party, with votes for others largely wasted. The current national electoral system favours the Conservatives (and has previously favoured Labour). However, if proportional representation were applied to national elections, Johnson would not have achieved a parliamentary majority in 2019.[54] A further manifesto pledge was to 'protect the integrity of our democracy, by introducing identification to vote at polling stations.' Who would not want to protect the integrity of democracy? However, there is actually very little voter fraud in Britain, and the danger is that voter identification can be used to deter voters and suppress the franchise, again a feature of US politics.[55]

These pledges by and large work in favour of government, at the expense of Parliament and voters for smaller parties. They appear to reduce the potential of Parliament to act as a check on government.

[52] Available at www.conservatives.com/our-plan/conservative-party-manifesto-2019.

[53] See further, 'Electoral Map Bias May Worsen as U.S. Gerrymandering Battle Shifts to States', *Reuters*, 29 June 2019.

[54] 'Hung Parliament and 70 Lib Dem MPs: What the General Election Result Would Have Been If We Used a PR System', *The Independent*, 14 December 2019.

[55] E.g. S Halpern, 'America's Redistricting Process Is Breaking Democracy', *New York Times*, 25 May 2022; also *Voter ID: Securing the Ballot or Suppressing the Vote*? House of Commons Library, 23 October 2019.

9.3.2.3 Dominance of the Executive

The UK has a fused system, whereby government is nested in Parliament, and government ministers must be members of one or other House. There is no strict separation of powers. Although the principle of parliamentary sovereignty applies in the UK, this usually takes the form of the government acting through Parliament to implement its programme of legislation, and so the executive dominates. Apart from rare chances, such as Private Members' Bills, the legislative initiative lies with the executive, which has also striven to control the legislature, through patronage or the party whipping system. Without government support, it is very difficult for backbenchers (parliamentarians who are not members of the government), even with cross-party support, to get legislation of their choice through Parliament. Government ministers have considerable powers, many of which are not statutory in nature but exercised under the royal prerogative (including foreign affairs, and until 2010, regulation of the Civil Service), which is often vague and untransparent. The royal prerogative is a form of binding, non-statutory, law-making by the Crown, now usually exercised by government ministers. Lord Roskill famously said that with prerogative he could hear 'the clanking of medieval chains of the ghosts of the past.'[56]

Thus, government ministers, especially the Prime Minister, have inherited powers formerly exercised by the Monarch using the prerogative. Here accountability is weak and few checks and balances apply. In the UK parliamentary system, where the government is vested within, and must retain the confidence of, Parliament, there is a less than clear cut separation of powers, and the ability of backbenchers to oppose government uses (or abuses) of power may be limited, especially where the government has a large majority. The ability of Parliament to curb the exercise of the prerogative is contentious. There now seems to be a weak precedent requiring that the government obtain parliamentary consent before committing British armed forces to military intervention, but this is not very well-established.[57] Additionally, Britain's uncodified Constitution leaves many key constitutional issues unsettled. In the UK, treaty making, and foreign affairs, are usually managed by the executive, but often with some sort of participation by the legislature. Brexit revealed the prerogative's status as particularly ill-defined, and potentially wide-ranging, in the UK. It is not unusual for the executive to control most of foreign affairs, and it took litigation to establish that the government could not use the prerogative to trigger Article 50 TEU (and so initiate the process of leaving the EU) without Parliament's consent – a principle established in the first *Miller* case.[58]

[56] Lord Roskill in *Council of Civil Service Unions* v. *Minister for the Civil Service* [1985] AC 374, 417, quoting Lord Atkin in *United Australia Ltd* v. *Barclays Bank Ltd* [1941] AC 1, 29.

[57] Research Briefing, *Parliamentary Approval for Military Action*, House of Commons Library, 17 April 2018.

[58] *R (Miller)* v. *Secretary of State for Exiting the EU* [2017] UKSC 5.

Miller acknowledged the crucial role of Parliament in protecting rights, as well as underlining that a UK statute may not be repealed by prerogative alone.

After the *Miller* decision, Parliament enacted legislation consenting to Article 50 being triggered and the Brexit process set in motion. This took the form of the EU (Notification of Withdrawal) Act 2017, a miniscule piece of legislation, with only one brief provision: 'The prime minister may notify, under Article 50(2) of the Treaty on European Union, the United Kingdom's intention to withdraw from the EU.' This legislation has been subsequently criticised as giving the government 'a blank cheque'. As Mark Elliott writes,

> At that point, parliament could have opted to put itself, at least to some extent, in the driving seat. It could, for instance, have legislated so as to give the government only contingent authority to trigger Article 50. The exercise of that power could have been made conditional upon the government presenting parliament with a set of negotiating objectives that met with parliamentary approval.[59]

This did not happen. But nonetheless, especially during the minority conservative government from 2017 to 2019, Parliament sought to exert itself and MPs tried to take greater control of affairs to shape the form that Brexit took, most particularly after May's Brexit deal had been voted down (by the largest majority in parliamentary history, on 15 January 2019). However, because the government controlled the agenda for Parliament, it was very hard for backbencher MPs to take action. As a result, some of the most crucial parliamentary happenings were forced to take place in the margins of parliamentary affairs – over procedures, motions, amendments to motions or even to amendments, 'humble addresses', and references to standing orders. All of this, however, meant that the political process appeared arcane, opaque, and confusing. And in any case, alternative Brexit arrangements put forward by MPs – such as proposals for a soft Brexit, or for a second referendum – were unsuccessful, albeit some were rejected by only a narrow margin. It is much easier for the government to control parliamentary processes than for backbench MPs to assert authority.

9.3.2.4 Unlawful Prorogation of Parliament

In autumn 2019, UK Prime Minister Boris Johnson prorogued (suspended) Parliament for 5 weeks. This had the drastic result of closing down Parliament altogether at a crucial moment in UK affairs. During that time, Parliament could not sit. No legislation could be adopted, nor could Parliament call the government to account for any actions it was taking. The deadline under the Article 50 TEU process was soon to expire, and without a Withdrawal Agreement negotiated with the EU, there were fears that Britain would leave the EU with no deal at all, with all sorts of dire consequences. It was seen as essential that, in this

[59] M Elliott, 'Why on Earth Didn't Parliament Take Control When It Had the Chance?' *Prospect*, 16 January 2019.

crucial time, Parliament be able to sit, and call the government to account on Brexit. Many suspected the prorogation was an attempt by the Prime Minister to 'shut down Parliament' to prevent it scrutinizing his handling of Brexit. A political crisis looked in danger of turning into a constitutional crisis.

The issue of the royal prerogative again reared its head. The power to prorogue Parliament is a prerogative power, exercised by the Prime Minister with the consent of the monarch. Although the process of dissolution of Parliament prior to a general election had been put on a statutory footing by the Fixed Term Parliaments Act 2010 (meaning that the Prime Minister could no longer dissolve Parliament and call a general election at a time of their choosing) the power to prorogue was still in the hands of the executive, although it had never been exercised for such a long period of time.[60] A legal action was instituted,[61] to test the Prime Minister's ability to act by prerogative alone to shut down Parliament, which went to the UK Supreme Court.

In an unanimous judgement (in itself striking) the UK Supreme Court held that the prorogation was unlawful. The first issue was whether the actual issue itself was justiciable – that is, a matter that can be determined by a court, or instead a matter reserved for 'high policy and politics'. The UK Supreme Court found it justiciable, and, as if to stress the orthodoxy of this holding, cited caselaw going back to 1610 in support ('the King hath no prerogative but that which the law of the land allows him'[62]). As was stated in the *Miller/Cherry* judgment: 'Although the courts cannot decide political questions, the fact that a legal dispute concerns the conduct of politicians, or arises from a matter of political controversy, has never been sufficient reason for the courts to refuse to consider it'.

The Supreme Court then held that:

> a decision to prorogue parliament will be unlawful *if the prorogation has the effect of frustrating* or *preventing*, without reasonable justification, the ability of parliament to carry out its constitutional functions as a legislature and as the body responsible for the supervision of the executive. In such a situation, the court will intervene if the effect is sufficiently serious to justify such an exceptional course.

Having established the legal test, the Court found prorogation did have the effect of frustrating or preventing Parliament from carrying out its constitutional functions. This prolonged suspension of parliamentary democracy took place in quite exceptional circumstances: the fundamental change due to take place in the UK Constitution on 31 October. Parliament had a right to a voice in

60 It is usually just exercised to suspend Parliament briefly for agreed recesses, such as the summer vacation.

61 *Miller/Cherry* v. *Prime Minister* [2019] UKSC 41. Two separate actions were brought – one in the Scottish courts (by Joanna Cherry QC, a Scottish National MP) and another in England (by Gina Miller). Both actions were consolidated in the UK Supreme Court.

62 This statement was famously made by Sir Edward Coke CJ, in *The Case of Proclamations* [1610] EWHC KB J22.

how that change came about. As the Court stated, 'The effect upon the fundamentals of our democracy was extreme' but 'No justification for taking action with such an extreme effect has been put before the court.' The government had not supplied any witness statement setting out reasons for the prorogation, 'The Court is bound to conclude, therefore, that the decision to advise Her Majesty to prorogue parliament was unlawful.'[63] This meant that Parliament must be recalled immediately and it was as if Parliament had never been prorogued.

Some described the judgment as unprecedented, and it was unprecedented, because there has been no attempt to prorogue Parliament for such a length of time before, at a time of national importance. Courts have found against governments before in the UK, but never found a Prime Minister's advice (to the Queen) to be unlawful as here. But the principles on which the Court relied to make its judgment could not be more central – parliamentary sovereignty, accountability, control of the exercise of the prerogative. If the Courts are not able to police and uphold these, who else could, given that Parliament was disabled? In upholding the fundamental principle of parliamentary sovereignty, the Court was hardly setting itself up as a proponent of some new judge-made Constitution.

There were critics of the *Miller/Cherry* judgement, among them the Judicial Power Project (JPP). The day after *Miller/Cherry*, the *Daily Mail* carried an op-ed article by Richard Ekins, an Oxford Law professor, and head of the JPP, against the judgement, which read – 'Bad for democracy, Bad for the law and Bad for the judges'.[64] The JPP ran a series of articles on 'the unconstitutionality' of the *Miller/Cherry* judgement.' Another Oxford academic, John Finnis (famous for his works on natural law rather than on UK constitutional law) writing for JPP, claimed for example that 'The Judgment was wholly unjustified by law.'[65] Although the JPP claims to emphasise the importance of parliamentary sovereignty in the British Constitution, stressing that courts have no place to question Parliament's decisions, critics of the JPP argue its thrust is rather to strengthen the executive. Thomas Poole for example, claims that:

> ... its targets seemingly include any institutional check on executive power, political as much as legal. This is not, to my mind, a programme of constitutional

[63] All extracts from *Miller/Cherry* v. *Prime Minister* [2019] UKSC 41.

[64] Available at www.dailymail.co.uk/news/article-7501071/Oxford-professor-RICHARD-EKINS-locks-horns-PETER-OBORNE-Supreme-Courts-verdict.html

[65] John Finnis, 'The Unconstitutionality of the Supreme Court's Prorogation Judgment', available at https://policyexchange.org.uk/wp-content/uploads/2019/10/The-unconstitutionality-of-the-Supreme-Courts-prorogation-judgment.pdf.

It was also John Finnis, who had initially raised the possibility of an extended prorogation in a newspaper article in April 2019. Finnis has been described in the following way:

'John Finnis is not just some ordinary law professor: the Australian legal philosopher and student of H.L.A. Hart has until his retirement held a prestigious chair at Oxford University for many years and now teaches at the Catholic University of Notre Dame in the USA.... Another, even more famous scion of Finnis's academic progeny is the US Supreme Court judge and Trump nominee Neil Gorsuch.' (M Steinbeis, 'Right Wing Crits' available at https://verfassungsblog.de/right-wing-crits/.)

> conservatism in the spirit of Blackstone or Burke. It is an anarcho-conservatism more familiar from the work of counter-revolutionaries such as Carl Schmitt. Authoritarian rather than conservative in disposition, it treats established constitutional forms and norms as fungible, even disposable, and presses exceptional moments in the direction of a central authority delivering the 'will of the people'.[66]

Such an image of a strong executive presence, delivering on the 'will of the people' was further emphasized in Boris Johnson's first statement after the General election in December 2019, in which he referred to 'members of our new one nation government – a people's government'.[67]

9.3.2.5 Attacks on Judicial Review

The different reactions to these two Supreme Court judgements (*Miller I* and *Miller/Cherry*) illustrate two very disparate sets of attitudes. On the one hand, is the view that sees the government implementing the referendum result, the mandate of the will of the people, deriving legitimacy from it. On this view, an obstreperous Parliament's role is eclipsed and judicial review unwarranted, a constitutional coup even, and judges may be 'enemies of the people'. On the other side, the two judgements are viewed as robustly upholding the Constitution, resting on old and venerated precedents. Judicial review is an important check on an overreaching executive, which had exploited populist sentiment to weaken Parliament.

Limiting judicial review clearly reduces an important check on government. This is especially concerning, given that the vast changes in the UK's legal landscape wrought by Brexit look all too likely to lead to legal challenges. The post-Brexit legal system will be governed by the UK's EU Withdrawal Act 2018 (the sprawling constitutional legislation transferring much EU law into national law), EU Withdrawal Agreement Act 2020 and EU (Future Relationship) Act 2020, all of which are very long and complicated statutes, much of which were drafted and adopted in haste. They contain huge scope for 'Henry VIII' clauses (namely, provisions allowing ministers to *repeal* statute law). If judicial review is constrained, there will be few effective checks on ministerial abuse of power. There is also of course the devolution dimension, which became more complicated with Brexit. For example, the UK Supreme Court already examined the Scottish Parliament Continuity Bill, under s33 Scotland Act 1998 (and in 2022 determined that a referendum on Scottish independence was outwith the competence of the Scottish Parliament).

But the need for judicial review extends well beyond Brexit, as is illustrated by a case from 2020. The UK government attempted to deport to Jamaica 50 individuals who had served sentences for criminal offences, without ensuring their access to legal advice prior to deportation (in breach of human rights laws). Many had spent their lives in the UK. An emergency ruling was made

66 T Poole, 'The Executive Power Project', *LRB blog*, 2 April 2019.

67 Available at www.gov.uk/government/speeches/pm-statement-in-downing-street-13-december-2019

by the Court of Appeal, ordering no deportation until it could be certified that the detainees could contact their lawyers. What made this an especially sensitive case was that it had clear echoes of the 'Windrush' scandal.[68] However, the Court of Appeal order prompted fury from the government. This government reaction was in turn met by criticism pointing out that judicial review underlays the rule of law and is a vital check against government abuse.[69]

Politicians have suggested curbs on judicial power and the instigation of US style political vetting for senior judges. After the prorogation decision, Iain Duncan-Smith, former conservative party leader, was quoted in the *Daily Telegraph* saying of Lady Hale, 'Given the radical judgment she's just made – inventing a law – if we're going to get this kind of stuff from her, is it not time for parliament to scrutinise appointments to the Supreme Court?'[70] Geoffrey Cox, (then) Attorney General, also suggested overhauling the appointments process to resemble something like the US system. But one might query whether this might render judges subject to political or populist influence rather than giving judicial appointments greater democratic legitimacy.

In any case, judicial independence can also have different resonances in different jurisdictions. An article in *The Daily Telegraph*, commenting on the *Miller/Cherry* judgement, stated: 'The very title [Supreme Court] implies ultimate judicial power of a sort that refashions our constitution along continental or American lines incompatible with our own belief in the supremacy of the voters' elected representatives.'[71] This is inaccurate and misleading. The UK Supreme Court has no power of 'hard judicial review' to strike down legislation and does not function in the same way as the US Supreme Court. Judicial review in the UK does not permit courts to replace government decisions with their own, but instead is a supervisory mechanism reviewing the lawfulness of decisions taken by public bodies. As Lady Hale stated, in a 2016 speech in Malaysia:

> We cannot strike down Acts of the UK Parliament. But please do not think that I – or any of my brethren – want us to be able to do that. We are, I think, very comfortable with the role that we do have. This includes the various rules of statutory interpretation which govern the way in which we read legislation and enable us to safeguard fundamental rights and the rule of law.[72]

[68] This involved Commonwealth nationals who had come to the UK on the ship 'Windrush' in 1948 (and their children) whose rights as British citizens were guaranteed under the Immigration Act 1971. However, under the Immigration Act 2012, they were forced to prove their continuous residence in the UK since 1973, which many lacked detailed records to do. As a result, many were threatened with, or actually deported, and lost access to work, healthcare and housing in Britain.

[69] Including from the President of the Law Society. See further, 'Deportation flight concerns coming from 'Westminster bubble', says No 10,' *The Guardian*, 11 February 2019.

[70] Lady Hale 'revelling' in Supreme Court judgment, say critics, in row over 'girly swots' remark. *Daily Telegraph*, 4 October 2019.

[71] Charles Moore, 'Fixing the Supreme Court should be Boris Johnson's Constitutional Priority', *The Daily Telegraph*, 8 February 2020.

[72] Lady Hale, 'The Supreme Court: Guardian of the Constitution?' (Sultan Azlan Shah Lecture, 9 November 2016).

The UK Supreme Court is a new creature, replacing the former judicial committee of the House of Lords, and was set up by the UK Constitutional Reform Act 2005. A separate Supreme Court, outside of the House of Lords and Parliament, makes clear that the court is independent, separate from the legislature and government, and that there exists in the UK an independent judiciary and a separation of powers.

Nonetheless, even with no strike down power of statute, the UK Supreme Court can be bold. In the *Unison* case, the Supreme Court nullified a ministerial order that would have introduced high fees for employment tribunals. Lord Reed (now the Court's President) then stated, 'The constitutional right of access to the courts is inherent in the rule of law.'[73] The Supreme Court seems even to have set a marker for what it might do if exceptional circumstances were to arise and were an *Act of Parliament* 'to abolish judicial review or to diminish the role of the courts in protecting the interests of the individual'.[74] Although there are no definitive statements from the Court, obiter statements suggest that such a truly exceptional statute might not be legally enforced.

The 2019 Conservative manifesto proclaimed that, 'Our independent courts and legal system are respected throughout the world.' However judicial independence was afforded little respect when Johnson openly disagreed with the Supreme Court's prorogation judgment in September 2019, nor was it in *Miller 1* in 2016, when the Divisional Court were declared 'enemies of the people' by the *Daily Mail*. Judicial independence continues to be under attack across the world, by authoritarian regimes such as Poland and Orban's Hungary. Britain is not immune.

This episode closes with a reminder from Justice Suzanne Baer, of the German Constitutional Court, of the important role that courts play in protecting democracy: 'constitutionalism connects democracy and human rights, by the rule of law, and installs courts as the backup to make it work if all others do not comply anyway. Courts, then, do not replace politics, but are the safety belts for democratic politics that do not hurt anyone.'[75]

9.3.2.6 The Role of the House of Lords

Many, indeed most States, have a second Chamber, which plays its role in the legislative process. However, the British House of Lords is in an anomalous position, a partially reformed relic of a former pre-democratic era. It was deprived of its absolute veto in the 1911 Parliament Act (and subsequent 1949 Parliament Act) and the House of Lords Act 1999 removed all but ninety-two hereditary peers. So, some of its worst undemocratic features have been removed. But it still remains unelected, with appointments made under the

[73] *R (UNISON)* v. *Lord Chancellor* [2017] UKSC 51.

[74] Per Lord Hope (obiter) in *AXA General Insurance Limited* v. *The Lord Advocate* [2012] 1 AC 868.

[75] S Baer, 'The Rule of – and Not by Any – Law. On Constitutionalism' (2018) Current Legal Problems 339, 357.

prerogative exercised by Queen on the advice of the Prime Minister, and reforms have stalled. Its legitimacy is questionable. Even if there is considerable expertise among its members, attendance is voluntary, many of its members are appointed simply as a result of patronage, and play very little part in the legislative process. Tony Wright pithily commented that: 'What kind of democracy is it that still has something called a House of Lords and an obsession with titles?.... The fact that we put up with this Ruritanian nonsense is a mark of a country which has not yet quite grown up democratically.'[76]

9.3.2.7 Corruption/Tax Evasion

Although Britain scores relatively well on the corruption scoring of the World Bank, and in Transparency International's Corruption Perceptions Index, it performs less satisfactorily when it comes to tax evasion and money laundering, and has one of the lowest scores on the Tax Justice Network's Financial Secrecy Index. Indeed, Britain has gained a reputation as a money laundering capital, and for its relations with offshore tax havens.[77] This means that there exist great discrepancies of wealth – particularly in London – and social justice suffers. This has been condoned by the political system. Corporate lobbying has flourished. Great inequalities continue to exist and this distorts politics and democracy.

9.3.2.8 Human Rights

Most Constitutions today, as well as sharing and balancing power, protect human rights, which must sometimes be enforced against popular, but unlawful, prejudiced views. This is especially so, given Britain's 'first past the post system', where legislation prejudicing minority groups (especially groups lacking electoral rights) could be passed by parliamentary votes not even representing a majority of the electorate. The threats to EU citizens after Brexit, or to the Windrush generation, come to mind. However, Britain only adopted the Human Rights Act, which incorporated the European Convention on Human Rights, in 1998, and the current Conservative government has plans to repeal or amend it. The next chapter will cover the issue of human rights, but suffice it to say that human rights are an important feature of democracy, a bulwark against majority prejudices, and a means of ensuring equality and pluralism. If human rights are not adequately respected and enforced, the ability for some individuals to play their part in society is diminished.

Notably, the 2019 Conservative manifesto committed to 'champion freedom of expression and tolerance.' But will this commitment apply to the media? In the pre-2019 election TV debate on climate change, when Johnson did not participate, Channel 4 'empty-chaired' him and replaced him with a melting

[76] Wright, 'Democracy in Britain', 194.

[77] See e.g. O. Bullough, 'How Britain Can Help You Get Away with Stealing Millions: A Five-Step Guide', *The Guardian*, 5 July 2019.

ice block. In response, the Conservative Party threatened to revoke Channel 4's licence if in government, and has since then initiated plans to privatise it. Post-election, the BBC has been warned that the government is considering decriminalizing non-payment of the licence fee, and would boycott the Radio 4 *Today* programme over perceived anti-Tory bias. On 3 February 2020, 10 Downing Street provided that it would admit only preselected media into selected briefings, thus excluding others – something which occurred during Trump's tenure at the White House. Yet, a free and independent media is a bulwark of a tolerant, democratic society, and its restriction or absence notable in autocratic states such as Orban's Hungary.

9.3.2.9 Unlimited Parliamentary Sovereignty

This subject has already been extensively covered in another chapter. However, it should be stressed that parliamentary sovereignty is not so much the sovereignty of every MP, but instead legislative sovereignty, which is very often simply *executive* sovereignty, which enables a government, often elected on a minority vote, to enforce its legislative agenda in the House of Commons. But once in this position, the British Government has considerable powers, as noted by a former American ambassador to Britain:

> An American arrives on British shores astonished to discover how unfettered a modern British government is. When I first lived here, in the mid-1970s, it took me a long time to understand that a British government, with a simple majority in the House of Commons, can do pretty much what it wants to. If the party in power can count on having one more warm body in its lobby than all the other bodies combined in the other lobby, there is nothing to prevent the government having its way. I kept looking for constitutional checks and institutional balances that could stay the will of a British government. But I could find none. In face of such arbitrary omnipotence, I could suddenly imagine myself as an American revolutionary ...[78]

Not only is there a lack of checks and balances on executive sovereignty but there has also been a great unwillingness reluctance to share sovereignty. This was evident in Britain's relations with Ireland up to the Anglo-Irish Treaty of 1921, in Britains' relations with the devolved nations, and its relations with the EU. But the result is that power rests in the hands of a few, usually elected by a minority of the population.

9.3.3 Direct Democracy and Representative Democracy; Popular Sovereignty and Parliamentary Sovereignty

UK constitutional law (Scotland may be a different matter[79]) does not acknowledge a principle of popular sovereignty. Instead, sovereignty is seen as resting with the Crown in Parliament, and UK politics is based on representative

[78] R Seitz, *Over Here* (London: Phoenix, 1998) 256. [79] See Chapter 1.

democracy. In 1653, Oliver Cromwell's *Instrument of Government* declared legislative power resided in the Lord Protector 'and the people', but this document did not survive the fall of Cromwell. England, and later the UK, did not develop a tradition of popular sovereignty in constitutional terms, even if there were sometimes talk of a 'sovereignty of the electorate' in political terms. However, such a sovereignty of the electorate only allowed the electorate to choose the government, it did not ground the British Constitution in the authority of the people.[80] This is unlike written Constitutions, such as the US Federal Constitution, whose legitimacy is explicitly stated to be based on the authority of 'We the people'. Referendums have not traditionally been part of the British political system. Instead, the British political system has been based on the theory of representative democracy, as expressed by Burke. This means that MPs' actions have been driven by their judgements as to the best interests of their constituents, their party, and the UK.

Notwithstanding, the view has been expressed that, since the Brexit referendum, Britain has mutated into a system of direct democracy. For example, Vernon Bogdanor has argued that 'the sovereignty of the people is trumping the sovereignty of parliament' and that 'the referendum has now established itself as a third chamber of parliament, issuing legislative instructions to the other two'. And the Tory MP, Bernard Jenkin, announced that 'We've grown up in a representative system of democracy. Now we have direct democracy. If you have direct democracy it trumps representative democracy.'[81] But these views are surely incorrect. In the first *Miller* case, the Supreme Court stated that '[t]he referendum is a relatively new feature of UK constitutional practice' and that 'The effect of any particular referendum must depend on the terms of the statute which authorises it.'[82] *Miller I* established that the referendum decision had no automatic legal effect, and that Parliament must give its consent to the triggering of Article 50 TEU to commence proceedings for the UK to leave the EU. The next section will examine the Brexit Referendum in detail and argue that its use has not transformed Britain into a direct democracy based on popular sovereignty.

Bogdanor also accuses 'liberal minded people' of being 'uncomfortable with the doctrine of the sovereignty of the people.'[83] However, evidence for this is lacking, and, on the contrary, there are many reasons to embrace greater

[80] Dicey described the electorate as the political sovereign, but stressed their powers were limited: 'The sole legal right of electors under the English constitution is to elect members of Parliament. Electors have no legal means of initiating, of sanctioning, or of repealing the legislation of Parliament. No court will consider for a moment the argument that a law is invalid as being opposed to the opinion of the electorate; their opinion can be legally expressed through Parliament, and through Parliament alone'. AV Dicey, *Introduction to the Study of the Law of the Constitution* (10th ed., London: Macmillan, 1959) at 59.

[81] V Bogdanor, 'Europe and the Sovereignty of the People' (2016) 87(3) The Political Quarterly; also V Bogdanor, 'After the Referendum, the People, Not Parliament Are Sovereign', *The Financial Times*, 9 December 2016. Jenkin, Interview, BBC Radio 4, World at One, 28 June 2016.

[82] *R (Miller)* v. *Secretary of State for Exiting the European Union* [2017] UKSC 117.

[83] V Bogdanor, 'Constitutional Reform: Death, Rebirth and Renewal', in A Gamble and T Wright (eds.), *Rethinking Democracy*, 53.

public participation, as this chapter has so far argued. Britain suffers from a democratic deficit, so an increase of democracy is to be welcomed. But democratic reform in Britain has been piecemeal, unprincipled, ad hoc, partly due to Britain's lack of a codified Constitution. The result of the EU referendum, decided on a narrow majority, does not transform Britain into a direct democracy, and there are also reasons, discussed in the next section, to be concerned about the lies and irregularities of the Brexit referendum.

But, in any case, avowing that the British Constitution does not rest on popular sovereignty does not lead to accepting unbridled parliamentary sovereignty, which may also be subject to as much short-termism and particular bias, as any populism. Surely the antidote is to require constitutional principle – which most countries have set in written Constitutions to control major constitutional change – whether instituted by referendum or other form. Without a codified or more substantive Constitution, the UK lacks any clear such principles, and 'taking back control' may mean its very opposite.

9.4 The Brexit Referendum

9.4.1 Previous Use of Referendums in Britain

Referendums have not been a highly significant feature of UK constitutional law. There is considerable uncertainty as to their place in the UK Constitution,[84] and how they accord with a constitutional tradition based on parliamentary sovereignty and representative democracy. UK-wide referendums were not used until the later twentieth century, and notably, many important issues such as decolonization, abolition of capital punishment, legalization of homosexuality, the welfare state, royal abdication, measures limiting powers of the Crown and House of Lords, and the introduction of the Human Rights Act, were not subject to referendums. Although there exist democratic arguments for referendums, their use might appear to undermine parliamentary sovereignty, if the popular vote goes against the preferences of the majority of MPs (as was apparently the case in the 2016 EU Referendum[85]). And notably, many Constitutions, even those expressed to derive their legitimacy from the people (such as the US and German Constitutions) do not permit country-wide referendums at all.

Since the 1970s, however, referendums have become more common in the UK, most notably perhaps, in the case of devolution to Scotland, Wales, and Northern Ireland,[86] the 2014 Scottish independence referendum, and referendums on EU membership. There have also been regional and local

[84] However, it should be noted that plebiscites were reasonably frequent in the British colonial context.

[85] See e.g. 'EU vote: Where the Cabinet and Other MPs Stand', *BBC News*, 22 June 2016.

[86] Scotland Act 1978; Wales Act 1978; Referendums (Scotland and Wales) Act 1997; Northern Ireland (Border Poll) Act 1972; Northern Ireland (Entry to Negotiations, etc.) Act 1996; Northern Ireland Negotiations (Referendum) Order 1998.

referendums – such as in London on the creation of a directly elected Mayor and Greater London Assembly in 1998,[87] and in North-East England on whether to establish an elected Regional Assembly in 2004.[88] But there have only been three UK-wide referendums: in 1975 on the issue of continued EEC membership, in 2011 on whether to adopt the Alternative Vote system for general elections, and the 2016 Brexit referendum.

There are also specific UK Acts of Parliament that have introduced referendum requirements. The Northern Ireland Act 1998 requires the Secretary of State for Northern Ireland to enable a border poll or referendum, 'if at any time it appears likely to him that a majority of those voting would express a wish that Northern Ireland should cease to be part of the United Kingdom and form part of a united Ireland.' The 2011 European Union Act required that any extension of certain EU competences be approved both in primary legislation and by a national referendum. Neither provision has been used, and the EU Act 2011 has in any case been repealed.

Notably, the use of referendums has not always been due to a desire for direct democracy. They have sometimes been used instrumentally by governments. In 2010, the House of Lords Constitution Committee, declared that 'we regret the ad hoc manner in which referendums have been used, often as a tactical device, by the government of the day.'[89] Referendums have been held to overcome government divisions, as in 1975, when Harold Wilson held a referendum over EEC membership to deal with divisions in the Labour party. The 2011 Alternative Vote system (AV) referendum sprung from promises and deals made within Coalition government. The 2016 EU Referendum was a response to fractious dissent within the Conservative party, and also to external pressure posed by UKIP (the UK Independence party).

9.4.2 The Brexit Referendum

The UK is the first state to leave the European Union. On 23 June 2016, a Referendum on EU membership was held, and the UK overall voted to leave the EU,[90] by a majority of 51.9–48.1 per cent,[91] in response to the question: 'Should

[87] Greater London Authority (Referendum) Act 1998.

[88] Regional Assemblies (Preparations) Act 2003.

[89] House of Lords, Select Committee on the Constitution, 12th Report of Session 2009–10 'Referendums in the United Kingdom', at para. 62. This view was supported by a Constitution Unit report: M. Russell, 'Take More Care with Referendums; Democracy Depends upon It', *Financial Times*, 10 July 2018.

[90] In fact, as only 37 per cent of those eligible to vote in the EU referendum voted to leave (many eligible to vote did not do so), there was no majority for Leave over the total eligible franchise. The 2016 Referendum result would have failed the threshold test of 40 per cent set in the 1979 Devolution referendums. See further AC Grayling, 'The EU referendum was gerrymandered', available at https://blogs.lse.ac.uk/brexit/2017/09/28/the-eu-referendum-was-gerrymandered/

[91] Electoral Commission, UK Referendum results: www.electoralcommission.org.uk/find-information-by-subject/elections-and-referendums/past-elections-and-referendums/eu-referendum/electorate-and-count-information

the United Kingdom remain a member of the European Union or leave the European Union?'[92]

The EU Referendum came about as a result of the UK EU Referendum Act 2015. Notably, there was no requirement in the Act that the UK Government implement its results. It was an advisory referendum, enabling the electorate to express its opinion before any legislation might be introduced. This is in contrast to the AV ('Alternative Vote') referendum[93], instigated by the Parliamentary Voting System and Constituencies Act 2011, s8 of which provided that alternative vote provisions would come into force if there were a majority of 'Yes' votes cast in the referendum. In the event, there was a No vote and so this did not happen.

The Referendum franchise was roughly the same as that for a UK General Election. Notably, EU citizens settled in the UK (over 3.5m), UK citizens resident in other EU countries over 10 years, and 16 and 17 year olds were excluded from voting in the Referendum[94] – although arguably, these were the groups most likely to be affected by its outcome. Therefore, some crucial groups were disenfranchised.

9.4.2.1 Implementing the EU Referendum Vote

Implementing the EU referendum vote has instituted major constitutional change in the UK. Because of its uncodified Constitution, the UK lacks specific mechanisms for constitutional amendment, in contrast to many other jurisdictions that make special provision for it. In many jurisdictions worldwide, specific constitutional constraints are set on referendum use, such as voting thresholds, requirements for supermajorities, protection of devolved regions, and so on, in order that Constitutions not be subject to tactical political purposes. Bruce Ackerman has suggested that major constitutional issues should be put to the voters twice before enacted into law, and that this would help the thoughtfulness of voters' decisions.[95] Ackerman also warned of the dangers of referendum systems: 'a poorly designed system could serve as a platform for pandering to the worst instincts of the public, as countless demagogues have shown since Napoleon first demonstrated the abusive potential of referendums in the aftermath of the French Revolution.'[96] Indeed, in the UK, referendums have sometimes required forms of special majority, such as a specified level of support in terms of votes, or a specific turnout, as was the case in the Devolution referendums of 1979[97] (which failed to achieve these requirements). However,

92 S1(4) EU Referendum Act 2015.

93 This was an attempt to introduce a (roughly speaking) proportional representation system into the UK, held as part of the conditions set up for UK Coalition government 2010–2015.

94 S2 EU Referendum Act, 2015.

95 B Ackerman, 'At the Crossroads', *London Review of Books*, 9 September 2010, 32–33.

96 Ibid., at 32.

97 'The 1979 Referendums' available at: www.bbc.co.uk/news/special/politics97/devolution/scotland/briefing/79referendums.shtml.

the EU Referendum Act contained no such provisions. It may be added that, since governments tend to dominate the House of Commons with their majority, and UK courts cannot overrule Parliament, few checks and balances exist to protect against hasty amendments. Most other States have codified Constitutions, with protections against abuse, and constitutional regulation of referendums. It was therefore important that the follow-up to the Brexit referendum should not be instrumental and unprincipled. This was not the case.

9.4.2.2 Can the Popular Vote be Legitimate if Half of Britain's Nations Voted to Remain?

Notably, two out of the four of Britain's nations produced majority votes for remain. If Gibraltar is included, three out of five territories voted to remain in the EU.

Notably, the SNP had tabled an amendment to the EU Referendum Bill, requiring that for the UK to leave the EU, each of the four constituent nations – England, Scotland, Wales, and Northern Ireland – would have to vote to do so, not just the UK as a whole – a call for a 'double majority lock' confirmed by Scottish First Minister, Nicola Sturgeon.[98] In making this point, the aim was to ensure that none of the UK nations would be removed from the EU against their will. However, Sturgeon was also emphasizing a point made by Westminster leaders during the 2014 Scottish independence referendum campaign – that the UK is a 'family of nations', with equal status for each of the family members.[99] Sturgeon's point was that to withdraw the UK from the EU, against Scotland's will, would be 'democratically indefensible'.[100] However, the SNP amendment requiring was rejected, and (then) UK Prime Minister David Cameron stated in the House of Commons in 2014 that: 'We are one United Kingdom, there will be one in/out referendum and that will be decided on a majority of those who vote.'[101] But, as this book contends, the UK is not a unitary State, but a union State, with a considerable amount of devolution. There also exist rules about the need for consent of the devolved parliaments where UK legislation affecting them is contemplated. But the Sewel convention was ignored on a number of occasions in Brexit legislation.

9.4.2.3 Could the Referendum Vote be Ignored?

The EU Referendum was advisory in nature. Legally, both the UK government and UK Parliament could have ignored it. That would have been both lawful

[98] 'SNP Bid for "Quadruple Lock" on EU Referendum Vote Rejected', *BBC News*, 16 June 2015.

[99] 'PM Begs Scots Not to Break Up "Family of Nations"', *Reuters*, 10 September 2014.

[100] In making this case, Sturgeon drew some comparisons: 'If you look at states like Australia and Canada there are some circumstances where changes to their constitution requires not just a majority across the country but in each of the provinces as well.... Germany requires its Länder to sign off on changes to the Basic Law, through a two-thirds vote in the *Bundesrat*. So you can see that such double majorities do exist.' N Sturgeon, speech, 29 October 2014, discussed at www.heraldscotland.com/ comment/ columnists/ a- federal- bomb- is- dropped- into- more- powers- debate.25721371.

[101] Hansard, Commons Debates, 29 October 2014, Column 301.

and constitutional. According to classic, Diceyan notions of sovereignty, if Parliament is actually sovereign it can legislate to do anything, including to ignore a non-binding referendum.

However, it became commonplace to add that politically, it would be highly inadvisable for the government to ignore the referendum result. Yet there exist many examples where governments have done just that. For example, in 2008, Irish voters rejected the Lisbon Treaty, but in 2009 a second referendum was held in Ireland, with 67 per cent of voters instead now backing the treaty.[102] And in July 2015 the Greek people voted by a roughly 20 per cent majority to reject austerity conditions that would be imposed by EU and other international institutions in return for a large bailout. Notwithstanding, the Greek government agreed soon after to perhaps even tougher measures.[103]

Yet, the UK government did not ignore the referendum result and stated in the policy paper, 'The Process for Withdrawing from the European Union', in February 2016, that it was under a 'democratic duty to give effect to the electorate's decision.'[104] (We might compare the attitude of an earlier conservative MP, Edward Short, Leader of the House of Commons, who, shortly before the first country-wide EEC referendum in 1975, stated, 'This referendum is wholly consistent with parliamentary sovereignty. The Government will be bound by its result, but Parliament, of course, cannot be bound.... Although one would not expect honourable members to go against the wishes of the people, they will remain free to do so'.[105]) In the *Cherry/Miller* case the Supreme Court stated, of the 2016 EU referendum: 'Technically, the result was not legally binding. But the Government had pledged to honour the result and it has since been treated as politically and democratically binding. Successive Governments and Parliament have acted on that basis.'[106] Such a strong political obligation tends to undermine the sense that the referendum was advisory only.

9.4.2.4 What Was the Nature of the Mandate?

But then the question was – what was required to follow up the Referendum result? Prime Minister Theresa May stated again and again that 'Brexit means Brexit'[107] – but what did this mean? Neither the referendum legislation, nor the vote itself, provided any guidance as to what the UK's future relationship should be with the EU, nor with other States. The question put to the electorate was in

[102] 'Ireland Votes in Favour of Lisbon Treaty', *The Observer*, 4 October 2009 at www.theguardian.com/world/2009/oct/04/ireland-votes-yes-lisbon-treaty.

[103] 'Greek Debt Crisis: What Was the Point of the Referendum?' *BBC News*, 11 July 2015.

[104] 'The Process for Withdrawing from the European Union', HM Government, 29 February 2016, at 7, para 2.1.

[105] Hansard, EEC Membership (Referendum) vol. 888 col 293: debated on Tuesday 11 March 1975.

[106] *(Miller)* v. *The Prime Minister; Cherry* v. *Advocate General for Scotland* [2019] UKSC 41 [7].

[107] See e.g. 'What Does "Brexit Means Brexit" Mean?' at www.bbc.co.uk/news/uk-politics-36782922

binary form: 'Should the United Kingdom remain a member of the European Union or leave the European Union?' The electorate voted only to leave the EU. They did not agree to any particular exit agreement. Some of those who voted Leave may have desired a 'Norwegian style' arrangement, which would mean EEA membership involving access to the Single Market, and associated freedom of movement – colloquially known as a 'soft Brexit'.[108] For other 'Leave' voters, however, terminating freedom of movement for EU citizens, and thus reducing immigration, was crucial. However, these issues were not put to the electorate in the Referendum. Nonetheless, the UK Government determined that the UK would leave both the Customs Union and Single Market, thus opting for a so-called 'Hard Brexit', and a more distant relationship with the EU.

9.4.3 The Referendum Campaign: Irregularities and Illegalities

The EU referendum cost £129m.[109] This included expenses incurred running the poll, grants to designated lead campaign organizations (up to £600,000), and delivery by Royal Mail of mailings from those.

However, the EU referendum result was tainted by allegations that both the official Leave campaign ('Vote Leave', fronted by Boris Johnson MP and Michael Gove MP) and the unofficial campaign ('Leave.EU', headed by Nigel Farage and Arron Banks), committed irregularities and even illegalities during their campaigns.[110] Both Leave campaigns were found to have broken the law by the UK Electoral Commission, and to have committed serious data breaches. There were many instances of this – for example, Vote Leave was fined by the Electoral Commission in July 2018, for exceeding its £7m spending limit.[111] Most of the overspend was used for online advertisements, which according to Vote Leave campaign director, Dominic Cummings (sometime advisor to Prime Minister Johnson), targeted 'roughly 7 million people, who saw something like one and a half billion ads.'[112] Vote Leave was found to have broken the law by channelling money to Canadian firm Aggregate IQ (connected with Cambridge Analytica), which used micro-targeted political advertisements on Facebook.[113] Leave.EU was founded by UKIP donor and businessman Arron Banks and backed by UKIP's Nigel Farage – the self-styled 'bad boys of Brexit' – the title of Banks's book on the campaign. Leave.EU was

[108] See e.g. 'What Does "Hard" or "Soft" Brexit Mean?' at www.bbc.co.uk/news/business-37500140

[109] Jim Pickard, 'EU Referendum Cost Taxpayers £129m', *Financial Times*, 14 December 2018.

[110] Allegations that the Remain campaign broke the law were dismissed: 'Remain EU Referendum Campaign Spending Claims Rejected', *BBC News*, 2 August 2018.

[111] 'Vote Leave Broke Electoral Law Says Electoral Commission', *BBC News*, 17 July 2018.

[112] R Darbyshire, '"We Dumped Our Entire Budget in the Last 10 Days": Inside the Behavioural Science Strategy of Vote Leave' (*The Drum*, 13 June 2017).

[113] 'Brexit ad blitz data firm paid by Vote Leave broke privacy laws, watchdogs find', available at https://techcrunch.com/2019/11/27/brexit-ad-blitz-data-firm-paid-by-vote-leave-broke-privacy-laws-watchdogs-find/

also found to have broken the law by overspending and other irregularities, most notably in conjunction with Arron Banks's firm, Eldon Insurance.[114]

In *Wilson* v. *Prime Minister & Electoral Commission*[115] the lawfulness of both the Referendum itself and the subsequent decision to trigger Article 50 TEU were challenged, on the basis that the referendum was a result of corrupt and illegal practices. But the challenge failed. Notably, unlike a general election (and ludicrously, given the serious consequences for the UK of the 2016 Referendum), the victory in the referendum could not be challenged in an election court because the vote was not legally binding.[116] The 2016 referendum has often been described as an 'instruction' from the British people to the government. But there is a question as to what a responsible government or Parliament should do when faced with an instruction tainted with illegality?

9.4.4 The Referendum Campaign and Lies

However, the irregularities and illegalities of the campaign were compounded by political slogans, often employing images in a particularly powerful manner, including cakes, cherries, walls, maps, and flags (e.g. the Union Jack and the EU stars), and terms and metaphors such as divorce, fights, and 'hard' and 'soft', or even 'red white and blue' Brexit. The combination of slogan (whether true or not) and image proved to be a particularly winning phenomenon.

9.4.4.1 'Brexit Battle Bus'

For example, a major icon of the EU referendum was the 'Brexit Battle Bus,' with its slogan 'We send the EU £350 million a week. Let's fund our NHS instead. Vote Leave'. Indeed, this 'Battle Bus' became a symbol of the Leave movement. By deploying the sign on the side of the bus, the advertisement could be viewed all over the UK, providing an enduring and eye-catching setting for Boris Johnson's speeches.

However, this slogan on the Battle Bus was deeply deceptive. The £350m figure was inaccurate, because it failed to account for the UK's rebate, meaning that the UK pays only £276m per week. Even then, most of that lower sum was actually returned to Britain – for example, in farming subsidies, for the development of poor regions, for science and universities, and so on. The UK Parliament Treasury select committee chair, Andrew Tyrie MP, informed the BBC that the £350m figure was 'not true',[117] adding that Vote Leave should repaint the bus immediately. But this did not happen. However, the pledge was

[114] 'Brexit: Leave.EU and Arron Banks' Firm Fined £120,000 over Data Breaches', *BBC News*, 1 February 2019.

[115] *Wilson* v. *Prime Minister & Electoral Commission* [2019] EWCA Civ 304.

[116] The Representation of the People Act 1983 prohibits certain unlawful practices and makes provision for challenges to the legality of a campaign. However, given the EU Referendum outcome has no legal status it is not possible to rely on the 1983 Act.

[117] '£350m Brexit Dividend Was an Illusion Tyrie Warns', *The Times*, 3 September 2016.

dropped by Brexiteers after the EU referendum, although Vote Leave campaign director, Dominic Cummings, went so far as to suggest that Britain would not have voted to leave the EU if the Battle Bus pledge had not been made.[118]

So, undoubtedly, this was a memorable and influential icon in the Brexit referendum. This simple, but false image outweighed the complex truth of the UK's financial contributions to the EU. Notwithstanding its huge influence, there was little to no accountability for its inaccuracies. It is not unusual for buses to carry advertisements – but normally, these must comply with standards laid down by the UK Advertising Standards Agency. However, these standards do not apply to political advertising, 'where the purpose of the advertisement is to persuade voters in a local, national or international electoral referendum.'[119] So while an advertisement may not mislead the public by claiming falsely, for example, that a face cream will make you appear 20 years younger, misleading statements such as those on the Battle Bus are permitted in UK political advertising. And the Battle Bus slogan very effectively bolstered, emphasized, and took advantage of myths[120] already in general circulation in the UK about the EU – that Britain was exploited in the sums demanded from it by the EU Budget. The Battle Bus slogan demonstrated that images and objects possess power and agency – in this instance to generate historic political change. Those campaigning for Remain, including the UK Government, were unable to offer anything comparably memorable or striking. The damage had been done. And even although the UK has now left the EU, £350 per week has not been paid to the NHS.

9.4.5 The Brexit Campaign and Immigration

Brexit has provoked intense emotional reactions. A good example is the anti-migrant emotions deliberately stoked by sections of the Leave campaign. In May 2016, polls indicated the Remain campaign was gaining ground. At this point, the Leave campaign changed tactics, and shifted its focus to immigration, which polling had revealed as a key concern for many voters.

The anti-migrant poster 'Breaking Point,' unveiled by UKIP leader, Nigel Farage, in June 2016, showed a large queue of brown-skinned migrants extending into the distance, with the caption 'We must break free of the EU and take back control of our borders.' This implied those queueing were coming to the UK, and played on some voters' fears of immigrants. But the poster was

118 https://blogs.spectator.co.uk/2017/01/dominic-cummings-brexit-referendum-won/ Also in October 2018, *The Independent* newspaper reported that 'Nearly half of the British public still believe the false claim from the Brexit referendum that the UK sends £350m a week to the EU, despite persistent attempts to debunk the myth.' *The Independent:* 'British public still believe Vote Leave "£350million a week to EU" myth from Brexit referendum' 30 October 2018.

119 See information on the Advertising Standards Agency website, available at www.asa.org.uk/about-asa-and-cap/the-work-we-do/what-we-cover.html#Outside%20remit.

120 E.g. Barthes: 'myth acts economically: it abolishes the complexity of human acts, it gives them the simplicity of essences'. Roland Barthes, *Mythologies* [1957] (Annette Lavers trans., Hill & Wang 1972) 2.

Figure 9.1 'Breaking Point'

extremely deceptive. The photograph was actually of refugees, mostly Syrian (i.e. non-EU), crossing into Slovenia, not coming to the UK at all.[121] However, accuracy was not paramount, as the poster's aim was to incite fear – of an unmanageable invasion of immigrants, and it was quickly pointed out,[122] on Twitter, among other media, that the poster was remarkably similar to Nazi propaganda.[123] Tragically, very soon after the poster was unveiled, Labour MP Jo Cox was murdered by a right-wing extremist[124] who repeatedly shouted 'Britain First.' The poster was also subject to complaints (from tens of thousands of people) to the police that it incited racial hatred and violated UK race laws.[125] But the poster did its intended work. However unattractive its message, after its appearance the Leave campaign's fortunes improved, and some attribute the Leave majority in the Referendum to voters' fears of immigration.

Images such as 'Battle Bus' and 'Breaking Point – both manipulations authorized by politicians – tell the story of Brexit's motivations and meaning for ordinary people as much as the platitudes of politicians, or laconic legal provisions. They also reveal that, sadly, the story of Brexit is not very inspiring, logical, nor much rooted in truth.

[121] www.theguardian.com/artanddesign/2016/jun/22/jeff-mitchells-best-shot-the-column-of-marching-refugees-used-in-ukips-brexit-campaign. The original photograph was taken by Jeff Mitchell, who won Photographer of the Year 2016.

[122] www.theguardian.com/politics/2016/jun/16/nigel-farage-defends-ukip-breaking-point-poster-queue-of-migrants

[123] Later convicted and sentenced.

[124] I have not been able to find any evidence of actual prosecution.

[125] Such footage was included in Auschwitz: The Nazis and the 'Final Solution' (2005), a six-part BBC documentary.

9.4.6 Conclusion

The EU referendum injected a relatively unfamiliar process into the UK Constitution, giving rise to issues of popular sovereignty and 'the will of the people' as legitimating devices, but leaving unsettled their status in UK constitutional law. Although the Referendum was set up through a legal process (by statute) and therefore lawful, its result was not legally binding. There were illegalities committed in the course of the campaign by both Vote. Leave and Leave.EU, both of which organizations were fined as a result. But these illegalities did not have the effect of nullifying the result, or setting aside the triggering of Article 50, although, had they occurred in the course of an ordinary election, they would have done so. These illegalities were compounded by a striking use of (sometimes false) slogans and images and playing on some peoples' fear of immigration.

9.5 The Future of Referendums in Britain

9.5.1 The Absence of a Consistent, Principled Approach to Referendums in the UK

Referendums may have become a more familiar part of the UK constitutional toolbox by the twenty-first century, but there has been a notable lack of consistency regarding their use. Referendums have been held in some cases and not others – for example, a referendum was held in 1997 on whether to introduce devolution for Scotland and Wales, but not on whether to approve expansion of devolution in Scotland in 2012 and 2016. No referendum was held on implementing the EU Lisbon Treaty, nor on House of Lords reform in 1999, nor on the introduction of EVEL (English votes for English laws) in 2016.

The holding of referendums in Britain has been casuistic and inconsistent. This is particularly serious given referendums have recently been held on matters of urgent public interest, such as the 2014 Scottish independence referendum with the 2016 EU referendum. Both were high profile, high stakes referendums, albeit that the Scottish referendum was not a nationwide poll and only residents of Scotland could vote.

There was a high turnout in both cases (although the turnout in the Scottish independence referendum was higher at 85 per cent compared to the 72 per cent of the Brexit referendum). Although there was a certain amount of verbal assault and misinformation in both cases, it is generally acknowledged that the quality of debate and information was higher in the Scottish campaign.[126] In 2013, both sides attempted to provide a more complete statement of their case. The Scottish Government published a 600-page *White Paper* setting out its proposal for independence, and the UK Government produced

[126] See further, Tom Mullen, 'A Tale of Two Referendums', (2016) OUP blog.

18 papers on a variety of topics in its *Scotland Analysis*.[127] In contrast, in the Brexit referendum, the debate was fiercer and more acrimonious, and there was more misinformation. Although both sides were at fault, greater blame rests with the Leave campaign which consistently conveyed untrue or misleading information (such as claiming the UK sends £350 million to the EU each week). In 2016, neither side presented a clear statement of the UK's future outside the EU.

However, it would be hard to conclude that the Scottish referendum was more legitimate than the EU referendum. Although Cameron's reasons for calling the EU Referendum may have related to a feud in the Conservative party, the Brexit referendum concerned a matter of secession and the UK's EU membership was a clear constitutional issue, concerning UK sovereignty. The earlier 1975 EEC referendum also provided a precedent. Nonetheless, the EU referendum and its outcome has led to Britain becoming a deeply divided country, between remainers and leavers. These two referendums illustrate the importance of accurate reliable information and trustworthy debate for democratic deliberation.

At present, there is no clarity, in UK law and politics at least, as to whether, and on what basis, a second Scottish Independence referendum could be held. In the May 2021 Holyrood elections, a majority of pro-independence parties was elected to the Scottish Parliament, and a mandate claimed by the Scottish government to hold a second independence referendum. Should this be a sufficient reason for the holding of a referendum, or indeed, does UK withdrawal from the EU, contrary to the wishes of a majority of Scottish voters already provide sufficient reason?[128] Or does the UK Government's present (at time of writing) stance, of refusing to engage in any negotiations, insisting that the 2014 referendum was a 'once in a generation event', constitute a satisfactory reason to reject the holding of a referendum?

The problem of course is the lack of any authoritative test to determine when a referendum should be held. Their use appears to be 'driven by political pragmatism, not constitutional principle.'[129] Although the Political Parties, Elections and Referendums Act (PPERA) 2000 supplies a basic framework for the conduct of referendums, there are still no constitutional parameters to guide when a referendum should be held, despite the regret expressed at the ad hoc nature of referendums by at least two investigatory reports in Britain.[130]

[127] *Scotland's Future: Your Guide to an Independent Scotland* (Scottish Government, 2013); *Scotland Analysis* (Office of the Secretary of State for Scotland, 2013).

[128] See *Scotland's Right to Choose: Putting Scotland's Future in Scotland's Hands* (2019) 11–18.

[129] Report of the Independent Commission on Referendums, UCL Constitution Unit, July 2018, 46.

[130] House of Lords, Constitution Committee 'Referendums in the United Kingdom' (2010). Report of the Independent Commission on Referendums, UCL Constitution Unit, July 2018.

9.5.2 Politically but not Legally Binding?

Sometimes the view is expressed that nothing can be done to regularize the status of referendums in the UK, because of the principle of parliamentary sovereignty – meaning that a constitutional framework for their use would demand a codified Constitution, in which parliamentary sovereignty was no longer the overriding principle.[131] The point being that, at present, any provision for referendums could be overturned by a future Act of Parliament. Yet, this approach is somewhat disingenuous and inadequate in the face of the current situation, whereby referendums are expressed as advisory and constrained by parliamentary sovereignty, yet seen as politically binding, constituting a democratic mandate that must be honoured. If referendums are to be treated as subject to such a strong political obligation then surely their regulation should be more principled and less casuistic.

9.5.3 The Broader Impact of Referendums

Michael Gordon noted that referendums can have key constitutional impacts, most especially regarding authority, sovereignty, and democracy.[132] Referendums have an irregular authority, deriving directly from the electorate, rather than traditional sources of power under the Constitution. This increases their ability to disrupt the regular political establishment. This also impacts our understanding of sovereignty – with commentators, such as Bogdanor even suggesting that referendums validate the sovereignty of the people,[133] thus presenting a clash between two different understandings of sovereignty. Yet it cannot be concluded that popular sovereignty has replaced parliamentary sovereignty. The *Miller I* decision confirmed that, in spite of the referendum result, Parliament had to consent to the triggering of the formal Brexit withdrawal process.

Their function in democratic decision making processes is also important. Even if popular sovereignty has not supplanted parliamentary sovereignty, nonetheless, the UK does suffer a democratic deficit, and any device that increases popular participation in political life can be welcomed. If conducted fairly and in compliance with human rights, referendums can be beneficial and complement representative democracy. But of course, the key issue is *how and when should referendums be held.*

9.5.4 *When* Should Referendums Be Held?

Many commentators have suggested that referendums should only be held on important constitutional matters – for example, the House of Lords Constitutional

131 E.g. the Independent Commission report at 76.

132 M Gordon, 'Referendums in the UK Constitution: Authority, Sovereignty and Democracy after Brexit' (2020) 16 European Constitutional Law Review 213.

133 V Bogdanor, 'After the Referendum the People, not Parliament, are Sovereign' *Financial Times*, 10 December 2016.

Committee suggested that 'if referendums are to be used, they are most appropriately used in relation to fundamental constitutional issues' and offered a non-exhaustive list of examples of such issues, including: 'to abolish the Monarchy', 'to leave the European Union', 'for any of the nations of the EU to secede from the Union', 'to abolish either House of Parliament', 'to change the electoral system for the House of Commons', 'to adopt a written constitution', and 'to change the UK's system of currency.'[134] While there is room for disagreement over how to define a constitutional issue, this justification for referendums rests on the premise that fundamental constitutional change requires the endorsement of the people. Broadening the field to include non-constitutional matters risks opening the door to an overwhelming array of potential referendums. So, it makes sense to limit a major constitutional issue to something which fundamentally alters the nature of the State. In Ireland, for example, referendums are only required for amendments to the Constitution.

A related and important question, however, is who should determine whether something is a major constitutional issue such that a referendum is required? Surely to leave this decision to the government of the day would be to open the process to charges of political expediency that have already been made? The alternative, of a Parliamentary vote on the issue, would satisfy the need for open debate in democratic politics but again, be subject to accusations of bias and expediency. However, to put the matter on a more independent, principled basis might trigger arguments on the need for a written Constitution, which would overtake the issue of referendums with much larger concerns.

But referendums could be constrained in a further way other than limiting their use to constitutional matters. It has been suggested that it might make sense that only those changes which already have a parliamentary majority be subject to referendum. Bogdanor argued that 'some decisions are so fundamental that a decision by Parliament alone is not sufficient to secure legitimacy for them. They need also endorsement by the people.'[135] In this way, referendums could serve the function of a popular veto. Dicey expounded such a theory in several works, including his article 'Ought the Referendum to be Introduced into England?' His argument was that the referendum could function as a surrogate second chamber; a device whereby the 'prerogatives of the crown' could be turned into 'the privileges of the people.'[136] Dicey's motivation for recommending the referendum (given his insistence on parliamentary sovereignty as a fundamental principle of the British Constitution) was his disquiet over the Liberal government's aim to introduce Home Rule for Ireland. His theory gained some support from conservative politicians, such as Arthur

[134] House of Lords Constitution Committee 'Referendums in the United Kingdom' (2010) 62, 94.

[135] Bogdanor, 'Constitutional Reform', at 52.

[136] AV Dicey, 'Ought the Referendum to Be Introduced into England?' (1890) Contemporary Review, see also Dicey's sixth edition of *An Introduction to the Law of the Constitution*, 503.

Balfour, who described this as the referendum functioning in 'a Conservative sense' as a constraint on change.[137] Used in this way, a referendum might be seen as supplementing representative democracy.

Many comments could be made about this restrictive 'Diceyan' view. Would this be furthering democratic decision-making or putting a brake on some issues? It might rule out policy change where a conservative electorate vetoed certain changes – such as the abolition of capital punishment or of criminal penalties for homosexual conduct, thus rendering law unnecessarily static, and allowing majorities to override minority rights. However, it could also exclude referendums in cases of secession/transfer of territory. Although Dicey recommended the referendum as a device to prevent the Home Rule in Ireland favoured by the Liberal government of his time, in the twenty-first century, it is more likely that a majority of unionists in the Westminster Parliament would reject any further independence referendums for Scotland, if there is a requirement that referendums be held solely after Parliamentary approval. Therefore, the 'double lock' of prior parliamentary approval and popular referendum could operate to inhibit change.

9.5.5 *How* Should Referendums Be Held?

This brings us to a final crucial point – as Gordon puts it, 'how to embrace the advantages of referendums while avoiding the pitfalls.' Gordon suggests that 'The most obvious way this could be done would be through a new Referendums Act.'[138] Such legislation might stipulate certain threshold requirements. These could take the form of turnout requirements; requiring a specific percentage of the electorate to vote for change; multiple majority thresholds for specific geographical territories, such as the 'quadruple lock' proposed by the SNP to the Brexit Referendum Act; or there could be a requirement to hold two separate referendums on the same question, separated by an interval. Threshold requirements such as these can promote stability and prohibit major constitutional change that only has limited support. But none of these were applied for the Brexit referendum.

Even if a Referendums Act proved unachievable, there are some crucial steps that could be taken to improve the process. Renwick and Russell usefully suggest a number of such steps.[139] First, that greater attention should be focussed on preparing for a referendum. This means that the effect of a vote either way should be clear to the electorate in advance, so they know what they are voting for. This was not the case with the Brexit referendum, although much

[137] Quoted in BEC Dugdale, *Arthur James Balfour, 1848–1905* (London: Hutchinson, 1939) 64. Arthur Balfour was conservative Prime Minister from 1902 to 2005.

[138] Gordon, 'Referendums in the UK Constitution', 244.

[139] M Russell and A Renwick, 'Five Ways to Improve Referendums after Brexit', The Constitution Unit, 24 June 2021.

more effort was made before the Scottish 2014 referendum. However, if it is not possible to detail policy outcomes in advance, then at least the procedure for reaching agreement after the referendum should be unequivocally set out. Again, this was not the case with the Brexit referendum, where, for example, the role of Parliament was unclear form the outset, and litigation was necessary to establish that Parliament must consent to the triggering of Article 50 TEU. It is also crucial that voters have reliable information. Again, this was not the case with Brexit, as the 'Battle Bus' episode illustrates. Finally, regulation of campaigning needs to be updated for the present age to deal with issues such as bombarding certain voters with negative and untransparent messages. The point is this – as Renwick et al stress, 'If politicians want to legitimise a decision through a referendum – particularly one on a contentious question such as Brexit or Scottish independence – they have good reason to want a referendum process that is unimpeachable.'[140]

9.6 Conclusion

It may seem a long way from the analysis of the basic function of democracy to the concretization of future referendum requirements in the UK. Yet, as I hope this chapter has demonstrated, there is a clear link between the conditions for actualization of democratic government and lessons to be learned from the Brexit referendum. Democracy performs an essential function in ensuring that people are significantly involved in the government of their society – and equality and liberty are enhanced in this way. Analysis reveals that the UK suffers a democratic deficit, especially on account of its 'first past the post' electoral system, and the lacks of checks and balances in its uncodified Constitution. However, referendums as such are neither democratic nor undemocratic. It depends how they are used. Although referendums may increase democracy, by allowing more direct popular participation, they can also exacerbate the democratic deficit if ill thought-out – if, for example, they allow a minority to impose major constitutional change at the expense of human rights, promote opposition and discord between nations and regions of the UK, or involve illegalities.

I conclude with a quote from the author Robert Harris, who probably reflected the views of many, when he wrote on twitter: 'How foul this referendum is. The most depressing, divisive, duplicitous political event of my lifetime. May there never be another'.[141]

140 A Renwick, M Palese, and J Sargeant, 'Discussing Brexit – Could We Do Better?' (2018) 89(4) Political Quarterly at 551.

141 http://twitter.com/robert_harris/status/743440375981936640?lang=en (16 June 2016).

10

Human Rights

10.1 The Mystery of Human Rights

Most States declare their respect for human rights. This includes the UK, which adopted the Human Rights Act (HRA) in 1998 and is also a member of the European Convention on Human Rights (ECHR) and some other international human rights treaties. Human rights seem to have become a 'secular religion'[1] for our times, and it is hard to disparage the idea of human rights (as opposed to less than optimal applications of them). Therefore, it is important that the UK complies with human rights in actions such as Brexit.

To be sure, sceptical accounts of human rights exist, including Karl Marx's critique, which contended that rights had become ideological tools of the capitalist bourgeoisie, as well as the English tradition of scepticism propagated by Jeremy Bentham. Nonetheless, human rights continue to offer a promise of universality, inalienability, and self-evidence – of 'values for a godless age'.[2]

10.1.1 The Emergence of Human Rights

But how can human rights be recognized as universal in nature if they were not identified as necessary before the modern era? Oppressed Europeans in the Middle Ages, for example, would have been more likely to look to a patron saint for relief. Prior to the eighteenth century, such rights as were legally recognized were conceptualized as particularistic in nature, for example as the rights of Englishmen, not as self-evident and universal.

Yet, as Lynne Hunt[3] remarks, somewhere between 1689 and 1776 (the latter being the date of the American Declaration of Independence, with its claim for 'self-evident' rights) a shift took place, and rights which had previously been viewed as pertaining only to particular persons, under particular traditions, transformed into human rights, which all could lay claim to. The second half of

[1] E Wiesel, 'A Tribute to Human Rights', in Y Danieli, E Stamatopoulou, and C Dias (eds.), *The Universal Declaration of Human Rights* (New York: Baywood, 1999).

[2] F Klug, *Values for a Godless Age: The Story of the United Kingdom's New Bill of Rights* (London: Penguin, 2000).

[3] Lynne Hunt, *Inventing Human Rights* (New York: Norton, 2007).

the eighteenth century saw not only the 1789 *French Declaration of the Rights of Man and the Citizen* and the US 1776 *Declaration of Independence*, but also other American documents asserting the existence of human rights superior to State law – including the federal Bill of Rights of 1789.

The expression 'human rights' is usually understood to derive from what John Locke meant by 'natural' rights – that is, those entitlements held simply by reason of being human beings. These rights are 'natural' because their source is human nature. Locke himself asserted that humans had natural rights to life, liberty, and property.[4] These rights were pre-societal, and possessed by humans in a state of nature, prior to any government. But Locke argued that government was nonetheless necessary to secure these inalienable, natural rights, which could not be adequately protected in the state of nature. And so he posited a (hypothetical) social contract, between government and the ruled, deemed necessary to protect natural rights. Locke's theories were influential in North America, and his influence can be seen on the American Declaration of Independence, which famously proclaimed: 'We hold these truths to be self-evident, that all men are created equal, that they are endowed by their Creator with certain unalienable Rights, that among these are Life, Liberty and the pursuit of Happiness'.

Social contract theory posits free and equal individual beings who can rationally bargain in order to ensure the benefits of government. The rights it tends to give rise to – such as free expression, liberty, property – are premised on autonomy. But note that, in the forming of the contract that is the US federal Constitution, many parties were quite definitely excluded from this process – notably women, slaves and native Americans.

It also seems that a greater focus on human rights in the eighteenth century relates to a changing notion of the self in that period. Liberal theories tend to identify human rights with rationality, agency, and autonomy. Rights are linked to a recognition of persons as separate individuals who are capable of moral judgement. This emphasis was partly a product of seventeenth-century revolutions of political thought, ranging across the Levellers, Lockean philosophy, and Grotius' juristic work. However, Hunt highlights not only this definition of self in terms of autonomy but also in a growing *empathy* – an increased awareness that others were like oneself. It might seem unrealistic to trace a growing empathy to the eighteenth century which witnessed penal practices such as torture, and the Bloody Code in England, in which capital punishment could be imposed for minor offences. Yet, torture had been a focus of critique since Montesquieu's criticism of it in *The Spirit of the Laws* in 1748, which was followed by Beccaria's rejection of the death penalty in his 1764 Treatise.[5]

[4] Locke, *Second Treatise of Civil Government* (1690) section 124.

[5] Cesare Beccaria, *Treatise on Crime and Punishment* (1764).

To be sure, empathy did not spring from nowhere in the eighteenth century – it is apparently a capacity of biological origins rooted in our brains.[6] Notably, Adam Smith, best known for *The Wealth of Nations*, was also the author of the earlier *Theory of Moral Sentiments*, a work of a quite different nature. In this work Smith explained, using the example of torture, how we identify and sympathize with another, even if they are a stranger: 'we enter as it were into his body and become in some measure the same person with him.'[7] As spectators of others, we imagine how we would feel in their situation. If we might share their motives, we approve of their action. If not, we disapprove. That knowledge forms conscience, an imagined 'impartial spectator' who informs us whether an action is right or wrong.

This openness to empathy, and the ability to imagine oneself in another's place, then opened the door to the possibility of a wider ranging body of rights, extending beyond one's own countrymen and class, and – even if neither the US nor the French eighteenth-century Declarations went so far as to open up rights to women, or in the case of the US, slaves – many groups who had previously been denied rights, that is, Jews and Protestants in France, were now able to be conceived as rights holders. Therefore, the eighteenth-century mindset is an important backdrop to the growth and dissemination of human rights and underlines their singular historical and western origins.

10.1.2 Why Are We *Still* So Preoccupied with Human Rights?

We are of course no longer living in the eighteenth century. A growth of nationalism (with a focus on ethnic ties rather than a universally shared humanity) explains why human rights as a doctrine was somewhat eclipsed in the nineteenth century and beyond. Although the horrors of twentieth-century totalitarianism may account for the impetus to draft Rights Charters in the post-war period, such horrors might just as easily have convinced us that 'inalienable' and 'universal' rights are incapable of mitigating human cruelty and serve no purpose. Why then does our preoccupation with rights continue?

If a combination of rational theorizing and a greater recognition of empathy help explain their origins, then perhaps a different philosophical and factual turn helps explain the continued obsession with rights. That framework is one of nihilism and disappointment. When social and religious motivations are absent, for many people human rights are the closest many possess to moral motivation. The contemporary world displays a breakdown of order, and a dearth of any basis for objective value. Likewise, the political realm manifests injustice and a corrosion of political structures. Secular liberal democracy exerts too little motivating force. Law is too often experienced only as externally binding by coercion and not internally compelling.

6 C Gearty, *Can Human Rights survive* (Cambridge: Cambridge University Press, 2006).

7 Adam Smith, *The Theory of Moral Sentiments* (London, 1759) Chapter I 'Of Sympathy', para. 2.

In this situation, human rights provide a counterbalance and can appear the nearest thing to religion, gaining at least a partial consensus across the political spectrum. Jacques Maritain, for example, in his 1954 'The Rights of Man', described how 'proponents of violently opposed ideologies' would announce at UNESCO meetings that '[w]e agree on these rights providing we are not asked why.'[8] Yash Ghai has highlighted the way in which human rights can appeal to a great variety of cultures and legal systems, and be successfully used to mediate complex ethnic and cultural claims, despite their apparent origins in eighteenth-century Europe. Ghai remarks that:

> For multicultural states, human rights as a negotiated understanding of the acceptable framework for coexistence and the respect for each culture are more important than for monocultural or mono-ethnic societies, where other forms of solidarity or identity can be invoked or minimized to cope with conflicts.... And most states are today multicultural, whether as a result of immigration or because their people are finding new identities.[9]

Whatever the source of conflict, human rights provide the essence of a common language, a currency that all can understand, a means of importing morality and ethics into law, and a reminder that we should not tolerate the intolerable, nor suffer the insufferable.

10.2 Human Rights in the UK

10.2.1 Introduction

In the past, Britain believed itself to be the home of liberty. Documents such as Magna Carta, Habeas Corpus, and the 1689 Bill of Rights were proffered as illustrations of British, and formerly English, constitutional arrangements that favoured liberty. Dicey chronicled how, when 'Voltaire came to England – and Voltaire represented the feeling of his age – his predominant sentiment clearly was that he had passed out of the realm of despotism to a land where the laws might be harsh, but where men were ruled by law and not by caprice.'[10] Many eighteenth-century North American colonists claimed English liberties for themselves.[11] Blackstone had praised English liberties, contrasting them with continental despotisms:

> The idea and practice of this political or civil liberty flourish in their highest vigour in these kingdoms, where it falls little short of perfection.... Very different from the modern constitutions of other states, on the continent of Europe,

[8] J Maritain, 'The Rights of Man', in *Man and the State* (Washington DC: Catholic University of America Press, 1998).

[9] Y Ghai, 'Universalism and Relativism: Human Rights as a Framework for Negotiating Interethnic Claims' (1999) 21 Cardozo LR, at 1102.

[10] Dicey, *Lectures Introductory to the Law of the Constitution* (1885) 174.

[11] As detailed in the chapter on the loss of the North American colonies.

> and from the genius of the Imperial law, which in general are calculated to vest an arbitrary and despotic power of controlling the actions of the subject in the prince, or in a few grandees.[12]

Blackstone, like John Locke, asserted the existence of 'natural rights' and the necessity of government to protect them. However, unlike the direction taken in the US, Blackstone believed the preservation of liberty to be so effective in Britain that formal Bills of Rights were not needed. Moreover, Blackstone asserted the sovereignty of Parliament, and did not adhere to the older tradition of the 'fundamental' constitutional laws of England, unchangeable by Parliament.[13] But what if a sovereign Parliament were to abolish rights? According to Blackstone, such a diminution of freedom was not possible, as the very structures of the British Constitution ensured liberty,[14] and its institutions operated as checks upon each other.

However, arguments for English liberty began to take a different turn over the next 100 years or so. Following after Blackstone came Burke, who although sympathetic to the case for the American colonies, was highly critical of the developments of the French Revolution, including its language of liberty and emancipation.[15] A little later, the utilitarian reformer Jeremy Bentham criticized English law for its unnecessary delay, cost and complexity. Yet, Bentham did not recommend Bills of Rights as remedies – indeed, he famously described the *French Declaration of the Rights of Man* as 'nonsense on stilts.'[16] He and his follower, John Austin (who was to become highly influential over subsequent generations of English lawyers) were traditionally seen as founders of the English legal positivist school, with its emphasis on law as 'posited' by the sovereign, rather than on any rights inhering in the individual.[17] This left little room for the development of any human rights law in England.

10.2.2 Dicey

Dicey followed in this positivist tradition and was extraordinarily influential in his late nineteenth-century writing on the British Constitution, and in his derision of Bills of Rights. Dicey identified parliamentary sovereignty as one of the pillars of the British Constitution, along with the rule of law which was supposedly protective of liberty. Human rights did not figure in this constitutional analysis.

[12] Blackstone, *Commentaries*, vol. I, 119–141.

[13] JW Gough, *Fundamental Law in English Constitutional History* (Oxford: Clarendon Press, 1955) *passim.*

[14] Blackstone, *Commentaries*, vol. I, 142–151.

[15] Burke, *Reflections on the Revolution in France* (London, 1790).

[16] J Bentham, 'Anarchical Fallacies', in *The Collected Works of Jeremy Bentham*, vol. II, John Bowring (ed.), 489 (1843).

[17] J Austin, *The Province of Jurisprudence Determined* (Cambridge: Cambridge University Press, 1995 ed W. Rumble).

Dicey's rule of law, as detailed in the *Introduction to the Study of the Law of the Constitution*, had three elements. First, that 'no man is punishable or can be made to suffer in body or goods except for a distinct breach of law established in the ordinary legal manner before the ordinary courts of the land'. 'In this sense', he maintained, 'the rule of law is contrasted with every system of government based on the exercise by persons in authority of wide, arbitrary, or discretionary powers of constraint'. Second, '... every man, whatever be his rank or condition, is subject to the ordinary law of the realm'. This was meant to contrast with other legal systems, such as Administrative law in France. But Dicey neglected the peculiar status of the Crown in English law, which rested on a great deal of prerogative powers for the government, even in Dicey's day. Third, according to Dicey,

> the constitution is pervaded by the rule of law on the ground the general principles of the constitution are with us as the result of judicial decisions determining the rights of private persons in particular cases brought before the courts; whereas under many foreign constitutions the security (such as it is) given to the rights of individuals results, or appears to result, from the general principles of the constitution.[18]

Dicey's conception is generally interpreted as a formal or thin conception of the rule of law.[19] For Dicey, the Constitution existed as a corpus of generalizations mainly derived from common law cases. Dicey's position, in so far as it left any room for rights, viewed them as residual liberties rather than as positive entitlements.[20] This meant that liberty was what remained after various actions were declared illegal. Ewing and Gearty denigrate this as a 'subordinate status' for rights, Simpson as an 'impoverished' account.[21] Yet, Dicey refused to admit any advantage for 'foreign' Bills of Rights declared in a Constitution, writing that the Habeas Corpus Acts: 'declare no principle and define no rights, but they are for practical purposes worth a hundred constitutional articles guaranteeing individual liberty.' Furthermore, because English rights were ingrained in the general common law, this meant for Dicey that the right of personal liberty 'is one which can hardly be destroyed without a thoroughgoing revolution in the institutions and manners of the nation.'[22] But nowhere did Dicey list any of those rights that he considered fundamental. The problem with Dicey's conception is that there exists no concrete core of protection, no positive measure

[18] *Law of the Constitution*, 195.

[19] See Paul Craig, 'Formal and Substantive Conceptions of the Rule of Law: An Analytical Framework' (1997) PL 467.

[20] E.g. K Ewing and C Gearty, *Freedom under Thatcher* (Oxford: Clarendon Press, 1990) 'Introduction'.

[21] K Ewing and C Gearty, *The Struggle for Civil Liberties: Political Freedom and the Rule of Law in Britain, 1914–1945* (Oxford: Oxford University Press, 2001); B Simpson, *Human Rights and the End of Empire: Britain and the Genesis of the European Convention* (Oxford: Oxford University Press, 2004) at 37.

[22] *Law of the Constitution*, 199 and 77.

that can be asserted in response to any repressive law or court decision. Unlike Blackstone, Dicey did not believe in natural, innate rights, and instead, following Bentham and Austin, took a positivist approach, based around actual existing laws. But the existing laws in his time offered very little concrete rights protection. Nor did Dicey want any. Although both the draft 1886 and 1893 Government of Ireland Bills contained some limitations on legislative power to restrict liberty, neither Bill was implemented and Dicey's attack on Irish Home Rule is well known. For example, in *England's Case Against Home Rule*, he attacked the 1886 Home Rule Bill, writing that formal guarantees of rights were: 'nugatory; they are worth neither more nor less than the pompous securities for every kind of inalienable right which adorned the most splendid and the most transitory among the Constitutions which have during a century been in turn created and destroyed in France – that is, they are worth nothing'.[23]

10.2.3 A Constitutional Heritage of Rights Scepticism

This Diceyan legacy continued well after his death. Although, after the Second World War, international discussion began over the introduction of Bills of Rights, this was a concept alien to English law. There existed no treatise analysing what rights were protected under English law, and little, if any, scholarly interest in the international protection of rights.[24] There was, however, a great deal of complacency as to protection of liberty in Britain. For example, in 1946 Sir Cecil Carr (Counsel to the Speaker of the House of Commons) writing for the first UN *Yearbook on Human Rights* declared that British liberty was secured by 'the good sense of the people and in the system of representative and responsible government which has been evolved.'[25]

Such complacency about British liberty was underpinned by the notion that the British system of government had survived the extension of the franchise in the nineteenth and twentieth centuries. Very little had changed constitutionally. However, as a result of this franchise extension, in order to survive, political parties had become much more disciplined, and the power of back-bench MPs waned, with the result that the Executive dominated Parliament. But it is in just such circumstances that rights are needed as counterbalances to an overbearing Executive.

Dicey had vaunted the common law and the judiciary as guardians of British liberty. Yet, until quite recently, British judges tended to defer to the Executive.

[23] *England's Case against Home Rule* (London, 1886) 260.

[24] Simpson remarked that 'the first book on the general protection of human rights by an English writer, albeit an immigrant from Poland not brought up as a common lawyer, was Lauterpacht's *An International Bill of the Rights of Man* (1945).' [Simpson, *Human Rights and the End of Empire*, 38.]

[25] Simpson, *Human Rights and the End of Empire*, 47.

Authors such as John Griffith, Keith Ewing and Conor Gearty[26] argued that the record of British judges was not a salutary one. The courts consistently upheld repressive Government measures – such as wartime restrictions of liberty,[27] measures taken against Irish nationalists,[28] against suffragettes,[29] and the sweeping restrictions of the Public Order Act 1936.[30] Courts were particularly deferential in cases where 'national security' was cited – this attitude extended to later twentieth-century litigation such as *GCHQ*, and *Spycatcher*.[31] Cases such as *Entick v Carrington*,[32] in which John Entick successfully sued the King's Secretary of State for trespass, are held up as beacons of British liberty defended by the courts. Yet, the case rested on Entick's property right – that the King's messenger might not enter his private dwelling on a general warrant. It did not establish Entick's freedom to publish independently of his property rights. Even *Beatty* v. *Gillbanks*[33] of which Dicey enthused, 'No better instance can be found of the way in which in England the constitution is built up upon individual rights than our rules as to public assemblies'[34] is more limited in ambit than Dicey's enthusiastic description might suggest. The case was an appeal against an order binding over Salvation Army members to prevent them parading for fear of provoking violence by a rival group. Their appeal succeeded on the basis that to stop the Salvation Army marching would be to punish them for doing a lawful act. But there was no assertion of a right to political liberty, which, as Ewing and Gearty assert, 'is a very insecure base on which to build a theory of political liberty, particularly as there is no fixed definition of what constitutes unlawful action, so that the general principle can readily be swallowed in the shifting sands of its exception.'[35]

A change in judicial attitude would only come later in the twentieth century, after Britain had become a member of the ECHR, and also introduced its own Human Rights Act in 1998. A new generation of judges appeared more willing to embrace the concept of a right.

[26] K Ewing and C Gearty, *Freedom under Thatcher*, and *The Struggle for Civil Liberties;* JAG Griffith, *The Politics of the Judiciary* (2nd ed., London: Fontana, 1997).

[27] E.g. *Liversidge* v. *Anderson* [1942] AC 206, in which Lord Atkin, in a famous dissent at 244, stated that the judges, 'show themselves more executive minded than the executive.'

[28] E.g. *O'Kelly* v. *Harvey* [1883] 15 Cox CC 435, in which an Irish Land League meeting was banned and the right to peaceful assembly denied.

[29] E.g. *R* v. *Hewitt* [1912] 28 TLR 378; also *Nairn* v. *University of St Andrews* [1909] SC 10, in which the House of Lords notoriously held that women did not qualify as 'persons' for the purposes of voting for MPs for the universities of Edinburgh and St Andrews.

[30] This Act was in principle drafted against the British Union of Fascists and prohibited wearing political uniforms in any public place, but was widely used against IRA demonstrations in Britain in the 1970s, and during the 1984/5 miners' strike.

[31] *Council of Civil Service Unions* v. *Minister for the Civil Service* [1984] UKHL 9, often known as the 'GCHQ' case. There were many cases in the 'Spycatcher' saga, including *AG* v. *Guardian Newspapers Ltd. (No. 2)* [1988] 3 All ER 545 (HL).

[32] *Entick* v. *Carrington* [1765] EWHC KB.

[33] *Beatty* v. *Gillbanks* [1882] 9 QBD 308.

[34] *Law of the Constitution*, at 271.

[35] *The Struggle for Civil Liberties*, at 31.

10.3 The UK's Role in Establishing the ECHR

Yet, the account so far raises a salient question. Why was Britain willing to sign up to the ECHR when it had no domestic tradition of a Bill of Rights and believed its own rights protection to be satisfactory? Human Rights Conventions, at least if they contain the enforcement mechanisms of the ECHR, constrain what States may do to those within their own territories. Why would the British Government willingly undertake these obligations?

Brian Simpson provides a salient explanation – that Britain's engagement with the Convention was 'a product of British foreign policy not of the British legal tradition, much less of British domestic policy.' The UN was already taking initiatives in the human rights field, and had produced the Universal Declaration of Human Rights in 1948 (described by Eleanor Roosevelt, one of its prime instigators, as a 'Magna Carta for mankind') and, as Simpson writes: 'unless the British Foreign Office was willing to stand aside from the work of the United Nations it had little choice but to break with the Diceyan tradition of opposition to formal statements of rights.'[36] Foreign policy dictated action in the face of a growing Soviet threat. UN activity increased the momentum for greater cooperation in Europe, and the ECHR was generated by the Council of Europe, with its driving force the protection of western Europe from Soviet power. These were Foreign Office responsibilities, and Foreign Office officials, rather than those with domestic legal training, took a primary role.[37]

However, although the ECHR might be seen as just the sort of continental Bill of Rights deprecated by Dicey, in fact Britain went further than passively accepting it. The UK played a key role in its genesis (as described in the chapter on Britain and Europe). David Maxwell-Fyfe's important role, and his insistence that the ECHR be not just 'a declaration of moral principles and pious aspirations', but 'a binding convention', has already been noted.[38] Indeed, the UK was the first country to ratify the ECHR, in March 1951.

Nonetheless, the ECHR is very different in structure and philosophy from the British common law approach to rights. The Convention asserts the existence of its rights, rather than leaving them with a residual or interstitial status, as the traditional Diceyan approach would have. Under the Convention, rights such as freedom of expression are asserted to exist (e.g. under Article 10(1) ECHR), and governments may only justify restricting them by clear laws in certain limited, specified situations (as under Article 10(2)). The ECHR also provides specific judicial mechanisms and requires its member States to

[36] Simpson, *Human Rights and the End of Empire*, both quotes at 39.

[37] Simpson details the key role of the foreign office legal advisor, Eric Beckett, who had an enthusiasm for human rights.

[38] 'First session of the Consultative Assembly at Strasbourg 1949' [in *Travaux Préparatoires Vol 1* (Martinus Nijhoff, 1975)].

recognize the jurisdiction of its Court and to permit the right of individual petition[39] (structures that the British Government initially opposed).

Notably, the UK, when it ratified the ECHR, also extended its application to UK dependencies, unlike most other European colonial powers. As a result, the UK soon found its conduct challenged under the ECHR – as in proceedings brought by Greece against Britain in 1956 and 1957 over Cyprus.[40] It seemed that the British tradition of liberty might not thrive in all of the UK's dependencies. This came as rather a shock in some quarters, and there was even a suggestion of denouncing the Convention, but, as Sir Hilton Poynton of the Colonial Office concluded in a minute written in 1956: 'we have got ourselves committed to this wretched Covenant and can't get out of it now …'[41] However, Brian Simpson's characterization – that 'it was as if ratification and extension to the colonies had all been a horrible mistake, or the consequence of some bizarre fit of absence of mind'[42] – reads very familiarly in the larger context of Britain's imperial actions. 'Absence of mind' seems to have been a common condition in the UK's relations with its colonies and dependencies. This might, however, go some of the way to explain Britain's present day conflicted approach to the ECHR, whereby some still apparently perceive it as this 'wretched Covenant'.

10.4 'Liberty Is Ill' in Britain

10.4.1 General

The ECHR has been dealt with quite extensively in the chapter on Britain and Europe and will not be analyzed further here. We will instead return to the domestic scene, to see how human rights protection fared in Britain in the post-war years.

For many, all was not well. In majoritarian political systems such as the UK, minorities risk being subject to discrimination and other unjust and irrational treatment, which is why Bills of Rights are often established as checks on the Executive. Although the common law is a source of some rights in Britain, these are mostly administrative in nature, being a component of a supervisory judicial review jurisdiction exercised by the English High Court over all 'inferior courts and tribunals' – which includes administrative decision-makers in all public bodies except primary legislation. Additionally, shortly prior to the 1998 Human Rights Act, courts had also established the existence of a very few common law 'constitutional' rights of especial significance – mostly concerned with access to justice – which could only be overridden expressly, and not impliedly, by Parliament.[43] Nonetheless, in 1988, on the tercentenary of

[39] Made compulsory with the 11th Protocol to the ECHR in 1998.

[40] *Application of 7 May 1956* (176/56) and *17 July 1957* (299/57).

[41] CO 936/296, Sir A Hilton Poynton.

[42] Simpson, *Human Rights and the End of Empire*, at 13.

[43] E.g. *Raymond* v. *Honey* [1983] 1 AC 1; *ex parte Leech*, [1994] QB 198; *ex parte Witham*, [1998] Q.B. 575; *Pierson* [1997] 3 All ER 577, HL; *ex parte Simms*, [2000] 2 AC 115.

the 1688 Bill of Rights, academics and intellectuals formed 'Charter 88' to campaign for a UK written Constitution. Ronald Dworkin famously published an article in *Index on Censorship* stating that 'Liberty is ill in Britain'.[44] The general thrust was that the Executive was insufficiently balanced by Parliament or the courts. Britain might have had a 'culture of liberty' but there existed no Bill of Rights to enforce particular liberties.

Many argued for a new Bill of Rights for Britain, or for incorporation of the ECHR (i.e. its domestic implementation). While unincorporated, the ECHR could not be directly enforced in UK courts, and if the language of a UK statute was in clear conflict with the ECHR, the statute rather than the ECHR had to be applied by the courts. According to Jonathan Cooper,

> the common law provided hotchpotch protection. The rule of law worked efficiently in respect of issues such as legality, but the notion of the rule of law could not actually guarantee rights. Civil liberties were flimsy and stood no chance against the doctrine of Parliamentary Sovereignty.... By the mid-90s, uniquely at the time across the Council of Europe, the UK had been found to violate all of the substantive ECHR rights except [freedom from] slavery, and a violation of that right was to follow.

Cooper concluded that the introduction of the 1998 HRA 'was a necessity.'[45]

However, not everyone was in favour of a new court-enforced Bill of Rights for Britain, nor of incorporating the ECHR. This included both conservative and progressive commentators. For example, Ewing and Gearty, in *Freedom under Thatcher*, counselled against judicially enforceable Bills of Rights in the UK. Their primary argument was that it would confer enormous power on judges. To support this argument, they analyzed decisions of British judges over the past half century, noting for example that in the *Spycatcher* case, 'They have accepted that Government can avoid scrutiny of its conduct by calling to its aid a concept, "national security", the definition of which the judges are content to leave to the executive.' They also considered the record of the Privy Council on constitutional rights (in its capacity as final Court of Appeal for Commonwealth cases) and found it wanting. Their recommendation was instead 'to introduce some real and effective political constraints on the power of the Prime Minister.'[46] To be sure, scepticism of Bills of Rights is part of a long tradition in Britain. As soon as the eighteenth-century Declarations of Rights came into being, critics such as Bentham and Burke were voicing their opposition to them. Bentham remarked that:

> Give the judges the power of annulling [Parliament's] acts; and you transfer a portion of the supreme power from an assembly which the people have had *some*

[44] *Index on Censorship*, 8 September 1988.

[45] J Cooper OBE, 'The Human Rights Act: Delivering Rights and Enhancing Dignity', in K Dzehtsiarou, S Falcetta, D Giannoulopoulos, and P Johnson (eds.), *Human Rights in Action: Assessing the Positive Impact of the Human Rights Act 1998 in the UK* (Submission to the IHRAR March 2021).

[46] *Freedom under Thatcher*, Conclusion.

share, at least, in choosing, to a set of men in the choice of whom they have not had the least imaginable share.[47]

Nonetheless, not everyone shared this distrust of British judges. Support for a Bill of Rights was to be found across major political parties – for example, both Dominic Grieve (former Conservative Attorney-General) and Harriet Harman (former Labour front bencher) were prominent Bill of Rights supporters during the 1990s. In any case, a new generation of judges were in place, replacing earlier judges such as Lords Widgery, Lane, and Denning. These newer judges were arguing for incorporation of the ECHR into domestic law.[48] According to Conor Gearty, 'You only have to name them to see how different the atmosphere is now.'[49]

10.5 The 1998 Human Rights Act

In 1998, Parliament adopted the UK Human Rights Act (HRA). The key aim of this legislation, according to the 1997 Labour Government *White Paper*, was that of 'bringing rights home',[50] empowering UK courts to enforce the ECHR domestically, and enabling litigants to avoid the expense and delay of going to Strasbourg. Thus it did not aim to introduce a specifically British Bill of Rights. The HRA implements most but not all ECHR rights into domestic law.[51] Under s6 HRA, all public authorities, including courts, and devolved parliaments, must comply with ECHR rights. All new UK laws should also be compatible with Convention rights and, under s19 HRA, the Minister in charge of a Bill is required to make a statement that its provisions are compatible with Convention rights. However, the sovereignty of the UK Parliament means that it can nonetheless pass laws which are incompatible with the ECHR. Notably, the HRA is not entrenched, so Parliament may amend or repeal it. In this way, and by excluding any 'hard' judicial review with a strike down power of statutes, parliamentary sovereignty is maintained, and ultimately human rights protection remains conditional on parliamentary will and acceptance.

Section 2 HRA 1998 requires UK courts to 'take into account' the jurisprudence of the European Court of Human Rights (ECtHR). Although initially, judges were urged to 'mirror' Strasbourg jurisprudence,[52] this approach was

[47] J Bentham, 'Fragment on Government' (Cambridge: Cambridge University Press, 1988) ch IV, para. 32.

[48] E.g. Sir Thomas Bingham, 'The European Convention on Human Rights: Time to Incorporate' (1993) 109 LQR 390.

[49] C Gearty, 'I've Changed My Mind about the Human Rights Act', *The Guardian*, 30 December 2009.

[50] 'Rights Brought Home: The Human Rights Bill' (1997).

[51] The HRA does not incorporate Art. 1 ECHR nor Art. 13. The view was that the HRA itself was the fulfilment of both of those Articles. But in *A* v. *UK*, 2009 at [158] the ECtHR held that the declaration of incompatibility is not an effective remedy.

[52] *ex p Ullah* [2004] 2 AC 323 para. 20 per Lord Bingham.

abandoned for a more nuanced one, and, on some occasions, UK courts have departed from ECtHR jurisprudence.[53] Notably, the HRA does not enable judges to invalidate incompatible primary legislation, as is the case with the US Federal Bill of Rights, and in Germany, South Africa and Canada. However, s3 HRA requires courts to interpret all statutes 'as far as possible' compatibly with ECHR rights,[54] and if this is not possible, superior courts (i.e. High Court or above) may adopt a 'declaration of incompatibility' under s4 HRA.[55] In this way, the HRA reconciles human rights with parliamentary sovereignty (by in fact leaving parliamentary sovereignty unconstrained) and it is up to Parliament to decide if to repeal incompatible legislation. It does not have to do so.[56] This contrasts with the 1972 ECA, which required UK law to be set aside if it conflicted with directly effective EU law. Thus, it has been said that the HRA adopts a 'dialogue' approach between Parliament and the courts.[57] In fact, relatively few declarations of incompatibility have been made, and almost all have been complied with.[58] One notable exception was where Parliament ignored the declaration of incompatibility regarding the ban on prisoner voting for over a decade, although did finally take measures to rectify the Strasbourg judgement.[59]

One high-profile occasion in which a declaration of incompatibility was issued was *A and others* v. *Secretary of State for the Home Department*,[60] which dealt with the legality of detention of suspected terrorists. The House of Lords found that s23 of the Anti-terrorism, Crime and Security Act 2001 was incompatible with the HRA because it discriminated against non-nationals, permitting their indefinite detention. The House of Lords also found that the UK was not entitled to derogate from Article 5 ECHR (the right to liberty) as the Government had not proved that the exigencies of the situation warranted such a derogation, although only Lord Hoffmann found that there was no 'public emergency threatening the life of the nation.' In so finding, the House of Lords disagreed with the Court of Appeal and refused to defer to the Secretary of State. In particular, Lord Bingham stated that 'The Attorney General is fully entitled to insist on the proper limits of judicial authority, but he is wrong to stigmatise judicial decision-making as somehow undemocratic,' continuing that the HRA 'gives the courts a very specific, wholly democratic, mandate'.[61]

[53] E.g. *R (Hallam)* v. *Secretary of State for Justice* [2019] UKSC.
[54] E.g. *Ghaidin* v. *Godin Mendoza* [2004] UKHL 30.
[55] E.g. *Bellinger* v. *Bellinger* [2003] 2 AC 467. [56] See s10 HRA.
[57] See Alison Young, *Democratic Dialogue and the Constitution* (Oxford: Oxford University Press, 2017).
[58] 2015 JCHR report.
[59] UK courts issued a declaration of incompatibility in *Smith* v. *Scott* [2007] SC 345, following the ECtHR decision in *Hirst* v. *UK*. Eventually, the UK Government introduced measures to allow prisoners on temporary licence to vote. On 6 December 2018, the Council of Europe Committee of Ministers adopted final resolution CM/ResDH (2018) 467.
[60] [2004] UKHL 56. [61] Ibid., para. 42.

The *Belmarsh* (as *A* v. *Home Secretary* is often known) decision illustrates how the judiciary scrutinized violations of rights, even in national security contexts – a clear move forward from the earlier approach in *Spycatcher*. The Government swiftly responded to the Court's judgement with new legislation – the Prevention of Terrorism Act, 2005 – which replaced detention with the control order system, which did not discriminate against foreign nationals (but raised other issues, which were subsequently litigated[62]).

Reaction to the HRA in the UK has been a bit mixed, although generally favourable.[63] The HRA has enabled individuals to litigate their rights claims in UK courts, and gain an effective remedy there, rather than spending time and money going to Strasbourg. However, the HRA was never welcomed by certain elements in Britain. These included right wing politicians and the press. The criticism usually accuses the HRA of 'mission creep', of being too foreign, or of infringing parliamentary sovereignty.[64] Many particularly disliked what they perceived as the strengthening of the right of privacy by English courts at the expense of the press (who were finding it more difficult to report sensational details of celebrities' private lives). This perception was coupled with the assertion that the Human Rights Act, along with the creation of the UK Supreme Court by the UK Constitutional Reform Act 2005, had led to an increase in judicial power and judicial review.

10.6 The Critique of Judicial Enforcement of Human Rights

It has been complained that the HRA has had an overly intrusive effect, and empowered judges. But human rights litigation frequently involves controversial moral or policy issues. Have UK judges acted inappropriately, become too activist? Judges do not, unlike Plato's fictional guardians, have any especial knowledge of justice, and *pace* Dworkin's ideal judge Hercules, they are not philosopher kings – and recent decisions of the US Supreme Court may be giving judicial review a bad name. No doubt examples of regrettable, poorly reasoned, judgments can be found.[65] But so can the opposite, as illustrated by former South African Constitutional Court judge, Albie Sachs, in *The Strange Alchemy of Life and Law*. Sachs conveys the sincerity of a judge

[62] E.g. *Home Secretary* v. *AP* [2010] UKSC 24 – challenging length and conditions imposed by control orders.

[63] For academic responses e.g. A Kavanagh, *Constitutional Review under the Human Rights Act* (Cambridge: Cambridge University Press, 2009); T Hickman, *Public Law after the Human Rights Act* (Oxford: Hart, 2010).

[64] E.g. 'Protecting Human Rights in the UK: The Conservatives' Proposals for changing Britain's Human Rights Laws', www.conservatives.com/~/media/Files/Downloadable%20Files/HUMAN_RIGHTS.pdf.

[65] My personal choices might be, from the UK House of Lords, *Bromley LBC* v. *GLC* [1983] 1 AC 768; the US Supreme Court, *Bowers* v. *Hardwick* 478 US 186 [1986]; and the ECtHRs *Otto Preminger-Institut* v. *Austria* [1994] ECHR 26.

grappling with crucial, value laden questions.[66] And the late Lord Bingham, speaking extra-judicially, remarked that it is inevitable and even: 'desirable that judges should on occasion give decisions that are deeply unwelcome to the powers that be. There are … countries in the world where every judicial decision finds favour with the government, but they are not places where one would want to live'.[67]

The 2019 Conservative party election manifesto declared, 'We will ensure that judicial review is … not abused to conduct politics by another means.'[68] This manifesto appears to suggest limiting judicial review, especially where perceived to be 'political.' Apart from anything else, what is meant by 'political' here? Although all legal issues might, following the lead of John Griffith or the Critical Legal Studies movement, be cast as 'political' (e.g. who should bear the risk of defective products) public law contains an inherently political element, because it deals with the workings of the Constitution, frequently operated by politicians. But there is a difference between courts making political judgements, and judges determining legal issues that arise in cases that have political dimensions – and it is the latter that were at issue, for example, in the *Miller* cases.

10.6.1 The Sumption Critique

In *Trials of the State: Law and the Decline of Politics*,[69] former Supreme Court Justice, Jonathan Sumption, criticized what he perceived as judicial activism, arguing that judicial decision-making had undermined legislation and the political process in the UK.[70]

Sumption's interpretation of the rule of law is a minimal one, which includes only a very limited range of human rights, leaving little room for judicial discretion. This contrasts with many current rule of law standards, such as those of the late Lord Bingham and the Venice Commission, which include a broader, more substantive spectrum of human rights. Sumption argued that to go beyond basic legal rights (i.e. rights to life, liberty and property, and those rights essential to democracy, namely freedom of expression and the right to vote) allows too much of a role for judicial legislation. Sumption was particularly critical of Article 8 ECHR, regarding it as vastly overexpanded by judicial activism into a more general right of personal autonomy which now

[66] A Sachs, *The Strange Alchemy of Life and Law* (Oxford: Oxford University Press, 2009).

[67] Tom Bingham, *Lives of the Law* (Oxford: Oxford University Press, 2011) 146.

[68] The Conservative Party election manifesto 2019: www.conservatives.com/our-plan

[69] *Trials of the State: Law and the Decline of Politics* (London: Profile Books, 2019) – developing Sumption's 2019 BBC Reith lectures.

[70] Sumption's approach was robustly rebutted by retired senior judges (e.g. Baroness Hale, *Law and Politics: A Reply to Reith*, 8 October 2019; Sir Stephen Sedley, 'A Boundary Where There Is None' *LRB*, 12 September 2019).

includes same sex relations, transsexuality, abortion, and 'much else besides'. But why should Article 8 be given the narrow interpretation Sumption proposes, given that its ambit, as drafted in Article 8(1) is broad, encompassing 'private life', 'family life', 'home', and 'correspondence'. Sumption was also critical of *Hirst* v *United Kingdom* (in which the ECtHR found blanket bans on prisoner voting incompatible with the ECHR) seeing this as an example of courts developing a rival notion of democracy to that of representative politics. Yet this matter has now been resolved by limited changes in the UK, such that only approximately 100 inmates were enfranchized as a result – hardly a threat to parliamentary politics.

Sumption did not go as far as recommending repeal of the HRA, nor UK secession from the ECHR, although he did argue that the 'only effective constraints upon the abuse of democratic power are political'.[71] But this cannot be right. The HRA itself legislates that the *courts*, Parliament and the Government work together to protect human rights. In any case, governments cannot always be trusted to protect human rights, and Parliament does not necessarily have the means to combat a strong Executive and act as a constraint on the abuse of power.

10.6.2 The Judicial Power Project

Further criticism of the HRA has come from the *Judicial Power Project* (JPP) (part of Policy Exchange,[72] a right-wing UK think tank) which claims on its website that, 'Judicial overreach increasingly threatens the rule of law and effective, democratic government.'[73]

The JPP has been fiercely critical of the HRA. For example, Richard Ekins (listed as head of the JPP on their website) has argued that that the 'courts are responsible for extending the [Human Rights] Act beyond its intended scope.'[74] Ekins cites judicial interpretation under s3 HRA as an especially serious example, contending that it has been wrongly understood to establish the power to change the meaning of legislation. But Ekins' claim is unsustainable. UK courts have stressed that rights-compatible interpretation under s3 HRA must 'go with the grain of the legislation', be compatible with 'its underlying thrust' and may not 'radically alter the effect of the legislation'.[75] The courts have also generally but not rigidly adhered to a concept of 'due deference' to

[71] J Sumption, 'Rights and the Ideal Constitution', in *Trials of the State: Law and the Decline of Politics*.

[72] Policy Exchange's funding is somewhat opaque – the 2019 UK 'Who Funds You' report rated Policy Exchange at E, its lowest rating. http://whofundsyou.org/org/policy-exchange

[73] https://judicialpowerproject.org.uk/about/. For a critique of the Judicial power project, see P Craig, 'Judicial Power, the Judicial Power Project and the UK' Oxford Legal Studies Research Paper No. 68/2017

[74] R Ekins, The Dynamics of Power in the New British Constitution (2017) Judicial Power Project, www.judicialpowerproject.org.uk/richard-ekins-the-dynamics-of-judicial-power/ 9.

[75] *Ghaidan* v *Godin-Mendoza* [2004] UKHL 30 [33]; *Poplar Housing* v. *Donaghue* [2002] QB 48, [73] Lord Woolf.

Parliament in matters of social and economic policy. For example, former Lord Chief Justice, Lord Woolf, expressed the courts' obligation of respect and comity for the democratically elected legislature:

> Legislation is passed by a democratically elected Parliament and therefore the courts under the Convention are entitled to and should, as a matter of constitutional principle pay a degree of deference to the view of Parliament as to what is in the interest generally in upholding the rights of the individual under the Convention.[76]

In any case, if UK judges are issuing declarations of incompatibility under s4 HRA, reading statutes compatibly with Convention rights under s3 HRA, or taking into account ECHR jurisprudence in their judgments, this is exactly what the Act – and Parliament which adopted the HRA – requires of them.

10.6.3 Rights Adjudication and the 'Political Constitution'

The UK is one of a tiny handful of countries not to have a codified Constitution. Yes, the UK has a Constitution, but it is a lot harder to determine its content in the absence of codification. Given that this is so, many people have subscribed to the theory of 'Political Constitutionalism'.[77] This view was famously expounded by John Griffith in his 1978 Chorley Lecture, 'The Political Constitution'. It was Griffith's view that the Constitution 'is no more and no less than what happens' and that, 'law is not and cannot be a substitute for politics.' Griffith conceded that:

> For centuries political philosophers have sought that society in which government is by laws and not by men. It is an unattainable ideal. Written constitutions do not achieve it. Nor do Bills of Rights or any other devices. They merely pass political decisions out of the hands of politicians and into the hands of judges or other persons. To require a supreme court to make certain kinds of political decisions does not make those decisions any less political.

Therefore, he continued, we should not assume that judicial review, nor legal controls, provide any deliverance, for '[o]nly political control, politically exercised, can supply the remedy'.[78] As we have seen, it is not only progressives such as Griffith, who have criticized a judicially enforced, legal Constitution. Those of a more conservative persuasion – including Jonathan Sumption, and the JPP – also do so.

There are however two problems with the theory of the Political Constitution. The first is that it does not accord with the legal system as it operates in the UK today. It is factually inaccurate. True, much of the British Constitution

[76] *R* v. *Lambert* [2001] 2 WLR 211, [16].

[77] E.g. A Tomkins, 'In Defence of the Political Constitution' (2002) 22 OJLS 157; KD Ewing, 'The Resilience of the Political Constitution' (2013) 14 German LJ 2111.

[78] JAG Griffith, 'The Political Constitution' (1979) 42 MLR, both citations at 16.

operates on the basis of political (i.e. legally unenforceable) conventions. But there are also many significant examples of 'legal constitutionalism', which means that Britain has a Constitution that is at least for some matters, controlled and enforced legally, by the courts. For at least 70 years, senior British judges have been issuing judgements, especially in the public law field, limiting the scope of the royal prerogative, reigning in ministers, upholding a separation of powers, and even questioning the extent of parliamentary sovereignty.[79] Both EU membership, while it lasted, and the Human Rights Act, strengthened human rights and empowered judges in those fields.

The second objection to the theory of political constitutionalism is that it is normatively unattractive. It relies over-heavily on the political process sorting out constitutional matters, rejecting the capacity of 'unelected' judges to determine what the Constitution requires. Maybe political constitutionalism appeared attractive at one time, when the UK finally achieved adult universal suffrage. Furthermore, Griffith's major work, *The Politics of the Judiciary*, linked his theory of political constitutionalism with a critique of the judicial conservatism and elitism of his day. However, given Britain's 'first past the post' electoral system, whereby a Government can achieve a majority in Parliament on a minority of votes (often well below 40 per cent), this winner-takes-all mentality all too easily permits a parliamentary majority to abuse its position, and to act contrary to the wishes of the minority (who may in fact be the majority of the total population). Further, because the doctrine of parliamentary sovereignty excludes the possibility of entrenchment in the UK Constitution, any law – however, fundamental – is only as protective as the parliamentary majority of its day permits it to be. The British Constitution is often vaunted for its great flexibility. But flexibility is not always a good thing, as when it enables repeal or amendment of any provision with the ease of a parliamentary majority of one. In this environment, there is a need for checks and balances, and the HRA and the judiciary can provide an important element of these checks.

10.7 Reform of the HRA?

In 2011, the UK Coalition Government established a Commission tasked with considering the creation of a Bill of Rights protecting 'British liberties'. It was suggested that a 'British' Bill of Rights might inculcate a greater sense of public ownership than the Human Rights Act.[80] However, the Commission failed to reach a consensus.[81] Two Conservative members argued for withdrawal from

[79] *CCSU* v. *Minister for the Civil Service* [1985] AC 374 (exercise of prerogative judicially reviewable); *M* v. *Home Office* [1994] 1 AC 377 (government ministers must comply with the rule of law); *ex p Fire Brigades Union* [1995] 2 AC 513 (rule of law and separation of powers); *R (Jackson)* v. *Attorney-General* [2005] UKHL 56 (parliamentary sovereignty).

[80] 'Commission on a UK Bill of Rights launched' (Ministry of Justice, 18 March 2011).

[81] *A UK Bill of Rights: The Choice Before Us Vol 1*, December 2012, para. 78.

the ECHR altogether.[82] In contrast, two other members opposed any change at all, stating that it had become 'clear to us that for some of our colleagues a UK bill of rights is a means towards withdrawal from the European convention,' and that 'We believe that such a path would be catastrophic for the UK, for Europe and for the protection of human rights around the world.'[83]

After the Conservatives won the 2015 general election, the Government declared its renewed determination to introduce a British Bill of Rights, although the demands of Brexit put these plans on hold. But the 2019 Conservative election manifesto stated, 'We will update the Human Rights Act and administrative law to ensure that there is a proper balance between the rights of individuals, our vital national security and effective government.'[84] And, in 2020, an Independent Human Rights Act Review (IHRAR) panel chaired by Sir Peter Gross (retired Lord Justice of Appeal) was set up to review the operation of the Act. At the same time, Parliament's Joint Committee on Human Rights (JCHR) launched its own inquiry into the operation of the HRA. In giving evidence to the JCHR in 2021, Baroness Hale, former President of the UK Supreme Court, stated:

> I do not think that the Human Rights Act causes a problem for parliament, because it is very carefully crafted [...] to ensure that parliament remains supreme and can take whatever action it deems fit, including doing nothing at all, even if the courts have said that a particular piece of legislation is incompatible with the convention rights. I do not think there is a problem or any need to fix it. I cannot myself think of a fix that would make things better as opposed to potentially making things worse.'[85]

Although the report of the IHRAR panel[86] suggested very few changes to the HRA, nonetheless, its report was largely ignored and in December 2021 the Ministry of Justice published its own consultation document, *Human Rights Act Reform: A Modern Bill of Rights*,[87] revealing a decision to replace the HRA with some other Bill of Rights. Nearly 12,000 responses were made to this consultation, mostly in favour of retaining the HRA. Nonetheless, in June 2022 (on the same day it published responses to its consultation paper) Secretary of State for Justice, Dominic Raab, introduced a new Bill of Rights Bill, to repeal and supplant the HRA 1998. The title 'Bill of Rights' suggests legislation of historic importance, but, as David Allen Green wrote:

[82] Lord Faulks QC and Jonathan Fisher QC, 'Unfinished Business', in *A UK Bill of Rights* 182.

[83] Baroness Helena Kennedy QC and Professor Phillipe Sands QC, 'In Defence of Rights', in *A UK Bill of Rights* 221.

[84] Conservative party election manifesto 2019 at 48.

[85] Available at https://committees.parliament.uk/oralevidence/1661/pdf/

[86] The report was published in December 2021 and is available here: https://assets.publishing.service.gov.uk/government/uploads/system/uploads/attachment_data/file/1040525/ihrar-final-report.pdf

[87] *Human Rights Act Reform: A Modern Bill of Rights* – consultation, available here: www.gov.uk/government/consultations/human-rights-act-reform-a-modern-bill-of-rights/human-rights-act-reform-a-modern-bill-of-rights-consultation

> the new legislation is designed not to confer new rights or expand existing ones, but to limit the practical effectiveness of rights already in existence. In clause after clause, complicated and detailed provisions seek to make it less possible for rights to be asserted … It is not a bill of rights, but a list of spoilers.'[88]

The Bill gave effect to the same catalogue of ECHR rights as the HRA, although in its clause 9 specifically recognized trial by jury as a fundamental component of fair trials in the UK. However, trial by jury is already recognized in English law, and, given the different laws on access to jury trial in Scotland, raises devolution issues – so its inclusion was both unnecessary and problematic. As with the HRA, superior courts might issue a declaration of incompatibility if they find a law contravenes a Convention right (clause 10).

However, in many other ways, the Bill limited rights protection. First, it mandated a 'permission stage', requiring applicants to show they have suffered 'significant disadvantage' (clause 15) before their claim will proceed. The Bill also required a high level of judicial deference to the Executive in many areas, including deportation, where, under clause 8, 'foreign criminals' could only rely on the right to family life if their deportation would cause 'exceptional', 'overwhelming' and 'irreversible' harm. Significantly, the Bill also removed UK courts' power to interpret legislation to render it compatible with the ECHR (i.e. s3 HRA). It also removed courts' requirement to 'take into account' ECtHR judgments (s2 HRA). Furthermore, the Bill instructed courts to ignore interim measures issued by the ECtHR – a stipulation which surely violates the UK's Convention obligations. This provision appeared designed to avoid rulings such as when the ECtHR issued interim measures[89] to prohibit deportation of an applicant to Rwanda (under the UK-Rwanda asylum agreement) until lawfulness of this agreement had been established. Additionally, clause 3(2) required domestic courts to have 'particular regard to the text of the Convention right'. This would deter 'dynamic' interpretations such as those of the ECtHR itself, and align UK judicial interpretation closer to 'originalist' 'textual' approaches, as in the 2022 *Dobbs* decision of the US Supreme Court, which overruled *Roe* v. *Wade*.[90]

Repealing the HRA, with its dramatic consequences for rights protection and the devolution settlement, would constitute a major constitutional change. As Merris Amos has stressed, in other democracies, this would take considerable time, involving 'constitutional conventions, public consultation, a referendum or special parliamentary majorities.'[91] Yet, the government presented

[88] David Allen Green, 'The Proposed Bill of Rights Is a Pointless Distraction', *Prospect*, June 27, 2022.

[89] Application no. 28774/22 *NSK* v. *UK* (14 June 2022).

[90] See *Tyrer* v. *UK* [1978] ECHR 2, for the ECtHR's use of dynamic interpretation. *Dobbs v Jackson Women 's' Health* 597 US [2022].

[91] M Amos, 'Why UK Approach to Replacing the Human Rights Act Is Just as Worrying as the Replacement Itself', *The Conversation*, 27 June 2022.

no solid reasons for repealing the HRA, nor is there evidence of any substantial demand for its repeal.

In June 2023, following the resignation of Dominic Raab, the Bill of Rights Bill was abandoned. However, there is no guarantee that it would not be resurrected at a future date. Moreover, given the Bill's clauses requiring UK judges to ignore ECtHR interim measures, and empowering them to depart from ECtHR rulings, there would be a strong likelihood that the UK would violate the ECHR. If this occurred sufficiently often, the Council of Europe could exclude the UK (as happened for Russia). If that were to occur, then AG Suella Braverman's proposal for the UK to remove itself from the ECHR[92] would have taken place, without anyone ever voting for it. The 2022 Bill of Rights Bill represented an atavistic and regressive step back to understandings of British liberty in former centuries – where judicial deference was extremely high, rights were narrowly defined, and 'foreign' sources of rights protection decried. It is hoped its provisions will not be resurrected.

10.8 Brexit: The Eradication of Rights

Given the UK's 'first past the post' electoral system, it has been possible for legislation prejudicing minority groups (especially those lacking electoral rights, such as EU nationals) to be passed by a bare majority in Parliament. Furthermore, it is very difficult, if not impossible, to give human rights guaranteed protection under the UK Constitution, because a later act of Parliament can always override an earlier one, under the 'implied repeal' rule. This makes substantive entrenchment almost unachievable in the UK. Therefore, under Britain's uncodified Constitution, human rights, even when set out in primary legislation, such as the UK HRA 1998, have a precarious status, leaving them vulnerable to repeal by ordinary legislation.[93]

10.8.1 Exclusion of the Charter of Fundamental Rights from UK Law

However, one exception to the difficulty of entrenchment in UK constitutional law was provided by EU law. While the UK was an EU member State, the principle of the supremacy of EU law over conflicting national law applied, meaning that rights guaranteed under EU law could be protected from implied repeal by a later UK statute – at the very least, a sort of semi-entrenchment.[94]

[92] E.g. 'Suella Braverman calls for UK to leave "political" ECHR in wake of Rwanda ruling', *The Telegraph*, 10 July 2022.

[93] Although the UK HRA has been classified by UK Courts as a 'constitutional statute', (*Thoburn* v. *Sunderland CC* [2002] EWHC 195, per Laws LJ, at para. 62) namely one that may only be repealed by express and not implied repeal by the legislature.

[94] Case 6/64 *Costa* v. *ENEL* [1964] ECR 585; s2(4) ECA 1972 and *ex parte Factortame Ltd)* (No 2) [1991]. Express repeal would still have been constitutionally possible, but contrary to EU law and membership.

And EU law provides individuals with many rights 'which become part of their legal heritage.'[95]

During the UK's EU membership, these rights took a number of forms. British citizens used their free movement rights under EU law to move to other EU countries to live, work, holiday and retire there. Other EU citizens likewise moved to the UK. However, the rights at issue are not only migratory in nature. British business enjoyed all sorts of rights of freedom to trade within the EU, without tariff or non-tariff barriers, as indeed did other EU traders with Britain. Workers derived many rights from EU law, such as equal pay, whether they migrated to another EU State or not, and consumers benefited from rights to consumer protection. The EU Charter of Fundamental Rights was legally enforceable in the UK, carrying the same weight as the EU treaties. While the UK was an EU member State, the EU Charter, and other rights in EU treaties, applied, and domestic courts were required, under EU law, to disapply incompatible national legislation. Post-Brexit, however, the EU Charter has been specifically excluded from UK law, and other EU rights are vulnerable to repeal by ministers using secondary legislation.[96] This removes the protection of a very large array of rights from individuals in Britain. The EU Charter is one of the most comprehensive rights documents in the world, protecting fifty different rights, encompassing civil, political, and socio-economic rights. To be sure, Charter rights apply only when a member State operates within the field of EU law, a somewhat murky area. However, the field of EU law is nonetheless wide, and covers much EU State action. So in leaving the EU, Britain has undergone a huge bonfire of rights. Not only have British citizens lost their EU citizenship, with attendant free movement rights, but also a large swathe of other human rights as well. It is hard to find a precedent for such a disengagement with human rights protection in the western world.

Now, to be sure, EU law did not vanish from the UK's legal system on Brexit day. Because so much UK law has derived from the EU since 1973, it was impossible to replace it with new UK legislation by 'exit day'. Therefore, the EUWA 2018 was passed, converting EU law into domestic law (where it becomes 'retained EU law') and then, where perceived necessary, allowing ministers to repeal or amend it. However, despite the general conversion of EU law into national law, s5(4) EUWA excluded the Charter of Fundamental Rights from domestic law from the exit date. The UK Government justified this exclusion by arguing the Charter is not a source of rights but only reaffirms existing rights which are protected by 'retained EU law', the common law, and the ECHR.[97] However this is inaccurate. Neither the ECHR, nor common law rights, match the full spectrum of rights provided by the

[95] Case C-26/62, *van Gend & Loos*, [1963] ECR 1.

[96] See further EUWA 2018, for provisions enabling UK government ministers to repeal or amend former (or 'retained') EU law by secondary legislation.

[97] UK Government, 'Charter of Fundamental Rights of the EU Right by Right Analysis' 5/12/2017. This analysis has been condemned for its superficiality – C Gallagher, A Patrick and K O'Byrne: *Report on Human Rights Implications of UK Withdrawal from the EU, An Independent*

Charter,[98] and effective remedies have been removed by the Charter's exclusion. Furthermore, the Government's position placed a heavy reliance on the UK HRA, which the Government has undertaken to repeal.

It is more likely that specifically omitting the Charter reflected a distinct political choice. In March 2017, when David Davis, then Brexit Secretary, declared the EU Charter would not be included in retained EU law, a report in *The Daily Telegraph* read: 'David Davis announced that the first EU law to be scrapped after Brexit will be a charter that helps criminals avoid deportation.' *The Telegraph* also quoted Sir Bill Cash MP (chairman of the House of Commons European scrutiny committee) saying 'Britain would immediately benefit when the charter was dropped because "it provides protection for people who have no right to be protected."'[99]

As Vernon Bogdanor has argued,[100] the EUWA (and Brexit more generally) achieves something unprecedented in the UK's constitutional history. For the withdrawal of the UK from the EU transforms a protected Constitution (i.e. one that contains entrenched provisions) into an unprotected one. While the UK was an EU member, neither the EU Charter, nor other rights provisions in EU law, could be repealed by the UK Parliament, and UK courts were empowered to disapply domestic legislation incompatible with those EU rights, as in the *Benkharbouche* case.[101] Ms Janah and Ms Benkharbouche, both Moroccan nationals, were employed as domestic workers by the Libyan and Sudanese embassies in London. They claimed they were paid below the national minimum wage, forced to work unlawful hours, unfairly dismissed and (in Ms Janah's case) discriminated against on racial grounds. The two defendant embassies argued State immunity (under the UK State Immunity Act) applied to their claims. The UK Supreme Court found for the claimants, and because the Embassies had infringed EU Charter rights, the relevant protections of the State Immunity Act were set aside by the Court. Under EU law, they had an enforceable claim and right to a remedy, but this no longer applies post-Brexit.

10.8.2 EU Citizens' Rights

For many, the issue of human rights and Brexit has been dominated by the status of EU citizens (namely, nationals of other EU States resident in the UK) but also UK nationals resident in other EU States – who are no longer EU

Legal Opinion, 2 March 2018, para. 3.47. See also J Grogan, 'Rights and Remedies at Risk: Implications of the Brexit Process on the Future of Rights in the UK' (2019) *Public Law* 683.

98 Which include for example the right to data protection, and also the right to be forgotten, as established in Case 131/12, *Google Spain SL*, v. *González* [2014] ECR I-000.

99 Both quoted in 'UK takes back the right to deport as Britain repeals powers from EU', *Daily Telegraph*, 31 March 2017.

100 Vernon Bogdanor, 'How Brexit Will Erase Your Rights', *Prospect*, May 2018.

101 *Benkharbouche* v. *Secretary of State for Foreign and Commonwealth Affairs* [2017] UKSC 62.

citizens. There are well over 3.5 million EU nationals[102] in the UK, and 1.2m British living in the EU, many of whom have made a permanent home there. EU law required them to be treated equally to host State nationals in many respects – a function of EU citizenship – but this no longer applies after Brexit. Prior to the 2016 EU referendum, some Brexiters insisted these rights would be guaranteed as 'acquired rights' (i.e. those rights not automatically revoked when a treaty no longer applies) under the 1969 Vienna Convention on the law of treaties. This has not been the case.[103] And, despite certain undertakings made to them during the referendum campaign, and pleas made by them not to be treated as 'bargaining chips', their rights were often ignored in the Brexit process.

It was the EU that insisted that EU citizens' status be protected and guaranteed under the EU Withdrawal Agreement. Under that Agreement,[104] EU citizens are granted 'settled status' if they provide evidence of UK residency for over five years. The settlement scheme has not, however, provided the 'automatic grant' of existing rights promised by many members of the Leave campaign, and there have been many unexplained delays in the application process.[105] UK citizens in other EU countries are little better off. They must also register, but will have no automatic right to move to other EU countries, as they will no longer be EU citizens.

Matters were hardly helped when, shortly before the UK general election in December 2019, Boris Johnson told *Sky News*: 'You've seen quite a large of people coming in from the EU – 580 million population – able to treat the UK as though it's basically part of their own country and the problem with that is there has been no control at all.'[106] This statement – met with widespread criticism – is clearly inaccurate. Contrary to Johnson's statement, such migration is not uncontrolled, because EU law makes provision for the expulsion of

[102] 3.8 million EU nationals according to the Migration Observatory Oxford in 2018: https://migrationobservatory.ox.ac.uk/resources/briefings/eu-migration-to-and-from-the-uk/

[103] The crucial point is that Article 70 Vienna Convention does not directly address individual rights. See further: A Aust, *Modern Treaty Law and Practice* (Cambridge: Cambridge University Press, 2007) at 266.

[104] *Agreement on the withdrawal of the United Kingdom of Great Britain and Northern Ireland from the European Union and the European Atomic Energy Community*, Brussels, 18 October 2019 (OR. en) XT 21054/19.

[105] As Stuart McDonald SNP MP said in the House of Commons in January 2020, 'Imagine a retired French lady and a young Polish guy.... The French lady has been here since the 1970s and had a permanent residence document under the old EU rules. Understandably, she thought she did not need to apply to stay, but it turns out that, of course, she did. The Polish guy was born here and because of that he believed that he was British, so he did not apply. However, it turns out that because his Polish mum and his UK father were not married at the time of his birth, he was not British after all, and he should have applied as well. Under the government's proposals, that French lady and the young Polish lad will be subject to the full force of the hostile environment.' https://hansard.parliament.uk/Commons/2020-01-07/debates/C5ADC5C3-0008-4CBB

[106] See 'Election 2019: Boris Johnson Vows End to Migrants "Treating Britain as Their Own"', *The Times*, 9 December 2019.

EU citizens who do not find work within 3 months of entry, or who commit criminal offences. And, of course, by no means all 580 million EU nationals came to Britain. And quite a few Britons exercised their free movement rights by going to other EU countries. This vilification of migrants has, however, been a feature of Brexit, dating back to the Referendum campaign. A further example was provided when, at the Conservative party conference, Prime Minister Theresa May labelled opponents of Brexit 'citizens of nowhere.' May said that '… if you believe you are a citizen of the world, you are a citizen of nowhere. You don't understand what citizenship means'[107] – a statement that had unfortunate echoes of the anti-semitic slogan 'rootless cosmopolitans' used as a term of abuse in the former Soviet Union.

10.8.3 The JPP and EU rights

An argument made by legal theorist John Finnis for the JPP at the time of the first *Miller* case illustrates how some conceive of rights in the UK. Finnis argued that the Supreme Court mistakenly assumed that EU rights are 'statutory rights enacted by Parliament' (and therefore the UK Government must not fall foul of the prohibition on using the prerogative to dispense with a statute).[108] Finnis argued instead that the ECA 1972 simply provided a means for making EU law rights enforceable in English law, and drew an analogy with double-tax treaties,[109] arguing that, although UK statutory provision was in both cases (i.e. the ECA and Tax Acts) a necessary condition for those rights' domestic legal efficacy, they were non-statutory in the sense that Parliament was not the original source for the rights. Finnis' argument seems to amount to the suggestion that EU rights are not rights in the relevant sense. Just as British railways have floundered and been delayed by the 'wrong kind of leaves or snow',[110] so Brexit was being held up[111] by the wrong kind of rights. The argument is that rights derived from the ECA are not rights in the full sense because their real authority derives from outside UK law, in an international treaty. It followed, then, that the rights that arose under the ECA could be eliminated by the exercise of the foreign relations prerogative without any need for Parliament's involvement. However, Finnis' analogy does not hold. Bilateral double taxation treaties are not comparable to multilateral EU treaties and do not give rise to rights comparable to rights acquired through EU membership.

107 But see further, 'Mrs May, we are all citizens of the world', says philosopher' *BBC News*, 29 October 2016 (the philosopher in question was Kwame Anthony Appiah).

108 J Finnis, 'Terminating Treaty-Based UK Rights', 26 October 2016, available at https://judicialpowerproject.org.uk/john-finnis-terminating-treaty-based-uk-rights/

109 E.g. the Taxation (International and Other Provisions) Act 2010.

110 E.g. 'LEAVES ON THE LINE: WRONG KIND OF SNOW', available at https://twsmedia.co.uk/2020/08/06/leaves-on-the-line-wrong-kind-of-snow/

111 In the sense that the UK Government could not trigger Article 50 TEU without Parliament's consent, and litigation was necessary to confirm the need for this.

In what sense are tax treaty provisions 'rights'? Double tax treaties are concluded to ensure people do not pay tax twice on the same income. But these tax treaties do not themselves impose taxes, nor create rights. EU treaties do create individual rights. Finnis' argument seems to suggest that there exist different classes of rights, and that rights only really count if they are properly homegrown and British in origin. But then, we might ask, how many homegrown rights actually exist in the UK? Not many. As I have argued, the common law had shown itself inadequate in the protection of rights. That is why the Human Rights Act was necessary in the first place, and why EU law also provided a valuable source of rights when the UK was an EU member.

10.9 Human Rights and Devolution

The UK is a plurinational state and the situation with human rights is complex across the devolved UK.

10.9.1 Scotland and Wales

The ECHR is written into devolution legislation. For example, s29(2)d Scotland Act 1998 provides that any Act passed by the Scottish Parliament is not law to the extent it is incompatible with any Convention rights covered by the HRA.[112] Devolved governments are also prohibited from acting inconsistently with the ECHR.[113] Repealing or amending the HRA would not remove these obligations but would necessitate amendment of the Devolution statutes. Indeed, it is likely that repeal, or even amendment, of the HRA by Westminster would violate the Sewel Convention, which requires that the Westminster government will not normally legislate with regard to devolved matters without the consent of the devolved Parliaments. Although Raab informed Parliament that the UK government would be 'seeking legislative consent motions'[114] for the Bill of Rights Bill, this seemed unlikely given that the Scottish and Welsh governments[115] made clear their opposition to HRA repeal.

However, the situation is more complex still. Although the HRA has UK-wide application, and is a reserved matter, human rights are partially devolved in Scotland and Wales. This means that devolved institutions have the power to promote human rights. For example, there exists a separate Scottish Human Rights Commission and also the Scottish First Minister's Advisory Group on

[112] s107(6) Government of Wales Act 2006 contains a similar provision.

[113] E.g. ss 29 and 57 Scotland Act 1998; similar provisions in the Government of Wales Act 2006 and Wales Act 2017.

[114] https://hansard.parliament.uk/commons/2022-06-22/debates/5736CBBA-A5F0-45B9-AA54-246FF57FB5EE/BillOfRights

[115] www.gov.scot/publications/human-rights-act-reform-consultation-scottish-government-response/; https://gov.wales/sites/default/files/publications/2022-03/human-rights-act-reform-a-modern-bill-of-rights_0.pdf.

Human Rights, established in 2017. In March 2021, the Scottish Government announced a new Human Rights Bill, whereby four UN treaties would be incorporated into Scots law, including legislation that enhances human rights for women, disabled people and minority ethnic communities.[116] In parallel, in Spring 2021, the Scottish Government introduced a Bill aimed at directly incorporating the UN Convention on the Rights of the Child into domestic law. It was this Bill that was challenged by the UK Government in the UK Supreme Court and found to be beyond the Scottish Parliament's competence – an example of intra-governmental conflict in the UK over rights protection.[117]

10.9.2 Northern Ireland

The situation in Northern Ireland reveals further complexity in human rights protection across the UK. Northern Ireland had a differentiated Brexit from other parts of the UK but it was already, pre-Brexit, subject to the distinct, enhanced rights protections of the Belfast/Good Friday Agreement[118] (B/GFA) which is a legally binding international treaty signed by the UK and Irish governments. The ECHR is also expressly recognized in the B/GFA. Any unilateral move by the UK to diminish rights commitments in the B/GFA would raise issues of bad faith, and breach of international law. The B/GFA also formed the constitutional kernel of the Northern Ireland Act 1998 (the major devolution statute for Northern Ireland). The HRA is expressly mentioned in the Northern Ireland Act, and the latter Act would have to be amended if the HRA were repealed or changed. The intention had been for Northern Ireland to develop its own Bill of Rights, but to date, none has been enacted, although the task has been taken up again more recently and would certainly be more appropriate for Northern Ireland than the 'British Bill of Rights' mooted by the UK Government earlier. ECHR and HRA protections are essential to the peace settlement and B/GFA. But the now abandoned 2022 Bill of Rights Bill emasculated the ECHR, reducing the protection that has accrued under ECtHR caselaw.

The B/GFA requires 'equivalence' between the human rights protection in both the Republic of Ireland and Northern Ireland, and the principle of 'non-diminution' requires that rights protection should not regress in either jurisdiction. Both Ireland and the UK incorporated the ECHR into domestic law – through the HRA in the UK and the ECHR Act 2003 in Ireland. The revocation of the EU Charter of Fundamental Rights by Brexit raises problems for Northern Ireland, as it is hard to see how rights protection may

116 'New Human Rights Bill', Scottish Government, 12 March 2021.

117 *Reference by the Attorney General and the Advocate General for Scotland* [2021] UKSC 42. See further chapter on Scotland.

118 *The Agreement reached in the multi-party negotiations 10 April 1998* 'Rights, Safeguards and Equality of Opportunity.'

remain equivalent between Ireland and Northern Ireland, when only one party enforces EU Charter rights.

Nonetheless, Article 2(1) of the EU/UK Withdrawal Agreement Protocol on Ireland/Northern Ireland[119] provides that there shall be 'no diminution of rights, safeguards or equality of opportunity' in the region as a result of the UK's exit from the EU, maintaining the commitment of the B/GFA. These arrangements are to be overseen by the Equality Commission for Northern Ireland, the Northern Ireland Human Rights Commission and the Joint Committee of the Human Rights Commissions of Northern Ireland and Ireland.

As a result of the Brexit Protocol, Northern Ireland has a different rights and equality system from the rest of the UK.[120] There has already been friction over rights in Northern Ireland, including disagreements over language rights, and post Brexit friction over Irish citizenship in Northern Ireland. The B/GFA allows people born in Northern Ireland to identify as British, Irish or both, but when Emma de Souza, born in Northern Ireland, claimed Irish citizenship, and requested a residence permit for her US-born husband, this was rejected by the UK Home Office, who deemed her British only, and required her to reapply as a British citizen or renounce her British citizenship and pay a fee to apply as an Irish citizen. Although de Souza's case was eventually resolved, this case revealed the complexity of identity and citizenship in Northern Ireland, and the failure of the UK government to recognize the B/GFA right for anyone born in Northern Ireland to identify as Irish or British.[121]

Therefore, in conclusion, human rights protection is not uniform across the UK. It is hard to see how a new Bill of Rights could function to improve human rights protection across the UK. Although the JCHR in 2008 described a national Bill of Rights as 'an expression of national identity' and 'potentially a moment of national definition'[122] it is hard to fathom how a human rights document could fulfil that function in the UK. This is perhaps why European rights protections, many now eradicated, were more tolerable in devolved territories. Divergent views of rights across the UK provide a potential source of friction and conflict.

10.10 Conclusion: The 'Monstering' of Human Rights

Many human rights have been eradicated in the UK as a result of Brexit. The post Brexit exclusion of the EU Charter from UK law, and the often fragile status of EU citizens' rights, means that rights protected under the HRA become even more important after Brexit. Yet this Act remains at risk of repeal in

119 *The revised withdrawal agreement and political declaration considered and agreed at European Council on 17 October 2019.*

120 See further chapter on Ireland.

121 See e.g. 'Northern Ireland-Born British and Irish Win EU Citizenship Rights', *The Guardian*, 14 May 2020.

122 Joint Committee on Human Rights, 'A Bill of Rights for the UK?' 2008, at 96.

future. This is hardly a fertile landscape for rights protection. The claim has been made that, in the UK, rights have been 'monstered.' Adam Wagner has described how: 'Human rights myths and fabrications have proliferated: the fleeing criminal suspect given takeaway fried chicken by police to protect his human rights; the prisoner granted access to hardcore pornography so as not to subject him to inhuman or degrading treatment; the illegal immigrant who avoided deportation because he had a pet cat'.

Wagner attributes much of the blame to the right-wing press that 'have enthusiastically promoted the narrative that the HRA is a charter for terrorists and criminals. Rather than a bulwark for ordinary people against the power of the State, the HRA is said to be a Trojan Horse which has brought terrorists to our shores and allowed convicted prisoners to live in luxury.'[123] All of this has resulted in a monstering of the ECHR, HRA, and EU, as well as of many of those who make human rights claims.[124]

Certainly, there has been too much misrepresentation of the HRA and too little public understanding of it. In late 2015, when it seemed at real risk of repeal, a public awareness campaign[125] (mostly crowdfunded) to save the HRA was introduced, using billboards, as well as short films, which focussed on those who had used the HRA to obtain justice, and did much to increase public understanding of the Act.

But will the HRA survive? Will rights once protected by the EU continue to be as robustly protected as previously? Time will tell. But, if as a result of Brexit, and attacks on the HRA, there is a regression to the view that 'a culture of liberty' (whatever that may mean) by itself, is sufficient to protect rights, then the outlook for human rights protection in the UK looks bleak.

[123] Adam Wagner, 'The Monstering of Human Rights', 19 September 2014, available at https://adamlcor.files.wordpress.com/2014/09/the-monstering-of-human-rights-adam-wagner-2014.pdf

[124] Similar points are made by Gearty, *On Fantasy Island* (Oxford: Oxford University Press, 2016); and Elspeth Guild, 'BREXIT and its Consequences for UK and EU Citizenship or Monstrous Citizenship' (Leiden: Nijhoff Law Specials, Volume 94, 2017) (focusing more on EU rights).

[125] 'Act for the Act', available at https://actfortheact.uk

Conclusion

As Lord Bingham once remarked, it has been all too usual for many to approach Britain's constitutional arrangements with a 'mixture of ignorance and insouciance'.[1] Lord Bingham continued that,

> This would not matter if the constitution were a peripheral feature of our national life. But the constitution is, after all, the body of rules and conventions which governs our life as a nation, the articles of association of UK PLC of which we are all members. Surely, therefore, it deserves more thoughtful consideration than the public seem inclined to give it.[2]

Such 'thoughtful consideration' is, however, notable mainly for its absence. We are in any case surely witnessing what Blick and Hennessey described as the end of the 'good chaps theory of government'.[3] Britain long prided itself on its 'unwritten' Constitution, viewing Westminster as 'the mother of parliaments.' However, as British Prime Minister, William Ewart Gladstone, stated back in 1879, the British Constitution 'presumes more boldly than any other the good sense and good faith of those who work it.'[4] This is because the UK, with no codified Constitution, heavily relies on political conventions and understandings. It also relies on the fact that those who work within politics – civil servants, politicians, and their special advisors – operate with self-restraint. That self-restraint has now largely vanished. The failure to observe the Sewel convention, and to continue legislating even in the absence of devolved consent, is a good example. The Blick/Hennessey article contains a long list illustrating other ways in which those engaged in the governance of Britain are no longer 'good chaps' (or 'chapesses') and cannot be trusted to observe unwritten conventions and understandings.

However, in addition to endorsing the demise of the 'good chaps' theory, this book has also stressed that deeply divided understandings of the British

1 T Bingham, 'The Courts and the Constitution', in T Bingham (ed.), *The Business of Judging* (Oxford: Oxford University Press, 2000) 225.

2 Ibid.

3 A Blick and P Hennessy, 'Good Chaps No More? Safeguarding the Constitution in Stressful Times' (2019) Constitution Society.

4 Gladstone, *Gleanings of Past Years 1843–78,* vol. 1, 243 (noted in Blick and Hennessey, 'Good Chaps No More?').

Constitution exist – which go beyond the more familiar distinction between legal and political constitutionalism – and, in many cases, are borne out of frustration with present constitutional inadequacy.

On the one hand, one view of the British Constitution, held by most recent UK governments, perceives the UK as a unitary, centralized State, with an omnicompetent Parliament. This view denies the possibility of any constitutional entrenchment – thereby rendering the Constitution flexible – but also placing fundamental principles, such as human rights, at risk, because of their lack of any entrenched legal protection. On this understanding, final authority remains with the Westminster Parliament. This view interpreted the EU referendum as a vote on a UK-wide basis, and afforded no protection, nor constitutional relevance, to different results in the devolved nations, in contrast to truly federal approaches. It also interpreted EU membership as a matter of foreign affairs reserved to the UK Government, and devolved nations were accorded no specific role in the EU withdrawal negotiations. It also, however, interpreted the formally advisory EU referendum vote as binding, thus requiring an implementation that introduced an unpredictable element into constitutional law, regarding when referendums would be enforced.

However, this view just outlined above contrasts with an alternative approach, which identifies the UK as a *union* State, rather than a unitary State. It interprets the UK as a union founded on treaties (e.g. the Treaty of Union 1707, Good Friday/Belfast Agreement 1998) and reliant on ongoing consent, as well as constitutional practice. This view also recognizes that the UK has been transformed by external developments (such as EU and ECHR membership) and restructured internally by devolution, but also by the Human Rights Act, and a desire for a more principled constitutional development than parliamentary sovereignty allows (such as the introduction of the House of Lords Constitution Committee and Joint Committee on Human Rights). It recognizes that the Constitution has also become much more legalized and susceptible to judicial review, especially in that murky area of the prerogative, as demonstrated in the *Miller* and *Miller/Cherry* cases. Furthermore, the Scotland Act 2016 and Wales Act 2017 (both Westminster legislation) declare the permanence of the Scottish and Welsh Parliaments, provisions which, if not simply redundant padding, fly in face of orthodox constitutional law's assertion of an omnicompetent Westminster Parliament.

Brexit brought these divisions into sharp focus, without, however, indicating any solution, and generally resulted in the imposition of resolute and unlimited parliamentary sovereignty. A serious and somewhat depressing question is whether continuing constitutional unsettlement may not be the 'least worst' solution in a contemporary Britain wrestling with so many constitutional problems?

I believe not. As this book has argued, there is no principled reason to continue to adhere to the Diceyan understanding of unlimited parliamentary sovereignty. Parliament's enactment of the 1972 ECA has demonstrated it is possible for Parliament to place limits on its own sovereignty, and having done so before, it may do so again. Even in 1978, KC Wheare noted that, 'parliamentary sovereignty, so often the obstacle to constitutional reform, has been made to look a little less formidable; and by this means it may be possible for reformers to advocate, and even to carry through, limitations upon sovereignty and authority which are one of the features of a good constitution.'[5] Parliamentary sovereignty may appear attractive, when contrasted with the overbearing urge of an executive wishing to exclude Parliament from the EU withdrawal process, or to prorogue Parliament altogether. However, the fusion of executive and legislature, which Bagehot deemed Britain's constitutional 'efficient secret', is all too capable of turning unlimited parliamentary sovereignty into parliamentary despotism. Moreover, without an insistence on unlimited parliament sovereignty, federalism, a codified Constitution and entrenchment all become possible.

Furthermore, there also exist, as this book has explored, interesting (and under-researched) options for the UK Union from comparative law and history. One such example is that of the *federacy*, which has much in common with UK devolution, because federacies comprise a smaller unit (e.g. Greenland) within a larger State (e.g. Denmark). However, although the smaller unit shares the benefits of association with the larger polity, it retains internal autonomy and self-government. There is thus considerable self-rule, but much less shared-rule than in federal states such as Germany or the USA. A further example may be found in the concept of the *Dominion* which provided practical autonomy and equality of status with Britain for some British colonies in the past. The Dominions of Canada, Australia and New Zealand were formally granted constitutional autonomy and equality by the Statute of Westminster in 1931, without any declaration of their independent status. Although the Dominion model has been criticized, partly because it has roots in UK's often (rightly) disparaged imperial past, it demonstrates the possibility of self-government, autonomous from London, even in the absence of a formal declaration of independence. Many legal elements of this device might be adopted constitutionally, without use of a name rooted in Britain's colonial past. One other possibility the book examined was that of an 'Autonomy Statute' for Britain's devolveds. In 2012, prior to the 2014 independence referendum, a Scottish Constitutional Commission discussion paper on 'Secure Autonomy' for Scotland argued that, whereas parliamentary sovereignty dictates that Parliament may not bind its successors, and so no devolution scheme may be safely regarded as permanent, Parliament can *renounce* its sovereignty. They cited historical examples of such a union, such as Austria-Hungary after the 1867 Compromise agreement. If there are unfortunate associations with a bygone, dead Empire, once again, key elements of the device might be recalibrated to construct an 'Autonomy Statute' for the UK's devolved nations today.

[5] KC Wheare, 'Does It Really Exist? Some Reflections upon the Contemporary British Constitution' (1978) Parliamentary Affairs.

However, one wonders if it is becoming too late to preserve the unity of the United Kingdom. It is indeed possible that Brexit has deepened existing divisions. Although issues such as Scottish independence and EU membership are not cut and dried, and allegiances cut across political boundaries, nonetheless, there now exists a large body who consider that Scottish independence, for example, provides the only solution for a flourishing future Statehood. Ultimately, Brexit may shatter the devolution settlement, and taking back control from one Union (the EU) may have destabilized another (the UK). If so, it will not be the first time in history that Britain's insistence on sovereignty in one area (in this case, in leaving the EU, but we might substitute for this the American colonies) has shattered its sovereignty over another – namely, the unity of the United Kingdom.

Alternately, some argue it is now time for Britain to adopt a codified and entrenched Constitution. There may be little historical basis for such a practice in Britain (excepting the 1653 Interregnum *Instrument of Government*, Britain's only ever written Constitution, which has been generally written out of Britain's constitutional history). But this need not matter, and the adoption of a codified Constitution would bring Britain in line with global practice, given that most countries have a codified Constitution, and even Britain's former imperial territories have chosen not to follow the British uncodified model. But even if it is desirable to codify the Constitution, how to bring that about? Hennessey and Blick offered a range of proposals to investigate major change. These included: a Royal Commission; a parliamentary inquiry; a Speaker's Conference or Commission; and a Citizens' Convention. But are people sufficiently motivated? Do they *want* written Constitution? Only a few years ago, the Commons Political and Constitutional Reform Committee published its report[6] on the prospect of a UK written Constitution. That report was the culmination of four years' work. But no codified Constitution came of all that work, and it is possible that the Brexit crisis, far from constituting a 'constitutional moment', has deepened existing divisions in society. It may be doubtful that the UK could reach a consensus on constitutional foundations that have eluded it in less disturbed times. Present turbulent circumstances may foster passion not reason. Yet, what is the alternative?

Anthony King proffered a striking and very apposite image in his book on *The British Constitution*:

> The old constitution possessed a certain monumental grandeur, a certain cruciform, cathedral-like simplicity. Its architecture and ground plan could easily be grasped, at least in their essentials. But that old building now looks as though it has been bombed from above and undermined from below. Parts of the roof have fallen in, at least one of the transepts has collapsed, and workmen have erected an untidy assortment of workshops and sheds inside the few walls still

[6] 'Consultation on a New Magna Carta?' Report available at https://publications.parliament.uk/pa/cm201415/cmselect/cmpolcon/599/599.pdf

> standing. Britain today has neither a brand new church, a postwar Coventry cathedral, nor a skilful restoration of an old church, like the Frauenkirche, Dresden, but something that looks a little bit like a bombed-out ruin left over from a major war.[7]

Britain needs a 'brand new Church.' This present ruin will not do. With Brexit behind but not forgotten, the Union in danger of fragmenting, and Britain suffering (in common with the rest of the world) the scars of Covid-19 and the looming climate crisis, the time is ripe for reassessment. After the death of a Queen who reigned for 70 years, the stability of that constitutional settlement looks further weakened. Britain faces a challenge, not just to its constitutional law and international relations, but also to its legal and constitutional imagination. Blick and Hennessey were notably accurate in their assessment that: 'From being a by-word for tedium the condition of the UK constitution has become a first order question cracking with political electricity.'[8] Maybe that excitement and interest can be commandeered in order to work on a new constitutional settlement.

[7] A King, *The British Constitution* (Oxford: Oxford University Press, 2007) 351.
[8] Blick and Hennessey, 'Good Chaps No More?'

Index

www.ingramcontent.com/pod-product-compliance
Lightning Source LLC
LaVergne TN
LVHW082021200926
848481LV00010B/2895